Programmable Calculators: How to Use Them

BY
Charles J. Sippl and Roger J. Sippl

Published by Matrix Publishers, Inc., Champaign, Illinois 61820
Portland, Oregon 97210

Typeset by Graphic World, Inc.
Printed by Strathmore Company
In House Editor: Merl K. Miller

Programmable Calculators: How to Use Them

Charles J. Sippl is a writer, educator and consultant in the computer, communications, and calculator fields. He is the author with his sons and others of more than a dozen books. Among them are: *Computer Dictionary and Handbook* (Howard W. Sams, Inc.), *Data Communications Dictionary* (Van Nostrand-Reinhold), *Microcomputer Handbook* (Petrocelli/Charter), *Microcomputer Dictionary and Guide* (Matrix Publishers, Inc.), *Personal and Home Electronics Buyers Guide* (Prentice-Hall), *Computers At Large* (Bobbs-Merrill), and others. He has taught at several California Universities and has conducted industry seminars and lectures around the U.S.

Roger J. Sippl is a Computer Science graduate of the University of California-Berkeley and a consultant in medical computer systems technology as well as a course-developer, teacher and seminar leader. He is the co-author with his father of: *Personal and Home Electronics Buyers Guide* (Prentice-Hall) and *2001 Things To Do With Your Home Computer* (Holt, Rinehart & Winston).

Acknowledgement: The authors wish to express their appreciation to all friends in the calculator clubs especially the major club founders, Richard J. Nelson and Richard C. Vanderburgh. Thanks also go to all the calculator companies that provided photographs and descriptions of their products, especially the fine people at Hewlett-Packard and Texas Instruments, Inc. Because a list of their names would be too long, and some would be inadvertently left out, appreciation to all is hereby noted.

Dedicated: To the grandchildren, Andria and Michelle Sippl, who started using their calculators in the first and second grades.

PREFACE

Tens of millions of people use calculators for numerous specific and worthwhile purposes. The most serious users now also find them to be very necessary tools in their work. For business people, engineers, scientists and others, calculators support their operations directly. They are actually participatory in the activities involved to increase productivity, improve accuracy, reduce costs, and speed better decision making. The wide range of software for the programmable units and the ease of original programming simplifies new application development. Jobs are up and running quickly; 'what if' ideas are calculated and explored, and trial and error solutions to problems are fast and easy with low-cost calculator devices.

But, calculators are more than tools of many trades. The development of a "How To . . ." book is principally a matter of topic priority selection. The modern calculator has many facets, capabilities, and challenging orientations. The advanced models introduced in late 1977 are so powerful and cost-effective that the word 'fantastic' is not inappropriate as a descriptive adjective for them. As noted on pages ahead they are being 'required' in many high schools and community colleges much like a basic text. Teachers of courses in accounting, business mathematics, statistics, chemistry, engineering, management and others expect their students to be proficient in the use of calculators. But, this sounds like professionals are the primary users which is not the real world case. Salesmen, clerks, housewives, trade people of all types, small business entrepreneurs, and students in every type of endeavor own and use their calculators heavily. Who doesn't use calculators? You'll lose trying to guess.

The thrust of this book is the analysis of personal or pocket 'programmable' calculators (PCs). The first programmables were very complex for new users and were designed by engineers for engineers. Now, however, programmables are very simple, very low-cost and are being used by all of the people noted above. They range from the Sinclair Cambridge for under $30 to the big desktop business and engineering 'system' calculators selling for up to $5000. Whereas in 1975 only three or four programmable models were available, today scores of models are selling extremely well and a dozen manufacturers including some of the largest electronics companies in the world back them up with excellent software and service policies. The subject matter of this book does not emphasize the very elementary four-to-six function $10 to $20 machines that tens of millions of people have purchased. Instead, the focus is on the trade-up models that a substantial portion of users of original 'four-bangers' will soon decide to purchase. It is obvious that the great majority of people, at least until now, had a distaste even fear for 'programs' and avoided these models. But, a totally new environment of digital electronics 'for every body' is changing those who were formerly inhibited by multiple function key boards. When electronic games became popular in 1975 and surged to sales of 3.5 million in 1976, keyboards and 'things electronic' began to be accepted as commonplace. Microwave ovens, TV sets, Videocassette Recorder/Players newer stereos, citizen band radios, customer bank terminals and scores of other devices now 'educate' all types of consumers on the use of multiple function keyboards. But, many people always feared 'programming' and still do

The 'gumstick' size magnetic cards containing 'ready-made' programs used by the HP-65 and then HP-67 and HP-97 as well as the SR-52 calculators by Hewlett-Packard and Texas Instruments provided users with 'ready-made programs of great utility, but these programmable machines sold for well over $200 and up to $800 which prohibited their mass use. A new generation of calculators has brought near miraculous computer-like power to hand-held calculators that now sell for less than $100. The TI-58 and TI-59 hand-held units introduced by Texas Instruments in mid-1977 provide 'snap-in' modules of Solid State Software™ — prewritten programs (generally 15 to 20) equivalent to 25 magnetic cards or 5000 program steps — all on a thumb-nail sized cube. Because the TI-58 sells at discount stores for under $100, this magnificent cost-performance achievement alone will move hundreds of thousands of new calculator users up into programmables whether they want to program themselves or simply use these plug-in modules to solve specific types or wide ranges of problems. The TI-59 uses these modules (Read Only Memory — ROM units) and/or mag cards — and both machines can use the PC-100A printers (about $150 to $175) for alphanumeric printouts for labels, headings, and plots or charts. No one need be afraid of programmables again — because of apparent complexity or high price. These machines 'break the ice' — and scores of competing products will follow. Chapters ahead provide details.

Because many hundreds of thousands of owners have 'fallen in love' with their now superceded Texas Instruments' SR-56, SR-51, SR-52 and Hewlett-Packard HP-25, HP-27 and other models, considerable discussion of these machines appears in the book. Also, because the revolutionary National Semiconductor 7100 hand-held ROM and RAM (Random Access Memory) insertable module calculator might possibly appear on the market, some abbreviated discussion is included in the book, principally for comparison purposes. The manufacturer canceled the project immediately before its marketing program seemed imminent. Some potential purchasers of the manufacturing/marketing rights were on the scene when National Semiconductor Corp. decided against increasing its line of consumer products. Certainly, a discussion of the total calculator scene must also include a rather extensive analysis of programmable desktop models. Several million of the older type four-function desktop machines will be quickly replaced with new, smaller super-efficient programmables from Burroughs, Monroe, Sharp, Victor, Wang, Olivetti, as well as TI and HP and others. Bankers, retailers, laboratory and wholesaler operations and many other types of managers already are jumping to card, cassette, and ROM-programmable units. Two chapters are devoted to these new more powerful calculating/computing machines. The compactness of the printing HP-92 Investor and HP-97 card programmable-printer make them most attractive, and the expansive capabilities of the Texas Instruments SR-60A at under $2000 but with interfaces to scores of peripherals make this an exceptional machine. These and others are analyzed ahead.

The organization and structure of this book is designed for amateurs and experienced users alike. The first few chapters establish the types of simpler machines, the environment of calculator/computer products, their uses in education and the professions, and then move the reader along into the first easy-to-use programmables. The middle chapters develop for the reader an understanding of capabilities of the most popular products and provide an introduction to elementary programming. Chapters 6, 7, and 8 explain the characteristics of the most advanced machines, but the reader is helped by being able to refer to an extensive glossary section at the end of chapter 3. Some rather extensive examples of programs and applications are developed to assist the reader in comparing his or her programs or following through on the user's own machine. Comparative examples of competing machines and alternate 'languages' appear in several sections of the book. Some serious but unavoidable omissions from the book are the many excellent applications contributions developed by members of the two largest calculator clubs. Space does not permit this luxury. But, each club publishes an excellent newsletter providing members with new capabilities discoveries, new member-developed exotic and pragmatic programs, absolute latest news of current and coming products. Members also benefit from other services and all of them quickly become sincere and dedicated calculator buffs. These guys and gals really put their machines to the test — and they have considerable power with the manufacturers. It is felt by many that these thousands of club members have been responsible for pushing manufacturers into providing machines of extraordinary power and versatility. Both clubs are recommended to all readers of this book. Although their names might change slightly, membership can be obtained by writing to either or both: HP-65 Users Club, Richard J. Nelson, Editor, 2541 Camden Place, Santa Ana, CA 92704 and SR-52 Users Club, Richard C. Vanderburgh, Editor, 9459 Taylorsville Road, Dayton, OH 45424. The magazine "Calculators/Computers," P.O. Box 310, Menlo Park, CA 94025 is an excellent 'beginner's guide' and 'asks' its readers to copy it and use it in schools.

The brief introduction to the book on the pages following provides the reader with the '1978' setting of the calculating/computing environment. As noted, the changes in this industry often reflect the leading edge of what's coming up in personal computers, in video games and recorder/players, in keyboard capabilities, in programmable appliances and other devices of an almost endless variety. Calculators have already become terminals for computers, for communications devices, for instruments, and many other devices and systems. They will soon interface to programmable mass memory, telephone systems, voice input-output, CRT or LCD multiline displays, and other peripherals. Thus, this entire book is really only a preface, a preview to imageproducing, low-cost computing pocket-sized communication and control devices. It's time to get ready . . .

Charles J. Sippl
Roger J. Sippl

CONTENTS

INTRODUCTION — Dynamic Change
is the Rule

The new advanced programmable calculators solve the programming tasks for those who want their applications techniques 'ready made' and also offer intriguing challenges for those who want to use their machines for developing solutions to complex engineering, financial, and scientific problems. And for the dedicated calculator buffs, they offer the capability to perform elegant programming techniques, discover and develop new features and uses, and 'output' fancy plots and charts with alphanumeric labeling and heads. The new machines offer strongly desired expandability features of thousands of program steps and an increasingly large number of available storage registers. And all this power is available for less than $100 on some machines and not too much more for added printer capability as well. The very large number of program steps is important because with more steps it is possible to create programs of expansive complexity and thus also new problem-solving capability. The increasing number of storage registers is important because they permit the user to handle very large amounts of data. This increases the already broad spectrum of user applications and satisfies a great number of requirements in professions, trades, education, research, finance, business, and all types of scientific endeavor. With plug-in software modules (ROMs), new users do not need to know how to program to solve either really tough problems or long and complex routine problems. The programs are pre-recorded, and a simple two-or three-key code brings any of them to immediate use with any type of data. The libraries of programs available from the manufacturers and clubs — and from the industry, educational and governmental institutions are endless. These new simple and fast capabilities mean enjoyable convenience, new speed and accuracy, decreased reliance on computers and faster turnaround time with reduced effort or need for special training.

In January of 1974 Hewlett-Packard shipped its first hand-held calculator with external memory, the HP-65. The era of personal computing began. In three years its successor, the HP-67, offered about three times its capability at less than half the price. Changes in the calculator industry occur rapidly — changes in size, performance, function, cost, design, technology, and coming soon, input and output.

Some of the design changes are pictured ahead with examples of the Texas Instruments' DataClip and their palm-sized shirt-pocket calculator. Intense competition has lead to dramatic price reductions. Research into improvements in unending The HP-19C printer pictured ahead is an example of high quality microminiaturization of powerful components — and of a printing

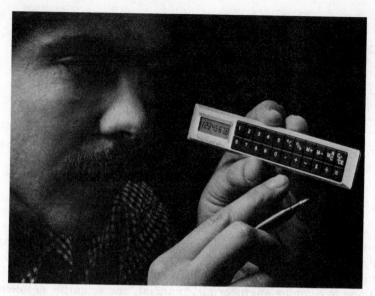

A unique carry-along calculator about the size of a six-inch ruler by Texas Instruments is called the DataClip™*. The model has five functions and a bright eight-digit liquid crystal display. DataClip operates up to 1000 hours on a set of batteries. It sells for about $30. It is pencil-thin, a little longer than a ballpoint and about an inch wide. DataClip slides easily into a pocket or purse. The four basic functions are complemented by a powerful memory that can be added to or subtracted from. Memory recall and clear memory can be executed, as well.

Shirtpocket Calculator — A palm-size calculator from Texas Instruments weighs less than three ounces, but can perform the most-needed arithmetic functions of larger, bulkier calculators. Designated the TI-1750, the miniature calculator typically can operate 2,000 hours on a set of batteries. It features a large, easy to read, eight-digit liquid crystal display (LCD). Designed for persons on the go, the slim TI-1750 fits easily into a shirt or coat pocket or purse to provide considerable computational power. Although it measures only 4-1/2 × 2-11/16 × 3/8 inches, the compact calculator has a four-key memory and can do add-ons, discounts, interest, square roots and percentages automatically. it sells for about $20 to $25.

Hewlett-Packard offers a pocket programmable calculator with an integral thermal printer. The keystroke programmable HP-19C has 98 fully merged program steps (that means as many as four keystrokes may be stored as one program step in memory), editing and programming functions, 30 data storage registers, a quiet thermal printer, and non-volatile storage for programs and 16 of the 30 data registers. It's a printing version of the HP-29C. Both were designed for engineers, scientists, surveyors, technicians, and students. The calculator comes with a 164-page applications book which includes common application programs in statistics, surveying, navigation and numerical methods. The HP-19C often sells for under $300 and the HP-29C for about $160.

mechanism as well. Calculators are available as parts of telephones (Figure-phone — see Chapter 5), as parts of alarm clocks, wallets, watches, even CB radios and tape recorders. At the low end of the market changes will continue to demonstrate cosmetics and specialized machines. In the high end, competition to the ROM-insert programmables is bound to occur. The microprocessor chip used in the $65 to $75 TI-57 programmable is ¼ inch square and carries over 30,000 transistors. It is thus more complex than many microprocessor chips used in microcomputers; some of these types average only 12,000 transistors. The amazingly low-cost TI-57 has eight addressable multi-use memories to store data, intermediate answers or results, and up to 150 keystrokes can be stored based upon 50 multi-key program steps. Six conditional and three unconditional branches and 10 labels for selective repetitive problem solving are also offered to optimize programs. The TI business machine comparable to the 57 is the MBA which has 32 steps of programmability but is also pre-programmed with many financial functions which can be string-programmed together to obtain complex financial manipulation. In effect, it is the equivalent of having the ability to program subroutines, not just steps. We have already noted (Preface) that the TI-58 and TI-59 can use 5000-step insertable (in the lower back of the machine) ROM modules. Among the most popular of the library modules is the Leisure Program module. it has 20 different programs for golfers, bowlers, chess players, football fans, bridge players, photographers and others interested in using the calculator for entertainment. Other programs can calculate biorhythms, land a spacecraft safely on Mars, simulate sea battles, and play blackjack, Acey-Deucy, Craps, Nim, and other games. Computer programmers might make special note of the excellent 'Hexadecimal Calculator' pictured below, called the TI Programmer. It can save computer users many hours of program drudgery and accuracy headaches as well.

For the elementary school kids, competition is fierce between TI's Little Professor, and DataMan™ and National Semiconductor's Quizkid I and II and the Quizkid Racer. A brief description of the utility which is comparable to the DataMan follows:

Quizkid Racer — Competitive Set

Once the basics have been mastered, Racer can add a competitive flavor to the QuizKid way of learning math.

QuizKid Racer retains all of the features of the QuizKid II and adds two keys

HEXADECIMAL CALCULATOR
The TI Programmer, a $40 to $50 handheld calculator from Texas Instruments, does arithmetic in three different number bases, and converts to and from these bases: hexadecimal, octal, and decimal. Among other applications, the TI Programmer will convert memory address to decimal form, add relative address to a base address to find specific computer memory locations, or determine if there is enough space in the computer's memory to hold a new block of data. The calculator can also perform bit-by-bit logic operations on numbers in hex or octal, including AND, OR, Exclusive OR and SHIFT operations.

that can expand the complexity and variety of 10-problem quizzes. The "PRO" key increases the difficulty of the questions and is used when the child has mastered the basic arithmetic operations.

The "COMPLEX" key adds another dimension to Racer. When this key is pressed, the child is required to supply one factor of each problem rather than the answer — for example, instead of the problem appearing as $2 + 4 = $ _____, the problem may appear as $2 + $ _____ $ = 6$.

Another added feature of QuizKid Racer is its ability to be linked to a second unit by a game adapter cable and allow two children to compete for the right answers to 10-problem quizzes that appear on both units. The first child to enter the right answer receives two points. If the other child also enters the right answer, he or she receives one point. At the end of the quiz the number of points each child has earned is displayed. A maximum of twenty points is possible.

It is ideal for parents to review fundamental mathematics with child.

Quizkid Racer is available in two different packages: one machine or two machines and game adapter cable.

Besides the several entries from National Semiconductor and TI, APF offers the Mark 1500 MATHEMAGICIAN that can be played by children and adults of all ages. It is a teaching calculator and device for game playing. It can be a competitive game with individual scores — and it offers Lunar Lander, Gooey Gumdrop, Numbers, Football, Walk the Plank and Countin On. Another large game manufacturer, Coleco, offers its model 2000 Lil' Genius™ calculator for problem solving and fun including buzzers, LED lights and a "Big Book of Math Facts" with complete instructions, pages of math problems, puzzles, games.

Although the HP Users Club and the TI Users Club have no affiliation with either manufacturer, they are able to 'teach' the designers more about their machines than they originally knew. For example, they have discovered how to make the HP-67 display words such as "I deal," "roll dice," "cards are," and "Colorado," to mention just a few of the literally hundreds contained in the club's word and phrase library. Not only that: with the use of a [gimmick] code, f LBL (i), minds will bend watching "Coca-Cola" ticker-tape across the screen in animation, for example. One member has discovered how to make the calculator display the internal program pointer register's contents, as well as other internal register contents. There are many more practical uses for these techniques.

Other 'unsupported' capabilities discovered by, especially the older HP-65 Users Club, are keyboard overlays for development of more alphanumeric utility than noted above, use of non-normalized numbers, exotic programming techniques, and the list goes on and on.

Calculators in Education and the Simplicity of Elementary Programming on the Sinclair Cambridge

On pages ahead we discuss the pros and cons of the use of calculators in classrooms. One interesting experiment was conducted at Pennsylvania State University where 60 volunteers in a college-level introductory course in statistics worked both easy and difficult problems. One group did them manually, a second with a simple four-function calculator, and a third with an advanced calculator that had both memory and square-root functions. Upon completing the problems, the students answered a series of attitudinal questions about themselves; they worked individually at both tasks. The subjects who used calculators solved their problems faster and with fewer errors than those who did not, but this was expected. More importantly, they perceived themselves as more energetic, interested, and emotionally content than did the others who used pencils only. It is to be presumed that the users of calculators experienced comparatively less "cognitive strain" (i.e. they didn't have to think as hard). The students who used calculators also rated themselves as more competent than did their less fortunate colleagues; they perceived the problems they had solved as easier and more meaningful. The administrators of the experiment believe that the results provide strong support for those who advocate the classroom utility of calculators. Many people are afraid to work with num-

THE FEATURES OF THE SINCLAIR CAMBRIDGE PROGRAMMABLE

The Cambridge Programmable is genuinely pocketable. A mere 4½″ × 2″, it weighs about 2 oz. Yet there is absolutely no comparison in the package of functions it offers. Because the Cambridge Programmable is both a scientific calculator with memory, algebraic logic and brackets (which means you enter a calculation exactly as you write it), and a programmable calculator, it offers simple, flexible through-the-keyboard program entry and operation. The Cambridge Programmable has a 36-step program memory, and features conditional and unconditional branch instructions (go to and go if negative). There is also a step facility, which allows you to step through the program to check that it has been entered correctly. If there is any programming error, the learn key allows you to correct single steps without destroying any of the remainder of the program. To achieve this, each program key-stroke has an identifying code, or 'check symbol'. (The symbols for the digit keys are the digits themselves, while the symbols for the operator keys are letters printed beside the keys. The check symbol for ⊟ , for example, is F. So if, as you step through the program, the display shows

check symbol   step number

F.0000 25

it means that ⊟ is programmed as step 26. If step 26 should have been ⊞ , all you have to do is press

learn

puts machine into
'learn' mode.   the correct step

It's as simple as that!

These facilities make the Cambridge Programmable exceptionally powerful, whether it's running programs you devise for yourself or the programs in the Program Library.

bers and feel threatened by them — and hand-held calculators definitely ease this computational anxiety and can thus have a major impact on human quantitative performance. The use of calculators by women for solving mathematical problems might be especially rewarding to them because, as many recent articles in the press have indicated, a great many are precluded from taking advanced scientific courses due to their sometimes (they think) inherent distaste for taking courses in mathematics, many of which are prerequisites. Some colleges recognize this problem and are doing something to help resolve the enigma. Mills College in Oakland, CA operates precalculus workshops and courses designed to give college women "positive experiences" in math. Since the program began, enrollment in math courses by women has tripled at Mills College. Calculators can certainly help. But it is the contention of the authors that the programmable aspects of new calculator users are most important. One of the lowest cost and easiest machines to use in initial learning steps is the "below $30" Sinclair Cambridge as shown below. Extensive discussion is developed on pages ahead about this unit and the very similar Litronix 2290 below $30 unit.

The reader can study the photos of the Sinclair Cambridge Programmable for $30 and then compare-read the information on the caption of the photo of the Texas Instruments' SR-60A. The relative merits of each show the basics of the simplest programmable and then jump to one of the most sophisticated. Everything in between can be found in the chapters ahead, because this is the range. Although this is only a brief introduction to the world of calculators and judged to be quite necessary for the reader to note in order to develop a full perspective on the industry and products, it would not be a proper introduction without some projections of 'what's coming next.' It certainly is most difficult to predict what manufacturers plan to market or to try to 'divine' what's on designer's minds. However, some observers have made a few judgements concerning the future. The success of card-programmables such as the HP-67/97 units and the TI-59 has enticed competition. APF Electronics officials have stated they have a model 'Mark 90' Keyprogrammable with 72 steps of programming capability to market as a competitor to the TI-57 and in the same $70 to $80 price range. It is a good guess that it will be followed by a card programmable to undercut the HP models and do battle with the TI-58 and TI-59. Certainly more solar-powered units will appear rapidly and so also will many non-volatile memory types (memory stays with power off). Teal Industries, for example, makes a calculator that can operate off the light generated by a candle, has no on/off switch and uses an LCD (Liquid Crystal) display. The officials of the Japanese company suggest that all their models will soon be solar-powered. And HP is so sold on their "Continuous Memory" models that most of their line might soon have this capability. Commodore Business Machines has marketed its PR100 keyprogrammable unit with 76 steps and is said to be flooded also with production and marketing tasks of its $600 PET the finest of lines between advanced calculators and home computers. But that little powerhouse hand-held programmable still has many price and perfor-little powerhouse hand-held programmable still has great price and perfor-mance advantages over the larger and more complex $500 'plus' home computers.

With more and more Japanese companies opting for programmables, observers perceive rapidly expanding markets for them particularly in schools. And, those school population numbers are very big and very enticing. Sharp Electronics, one of the major Japanese manufacturers, is offering its PC1201 for about $90 which has 128 program steps and 12 memories. It has non-vola-

PERSONAL COMPUTER/CALCULATOR FROM TI

Like the model SR-60 personal computer/calculator, Texas Instruments' SR 60A, serves as the heart of a business system. It provides the power of a computer with the usage simplicity and low cost of a calculator. An ideal problem solver for small business, SR 60A uses a microprocessor to control an optional letter quality typewriter with full input/output capability for full-page reports and multiple-copy forms printouts. The microprocessor can also control up to two digital quality cassette tape drives with file management capability for on-line storage and retrieval of payroll records, inventory status and sales orders. Serial communications capability is also available, allowing the SR 60A system to communicate with computers and other devices.

A broad range of business problems can be handled with the SR 60A, including inventory, payroll, general ledger, accounts receivable, income tax and pensions. What makes the SR 60A especially suitable for business situations is its large display that "asks" questions or gives instructions in plain English. Answers are given by pressing the appropriate response keys — Yes, No, Not Apply, Not Known — or the instrument will give instructions to enter information which is available, such as hours worked or number of shares. The user enters the number asked for and presses the "enter" key; the SR 60A then asks for this information in the proper sequence to process it and gives the answer in seconds. Throughout this process, the built-in 20-character alphanumeric printer identifies pertinent data with words for additional ease in analysis. The basic machine, which weighs 16 lbs., provides up to 2640 program steps or 330 data registers, expandable to 7920 program steps or 990 data registers with optional memory modules. A special partitioning feature allows the user to allocate program step/memory resources to fit his specific program. Over 250 programs are available, and custom programs to solve special problems can be created right on the keyboard by the user or by a TI dealer. Calculations are further simplified by TI's AOS™ algebraic operating system, which allows equations to be entered left-to-right, as normally written. The SR 60A, which replaces the SR 60, has a suggested retail price starting at $1995. (see Chapter 6) tile storage capability with the inclusion of two silver-oxide batteries. A program library of over 60 routines and games was immediately available. The unit incorporates a vacuum fluorescent display and uses an audible signal, a beeper, to indicate when keys are depressed during programming. This beeper can also be employed by the user, under program control, to give an audible indication of any kind to alert the user that he must do something, e.g. a prompting capability. The PC1201 is a full scientific version with all standard functions found on most advanced scientific models. A lower cost model uses a six-position thumbwheel switch that changes the function of four calculator keys. The EL5001 (at below $50) thus has a convertable keyboard enabling the machine to perform calculations in statistics, equations, vector analysis, coordinate conversions, plotting and integration. The thumbwheel eliminates 15 extra keys.

Casio calculators will use CMOS chips, like HP, to conserve battery power — one machine boasts a battery life of 13,000 hours. Another can operate continuously for 1800 hours on two silver-oxide batteries. The example given is that if a person uses the calculator for an average of 20 minutes daily, the batteries will have to be replaced every 15 years. The Casio FX201P that sells for less than $200 is an advanced scientific unit that is both keystroke and magnetic card programmable and can accommodate 144 program steps per card. Practically all observers agree that the next steps in advanced hand-held programmable units will be the addition of video displays of multiple-line and graphics capabilities. Sinclair already makes a 'pocket' TV set and might be in the forefront with a calculator capability add-on. A second point on which there is much agreement is that future units will have high level language capability — perhaps a 'Tiny Basic' compiler or interpreter in a ROM module.

Big competition to Advanced Desk-Top Calculators: $600 Personal Computers. A personal microcomputer for your home is being offered by Radio Shack, the nationwide electronics store chain. For about the price of a color TV, the new Radio Shack TRS-80 Microcomputer System can be used for personal finance management, storing recipes, menu planning and to play an ever-increasing number of computer games, including blackjack and backgammon.

This necessitates an alphanumeric keyboard — and thumbwheels is one way to handle this. Also, for the novice (anti-programming) users, prompting instructions are bound to be a key item for pocket models; TI already does this on their SR-60A desktop. Certainly, easily insertable modules such as the TI ROMs are leading thrust — and with the exciting games in the 'Leisure' module leading the way, anybody and everybody can have real fun — and receive a great education in problem-solving with these excellent "under $100" machines. And, these price-performance calculator miracles will probably never cease in happily startling the always curious 'try anything once' consumer — if the price is right. And, it certainly is now — as the pages ahead prove. . . .

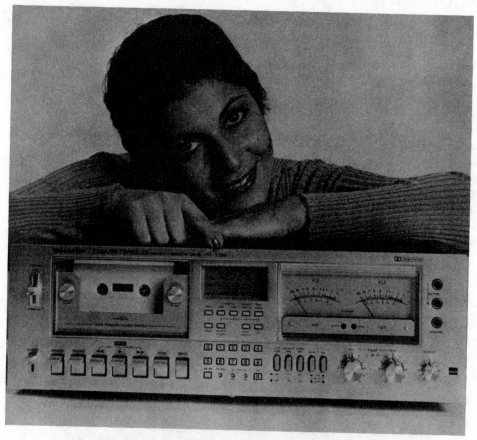

CALCULATOR-KEYBOARD MICROPROCESSOR CONTROLLED CASSETTE TAPE DECK BY SHARP ELECTRONICS CORPORATION — AND MORE PROGRAMMABLE APPLIANCES COMING

Sharp Electronics Corporation in late 1977 introduced the audio industry's first microprocessor-controlled cassette tape deck. Officially called, "Computer Controlled Stereo Cassette Deck RT-3388", it has five forms of memory. It can be directed to find the start and automatically play any song on a cassette by going either forward or in reverse. It can be programmed to turn itself on and off, and has both rewind and tape counter memory. It can even be programmed to repeatedly play a certain segment of a tape. Heart of the microprocessor unit is a Liquid Crystal Display digital quartz clock and "command post". Not only is time displayed, but the "command post" shows the user what other functions the cassette deck is performing. The RT-3388 carrys a suggested retail price of under $300.

CALCULATOR INCLUDED IN BALLY VIDEO GAME —
CASSETTES INCLUDE MATH EDUCATION AND ART . . .

The Bally Professional Arcade has commercial arcade excitement and fun, and that all begins with Professional-arcade games. The computer-like console comes with the popular Checkmate, Gunfight games and a sophisticated 4-function, 10-memory printing calculator built in. The Bally Professional Arcade works for its owner as well as entertains him. It's a sophisticated 4-function, 10-memory printing calculator with scroll button and entry correction, capable of reconciling bank balances, computing taxes and the like.

CHAPTER 1

THE CALCULATOR — ITS PROGRESS: PAST AND PRESENT

INTRODUCTION TO CALCULATOR CAPABILITIES AND PROGRESS

The Competition for Market Shares for the Hand-Held Programmables . . . With or Without Printers

Markets in the calculator industry have been multiplying. The recent advances in hardware technology reflect the strong trends toward programmables and special-purpose calculators in engineering, business, and industry. Advances in hardware technology have increased the performance capabilities of programmable calculators to the point where they rival and sometimes beat minicomputers. The more pragmatic designers of calculator products have historically been more user-oriented than minicomputer designers; the more advanced programmable calculators are far easier to use than minis and often offer equivalent or higher performance at less cost. The enhanced calculator capabilities in internal programming and memory, as noted in chapters ahead, have resulted in full system machines in the broadest context. Also manufacturers have rushed new designs of special application calculators with distinct capabilities for the individual markets, as for accountants, brokers, architects, inventory control, etc., all with alterable programmed controls and capabilities, and all at relatively low cost. And the trend toward even lower prices for the vast range of machines continued through 1977. Various models, Texas Instruments units and Hewlett-Packard units, are shown here but are discussed in detail in Chapter 4. (Pictures of other manufacturer's many hand-held programmables are displayed in other sections of this book.)

These developments in the calculator field mean great savings in time and cost to the ultimate consumer, both for personal calculator use and for *office* use in the business, scientific and industrial communities. The buyers of calculators in 1977 got more for their money than ever before, and this should continue as more years pass and competition remains intense. New innovations in both product capability, quality, and design, coupled with new emphasis on product utility, reflect consumer demands for greater reliability at all price levels. The point where a $5.00 throw-away calculator will be acceptable might even be reached very soon. The industry today has reached a point in sophistication where it can provide programmables or offer machines tailored to any individual needs. The customer need not fit his needs to the machines available. Many manufacturers have happily and very successfully designed custom machines that will fit any customer's individual need. One might almost say they can purchase a **tailor-made** machine, but at costs like suits off the rack . . . and the racks continually fill with newer and better models.

Most People Like Calculators and Still Fear Computers

The cost of computer equipment, time, the inconvenience of waiting for turns at terminals, plus the problem of having to learn, remember, and use special machine languages, special procedures and rules, are just a few reasons that push people to individual programmables or **systems** calculators. And this is true for businessmen, professionals, teachers, students and especially engineers and scientists. Calculator designers have been able to almost completely remove the machine language-special rules barriers. Instead of forcing users to adapt to the complex machine, calculators have been adapted to users, and they use the math language most grew up with or can quickly learn. The simple BASIC language, is also used on some models as noted on pages ahead. The calculator *systems* are also designed for the easiest interaction between user and machine. There are generally no tough or easily misunderstood machine *system* rules or difficult *coding-type* languages to learn for this processing either . . . just natural, English-like programming, special function keys and a simple keyboard. These units automatically do math, statistics, invoicing, inventory control, or solve hundreds of other problems exactly the way users would ordinarily write them down . . . and these capabilities are *expandable* through programs . . . not hardware.

The greatest challenge to manufacturers of calculators today is to develop ranges of low cost peripherals which match their units in low price, pragmatic performance, small size and steady reliability. The consumer step-up is from very low-cost 4-6 function machines — usually to programmable pocket-sized units, then to pocket desk calculators that print and display, then to even more sophisticated key-changing, ROM/RAM computer types. The last type offers as much memory as needed and as many peripherals as the user desires. They perform tasks similar to the problems resolved by many standard computers — automatically, accurately, and with special easy-to-use keys, tape cassettes or *slip-in* strips, cards, etc., and even complete **interior-insertable** microprocessors. The typical low-cost **fully** (exterior media) programmable calculator (hand-held) permits storage of up to 480 computation (program memory) steps and requires entry of nothing but the numbers for each problem. User-developed programs recorded on magnetic cards or strips are easy. ROM chips, cartridges, or cassettes, etc., are developed and maintained by manufacturers, and whole libraries of them have become available free with machines or commercially for rent or purchase. The X-Y plotters, typewriters, printers, etc., at very low cost permit engineers and scientists to type in or plug in graphic output problems for immediate preprogrammed solutions and with output of even *devilish* formats from and/or with complex programs formerly requiring costly large system processing. This chapter *opens the door.* . . .

The TI Programmable 57 calculator has product features and associated learning materials for students and others who want to learn programming fundamentals.

The TI Programmable 58 calculator is shown with the PC-100 A printer.

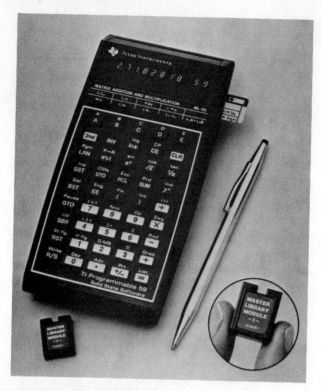

The TI Programmable 59 calculator is shown with a Master Solid State Software Library module.

Texas Instruments' key programmable business calculator, the MBA, offers excellent financial capabilities with a 'learn' key that remembers the user's own program sequence of up to 32 steps, repeatable with the push of a single key.

POWERFUL PAIR: New, fully programmable personal calculators from Hewlett-Packard have as much as three times the program memory capacity as predecessor, the HP-65. The HP-67 pocket-sized calculator and the HP-97 printing calculator both perform the same functions, and programs recorded on tiny magnetic cards on either machine will work on the other. HP-97 provides printed record of calculations, operations, memory and program registers.

APF ELECTRONICS, INC. OFFERS A POWERFUL LOW-COST
PREPROGRAMMED AND PROGRAMMABLE UNIT — AND NA-
TIONAL SEMICONDUCTOR A FINE CALCULATOR-WATCH.

CALCULATOR/WATCH in the timekeeping mode: continuous read
display of hours, minutes, seconds counter; month/date calendar;
dual night viewing lights and AM indicator. In the calculator mode:
Algebraic logic; Scientific notation; trigonometric and logarithmic
functions; store/recall memory; pi; powers of numbers keys; register
exchange and reciprocal keys.

Caught up in the data deluge, scientists, engineers, managers and researchers of all types have found better, faster, more accurate and economical ways and means of acquiring and handling data. They have discovered and fallen in love with their calculators. Most of these happy *personal* data processor owners are not content with four-to-six simple function machines. The fast, accurate arithmetic functions are fine — even the *scientific* models with *special function keys* (SFKs) or the specially *tailored* professional models designed precisely for statisticians, brokers, realtors, bankers, engineers, surveyors, and a score or more of other specialists still don't have enough *power* and versatility, or indeed, challenge. The magic and the real power of the calculator world is *programmability*. The more than 100 million calculator users in the world seem to be continually amazed at the great performance variety and extra utility that they can purchase for such small amounts of money when they buy programmable calculators. But, weren't they complex and difficult to use? Not at all! During the year 1976, an expanding number of constantly curious potential users became even more pleasantly surprised when they became aware of new *consumer* **programmable** calculators for as little as $30. And other programmables with wide ranges of remarkable professional capabilities are also selling for under $100.

Most amazing and satisfying of all, however, were the very significant 1976 price reductions of exterior or *fully* programmable 224-step hand-held units that began selling for $300 to $400 by such excellent-reputation manufacturers as the Texas Instruments, Hewlett-Packard, National Semiconductor and other companies. Many calculator users, especially accountants, statisticians and scientists, were made even happier when they discovered that their programmable hand-held units, or small desk-top units also had printing capabilities and yet retailed for less than $600 to $800. Other 1976 developments included the highly competitive mass marketing of many of these units with *nonvolatile* memories and solar cell power. Programs and data stored in these calculators no longer *disappear* when the units are turned off — and the worry is gone of accidental erasures of hours of important work. Alphanumeric and two color displays appeared. The great calculator year of 1976 also offered far greater ranges and availabilities of software — very pragmatic, easy-to-use, and most valuable and versatile programs. And these became widely available in various media, as: magnetic strips, cards, cassettes, cartridges, disks, and plug-in *Read-Only Memories* — the very fast, high capacity, and low-cost PROMs. But the axiom of the calculator industry remains — " . . . whatever the manufacturers are offering in the calculator lines today, something better will be available tomorrow. Neither the designers nor the manufacturers can specify for any set length of time what they intend to bring out . . . this year, or even this month." This is indeed a vigorous and volatile industry.

Some Brief Historical Notes

Some researchers date the origin of the modern electronic calculator to an Electronics show in Boston in 1963 when a $5000 novel all-electronic calculator was exhibited and labeled the *Mathatron*. It was judged by the new entrepreneurs to be the perfect compromise between the electromechanical standard four-function ("adding") machine and the (then) small $20,000 computer. A new niche in the field of computation was thus opened and the start of massive competition against all the *old reliable* adding machine manufacturers (Friden, Monroe, Olivetti, Victor, etc.) began. Unfortunately Mathatronics no longer exists as a company to reap the rewards of its founders foresight. But such enterprising companies as Wang Laboratories, Victor, Sharp, and a few other early pioneers and (in 1968) Hewlett-Packard joined in early fiercely competitive battles. Several hundred companies quickly followed and many exited when the pace quickened.

At first these calculators were market-aimed almost exclusively at engineers and users of calculator-controlled instrumentation systems. Hewlett-Packard blazed a trail, with Wang, by offering a few calculator-controlled network analyzers and computing counters, and these battles were quickly joined by Tektronics, Inc. In such systems, calculators act as the control brains collecting and analyzing data from measuring instruments, and by directing programmable generators to force functions onto the system under test. Hewlett-Packard developed a commanding lead by exploiting this technology into programmable hand-held calculators and by constantly widening the range and specialized capabilities of desk-top units. Many other American and several Japanese, Hong Kong, Taiwan, and British firms began a deluge of consumer markets with low-priced units, bringing rather fantastic calculator capabilities down into the $20 and now *below $10* price ranges. The prediction of electronic calculators *as common as the pen* might well come true. Texas Instruments, with a very large share of the market, selling to more than 30,000 retail outlets, noted in early 1976* that the 1975 calculator market had increased to 45 million units, or 51 per cent over 1974 ". . . and that sales in 1976 were expected to total 58 million units at a $1.7 billion selling price."

Calculators became so low-priced, due to their near fully-automated mass production, that they became premiums for thousands of contests, attendance prizes, etc.; they are given away with store coupons and sold in photographic stores, stationers, appliance dealers, department and discount stores, electronics and the new *computer* stores, radio and phonograph shops and through dozens of mass marketing catalog houses. An executive of a leading calculator chip manufacturer, Rockwell International, recently stated, "The market for calculators which was originally predicted as substantial, turned out to be enormous." Calculator components and *package* designers have now become very consumer-oriented. And in 1976, with hundreds of companies *shaken out* of the markets by the strong competitive production and marketing efficiencies, the remaining stalwarts began to use closely-defined marketing programs of *trading up* the existing 100 million users to new products. The $1.7 billion 1976 figure will reach well over $2 billion quickly as the newer, more versatile, powerful programmables, with printers, cassettes, cartridges, disks, ROMs, etc. bring the former users of lower-cost units "up" into the *2nd generation* units with nonvolatile memories, and fancy displays. They also offer massive **exterior** data and program storage media, devices, and facilities, and scores of new calculator output peripherals. And all of these items are offered at very surprising low customer costs, and with consumer-oriented easy-to-use capabilities, "everybody is becoming his own programmer."

The bewildering array of more than 400 calculator brands and models in 1974 from up to 100 manufacturers and fabricators have settled now down to under 200 major mass sale units from 30 to 40 world-wide marketing manufacturers. Happily also, a degree of standardization and price/function comparison is being achieved. Most discreet components formerly *off the chip* are being placed *on* single or fewer chips, cutting the cost of manufacturing and assembling of calculators. Generic (lines of) chips are developed with relatively inexpensive change of (manufacturing) mask, and features are now incorporated to

---

*Electronic News, April 26, 1976, p. 6.

prevent erroneous entry of digital data through bouncing of key contacts, or from electrical noise, or accidental depression of more than one key. Many units now have multiple-colored (multi-function) keys, many with indicia on tops, sides, and below key position. New component techniques have tripled and quadrupled the life ("trickle power") of batteries for portables. And thousands of users are learning a great deal from each other as to which models are better, faster, more convenient, and they purchase on these recommendations. But, the technology is advancing so rapidly that without advice or *guide* books, practically all other new users are at a loss or are totally confused when looking at the calculator marketplace. This is principally due to the new jargon — almost totally foreign to most amateur buyers . . . and this also includes the noncomputer-oriented engineers, a dying-out breed.

CALCULATOR CLASSIFICATION SYSTEM

The maze of the calculator marketplace can be organized into a relatively basic structure of calculator types, their components and capabilities. On a rather primitive but functional basis the classifications fall into groups of three — three general *classifications* of calculating instruments; three *types of operating units* in each classification; three primary characteristics of each type of unit, three types of memory; three types of logic; three types of software (programs) and 3 general classes of peripherals. This organization system hopefully will provide a pathway for the eager calculator purchaser — whether he or she is a high school student, a manager of a large bank or industry, or an engineer, office worker, salesman or practically any other type worker or hobbyist.

Practically all calculators are: Hand-Held (pocket); Desk-Top (display or printing, or both) or computing (control systems). These are the basic and broad classifications, and within *each class* the calculator will either be: (A) Basic — Four-to-Six Function; (B) Preprogrammed (Basic or Advanced) and (C) Programmable (Basic or Advanced).

CALCULATORS: CLASS AND FUNCTION STRUCTURE

CLASS

I. HAND-HELD	II. DESK-TOP	III. COMPUTING
A. Four-Six Function	A. Four-Six Function	A. Prompting/ Peripherals
B. Preprogrammed	B. Preprogrammed	B. Exterior Memories/ High Level Languages
C. Programmable	C. Programmable	C. CRT Computing Systems

TYPE

A. FOUR-SIX FUNCTION	B. PREPROGRAMMED	C. PROGRAMMABLE
1. Arithmetic	1. Slide-Rule/Scientific	1. Keyboard/Temporary
2. Memory	2. Business/Financial	2. Card, Tape, ROM (Permanent)
3. Special Function Keys (SFKs)	3. Professional/Specialist	3. Language/Interactive

MEMORY TYPES

1. Intermediate Storage
2. Addressable Storage (direct/indirect)
3. Automatic Input-Output Storage

LOGIC TYPES

1. Arithmetic
2. Algebraic
3. Reverse Polish Notation (RPN)

SOFTWARE (PROGRAMS)
1. Simple Formula
2. Decision-making
3. Interactive/microprogrammable

PERIPHERALS
1. Input-Output
2. Communication
3. Control (Remote)

The Hand-Held, Preprogrammed, and Programmable Classes all carry subgroups as either: Basic or Advanced.

Thus a Desk-Top (Class) Type B-2 would be a: Desk-Top Preprogrammed Business/Financial Calculator. Because its preprogrammed and not programmable, it would have no exterior software capability. But, it could have Memory Type 2, Indirect Addressable Storage, and Type 3 Logic, RPN, and Type 1 Peripherals, i.e., Input-Output (printer, or voice output).

It will be difficult to discover any calculator that does not fall within these three Broad Classes, Functional Types, or Memory, Logic, Software or Peripherals groups.

An example of the *confusion* of the calculator marketplace follows: One research firm, the Buyers Laboratory, Inc., of Hackensack, NJ, completed the BLI 1974 and 1975 Electronic Calculator Reports. These reports covered more than 200 selected machines, and presented the lab's recommendations in each of 13 categories of electronic calculators. The categories and numbers show the extensiveness of the field at these times. They were as follows:

Battery operated mini-calculators (39 machines; included in 1975, 65.)
Non-memory display machines (15 machines; included in 1975, 16.)
One-memory display machine (28 machines; included in 1975, 37.)
Two or more memory display machines (11 machines; included in 1975, 37.)
Printers with display (24 machines; included in 1975, 23.)
Non-memory printers (7 machines; included in 1975, 18.)
One-memory printers (41 machines; included in 1975, 52.)
Two or more memory printers (15 machines; included in 1975, 16.)
Financial machines (9 machines; included in 1975, 9.)
Statistical machines (12 machines; included in 1975, 10.)
Commercial machines (8 machines; included in 1975, 5.)
Engineering machines (22 machines; included in 1975, 43.)
General-purpose programmables (18 machines; included in 1975, 13.)
(See "Calculator Classification System".)

An initial trend of many manufacturers was to produce and sell many different models. A popular marketing photograph by Rockwell International, for example, showed 11 versions of the same basic electronic calculator being produced by simple changes in the microprogram of the same generic chip. But, early in 1976 even Texas Instruments cut its extensive line down to 12 models, requiring less parts overall, and new designs cut costs for individual units. New models continue to be introduced, but more *older* types (2 or 3 year life) are dropped. Hopefully, the industry might soon standardize on much more of at least the basic technology and terminology, such as: functions, keys, memories, instructions, etc. Currently, what one vendor calls a storage register is called a memory by another and an automatic accumulating register by a third; still another vendor calls it simply a register, or even an **accumulating** memory. One can hardly blame customers for their complaints of *jargon* confusion.

The Programmable Calculator Market: A Brief
Analysis and Some Projections

The electronic calculator market, we have noted earlier, burgeoned to an estimated billion dollars in 1973, more than doubled in units and practically doubled in dollars in 1976 as the calculator and its peripherals moved to more business offices and into schools and the home. The electronic calculator market now is characterized as having: (1) significant size, (2) speeding technological progress, (3) many new customer segments, (4) continuing growth potential, and (5) one that is forging new large markets in all countries around the world.

The calculator markets are subdivided into many segments (see chart) but basically into **programmable** (hand-held or desk-top) and **non-programmable** units. Programmable-type calculators were initially sold almost solidly in the scientific, engineering, and a few business markets. Now, programmability is the choice of teachers, students, many types of professionals, government and office workers, and an absolute must for all engineers and math people. They have now become a large and growing proportion for all 50+ million-per-year calculator sales. Initially, some relatively expensive products had capability too tightly tailored to a particular profession such as *slide-rule* types for engineering people or *payment schedules* for financial people. But now the wide consumer, and total scientific and business markets utilize programmable **general-purpose** display and printing calculators, priced and merchandised with great ranges of software availability on cards, strips, tapes, ROMs, etc. (The H-P Users Club has 5000 programs for H-P units alone.) The electronic calculator market's annual growth rates have been 30% to 40% over the past three years and should continue at these rates to thereby increase substantially in numbers and dollar sales for another several years at least. Some as yet nearly untapped very large markets, especially primary and secondary teaching aids, will significantly enhance the sociological importance of the electronic calculator.

The earliest professional machines used TTL (transistor-transistor logic), were programmable, and in most cases were intended for scientific or statistical applications. In 1969, however, the Japanese and others introduced very low-cost four-function calculators based on metal oxide semiconductor/large scale-integrated (MOS/LSI) circuit technology. This forced the U.S. to offer competitive electronic units to protect market positions. By purchasing the more advanced U.S. semiconductor technology the Japanese, using their historical low-cost manufacturing capabilities, began to drive aggressive pricing into the markets. In late 1971, however, the U.S. share of the calculator market had grown dramatically, due to breakthroughs and the consequent rapidly lowered prices for American semiconductors, displays, and keyboards. Americans also developed the drastic reduction in assembly costs attributable to the availability of unique two- and three-chip calculator designs and mass-production techniques for microprocessors. One-chip, hand-held calculators were also introduced in the U.S. in late 1972. The U.S. quickly regained sales leadership but again lost it for the domestic 4-6 function calculator market. But, it practically controls 80% of the world market for programmable types. The giant American semiconductor suppliers of MOS/LSI calculator chips now integrated them into the manufacture of other types of finished games, devices, and machines. A major portion of the cost of a small calculator is in the semiconductor processor chip and the LED (Light Emitter Diode) displays. Labor is now minimal. In 1974 calculators in the $20 to $30 retail price range were plentiful and sales were brisk. But, also during the 1971-76 5-year period, many purchasers of electronic calculators in the United States began to *tradeup* to fully programmable hand-held types. In 1976, prices for the best units decreased from $800 to around four hundred dollars and less. Even at the higher prices in 1974, this *programmables* market began to take off strongly and in many directions. Today the tremendously versatile programmables are near *miracles of personal computing power.*

The scientific and business *old time* calculator markets quickly showed a distinct and full transition from slide rules and "adding" machines to **all-electronic** calculators. The wide variety of scientific problems to which the programmable scientific calculator can be applied has resulted in sophisticated but easily mastered programming techniques as well as low-cost, small-sized peripherals such as tape cartridges and cassettes, tape and card readers, printers, disks, ROMs, and plotters, plus others coming. The scientific and programmable calculator markets originally, and still, dominated by pioneering U.S. manufacturers such as Hewlett-Packard, Tektronix, Litton-Monroe, Wang, and others now find that Rockwell, Olivetti, Victor, National Semiconductor, and Texas Instruments also offer fierce competition. Worldwide sales of fully **programmable** scientific or general purpose calculators supplied mostly by U.S. manufacturers totaled over $200 million in 1976 and are growing at a rapidly expanding rate with American firms expanding their lead in units and **systems** selling at prices from under $200 to $8000.

Hewlett-Packard was one of the first to combine the features of a low-cost hand-held unit with those of the original programmable scientific instrument control calculators. Several large firms, including Texas Instruments and National Semiconductor, then introduced families of competing hand-held machines aimed, initially again, at the engineering and scientific professions. This was soon followed by wide acceptance and use by the accounting and financial professions as brokers, bankers, insurance company personnel, etc., bought them. Then came general educational use of programmables. However, many still choose between *fully* programmables or highly specialized machines. Although the former are more versatile, the latter are specifically preprogrammed or key alterable with ROM.

With microprogramming technology it is feasible to build special-purpose desk-top portable but key-alterable calculators for a great variety of professionals such as surveyors, pilots, or civil engineers. The striking improvements in device complexity, lower prices, and production expansion capability provided by the semiconductor industry is causing the replacement desk-top mass market for calculators to flower also. With programmability, these units become excellent computer terminals, as noted on pages ahead.

The three major semiconductor products used in a typical calculator are the microprocessor, the display driver chips, and the LED display. Since 1970, the price of calculator processor chips had fallen from $30 to around $5 in 1973, and $2 and lower since then. During this same period, prices of LED displays have dropped to well under $.50 per digit. This was followed by the elimination of the display decoder/driver chip formerly required in many calculators. As we will note further in chapter 2, calculators use serial microprocessors operated under microprogram control in the form of read-only memories incorporated on the chip. Other complex program and data memories are added along with registers and interfaces for major operation units and systems. Modularity and micro-programmability make it possible to make families of processor chips that are applied to wide ranges of applications. Recently N-channel and CMOS devices have resulted in nonvolatility in some units (no loss of programs or data when the unit is turned off), and many circuit densities and chip power are being increased dramatically. There is now a wide availability of programmable microprocessor chip sets that are configured to bridge the computational gap between calculator and mini-computer, thus permitting many types of calculators to perform wide ranges of automated instrumentation, processing control, and simulation functions. Some printer mechanisms use drum type impact printers with a price of about $50 in large quantities. Thermal printers of improved reliability, in large volume purchases were about $35, and lower cost units and many other media and peripheral items are now also very common.

Future Prospects for the Late 1970s

Despite the rapid growth and its prior attendant appearance of chaos, the current somewhat *settled* future of the calculator market appears bright but challenging. Programmable calculators will continue to grow in sophistication and general purpose computational ability and will find an ever-widening group of students and other new users. Software support will make these new calculators an alternative to big computer time-sharing in many business and industrial environments. These desk-top programmables will spread calculator utilization because hundreds of thousands of clerical use calculator terminals for processing systems will be in use — many supporting or requiring networks. Business, financial, and scientific calculator users will concentrate over the next few years on replacing their millions of electromechanical units still in the field, most often with programmables. More than a million new electromechanical units were formerly being built each year for sale in the U.S. market. Their production has stopped. Thus, this considerable potential exists for the new *below $1000* programmable printing calculators. By 1978 they should be able to completely replace the entire market. Out with *adding machines* and in with programmable calculators . . . the business, financial, and research offices will never be the same. The challenges are enormous. The experienced users have little difficulty in justifying the replacement since greater capability is now available at the same or a lower price than their original units. The U.S. professional and technical work force is at least 12 to 15 million people. This covers hundreds of old and new job classifications. The potential for also expanding the professional calculator markets with many new users, appears very good, specifically because millions of student users would be *lost* without their *trusty* calculators.

Consumer programmable calculators should continue to experience annual unit growth rates in excess of the former 30 to 40% range. Increased awareness and student education is needed. The burgeoning 4-6 function consumer market had just started to open up with the capability upgrades of $30 to $40 low-cost units, but it then exploded with many millions of $10 and $20 units. It is now continuing to expand with *electronic* check books, wrist calculators, and scores of $60 to $70 electronic *slide-rules,* now with programs. The United States has more than 60 million families. Many forecasters see two or three calculators per family. The dimensions of this consumer market added to the great potential of over 15 million high school students are well known to semiconductor manufacturers, calculator manufacturers, and to mass merchandizing retailers. All are excited about the massive hand-held consumer markets and the programmable calculator market surges. Up to mid-1974 relatively little consumer education or hard sell had been necessary to move large quantities of single calculators. There is no longer any reluctance on the part of educational institutions to permit widespread use of these handy and accurate educational appliances. A growing number of universities and community colleges offer credit for "How-to" classes in calculator applications courses. A great many students no longer use slide rules for their math operations. Practically all teachers now also permit the use of calculators in classwork and examinations (see *Points of Progress* below). Personal calculators are big sales items in department stores and are made bigger by distributing through traditional college book store outlets and through direct mail sales by many manufacturers. There already exists a large and growing used calculator market. Most calculator suppliers are strongly encouraging and stimulating the *upgrade* markets. The obsolescence factor has caused a *throwaway* psychology for many types of personal and old-fashioned professional calculators. New calculator units with mass memory, or specific data base assistance are being used in teaching machines, and this plus their use as "home computer (hobbyist) terminals" takes on new sociological implications. Calculator-based, self-instructional automated machines have come into widespread experimental educational usage. The impact on teachers, unions, and teacher associations of low-cost massive, easy-use remote two-way or stand-alone calculator-terminal applications in homes is exciting. As stressed in Chapter 4, calculator *million word* memories on cartridges and cassettes are the biggest value around in *computing* calculators.

Many scientists, engineers, and managers who would like to fully automate their complex measurements, or widespread, remote entry information systems, most often do not require all the complex capability offered by the standard or mini-computer systems. And they very often are working on strict and limited budgets. The speed and memory capabilities of the current programmable calculators enable them to solve these automation **system** requirements without destroying their tight budgets. The key to the problems is now very often the rapid development of calculator-based systems. The end user can often design and construct these himself without significant interface design or large consultant fees. These units and their put-together systems allow the end-user to buy the specific internal processor of his choice. The calculator *shell* he desires and the other system components of his preference, can simply be plugged all together . . . "and go." Often this whole procedure is accomplished with minimum "free" consultation with supplier engineers over a very brief time period . . . and with **no** *computer-scared* employees.

The Use of Calculators in Schools

Some years ago the use of calculators by some students and not others for class work, home work, and especially examinations became a very fiery issue among both teachers and students. In some areas of the U.S. and several foreign countries the conceptual and pragmatic battles still run. There are many arguments on both sides, and a brief summary of some of them might profitably be developed at this point. The general conclusion by the majority of the people who have debated the issue at length is that, yes, calculator use should be permitted by students in schools, but that several very significant problems must be resolved first . . . especially before they're permitted during examinations.

It is admitted by both sides that the dramatic drop in the price of hand-held units places them within the buying power of practically all students. In many sections of the U.S. it is equally likely to find them in school bags as it is in business briefcases. College students especially are opting for speedier, easier, more accurate calculator procedures for solving lengthy mathematical, business, or scientific problems. And both parents and teachers are being *bugged* very doggedly now about the fairness of some students having and using them and not others. These conflicts are most vociferous in most high schools and a growing number of grade schools. Although the use of the *magic* problem-solvers in either secondary or elementary schools is growing, the former small percentage of users has kept the problem from major parent-teacher-student clashes or school board decisions, but the *get ready* sign is definitely up. And with low level *consumer* programmables selling for under $30; excellent *scientific* key programmables costing well under $100, and fully programmables at $200 and $400, the determination of *allow or not allow* becomes a bit more complex. And the numbers of students involved are becoming astronomical . . . current and future. The problem won't disappear; instead, it will grow in intensity.

The Points of Argument Enumerated

Although most points below relate to fairness to individual students, others definitely imply major problems for school boards, principals, and individual teachers . . . and to teachers of many different classes. (1) All students cannot afford calculator units despite their low prices, and even if so, they often become broken, lost, stolen, or forgotten. Allowing full and general use of them in class, at home, or for tests then would obviously place the poorer or otherwise unequipped student at a disadvantage, and unfairly so, and many teachers, parents and students object strenuously. (2) If a basic type model is permitted and/or furnished to those without them for temporary use, isn't it also unfair to forbid the more industrious, wealthier, or highly challenged students to own and use a higher capability, more expensive and sophisticated machine? The fairness doctrine works both ways, and the very clever elementary and secondary school students are not only using these, but an increasing number are computer club members as well. (3) If some school boards, specific schools or teachers stipulate exact capabilities or models to be permitted, it might easily appear they were endorsing or advertising for certain manufacturers. (4) The problem of numbers is immense, precluding the distribution or forced charge of *school units,* at least in a great many environments. During examinations at some schools and colleges, between 40,000 to 60,000 printed numerical tables and charts are furnished. Consideration then must be given not only to initial costs of furnishing, but also to the problems of maintenance and obsolescence. (5) The competitive "equal-less than equal" school facilities battles are already very hot in the U.S. If some schools furnish calculators to their students — or even *allow* them, other Parent Teachers Associations, Teachers Unions, etc., could easily scream justifiably about unequal systems, facilities, grades, and opportunities. (6) Many textbooks are now available and in demand, especially in Mathematics, Statistics, various sciences, and engineering disciplines that are structured around the use of calculators, just as slide rules were previously and in some cases still are. Are there to be sets of rules as to specific machine capability levels, some programs permitted while others are forbidden? What about capabilities such as the exotic mass-memory, high-level languages, desk-tops? (7) A significant number of schools now offer courses in calculator operation. Certainly those students who become taught, exposed to, or who have gained expertise or proficiency in the operation of the better units will have advantages over students who must dig out these *complexities* themselves . . . the former getting great math and stat grades, the latter poorer ones. Is *Calculator 1* to become a required Freshman (high school or college) course . . . and what about those 7th and 8th grade calculator *geniuses?*

The Philosophical Argument on Calculator Use at School

One school superintendent was quoted along these lines, ". . . they are going to have a tremendous part to play in education. In a few years time we will be throwing away our slide rules and logarithm tables and every child will have a calculator . . . and I must say I'm looking forward to that time." Another school leader issues a warning about lethargy as regards the problem, ". . . we don't want to just drift willy-nilly into using calculators — we must decide whether to use them, and when and how to use them." Many teachers note that they are not only being used as adjuncts to the various course syllabi, like the slide rule, but in many cases, they are being **structured** into the teaching situation and the curriculum. Time for indecision, even for experimentation is now past in many institutions and localities. In summary of a lot of arguments pro and con, one leader suggests that children should not be **used** as calculating machines — rather let **them** use the machines.

The basic arguments against their use center around the concept that the calculator will become some sort of crutch and children will forget how to perform even the simplest calculations. Another way of stating this, "If you use calculators too much, you would be lost without them." These thoughts are countered with (in the case of a child from a Hongkong school), "Nobody would dream of swimming across the harbour when there are ferries." He further felt, echoing the thoughts of many classmates, that students, especially in high school, should be encouraged to use calculators in schools "because not only are they more accurate and time-saving — they would also provide training and practice for what some students might one day use in their work." He continued. "In an age where mechanisation and specialisation are the main themes, we need to become specialised ourselves, and if a machine can relieve us of the burden — we should use it." A retorting grumbler, remarked, ". . . calculators give one a false sense of security."* Thus, the problems are formidable, increasing; will the students force the issue?

Some Innovations, Products for Teaching Calculator Operations

As an introduction to this specific topic, a letter asking for assistance is reprinted from the publication, "People's Computer Company" (Vol. 4, No. 5, Mar.-Apr., 1976, p. 33), which is self-explanatory.

Calculator Curriculum Study

Dear Mathematics Educator, In just three years, more than a hundred million electronic calculators have come into common use. Millions more are on the way at prices almost anyone can afford. Clearly a fundamental change is occuring in the application of mathematics to everyday problems.

Such a large-scale innovation has implications for those of us involved in mathematics education. At the same time many research studies just being published, reveal an alarming decline in mathematics computational skills, concept understanding and problem analysis. An important area for all of us to examine is the role of the calculator in meeting the challenges revealed in these studies.

We are searching for answers to the question, will the hand-held calculator become a part of the problems or can it be the key to solving many of them? We need your help. Will you please permit us to

---

*Guterres, Halima, "Calculators: Should Students Use Them?", SOUTH CHINA MORNING POST (Hongkong), April 26, 1976, p. 3.

send you a copy of our Calculator Curriculum Study Question-
naire, along with our postpaid return envelope? We would appreciate
your time.

Sincerely yours,

DR RUTH HOFFMAN
Mathematics Laboratory
University of Denver
Denver CO 80210

The next issue (July, 1976, p. 41) of the publication contains an announcement
of a visual aid for calculator class instructors, as follows:

"A CALCULATOR FOR YOUR OVERHEAD PROJECTOR
Now available, a four-function calculator modified for use with an overhead
projector. Put it on your overhead projector and compute. Results appear in
large numerals on the screen, clearly visable to everyone in your classroom
or auditorium. For info, contact Stokes Publishing Company, P.O. Box 415,
Palo Alto, CA 94302."

The same issue continued the National Semiconductor QUIZKID announcement below.

CAI For $24.95

Now! For $24.95 you can free up a port on your HP 2000 or other
CAI drill and practice machine.

QUIZKID II — A timed series of 10 arithmetic problems appear
automatically in the display. The child, dragon or other learner is required to key in the answer to the problem shown in the display. Over
1200 problems are automatically generated by the calculator. A slow/
fast speed control key adjusts time allowed for the user to enter the
answer. Suggested retail, $24.95. Also available is an optional game
adapter which connects two QUIZKID II's for a contest.

National Semiconductor QUIZKID III — Has all the abilities of
QUIZKID II plus games for over 6,500 additional problems. Contains
amateur and pro keys for adjusting complexity of problems, and a
complex key for problems to be automatically displayed with one of
the factors missing but with the answer given. This model is being
test marketed.

For info, contact National Semiconductor, 2900 Semiconductor Dr.,
Santa Clara CA 95051, (408) 737-5000. (July '76 p. 41 PCC)

The EduCALC

An enterprising teacher is successful with his invention. **It's an EduCALC,
a teaching calculator with two display units.** It has the usual small, red
numerical readout facing you as you operate it, and also it has another BIG
display unit showing the same number in the opposite direction toward your
audience or class. Its big, bright neon digits have that same twinkling fascination for the viewer that has attracted him to his own calculator.

Compared to computers, the EduCALC plus students' calculators equals a teaching system which costs very little indeed, yet gets more student involvement. Much of EduCALC's success is due to its ease of use (no professional operator required) and low cost (every school can afford it). It can be employed concurrently in many different courses; its general purpose is to remove an overburden of calculation and reveal concepts.

Anyone who has tried to communicate numbers and calculations to other people knows the problem. The display digits are just too little to be read if you hold the calculator up to be seen, even before a small audience. Yet reading of the numbers loses attention and interest, and so does writing them on a blackboard. The EduCALC gives us a way to really hold an audience, a way to give our calculations "sex appeal".

This important new visual aid for teaching is in use at the University of California, for example. Users have found that it captures the attention of students all the way to the rear of a large, well-lit lecture theater.

The "Master" Calculator: Each EduCALC has its own built-in calculator. These calculators are made by Hewlett-Packard. Three different EduCALC models are available:

Model	Master
21 GD	HP-21 Scientific Calculator
22 GD	HP-22 Business Management Calculator
25 GD	HP-25 Programmable Scientific Calculator

Other models for the HP-67 became available later in 1977.

The "Slave" Display: When 115 VAC is supplied, the big display lights up toward the audience. This display is formed of planar gas discharge digits made by Beckman Instruments. They have a wide viewing angle of 130°, a spectacular legibility at 60 feet (18 meters) distance, and a life expectancy of ten years or more.

The Cabinet and Accessories: The EduCALC cabinet is an oak lectern which contrasts with the black face of the big display. It comes complete with a carrying case that doubles as a pedestal with which you can elevate the lectern above desk height. Also included with each EduCALC are the Owner's Manual and/or Application Handbook which are normally supplied with its master calculator.

The Interface Electronics: The EduCALC needs to electronically modify and amplify the signal levels and format of the pocket calculator display before they can be used to drive the big neon display. Medium Scale Integrated (MSI) circuits are used to demultiplex and buffer the calculator output. The engineering is conservative; each EduCALC is built and tested to function reliably for many years.

The Warranty: Each EduCALC is warranted against defects in materials and workmanship for one year from date of delivery.

Compared to computers, the EduCALC gives a really inexpensive teaching system. Students buy their own calculators, so the only expense is the EduCALC itself. Yet this system gets even more student involvement, more excited interest in the math.

This is a dramatic new sales, lecturing, and teaching tool. It costs no more than a good office typewriter. Many teachers have found that the money was readily available to them in budgets marked for "Innovative Projects" or "Curricular Development", as well as in the more customary "Audio Visual" or "Supplies and Equipment" accounts.

The price for the programmable model, the 25 GD, is $950, including delivery in the U.S.A. The 21 GD is $855, and the 22 GD sells at $920. There is a 15-day trial period during which you may return the machine to obtain a full refund if you are not satisfied.

To order one or to receive further information, write the manufacturer:

> Educational Calculator Devices
> P. O. Box 974
> Laguna Beach, CA 92652   (714) 497-3600

Texas Instruments Introduces Line of Special Calculator Products for Fun, Entertainment, Education

Calculators are now routinely used by families to figure gas mileage, bank balances, interest earned, mortgage costs. Others use them to have more accurate information to buy groceries, carpet a room, build a playhouse or to do homework assignments or find a faster, better way to figure Little League batting averages. Americans and calculator users around the world are doing all of these tasks and more—even playing games and having fun—with calculators. In fact, more than 100 million calculators are now in use worldwide and about half of U.S. households own one.

To help to fulfill a growing demand for calculator products that do more, Monroe National Semiconductor Corp. and Texas Instruments have announced new lines of calculator-based family gift products which include special extra materials for added utility. The new materials combine new learning experiences with fun and entertainment for both adults and children. A strong and expanding effort is demonstrated by the new calculator-associated materials, produced by Texas Instruments Learning Center in cooperation with leading educators. They include a special "how-to" book for household mathematics, student math kits for junior high up through college students, learning activities for elementary-age children and calculator board games for the family. The products became available through participating TI retail outlets in September, 1976.

Some of the new products are:

"Family Math" is a 52-page pocket-size book designed to be offered by retailers as a bonus value along with TI's new ultra-slim TI-1600 and TI-1650 calculators. These models have a suggested retail price of $24.95 and $29.95, respectively. The book is designed as a quick reference solution to everyday-life math problems in home finance, hobbies, do-it-yourself projects, sports, travel and consumer economics.

"The TI-1270 Student Math Kit" includes a calculator designed specifically for the needs of junior and senior high students, a special 80-page "how-to" book as an aid to classroom problems and personal student finances, a student carrying case with orange "racing stripes" and an A-C adapter. Suggested retail price is $18.95.

"The TI-30 Student Math Kit" includes a calculator designed specifically for high school level mathematics and beyond. Included in the student kit are a 200-page "how-to" book for classroom and everyday-life math problems plus a youth-oriented denim vinyl carrying case. Suggested retail price is $29.95.

"The Little Professor" is a learning aid for children five years and up. The Little Professor automatically generates a sequence of preprogrammed problems—more than 16,000 of them—and involves the child in an "instant feedback" learning experience. It allows the child to select problems geared to his level of skill. Included is a colorful, child-centered 32-page book of activities which motivate and teach through enjoyable involvement in mathematics games and exercises. Suggested retail price is $19.95.

"Check Out" is a new calculator board game incorporating a TI-1400 calculator. Developed with the aid of home economists and nutritionists, "Check Out" challenges two to four players to buy the best food values to win. The game and a special book help children and adults understand facts of good nutrition, improve ability to shop on a budget, sharpen skills at calculator math, and practice counting money and making change. For ages 11 and up, it has a suggested retail price of $19.95.

"Calculator Squares" is another new calculator board game which can be played with two to four people, age 12 and up. A strategy game involving luck, skill and suspense, "Calculator Squares" also includes a TI 1400 calculator. Suggested retail price is $17.95.

Texas Instruments, earlier in 1976, introduced a broad line of calculator-associated learning materials for use in classrooms from Kindergarten through high school. These institutional classroom products were developed by educators at leading universities in conjunction with the TI Learning Center, an organization specifically devoted to educational products.

Both the classroom calculator products and this new line of retail products provide added value in the form of learning experiences, solutions to everyday-life problems, interesting activities, entertainment and fun. One objective, is to provide more successful, more pleasurable experiences with mathematics to people of all ages in all walks of life.

Little Professor Helps Children Explore Math

The Little Professor is a calculator-based learning aid with more than 16,000 pre-programmed math problems. Children can choose problems geared to their individual level of skill. As they become older and more proficient, they can select three higher levels of progressively more difficult arithmetic

The "Little Professor" calculator (shown above) has 16,000 prepro-grammed arithmetic problems for personal tutoring and is an electronic successor to flash cards for children 5-9 years old. (Texas Instruments)

problems. After the type of problem and degree of difficulty is chosen, the machine presents a problem in its large lighted display. For example, if a 5-year old wants to practice addition, he or she presses keys marked "+", "SET" and "GO" to generate the first problem. On the display, an equation such as 2 + 4 = would appear. The child gets three chances to key in the correct answer. If he or she inputs the wrong answer, an error indication, "EEE" will be displayed and the child gets two more chances. If the answer is right, the completed answer is shown and then a new problem is displayed automatically. If, after three tries, the correct answer is not given, the completed equation will be displayed and the child presses the "GO" key to move to the next problem. As an added feature, the Little Professor automatically displays a score showing how many of 10 problems were answered right.

The Little Professor functions as a personal tutor in basic math for children aged 5-9. It presents addition, subtraction, multiplication and division sequences, all in variable degrees of difficulty. Children work at their own speed and usually consider the machine a game as well as a learning instrument. Educators have long used flash cards for drill and practice to help students gain proficiency in math. The Little Professor presents this drill in a new, motivating manner, providing an electronic successor to the flash card. The Little Professor is packaged with "Fun With Math Facts," a colorful and stimulating booklet with a panorama of problems, pictures and activities for children —and helpful hints for parents. It opens a wealth of math exercises for children to do alone, or in competition with friends.

TI Calculator Board Game Operations

"Calculator Squares" and "Check Out," are two creative games with one thing in common—the "zip" added by electronic calculators. *CALCULATOR SQUARES* is a fascinating and challenging game of luck and strategy, where two to four players aged 12 and up attempt to build a straight-line path from start to finish. Much like traditional games, each player can play aggressively against his opponents as well as working toward his own goal, and defending against the moves of his adversaries. The electronic calculator is used to try various number alternatives each turn, allowing the selection of a "best" alternative each time. Each time an opponent changes the conditions, the alternatives need to be re-evaluated. Excitement mounts as one strategy after another is foiled, then re-thought, and repositioning occurs. The calculator makes it possible for alternatives to be quickly tried before a decision is made. This provides math practice, and reflects the way decisions should ideally be made—based on examining alternatives and selecting the most plausible.

CHECKOUT combines the elements of nutrition, budgeting and smart shopping into a very interesting game for from two to four players ages 11 through young adult. It is a family game, and teaches younger members to handle and count money. In addition to a Texas Instruments calculator, "Check Out" includes a center organizer/tray for cards and spinner, and four separate boards called "shopping baskets"—one for each participant.

The calculator is used to work out unit prices, compute percentages, and assist in budgeting. There are additional features that can be added after the basic game is mastered by adding "people" cards and measuring calorie intake along with other factors. (The games, with calculators were priced less than $20.)

TEXAS INSTRUMENTS, MAJOR UNIVERSITIES HAVE WORKED TOGETHER ON MATHEMATICS EDUCATION PROGRAM USING CALCULATORS

A line of calculator-oriented mathematics learning materials, developed in cooperation with the Lawrence Hall of Science of the University of California at Berkeley, Syracuse University, and the University of Denver was offered in late 1976 by Texas Instruments Incorporated. A research group at the Lawrence Hall of Science is developed a system of student and teacher materials aimed at Kindergarten through grade six called Elementary Mathematics Concepts with Calculators. These materials were independently evaluated by Syracuse University. The University of Denver prepared materials for grades seven through 12, and tested them in classroom situations. Student and teacher feedback was received by the developing universities directly from test sites. The product line, part of which has been under development for more than two years, was ready for classroom use in the 1976-77 school year. It is designed to utilize the calculator as a positive influence in the learning of basic mathematics concepts in Kindergarten through high school. Student and teacher materials, with calculators, form an integrated system for teaching mathematics.

The program materials for Kindergarten through grade one were initially implemented and evaluated in 35 classrooms in four states covering a cross section of American life ranging from mid-city schools to sites in small towns and suburban areas. The evaluation program included nearly 800 students. Teachers in the Kindergarten through grade one test site program have been enthusiastic in their evaluation of the program, calling it both educational and motivational. Often the children use the materials as spare time activities instead of playing games or using the playground. Peer teaching is encouraged. One child, who has been taught an activity, will in turn teach it to some of his classmates so they can work together in a learning situation. The high interest level of these supplemental materials has made teaching easier by helping make mathematics learning more enjoyable, according to test site teachers. The Kindergarten through grade one learning system employs special "ABLE" calculators with interchangeable limited-function keyboards.

(ABLE is an acronym for ABstract Linking Electronically.) These snap-out keyboards allow the teacher to adjust the ABLE unit to the child's mathematics skills. These units are designed to enable the child to link experience with concrete objects, such as plastic frogs, with abstract numeral representations. Each ABLE unit includes six interchangeable keyboard "faces" ranging from 0 and 1, + to 1 through 9, +, −, ×. With the ABLE units, children can "make" numbers before they have learned to write numerals with pencil and paper. Materials for secondary school use also underwent student and teacher test in a variety of junior high and high school classrooms.

In just a few years, calculators have become pervasive in our society, and sales of a second one-hundred million more are on the way—at prices virtually anyone can afford.

They have brought fundamental changes to the way mathematics can be applied to everyday problems. The implications are profound for education at all levels. The focus of this program is to provide a professionally planned, orderly and tested alternative for mathematics educators considering introduction of calculators in their classrooms. The new materials began to be introduced through teacher workshops in 13 major cities in the Spring of 1977. Many teachers became actively involved with the materials at the National Council of Teachers of Mathematics (NCTM) annual meeting in April of 1977.

A similar enrichment system was being readied for immediate use in high school introductory algebra courses. This unit will follow the scope and sequence of commonly taught algebra curricula, and will incorporate a teachers' guide, classroom visual aids, student workbook, a more advanced calculator, and more than 50 activities, including worksheets and manipulatives. The algebra activities contain carefully sequenced algebraic concepts utilizing the calculator as a powerful learning force in such areas as signed numbers, variable expressions, order and equality, and basic equations and formulae.

All teachers' guides will include brief cross references to the popular current textbooks, allowing their easy implementation into existing programs. Since calculators were increasingly being used in schools, the TI approach is one of providing materials to carefully integrate calculators into the curricula which will enhance students' learning experiences. Within Texas Instruments, the program is under direction of the TI Learning Center, an organization that produces and markets textbooks, instructional videotapes, audio-visual teaching materials, seminars, workshops and other related educational materials. With this approach to mathematics learning, students are encouraged to discover, explore, share and explain their solutions. According to the director, "They can become very involved: Younger children even with such things as simple estimation in Kindergarten; older students in applying mathematical skills and concepts to analysis and problem solving. This is just the beginning. The calculator enables the student to engage in true analysis and problem-solving in a way never before possible. Today, problem-solving is becoming more relevant in the classroom because the calculator allows use of real-life data for computing solutions. In the future, understanding subjects such as the basics of programming and its elements will be enhanced significantly through the use of calculators."

West coast college packs pocket calculators

Pocket calculators in the classroom — we have noted above that hot debate rages among academicians with critics denouncing the hand-held gadgets as debilitating crutches, spawning a generation of mathematical cripples. Proponents, meanwhile, laud the devices as legitimate learning aids which actually increase understanding. Though the number of advocates appears to be on the rise, rare is the educational institution that actively encourages classroom use of pocket calculators.

One that has is Menlo College, in Menlo Park, CA. Menlo's math and science professors feel so certain of the potential of pocket calculators as learning tools that in 1975 they equipped an entire classroom with them, revamped teaching methods and altered subject matter to match the capability of the calculators.

After a full academic year of use, the program was an unqualified success. In the following year, Menlo placed greater curricular emphasis on the calculators, involving more number-oriented courses, more students, more teachers.

Soon after, six professors teaching nine mathematics, science and business classes used the school's Computation Center. The Center was furnished with 20 Hewlett-Packard HP-45 pocket-sized scientific calculators, one to each student. About one-fourth of Menlo's 550 students used them in at least one class.

Outfitting a classroom with calculators affords all students equal learning opportunity, according to the teachers and chairman of the mathematics department. This overrides the objection of some critics that the calculators give unfair advantage to those who can afford them while penalizing students who cannot.

"Although no formal study has been made, all are convinced that students actually learn more, not less using calculators in the classroom," was the quote from the chairman of Menlo's computer science department.

The Progression of Many Users — From Hand-Held Units to Complete Systems . . .

In these introductory, *what's ahead* chapters, a very brief analysis of calculator *computing* systems is appropriate. These extensive capability systems are analyzed in significant applications and operations depth in the latter chapters of the book. However, a flavor of their capabilities can be discerned at this point to provide some perspective to the full range of the concepts of the Class 3 systems as noted on the calculator classification chart. As the reader moves through Part I, he perceives the majority emphasis to be the contrast and comparisons of construction, capabilities, and variable uses of: (1) basic, (2) special-purpose, (3) preprogrammed, (4) key-programmed and (5) card-programmed systems. These few notes of major calculator (6) *computing* systems will provide a basis of the considerably more exotic and powerful systems. The reader might thus develop his own strong set of concepts of what future peripheral capabilities are in store for the first five level low-cost, portable, personal calculators. How soon will these be achieved? What lies ahead as all electronic costs continue to slide? The individual unit's power and versatility will continue to expand even for low-cost units. This can be discerned *along the way* as the reader becomes aware, in the first few chapters, of the basic principles and procedures of manufacturing and calculating with the current relatively simple programmable instruments.

We will note ahead, for example, that some units, for under $800, offer 100,000 steps of programming. This is expandable with additional tape cassettes, and one unit offers 100 preprogrammed functions, all contained in a 6.5 lb. machine. We will also note that a *floppy disk* replacement for cassettes is available for the Hewlett-Packard 9830 *computing* calculator system — the unit storing the equivalent of five to seven cassettes at the cost of one cassette, and with the capability of being fifty times faster, providing 305 K (thousand) bytes (characters) of user area. It is only 4 inches high and fits neatly into place

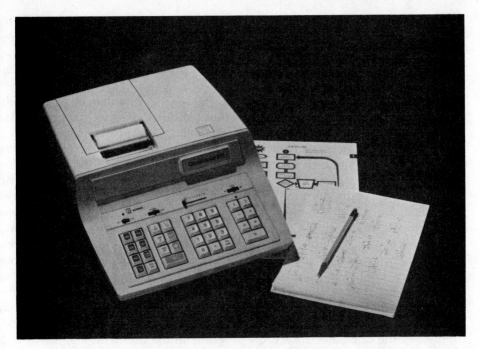

**Computerized Math Drill and Practice Achievement Program
by Monroe Education**

A unit offering computerized mathematics drill and practice programs has been announced by Monroe's Calculator Division. Called the Classmate 88, and costing less than $2.00 a day, the operation achievement program designed and approved by educators uses an individualized instruction approach which enables students to generate unlimited drill and practice routines in over 70 computational skills. Addition, subtraction, multiplication, division, fractions, decimals or number-concept exercises are provided the students at their own learning pace.

Simple flow chart instructions and a completely self-contained machine allow students to work without supervision. All drill and practice programs are hardwired into the machine so that with the touch of a key, the student or teacher can select the subject area and generate an unlimited number of exercises in any one of the 70 skill areas. A complete software support program includes a Diagnostic Placement Test and a flow chart operating instruction for each skill. Another feature of the program provides automatic scoring to enable the teacher to readily evaluate student progress.

between the calculator and printer . . . users just plug in the Input-Output (I/O) connector and power cord, and it is ready for use. The unit, the FD-30 from Infotek Systems, stores a 10,000-word array in only five seconds. The applications of the newest technologies in the traditional jobs of measuring, controlling, and communicating seem to appear early and most pragmatically in the larger computing calculators first, and they then appear relatively quickly thereafter in low-cost hand-held or convenient small desk-top units. These and other capabilities then also appear in or act as low-cost terminals — as stand-alones, or as part of clustered, *distributed intelligence* systems, linking people and machines in remote locations to a central processor or a centra data base. **Computing** calculator systems are rapidly being accepted, becaus of the favorable prior calculator experience of millions of users, and as a speed way to include more people faster (without difficult computer training) int these *processing-communicating loops.*

Computers and transmissions, in many cases, have become overloaded, an *big system* users then begin to explore the possibility of not only collecting dat at the terminal but also of sorting, organizing, and processing it *locally* t minimize computer time. Thus, *intelligent terminals,* many of them true cal culators, preprogrammed or programmable, permit this *on the spot* pre- o post-processing or completely stand-alone total processing. Calculators the come to be the actual terminals of the network. This provides the capability (*distributed intelligence* time-sharing of a larger system, using a minicompute with calculator terminals or allows the calculators to act as remote batc terminals to huge systems, but with a great portion or all of the actual proces ing being completed by the people who know most about the data or informa tion. These are the calculator people who assemble, enter and/or actually us that data and information. Thus, much of the computation is being performe at these users' desks — on calculators acting as terminals. The computer ca send unformatted data to these calculators with the final format being deter mined by the calculator-insertable program on the user's desk or site. Or th calculator may send messages or data to another calculator user or transmit i to the main computer, often with added worldwide communications capabilit for large user operations. Protocols, interfacing, etc. can be stored or inserte by tapes, cassettes, floppy disks, etc. directly into the calculator itself. A close description and analysis of one or two of these *computing* calculators at thi point will suggest to the reader that many of these *terminal* capabilities ar already also built into their hand-held units, or soon can and will be. Note below show that they might also well become parts of telephones, TV sets an hobbyist home microcomputers. A little futurism at this point, with simplifie and abbreviated discussion can't be too harmful — and might add some in trigue to what the next few chapters develop.

BASIC Language Calculators Provide Business, Industrial, Scientific Users Extra Benefits

In a brief preview of major calculator systems capabilities, the H-P 9830B i a good example because it has mass-memory capacity, uses the BASIC lan guage, and very often serves as a terminal in *distributed intelligence* system It operates with a line or thermal printer, data communication interface, car readers, tape readers, Read Only Memory (ROM) Input-Output, and/o Modem, and other control programs. It uses external cassette and dis memories (as noted above) and other peripherals, as plotters, etc. It has tw very powerful terminal program editing systems, one for the cassette-oriente batch terminal and one for the mass memory-oriented batch terminal. Eac allows users to add, delete, and insert 80-column, card-image data into a existing data base, on the cassette or the mass memory. This provides a fas convenient medium for data storage before the information is transmitted ove the data communications link. Users can thus eliminate punched cards o paper tape as their data storage medium when and if desired. These system are often used for Remote Job Entry (RJE), preparing numerical control tape for manufacturing or process control machine automation, payroll, inventor control, structural design, instrumentation control, and hundreds of other ap plications, many of which are analyzed in Chapter 9.

The H-P 9830-B recently added matrix manipulation and alphanumeric text and labeling capabilities to its power range. Despite these expansive capabilities and an increasing line of peripheral equipment, in most cases, users simply plug in the devices they need, load their program and go . . . all without help from computer experts or complex, expensive programming and interfaces. Such systems, the H-P 9830 A and B and several other brands of competing systems, are often all the computing power a small company needs for its: .accounting, research, production, marketing, design, payroll, inventory, and other functions. Random access data bases can be created, including management information systems, with HP-supplied (or competitive brand) programs for hundreds of basic operating functions. These low-cost, proven programs include commercial, financial, industrial, engineering, data acquisition and control, etc. and additional ones can easily be originally written even by non-computer people, either in the language of mathematics or by using BASIC, which can be learned by practically anyone within a week or so. Thousands of users of these type *computing systems* from H-P, Wang, Tektronics, Commodore, Rockwell, Olympia, Olivetti, Monroe, and others are experienced in applications as varied as quadratic equations, budget preparations, statistical analysis, report generation, etc. generally without professional programmers, central or time-shared computers.

How Many Calculators Are Really Being Sold? Where Do They Come From?

Perhaps the best (though not the clearest) way to explain how many calculators are sold around the world and who makes them is to reprint some of the typical news stories that are reported in the professional journals "quoting the experts." Some clarifying comments about each item used and a conclusion will attempt to tie together the *facts* presented. However, some introductory notes are in order to provide the environment for the answers to the *how many* and *where from* questions before the discussions begins. Although the detail of calculator components and construction is more thoroughly presented in Chapter 2, at this point it should be noted that calculators are primarily *modules* of chips and assemblies. For example, General Instrument's Microelectronics division in Hicksville, N.Y. in 1975 supplied 37 calculator chips to major calculator assemblers. Recently they offered many more modules, competing against Texas Instruments, MOS Technology (Mostek), Rockwell International, National Semiconductor, Electronic Array, Inc., and several other American and Japanese firms. Generally, each module contains the electronics required to produce a total calculator, including: an MOS LSI Arithmetic-Logic Unit (ALU) chip, a light-emitting diode (LED) or other type display, a (sometimes) driver chip, and when necessary, passive components. Typically, then, the assembler adds a 9-volt battery (or three AA cells 4.5V, see below), keyboard, and case. Such modules can then, for example, supply four functions (+, −, ×, ÷) and percent; four functions with memory; five functions plus memory; a slide rule calculator; etc. Some primary suppliers or other fabricators add impact or thermal printers, larger digit and other type displays, and other special function capabilities. But, in essence, these are the components of modules and assemblies.

The Metal Oxide Semiconductor Large Scale Integrated (MOS LSI) chips — their density, power drain, size, integration techniques, etc. and the efficiency with which they are manufactured, tested, and marketed (in huge quantities) can be referred to as the *advanced technology* of the calculator industry . . . much of the best of this is *owned* by American companies and is licensed *(second sourced)* by them to other firms. Only a few firms both manufacture and assemble all components, such as Texas Instruments, National Semiconductor, etc. while others buy only one or two components and do the rest of the work *in house.*

Calculator Distribution Progress — From Basic Engineering Tools To Mass Markets

Microelectronics, the microminiaturization of components and the integration of them in silicon chips, is doing very well. In fact, *chip* devices centering around microprocessors, the arithmetic-logic units (ALUs), and the combining of these chips with exterior memory devices, is by far the hottest industry around. For research, design, and new product implementation this is greater than anything else since the invention of the computer itself. The true consumer market for these products is only now beginning to emerge. An example of one *item* alone was the prediction of sales of from 2.5 to 4 million *computerized* games for the Christmas Season, 1976 (see discussion: Chapter 2). As many people noted in early 1976, the top executive of Texas Instruments predicted total 1976 calculator sales would reach 58 million units worth approximately $1.7 billion. This data is both supported and segmented in discussion below. There are many reasons for this on-going success. The most obvious factor is price-performance. Practically no other product, with the possible exception of the $5 transistor radio, offers more pragmatic power for such low prices as calculators — and in ranges from $8 to $8000. Technological advances in logic types, fabrication and assembly techniques, and strong mass-selling competitive marketing resulted in the economics associated with the success of this industry.

Perhaps the most significant factor to the amazed consumer is that while prices keep falling, capabilities continue to increase. An excellent and popular $800 calculator is suddenly (within 3 years) supplanted by one that is almost twice as powerful and versatile but at about half the retail price — and from the same company. Today's $60 calculator is more than twice as useful and valuable as many that sold for $150 to $200 only a year earlier . . . and the trend continues for both small and large systems. And equally as important, excellent software — programs of thousands of types — are available at very low cost, making the already easy-to-use devices even more fun and profitable to use. Today practically all the lowest cost calculators have memory, rounding capability, fixed and floating decimal, and a host of special function keys. The user keeps getting more for less . . . the customer couldn't be happier. Now, programmability is just as low cost as the $30 simple-function machines. The Litronix 2290 and others is an excellent value in a programmable consumer calculator, but it's also good for businessmen, students, and anyone with simple repetitive computation requirements, and any number or type of them.

User-programmable calculators will undoubtedly have the largest rate of sales increase in both unit volume and certainly dollar amount . . . approaching and passing one-fifth of the market in units and perhaps 30% in dollars in 1977-80. The larger calculator *systems* easily rival micro and minicomputers in performance and are certainly a happier combination of ease of use and minor software expense. Fortunately also, parts inventories, product lines, product literature, and other items are beginning to show a significant degree of worldwide acceptance. But much more standardization is needed to take the confusion out of the marketplace. The industry is relatively young. As late as 1971 there was little or no consumer market for calculators — and, as late as 1974, programmable calculators were still a distinct luxury. More than

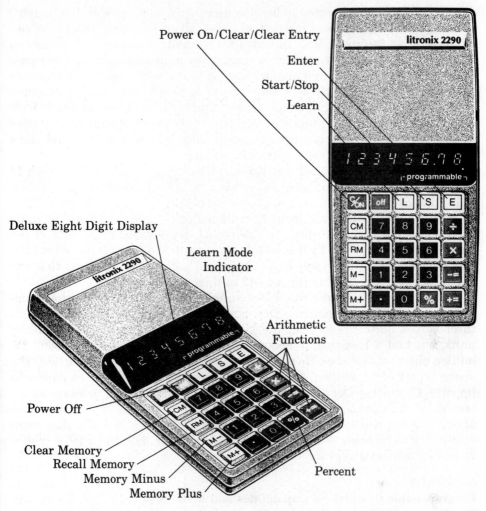

Power On/Clear/Clear Entry
Enter
Start/Stop
Learn

litronix 2290

Deluxe Eight Digit Display

Learn Mode
Indicator

Arithmetic
Functions

Power Off

Clear Memory
Recall Memory
Memory Minus
Memory Plus

Percent

A $30 hand-held programmable calculator. The Cambridge is a similar below $30 — programmable offered by Sinclair Radionics, Ltd.

$500 million worth of calculators were sold in 1973; most are now ready for replacement — and a whooping $3 billion market is anticipated for 1979 or 1980. The majority of the early calculators sold went to the U.S., Canada, Japan, and West Germany, with other European countries receiving only a *sampling*. Now the rest of the world is beginning to catch up — and even the pioneering countries are less than 20% to 25% saturated. So, the mass marketing — now of programmables as well — continues.

In the first ten months of 1973, Japanese shipments to the U.S. totalled 2,270,000 vs. 867,000 for the same ten months in 1972. The total Japanese 1973 production was 4,758,000, thus the U.S. was then buying roughly half of Japan's output. U.S. production of all types of calculators reportedly exceeded 9 million for 1973. Japan equalled that in 1974; one of the Japanese manufacturers alone, Sharp, was producing at 150,000 a month of low-end $39 to $49 units in late 1973. Rapid and steep price erosion had then just begun to open the market to junior and senior high school students. This market segment is now wide-open, and a significant number of the 15 million American students in this category are expected to become users very soon . . . with the (maybe) blessings of many or most instructors. Also, about this time hand-held calculators — at $40 to $150 — intended for specialized use by such groups as stockbrokers, machinists, salesmen (insurance, real estate, etc.), surveyors, etc. began to proliferate in a manner similar to the way consumer calculators mushroomed in sales in 1973-74. Small desk-top models are now fully accepted in all offices — and the huge replacement market of old *office adders* is wide open . . . thermal printer units are appearing everywhere. A semiauthoritative report is quoted below concerning recent Japanese production, and some specific company data is especially enlightening.

The 1975 production from Japan was noted as about 32 million units with 14 million units coming from Casio; Tokyo Electronic Application, about 5 million units, and Systech's production was expected to match Casio, for another 12 to 14 million units. This totals about 32 million alone — and the 11 million units exported to the U.S., according to this report, represented about 52% of the American market, which by this calculation, meant the American market then was at least 22 million total units. A special note to remember is that the Japanese alone expected to produce 40 million units in 1976.

A report from the American **Electronics** magazine* quotes various suppliers and the U.S. Commerce Department statistics. One major manufacturer agrees quite closely that the U.S. 1975 market was about 20 million units, but had a lower *guess* about American production . . . only about 4-5 million units (vs. 9 above). He also saw only 6 million Japanese imports vs. the above report of 11 million; his figures suggesting 10 million non-Japanese imports. Commerce Dept. figures were all lower. (Japanese shipments as reported by the Japanese Finance Ministry for the months of February and March are noted below: 11,074,779 exported to the U.S. in 1975; they were continuing to increase — 2.5 million for the first two months in 1976 or at a rate of 15 million a year.)

SUMMARY
Programmable Calculators: Capabilities and Systems —
The Expanding Marketplace

The electronics industry by mass-producing low-cost programmable and *computing* calculators is bringing a new way of life for people of all nations. The innovative, fiercely competitive electronics components industry has already made real progress stalking for entrenched world-wide, simply-operated calculator distribution. The current explosive growth of programmable calculator capabilities detailed throughout this book is a most powerful example of personal-life electronics-related changes occurring and to come. These units, unlike earlier ones that served only the professional and business markets, have created wide ranges of entirely new customers — the man on the street, at work, or at home despite his profession, business, hobby, or endeavor.

Low-cost electronic calculators have become an impulse buy in department stores, direct mail sales, *coupon* premiums, etc. But innovations in solid-state mass-produced consumer electronics have just begun. More and more calculator-type products are in the consumer's future as costs continue to fall and capabilities increase. The design industry is finally cracking the huge machine and process-control equipment markets with $10 microprocessors buried within hundreds of products, and microprocessor-controlled devices are getting into peoples' homes in a big way. Electronics people have learned to

---

*"Calculators Take Offshore Trip," **Electronics,** February 5, 1976. p. 75.

design automated instruments for the doctor; information retrieval for lawyers; delivery systems for hospitals; word processing for business offices; automated tests for the steel mills; paperless records for the city government and whatever. Products are moving into a thousand avenues that electronics people have never envisioned before. They are now thinking and planning *outward*. The days of electronics companies growing by trading and selling primarily to one another in the industry are gone. Hundreds of new entrepeneur firms now go directly to user markets with pragmatic but untried marketing of products because risks are low, development time is fast and production costs are minimal. (And giant IBM is not in this battle . . . yet). An important shift on emphasis in marketing is taking place. Examples of the change are evident in the examination of the calculating and information control products on the pages of following chapters.

It has been noted that primitive programmables but significantly sophisticated scientific electronic calculators were introduced to the business markets in 1969. Now business programmables have swiftly risen to a new class of data acquisition and process control devices since that time. This was accomplished by first adding new type *memory chips* and then simple microprocessor devices to many hand-held units. New sophisticated microprocessor systems are within all major desk-top models. Because the Read-Only Memory (ROMs) could be *altered* and thus are programmable (PROM), and because the microprocessors can quickly be programmed or redesigned with wide versatility, the advanced programmable calculator has now become a true computer with both specialized and almost unlimited ranges of capabilities. The primary characteristic that is now pushing the sale of these remarkable devices into the tens of millions annually is that they are exceptionally cost-effective. Although hardware costs are somewhat similar to many *bare bones* microcomputer systems, the programming costs are substantially smaller because of the simpler keyboard-oriented instruction set of the calculator. Installation costs are a low minimum due to the *plug-in* nature of low-cost interface and peripheral equipment. (See Chapter 4: *Interfaces* and *Use of ROMs* in PCs.)

It is extremely simple to expand the memory capability of programmable calculators with more memory chips (ROMs or Random Access Memory [RAMs]), or with low-cost peripherals, such as high-speed magnetic tape, cassette systems, cartridges or other external semiconductor or even *add-on* core memory devices, disc drives, etc. Calculator manufacturers design their units to be very practical, not only for conventional and *prompting* processing but also for supervisory control of processes, *sensing* instrumentation for equipment control, and highly specific or distinct problem solving, such as, esoteric statistics, real estate detail computing, all types of engineering, finance and other technical problems. Special plastic overlays for all keys or for individual or banks of keys of the calculator can change the basic performance on some units to practically any specialized computing device imaginable when they are designed to signal (connected to) programs contained in specific ROMs or RAMs which can be built in originally or added externally as *plug-in* printed circuit (PC) or special magnetic cards.

Most programmable calculators use external memory transfer instructions by having a simplified *program step/data register* orientation of the straightforward calculator language which is preserved and insures a low programming cost. The number of programmable calculator manufacturers is expanding rapidly and, each of them it seems, is bringing to the markets ever more powerful calculators, many with high-level languages, such as BASIC, FORTRAN, and others. Some of these new large units have multiple-line, multi-color alphanumeric displays and can be operated in the *conversational* mode. Some of those with CRT displays, which are parts of the *computing* calculator systems can be used for alarm signals, ennunciator panels, editing versatility, report-format checking, *hand shaking* procedures for training beginners on *how to use* them, etc.

The BASIC language is a terminal or time-sharing language, learned by practically anyone within a week's time, and is easily used for telecommunication applications. Most calculators have serial input-output capabilities which allow data communication or process control, using simple *twisted pair* wires, simple low-cost modems, and the telephone system. The basic compiler on many advanced systems is hard-wired with the built-in ROMs, and program execution by calculator is very often faster than that by some minicomputers. Most of all, the calculator is easier to use by far, and practically no one is *afraid* of the programmable calculator, but as noted, millions are scared to death of regular computers. Several new types of calculators using BASIC are ideally suited to many types of in-house data transmission systems and are very practical for the industrial user who can install rather complex communication systems using their own in-house electricians.

All this is causing a *Microprocessor Trauma* in the computer and components markets. Most large LSI or semiconductor manufacturers see the clear bright light and are moving into the processor market briskly. On the other hand, all standard computer manufacturers are also swiftly developing an LSI capability for more microprocessor-calculator-like products. A brand new microcomputer device or new calculator product can be conceived and developed in six to eight months. Dollar and time investment requirements are small, and the design-implementation feedback circle operates in a shorter time frame. The shortened development cycle of the microcomputers and calculators, has served to accelerate many advances in technology, software, peripherals, and applications, leaving society to ponder how to catch up. Many observers suggest that we seem to have more and better technology than we know what to do with.

CHAPTER 2

TODAY'S CALCULATOR/ MICROCOMPUTER TECHNOLOGY ENVIRONMENT

Computing Solutions Using Calculators — The Philosophy and Pragmatics

Calculators are available for routine, basic statistics, or the most subtle and complex analysis. Calculators help derive the essential truths from data. And they do it at a price most can afford, both in terms of their very small capital outlay and almost non-existant operating overhead. There are many varieties of calculators — hand-held, pre-programmed and/or programmable are top sellers — most of the advanced systems can couple with an incredible range of options and peripherals. Users can pick the precise combination of functions, memory, input, output, and storage features that fit specific utilities, problems and budgets.

Typical examples: A *standard $25 machine* does sums, means, and percentages at a touch of a single keystroke. Sophisticated desk-top units handle a 30-variable, multiple-linear regression with transformations in a matter of minutes. Manufacturers offer comprehensive libraries of math, scientific statistics and other software to the delight of every researcher. Thirteen volumes are available from H-P, for example, for one calculator; hundreds of programs, ranging from quality control assurance to complex modeling; from non-parametric statistics to high-level chemical or financial analyses are also available. Each is fully documented; ready to put programmable calculators to work. Special features, insertable or read-in data storage, programs, etc. match solutions to problems. Anyone, everyone can use these low-cost electronic programmable calculators.

Wrist Watch Calculators: A Common Tool/Appliance Soon?

Within ten years practically everyone will be carrying an electronic calculator no larger than a wrist watch that can handle virtually all his mathematical problems, according to a New York University researcher. (Two wrist calculator models appeared in 1975; many types were popular in 1976.) He spoke at NYU's Courant Institute of Mathematical Science during a seminar on electronic calculators in May, 1974. He maintained that they will be so inexpensive even grade school children will wear them as they now wear wrist watches. He further stated that the low-cost calculators will not make children too mentally lazy to do mathematics in the traditional way. He believes the contrary is true. By taking much of the drudgery out of math, they will make children more interested in science and other fields of learning where math is necessary. Many will begin by using calculators purchased or leased by the schools. (See photos of some "wrist-clock calculators ahead.)

The question has arisen many times — at what age or grade level does one start to teach children the use of calculators. Some have had great fun with 3 to 5 year-old children and their calculators. Others are very worried about these procedures as being *too novel* — even dangerous to children's mental health. But, this is sheer foolishness. The *calculator/microcomputer* environment in which we live today becries the need to introduce the children of this age to their working tools as soon as they are able to use them — not understand them. The experiments conducted all around the states thus far have been fruitful and fun. Problems presented on calculators operationally for primary school children are so simple that there can be only slight semantic confusion. Even very young children not previously taught how the calculator works can use them quickly. (See National Kuiz Kid units, Mickey Math, others.) Even slightly older children, who can only handle additions and subtractions without the calculator, are capable of performing multiplications and divisions perfectly and higher level arithmetic easily using their calculators. They must, however, be taught the basic concepts of multiplying and dividing up through double integers. The *game type* teaching calculators really prove to be a help in saving time, improving accuracy, and assisting in instruction.

Independent of these first limited results, what insight that has been gained and what impact seen is very impressive. The insight seems to be that all teachers must consider the new children's calculators now in all mathematics education. This is going to be terribly difficult not only because of teacher resistance caused by expected productivity increases but more importantly because much of our mathematics educational system is based on mental alogrithmic competition. In our affluent age, are the values of conservation and competition taught by the recent shortages and recessions still valid or can we spend a little money to get better, faster and more correct answers for all arithmetic, geometry and trigonometry problems by even fourth grade students and spend the teacher-hour savings on personal economics, for example?

The impacts seem huge. Alert and eager students freed from the drugery of grinding out mathematical alogrithms may be propelled into conceptual mathematics and, as a minimum, will be better trained as future calculator and computer users. That miniscule fraction that must learn how the calculators and computers work inside may well develop a hierarchy of progress goals great inventors set for themselves. Certainly we must face the fact that the great majority of users want answers, not methodology. Another impact still untested is in the storage of mathematical tables, etc. One observer, as a matter of reference, consulted his high school trigonometry texts. They generally include about 120 pages of tables of functions, mainly trigonometric and logarithmic. These tables are mostly 4 place tables, at least alogrithmically, and out to 10 places. That means that some calculators are the equivalent of a set of tables a million times larger than that in the trigonometry book. This capability, he suggests, may not be commonly required right now but the impact is striking when further application of the teaching calculators is made to more specific areas of educational endeavor.

Most observers feel that the environment of the times is the most important relevancy to the books written as teaching texts in the schools. This chapter is an attempt to explain some of this *electronic tool* environment before a beginning and progressive steps are made in other instruments of this environment.

The Widening Range of Calculator Novelty Products

As previously noted, continued advances in microminiaturization technology and excellent mass production techniques forced price reductions of calculator chips to less than $1.50 and modules to below $5. Even when encased, the less than $10 units are profitable. Their tiny size, excellent reliability, and popular acceptance entice many eager innovators. They have been tempted to *package* the calculator in scores of devices. Many of the items are very practical; others are clever prestige items, and some are simply ornamental. The calculator *checkbooks, wallets,* pen, biorhythm output units, etc. are very briefly described below. More significant than the others are the increasing range and capability of calculator-watch combinations. It is interesting to note that the competition in this latter field has spawned development of some quite valuable components which may appear soon as tiny control units in other products. The reader's attention is directed to notes below about *solar cell* calculator power, alphanumeric readouts, as well as bicolor Light Emitting Diodes (LEDs). All these items and many more to come are part of the *calculator environment* in which we live and which forms a base for the introduction of the more complex and expanding ranges of programmable calculator-type instruments and the very powerful advanced desk-top calculator systems and networks.

For whatever reasons, the **ultra-thin** 1/4-inch to 11/16-inch calculators have been selling well, generally as *shirt pocket* units. One of these is the Hanimex that weighs only 2½ ounces.

Users can keep it in their pocket comfortably all day long — at lunch, on the airplane and during all those times when they wish they had a calculator with them. The Hanimex is an eight-digit, 4-function, percentage calculator. There's an automatic constant on all four functions. The unit features algebraic logic (users perform functions exactly as they think), and the LED display has overflow indicators and a floating negative sign. The clear key doubles as a clear entry key, and the unit measures 11/16″ × 2⅛″ × 4⅜″ — convenient for any pocket.

Calculator/Wallet — Some manufacturers offer desk-top calendar-calculator combinations for business gift giving. Rockwell offers a combination wallet and built-in ultra-thin five function calculator, priced at $40. The unit includes a ballpoint pen, check or notebook pocket, and transparent credit card inserts. The calculator has a full four-key memory and functions include percent with automatic add-on and discount, square root and change sign. The 24K operates in algebraic logic and maintains trailing zeroes in add and subtract for monetary calculations. It positions the decimal point automatically and also performs chain calculations. Fairly impressive for a product that weighs less than half a pound and measures 5½ × 2¾ × ½-inches.

Mostek Calculator for Check Accounts — A semiconductor manufacturer, Mostek Inc. has introduced a purse-size, two-function calculator which is designed for computing checking account balances and is aimed at the female consumer market. Called the Checkmaster, the $39.95 unit, with a keyboard and six-digit LED display, automatically adds deposits and subtracts checks. The machine features a memory which retains the correct checking account balance even after the unit is turned off.

The battery-powered Checkmaster incorporates a single modified P-channel MOS chip and LSI circuitry. Also, the unit is designed in a case which opens and closes and holds a checkbook. The system automatically shuts off when the case is closed.

Initially, the unit was marketed by the JS&A National Sales Group, a Northbrook, Ill., mail-order distribution firm. In addition, the Checkmaster was marketed under the Corvus trade name by banks as a bank account premium and by retailers. Mostek, a Dallas-based firm, expected to sell about 250,000 units during the year 1976.

Here's how it works. — Users open their checkbook holder and turn on the built-in computer. Press the "Balance" key, and their bank balance is recalled on the display. The CheckMaster memory never forgets their balance — even months after they last recall it.

They enter the amount of their check and press the "Check" key. The check amount is automatically deducted from their balance, and their new balance is displayed — and all with just one key stroke. Or they enter the amount of a deposit, and press the "Deposit" key. Their deposit is automatically added to their balance, and again, their new balance is displayed.

Biorythm Calculator — The BIOLATOR is a dual function machine. It is an 8-digit, four-function calculator. Plus, it calculates a users biorhythm status for the day. They key in their birthdate, and the machine will automatically compute their physical, emotional, and intellectual condition for the day. A built-in 99-year calendar does it, can also be used for computing loans and interest.

For past, present or future, the Biorhythm information is based on the theory that an individual's biological condition fluctuates in cycles, beginning the day he is born. One's physical condition follows a 23-day cycle, sensitivity (emotional), a 28-day period, and intellect, a 33-day interval. All a user needs to do, according to a spokesman for the Fairfield, NJ, company, is to key in his date of birth, followed by any desired date. The calculator then immediately displays three numbers, which when checked with a chart mounted on the back of the unit, give the three facets of a person's biological state on that date.

The calculator can also be used to compute the number of elapsed days between any two days in the 20th century, for financial work. The Biolator can also perform the usual functions of addition, subtraction, multiplication, and division, all in floating-point decimal. Results appear on an eight-digit green Digitron (gas-discharge) display. The calculator provides an additional feature. When using any of the four arithmetic functions, the second number entered is automatically held in an additional register. This can be a great convenience, even for amateur users, for repeated calculations where one number is used over and over. The Biolator operates on two AA batteries or an ac/dc (with optional adaptor) and is marketed in the U.S. at $29.95.

School-Box Shaped *Mickey Math* Calculator

Mickey Math is only 1″ × 7½″ × 7½″ with a hand-grasp handle as a cutout to the case. It is so thin it fits conveniently in school bags (or briefcases) or car glove compartments. It weighs only 14 ounces and its built-in keyboard is colorful and easy-to-control. The readout has six large digits; full floating decimal, four-function constant and algebraic logic (users perform functions as they normally think) and makes working even quite complex problems very simple. Users can perform chain calculations, derive negative balances, etc. The Mickey Math calculator was designed for children and comes with a colorful pictured booklet with clear examples designed to stimulate math interest in grade school children and make them appear like little geniuses. Many **executives** use it as a "fun" item even when they calculate very large *deals*.

Calculator Pen — Full Calculator Side Input and Readout and a Fine Writing Instrument

Calcupen was the first writing instrument with a built-in calculator. It is designed to give users immediate, accurate answers almost as they write them down. It is definitely a prestige item but is also quite practical — many unknowing observers are mystified when users with only a pen apparently visible, are able to come out of discussions with great mathematical answers although they seem to be only playing with their pen. (Students prohibited from using calculators at exams are known to have carried such *strange* pens with them.) "Calcupen" is distributed by the Keith Ian Co. (W. Long Branch, N.J.) and performs addition, subtraction, multiplication, division, squares, powers, percentages . . . by simple right, left, up, or down touches of the sides of 5 square pressure buttons along the side of the metal pen. All numbers, functions, etc. are clearly indicated on these pressure squares, and the direction of the push activates the calculator unit to that number or function. The answers appear in the 8 digit plus sign indicator window at the lower side of the pen. The Calcupen uses its unique trademark *teetertouch* keyboard effectively, and because it is finely crafted, it is an instrument practically in a class by itself. Available with battery, pen refill, 90-day warranty.

1975 Watch/Calculator — A hit of the 1975 Christmas season, Time Computer Inc. introduced a solid gold Pulsar watch-calculator combination with a six-digit LED display. The calculator has five functions, plus memory, floating decimal, and display overflow. Originally priced at $3,950, its designed around two C-MOS chips, one each for time and calculation. The watch uses four battery cells that should last for a year for 25 calculations and 25 time readouts a day.

The big drawback to the Pulsar calculator — in-addition to its price — is that users have to use a special plastic stylus to key in information. Even though Time Computer supplies the retractable stylus mounted on the top of a ballpoint pen, the fact that the calculator can't be operated with an ordinary ballpoint tip means a user's $3,950 calculator isn't usable if the wearer forgets the stylus. But this problem probably will be overcome with later models, and certainly by competitors, which included a dozen companies in 1977.

The Optel I Calculator/Watch — Multiplexed circuits connecting the display segments have helped cut the size of one calculator/watch combination so that it fits on the wrist. The all-electronic calculator/wristwatch was exhibited by Optel Corp., Princeton, N.J., in Switzerland at the Basel watch and jewelry fair in 1975. Prototypes were ready for sampling and small production quantities were scheduled. Called the Optel I, the calculator/watch is designed around complementary-MOS circuits and a field-effect liquid-crystal display. It uses multiplexing to wire the display segments, simplifying the design. The display has eight digits, six of which are used in the normal time-keeping mode to show hours, minutes, and seconds. All eight are operable when the device is switched by pushbutton to the four-function calculating mode.

Succeeding versions have memory and many calculator functions for scientific applications. Prices for the first two models were between $500 and $550 for the standard version and $975 for the fancier one. The Optel I packs three C-MOS chips into its case, measuring 3.3 by 4.57 by 0.953 centimeters. One chip contains the countdown circuitry for time-keeping, the second integrates the calculator circuitry, and the third the buffer and driver stages for the display. The 1-second time pulses are derived from a 32-kilohertz crystal oscillator whose frequency is counted down by a 15-step divider network. The power pack consists of four 1.5-volt silver-oxide batteries, each about 15 millimeters in diameter and 4 mm thick.

Wrist-Watch Size Calculators — An example is a handy calculator with a 17-key unit. Its tiny keys and readout use a layer of conductive rubber. The trend toward micro-miniaturization in electronics has been pushed ever further by the watch industry. Chomerics Inc. of Woburn, Mass. responded by introducing a keyboard measuring only ¾ × 1 inch with 17 keys of 5/32-inch centers. The key array includes a moving decimal point, constant, clear, multiply, divide, add-equal, and subtract-equal keys that are as easy to read as a watch face. The full calculator would probably have either a four-digit liquid-crystal display or a six-digit light-emitting-diode (LED) readout.*

This pencil tip or stylus keyboard makes use of Chomerics' materials technology in conductive elastomers, paints, and inks, and its capability in full-size keyboards. The miniature keyboard uses the same materials as the large subassemblies, but they are put together differently. The keyboard consists of a tiny printed-circuit board, screened with a silver paint that provides a permanently conductive contact surface. Over this is laid a 0.005-inch-thick Mylar spacer with holes directly under the keys. A layer of conductive rubber, and a Mylar legend sheet has the keys on it. When the Mylar is deflected, an electrical impulse that is set up in the conductive rubber travels through the holes in the Mylar spacer to the printed-circuit board. The keyboard was developed as a result of inquiries from watch companies, and samples were supplied to at least 10 of them for ordering. In volume the manufacturer says the keyboards could sell for less than $2 each.

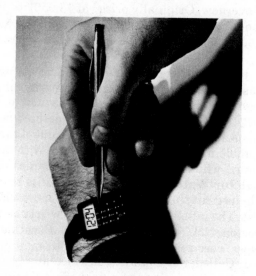

Calculator-Watches for Men Abound In 1977! — Many calculator-watches combinations that can be worn on a man's wrist have been developed by several firms. Calcron, a new product, is a scientific calculator and a man's digital wrist watch combined in a 1.5-inch-square case and less than 0.5-inch thick. The 40 functions of the keyboard — including trigonometric, logarithmic, exponential functions, square root, memory, chaining degrees and radian — use 20 buttons and operate by the use of a shift key like a typewriter's. Rechargeable nickel-cadmium batteries supply power for about 20,000 calculations. Retail price of the system is $500, including a battery charger. The calculator portion is priced at $300. The unit is said to have 40 functions in

---

* Slightly larger readout areas could accommodate several 'answer' lines, using an attached magnifier for improved clarity.

a 20-button keyboard through use of a shift key. Buttons on right give hours, minutes, seconds and data in the same 9-digit LED display used in calculators. The company also began working on a wrist watch for women to be called Femcron. Major companies have multi-function units on the market.

Hughes Aircraft Company Enters Calculator-Watch/ Alphameric Readout Devices

With the success of several calculator-watch devices described above, Hughes AirCraft, using some of their developed space technology, began selling in mass market volume modules which other fabricaters and marketers eagerly sought to offer in several new gift and prestige markets. Two stories reprinted from Hughes News (May and June, 1976 issues respectively) explain the development and capabilities.

Coming up: You can get messages on digital watches

A new five-function digital electronic watch module, featuring a pre-programed fixed message of up to four words in addition to the usual time and date readout, has been introduced by the Solid State Products Division of Hughes Industrial Electronics Group.

The solid state module can display a message comparable to an inscription on a watch case. Messages planned for the first units include holiday and birthday greetings, affectionate remembrances, political slogans, and class, group, and club identifications.

The fixed message is programed onto the MOS chip, which controls the watch readout, in a separate masking stage during manufacture. Five nine-segment light-emitting diodes provide alpha-numeric readout of up to five letters or digits per word. In addition to the four-word message, the watch also displays the customary month, date, hour, minute, and second.

The new module is offered as either a one or two-button model, and shipments began in volume in mid-1976. Initially, it was offered only to present customers of Hughes modules, and then carried a nominally higher price than existing five function modules.

Sample messages offered by Hughes include "HAPPY BIRTHDAY," "LOVE YOU DAD," "GRAD CLASS OF 1976," and similar remembrances. Jewelry and department stores are expected to market the new watches, as well as merchandising companies that sell through catalog, credit card, and direct mail promotions.

In addition, custom modules with special commercial and advertising slogans will be offered to businesses for use as merchandising devices.

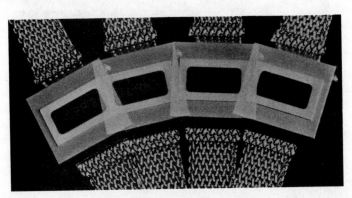

Calculator Module Joins Newport Beach Watch Line

Solid State Products Division in Newport Beach has started production on a new electronic watch module, featuring a nine-function calculator in addition to a standard four-function digital watch.

The new solid state-module, measuring 1.4 × 1.25 inches, has a standard calculator keyboard on its face, along with an eight-digit light-emitting diode (LED) display for readout of the calculator and watch functions.

Keys are easy to operate with the point of a pencil or ball-point pen.

The calculator operates with a floating decimal and provides the following functions: Addition, subtraction, multiplication, division, per cent, memory, reciprocal, squares, and constant for multiplication and division.

The watch portion displays hours, minutes, seconds, and date.

The calculator memory retains entries even when the unit is in its time-display or non-display mode. This feature, called a non-volatile memory, permits the user to call out the time without losing the figures in his calculation.

The display uses .08-inch LEDs magnified to .10 inches. When in the calculator mode, the display automatically turns off after a few seconds. Errors in the entry or function are indicated on an additional LED, located at the extreme left of the display.

Four batteries are used — in two sets of two each — permitting the two that power the display to be changed without affecting either the timekeeping or calculator memory. In this way, the display batteries, which must be replaced more frequently, may be changed without requiring resetting of the watch or reentering of data in the calculator.

The company stated initial production of the new module is committed to one of Hughes' existing customers, North American Foreign Trading Company, of New York, which sells under the Compuchron label.

Hughes, which supplies many name-brand and private-label watch companies with modules for digital electronic watches, does not market a watch to consumers under its own name. Competition is building, but published industry statistics have identified Hughes as the largest producer of these modules.

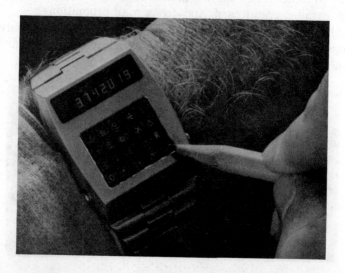

Also in May, 1976, Texas Instruments began to offer samples of bicolor LEDs. The firm's optoelectronics team designed a single chip that changes colors at different current levels. The company has chosen to go with two-chip packages, in which the polarity of the current determines which of two differently colored LEDs, wired in reverse parallel, will turn on. Litronix also in May, 1976, announced an alphanumeric LED display with four 0.16-inch characters preassembled for multiplex operation on a Printed Circuit board. Applications include hand-held and table-top calculators, instruments, data terminals, appliances, and auto dashboards. The characters are readable in daylight at distances up to 5 feet within a 20-degree half angle. Luminous intensity is 0.5 mcd per digit at 5mA current per segment. Initially, the price of the DL-416 display in 1,000 piece quantities as $15 per four-character module.

About the same time Motorola's Semiconductor Products group entered the commercial solar energy field with cell arrays for powering battery-charging equipment. Earlier, at the April, 1976 Hanover, West Germany Fair, a Triumph-Adler group (Div. of Litton Industries in the U.S.) introduced a pocket calculator powered by solar cells. It is called the Solar 1980 and has a liquid-crystal display. It is only one centimeter thick and was made to sell for about $120. It offers floating decimal point, square root, memory for positive and negative input, and single or total clearance.

Wristwatch of Tomorrow Predicted to Contain Phone and Memory

At a March, 1976 *Centennial of the Telephone* convocation jointly sponsored by AT&T and Massachusetts Institute of Technology, Arthur C. Clarke, the well-known science fiction author, predicted that the wristwatch-telephone of tomorrow will be a personal transceiver with information retrieval circuits. He stated that it will also have a memory to hold a few hundred most-used phone numbers. The envisioned portable unit was described as something like the watch-calculators discussed above but with RAMs, ROMs, etc. to combine with data banks, including information processing circuits. The unit was predicted to have capability of acting as a constant companion serving much the same functions as *a human secretary.* Clark called it a "Minisec," and stated that it would provide more and more services until it finally developed its own personality. Mr. Clarke also had much to say about personal use of communications satellites to *unite mankind,* and compared them to the uniting force in America of the railroad and telegraph of a century ago.

The very rapid progress of these and other communications devices is based primarily on the lowering of costs of microcomputer power and the developed versatility of these tiny powerhouses. The lower the cost of the computers-on-a-chip, the wider their product application is likely to be. Crucial to cost reduction of more and more control products is how to plug components of smart machines together. Thus, most of us will be concerned with how to manage the interface or interconnection problem. Some observers have labeled this the *connector confrontation.* Manufacturers who deal successfully with interconnections early in a project development will reap tremendous cost advantage. Not only product innovators, hobbyists, etc. but also the basic design engineers who solve beforehand, the interface problem, can lead their companies and their industries into front positions in the microcontrol revolution.

Calculators and Microcomputers That *Speak*

Much development has taken place and several quality calculator products have been produced to assist the blind and visually-handicapped persons. These *voice* applications are now being developed to also considerably assist people without these handicaps. For example, current voice recognition/ response systems now allow verbal electronic communications through calculators and computers — with ease and at low costs. Voice control systems are currently being used in collection of inspection data; security access through voice identification; in materials handling equipment; on assembly lines; and in numerical control (automation) programming and systems, to list only a few industrial applications. We are all aware of the *computerized* answers we receive from *wrong number* phone calls and in many sections of the U.S. from *long distance operators, information operators,* and other similar response systems. Computer-controlled voice systems are also used for airline baggage handling, telephone talk-back systems, computer aided instruction, (CAI) systems to aid the handicapped and with systems for translating English to foreign languages, vice versa, and other applications. The importance of these systems, and especially their simplicity and low cost, are expected to become fully realized as these systems find their way into many new and varied personal systems as well; home terminals, etc., as offshoots of the industrial and other systems noted above. One distinct advantage to those office workers, engineers, etc. who use audio calculators is to permit them to concentrate full visual attention on the columns of printed figures of work being calculated while listening to the audio input and output, without having to shift attention back and forth from the work to look at the visual display. This capability alone can greatly increase speed and efficiency.

Specially-designed Calculators Assist Professional Development for the Blind

The American Foundation for the Blind has introduced two calculators — one braille and the other an audible unit — for blind and visually handicapped persons. The braille calculator was adapted by AFB's engineering division from a standard portable calculator. It is a five-function unit with floating decimal point, mounted in a box and equipped with a single braille cell. The cell, which uses four dots of the basic six-dot braille notation, is activated by depressing the "read" button at the front of the instrument. The digits and decimal point displayed on the visual readout are presented in sequence in the form of small pins which pop up to form a braille digit. The audible version has a 24-word vocabulary which announces every entry and result. It has six basic functions, accumulating memory, automatic constant, change-of-sign key, floating decimal point, and 8-digit display. The speech key can be pressed repeatedly to announce what is on display without initiating further calculations. The speaker is loud enough for small classrooms and there is an earphone for private listening. AFB's catalog, "Ideas for Better Living," describes these units along with several hundred other devices designed for the blind. Write to Aids and Appliances Division, AFB, 15 W. 16th St., New York, NY 10011, for a free copy.*

Several other companies manufacture *talking calculators* designed to assist the visually handicapped and to perform in other applications. A *Speech Plus* talking calculator was developed by Telesensory Systems, Inc. with a 24-word spoken vocabulary that is electronically synthesized by a custom LSI microcontroller in conjunction with a single 16K ROM. The speech synthesizer is expandable to 64 words and is entirely contained on a single 4 in. × 6½ in. printed circuit board. The unit includes batteries, volume control, and loud-

---

* "Calculators For the Blind", Popular Electronics August, 1976, p. 30.

peaker. Silicon Systems, Inc. of Santa Ana, CA. also produces a microcomputer chip containing output for speech synthesis in addition to normal outputs. A keyboard strobe sets up the outputs of the calculator chip. These signals function as inputs to the SSI microcontrol chip, which in turn takes these inputs and fetches control information stored in a ROM chip. It also determines the addresses needed to access data stored in the ROM. Sound is produced from data stored in the large ROM. The SSI control chip selects the addresses to be read. Speech is produced from data stored in a given location. Each speech sound is made up of many digital bits, each one an increment of the analog audio signal. Synthesized analog speech is then filtered to make it sound more like natural speech. The audio output from the control chip is amplified and reproduced by a loudspeaker built into the calculator. Another system that uses standard-sized keyboard and offers natural-sounding voice with amazing clear fidelity can probably be more clearly explained using the literature from the company.

Master Specialties Company of Costa Mesa, CA. was the first to introduce a Talking Calculator with solid-state voice. This Audio Response Calculator was originally used in vocational education for the blind and continues to be used in this important field. Recent technological advances have permitted both cost and size reductions to extend its use into other applications.

The MSC ARC 9500 is an 8-function calculator that provides both an 8 digit visual display and voice readout for the basic four functions plus all numeral entries and results. Each spoken word is digitized and stored permanently in its own individual Read-Only Memory (ROM) for a clear, natural-sounding voice readout. The solid-state operation of the system provides years of maintenance-free operation and audio output.

In addition to the numeric-words zero to nine, the voice system in the calculator includes the words "plus", "minus", "times", "divide", "equals", and "point" for decimal point. The operator inputs the data through a standard keyboard with easily-learned key positions with touch sensitivity. In the learning mode, as each key is depressed, the number or word associated with that key is announced through a speaker in a natural-sounding male voice. When the "equals" key is depressed, the voice announces "equals" and then voices the number of the total that has been calculated by the arithmetic section of the calculator. A "point" is included in the numeric callout for the decimal point when required.

The ARC 9500 is human engineered to insure ease of efficient operation. All number keys are in a separate group, the arithmetic and percent key in another group, and the additional function keys in a third group to simplify location. The numeric displays utilize large, bright, sharp digits that can easily be seen in most ambient light conditions.

Vocational Education for the Blind

The MSC Audio Response Calculators have already proven to be of immense value in vocational education for the blind. One of the major obstacles to a blind person finding gainful employment is in their inability to use a typical office calculator, which is equipped only for sighted readout. Persons blind since birth also have a particularly difficult time developing an understanding of and skills in basic mathematics. The MSC Audio Response Calculator is a valuable tool in the development of such skills. It permits the operator to hear both the input and the output in a loud, clear voice. The recent cost reduction in this unit is expected to open up a whole new field of vocational opportunities for the blind.

Electronic Games — From Puzzles to Eye Response/Touch Dexterity to Mental Skills and Intellectual Contests

The immense popularity of pocket calculators and the *handiness* with which they manipulate numbers, quickly brought the challenges and fun of number games and puzzles. They were invented by the hundreds and within two years more than a dozen *calculator games* books hit the market. New programming discoveries, games, puzzles appear almost weekly in the dozens of well-read periodicals of the hobbyists, engineers, radio *hams* and scores of other calculator cultists. As one would expect, several clubs and American and foreign country chapters of clubs have sprung up, the largest being the H-P Users Club, headquartered in Santa Ana, California with 2000+ members in 15 countries as of early 1977, with a fine newsletter, *Share-A-Program* system; new and expanding local chapters. They are demonstrating much more versatility and applications progress in calculator capabilities than the manufacturers' educational efforts. (More details of clubs on later pages.)

The dedication of thousands of calculator users is very intense, and many of the games, tricks, puzzles and super-programs developed have already become classics. Many of the newest and best are interactive contests, and all involve elements of conflict and competition, with rules for making moves, timing, and ending of games. Most are playable by owners of the inexpensive *four bangers* with 6-digit displays. Those owners of more sophisticated units can come up with many variations, providing more exciting options. Players need not be expert mathematicians, and multiple calculators are seldom needed. Individual turns and game-plays are fast-paced. Dozens of games have sufficient variety to intrigue people who love numbers as well as those who hate but must learn to master them. Elements of chance, strategies and excitement and personal *touches* are the principal variations and combinations that continually add sporting chances for all players.

Games help sell calculators, and now also, it seems, calculator users are becoming the vanguard of the more exotic computerized TV game purchasers. A few of these games are noted below, but emphasis is placed on the way former *non-intellectuals* very suddenly and happily become acclimated to digital concepts, capabilities and interfaces — through the use of *interactive, real-time response* games at their TV sets. Thus, whereas the familiarity with calculators helped reduce the fear of *things electronic* of the general public, the demonstration through games, that programmability is NOT complex, is significantly aiding in the mass public purchases of "advanced" programmable calculators.

One of the video game pioneers, Magnavox, introduced its Odessey TV game in 1972. Many consumers were very interested but many thousands more were also very soon fascinated with later lower priced units and the many *add-on* devices and extra variety. Single game units were quickly followed by triple-game units and these by game **systems** with sound and color but with retail prices well below $100. In fact the largest supplier of TV game chips in mid-1976 was General Instrument Corp. which offered a "six-on-one" TV game chip that broke the TV game industry wide open. It offered: 4 paddle games and 2 rifle games, all on one chip, (as advertised) . . . "With a fast ball and a slow ball." The ad continued, "at a steep angle and a shallow angle. With a long paddle and a short paddle. And the option to use other variables in any combination . . . (and with) true color. Colored balls that don't change color. Team colors for the paddles. And if you want to play your tennis on grass, just color it green . . . the *Six-on-one* uses only 30 milliamperes . . . players have an option of a rechargeable battery-powered unit. Scoring is automatically displayed on the screen. External electronics required are minimal. Interfacing is simple, through the antenna. The *six-on-one* chip is a standard 28-pin, plastic, dual-in-line (DIP) package . . ." And, one might add, the chips were very cheap, getting cheaper as quantities built into the millions. The competitors quickly jumped in with vicious price-slashing to ensure their own early large shares of this practically unlimited market for the masses. The market size was initially estimated at 2 million units for 1976-77, then 2.5 to 4 million, and finally to 7 million for 1977-78.

With those figures, giant RCA jumped into the market with *high-end* products based on the company's 1802 single-chip microprocessor. The RCA game is microprogrammable, like the Fairchild and Rockwell games mentioned below, with cartridges. The relatively simple "Pong" and other paddle and target games, originally selling for about $80, were expected to be available very soon "after the (1977) holiday season for $30 and $40." The major semiconductor and microcomputer manufacturers sought to avoid this price erosion with the *fancier* microprogrammable — endless variety — types. The main market units were priced from $50 to $150, but a large and growing market from $250 to $1000 was expanding fast. Microprocessor-controlled electronic pinball machines and coin-operated video-display games worth $250 million brought the total electronic games market to near $1 billion for 1976-77, from a start of a few hundred thousand dollars 3 years earlier.

Atari, one of the makers of the Pong game, successfully sold in mass through Sears, Roebuck & Co., unveiled a line of new video games and an estimated 30 companies were in the field with competing units in mid-1976. The variety extended to airplane *dog* fights, sea skirmishes, tank battles, and a seemingly unending variety with new intrigue popping up weekly. For example, Fairchild's Exetron Division demonstrated five games at the Consumer Electronics Show, in 1976, and displayed some of the 10 or more $19 to $25 cartridges that plug into one game console to *program* different games, the base game selling for from $100 to $150. Other companies purchasing the same F-8 microprocessor offered chess games *matched against the microcomputer* at several levels of complexity, using hand-held units that have only an alphanumeric display. The head of one firm, Executive Games, Inc. suggested that the type and variety of games were limited only to the imagination of the individual company.

Names such as Bally, Ramtek, Micro Inc. and others were certain to become household words as the competition expands. Microprocessors are again, like they are in advanced programmable calculators, the *magic* since they permit game controls to be programmed and reprogrammed quickly when developing the original game concept; when offering multiple options for the user, and when building in more features for use with cartridges and tapes. Such expandable capability allows some of the suppliers to program into home games the ability to make the better games progressively more difficult as the players become more accustomed to the variable formats. This adaptability heightens the players interest longer and increases his challenge — not only to the games but also to the tools and digital products, very similar in operation and control, to these he uses at work — programmable calculators.

It was interesting to note that just as the electronic game onrush occurred, Sony (not in the games business) announced its home video cassette recorder that works with both tape and a paper-like sheet storage medium, Mabica, the potential being greater than tape or disks because it costs less than tape and is erasable, unlike disks. West Coast consumer import sources believe Sony could market versions of its Betamax recorder equipment, first sold in the U.S. in

November, 1975, that would work with both kinds of media in early 1977. Sales of the existing plastic tape Betamax were so strong in 1976, Sony was many months behind in orders. Sony executives estimated that 100,000 sets would be sold in 1976, about 30,000 in the U.S., escalating to 200,000 in 1977 and 400,000 in 1978. A console version including a 19-inch TV lists for $2,295 in Los Angeles, while a video deck without TV set was selling for $1,295. All suppliers, dealers, etc. involved are certain prices will fall quickly with the ultimate market seen, at least by Japanese leaders, as . . . "one recorder with almost every color TV." Sony's American tape plants were under construction in mid-1976. (Matushita Electric Ind. Co., Victor Co., Hitachi Ltd., Sharp Corp., and Mitsubishi Electric Corp. were some of the Japanese firms offering units, some well below $1000 in 1977.)

Because of the similarity of technology between games and programmable calculators, especially the media — magnetic cards, cassettes, tapes (and paper-like *Mabica*), as well as programmability of the chips — each type of electronic device assists and enhances the capability and certainly the customer familiarity of the other. This results in better, faster customer education and acceptance of electronic devices, and especially programmable products. Perhaps the best example of this is the *new intelligence* of programmable video games. As late as 1975, suppliers did not dream they could interest even electronic enthusiasts with *open market* introduction of *pocketfuls of programs* in any media. Now, they are rushing what was recently considered *far too complex for the public*. These are the quite exotic software products, devices and media they are marketing with full expectation that the public will quickly pick up the jargon and use many types of microelectronics like veterans in just a few years. And they may well be correct in their judgment of the public's insatiable curiosity and basic intelligence.

Although the paddle-target type video games will initially dominate, the game industry's next generation did not wait long. As noted, the early 1977 season offered the more sophisticated customers programmable games like new models of Fairchild's Video Entertainment System (VES), Rockwell's microprocessor TV system, called, Videorespond, and others. The former will highly promote the programmability *play value* of the four-chip F-8 microprocessor set with additional random-access memory (RAM) and video-modulator circuits, with improved processors also on the quick "drawing board-to product response" cycle. The VES consists of a console for the top of the TV set and attached joystick controls, with a competitive pricing program to get the units quickly to the users. The main feature and the more profitable element, that competitors envy, is the Videocart™ cartridges, which are digitally encoded tapes that program the various games. Five videocarts offering 10 games were originally available including four mathematics quiz games. In addition, VES contained two games built into the console: tennis and hockey, but these two, due to the microprocessor, were far more challenging and intriguing than the low-end video games. The joystick that controls the paddles rotates players, moves them anywhere on the playing surface, offers on-screen scoring, plus time limits on play (hockey mode), overtime periods, with elapsed time showing during the play. A definite hobby-craft educational aspect is the first supplied Videocart *Doodle*. The joystick is used to control a four-video-line cursor to actually *draw* with three colors, red, blue, green, as selected on the console. Also, offered is Quadra-Doodle, the processor forming random, kaleidoscopic patterns on the screen. The game permits *freezing* of the action indefinitely if players are interrupted or decide to watch something on the TV and continue later, even weeks later.

Rockwell's processor (the PPS-8) controls a larger, more complex system of games and is in effect, a true "home computer." Many games are offered but, since the system is interactive, Videorespond, with its joysticks and keyboard, operates in two modes for inputs. It is also programmed by exterior devices, first with digitally encoded audio cassettes, which are also used to record, store and playback information. Other cassettes, *anybody's imagination, again,* are used for programming the microprocessor. In demonstrations, Videorespond performed in four distinct modes: information storage; programmed instruction; information storage with text editing, and *prompting calculation,* such as figuring out diet programs, drawing color pictures on the screen and completing thought games played against the microcomputer. Whole *palettes* of colors can be programmed for composing pictures, and the system offers rudimentary animation capability accompanied by audio-commentary. One commentator thoughtfully mused that we are now certainly on the threshold of the true computerized *home entertainment and educational center.* Certainly the microprocessor with even more capability supplied by competitors and fabricated by imaginative enterpreneurs will do many home chores, control, and surveillance duty very soon — from a library of low-cost program tapes. And, people might soon catch up to the challenges of present high technology. . . .

TODAY'S PROGRAMMABLE CALCULATOR ENVIRONMENT
MESHES WITH HOBBYISTS AND HOME COMPUTERS

Who are the people most enthused about these latter *programmed control, information storage, sensor and response* capabilities? The ones most familiar already with the technology and these capabilities. The programmable calculator (PC) users, several hundred thousand have already painstakenly gained the experience, and some millions soon will gain that experience at schools, offices, factories, laboratories, executive suites, and *in the field* as the programmables become completely commonplace due to their low costs. A great many PC owners who already know what ROMs, RAMs, stacks, bit-slice chips, etc. are and who use this technology have become the base for an estimated 100,000 microcomputer *Club* members in more than 100 American cities, and more clubs pop up almost weekly.

Seven new *slick-paper* exclusively microcomputer periodicals have jumped into the almost frenzied microcomputer hobbyist marketplace. A few years ago microcomputer do-it-yourself kits sold for from $400 to $1000. The most popular was the Altair kit which brought real computer power to the amateur for only $439 in 1975. The then small MITS company of Albuquerque, New Mexico quickly sold more than 8000 of them, much to the surprise of everybody, especially the executives at MITS. Some club memberships number in the thousands (one claiming over 5000 members) and many start with *first meeting* attendance of several hundred. Suppliers present their wares; programs and equipment are sold, exchanged and bartered, and practically any speaker with a few new exotic microcomputer applications can whip up wild enthusiasm from the crowd, especially if the *parts* to complete the task are cheap — and, almost without exception, they are — even 100,000 word disks, display terminal kits, etc.

Hobbyists make things very easy for themselves by copying the innovators, by using almost give-away programs developed by club members, and by reading everything in print about microprocessors, the newest darling of the engineers, ham radio operators, scientists, business and industrial calculator users, students, teachers — and thousands of high school kids, especially the Boy Scouts, who have several computer *merit badges* to earn. They really don't have to struggle through tough coding; *Tiny BASIC* is a very simple language to learn in a few days — and its available for $5 from some sources, $10 from others. The entire system uses only 2000 words of memory, and it works on practically all the models of micros — about 60, in 1976, the number sure to grow into the hundreds. Some microcomputer kit prices in 1976 were slashed to $99 for very good systems. A description and picture of one of them is described below.

$99 Computer

"For less than the cost of many scientific calculators, you can now get your hands on an eight-bit microcomputer kit that can be assembled in something less than an hour (if you aren't all thumbs). The price is even more amazing when you see how the product comes "packaged." It comes in the form of a notebook with instructions on how to get the job done.

"Each notebook includes an SC/MP microprocessor, a single-chip cpu housed in a 40-pin dual-in-line ceramic package, and featuring static operations, forty-six instructions, single-byte and double-byte operation, software controlled interrupt structure, built-in serial I/O ports, bidirectional eight-bit parallel data port, and a latched 12-bit address port. Also included are a 4K-bit ROM organized into 512 bytes and pre-programmed to contain "KITBUG," which is a monitor and debugging program that assists in the development of the users' application programs. "KITBUG" even provides teletypewriter I/O routines and allows examination, modification, and controlled execution of the user's programs. Also included are two 256 four-bit words, a voltage regulator, an eight-bit data buffer, a timing crystal, tty interface, a 72-pin edge connector, a 24-pin IC socket, a 40-pin IC socket, a printed circuit board, eight capacitors, and seven resistors. Large quantities of the "SC/MP" kit are immediately available from the factory and franchised distributors." NATIONAL SEMICONDUCTOR, Santa Clara, Calif. (*Datamation*, July, 1976, p. 130.)

Of course, the more capable *deluxe* home computer systems with lots of memory, visual display terminals, special alarms, device controls and data bases cost upwards of $2000. As more and more microcomputers are used by business, production and process control industries, laboratories, and financial and service institutions, the mass manufacturing and widespread marketing reduces unit costs still further. This aids the computer hobbyist with lower prices, increased versatility and more new ideas for additional applications.

The heart of the microcomputer is the tiny programmable microprocessor. Besides its successful use in millions of advanced calculators, the microprocessor is routinely used in scores of commercial devices. Some examples are: taxi meters, it keeps track of five passenger fares at the same time; in car phones, it records and automatically dials stored phone numbers at the touch of one button; (see below) it calls up on demand from plug-in cassettes the play for as many as 200 video games; in watches with alphameric keyboards, it permits the wearer to enter a date — such as his anniversary, and months later to watch it flash a reminder on its face in time to buy a present; in factories as controllers for individual tools, it directs the metal-cutting and welding machines and feeds data to recorders on the number of good and bad cans; and it is a godsend to thousands of eager inventors and innovators who now can plan, design and implement new control in thousands of new and old tools, instruments, toys, appliances, etc. in industry, science, education, communication and many other endeavors. Some leaders proclaim that it multiplies man's brainpower with considerable more range and capability than the first industrial revolution multiplied man's muscle power. One manufacturer alone,

Rockwell International, produced more than 1 million microprocessor chips by mid-1976, and it has 20 or more competitors in the U.S. alone, several with equally as large or larger production capacity. And more manufacturers are either entering the microprocessor world or are rapidly expanding their facilities. The key to the huge sales totals is simply price — a very sensational drop in prices of practically all electronic control raw material and finished products. Within a single year, high quality, multifaceted microprocessors fell from $100 to $20, and new more versatile, faster units came out in competition until prices went below $10 making microcontrol the cheapest thing around.

One manufacturer suggests that "computer power today is essentially free," only the memory, peripheral devices, and input-output units to gather and distribute the information, issue control orders and develop analyses represent costs, and those are falling as more and more formerly electromechanical devices become all-electronic." Old products now have new, far better capabilities; new customized products can be made efficient and versatile very quickly and relatively simply. Once a microprocessor is designed into or added to a product, tremendous marketing advantages accrue and can be quickly exploited. A product's functions can be programmed (altered) not by a costly and time-consuming redesign of its electronics but simply by adjusting or changing the instructions (programs or software) stored within or as enterable to the microprocessor. New features can be added with very little increase in cost; dumb products can be made *smart,* like the 12 to 20 automated functions, special timing and signaling now available on most microwave ranges, and the multiple *magic capability* of new model sewing machines, etc. Ultrasmart postage scales are saving some companies tens of thousands of dollars in *exact* postage costs yearly from the inferior scales, and formerly *guess-at* complex rates, etc. Microprocessors *hear* voices, digitize numbers and words, store, translate, and transmit prices over stock *tickers,* provide voice answerback to phone callers, accept voice commands from machine operators who must use both hands but require changed machine or feed operations, etc. Airline pilots use microprocessor *black boxes* to calculate the altitude, weight, outside air temperature, and engine pressure ratios and the interaction of these factors automatically. The output supplies the proper altitude, speed, headings for the specific aircraft's weight to save fuel, provide more comfortable trips, and increase safety.

Microprocessors have decreased the costs of Optical Character Readers (OCRs) so that they are now cost-effective. They are used to machine-read printed and hand-written prices, stock numbers, and special codes on merchandise tickets, invoices, messages, etc. New systems are using small tabletop readers, penlike *wands* and other read/transmit devices. Consumers notice more and more microcomputer-controlled home appliances, electronic point of sale (POS) systems at supermarkets, fast-food restaurants and hundreds of other cash and credit transaction points. Executives of microcomputer manufacturing companies predict that between "7 and 10 microprocessors will be in each home by 1980." They are already especially effective in homes and industry as energy managers, security and safety control devices, and they are automating hundreds of communication devices, particularly the end devices of telephone and television systems. Several foreign and domestic automobiles have them integrated to sensors as automated diagnostic controllers, emission test and control devices, controllers of the engine spark advance, and no end is in sight.

As to further assurance of the *home computer,* every home (practically) has two terminals — a telephone and a TV set; the mere coupling of either of these two devices with a simple microprocessor provides a rudimentary home computer — ready and waiting to be used for scores of calculating, communicating, control, and analytical applications. RCA and a half-dozen other major microcomputer makers have already announced or hinted at production schedules for data input, calculator-like keyboard TV sets. They will supply users with many types of information processing capabilities, even customized *hard copy* newspapers produced directly from TV set attachments. Much talk and many articles already speak of totally automated factories and the socially-explosive implication on disemployment of workers. (They become **dis**-employed when the job function they performed disappears rather than **un**employed because there is less need for them to perform that function.) To say that the microprocessor will speed automation is indeed an understatement. Microprocessors have already revolutionized the instrumentation industry. Without new microcontrol devices (several of them) to reduce size, increase speed and accuracy, they remain securely on the shelf. But with them, the sales are phenomenal. Micros in offices, stores, factories, laboratories, etc. mean significant change. In some operations, the change has become all encompassing, and a large number of companies feel they must rush to microcomputers as fast as possible or lose out drastically to competitors.

Many observers are concerned about both the lack of supply and difficulty of handling microcomputer software. But the experience with millions of people quickly solving their programmability problems with calculators suggests very rapid supply and utilization of microcomputer programs. Microcomputer industry people suggest the technology will permit the great majority of capabilities in *firmware* — wired-in or *dedicated* microprocessors (like calculators). And the efficiency of BASIC and other languages is such that anyone will be able to program micros and the products that contain them. "A million devices (transistors, etc.) on a single chip" with all the necessary memory are promises being made by designers. Obsolescence is assured for those products without micros — and the *wrist-radio-phones,* billion dollar microprocessor industry predictions and projections go on and on . . . and they are not being dismissed or doubted.

Microprocessors vs Microcomputers

The terminology surrounding microprocessors and microcomputers is often very confusing. A small attempt will be made at this stage to make some points of clarification. Much more detail is given later in the text. Most readers are more concerned with what can be done with microprocessors than how they are built and how they operate per se. However, fundamental concepts must be understood. Basically, the microprocessor contains all the foundation elements necessary to manipulate data encoded in binary numbers. It thus stores a program and controls the execution of it even though its total operating components are contained on a single or pair of very tiny, complex semiconductor chips (of silicon, usually). Most are MOS-LSI chips — Metal Oxide Semiconductor, Large Scale Integrated chips or *sandwiches* of planes of these binary electronic switching arrays. This makes them programmable by using *machine* codes or languages, the microprocessors, and a few other associated chips (memory) can contain interpreters or compilers so that programmers may use higher-level (simpler to understand and use) languages. And many of these are rapidly being used, such as, BASIC, APL and perhaps a dozen others.

To become a microcomputer, the microprocessor chip requires, on the same or associated chips, power supply circuitry, memory (usually Read Only Memory (ROM)), input-output ports (pins), and control interfaces (circuits) for these. And all of this often is mounted on a printed circuit board that may include from 10 to 200 various chips or DIPs, which stands for the most common mounting of chips and pins, Dual In-line Package. These look like tiny bugs with 30 or 40 metal legs, with the microprocessor chip as a *hump* in the middle of its back). See photos on next few pages.

The power of the majority of microcomputers derives, to a large degree, from the multiplicity of data paths connecting its basic elements. Micros, or microprocessors become full-fledged microcomputers with control, I/O, memory, interfaces, etc. They are used within many peripheral devices to obtain great advantages because of tiny size, very low power requirements, low cost and tremendous flexibility they substitute for attributes of *regular* computer processing power. Micros are true stored program computers now mass-produced with near total automation. Until recently the greatest use of microprocessors was in calculators, computer terminals, communication devices, computer peripheral devices, components for large computers and in games. Now they are spreading everywhere, as noted above. And *stacked* microcomputers in units of 32, 162 or even 512 make very powerful systems.

Finger tip Microprocessor Chip on DIP-Dual In Line Package replaces complete PC board.

THIMBLEFULL OF ELECTRONICS

A thimble holds over 500 microcircuits, each one-tenth of an inch square. They are the equivalent of more than a million transistors. The tiny electronic circuits are manufactured by NCR Corporation's Microelectronics Division in Dayton, Ohio. Used in NCR computers and data terminals, they reduce the electrical interconnections in a typical data terminal from approximately 70,000 to 1,000.

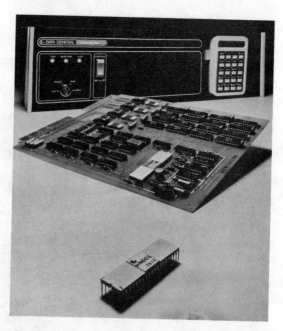

Data General's microNOVA family puts 16-bit NOVA architecture into a microprocessor, a computer-on-a-board, and an MOS mini-computer, to give OEMs a complete packaging range.

Event Driven Systems That Expand Home Computer and Terminal Markets

Minicomputers are the big brothers of microcomputers. More than 100,000 have been sold, the majority of them for dedicated control systems. In the drive for true automation, costs and computer size had to be further reduced — and most of all, the result would have to assure easier user-oriented management. In most cases this means event-driven systems would be required to originate, drive and terminate user-oriented transactions. Examples of these are banking equipment, specifically check authorization equipment that allows consumers to operate the terminal instead of a teller or supermarket store employees. Research has shown that customers enjoy operating cash dispensers that are easy to use and that, more importantly, create a pleasant image so the consumer is not graphically reminded he is dealing with a dominant machine. Vendors have found that sensitivity to the concerns of the user will have long-run beneficial effects for both vendor and user. It is especially important to design in pleasant or at least acceptable *human factors* to hasten the evolution of terminal equipment into the customer's life-style without difficult sociological problems. Proper consideration may also finally begin to dispel many of the deep suspicions and insidious types of distrust and jealousy of computer systems by a large share of the public.

As will be noted in chapters ahead, many advanced programmable calculator users will graduate up to the control of distributed processing terminals, instruments and systems, using basically the same keyboards, techniques, and capabilities they mastered in their earlier calculator training days. With the proliferation of the distributed processing concept, *the intelligent terminal* looms as the dominating device in offices, schools, laboratories, factories, and other information processing inquiry and termination points. Many become in effect, stand-alone communications processors — with highly customized end-product formatting and specialized reports as net results. In these type instruments and devices, the microcomputer and minicomputer are apparently merging. In terms of price/performance, the reports of research companies show the effects of the economics of integrated circuitry on minicomputer DP functions. The price of a quite standard 4K (4,000 word) minicomputer, for example, dropped from close to $18,000 in 1965 to less than $2,000 in 1976. Multiminicomputers and stacked microcomputers are very powerful, and when enough of them are placed in parallel, the overall performance can outpace even the giant IBM 370/168 on certain problems, according to several reports. People at Gruman Research (Gruman Aerospace Corp.) suggest that 10 to 20 microprocessor modules and a minicomputer can cut the time needed to solve a complex problem from several hundred hours on the 370/168 to a more manageable 2 to 20 hours, cutting the cost dramatically as well. Similar systems are developed with programmable calculator systems integrated with a minicomputer programmed in a high-level language. In operation the calculator modules are programmed to carry out the repetitive calculations on command from the minicomputer. These calculator systems capabilities and applications are reviewed in significant detail in the last few chapters.

Programmable Calculator Users: Vanguard to Home Computer Popularity

A basic theme developed throughout this book relates to the rapid acceptance of home computers and computer terminals as a result of the leadership of the hundreds of thousands of programmable calculators and *ham* radio operators. Big pushes by such strong periodicals as: POPULAR ELECTRON-ICS, *73*, BYTE, PEOPLE'S COMPUTER COMPANY, INTERFACE AGE, MINI/MICRO SYSTEMS, CREATIVE COMPUTING, MICROCOMPUTER DIGEST, COMPUTER HOBBYIST, and a score of others are important moving forces. The H-P Users Club with its very dedicated and energetic members throughout the world, its educational and updating member contributions to its newsletter, share-a-program system and calculator manufacturer program library etc. and contributions of the TI Calculator Club and periodicals have given enthused calculator entrepeneurs *a place to go* with their ideas, innovations, and craving for associationship. Practically all hand-held programmable calculator users well realize that the widening lines of peripherals for **desk-top** programmable calculators quickly (a year or two at most) become available to them for their personal hand-held calculating fulfillment. Printers, tape cassettes, insertable ROMs, typewriters, floppy disks, etc. are now being offered in volume as adaptable (with low cost interfaces) to hand-held units. These same users further realize that the advanced large screen programmable calculator systems (full capability standalone computers in most cases) will soon be within their own price environment and thus available as very versatile home information and control systems.

Terminals are the Tentacles of Systems; Calculators Are Excellent Terminals

Business, industrial, educational and research users of computer systems now demand remote terminal capability but they hate large, complex, expensive systems and their inherent delays — and they dislike the high costs, strict rules, and inconvenience of hiring outside timesharing services, and the inherent delays in these systems also. Now with increased terminal power and versatility of desk-top calculators (due to the inclusion of microprocessors) and the severely reduced costs, many more purchaseable options are available to them — and with immediate, local and total control. They can maintain local databases, complete most of their processing in their own offices, on their own desks. And the very rapid and unproblemmatical *human acceptance* of these *smart* terminals is due in great part to the fast rise, experience, and popularity of electronic calculator users.

Managers now realize that tiny, inexpensive calculators can not only calculate, process, and print extremely fast and accurately . . . but they are also fun to most users. They also now realize that slightly larger machines can remember more, arrange it in proper order and format and print it out, even after visual editing, also for very low cost, i.e., only slightly more than a good office typewriter. And this is true today, and the good calculator *man-machine* relationship continues to get even better. What alert college-educated staff man or woman cannot run or learn to run a programmable calculator? Practically none. Then also it can be surmised they should adapt in a friendly fashion to similar keyboard calculator-type on simple programmable terminals. Adding disk memories, plug-in ROM or cassette programs, etc. gives these units *big system* power. These then become *small time,* small size, small priced systems. They are actually replacing larger in-place computer systems, and happily so for most all concerned. And the self-taught or formally calculator-educated people are most acclimated and ready to take over, often with great pleasure and promise.

Perhaps an even greater *total population* impact of the use of calculators by the millions relates to their acceptance by even the smallest shops, stores, professionals and service firms. These two-to-ten person *shops* have shunned computers and even *smart* terminals as being too expensive and complex. But, a great many of them now heavily and heartily use and/or most soon will purchase calculators. And the low costs and versatility of programmables make them most enticing. These small shop operators do indeed require computational capability and they really need good control in the systems they operate. The step-up from hand-helds to desk-top programmables is easy for them to make . . . mentally, emotionally, and economically. Most calculator manufacturers see this huge market unfolding for them as do scores of new PC peripheral companies.

With the advent of built-in microprocessors, the toughest terminal hardware interfacing problems have been all but eliminated. One research report suggests that by 1978 all smart terminal manufacturers will be able to offer devices which are compatible with all mainframes. Thus, programmable calculators operated as communication terminals and as smart terminals will not only not obsolete others but they can become part of growing systems, despite the brand name of the old or additional units. And practically all advanced programmable calculator and smart terminal systems are moving from tape cassettes to the larger capacity floppy disk drives, and in displays, new sharper plasma units may replace cathode ray tubes (CRTs), but basically or at first, in applications where counter space is at a minimum. Some examples of the use of microprocessors in terminals to make them smarter, smaller, and cheaper are summarized:

Tektronix designers were given the challenge of developing a lower-priced, locally controlled compact computing system combining convenient storage, large-screen graphic display, and a general purpose interface bus (connector line or highway system for multiple devices). They achieved these goals (for their 4051 BASIC Graphic Terminal) by using a Motorola MC6800 microprocessor for the central processing unit (CPU) of the terminal control.

Fasfax was looking for the way to package their Point of Sale (POS) system more compactly with a smaller power supply and fewer inside components, yet increase system capability. They also used the M6800 microprocessor family to produce "Stanley." They were satisfied that it become one of the most cost effective, most adaptable POS systems available for the restaurant business. The microprocessor controls up to six units.

Codex Corporation's series of intelligent network processors required a microprocessor to perform network management and centralized control, terminal intermix, data compression and several additional functions in a uniquely executed microprocessor architecture. Again the M6800 family provided excellent performance with its compatible I/O, ROM, and RAM (Random Access Memory).

Hewlett-Packard recently offered a CRT terminal which has 220,000 bytes (characters) of built-in mass data storage. The Model 2644A can perform on a stand-alone basis many operations normally requiring connection to a computer. Two fully-integrated tape transports provide enough data storage for a normal day's work. For data entry, forms can be stored on one cartridge and selectively retrieved in seconds. Program preparation, editing, tape copying, and tape-to-printer operations are all within the stand-alone abilities of the microprocessor-controller. The enhanced display of the unit contains 1,920 characters that can be displayed in a 24-line by 80-column format. Inverse video, blinking, half-bright, and underlining can be employed in all of their possible 16 combinations.

Texas Instruments Co. firmly believes there will be a huge consumer demand for portable computer terminals — much like the demand for pocket calculators. Its Model 745 is pegged to sell in the tens of thousands for under $2000 (with big reductions for large distributor orders). It weighs less than 13 pounds and is expected to sell in volume to insurance, real estate, wholesaler, manufacturer and educational markets. There are more than 450,000 insurance agents in the U.S., and the 745 is capable of talking to a central data base in the home office. Contract closures can be made on the spot instead of having to pack up and leave and get back to the potential buyer — who often changes his or her mind in the interim. The 745 is part of the *Silent 700* series of non-impact thermal printers, running at 10-30 characters per second with a built-in acoustic coupler (with use by ordinary phones), standard ASCII keyboard complete with embedded numeric pad. The microprocessor-controlled unit uses programmable read only memories (PROMs) and can easily be equipped with special keyboards. Lower cost versions are available.

Low-cost PCs, Microcomputer Kits, Smart Terminals Lead to Home Terminal Acceptance

Within one 12-month period beginning in late 1975, more than 10,000 microcomputer kits were sold to hobbyists, designers, schools and pure amateurs. The micros almost burgeoned their way into the vast build-it-yourself hobby markets. *Black markets* sprung up in duplicated software *packages* and for several components in short supply. Within the first two years, ease of use attributes demanded by users forced microcomputer manufacturers and fabricators (those who take parts and fashion them into unique designs and special capabilities) to sell both kits and finished units with calculator-like keyboards. Just as with the dedicated innovators of the PC users and club members (many of them the same customers), the microcomputer unit (MPU) hobbyist users controlled home heating systems, burglar and smoke alarms; developed information retrieval systems (recipes, tax items, medical and vital records, special dates, etc.). Users monitored inside and outside temperatures, humidity, etc. and invented or brought home special programs that allowed many of them to do a considerable amount of their office *desk* work at home. They rigged sensor-photocells to signal weights, heights, and *diameters* to identify friends at their doors. New input and output devices are becoming very economical and efficient; communication systems are being simplified; mass-storage systems are capable of on-line remote recall (trillions of bits of data at microsecond speed — 1 millionth of a second), and more and more homes have their remote terminals on-line to offices — client, customer, vendor, etc. They have become increasingly valuable for business purposes to save considerable travel time and costs.

These home microcomputers and terminals cost little more than a major appliance and are small enough to fit in or on a desk. Some hobbyists have programmed their systems to care for their homes while they are on trips — to reduce temperature at certain times of the day, turn on lights at certain hours, answer the phone with prerecorded messages. Some, with terminals phone-line connected or connectable to their company's office computers, send in their work over leased telephone lines and receive assignments back. Others develop files of their hobbies, profession, literature, friend's interests, etc. for instant recall on demand. Others are building their own rather complete *personal interest* libraries from books, periodicals, newspapers with abstracts, references, etc.

An example of a hobbyist terminal kit that interfaces to a TV set follows. One major hobbyist supplier offers a kit to be used to hook up an electric typewriter to a TV set. The user can convert both units into a computer terminal by assembling the kit. The CT-1024 from Southwest Technical Products Corp., San Antonio, TX has a ROM (insertable control program) that generates the standard ASCII characters and 1000 words of memory to store information for display on the TV screen. The input is an ASCII keyboard, and the output is connected to the TV's amplifier by a 75-ohm coaxial cable. Some typewriters are connected to the television receiver through the antenna terminal. The terminal can display a page of information, consisting of 16 lines of 32 characters each. The unit's memory can store up to two pages of information or 1024 characters. The unit also comes with an optional cassette recorder adaptor, so that information can be entered on or retrieved from standard cassette tapes, thus, providing unlimited storage. The complete computer kit ranges in price from $200 to $300 depending on options.

These terminals, kits, interfaces, memory devices, and scores of other accessory and peripheral products have become available at *computer stores* that began springing up by the score in 1975 and by the hundreds in 1976. Very soon after the large electronic catalog houses, (Heathkit, Edmund's Scientific, Chafitz, etc.) chain stores (Radio Shack, Olsen's, etc.) which have thousands of branches planned sales of hobbyist computers, kits, and terminals with associated equipment. Department stores with *Electronics Departments* for Electronic Games, Calculators, CB Radios, etc. began selling computer terminals as well. And several large manufacturers quickly developed models specifically designed for this *amateur* market. These marketing outlets are also watching several other electronic equipment products that are very promising. Many *home* computers are designed to respond to a wide range of spoken instructions, as are calculators noted above. Industrial robots have a history of slow development and high cost, but this is rapidly changing as small entrepreneurs are now using microprocessors provided with decision making ability. As they are given input information from sensors they form output commands based on resident programs acting on these data.

Many amateur *computer artists* and *computer musicians* are having significant successes with their products. Amateur solar systems for the do-it-yourselfers are being marketed, and their systems for producing heating and cooling plants are very close to cost effectiveness. (Sun-powered calculators, pop-corn poppers, TV sets, portable radios, toys and watches are among the endless products being marketed.) The concepts of *biorhythm* control and analyses by calculator and computer are bringing in whole new branches of hobbyists, and very large ones, to computer concepts and the implementation of systems specialized in their knowledge disciplines. Many advanced calculator users and home computer hobbyists well realize that electronic mail is not too far away. Long distance videofax has become very cheap both in equipment and service, with hard copy messages now available in less than 1 second per page. And computerized word processing systems in offices are claiming a huge market. In effect, with any of the various types of electronic document-preparation terminal and point-to-point communication links, an electronic mail service is *in being*. With these new fast, low-cost, and simpler systems, users could deliver business letters across the land electronically. And several companies, not supported by but in cooperation with AT&T, offer combination micro-wave local lines individual *packet* message services.

IBM's new satellite company, SBS, Satellite Business Systems, Inc. in association with Comsat and Aetna Insurance, will soon offer businesses individual rooftop-antenna satellite services, in effect, practically circumventing the phone lines with lower cost, more convenient service. And its competitors, RCA, Western Union, American Satellite, AT&T, and General Tel., plus others with satellites of their own or leased are striving to beat SBS to much of its projected punch. Bell Canada, in August of 1976, stole a march on the rest of the world, when it scattered 200 of its E-phones (for all-electronic) across Canada for field tests. Even the ring was electronically generated. The wide use of LSI circuitry permits all circuitry to be installed in the handset itself, leaving the base free for added features such as tape recorder, calculator, numbers memory, and a score of other devices. Alert hobbyists, and most of them are avid readers of latest electronic developments, also are knowledge-able about the experiments in twoway TV cable systems and the new low costs of such equipment and services. First-run movies are offered by one typical system at 29¢ for each family member for a typical family of four, this low price is due to the cable system's use of satellite-shared facilities with other Cable TV systems.

Calculators vs. Computers — Differences and Advantages

Until 1976 there were considerable differences between microcomputers and electronic calculators, certainly in outward appearance. The modern cal-culator's primary outward characteristics were a keyboard, single line display — and on several types, a roll tape printed output. Entry of numbers was direct and immediate as were the displayed or printed decimal or scientific notation answers. Calculators are specifically designed for human convenience and ease of continuous interaction. Early microcomputers were chips mounted on cir-cuit cards with strings of wires attached in every direction and with input and output from teletypes, punched tapes, etc. In 1976, however, a great number of the hobbyist type microcomputers were available in neat boxes (card cages) with calculator-type pads (keyboards), LED or other display readouts (includ-ing TV sets), some even with typewriter input and printer output. It seems that the *ease of use* characteristics of calculators was being demanded by hob-byists, and the fabricators of micros were acceding to those demands.

At the same time, advanced desk-top calculators were already using computer-like peripherals as CRT displays, printer output disk memories, al-phameric (typewriter) input, BASIC and other high level languages, plotters, programs on many media — paper or magnetic tape, magnetic cards, insert-able ROM or Programmable ROM (PROM), cassettes and cartridges. The users of hand-held units were aware of their desk-top *bigger brother* capabilities and were not overly surprised as practically all of these capabilities became avail-able for their smaller *belt-strap* powerhouses. Thus, while many microcomput-ers are beginning to look and act more like calculators, calculators are per-forming more and more like computers. For example, common computer-like calculator capabilities are: Write, Edit, Internally Store, Preserve, Display Programs; Numerous Data Storage Registers, Labels, Flags, Addressing Types, Subroutines, Nests, Loops; plus Tests, Pauses, Decisions, Branches, Online Graphics Instruments and Peripheral Commands, and the list goes on. What then are the primary differences — and secondary ones.

There are at least a half dozen in the first category and scores of incidental or secondary differences. Keyboard inputs, display outputs and even slower speeds must now be dismissed as primary differences. Microcomputers use the first two characteristics, and the most advanced models of desk-top calculators operate in low microsecond (very fast) speeds. Although microcomputer kits sell from $100 to $500, generally this former low price advantage is matched and exceeded by fully programmable calculators. This is especially true now that National Semiconductor, (NS), Hewlett-Packard (H-P) and Texas Instruments (TI) offer excellent hand-held units, the H-P 67, and TI 57, 58 and 59, with most of the capabilities listed above, for common (discount house) selling prices of from $70 to $350 in the Los Angeles area and around the U.S. National Semiconductor with other models, Casio and Sharp units with similar capabilities and prices, are pushing the "Big Two" leaders very hard for their own increased shares of these markets.

Although similarities do appear between calculators and computers as regards price, speed, and appearance, technically calculators ARE slower, even at the high end, than the now prevalent nanosecond (billionth of a second) micros. Again, also at the high end, microcomputers ARE cheaper especially as regards their ability to handle data transfers to and from memory at megabyte speeds; the handling of really large 10 million-bit data memory without back-up storage; the ability to use many computer languages, develop ultra high speed control processing, and handle extremely complex programming. Primary difference #1 then is: As regards very high level capabilities, microcomputers are faster, more versatile and cheaper for these special applications. (See Box: SC/MP.) Contrasted with this, however, calculators at the lower end capabilities are much simpler, easier to use, considerably less expensive and troublesome; they require little or no education in areas such as languages, internal operation and control, and perform very efficiently without awkward or expensive peripherals or programming. Calculators are friendly and fun; microcomputers are often complex, challenging and sometimes fierce.

Fundamentally, calculators are NOT to be considered scaled down or miniature computers. There are many basic and very distinct differences in design. Difference #2: With few exceptions, calculators are specifically designed for total and continuous calculator-human interaction. Computers, except new personal types, are designed for automated nonhuman interaction; computers communicate with each other and other machines. Primary difference #3: With exceptions of only the most sophisticated calculators, internal operation and output of calculators is decimal (internally, binary-coded decimal) with conversion to scientific notation when desired or necessary. Computers work with straight binary, often using interpreters and compilers, and output is in an endless variety. Perhaps the most significant difference between the two information control instruments is in the internal structure. Difference #4: Computers are structured to operate as word-oriented binary machines. Although there are exceptions, arithmetic and data transfers and operations take place in parallel with busing architecture (busses are *paths* or *highways*). For example, a 16-bit *word* machine carries data and addresses, say on 16 wires. Calculators are character-oriented decimal machines, using binary circuit internal logic, but representing numbers one decimal digit at a time, and as binary-coded decimal or with similar schemes.

The simpler calculator machines are 4-bit (one number) machines. The H-P 65 fully programmable machine was developed around a 6-bit word. Each step of program memory was represented internally, and on the magnetic card, by 6 ones and/or zeroes. This scheme allowed only 64 (or 2^6) possible one-step instructions. With those 64 instructions, it was possible to merge the most important multiple keystroke operations — such operations as recall, store, and stack manipulation. However, other multiple keystroke operations required more than one step in memory. In the H-P 67/97 systems, all operations were merged into single program steps. This required a larger, 8-bit word for internal representation of each program step. This made direct compatibility with the 6-bit system, or the H-P 65 impossible. H-P 65 programs had to be rewritten (converted) for use on the new, expanded-capability H-P 67, the H-P 97 (a *desk-top* 67) has a built-in printer. The NS 7100, however, has a microprocessor in it and is, in effect, a hand-held microcomputer. The internal operating differences (bit *slice* systems, etc.) are far more substantial and significant than this and are discussed more fully in chapters ahead.

At this stage of the book the simpler concepts of differences and advantages can quite well be summarized as: Calculators are friendlier, simpler, handier and can be used immediately by switching them on for great varieties of spontaneous answers — all without special training in complex languages, equipment and program utilization. But also at this point, it might be noted that because several calculators are now available with more complex PROM programming, special PROM development (assembly) services are available. One of these shops summarizes its operations as follows: "The program is submitted to us on coding sheets; we run an assembly on our development system and return the programmed PROMs and listings to the customer. Advantages of this system are: low cost, no capital investment, and the use of our library of proven subroutines. In addition, we can run simulation on the actual microprocessor or calculator and provide assistance in programming if required."

It is obvious there is a merging of advanced programmable calculator users and microcomputer hobbyists — and that the distinctions between the two are at least *blurred*. Programmable calculator users cover practically every range of businessman, engineer, manager, student, teacher, professional, office worker, salesmen, etc. But, who are the microcomputer hobbyists? A composite of the membership of the hundreds of computer clubs and thousands of customers of *computer* stores suggests the following member groups. (1) The dedicated and challenged programmable calculator user is a natural for seeking more adventure in the wider versatility of microcomputers, specifically the superspeed and the ever-widening device control capabilities. (2) Engineers, radio *hams,* electronically oriented people with strong background in *hardware* find the design and control capabilities intriguing. (3) Computer system employees are now becoming quite curious about their machines since they are no longer only available as $25,000 to $1 million monsters; at $500 to $1000 for all that power, they are looking into micros — to develop a steadier hold on their jobs, be more aware of developments, and get hold of the whole machine themselves. (4) Most programmers seldom get a chance to *do the whole job* or completely run the system, and they really are not *hardware* people; micros offer them the opportunity to really expand their capabilities, to test their ideas, pet programs, new applications, themselves on their own hardware. (5) The mighty army of do-it-yourselfers will certainly not let the computer kits alone; they've dealt with everything from home furniture to solar heating systems and the computer, now at below $500, will be just one more gadget to build and master. (6) The inquisitive and interested rank amateur even with no experience whatever in hardware, software or programmable calculators, such as: accountants, students, Boy Scouts, businessman, teacher, electrician or garage mechanic all are known to be members of computer hobbyist clubs; they have always had an interest in *the thing* but didn't know where to turn or how to start *getting at it* — now they know.

Basic Computer Components

Most modern computers are fundamentally the same in design and operation. This statement generally holds true whether the computer is a giant multi-billion dollar supercomputer or a lowly $30 microcomputer. The Central Processing Unit (CPU) is its heart; in microcomputers this is called the microprocessor. Many observers suggest that the major components of all computers are five: the Arithmetic-Logic unit (ALU), Control Circuits, Storage or Memory (for both data and instructions), Input Ports or Devices, and Output Devices or Media. It has now become more common, however, to group the first two and call that single chip (in many hobbyist microcomputers) or chip system or board, the microprocessor. The microprocessor thus performs the arithmetic and logic, as the instructions (which it calls — *fetches*) dictate and also controls the memory and input/output (I/O) transfers. Although the single chip microprocessor (cheaper, smaller, simpler) has become the vogue for calculators, games, simple control devices, etc., the more complex, larger, and powerful microprocessor capabilities are often on a microprocessor or CPU *board* providing for more control programs (usually integrated in ROM or PROM), and with clocks and other switching, I/O, and special integrated operating system (OS) program *chunks* or macroprograms. Thus, depending upon whether one considers the ALU and control separate components, i.e., a two-part CPU or microprocessor, the four or five elements with the input and output of storable programs also define how a computer works. The control portion directs the operation of the ALU, and the traffic into and out of memory, holding intermediate *(scratch-pad)* results until needed. That input can be single commands (1 or 0 — on or off) from individual sensors or long subdivisions (subroutines) of massive programs conducting data base searches or controlling communication networks. One must remember that despite this quite awesome power, due to Large Scale Integration (LSI) of several thousand Metal Oxide Semiconductor (MOS) devices as sandwiched on a single microscopically tiny silicon chip, microprocessors can be *stacked* to build very economical, massive capability machines — still contained in very small *black boxes*. Hobbyists start with micros as *answer machines,* environmental device controllers, game players, but the intrigue is with the expandability of this power through program and stacked micros. Some sociologists are not too happy about where some imaginations might run.

Below is National Semiconductor's published description of SC/MP, one of its units. Distributors began marketing the basic unit 'kit' at $99.95 in mid 1976. It is compared with a quick description of a competing Motorola M6800 system (chip set) as fabricated (integrated with other parts and 'packaged') by another firm and selling for $1050, but containing a keyboard and other 'quite necessary' I/O devices. To further demonstrate the range of calculator vs microcomputer products, brief descriptions are given of National's $9.95 CPU as related to two calculator chip offerings — the very simple one offered for $4.50 and the more advanced one with various interfaces, RAMs, etc. (The latter two prices are for large quantity orders.)

SC/MP: a Simple to use Cost-effective/Microprocessor

National's single-chip SC/MP marks the birth of a new generation of microprocessors. As an early, *low-cost* true microprocessor, SC/MP needs only one memory chip (any standard ROM, PROM, or RAM) to form a complete, fully programmable, general-purpose microprocessor system.

And this system, because of its low cost, is ideally suited to replace "sheet metal" logic in toys and games, traffic controls, home appliances, vending machines, home and building security and environment controls, on-board automotive computers, and so on.

SC/MP's features make it all happen: 8-bit data handling is combined with 16-bit addressing; an on-chip clock simplifies system design; a serial I/O port makes for easy interfacing; built-in flags and jump conditions simplify control tasks; an interrupt structure that gives fast response to asynchronous events; a delay instruction to simplify timer systems. And all of these are supported by a set of 46 control-oriented instructions.

Getting started with SC/MP is quite simple. Aside from the CPU chip itself, two kits are offered. The basic kit includes all ICs, firmware, discretes, and mechanical hardware to let you explore SC/MP's capabilities. The SC/MP LCDS (Low-Cost Development System) goes further, and includes a keyboard, a display, more memory, etc. — it's a complete microcomputer, in fact, which lets you rapidly develop and debug programs, and experiment with interrupts and interface structures.*

M6800 μC Comes with 8k Memory, Power Supply

A complete microcomputer built around the Motorola 6800 microprocessor chip set, the Expanded-68 is designed for system prototype development use and comes with an 8k memory and power supply. Also included in the package is a 16 digit keyboard, Teletype adapter, hex LED display, expansion cabinet, application manual and programming manual. ($1050 — **Electronic Product Associates**)

μ Computer, RAM, ROM Fit on 4½″ × 6½″ Card

One small complete 8 bit microcomputer (4½″ × 6½″ card) has a Fairchild F-8 chip. The Model 810 F8 based system is fully assembled and tested, and operates with an instruction time of 2 μ sec. Besides the F8 microprocessor, the system comprises 1k byte RAM, 1k byte of firmware, and 32 bidirectional latched I/O ports, all TTL compatible. The microcomputer features two independent external interrupt inputs, two independently programmable interval timers, and a data terminal interface. Memory is expandable with PROM, RAM and cassette program loader modules. ($179 — stock.) Pronetics

Our $9.95* CPU is Actually Less Than Half the Price of the 8080 or 6800 CPU.

And it's just the beginning of your saving. On-chip RAM, ROM and timers make an even bigger difference. Difference in cost. Difference in reliability and difference in manufacturing time. The following is the whole price/performance story of our F8 system, from minimum configurations to expanded systems.

Lowest Cost Configuration

Our minimum configuration F8 is perfect for controlling home appliances, braking systems, vending machines, ignition systems and other uses with modest memory and I/O requirements.

---

*National Anthem — National Semiconductor Corp. Newsletter, No. 3, May, 1976.

Two chips do it all — a $9.95 PSU (Program Storage Unit) and F8 CPU (Central Processing Unit) for $9.95. The CPU is an 8-bit device, with a cycle time of 2 microseconds. It's the heart of all F8 microprocessors. It includes 70 instructions, 64-byte RAM (Random Access Memory), instruction register, accumulator, 16 individually controllable I/O lines, power-on reset, on-chip clock and control lines to other devices.

The PSU features a 1K byte ROM (Read Only Memory), program counter, 16 individually controllable I/O lines, 8-bit data port, stack register, incrementer/adder, and programmable timer and interrupt.

We're the only manufacturer in the world to offer this 2-chip performance. The 8080 requires 7 chips (9 chips with timer) to do the same thing.

Double the Program Storage

If you need more program space, just substitute PSU's. Our new 2K byte PSU offers twice the ROM for only $14.95.

Built-in Interface to External Memory

But suppose you need a couple of RAM's added to your CPU and 2K/PSU. Again, substitute PSU's for one with a built in memory interface. Avoid paying for extra chips. Order our new 2K/PSU-MI for $14.95. This is super microprocessor power on 4 chips. (Fairchild) *Electronic News*, July 12, 1976, p. 12.

Calculator Circuit Has Direct Digit Drive

The Model MK (Mostek) 50321N is an eight digit, eight function, full memory calculator circuit with direct digit and segment LED drive. The circuit features the standard four arithmetic functions along with % $\sqrt{x}$, $1/x$, x^2 and a six key memory. The user can select either a m + = or an m + mode of memory operation. Other capabilities include percentage add-on/discount, five function automatic constant, and repeat add/subtract. A floating negative sign and seven digit negative numbers eliminate the need for a ninth digit. ($4.50 ea/100 — in mid 1976.)

Processor is Calculator-Oriented

Looking for a versatile, low-cost, dedicated or custom-programmable calculator or control system? We've got it! Our MM5799 contains all system timing functions, all arithmetic and logic functions, all RAM functions (384 bits), and all control ROM functions (1536 microinstructions 8-bits wide, 10-μs/microcycle) that you'll need to implement a variety of small control and microprocessor systems.

A single MOS/LSI chip, the MM5799 can scan 56 keyboard switches, or you can enter BCD data words. Its eight outputs present information in either a BCD or a seven-segment-plus-decimal-point format, and four additional latched outputs give you encoded digit-timing information. Further, a serial-in port and a serial-out port let you expand the basic RAM store and interface to peripherals.

And speaking of peripherals and extra storage, our MM5788 printer interface, DS8664 Series oscillator and decoder/drivers, MM5785 RAM interface, and MM2102 and MM74C930 1-K static RAMS are a perfect match to an MM5799-based system.

> A special purpose microprocessor, our MM5799 uniquely bridges the gap between the overkill of general purpose processors and inflexible, costly, custom LSI. (National Semiconductor Corp.)

Conclusion: Programmable Calculators, Microcomputers, Home Terminals — Where We are and Where We're Going . . .

It was no great surprise to calculator industry people, but it might be an interesting note to people now very enthused about the electronics industry — the division manager of the Microelectronic Device Division of Rockwell International, in Anaheim, California announced that in January of 1976 his company had the highest monthly output of LSI semiconductors, the basic components for calculators and microprocessors. The monthly total was more than 2 million chips, three times that of January, 1975. Equally as noteworthy, although the two million confetti-sized *chips* of LSI semiconductors contained the equivalent of 20 billion transistors, they weighed only 62 pounds. The microprocessor chip, as noted, is the heart of millions of calculator modules and is the principal component of the hundreds of thousands of microcomputers now *revolutionizing* practically all ranges of electronics. A considerable number of the pages ahead will provide rather thorough analyses of microprocessors and associated chips.

Forecasts have been made that there will be at least one microprocessor for each 20 people in the early 1980s. One expert has compared the invention of the microprocessor to the Gutenberg press. At least in terms of impact on the population mass, that analogy seems justified. Printing made information available around the world and at almost negligible cost. The microprocessor already offers wide ranges of information processing, device control, and communications capabilities now with chip sets as low as $10.00 to $12.00 in mass quantity for use within thousands of types of appliances to increase mankind's awareness and extend his intellectual powers.

To *actively* demonstrate the striking cost reduction of computing power, one of the top officials of Fairchild Camera & Instrument Corp., addressing the Electro 76 Conference in Boston, tossed into the audience computing power equivalent to that valued at $18 million in 1953. The speaker threw 18 of Fairchild's F8 microprocessor chips and observed that each $10 chip contained roughly as much power as IBM's 701 machine when introduced. As another example of the declining cost of electronics, he compared the Friden electromechanical calculator, which sold for $800 or more and handled four functions, with the simple $10 one-chip calculator being sold now by the millions.

Besides the rapid price reductions for new electronic products, one of the other significant elements of the LSI revolution is the reduction in engineering design time for a product when one uses a microprocessor as a component. In the early 1960s it required perhaps 50 man-years to put together a complete working system with transistors, etc. Now this can be done in about nine man-months with microprocessors, and the capabilities are several magnitudes more versatile. This shortened design phase has several other advantages: new devices can be developed, tested, and marketed very rapidly; the ease of finding capital for such products has enticed tens of thousands of new entrepreneurs into the applications areas, and ideas based on microprocessors are causing *ripple* revolutions in offices, homes, factories, entertainment, and almost anywhere fast, accurate control can substitute for electromechanical devices or can make any product more cost-effective.

The Fairchild executive predicted that by 1980 there would be a microprocessor in every home and every car, and that his company was very excited
about electronic games. Initially, it was stated, games will be installed and
linked to TV sets. Children (and their parents) will become inquisitive, familiar and soon expert concerning the interfaces and capabilities that will proliferate, and gradually the entire family will use these and other low-cost systems for increasing pleasure and profit. It was felt that the consumer market
will jump well ahead of the industrial market for microprocessors because of
this mass enthusiasm for the tremendous variety of computerized fun at such
low cost. Consumers have been voracious buyers of electronic wares ever since
the days of crystal radios, then calculators, then electronic-controlled microwave ovens, sewing machines, and now TV sets, soon telephones, etc., etc.

The *home computer* hobbyist market is, as noted, an astounding new twist
to ponder. It is giving consumers control of computers, a concept totally incon-
ceivable just a few years ago. A great many of these enthusiasts are shortwave
radio hobbyists; this is a strong communication upgrade, but especially so with
coming TV-sized satellite-roof antennas and two-way TV capabilities being
tested in England, France, Germany, Japan — and belatedly, the U.S., who
knows what's next?

Most calculator designers feel the problems they face are not related to
electronics but rather they are due to the fact that change is occurring at a rate
too fast for people to fully assimilate it by any conventional means. Silicon
transistors did not exist 25 years ago and integrated circuits are only 16 years
from their introduction. The pocket calculator alone (since 1973) has lead and
will continue to cause widespread change and an evitable impact on the education and consumer attitudes of our current generation, because low cost power
makes them almost a necessity for everyone. Large Scale Integrated circuits,
their derivatives and extensions will penetrate and cause change in virtually
every facet of our society. The constant drive of microprocessor device manufacturers and designers is to simplify what the user has to do in order to use the
new consumer fingertip automation. For example, one of the main thrusts and
cause for popularity of programmable calculators is to continue to use the
concept of performing **in hardware** what currently in microprocessors is done
with software. The next generation of calculators (and microcomputers as
well) will feature data bases on a half-dozen types of low-cost, super-dense
media that have their own controllers built from bit-slice microprocessors.
This is a good way to develop add-on, extremely high-capability easily-pro-
grammable control or built-in specialized *dedication,* with no *worries* or bother
by the user about *how* it all works. (Bit *slices* are add-ons to CPUs.)

The chairman of the board of Intel Corp, whose company is credited with
the *invention* of the microprocessor and a considerable amount of the pioneering work, suggests that we've only begun to scratch the surface of what's going
to happen with all of this. "It will just sneak into every mode of life that we
have." Even in the big computers, the new microprocessor architecture is causing considerable havoc. For example, for its new 1976 models 138 and 148 in
the IBM System 370, IBM has almost doubled the performance of predecessors
135 and 145 — but kept the same price. Although these are items of study for
other readers, the basics — the ubiquitous, innocuous and inexpensive chips
are the basis for many devices besides pocket and desk calculators. And as we
note ahead, thousands of new products are now building on calculator technology — an industry that plows ahead with success.

This *perspective* chapter has provided relative information concerning designers who are progressively using calculator technology for noncalculator

devices and applications. The adaptions and innovations based on calculator device success is extremely extensive. Some calculator chips have such powerful capabilities, in fact, that a number of original equipment manufacturers (OEMs) are using them in specialized instrument and control systems in place of microcomputer subsystems and the more expensive minicomputers. One industry executive had predicted that in 1977 not less than 20% of the total calculator chips manufactured would be used in commercial equipment and systems rather than in conventional calculators. For example, already in 1976 calculator chips were used: to assemble micro controllers for specialized types of watches and clocks; laboratory, industrial and service test equipment; medical instruments; process monitors; communications equipment; surveilance and security systems; and automobile, appliance and industrial controls. Under development and scheduled for early release were types of *wrist* game units, telephonic devices, etc., much of this based on the initial successes of combination wristwatch-calculators.

The major new consumer electronics products in entertainment, communications, and education that are building on calculator technology and its specific progress, are also following the road to success denoting the marketing skills derived from *new electronics* merchandiser leaders. A company called Phone Devices Corp., Chicago, Illinois, has introduced *Figure Phone,* which is a push-button telephone that includes LED display, an eight-digit calculator, digital clock, and daily calendar. This new instrument allows the user to phone and calculate. Other chips related to telephone attachments help performances of answering devices, call diverters, automatic dialers, voice inquiry and response, and other services. As more students continue to *enjoy* their calculators and their teachers will reduce their fears of *ominous* change in their teaching devices — those which employ CRT displays, cassettes and cartridges, audio feedback, displayed instructions and answers, immediately corrected tests, automated scoring and remedial requirements, and the end is completely unforeseen for this application area.

CHAPTER 3

THE BASIC CALCULATORS — KEYBOARDS, SPECIAL FUNCTION KEYS, AND PREPROGRAMMED UNITS . . .

As the reader will quite quickly perceive, the wide range of calculator types, capabilities, keyboard designs, special functions, and dozens of other differentiating characteristics strongly suggests that the now widespread *calculator discipline* has already developed its own terminology. Although much of its scope and many of its specifics relate quite consistently to computer nomenclature and jargon, a great many of the initial terms and concepts and those continuing to evolve are strictly *calculator-related.* Many of the terms, phrases, and definitions are already well-accepted; others are in effect, *coined* almost daily as more and more games, tricks, puzzles, — more and more unique problem-solving programs, control applications, dedicated calculating (computing) devices, etc. become widely accepted and utilized around the world. No age-group is more inventive than the 15-to-25 year-olds — and this is the predominate age of calculator users. Their enthusiasm, dedication, and deep involvement is characterized by the development of more and more calculator clubs — within schools and internationally. A proving fact is that the largest club, the HP-Users Club, with more than 2000 members now (late-1977) collects and exchanges more than 5000 programs among its members. The previous *field* of only four models of hand-held programmables in 1975 expanded to more than a dozen in late 1976, with many more on the way. Casio, Canon, National Semiconductor (NS) and others joined Litronix, Hewlett-Packard (HP) and Texas Instruments (TI).

The problems of *communication* between and among calculator users because of a deluge of new terms and concepts are difficult to solve, especially in a teaching text. An attempt to cope with these difficulties, in this book, is to include a brief glossary — not *hidden* at the back of the book — but at the end of this, the first tutorial chapter. This small collection is only an *inside* aid to the reader; it is not a solution to the *new vocabulary* problems. A companion book, CALCULATOR USERS GUIDE AND DICTIONARY, (Matrix Publishers, Inc.) is recommended for use with this book because the glossary herein presented is inadequate for the readers who hope to master the concepts and explanations of the programmable systems presented later. The majority of the deeper topics relate to quite sophisticated calculator systems.

A *concept explanation,* browsing dictionary with more than 325 pages, as contained in the *guide* book noted above, should be used to grasp the fullest scope of the expanding *advanced* technology and more unique and complex but pragmatic product capabilities and applications.

No attempt was made, in the glossary listed at the end of this chapter, to define or explain any of the major concepts, procedures and products of the advanced programmable or *computing* class of calculators. The very brief definitions of terms that are used in the first few chapters of this book hopefully will serve to provide *quick look-up* reference only and for only those definitions that relate to the less complex four-six function, *scientific,* preprogrammed, and key-programmable machines. The chapters related to *fully* (exterior media) programmable units, advanced desk-top devices, and the specific computing capability models will contain, as much as possible, definitions of the new concepts within the chapters offering explanations of the products, procedures, and programming capabilities. It is possible to include a small minority of the definitions needed to master the details and wide range of these *system* product designs and applications within this book. The recommended simultaneous use of the CALCULATOR USERS GUIDE AND DICTIONARY with this book then will afford the reader considerably more intellectual penetration of the diverse and challenging segments of utilization and future system projections of these devices. The various calculator clubs and magazines will also assist the diligent student in his or her search for more adventuresque explorations of more exotic calculator applications and the onrushing progress.

As will be noted in this chapter, in particular, the textual material moves very rapidly especially as it concerns the simpler, very low-cost, 4-6 function calculators. (It does the same in later chapters with the discussion of the relatively unproductive non-preprogrammed or non-programmable desk units.) All evidence from marketing reports strongly projects that major manufacturers do not desire to compete in the *below-$10* machine pace. Most of them even shun the competition of the *below-$50* ranges. Research and sales returns also show that students and consumers are becoming much more interested in the engineer-scientist-businessman-oriented units. These machines then are the more capable **preprogrammed** units, many with **user-definable** keys. And more and more of these are also offering degrees or types of programmability. The entry of some of the giant calculator *chip* manufacturers such as National Semiconductor, Rockwell, Casio and others directly into the handheld *programmables* markets confirms the strong movement of major market groups (salesmen, high school students, clerks) into the *purchase now* segments of the more advanced or *sophisticated* products. Texas Instruments and Hewlett-Packard have held the very large shares of these markets for these *upgraded* hand-held units, but the competition is coming from many directions now and from other very stalwart innovative international companies. The *pioneer* advanced desk-top *computing* class manufacturers are also starting to reel from competitive *bombshells.* The *desk-top* calculator — Victor, Olympia, Olivetti, Tektronix, Wang, Sharp, Monroe, etc. already competing with TI and HP desk-top products are bracing for new products, technologies, peripheral devices, and full scale *computing* units with built-in communicating capabilities.

A few words are appropriate, however, for cheers to the makers of the four-to-six function units. They are heavily promoted as four-or-five function, *with memory,* with constants, fractions, chaining, etc., and they **now** usually offer percent, square, and root keys. Many also offer slide rule capabilities (limited), plus exchange of data in memory, discount, credit balance, clear and clear entry keys, etc. all of this is really self-explanatory, but it will be reviewed nevertheless. Cost-cutting is being achieved, even for advanced units, by the use of single-chip processors; one-piece LED modules, (providing as many as 14 seven-segment digits), and single-component keyboards. These manufacturing efficiencies have cut assembly (labor) costs to an almost negligible amount. Suppliers (and their promotion teams) seem no longer worried that consumers won't understand computer-like concepts as: addressable memories, programmability, stacks, labels, etc. The basic *four-banger* that only adds, subtracts, multiplies and divides has largely disappeared. Simple memories are now *standard* that allow users to park a displayed number in invisible storage with a stroke of a key, for as long as desired. The press of another key brings it back — and this technique or capability of the processor chip has led to the very low cost, key-programmables, such as the 10-step under $30 Litronix 2290. This, and the NS, Casio and Canon units are some of the best *stepping stone* units to lure users next to fully programmable units. The *hot* key-programmables, with added *scientific* or slide rule capabilities and *special function keys* (SFKs) are most intriguing, and while the simplest units sell for less than $100, others go to slightly over $200. They are tremendous values. Many of these units also add business and statistical functions to simple programmability. And, it is with these units that the following chapter opens. This chapter opens with nonprogrammables and moves quickly to *advanced* preprogrammed units in an attempt to *keep it simple.*

The calculator industry has become one of the most interesting, challenging and also, for some producers, most exasperating billion dollar enigmas of the total electronics marketplace. Offering great benefits to the consumer, the competitive efforts of the leading companies continue to bring price drops for ever more capable units. New technologies have brought automated calculator chip versatility, new methods of mass manufacturing, and individual chip computerized quality testing, excellent efficiency in component assembly, faster air freight distribution and highly spirited mass marketing strategic and tactical surprises. They combine to amaze and astonish practically all professionals, students, and consumers with the very high quality but low prices of all calculator products. Typical also is the mass selling done by many big chains, such as Sears, Penney, May Co., and other stores — mass sales catalog and direct mail houses, such as Contemporary Marketing, Inc., Chicago, Chafitz, others. For example, Contemporary Marketing had mass sales of the Commodore rechargeable model SR4190R. It offered, "A powerful scientific-business **preprogrammed,** high-quality **50-key** calculator with **106 directly accessible keyboard functions** . . . for $59.95," in mid-1976. Some of those preprogrammed (multifunction but single-key operations) include a unique "Hours-Minutes-Seconds in digital clock format . . . (users) can perform arithmetic operations such as time study and motion analysis in this mode as easily as in the decimal mode . . . combination and permutation operations are not hindered by the overflow which occurs when the factorial is larger than 10^{100} . . . among the direct entry functions are Poisson and Binomial Probability Densities; Gaussian Distribution; Linear Regression Analysis; Mean and Standard Deviation; and many more . . . most important, all are on the keyboard . . . several thousand preprogrammed steps put all of these functions at your fingertips . . . instantly. You needn't bother with preparing formulas, using tables, creating programs or maintaining an elaborate library . . . (this) broadest range of diversified applications is at your command." The definition of the capabilities of the 50 keys are an engineer/mathematician/statistician/businessman's dream. Such a 106 function, simply-operated $60 machine puts real decision pressure on the potential purchaser when he or she contemplates making the best buy, what is it to be — preprogrammed, key-programmable, or any one of an expanding number of *less than $200* to $400 excellent *fully* programmable units capable of using whole libraries of tested and proved programs. Thousands are prepared and available at very low cost, or new programs can be made available for users to **custom** program, all quite simply by using blank cards, cartridges, ROMs, or tapes. Many clerks are being enviously watched by their immediate superiors, as they develop new *better way* programs.

It becomes quickly obvious that most of these valuable extra capabilities, some of which even the alert professional or very sharp student has never known before, cost them nothing extra at all. And as many teachers hopefully point out, perhaps the users will endeavor to find out what these exotic math and stat functions are, and after understanding these new (to them) concepts, these users will begin to apply them, thereby significantly expanding their calculating (computing) capabilities. With a $60 unit as described, amateur (or hobbyist) engineers, electricians, mathematicians, etc. will display test them for *answers* and *play with* logarithms, trig squares and roots. Perhaps business people or students will use single keystrokes to display the sine, cosine, tangent, or the inverse trigonometric functions of any angle, or instantly find the reciprocal of a number, display pi with a single key, raise a number to any power, etc. While so doing, most people quickly see that such instruments can very fundamentally aid a bright youngster through high school and college, especially if his chief interests lie with engineering, statistics, physics, and this is also true even with economics and business management, etc. These students are already aware of the fact that their toughest problems involve solving complex statistical business and economic planning puzzles and playing *what if* with forecasting and mathematical resource allocation models.

The best advice, from teachers, fellow users, parents, etc. is to buy **all the calculator capability** one can possibly afford. This suggests that the student, professional, or even the alert consumer won't soon after one purchase be looking again for a unit with more capability to see him completely through school. Many realize that performing these extra calculations, though quickly learned, are also important . . . either in school, currently on their jobs . . . or on one of many types of jobs most will desire after graduation from either high school or college. As is easily discerned, the very extensive capabilities of some units, similar to the one described, beat the sliderule by performing in one operation what would take 6 or 7 normally. And the advanced calculator units beat the simple units in speed, fewer strokes, better accuracy and with many more statistical or mathematical calculations capabilities allied to or associated with the primary subject, professional school or endeavors sought by the user.

To make a strong point even more distinct, the unit described is a cost/ performance *bargain,* for a great number of potential users. However, is it the best for you? One of the first questions an associate or fellow student might ask is, "Let's see it do register arithmetic." To do this the unit must have several memories into which the user can store constants or other numbers that he might use more than once in a problem — one a previous answer, for example, that he can call back instead of making a pencil note. Experienced users know that having these extra storage registers allows them to directly add to, subtract from, multiply or divide into numbers so *saved* because they remain in the memories (the *stack* in some units) for later display (rolling the 4-register

(HP unit's) stack up or down). This capability provides for review or making new *what if* calculations, for example. National Semiconductor and others besides HP use this *stack* architecture. The stack is much like the automated picture slide projector-loader. A press of a correct button shows one entry, or the next, or the previous one, etc. The calculator can be directed to manipulate any one of those numbers stored in that register (interior location) or place another answer there, or another, for future manipulation of these answers or intermediate figures, when and if it becomes necessary. Or they can all be erased by simply overwriting them with the next calculation result. The vertical stack is a principal element of the RPN logic described several times throughout the book. Logic systems describe how users key in problems; how the calculator operates internally on these numbers. And the systems (methods) become very important when very complex problems are either presented to the calculator or are resolved through many steps by it.

The strongly competing system to RPN, and favored by many users, is the algebraic or AOS (Algebraic Operating System) used by Texas Instruments and a great many other manufacturers. Unfortunately, the use of the latter system sometimes requires restructuring the more complex problems before entry, although the **neat** use of parentheses does much to simplify most processes. If these more complex problems are used quite often in schoolroom classes or on the job, it is best to originally write, check and recheck a simple program for them — and then enter the program into the calculator. If the unit is a programmable type, then only the data need be entered from then on. The user need not ever worry about the order, problem structure, etc. again — at least for that particular problem. And this is why the decision for *What is the best unit for me ... my work?* becomes difficult. It's primarily a question of programmability or a great many often-used straight one- or two-key preprogrammed functions. If it is to be a programmable type — then the real alternatives of super capabilities of some machine arise. Not only is the fundamental question of *Should it be just key programmable?* involved — but it also must be determined if it is advantageous for the machine to be card, ROM, cassette, cartridge, or even disk programmable. And the wide-ranging criteria for these decisions follow in the next chapter.

**Beginning Calculator Users — How They Start and Progress . . .
the Challenges . . .**

The *four-bangers,* those $10 to $20 units that add, subtract, multiply, and divide, that come in checkbooks, as wallets, pens, as schoolbags, *owls,* etc. are quite simple instruments. Counter salesmen will quickly explain the differences — usually trying to trade the customer up to the ones with more preprogrammed functions. It is not difficult to move the $10 customer to a $30 *memory* unit or a $40 unit such as one that can use constants, percentages, discounts, etc. These capabilities are very briefly explained below. The first item to master, however, is the operation of the different *logic* systems. The counter salesmen will keep this as simple as possible, perhaps explaining them as follows:

The Algebraic Method — This is rapidly becoming the most common because it is the simplest and most natural. Texas Instruments and most other suppliers use and prefer it. The user presses the keys the same way he or she would write the problem down: $7 + 45 - 17 \times 12 \div 5$. The user then pushes the = button to receive his displayed answer, 84. The easiest way to recognize this method (logic) is to look for the operator signs, $+, -, \times$ and $\div$ and the simple = sign. As noted ahead, there is much more to the logic, such as merged functions, memory, parentheses, etc. (some units require a = after each operation).

The Arithmetic Method — This is slightly confusing. There are + = and − = keys that must be pressed after the user enters any positive or negative number into an equation. For the problem given above, a user would push the following keys in order: 7, + =, 4, 5, + =, 1, 7, − =, ×, 1, 2, ÷, 5, + =, to arrive at the 84 answer. It is a bit unnatural, and it might cause some inadvertant errors, but as a user handles the unit often, he becomes quickly proficient. Most users proceed two or three times — checking against the instruction booklet to be sure they understand the strict operational use of the + = and + − function. Litronix and many other manufacturers use this method.

Reverse Polish Method — This method (logic) can be immediately recognized by the lack of an = key. To use this method, users must press the + key or the −, ×, or ÷ keys AFTER they enter **each** additional number in the problem. This may seem a bit unnatural, but it is the favorite method for millions of dedicated users of HP units, who swear it is the easiest and fastest especially for long problems. (More thorough explanations on pages ahead.)

The next item the beginner must understand is the **floating decimal** that relieves the user of the necessity of entering decimal places for whole numbers. An example is: A user enters $10.95 as 1,0, . (decimal point) 9,5. To add $9.00, the user simply presses +9 . (point). On a more confusing **fixed decimal** machine, the user must add two more zeros. This can be and is a nuisance for those working with a long list of numbers with, say, many decimals, a lot of them with .00. Floating decimal machines permit users as many decimal places as they need for the calculation. Dividing 16 by 7 on a floating decimal machine answers 2.2857142, a number that should be rounded to 2.29. With a fixed decimal machine that allowed two decimal places and simply dropped the numbers that didn't fit, a wrong answer could easily be developed. This is especially true if that incorrect **answer** required further multiplication or division. Floating point machines provide answers accurate up to 8, 12, or 16 places depending upon the number of digits shown on the display. It is important to buy a display larger than 7 digits for many fractional calculations (necessarily first converted to decimals — except for the new units that handle fractions as fractions). If the unit is only a 6-digit fixed decimal machine, users will not be able to do even simple fractional (decimal) multiplication. The display will show E followed by a string of zeros, indicating that the calculation exceeds the unit's capacity, even though the answer might not. Users should also be sure the displays on the units they buy do not *wash out* in very bright light, and the displays should be readable at practically any angle. Few users have battery or charger problems — and adapters (to regular ac current) are very low-cost, so that long run operations are not damaging to batteries. Keyboards that click each time a key is pressed are preferred by some users, not by others. Usually, the major selling points for low-cost units are the addition of the following simple keys: **Percentage key;** it adjusts the decimal point (dividing exactly by 100) when calculating and on some units also calculates net answer discounts; **Memory key;** it permits users to repeatedly add, subtract, multiply, or divide by the same number without repressing it; **Clear key** allows users to *erase* an entire problem without shutting the machine off *(clear entry* key lets users erase only the last entry — often because they hit the wrong last key); Metric conversion keys permit immediate direct conversion for inches to centimeters, gallons to liters, etc. for example. Other keys are explained on pages ahead.

With these simple capabilities, users compute food costs, travel expenses, sales taxes, balance checkbooks, figure house and car payments, gasoline mileage, and other personal or small business finances. The *memory* units in the low-cost range saves users the task of writing down intermediate totals by storing them, providing a grand total at the end of long calculations, etc. Most simple machines now permit adding and subtracting to the memory as well as recalling and clearing it. Sliderule functions are, in the simpler units, single-key functions such as squares, roots, reciprocals, sign change — and the next step up often is to *scientific* units with more sliderule capabilities as logs, trig and exponential capabilities. The simpler preprogrammed business calculators offer one- or two-key functions to calculate mortgages, annuities, interest rates, etc. These are all quite basic features, but many more are to come.

A quick review of the simplest four-six function general features: A flip of the On/Off Memory Switch, and the automatic accumulator is activated. A press of the (=) key and the number on display is automatically entered into the memory. Recalling the memory is done by pressing the Memory Recall (MR) key. To "subtract" a number from the memory, press the (−) key before pressing the (=) key. When it's necessary to "save" the number in the memory while performing intermediate calculations, flip the memory switch OFF. On some units the memory will "freeze" whatever number is being stored at the time. To erase the memory entirely, press the Memory Clear (MC) key.

Automatic accumulators could be of service for invoicing customers . . . calculating payrolls . . . solving complex formulas with intermediate computations . . . estimating construction jobs . . . resolving discounts and markups, etc. Some units offer two additional built-in memories: CONSTANT MEMORY locks-in a fixed multiplier or divisor . . . there is no need to re-enter a constant for each operation. People traveling abroad are able to compute speedy dollar equivalents of unfamiliar currencies . . . convert liters to gallons . . . miles to kilometers with these conversion keys.

STACKING MEMORY allows one to add to or subtract from an original number. For example, when adding 7.5% tax to $24.95 item, after the tax of $1.87 appears in the display, press the "PLUS" for a total of $26.82. One can compute discounts the same way . . . by pressing "MINUS". "Memory Stack" also acts as a Clear-Entry key for automatic error-correction. When working with long lists of numbers, the user can make an unwanted entry vanish — even after it was totaled — by touching the "MINUS" key. There's a combination C and CE key on some units. Press it once to erase the previous entry only . . . twice to clear the entire display. One button does both. Automatic decimal precision operates for all functions. On many machines one can select the fixed dollars and cents decimal with roundoff to the nearest penny . . . OR allow the decimal to float to its proper position automatically. Many units now provide that audible click to indicate entries have registered properly and overflow signals to indicate an answer has more than 8 digits, also a minus sign to show negative results, and some offer a memory "occupied" light to indicate when the memory is in use.

The reader might gain more confidence by examining the operation of some specific relatively simple units. Two Casio machines and some examples could clarify elementary problem-solving procedures. Descriptions of these units follow:

Fractional Calculator With Simple Algebraic Logic — Casio AL-8

Users touch the keys as the figures and commands occur in the formula, then press the = key for an instant answer.

Another useful feature is that before calculating, users can select either the floating decimal for a full 8-digit answer, or fixed mode with cut-off or round-off

at 2 decimal places. The independent memory (M+, M−, MR, MC System) provides the capacity to solve a host of complicated problems. In grand total calculations, such as invoicing, users can obtain the horizontal total (quantity × unit price) and vertical total (sales amount and the total number of items) simultaneously in conjunction with the electronic memory. The AL-8 has a convenient % key for mark-up/discount. Users press the % key to have the answer for ×/÷ operations to 1/100 (a centuple). This makes price mark-ups, discounts, or any percentage calculation instantaneous. Also, the convenience of constants for doing repetitive figurework, powers, reciprocals, conversions saves lots of time and effort. Users touch +−×÷= as they appear in the problem.

Problem	Example		Operation	Read-out
Addition Subtraction	8.765 + 1234 − 258.78 = 983.985		8 · 765 + 1234 − 258 · 78 =	983.985
Multiplication/Division	1.23 × 45.6 × 789 = 44253.432		1 · 23 × 45 · 6 × 789 =	44253.432
	96.3 ÷ 1.47 ÷ 3 = 21.836734		96 · 3 ÷ 1 · 47 ÷ 3 =	21.836734
Percentage Calculation	6% of 159 . . . . .9.54		159 × 6 %	9.54
	Percentage of 25 against 500 . . . .5%		25 ÷ 500 %	5.
	15% mark-up of 1500 1725		1500 × 15 % +	1725.
	25% discount of 1960 1470		1960 × 25 % −	1470.
Constant Calculation	98.5 × 3.3 = 325.05		3 · 3 × × 98 · 5 =	325.05
	1265.5 × 3.3 = 4176.15		1265 · 5 =	4176.15
	Percentage of 30 against 200		200 ÷ ÷ 30 %	15.
	Percentage of 50 against 200		50 %	25.
	Percentage of 70 against 200		70 %	35.
Memory Calculation	123 × 456 = 56088	"F"	MC 123 × 456 M+	56088.
	−) 147 × 258 = 37926		147 × 258 M−	37926.
	18162		MR	18162.
		"F"	MC 74 M+ 63 M+	63.
	(74 + 63) × (23 − 56) = −4521		23 − 56 × MR	137.
			=	−4521.
	$\dfrac{(5.3 + 8.6) \times 9}{5.6 \times 2.3 - 8} = 25.635245$	"F"	MC 5 · 6 × 2 · 3 − 8 M+	4.88
			5 · 3 + 8 · 6 × 9 ÷ MR =	25.635245

Fractional Calculation — The World's First Calculator With This Unique Function

Users can work fractions, improper fractions, mixed numbers . . . . entering them directly as they appear in the written formulas. Answers are also given in fractions and they can be converted to decimal notation, if desired.

Example	Operation	Read-out	
$\dfrac{1}{4} + \dfrac{2}{5} = \dfrac{13}{20}$	1 P 4 + 2 P 5 =	1/4. 2/5. 13/20.	
$\dfrac{6}{24} \times \dfrac{5}{7} = \dfrac{5}{28}\ (=0.1785714)$	6 P 24 × 5 P 7 = P	1/4. 5/28. 0.1785714	(Automatic reduction) (Decimal notation)
$1\dfrac{2}{3} \times 4\dfrac{5}{6} \div 7\dfrac{8}{9} = 1\dfrac{3}{142}$	1 P 2 P 3 × 4 P 5 P 6 ÷ 7 P 8 P 9 =	1/2/3. 8/1/18. 1/3/142.	 (Answer of $1\dfrac{2}{3} \times 4\dfrac{5}{6}$)
$3\dfrac{456}{78} = 8\dfrac{11}{13}$ (Reduction)	3 P 456 P 78 =	8/11/13.	

Time Calculation (Angle Calculation)

Parking times and other time-related calculations, angle calculations, etc., can be directly entered as in the written formulas. Answers are given either as a decimal or in sexagesimal notation.

Example	Operation	Read-out	
1 hour 23 minutes 45 seconds + 6 hours 54 minutes 32 seconds = 8 hours 18 minutes 17 seconds	1 P 23 P 45 P + 6 P 54 P 32 P = P	1.3958333 6.9088888 8.3047222 8° 18° 17.	 (Answer in decimal) (Answer in sexagesimal)
Calculate the flying time of a plane leaving New York at 9:05 am and arriving in London at 15:50 (New York time).	15 P 50 P − 9 P 5 P = P	15.833333 9.0833333 6.75 6°45°0.	 (Answer in decimal) (Answer in sexagesimal)
(45° 56′ − 12° 23′) × 2.5 =83° 52′ 30″	45 P 56 P − 12 P 23 P × 2 · 5 = P	45.933333 12.383333 33.55 83.875 83° 52° 30.	 (Answer in decimal) (Answer in sexagesimal)

Statistics — One of the First Personal Calculators with a Built-in Standard Deviation Program.

The built-in standard deviation program is indispensable for statistical calculations. Just input the data and press the = key. This simple operation is sufficient for arithmetical mean, sum of value, sum of square value, number of data, as well as standard deviation.

Example	Operation	Read-out
	AC 55 = 54 · 1 =	
Compute standard deviation (σ),	51 = = 53 =	
arithmetical mean ($\bar{x}$), sum of values	52 =	
(Σx), sum of square values (Σx^2)	(σ=) P	1.6497474
and the number of data (n) for the	($\bar{x}$=) M+	52.683333
set of numbers 55, 54.1, 51, 51, 53, 52.	(Σx=) MC	316.1
Formula: $\sigma = \sqrt{\dfrac{\Sigma x^2 - (\Sigma x)^2/n}{n-1}}$	(Σx^2=) MR	16666.81
	(n=) M–	6.

Some other simple problems are solved as follows.

Square Roots — Given Instantly For Any Displayed Figure
Square roots are always available at just one touch of the key.

Example		Operation	Read-out
$\sqrt{2}$ = 1.4142135		2 P	1.4142135
$\sqrt{1.2 \times 14}$ = 4.0987803	F CUT 5/4	1 · 2 × 14 = P	4.0987803
		=	4.09
$\sqrt{5} + \sqrt{3}$ = 3.9681187		5 P + 3 P =	3.9681187

Grand Totals — Highly Advantageous In Totaling

It offers a great advantage to accountants, bookkeepers and salesmen. In combination with the independent memory (M+, M–, MR, MC), totals and a grand total can be obtained at the same time.

Even complex calculations can be handled easily.

Example				Operation	Read-out

Invoicing

Article	Q'ty	Unit price	Amount
A	250	$18.75	($ 4,687.5)
B	385	96.25	(37,056.25)
C	421	23.45	(9,872.45)
Total	(1056)		($51,616.2)

	Operation	Read-out
	MC AC 250 M+ × 18 · 75 =	4687.5
	385 M+ × 96 · 25 =	37056.25
	421 M+ × 23 · 45 =	9872.45
	MR	1056.
	P	51616.2

Remainder — One-Touch Answers For Division

A problem such as 15 ÷ 7 can be entered directly as in the written formula. The quotient of 2 is displayed and subsequent pressing of the P key gives the remainder of 1 instantly.

Example	Operation	Read-out	
123 ÷ 7 = 17	123 ÷ 7 =	17.	(Quotient)
Remainder: 4	P	4.	(Remainder)
456.789 ÷ 2.3 = 198	456 · 789 ÷ 2 · 3 =	198.	(Quotient)
Remainder: 1.389	P	1.389.	(Remainder)

CASIO FX-19 SCIENTIFIC CALCULATOR

Casio FX-19 Scientific Fraction Calculator

Users calculate in fractions without any need for figure conversions. The answer is also displayed in fractions. Improper or mixed fractions can be used without conversion in any arithmetic operation. Reductions can be performed readily. Numerous built-in functions, are simple to use. Almost all major functions are built-in. For example, sin, cos, tan, $\sin^{-1}$, $\cos^{-1}$, $\tan^{-1}$, log, ln, 10^x, e^x, x^y, $\sqrt{\ }$, $1/x$, ° ", π, exp. etc. All keys are independent, so operation is extremely simple. Also, the use of exponents makes possible calculations of up to 100 digits (exponent $10^{\pm99}$).

A built-in program function makes standard deviation calculations easy. Standard deviations (population standard deviations or sample standard deviations) can be found by the following simple operation: data = data =. Simple average, number of data, sum and sum of squares can also be found by merely pressing the required keys. Other features:

- Angles can be expressed not only in degrees, minutes and seconds, but also in Radians and Grade.
- The independent memory greatly facilitates mixed calculations and other functions.
- All basic calculator functions are included. For example, constant multiplication/division, upper rank priority function, etc., as well as an easy-to-see green display.
- Error check shuts out overflows (over $10^{\pm100}$) and impossible calculations.
- The compact size provides easy portability. Either AC or DC power sources can be used.
- Answers to troublesome fraction calculations and standard deviations found readily.

Examples of Calculations
Multiplied conveniences. New functions from Casio technology.

Formula	Example	Operation	Read-out
Fraction Calculations	$\dfrac{789}{45} = 17\dfrac{8}{15}$	789 $a\frac{b}{c}$ 45 =	17/8/15.
	$\dfrac{2}{5} + 3\dfrac{1}{4} = 3\dfrac{13}{20}$	2 $a\frac{b}{c}$ 5 + 3 $a\frac{b}{c}$ 1 $a\frac{b}{c}$ 4 =	3/13/20.
	$1\dfrac{2}{3} \times 4\dfrac{5}{6} \div 7\dfrac{8}{9} = 1\dfrac{3}{142}$	1 $a\frac{b}{c}$ 2 $a\frac{b}{c}$ 3 × 4 $a\frac{b}{c}$ 5 $a\frac{b}{c}$ 6 ÷ 7 $a\frac{b}{c}$ 8 $a\frac{b}{c}$ 9 =	1/3/142.
Standard Deviations	Data: 55, 54, 51, 53, 52. Population Standard Deviation (σ_n) Sample Standard Deviation (σ_{n-1}) Arithmetical mean ($\bar{x}$) Number of data (n) Sum (Σx) Sum of square (Σx^2)	"SD" AC 55 = 54 = 51 = 53 = 52 = ($\sigma_n=$) °'" ($\sigma_n - 1=)^{1/x}$ ($\bar{x}=$) MC ($n=$) MR ($\Sigma x=$) M– ($\Sigma x^2=$) M+	 1.4142135 1.5811388 53. 5. 265. 14055.

One-touch answers for scientific calculations

Formula	Example	Operation	Read-out
Sexagesimal/ Decimal conversion	63° 52' 41" =	"DEG"	63 °'" 52 °'" 41 °'"	63.878055
Trigonometrics	sin 30° =	"DEG"	30 sin	0.5
	$\cos\dfrac{\pi}{6} =$	"RAD"	π ÷ 6 = cos	0.8660254
	tan 78° 45' 12" =	"DEG"	78 °'" 45 °'" 12 °'" tan	5.0288684
Inverse Trigonometrics	$\sin^{-1} 0.456 =$	"GRAD"	· 456 arc sin	30.143661
	$\cos^{-1}\dfrac{\sqrt{3}}{2} =$	"DEG"	3 √ ÷ 2 = arc cos	30.
	$\tan^{-1}(-1.23) =$	"DEG"	1 · 23 +/− arc tan	−50.888609
Logarithmics	log 123 = ($\log_{10}$ 123 =) In90 = ($\log_e$ 90 =)		123 log 90 In	2.0899051 4.4998097
Exponentiations	$10^{1.23} =$ $e^{7.89} =$ $2.3^{4.5} =$		1 · 23 10^x 7 · 89 e^x 2 · 3 x^y 4 · 5 =	16.982437 2670.4439 42.439989
Square roots & Reciprocals	$\sqrt{2} + \sqrt{3} =$ $\dfrac{1}{3} - \dfrac{1}{4} =$		2 √ + 3 √ = 3 1/x − 4 1/x =	3.1462643 0.0833333

This 8 Digit Calculator With One Memory Performs Complex, Normal and Scientific Functions.

Formula	Example	Operation	Read-out
Basics	$(12 + 3.4) \times (5.6 - 78) =$ $[(1.2 \times 10^{18}) - (3 \times 10^{19})]$ $\times (4.56 \times 10^{23}) =$	MC 12 + 3 · 4 M+ 5 · 6 − 78 × MR = 1 · 2 EXP 18 − 3 EXP 19 × 4 · 56 EXP 23 =	−1114.96 −1.3132 43
Constants	$41 \times (-6.3 \times 10^{12}) =$ $52 \times (-6.3 \times 10^{12}) =$	6 · 3 +/− EXP 12 × × 41 = 52 =	−2.583 14 −3.276 14

$$\sqrt[n]{x} = x^{\frac{1}{n}} \qquad \sqrt[5]{456} = 456^{\frac{1}{5}} = \qquad\qquad 456\ x^y\ 5\ 1/x = \qquad 3.4024595$$

$$\sin\alpha \times \cos\beta \qquad \sin56° \times \cos23° = \qquad\qquad \text{"DEG"}\ \text{MC}\ 56\ \text{SIN}\ \text{M+}\ 23\ \text{COS} \times \text{MR} = \qquad 0.7631329$$

$$\sinh x = \frac{e^x - e^{-x}}{2} \qquad \sinh 1.2 = \frac{e^{1.2} - e^{-1.2}}{2} \qquad\qquad \text{MC}\ 1\ \cdot 2\ e^x\ \text{M+}\ 1/x\ \text{M-}\ \text{MR} \div 2 = \qquad 1.5094613$$

Specifications

Capabilities:

Normal functions — 4 basic functions, fractional calculations, multiplication/division with a constant, chain & mixed operation, automatic accumulation in four functions, direct access to the memory, true credit balance and various kinds of practical calculations.

Scientific functions — trigonometric/inverse trigonometric functions, common & natural logarithmic functions, exponentiations, square roots, reciprocals, sexadesimal/decimal conversion, π entry, statistical calculations including 2 kinds of standard deviation, and other applications.

Capacity:

	Input range	**Output accuracy**
Entry/basic functions	8 digits mantissa or 6 digits mantissa plus 2 digits exponent up to ±99.	
Fraction	Max. 3 digits for each integer, numerator or denominator and at the same time Max. 6 digits for the sum of each part.	
$\sin x/\cos x/\tan x$	$\lvert x \rvert \leqq 1440°$ (8π rad, 1600 grad)	±1 in the 8th digit
$\sin^{-1}x/\cos^{-1}x$	$\lvert x \rvert \leqq 1$	—"—
$\tan^{-1}x$	$\lvert x \rvert < 1 \times 10^{100}$	—"—
$\log x/\ln x$	$0 < x < 1 \times 10^{100}$	—"—
e^x	$\lvert x \rvert \leqq 230$	—"—
10^x	$\lvert x \rvert < 100$	—"—
x^y	$0 < x < 1 \times 10^{100}$ $\lvert y \rvert < 1 \times 10^{100}$	±1 in the 7th digit
$\sqrt{x}$	$0 \leqq x < 1 \times 10^{100}$	$\div1$ in the 8th digit
$1/x$	$\lvert x \rvert < 1 \times 10^{100}, x \neq 0$	—"—
o' "	up to second	—"—

Decimal point: Full floating mode with underflow.

Negative number: Indicated by the floating minus $(-)$ sign for mantissa. The minus sign appears in the 3rd column for a negative exponent.

Overflow: Indicated by an "E." sign, locking the calculator.

Read-out: Green Digitron tube panel and zero suppression.

Main component: One chip LSI

Power consumption: 0.35 W

Power source:

AC: 117V (±10V), 50/60 Hz with applicable AC adaptor.

DC: Four AA size Manganese dry batteries (SUM-3) operate abt. 16 hours continuously.

Four AA size Alkaline dry batteries (AM-3) operate abt. 35 hours continuously.

Usable temperature: 32° F ~ 104° F

Dimensions: 1-⅛" H × 3-½" W × 5-⅞" D

Weight: 9 oz. including batteries.

A Simple Story of Chips
The Basic Calculator is Simple

The basic calculator — particularly the mass-produced hand-held and desk units — is simple. It consists of six elements:
1. An IC calculator chip (or chips).
2. A keyboard & switches
3. A display LED (usually)
4. A display interface circuit or component.
5. A power supply (battery or ac or both)
6. A case.

Today chip manufacturers have developed generic, microprogrammed calculator chips that can be modified in function by changes in the information in memories on the chip. A simple mask change is all that is necessary. As a result, lines of calculators have been developed from each of the generic chips. For example, at least 11 different calculators have been produced from the same basic chip by Rockwell International Microelectronics Div. of Anaheim, Calif.

At Texas Instruments, Dallas, that company's basic TMS 0100 one-chip calculator has given rise to 30 different calculators. While most four-function calculator chips can, with proper programming, duplicate the functions of competitive chips, they differ in details. For example, TI uses an external clock while Rockwell International puts its clock on the chip. The trend, however, is to put more and more of the interfacing circuitry and components on the chip to reduce the calculator manufacturer's costs. Calculator chips are generally tailored to drive a specific display. The displays for the smaller machines are of three principal types: gas-discharge, fluorescent tubes and LEDs (Light Emitting Diodes).

'Rollover' — or more accurately, rollover protection — is a term specified by chip manufacturers. When incorporated in the keyboard logic system, this feature prevents more than one key from entering data at a time. For example, when one key is depressed, the rollover logic inhibits double entry of data if a second key is accidentally pressed at the same time.

The following major factors should be considered in selecting an electronic calculator: Calculating requirements; Display considerations; Power-supply considerations; Keyboard-function capabilities; Automatic-function (internally programmed) capabilities. Where complex scientific calculations involving trigonometric, logarithmic, angular, and nonlinear functions are a part of the day's work, specialized calculators — either hand-held, desk-type or large programmable machines — are the logical choice. However, with a simple four-function calculator — having an automatic or insertable constant and at least one memory — both chain and mixed calculations can be readily performed. Experience has shown that users of calculators — like slide-rule users — are continually finding shortcuts to solve fairly complex computations. Types of problems that can be solved with little difficulty include raising a number to the nth power, finding the power to which the number is raised or finding the nth root of the number. Evaluation of simple formulas, conversions of various dimensions and physical units, and calculations in preparation of engineering budgets are fast, simple operations with four-function calculators. All are microprogrammed for control. The internal program of the chip generates all the algorithms used in the computation. Computation time/display is controlled by the ROM, Read Only Memory Chip.

1. The heart of today's electronic calculators is a small micropro-grammable MOS-LSI microcomputer dedicated to calculating func-tions. The compartmentation of functions on Texas Instruments' TMS 0100 calculator chip, used in 30 versions, is shown above. The microprogram is contained in the program ROM.

Third Calculator Chip Adds Power

A new array lets scientific units compute complex functions in a few key-strokes. Solving advanced mathematical, statistical, or scientific problems becomes elementary with any hand-held scientific calculator designed around a new three-chip set from MOS Technology, Inc., Norristown, Pa. Basic calculating features plus a 14-digit display are handled by two chips, while the third extends the computational power of the system to include advanced functions. Designated the Senior Scientist, the set operates in conjunction with a 40-key keyboard. On these keys, factorials, binomial coefficients, probability integrals and other advanced functions are repre-sented in the 'upper-case' position, actuated by a shift key.

All three chips are involved in handling series expansions, vector manip-ulation, permutations and combinations, coordinate conversions, compli-cated statistical equations, and complex mathematical problems in general. But the first two chips of the Senior Scientist may also be used alone to provide a basic 40-key scientific calculator. This unusual option is provided by a system architecture common to all scientific-calculator array sets from MOS Technology: the master array of the system is programmed to recog-nize the presence or absence of the third chip, and no electrical change is required to change the functional level.

Included within the three chips of the set are 12 data memories and 2,560 words of program storage. The memories are allocated in such a way that three are directly usable by the operator with separate store/recall keys. An additional four memories are internally accessed for storage of statisti-cal group data, prior result data, and prior parentheses data. The remaining five are used by the system as working registers. A minimum number of external components is required for integration of the set into finished calculator designs, and power dissipation is kept at minimum levels, less than 300 milliwatts average. Price of the set was $50 in quantities of 100,000 (1974), but it fell to well below $10 in early 1976.

An Initial Concept of a 'Stack' — How It Helps

On some algebraic logic units, users must determine where to begin the problem. They also must be concerned with what is stored in memory, and they may be required to rearrange the problem to solve it. Machines with a *stack* architecture are claimed to provide consistent, unambiguous data entry and processing via *left to right* rules. Every problem is entered in exactly the same way — and all intermediate answers are shown, allowing the user to follow substeps with reassurance. The 4-stack machines have roll-up, roll-down and exchange (register) keys, and each of the stack registers can be displayed on the press of a specific key. On many algebraic machines there is no way to see the contents of some of the registers. On the other hand, algebraic system users claim that RPN or stack entry is often confusing, requires more keystrokes, etc. Throughout the two chapters ahead, advantages for both systems will be claimed, and individual preferences noted. In general, the systems *argument* is not winnable by either side — users who become accustomed to either will swear by its enhanced capabilities and ease-of-operation over the other. New users can quickly determine which system is being used — the RPN machines usually have a very large *enter* key and *no*-key; the algebraic system machines do not have the enter key at all.

The typical 4-register operational stack retains as many as 4 intermediate solutions in sequence, and automatically positions them for use on a last in, first out basis. At the proper time, the solutions are *automatically* entered into the calculation being performed, so users don't have to re-enter them manually. It's this automatic operation of the 4-register stack that makes RPN (Reverse Polish Notation) possible. The stack design also permits X and Y register exchange, and roll-down of any entry to the display for review or other operation.

The "Last x" *register* permits error correction or multiple operations. When a function is performed, the last input argument of the calculation is automatically stored in the "Last x" register. This argument can be quickly and easily recalled to correct an error, or to perform another operation using the same number.

Addressable memory registers make data manipulation easy. Users can store data (an intermediate solution, a constant, etc.) in any of these registers . . . retrieve it instantly . . . and even do register arithmetic $(+, -, \times, \div)$ using or modifying data in any register.

The more entries or intermediate solutions a calculator remembers for users the less remembering — or writing down — users have to do. And the less chance for error.

Potential purchasers then should consider at least the following as they judge merits: (1) type of logic used (2) number of registers (3) preprogrammed functions — number, type.

The Meaning of *Advanced* Calculators . . .

Throughout this book the adjective *advanced* (calculators) is used to differentiate between the simple four to six function units, even those that offer percents, chaining, operations with constants and several quite elementary statistical functions, and the units with far wider ranges of capabilities. The advanced units will generally include dozens of preprogrammed functions. Some of these with printers, for example, are:

Preprogrammed Operations:

Reset, clear entry, print switch (on or off), print key for selective printing when print switch is off, printed tape advance, set decimal point (0 to 9 digits to right of decimal point), exponent (scientific notation), enter and calculate with angles in degrees-minutes-seconds, enter and calculate with angles in decimal degrees or grads, decimal degrees to degrees-minutes-seconds, degrees-minutes-seconds to decimal degrees, square root, square, reciprocal, factorial, statistical summation (number of data items, sum, sum of squares), delete data from summation, mean, standard deviation, sine, arc sine, cosine, arc cosine, tangent, arc tangent, to polar, to rectangular, degrees (or grads) to radians, radians to degrees (or grads), base e logarithm, base e antilogarithm, base 10 logarithm, base 10 antilogarithm, integer, fraction, absolute value, pi, e, round.

Arithmetic Functions:

Add, subtract, multiply, divide, and a^x (raise a number to a power), left and right parentheses (nesting to four levels).

English → Metric
Metric → English
Conversions:

Degrees Fahrenheit to degrees centigrade, inches to centimeters, inches/second to centimeters/second, inches/second^2 to centimeters/second,^{2} inches^3 to centimeters,^{3} feet to meters, miles to kilometers, miles per hour to kilometers per hour, U.S. gallons to liters, U.K. gallons to liters, pounds to kilograms, ounces to grams, pounds/inch^2 to kilograms/centimeter,^{2} pounds/feet^3 to grams/centimeters,^{3} degrees to grads.

Other advanced capabilities relate to data and program memories (storage registers).

The hand-held units which offer the greatest value are those with from 24 to 35 and up to 50 keys. And through the use of *second function* (and third and fourth) capability, for most of these keys, they offer up to 100 and more preprogrammed specialized functions. To use these second function or *shift key* functions which offer greater versatility with little or no increase in keyboard of total instrument size, gold- and blue- colored prefix keys are utilized. Some of these are labeled f, g, and h. Primary functions are labeled directly on the keys, with alternate functions on the **space** immediately above the key. To utilize an alternate (second, third, or fourth) function, users simply press the gold, blue, etc. key first, then the appropriate key below their desired function same-colored designation. For example, the factorial function key lets users quickly calculate combinations and permutations. The users merely press the gold key, then the key with "n!" above it to quickly calculate the factorial of positive integers. Instead of spending many minutes and several steps on simpler 4-6 function units, such problems can be completed in one or a few seconds. Thus, means, factorials, percentages, metric or polar conversions, trigonometric functions, logs and reciprocals, etc. are generally one-key *preprogrammed* functions.

Those users about to spend up to or more than $100 for a pocket-sized calculator should choose carefully. Outward appearances often reveal little about the unit's true calculating power. Advanced units must be able to solve complex, real-world problems — problems which involve even more than log, trig, statistics, and business arithmetic problems. The best units, as noted, offer storage registers to hold constants and intermediate answers; they offer logic systems that are simple, consistent and are practical to use. New users must generally make a choice between the three different logic systems. Older users often have definite preferences — mostly because they have become *accustomed* to their first-use unit. The convenience, simplicity, and power (versatility) of each of these will be fully explained on pages ahead. At this point they may be again simply defined as follows: (1) Reverse Polish Notation (RPN) with 4-register operational memory stack and a minimum of one addressible storage register. This is the system used in all hand-held Hewlett-Packard units. (2) Modified algebraic notation without parenthesis key but with operational hierarchy, three internal working registers and one addressable storage register, and (3) Full Algebraic Operating System (AOS) with left-to-right sequence of entry, mathematical order of operations (functions, then powers and roots, then multiplication or division, then addition or subtraction) and often with 9 levels of parentheses. Advanced Texas Instruments units use this logic technology.

Whatever the brand, logic type, number of program steps, labels, flags, user-definable keys, stacks, nesting or subroutine levels, register reviews, etc. both preprogrammed and programmable hand-held calculators are available from dozens of suppliers that slip comfortably into pockets, weigh from 6- to 9-ounces and pack enough power to out-compute any sliderules made and practically all desk-top calculators more than five years old. Ideally, any thinking tool one uses should be an extension of one's mind. Users who know basic mathematics, some statistics, a bit of geometry, etc. can put in data and instantly receive important, needed results at very low tool cost, without waiting turns, remembering special languages or tight rules.

Some Philosophical Notes About Buying More Advanced Calculators — Especially for School

Should people buy calculators with extra capabilities that they might only seldom or perhaps never use. The price differential is now very small, and the answer must generally be, yes. The practice, play and even infrequent use of the extra trials, the tempting experiments, fun games, challenges and tricks will certainly not do tomorrow's students and consumers any harm. Indeed, as teachers have come to realize, advanced hand-held calculators have, almost without exception, promoted and encouraged the study and extended practice of mathematics. Some feel that the classroom of the future will have them built into desks. They have been reported to assist or steer many students and current workers to rationalize the average person's formerly adverse or *pained* attitude toward computers. These *little computers* used on the job or in school have helped people realize the importance of the accuracy of their own input data; they have come to realize that the mistakes, foulups, etc. are really the fault not of the computer itself but of the people who designed the software or those who control and input the original data.

As previously noted, some teachers, superintendents, or school board members have already located individual-student calculators in classrooms as regular tools, especially in math, statistics, and special education classrooms and laboratories. Most are being used as aids and *check tools* rather than as integral to total programs. Practically none anticipate prohibiting their use, though most governing functionaries have yet to establish firm policies concerning their use. Most are already cognizant of the encouraging reports being publicized in the journals from teachers who allow and encourage the use of the calculators for creating and promoting interest in development and organization of problem-solving techniques and procedures. The rapidly expanding proliferation of advanced calculators in business, the professions, and by consumers is making the need for answers to their use as teaching tools increasingly urgent. Their use is not a fad; they are not just fun, game, and puzzle items. Very soon perhaps a large majority of high school students will be using them at least for home work, if not for much classroom use. Certainly their use has a positive effect on students of mathematics — the better students solving problems faster, more accurately, and the slower students more easily grasping mathematical concepts and getting *some* answers, thus avoiding a total distaste for anything mathematical.

In general, most students accept the concept that they are already living in a type of computerized society and that they must learn to use, if not master these type machines, at least learn to cope with them. Most see the mastery of advanced calculators as a first step. Many, formerly afraid of the complexities — electronics and programming — now become inclined to see data processing in terms of personal career selection. Their attitudes, after using their own input and becoming very pleased with their own production, change markedly and positively toward their personal use of ever more capable computing products, procedures — and indeed, the latest electronic/gaming/computing/communicating innovations. There is a paucity of publically available information as to the very surprising *computing* game-playing, and educational capabilities of calculators — at least in relation to the mountains of articles, books, periodicals, etc. available about computers. More than a hundred million people own calculators, but less than 50,000 *people* **own and use personal** computers, though the number of *home* computers is growing rapidly.

The impact of hand-held calculators on higher education (colleges and universities) has been so swift that it is estimated that as many as 80% of the engineering, math and statistics students own some type or other. This has caused at least several scores of research projects in the secondary areas and a significant number in primary educational areas as well. Certainly the **Kuizkid, Mickey Math,** and other calculator games and the use of *computer* TV games with calculator-like keyboards plus the mother's *checkbook* calculator and the dozen or more other novelty calculator items now entering the marketplace in large quantities will *educate* more and more of the very young children to their operation and practical educational use. As students have been told almost endlessly, the *concepts* of problems are more important than the calculations themselves. Knowing *how* to solve problems by deciding what operation to use is more important than the actual computation. The calculator use is faster; more accurate calculating per se gives the teacher more classroom time to spend on the structure, meaning, and operations of mathematics. And the coming flood, plus the already existing *projection* teaching tools for calculator classes are immensely important.

Those individuals in business well realize that the decisions they are called upon to make and the preparation for them involve time and money. And most often they reflect on profitability of operations. Advanced calculators, hand-held or desk-top, provide many with ease of application of the necessary equations, interest and other tables, and the procedures for reaching rapid, specific answers. Engineers, researchers, and scientists require precise accuracy and the answers to many hundreds of *what if* questions through the use of scaled, ordered, or slightly changed data. And again time and money can be saved and the ranges of inquiry can be significantly increased through the use of advanced calculators. Oftentimes businessmen not formally trained in the *hard* sciences can solve quite complex mathematical and engineering problems, following the step-by-step directions found in most calculator owner's handbooks, and do so almost immediately even if they've had little or no specific training in these disciplines. And this same extra convenience applies to engineers and mathematicians who try to solve difficult business and financial models and problems, again by using programs and procedures supplied by calculator manufacturers. The procedural know-how is or can be placed inside the calculator. The concepts evolve from the problems themselves. Similar calculations would take hours and hours of pencil and paper work, if they were attempted at all in the very prevalent cross-disciplinary environments.

Businessmen and engineers must now concern themselves with economic and scientific problems that are becoming more consistently common to both. Many of these relate to the time value of money classifications or budgetary payout times of research and development prototype products. Both engineers and businessmen are very concerned with fast and accurate numerical answers of combinations of financial, mathematical and statistical plans, forecasts and decision analyses. For many of these people, sophisticated calculators that they can learn to efficiently operate in a few days, offer them services much like those achieved by having a true personal pocket computer. One major calculator company uses a nationally advertised slogan, "The waste of figuring over and over . . . is over." As is noted in pages ahead, calculators — whether preprogrammed or programmable — makes it easy to preserve and use these programs to solve problems, process data, plan and project with fewer errors, costs and inconveniences.

A Closer Examination of Preprogrammed Functions

There are several quite important attributes of hand-held calculators that potential purchasers should consider above others. Most of them will be mentioned or discussed in some detail in this and the following chapters. We have noted in previous discussion the importance of memory, percent key, floating-point decimal systems; metric conversions, automatic round-off, square root, reciprocals, squaring, etc. Because more than 10,000-plus transistors can be positioned on chips or wafers smaller than one-inch square, it is not difficult for designers to add more functions to the Arithmetic Logic Unit assembly — and the cost to do so, spread over millions of units, is infinitesimal. The reduction in size and the performance of these chips have continually improved and expanded. Many users will at least sometimes in their experience desire to convert various factors, use logarithmic functions, statistical routines and use the ability to raise numbers to powers. Thus, these and scores of other extra functions should be and are available very cheaply, and users should seek them out in the units they choose, remembering to *buy all the calculator you can* for now and in future use.

Generally, potential users ask two basic questions (1) What types of problems will my unit be used to solve, and (2) What quite difficult problems **might** I request my calculator to solve in the far-ranging future? Non-engineering people might suspect that they will never need to use, for example, rectangular-to-polar coordinate functions. Business forecast and operation models indeed often require such computations. Modern management science is loaded with necessary geometrical, statistical, and matrix calculations — plus the use of the calculus, all ranges of log, root, conversion, nonlinear algebra and exponential functions. It would be *dollar foolish* to avoid these capabilities in calculating instruments when only a few dollars or ten add dozens of them to keyboards. Modern operations research techniques include many math-heavy analyses, such as: Queuing Theory, Linear and Nonlinear Programming, Input-Output Table utilization, Game Theory, and many more. Many users will want printing capability with their hand-held units, a dozen or more models offering this are available. Many users will be able to choose between LED and gas discharge displays. Some units have liquid crystal displays (LCDs) and others fluorescent; even LEDs are now available as alphanumerical and multicolored output. Price/cost advantages are often individual preference.

Other primary elements of consideration that concern some of the first steps above straight *extra* function (single keystroke) are: a large number of storage registers; (all or most functions should be directly accessible from the keyboard) the ability to add, change or skip program steps at will; branching and unconditional testing, etc. But before these deeper functions listed below are sought, most users will be sure that sufficient preprogrammed functions — and the right type — are contained on or are within the capability of the instrument being purchased. Several types and brands are enumerated below. One typical heavily preprogrammed type description follows:

Pre-programmed calculators, financial institutions — Some programmed electronic printing calculators designed especially for commercial banks, savings and loan associations, and other financial institutions, used stored programs to provide simple and rapid solutions to the complex computations which are part of the everyday work of departments handling installment loans, commercial loans, mortgages, and savings accounts. The calculator's simplicity of data entry and rapid calculation eliminate the need for charts, rate books, tables and formulas. For example, computation of monthly payments of a conventional mortgage loan is performed by entering the principal amount, the annual interest rate, and the number of years of the loan. The automatic result shows the monthly payment, including principal and interest. Monthly payments on installment loans including credit life insurance and accident/health insurance can be computed quickly and can include "odd days" interest, frequently lost by an institution because of the number of references that must be made to rate books or charts. General financial applications include such routines as equity calculation on a mortgage loan, equivalent interest rate on discounted notes, calculation of periodic withdrawal from a known investment, and others.

As previously noted, efficient pocket calculators should have at least one addressable memory — to store constants or other numbers used more than once in a calculation. Performing register arithmetic (adding, etc. into, to, or from stored numbers) makes data manipulation exceptionally easy, even when working with problems involving three simultaneous linear equations (or 3×3 matrix inversions). Automatic memory (or operational stacks, or a four-register stack, etc.) is also important for re-entering numbers (intermediate answers) into the calculation at the appropriate time. This eliminates the need to write operating numbers, intermediate answers, etc. down, thus reducing errors and adding speed to projects.

A brief description of the number of preprogrammed functions that can be had in one of the under $60 quality calculators is summarized below — the 50 keys, 106 directly accessible keyboard functions are:

A Brief Summary of the Commodore SR4190R 10-digit Mantissa, 2-digit exponent with Variable Exponent Integer Increase and Decrease: MANT, EE, EE ↑, EE ↓
Register Keys: STO 1, RCL 1, Σ1, STO 2, RCL 2, Σ2, x ↔ y, Xn, Xi, Yi, $\alpha, \beta, \gamma,$ ( ).
One Real Variable Function Keys: In, log, e^x, 10^x, $1/x$, $\sqrt{x}$, x^2, SIN, COS, TAN, INV SIN, INV COS, INV TAN sinh, cosh, tanh, INV sinh, INV cosh, INV tanh

Two Real Variable Arithmetic Function Keys: $+ - \times \div$
Two Complex Variable Arithmetic Function Keys: $j+, j-, j\times, j\div$
Two Real Variable Analytical Function Keys: $\to P, \to R, P_m^n, y^x, \sqrt[x]{y}, \%, \Delta\%, C_m^n$
Statistical Function Keys: $x \leftrightarrow y$, SLOPE, INTCP, GAUSS, BINOM, POISS, x_s, y_s
Hours-Minutes-Seconds Mode: HMS
Unit Conversions: (°F) C, (d) dms, (d) gra, (gal) l, (oz) g, (lb) kg, (ft) m, (mi) km, (f oz) l, (in) cm, (BTU) J
Degree/Radian Conversion and Mode Keys: d/r, $d \leftrightarrow r$
Numerical Entry Keys: 0-9, π
3 Angular Units: radians, degrees, grads
Poisson and Binomial probability densities. Gaussian distribution.
Mean and Standard Deviation PLUS Linear Regression Analysis.
Power supply: Built-in rechargeable Ni-Cad batteries. AC adapter/ recharger included.
One Year Warranty

A competing HP-21 unit for perhaps $10 or $20 more offers the following:
• 32 pre-programmed functions and operations, including rectangular/polar conversion, register arithmetic and common log evaluation.

HP-21 performs all log and trig functions, the latter in radian or degrees. It permits users to:
• convert polar to rectangular coordinates, and back again ($\to P, \to R$);
• do full register arithmetic ($M+, M-, M\times, M\div$),
• calculate a common antilog (10x) with a single keystroke.

The HP-21 also performs all basic data manipulations ($1/x, y^x, \sqrt{x}, \pi$) and executes all pre-programmed functions in *one second or less*.

Full display formatting. The Display key (DSP) allows users to choose between fixed decimal and scientific notation and lets users control the number of places displayed. (The HP-21 always uses all 10 digits internally.)

When a number is too large or small for fixed decimal display, the HP-21 switches automatically to scientific, so users need not worry that the calculator will confuse a smaller number with zero.

Finally, if users give the HP-21 an impossible instruction the Display spells E-r-r-o-r.

RPN logic system. Users can evaluate *any* expression without copying parentheses, worrying about hierarchies or re-structuring beforehand. The calculator remembers what's where — automatically. Users can solve *all* problems their way — the way they first learned in beginning algebra.

Some Examples of the Preprogrammed Hewlett-Packard Units

Two different versions of extensively preprogrammed low-cost calculators are the HP-22 and HP-27. Some details are given below on each. Competition, with slightly lower prices comes primarily from Texas Instruments and National Semiconductor. Details of these products, in brief outline, are also given below:

HP-22 Business-Statistics Calculator

The new HP-22 pocket calculator is a management tool for anyone who needs to evaluate and analyze business problems quickly, easily and accurately. With the HP-22, users have the solution to virtually every calculation required for modern business management — literally at their fingertips. The knowhow is built into the instrument chip. And the keyboard legends clearly show capabilities. All the fundamental financial functions of the HP-22 are integrated with a comprehensive range of the statistical and mathematical functions needed in today's business world. It's like having three calculators in one compact body. With it, users handle everything from simple arithmetic to complex time-value-of-money computations including interest rates; rates of return and discounted cash flows (net present value and internal rate of return) for investment analysis; extended percent calculations; accumulated interest/remaining balances, amortization and balloon payments. You can even handle planning, forecasting and decision analysis. And users can approach business problems in a variety of ways to arrive at intelligent decisions and recommendations based on facts. All the financial equations, statistical formulas and mathematical functions are preprogrammed and stored in the HP-22. All users do is key in data, press the appropriate keys, and see answers displayed — in seconds. For example, users can project future sales, revenue or inventory requirements with ease. The HP-22 employs the same RPN logic system used in all Hewlett-Packard pocket calculators, regardless of price. This system, combined with the four-register stack, allows users to do everything from routine arithmetic to lengthy, complex business problems. All intermediate answers are displayed and stored automatically in the HP-22, so users seldom need a scratch pad.

The Financial Capabilities

The five keys in the top row of the HP-22 are the basic financial keys, preprogrammed to replace equations and interest tables. The gold key relates to the gold legends on the keyboard, giving access to three additional financial functions (plus fifteen additional mathematical and statistical functions). To use any of the additional functions, press the gold key first. To solve problems simply enter known data, press the appropriate financial keys and see answers displayed automatically. When users enter three known values with the financial keys, they can solve for another unknown value. For example: enter amount of present value [PV]; enter number of periods involved [n]; enter payment [PMT]. Then, push [i] and get interest.

12×	12÷	ACC	INT	BAL
n	i	PMT	PV	FV

Expanded Percentages Capability

Percentage is the common standard of measurement in the business and financial world. For this reason, the HP-22 provides three separate percentage function keys. The [%] key is used to calculate a percentage. For example, to calculate 4% of a displayed number, just key in 4 and press the [%] key. There is no need to convert the 4% to its decimal equivalent of .04. The [Δ%] key is used to compute the percentage difference (ratio of increase or decrease) between two numbers. The [%Σ] key is used to find what percentage one number is of another number or of a total sum. The HP-22 saves the base number for multiple percentage calculations on the same base number.

%Σ	Δ%
CHS	%

The Statistical Capabilities

In addition to the financial capabilities, the HP-22 gives pre-programmed statistical capabilities for planning, forecasting and analysis. Using the [Σ+] key, users can enter statistical data into five of the ten addressable memories, where it remains unaffected by most other calculations. With this data users calculate linear regression, linear estimates, mean/average and standard deviations. Using the [Σ−] key they can adjust or correct input data without having to repeat the entire calculation. For example, to project sales, key in past performance data, then press the [L.R.] key. Key in the number of the forecast period and press the [ŷ] key to obtain sales at that future point in time. To obtain an average, key in all data, then press the [x̄] key to obtain the average. The HP-22 automatically keeps track of the number of entries. To find standard deviation (a measure of statistical validity), key in your data, then press the [s] key for the answer.

| Σ− | L.R. | ŷ | x̄ | s |
| Σ+ | x ≷ y | r↓ | STO | RCL |

The Mathematical Capabilities

Occasionally, unique business or business-related problems may arise that cannot be solved by using the pre-programmed functions. For these situations, the HP-22 gives virtually all the math functions needed in business, such as logs, antilogs, exponentiation and root extraction so users may work out their own solutions to unusual individual problems.

| ln | e^x | y^x | $\sqrt{x}$ |
| − | + | × | ÷ |

The Step-up of the HP-22, the HP-80: The Businessman's Pocket Calculator That's Preprogrammed to Solve Hundreds of Time-and-Money Problems

The HP-80 financial pocket calculator is a highly sophisticated computer-calculator which provides 36 separate financial capabilities, including bond yield and price, compound interest, mortgage payment and analysis, trend lines, rate of return analysis, accrued interest, discounted notes, true equivalent annual yield, annual percentage rate conversions, mean and standard deviation. And the HP-80 has a built-in 200-year calendar.

In short, the HP-80 can solve almost any business problem without resort to cumbersome tables or expensive computer time. The HP-80 features a 200-decade operating range, and provides answers with an accuracy of up to 10 significant digits. Or, users can round the display and number of decimal places from 0 to 6. Numbers too large or small for conventional, fixed-decimal notation are automatically displayed in scientific notation. The HP-80 also provides a four-register operational memory stack, and a separate addressable memory register for storage of constants or other data.

Besides offering the capabilities of the HP-22, the HP-80 provides the following: Amortized (direct reduction) loans (ordinary annuity). Users can solve for: the number of payments; the number of payments to reach a specified balance; payment amount; annual percentage rate, with or without fees; principal amount; amortization schedules; remaining balance (remaining principal, last payment, balloon payment) and accumulated interest; payment amount for loan with a balloon payment; annual percentage rate with balloon payment coincident with, or one period after, the last payment; price and yield of discounted mortgages (prepaid or fully amortized), and the mortgage factor for Canadian mortgages.

Loans with a constant amount paid toward the principal — With the HP-80 users can prepare a payment schedule showing the interest portion per payment and the remaining balance, when a constant amount is paid toward the principal.

Sinking funds (ordinary annuity) — The HP-80 can calculate: payment amount, interest rate, number of payments and debt retirement amount.

Consumer loans — Users press the keys to calculate the monthly payment amount, or to convert the add-on interest rate to the annual percentage rate of interest. And, using the Rule of 78's, they can use the HP-80 to calculate rebates.

Also, they can convert the annual percentage rate to the add-on rate.

Savings functions (annuity due) — Users can calculate the number of deposits, the rate of interest, the deposit amount and the future value.

Lease and rent functions (annuity due) — The HP-80 can be used to convert the add-on interest rate to the annual percentage rate, or vice versa.

Users can calculate: the number of payments; rate of interest; payment amount; payment amount with balloon payment or residual value, and present value.

Discounted cash flow analysis — $\Sigma + \Sigma -$. Users can quickly and easily perform a discounted cash flow analysis and calculate the net present value of even, uneven or deferred payment streams.

The HP-80 can also be used to calculate the discounted or internal rate of return (iteration of the above.)

The HP-27: An HP-21 Step-up With Significant Functions
Used by Scientists and Financiers

The HP-27 Scientific/Plus is the most powerful preprogrammed pocket calculator Hewlett-Packard has built to date.

Five new functions never before offered by HP include variance, correlation coefficient, normal distribution, net present value and internal rate of return. Other items of significance:

28 Exponential, Log and Trig Functions — all Preprogrammed

The HP-27 gives all the most-used exponential, log and trig functions — including sines, cosines, tangents and their inverses in three angular modes; natural and common logs and anti-logs; pi; related arithmetic functions; coordinate conversions; angle conversion, angle addition and subtraction.

15 Important Statistical Functions — all Preprogrammed

Many statistical functions useful in both science and business are provided by the HP-27 — including three important functions: variance, correlation coefficient and normal distribution. Summations of data points are stored for easy access. Users can adjust or correct input data without having to repeat an entire calculation. Once data is keyed in, users can calculate the means, standard deviations and variances for two variables. They can also calculate linear regression, linear estimates and the correlation coefficient for two variables. Users also calculate the density function and upper-tail area under a normal distribution curve.

10 Valuable Financial Functions — all Preprogrammed

For convenience in solving both personal and job related business problems — such as mortgages, compound interests and sinking funds — all fundamental financial functions are preprogrammed into the HP-27 to eliminate the need for bulky books of equations and interest tables. Two new preprogrammed functions — net present value and internal rate of return for uneven cash flows — facilitate capital budgeting and resource allocation. In addition, the HP-27 provides three separate percentage functions for ease in calculating margins, markups, discounts, percents of totals, etc.

20 Memories Help Simplify Difficult Calculations.

In addition to the 5 financial memories, the 4 operational stack memories and a last-x memory, the HP-27 provides 10 addressable memories for data storage. This large memory capacity lets users make highly complex and lengthy calculations with ease and assurance. Displayed values may be stored in any addressable memory and later recalled to the display. In addition, register arithmetic can be performed on all ten addressable memories.

6 Clearing Options Give Users Flexible Use of Memories

With the CLX key, users can clear the display only. They can clear all four memories of the operational stack with the STK key. The last six addressable memories, which are used for statistics, are cleared with the Σ key. The REG key clears all ten addressable memories, all five financial memories and the last-X memory. Or users can clear the status of the financial memories with the RESET key. In addition, they can clear the prefix keys with the key labeled PREFIX.

The HP preprogrammed line also includes several printing units — the HP-46, HP-81, HP-91 and the new HP-95C. The HP-91 is similar to the above in functional capability. The HP-91 fits a desk environment and adds printing to the repertoire. It's small enough ($9 \times 8 \times 2\frac{1}{2}$ in.) to fit in a standard briefcase for travel — or a lockable desk drawer for security — yet weighs enough ($2\frac{1}{2}$ lb.) to sit firmly on the desktop. The HP-91 boasts many preprogrammed functions plus 16 addressable memory registers instead of 9; engineering notation; the ability to perform regression and linear estimates; 3 "%" functions instead of 2; and keyboard buffering 7 keystrokes deep.

Printing can be "manual" (prints only when "Print X" or a list function is pressed), "normal" (prints all entries and functions) or "all" (prints digit entries, functions and results). The calculator will print in fixed decimal, scientific notation and engineering notation. Separate numeric and function keysets, coupled with the 7-character buffer, let a "touch-entry" trained operator use the calculator without reducing normal speed. In addition the HP-91 has a "Last-X" register for error recovery or multiple operations and a 4-register automatic memory stack, combined with HP's RPN logic system for more efficient desk manipulation. A 220-pg. owner's handbook contains user instructions and a comprehensive application section that gives the most efficient keystroke sequences for solving problems in mathematics, statistics, finance, navigation and surveying. (The HP-95C is analyzed in Chapter 4.)

Calculators Now Essential in all Modern Enterprise

The growing complexity of statistical and mathematical tools has made managers' work more precise. Simultaneously, this mountain of information has also placed a tremendous burden of data analysis and interpretation on their desks, a burden that often requires them to work evenings, weekends, and even holidays. For some, big computers help — but unless the problem is extremely complex or involves massive amounts of data, using the big computer can be more of a hassle than it's worth. The time spent writing programs or waiting turns on the computer has to detract from the time spent on truly productive work.

Now managers can put preprogrammed or programmable calculators on their desks to greatly reduce their computational workloads. Replacing the big computer is not the purpose of calculators. But, they are designed to complement any computing tools presently in use — from adding machines to huge, general purpose computers. Various models allow users to fit the right machine to the right problem and greatly increase their utility.

The desk-top calculators decentralize and personalize the decision-enhancing powers of information processing systems — bringing to the individual what was previously only available to staff leaders or various top executives. Departmental managers, special research workers, project leaders, etc. can now cope with more data, explore with more insight, digest more facts, use more 'what if' techniques 'on the spot' and far more successfully than before with the recently offered preprogrammed or programmable desk-top calculators. Thus, better decisions are made — in the conference rooms, laboratories, in the field, . . . wherever decisions must be made; better decisions with more accuracy and more options considered, from broader data bases, the information being instantly recallable. The advanced calculator is a powerful personal mathematical resource, without the user being required to possess programming experience or computing system expertise. The entry and recall systems are easy to use, flexible, and expandable at low cost and with little if any inconvenience. Personal problem-solving techniques and styles can be introduced and followed, professional capabilities are being magnified and made adaptable for faster, better procedures through the use of advanced calculators.

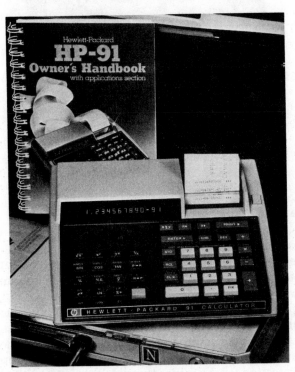

PREPROGRAMMED DESK-TOP CALCULATORS — PRINTERS AND NON-PRINTERS, SOME EXAMPLES
The above picture of the Hewlett-Packard HP-91 printing preprogrammed scientific calculator is a typical example of the display, printing, and expanded preprogrammed capability that has become available at very reasonable costs, below $500 for this unit.

Desk-top Preprogrammed Units: Alterability

There are many examples of preprogrammed desk-top units; one of the best that demonstrates 'alterable keyboard' and ROM-added capability is the Burroughs 6451. Many other brands and models imitate this procedure and capability.

THE BURROUGHS PREPROGRAMMED SYSTEM

The Burroughs C 6451 is an example of a general-purpose calculator — plus a unique application calculator. Burroughs, technologically sophisticated C 6451 is designed to handle time-consuming calculations involving units of measurement with a conversational simplicity never before offered in a desk-top calculator. The C 6451 features a Program Activator Panel. The user snaps the Program Activator Panel into place on the applicational keyboard of the C 6451.

The versatile Program Activator Panel . . .
- activates the measurement, liquid, or weight programs.
- combines the functions of the applicational keyboard with the computing and listing keys of the basic calculator.
- identifies the three common function keys (per, convert to and metric) and the nine unit entry keys which represent the units of measurement for the applications.
- permits computations and conversions for a broad range of liquid, weight or measurement applications.

Measurement, weight or liquid problems are entered on the keyboard in the same manner as they would be stated by the user. It's quite simple. The C 6451 also provides protection for the future through its ability to handle conversions to and from the metric system of measurement. The C 6451's simplicity is activated by combining a standard calculator keyboard with unit entry keys for the different measure systems. Problems involving units of measurement are entered on the keyboard conversationally in the same manner as they would be stated by the user.

Advanced large-scale circuit technology gives the C 6451 the versatility to add, calculate or convert in several measurement systems. The systems are weight (avoirdupois, troy and metric); liquid (US, imperial and metric); measurement (linear, area and volume); time; quantities (gross, dozens and singles, fractions and decimals); and temperature (Fahrenheit and Celsius). The values and functions of the different systems are stored in micro-programmed read-only memories which are accessed by three interchangeable program activator panels. These program activator panels fit over the unit keys and can be changed easily. In a matter of seconds, for example, the user may change the labels and functions of the unit keys from tons, pounds and ounces to hours, minutes and seconds or one of the other measurement systems available. The C 6451 is designed to handle conventional business calculations as well as measurement applications and gives the user the advantages of both display and printing output. The display-only mode saves paper in random calculations where an audit tape is not required. The display-and-print mode provides both the legibility of the large Panaplex® display and a printed tape which identifies each entry and calculation with symbols applicable to the measurement program in use. In 1976, purchase price of the basic C 6451 calculator with one program activator panel was $695. Prices range from $695 to $795 depending on the number of program activator panels provided.

One of the primary points stressed throughout this book is that users of hand-held units become quite specifically trained and happily experienced with their low-cost units. The descriptions of the desk-tops demonstrate that the capabilities, operational techniques, and utilization step-ups are very similar to those *first-used* hand-held units. This further strengthens the claim of the Hongkong student quoted earlier, that earlier school use of advanced calculators, especially for those students who do not intend to go on to college, does indeed prepare them for later life jobs, personal business or professional use, and often is their tried and trusted tool for practically any trade or endeavor. The use of ROM and RAM in preprogrammed models, particularly the NS 7100 *plug-in* characteristic, is obviously the direction of construction and utilization of an ever-increasing number of calculating instruments. The Burroughs' systems examples (the C6203 is custom-preprogrammed for commercial banks, saving and loan institutions, other financial institutions and the financial management of large specialized commercial enterprises) suggest expanding lines of *changeable intelligence* preprogrammed machines that could be practically endless.

Some other manufacturers with very complete lines of equally capable desk-top preprogrammed units are: Casio, Canon, Olympia, Olivetti, Monroe, Sharp, Adler, Underwood, Lloyds, and others. (The reader is invited to check latest edition of "Calculator Users Guide and Dictionary," Matrix Publishers, Inc. for specifics and operating details.) No attempt is made in this book to compare, contrast, or highlight any specific model or company product. Some units lend themselves to *example* analysis and are therefore described to indicate *trending* capabilities expected to be utilized by several other suppliers, or in effect, to become standard operating features. As the reader is already certainly very well aware, the calculator industry is perhaps more dynamic, more competitive, more innovatively challenging than any other in the total electronics or business equipment areas.

Some Texas Instruments Products — and Why They Scare Competitors. . .

One of the strongest, highly innovative, and fiercely competitive manufacturers of calculator products is Texas Instruments, Inc. Many financial analysts who closely watch the calculator scene suggest the price and marketing leadership of this electronics giant has done the most to spread calculator capability so rapidly and dramatically. It is obvious that any one firm that has more than 30,000 outlets for its calculator products and that quite consistently demonstrates uncustomary but powerful marketing bravado in pricing and new product introductions could well become a dominating force. Hewlett-Packard will, of course, fight any competitor to keep from taking a back seat in any aspect of this amazing industry. Certainly the many very large Japanese manufacturers must be counted as high up in the hierarchy leaders in the production of low-cost advanced calculator capability. And a dozen or more equally strong American and international companies continue to battle for their own diligently-fought market shares. And most continue to wonder, "Where is IBM?" Rumors continue to persist that RCA, Gillete, and others — all have completed extensive studies of markets, technologies, etc. — will soon enter the calculator marketing wars. All this keeps all producers alert and on the upbeat.

The low-cost calculator line from Texas Instruments (TI) has been strongly accepted by American customers and many more around the world. It is extensive and compelling — and expanding. Only a few of the models will be reviewed here to compare and contrast with other units already described. The principal units that relate to the capabilities that this author feels most strongly identify TI are those that are the most generally needed and sought. The Power of the TI line is represented by the SR-50A, SR51A, TI5050. The SR-56 and PC-100 printer option, the SR-52, SR-60 and other units are held for discussion of the Programmable chapter. The SR-60 is pictured below for comparison with the other competitive preprogrammed units, although the SR-60 is preprogrammed/programmable, **and** *prompting*. The PC-100 printer is a remarkable unit, sells at discount stores for about $230 and accommodates the two hand-held units; the programmable SR-52 and SR-56, and undoubtedly other models to be announced. The handy printer is a very convenient checking and proofing tool and is pictured near the front of the book.

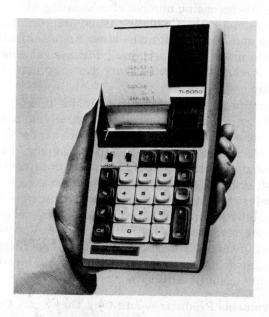

Texas Instruments TI-5050 Hand-Held Printing Calculator

The TI-5050 pictured above is a popular unit for those users who require only simple calculations. It has very little sophistication for engineers, businessmen, statisticians, or scientists, as do other Texas Instruments models. It is one of the best of the hand-held printers, however. Its competition, in 1976, was from the under $100 Casio, "Mini Calculator/Printer" using a narrow ¼" tape horizontally mounted within the case, and the Facit-Addo, Inc. unit model 1140 (1½ pounds), which uses a 2¼ inch tape (thermal) and has 8-digit capacity, floating decimal, automatic constant and percentage keys, permitting discount and markup calculations.

Operating Features

The TI-5050 performs chain calculations with all four functions . . . , press desired function key to use any result in next problem. Repeated addition and subtraction without re-entering the number. Number entries are cleared with the CE key. A # key (non-add) to print reference numbers. The ↑ key feeds extra paper for easy tearoff.

Percent

Calculations requiring percentage add-ons or discounts are easily solved with the % key . . . audit symbols "A" or "D" are printed beside the respective result. The TI-5050 will also print the ratio of two numbers as a percentage when the numbers are entered as a division problem and completed with the % key.

Chain/Constant Switch

The Chain/Const switch permits normal chain calculations or multiplication and division by a constant without re-entering numbers.

F/$ Switch

Choose full floating decimal (F) or add-mode ($) operation. In add mode, the decimal is automatically positioned at two places for easy entry of dollars and cents *without using* • key.

The Texas Instruments 'Prompting' SR-60A

The fully-programmable SR-60A offers users the ease of "Plain-language" programming that eliminates intermediate steps, yields immediate results. A "prompting" feature, properly programmed, displays words or phrases to "ask for" keyboard entries to solve a specific problem.

The SR-60A's 20-character display shows 10-digits for mathematical, power and root functions, 2-digit exponent plus sign, 13-digits for special functions and data registers. The algebraic entry format and parentheses let users enter data in the same order a problem is written. The calculator has 40 registers and 480 program memory locations, with optional memory expansion to 1920-step program memory and 100 data registers. The unit is further analyzed in the following chapter.

The Texas Instruments low-cost preprogrammed hand-held units are very high demand items for students and on-the-job professionals. Despite their extensive capabilities, as listed below, the SR-50A sells in many areas at a below $50 price, while the expanded capability, SR-51A, sells for only $10 or $15 more at many major calculator retail outlets.

The SR-50A

Complex scientific calculations are solved as easily as simple arithmetic with a full function, portable slide-rule calculator, ideal for student or professional use. The SR-50A features an algebraic keyboard and sum-of-products capability with single-function keys for easy problem solving.

In addition to simple arithmetic, the SR-50A performs all classical slide-rule calculations — roots, powers, reciprocals, factorials, common and natural logarithms and their inverses, trigonometric (sin, cos, tan) and hyperbolic (sinh, cosh, tanh) functions and their inverses — all in free floating decimal point or in scientific notation. (See chart for additional detail.)

The versatile electronic memory allows data to be stored and retrieved or added to memory. The SR-50A features a degree/radian switch which makes the calculator interpret the displayed angle in degrees (when set at "D") or in radians (when set at "R"). By pressing the angle change key (D/R), the calculator will convert the display angle from radians to degrees or degrees to radians.

The SR-50A computes and displays numbers as large as $\pm$ 9.999999999 $\times$ 10^{99} or as small as $\pm 1.0 \times 10^{-99}$ on the bright, easy-to-read 14-character display (10-digit mantissa, 2-digit exponent, 2 signs). Automatically converts to scientific notation when the calculated answer is greater than 10^{10} or less than 10^{-10}. Answers are calculated to 13 digits and displayed rounded to 10 significant digits; however, for maximum accuracy, the SR-50A uses all 13 digits for internal calculations.

The SR-51A

A professional calculator with special features for statisticians, businessmen, engineers, scientists, and students. In addition to simple arithmetic, the SR-51A performs:

- Functions of x — square root, square, reciprocal, y^x and $\sqrt[x]{y}$.
- Logarithmic functions — common and natural logarithms and their inverses.
- Trigonometric and hyperbolic functions — and their inverses.
- Linear regression — least-squares linear regression problems performed on two-dimensional random variables from a minimum of 2 to a maximum of 99 data points.
- Statistical functions — factorials, random numbers, permutations, mean, variance, and standard deviation.
- Decimal point — allows selection of the location of the decimal point from zero to eight decimal places — or full floating.
- % — performs add-on, discount, and percentage calculations.
- Δ% — calculates the percentage change between

$$x_1 \text{ and } x_2 \left(\frac{x_2 - x_1}{x_1}\right) \times 100$$

- Constant operations — allows repetitive calculations of roots, powers, addition, subtraction, multiplication, and division.
- Conversions — 20 preprogrammed conversions and their inverses, as listed below, by entering simple two-digit code:

The SR-51A features three user accessible memories for storing, recalling, summation, and multiplication of data to memory independent of arithmetic keys.

The SR-51A computes and displays numbers as large as $\pm 9.999999999 \times 10^{99}$ and as small as $\pm 1.0 \times 10^{-99}$, automatically converting answers to scientific notation when the calculated answer is greater than 10^{10} or less than 10^{-10}. Answers are calculated to 13 digits and displayed rounded to 10 significant digits; however, for maximum accuracy, the SR-51A uses all 13 digits for internal calculations. Provides sum-of-products capability without the use of special keys. Operates on fast-charge rechargeable battery pack (4 hours to restore full charge) or AC.

These two units have been so widely sold and continue to be accepted in many areas as 'standard' preprogrammed units, that several problems and their solutions are presented to demonstrate the simplicity of operation and extensive yet low-cost capabilities.

A reprint from Texas Instruments Literature Algebraic Entry vs Reverse Polish Notation ... A candid comment

"Most hand-held professional calculators use either algebraic entry or Reverse Polish Notation (RPN). There are two basic schools of thought on which is best — each manufacturer advocating his own.

"And, to make it more confusing, a good case can be made for both by the careful selection of sample problems. In truth, there is no ultimate answer. Either system can be operated with ease by the experienced owner. And either can be a boon to the simple solution of the most complex problems. Many practiced users of RPN now swear by it. But owners of algebraic machines can find RPN awkward and confusing. It boils down to individual preference.

"The case for algebraic is straight-forward: It lets you key the problem just as you would state it. Because it works the way you think, most people find it easier to master and more natural to use. That's why TI and most other manufacturers chose this method. For example, when we think in algebraic notation, we say, "Two times four equals eight." With RPN, we'd have to say "Two and four multiplied." An oversimplification, but it points up the fundamental difference.

"The TI SR-51A and SR-50A let you key the problem simply, just as you would state it. In addition TI offers a unique register system which provides a sum of products capability directly at the keyboard. This ability to store the first product while the second is being calculated is in addition to memories accessed by memory keys.

"Here's a typical problem to illustrate the difference:

$$(2 \times 3) + (4 \times 5) = 26$$

With Algebraic:

$$2 \times 3 + 4 \times 5 = 26$$

With Reverse Polish Notation:

$$2 \text{ ENTER } 3 \times 4 \text{ ENTER } 5 \times + 26$$

"Of course, *all* algebraic machines do not have the extensive capabilities of the SR-51A and SR-50A. With some limited-function algebraic calculators, it is necessary to write down intermediate answers and impossible to store numbers for review and later use. (RPN, as well, requires notation of intermediate results in complex calculations which might otherwise overload the stack.)

"Such limitations do not apply to the SR-51A and SR-50A. These are truly full-function slide-rule calculators designed for the most sophisticated, complex technical problems.

"The case for algebraic entry is strong — particularly in the light of the exceptional capabilities of the SR-50A and SR-51A. That's why Texas Instruments chose this method after thorough evaluation of the alternatives. If you evaluate the alternatives, we think you'll prefer algebraic too. But, even if you are already conditioned to RPN, the added value offered by TI is well worth the easy transition."

SR-50A CALCULATING POWER GIVES USERS FAST ANSWERS TO PROBLEMS SUCH AS . . .

Business — Investment Decisions

A decision must be made for a capital equipment investment. What is the maximum recommended purchase price Q of a machine with projected earnings for five years of $1200, $1500, $1700, $1300, and $900. Assume a value of zero after five years. Use an interest rate of 6.25%.

$$Q_{max} = \frac{R1}{(1+r)} + \frac{R2}{(1+r)^2} + \frac{R3}{(1+r)^3} + \frac{R4}{(1+r)^4} + \frac{R5}{(1+r)^5}$$

$$= \frac{1200}{(1.0625)} + \frac{1500}{(1.0625)^2} + \frac{1750}{(1.0625)^3} + \frac{1300}{(1.0625)^4} + \frac{900}{(1.0625)^5} = \$5601.84$$

Please note the use of the $x:y$ exchange key in the processing of this example. Each denominator is processed before division is performed. The numerator of each quotient is entered as the divisor. Pressing the $x:y$ key prior to the next function key exchanges the numerator and denominator values before the division is performed.

Enter	Press		Display
1.0625	STO	$\div$	1.0625
1200	$x:y$	+	1129.411765
	RCL	x^2 $\div$	1.12890625
1500	$x:y$	+	2458.131488
	RCL	y^x	1.0625
3		$\div$	1.199462891
1750	$x:y$	+	3917.117851
	RCL	y^x	1.0625
4		$\div$	1.274429321
1300	$x:y$	+	4937.182265
	RCL	y^x	1.0625
5		$\div$	1.354081154
900	$x:y$	=	5601.839622

Boating — Velocity Made Good

A sailboat sails an effective course into the wind by tacking back and forth at an angle to the wind. If the wind velocity and boat velocity are drawn as vectors, the component of boat velocity directly into the wind is the velocity made good, VMG. Using the vector diagram and quantities shown, determine the VMG of the boat.

V_W = apparent wind velocity, 17 knots
V_B = boat's true speed, 9 knots
a = apparent angle of wind, 28°

This problem can be solved using vector equations. Each upper case V represents a vector and each lower case v represents a vector magnitude.

$$V_A = - V_W$$
$$V_x + V_y = V_A$$
$$v_x + j v_y = V_A$$
$$v_y = v_a \sin a$$
$$= 17 \sin 28$$
$$= 7.981016567$$
$$v_x = v_a \cos a$$
$$= 17 \cos 28$$
$$= 15.01010908$$
$$v_D = v_x - v_B$$
$$= 15.01010908 - 9$$
$$= 6.010109079$$
$$V_T = v_D + jv_y = v_T \angle b$$
$$= 6.010109079 + j\,7.981016567$$
$$= \sqrt{(6.010109079)^2 + (7.981016567)^2}$$
$$\angle \arctan \frac{7.981016567}{6.010109079}$$
$$= 9.990897687 \angle 53.01840377°$$
$$VMG = v_B \cos b$$
$$= 9 \cos 53.01840377$$
$$= 5.414026187 \text{ knots}$$

Angle: Deg

Enter	Press			Display	Remarks
17	×			17.	
28	sin	=	STO	7.981016567	v_y
17	×			17.	
28	cos	=	−	15.01010908	v_x
9	=			6.010109079	v_D
	x^2	+	RCL	7.981016567	
	x^2	=	$\sqrt{x}$	9.990897687	v_T
	RCL	÷		7.981016567	
6.010109079	=	arc tan		53.01840377	θ
	cos	×		.6015584653	
9	=			5.414026187	VMG

Architectural Engineering — Girder Design

What is the total bending moment M in a 19.7 foot simply supported girder with a total uniform load W of 55,000 pounds and a wind load M_w of 110,000 ft lb?

The moment will occur at a point p feet from one end

$$p = \frac{2 \times 110,000}{55,000} = 4 \text{ feet}$$

$$M = \left(\frac{W}{2L}\right)\left(\frac{L}{2} - p\right)\left(\frac{L}{2} + p\right) + \frac{pM_w}{L/2} = \frac{WL}{8} - \frac{Wp^2}{2L} + \frac{2pM_w}{L}$$

$$= \left(\frac{55000 \times 19.7}{8}\right) - \left(\frac{55000 \times (4)^2}{2 \times 19.7}\right) + \left(\frac{2 \times 4 \times 110000}{19.7}\right) = 157,772.5254 \text{ ft lb}$$

Enter	Press	Display
55000	×	55000.
19.7	÷	1083500.
8	−	135437.5
55000	×	55000.

4	$x^2 \div$		880000.
2	$\div$		440000.
19.7	$+$		113102.4746
2	$\times$		2.
4	$\times$		8.
110000	$\div$		880000.
19.7	$=$		157772.5254

Chemical Engineering — Fluid Flow

What is the amount of flow of fluid across a weir with a V-shaped notch? The angle of the notch is 35° and the height of the liquid from the bottom edge of the weir is 4.5 feet.

$$Q = 2.505 \left(\tan \frac{\alpha}{2}\right) H^{2.47} = 2.505 \left(\tan \frac{35}{2}\right) \times (4.5)^{2.47}$$

$$= 32.43134362 \text{ cu ft per sec}$$

Angle: Deg

Enter	Press	Display
4.5	y^x	4.5
2.47	$\times$	41.06150933
17.5	$\tan \times$	12.94664416
2.505	$=$	32.43134362

Physics — Thrown Object

If a ball is thrown upward with a velocity of 86 feet per second, what is its velocity and height at the end of 1.75 seconds? Use $g = 32.2$ feet per sec^2.

Velocity,

$$v = v_0 - gt = 86 - (32.2)(1.75) = 29.65 \text{ ft/sec}$$

Enter	Press	Display
86	$-$	86.
32.2	$\times$	32.2
1.75	$=$	29.65

Height,

$$s = v_0 t = \frac{1}{2} gt^2 = (86)(1.75) - \frac{1}{2}(32.2)(1.75)^2 = 101.19 \text{ feet}$$

Enter	Press	Display
86	$\times$	86.
1.75	$-$	150.5
32.2	$\times$	32.2
1.75	$x^2 \div$	98.6125
2	$=$	101.19375

Civil Engineering — Time of Concentration

The total runoff of rainfall from an area to an inlet will be maximum at the time that the water from the most remote area contributes to the flow. Determine this time if the distance from the most remote area is 1350 feet, the slope is 0.15 foot per foot, and the rain intensity is 1.7 inches per hour. Use a coefficient of 2.5 for turf.

$$t = C\left(\frac{L}{Si^2}\right)^{1/3} = 2.5 \left[\frac{1350}{.15 \times (1.7)^2}\right]^{1/3} = 36.50801589 \text{ minutes}$$

Enter	Press	Display
1350	$\div$	1350.

.15	÷	9000.
1.7	x^2 $x\sqrt{y}$	3114.186851
3	×	14.60320636
2.5	=	36.50801589

Electrical Engineering — RL Equivalent Impedance

What is the equivalent impedance of a 560 ohm resistor and a 25.5 milli-henry inductor at a frequency of 2500 hertz?

$$\text{Zeg} = R + j\,X_L = 560 + j\,400$$

or $\quad$ $\text{Zeg} = A\ \underline{/\theta} = 688.5\ \underline{/35.6°}$

where $\qquad \theta = \arctan \dfrac{X_L}{R}$

and $\qquad A = \dfrac{X_L}{\sin \theta}$

and $\qquad X_L = 2\,\pi\,fL = 2\,\pi \times 2500 \times .0255$

Angle: Deg

Enter	Press			Display	Remarks
2	×			2.	
π	×			6.283185307	
2500	×			15707.96327	
.0255	÷	STO		400.5530633	X_L
560	=	arc	tan	35.57512944	θ
	sin	$1/x$	×	1.718892434	
	RCL	=		688.50763	

WITH THE SR-51A USERS SOLVE EVEN COMPLEX PROBLEMS LIKE THESE IN SECONDS . . .

Business — Trend Analysis

The linear regression feature is extremely useful in predicting trends. For example, over a five year period a certain company reported the following earnings per share. What is the predicted earnings per share for the next five years?

1st five years (known)	2nd five years (predicted)
1. 1.52	6. 3.53
2. 1.35	7. 4.03
3. 1.53	8. 4.52
4. 2.17	9. 5.02
5. 3.60	10. 5.52

What is the expected percent growth from the 9th to the 10th year?

Part I. Because we are performing a trend analysis, only the earnings per share need to be entered in sequence. Here is the calculator procedure:

Enter	Press	Display	Comments
	2nd CA	0	All registers must be cleared at the start of the problem
1.52	2nd y	1.	The 1 indicates data point 1 is entered
1.35	2nd y	2.	
1.53	2nd y	3.	
2.17	2nd y	4.	
3.60	2nd y	5.	

This completes the data entry. To find the extrapolated values enter the year and ask for the corresponding y' value. That is:

Enter	Press	Display	Comments
6	2nd y'	3.528	6th year
7	2nd y'	4.026	7th year
8	2nd y'	4.524	8th year
9	2nd y'	5.022	9th year
10	2nd y'	5.52	10th year

Part II. The predicted percent change from year nine to year ten is defined as

$$\Delta\% =, \frac{y'_{10} - y'_9}{y'_9} \times 100$$

Where y'_{10} = Earnings per share for the year 10
y'_9 = Earnings per share for year 9

The calculator solution is as follows:

Enter	Press		Display	Comment
	2nd	CA	0	Clear regression routine
5.022	**2nd**	$\Delta\%$	5.022	
5.52	**2nd** Fix Pt.	2 =	9.92	9.92 percent increase

The procedures employed in this example apply to many other areas. For example, we could use the steps described above to perform sales forecast or market analysis.

Physical Science — Regression Analysis

As another example of regression analysis suppose that two different kinds of measurement were made on the same population with the following results:

x	20.4	19.7	21.8	20.1	20.7
y	9.2	8.9	11.4	9.4	10.3

What is the equation of the regression line that best fits these points? We wish to find the following expression

$$y = mx + b$$

Where m = slope and b = y intercept. First we enter the data into the calculator:

Enter	Press	Display
	2nd CA	
20.4	2nd x	20.4
9.2	2nd y	1.
.	.	.
.	.	.
.	.	.
.	.	.
20.7	2nd x	20.7
10.3	2nd y	5.

The slope and y intercept are found as follows:

Press	Display	Comments
2nd SLOPE	1.22906793	Slope
2nd INTCP	− 15.40505529	y-intercept

Thus the equation of the regression line is

$$y = 1.23x - 15.41.$$

Statistics — Mean, Variance and Standard Deviation

When calculating these statistical parameters, the user may choose to represent his data in any one of several different methods. One way is to treat each datum separately or as *ungrouped data*. In this approach, the user assigns each datum its own value. He sums each datum and divides by the total number of such datum. From this approach comes the more common expression for the mean:

$$\overline{X} = \frac{\sum\limits_{i=1}^{N} x_i}{N}$$

where x_i = value of datum point i
              N = total number of data points

Another common method exists and is referred to as *grouped data*. In this approach, the range of data (total range of values of x_i) is divided into intervals. All values of x_i which fall into the same interval are assigned a common value, usually the interval midpoint. From this approach arises another expression for the mean:

$$\overline{X} = \frac{\sum\limits_{i=1}^{A} f_i x_i}{\sum\limits_{i=1}^{A} f_i}$$

where A = the number of intervals
              f_i = number of datum falling in interval i
              x_i = value assigned to datum in interval i

$$N = \sum\limits_{i=1}^{A} f_i = \text{total number of data points}$$

By performing some algebraic manipulation it is possible to show that:

$$\overline{X} = \frac{\sum\limits_{i=1}^{N} x_i}{N}$$

$$\text{Var.} = \frac{\sum\limits_{i=1}^{N} x_i^2 - \frac{\left(\sum\limits_{i=1}^{N} x_i\right)^2}{N}}{N}$$

$$\text{S. Dev.} = \left[\frac{\sum\limits_{i=1}^{N} x_i^2 - \frac{\left(\sum\limits_{i=1}^{N} x_i\right)^2}{N}}{N-1} \right]^{1/2}$$

By remembering the assignments to each memory when using the $\Sigma +$ key, it is possible to rewrite these expressions as follows:

$$\overline{X} = \frac{M1}{M3}$$

$$\text{Variance} = \frac{M2 - \dfrac{(M1)^2}{M3}}{M3}$$

$$\text{S. Deviations} = \left[\frac{M2 - \dfrac{(M1)^2}{M3}}{M3 - 1} \right]^{1/2}$$

Where M1 = Contents of memory 1
M2 = Contents of memory 2
M3 = Contents of memory 3

The SR-51A is programmed to handle ungrouped data. However, as the second example that follows shows, users can handle grouped data easily by using the algorithm that is developed.

Ungrouped Data: What is the mean and standard deviation of the following six capacitor values, 166.4, 167.0, 166.5, 168.6, 171.4, 167.8, drawn at random from a production lot.

Enter	Press	Display	Comments
	2nd CM		
166.4	Σ +	1.	⎫
.	.	.	
.	.	.	Enter data
.	.	.	
167.8	Σ +	6.	⎭
	2nd MEAN	167.95	Mean value
	2nd S. DEV	1.884409722	Standard deviation

Grouped Data: Here is an example to show how the mean and standard deviation of grouped data can be found. For this example we are provided with a set of observations and the frequency with which each datum is observed.

Observation	82	91	90	85
Frequency	2	3	1	7

The expressions we shall use are:

$$\overline{X} = \frac{\displaystyle\sum_{i=1}^{A} f_i x_i}{\displaystyle\sum_{i=1}^{A} f_i} = \frac{M1}{M3}$$

$$\text{S. Dev.} = \left[\frac{\dfrac{\displaystyle\sum_{i=1}^{A} f_i x_i^2 - \left(\displaystyle\sum_{i=1}^{A} f_i x_i\right)^2}{\displaystyle\sum_{i=1}^{A} f_i}}{\displaystyle\sum_{i=1}^{A} f_i - 1} \right]^{1/2}$$

$$= \left[\frac{M2 - \dfrac{(M1)^2}{M3}}{M3 - 1} \right]^{1/2}$$

The principle is to store data into the three memory registers in exactly the same format that the mean and standard deviation routines already preprogrammed in the calculator use them. In memory one we must store $\sum_{i=1}^{A} f_i x_i$, in memory two we must store $\sum_{i=1}^{A} f_i x_i^2$,

and in memory three we must store $\sum_{i=1}^{A} f_i$

Enter	Press	Display	Memory Contents M1	M2	M3
	2nd CM				
2	SUM 3 ×	2.	0.	0.	2.
82	= SUM 1 ×	164.	164.	0.	2.
82	= SUM 2	13448.	164.	13448.	2.
3	SUM 3 ×	3.	164.	13448.	5.
91	= SUM 1 ×	273.	437.	13448.	5.
91	= SUM 2	24843.	437.	38291.	5.
1	SUM 3 ×	1.	437.	38291.	6.
90	= SUM 1 ×	90.	527.	38291.	6.
90	= SUM 2	8100.	527.	46391.	6.
7	SUM 3 ×	7.	527.	46391.	13.
85	= SUM 1 ×	595.	1122.	46391.	13.
85	= SUM 2	50575.	1122.	96966.	13.
	2nd MEAN	86.30769231	(Mean Value)		
	2nd S. DEV	3.275785286	(Standard Deviation)		

Engineering — Aerodynamics

An airplane is in a steady coordinated turn. The true airspeed is 175 knots at a 50° bank angle. What is the turn radius in feet and the turn rate in degrees per second.

The equations used are

$$\text{Turn radius } r = \frac{V^2}{g \tan \phi}$$

$$\text{Rate of turn } W = \frac{g \tan \phi}{V}$$

Where V is in ft/s
W is in radians/s
$g = 32.2$ ft/s^2

The calculator solution is as follows:

Angle: Deg

Enter	Press	Display	Comments
	C 2nd Fix Pt 2	0.00	Two-place decimal
32.2	×	32.20	Value of g
50	tan = STO 1	38.37	
175	INV 2nd 05 ×	201.39	Naut. miles to miles conversion
5280	= ÷	1063320.21	Miles to feet
3600	= STO 2 x^2 ÷	87241.50	Seconds per hour
	RCL 1 =	2273.43	Value of r in feet
	RCL 1 ÷ RCL 2 =	0.13	Value of w in rad/s
	INV 2nd 15	7.44	Value of w in degrees/s

Electrical Engineering — Distributed Transmission-Line Parameters

Calculate the distributed capacitance and inductance per meter of a two-wire transmission line with the following characteristics.

Wire radius   a = 0.15 cm
Wire separation b = 2.5 cm
$$\mu d = 4\pi \times 10^{-7} \text{ H/m}$$
$$\epsilon d = 10^{-9}/36\pi \text{ F/m}$$

The necessary equations are:

$$C = \frac{\pi \epsilon d}{\cosh^{-1}\left(\frac{b}{2a}\right)} \qquad L = \frac{\mu d}{\pi} \cosh^{-1}\left(\frac{b}{2a}\right)$$

To solve using the calculator

Enter	Press	Display		Comments
	2nd CA		0	
2.5	÷	2.5		Enter value of b
2	÷	1.25		
0.15	= INV 2nd cosh	2.80979112		$\cosh^{-1}\left(\frac{b}{2a}\right)$
	STO 1 1/x ÷	.3558983417		
36	×	0.009886065		
1	EE	1 00		
9	+/− =	9.886065047-12		Value of C in farads per meter
	RCL 1 ×	2.80979112 00		
4	EE	4 00		
7	+/− =	1.123916448-06		Value of L in henries per meter

Mechanical Engineering — Cam Problem

What is the minimum base radius of a cycloidal cam having a maximum pressure angle of 25°, a cam angle of 75°, and a rise of 1.25 inches. The line of action passes through the center of the cam.

$$L = \text{stroke} = 1.25 \text{ inches}$$
$$\beta = \text{Total cam angle} = 75°$$
$$R = \text{Base radius}$$
$$\alpha = \text{Pressure angle} = 25°$$

By differentiation and maximizing the rate of change of the radius the following formula can be established:

$$R = \frac{2L}{\beta \tan \alpha} - \frac{L}{2}$$

where β is expressed in radians
Therefore:

$$R = \frac{2(1.25)}{\beta \tan 25°} - \frac{1.25}{2}$$

$$R = 3.470706523 \text{ inches}$$

Solution: Angle: Deg

Enter	Press	Display	
	2nd CA		0
2	×		2.
1.25	÷		2.5
75	2nd 15 ÷	1.909859317	
25	tan −	4.095706523	
1.25	÷		1.25
2	=	3.470706523	

SOME ALTERNATE TYPE OPERATING INSTRUMENTS AND SYSTEMS

The Casio preprogrammed desktop calculator demonstrates a slightly different type of keyboard and operating procedure. The reader is invited to follow through on whatever brand or model he or she uses by practicing on the simple problems described to note these different characteristics.

PROBLEM	EXAMPLE	OPERATION	READ-OUT	
Basic Operation	$(1.2 \times 10^8) \times (3 \times 10^{23}) = ?$	1 . 2 EXP 8 $\times$ 3 EXP 23 =	3.6	31
Sexagesimal$\rightarrow$ Decimal Conversion	$53° \ 45' \ 28'' = ?$	53° ' " 45° ' " 28° ' "	53.75777777	
Trigonometric	$\tan \dfrac{\pi}{5} = ?$	RAD $\pi \div 5 =$ tan	7.265425278 -01	
	$\sin \dfrac{1}{5} \cdot \pi \ (\text{rad.}) +$ $\cos \dfrac{1}{10} \cdot \pi \ (\text{rad.}) = ?$	RAD MC $\pi \times 5 \ 1/x =$ sin M+ $\pi \times 10 \ 1/x =$ cos M+ MR	1.538841768	
	$2 \sin 18° \cdot \cos 29° = ?$	DEG 2×18 sin $\times 29$ cos =	5.405447062 -01	
	$\sin^2 17° - \sin^2 8° = ?$	DEG MC 17 sin $\times$ M+ 8 sin $\times$ M$-$MR	6.611206169 -02	
Inverse Trigonometric	$\cos^{-1} 0.25 = ?$	DEG . 25 arc cos	75.52248781	
	$\tan^{-1} (-1.962) = ?$	RAD 1 . 962 +/$-$ arc tan	-1.099431568	
Hyperbolic	$\sinh 8.5 = ?$	8 . 5 hyp sin	2457.384318	
	$\sinh^2 2.5 - \cosh^2 3.6 = ?$	MC 2 . 5 hyp sin $\times$ M+ 3 . 6 hyp cos $\times$ M$-$ MR	-298.7529033	
Inverse Hyperbolic	$\tanh^{-1} 0.7 = ?$	. 7 arc hyp tan	8.673005277 -01	
Logarithms	$\log 41 = ?$	41 log	1.612783856	
	$\ln 4.56 = ?$	4 . 56 ln	1.517322623	
	$\log 65 - \log 32 = ?$	65 log $-$ 32 log =	0.307763378	
	$\ln (1.31 \times 10^{-3}) + \ln 68 = ?$	. 1 . 31 EXP 3 +/$-$ ln +68 ln =	-2.418220437	
	$\log (1.31 \times 10^{-3}) + \log 68 = ?$	1 . 31 EXP 3 +/$-$ log + 68 log =	-1.050219792	
Exponentiation	$e^{-1.2} \cdot \sin 46° = ?$	DEG 1 . 2 +/$-$ $e^x \times$ 46 sin =	2.166609842 -01	
	$\sqrt[5]{1024} = 1024^{\frac{1}{5}} = ?$	1024 x^y 5 $1/x =$	3.999999999	
	$44.44^{25.8} = ?$	4 . 4 x^y 25 . 8 =	5.040581362	16
Factorial	$58! = ?$	58 $x!$	2.350561331	78

Casio *fx-3* **Scientific Calculator**
- **Four fixed programs for polar coordinates, rectangular coordinates conversion, quadratic equation and standard deviation**
- **25 scientific functions**
- **A large, bright green 10-digit mantissa plus 2-digit exponent display to ± 99 digits**
- **Multi-purpose independent 4-key memory plus five data storages**

Polar to rectangular

Formulas:

$$x = r \cos \theta$$
$$y = r \sin \theta$$
(θ is in degrees)

Example:

If $\theta = 38°$ and $r = 6.2$,
then $x = \ldots$?
and $y = \ldots$?

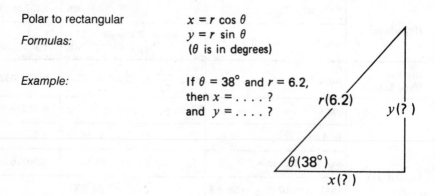

Operation:

6.2 [STO] [K₃],
(r)

38 [STO] [K₄],
(θ)

[ANS] [K₁] $\cdots$ **4.885666672** *(x)*
[K₂] $\cdots$ **3.817101146** *(y)*

Rectangular to polar

Formulas:
$$r = \sqrt{x^2 + y^2},$$
$$\theta = \text{arc tan}\left(\frac{y}{x}\right)$$

Example: If $x = 6.5$ and $y = 3.8$,
then $r = \ldots \ldots$?
and $\theta = \ldots \ldots$?

$r(?)$ $y(3.8)$

$\theta(?)$

$x(6.5)$

Operation:

6.5 STO K3 ,
(x)
3.8 STO K4 ,
(y)
ANS K1 $\cdots$ **7.529276193** (r)
K2 $\cdots$ **30.31121322** (θ)

Quadratic equations

Formula: The roots of $ax^2 + bx + c = 0$

are $\dfrac{-b \pm \sqrt{b^2 - 4ac}}{2a}$.

If $b^2 - 4ac$ is positive, the roots
are real; otherwise they are complex,

being $\dfrac{-b}{2a} \pm \dfrac{\sqrt{4ac - b^2}}{2a} i$.

Example: $3x^2 - 3x - 18 = 0$

Operation:

3 STO K3 ,
3 +/− STO K4 ,
18 +/− STO K5 ,
ANS K1 + K2 = $\cdots\cdots\cdots\cdots\cdots\cdots$ **3** (x)
K1 − K2 = $\cdots\cdots\cdots\cdots\cdots$ **− 2** (x)

* If $b^2 - 4ac$ is negative, the roots
should be read as follows;
$x_1 + x_2\, i$ or $x_1 - x_2 i$
(K1) (K2)   (K1) (K2)

Statistics

Mean, Standard deviation, and Sums (ungrouped data)

Formula:

Mean: $\overline{x} = \dfrac{\Sigma x}{n}$, Sum of items: n

Sum of values: Σx,

Sum of square values: Σx^2

Standard deviation: $S = \sqrt{\dfrac{\Sigma x^2 - \dfrac{1}{n}(\Sigma x)^2}{n-1}}$

Example:

Compute S, $\overline{x}$, n, Σx and Σx^2 for the set of numbers 58, 54, 56, 51, 53.

Operation:

[AC] 58 [ANS] 54 [ANS] 56 [ANS]
51 [ANS] 53 [ANS]

[K₁] ·········	**2.701851217**	(s)
[K₂] ·········	**54.4**	($\overline{x}$)
[K₃] ·········	**5**	(n)
[K₄] ·········	**272**	(Σx)
[K₅] ·········	**14826**	(Σx^2)

A Systems Calculator from Canon

The Canola F-11, from **Canon USA Inc.,** is a similar unit and has a 13-digit display consisting of an 11-digit mantissa (10 digits and a sign) and a three-digit exponent (two digits and a sign and 10 separate independent accumulative memories). Fifteen statistical subroutines do not affect or occupy the above memories. Common conversions are unnecessary with the Canola F-11. All fractions can be entered as fractions, without the need to convert them into decimals, by using the "/" key. Metric conversions and their inverses are programmed into special keys for instant equivalents. Degrees, minutes and seconds to decimal degrees can be converted by single-key entries, as well as exchanging polar coordinates for rectangular coordinates. A three- to twelve-level parenthesis system enables the user to place computations within other calculations. Designed for scientists, statisticians and engineers.

CONCLUSION: The Basic Four-Function Hand-Held Calculator — and How It Led to — "Personal Computer Power to the People . . ."

Most manufacturers judge the average service life of calculators to be four years. Of course, many will last for ten or even twenty years. But, in general, within a four year period, most units will have been dropped, broken through misuse, or in other ways *used up*. Very often, also, owners will move up to fancier, more capable models. The question of significance is, "Moved up to what levels?" A primary thesis of this book is that the use of calculators will become so pervasive throughout schools, business, industry, science, and government, that they will become a near universal data and information processor. Practically no one will be adverse to the use of processing or control devices that are based on or designed with a *calculator-type* input-output device. It has been noted that in some instances plans are being made to incorporate them semi-permanently into schoolroom desks — so that all students have the use of the same capable device; so that they cannot be removed or stolen, and so that school districts get full value because they can be used by hundreds of students moving to calculator-equipment rooms throughout the school day. It has also been noted that calculators are being incorporated into hundreds of scientific instruments. These intelligent devices signal time, measure, place, position and in many other ways control, process and report — visually or audibly and also remotely or locally to other devices or humans. Already the advanced programmable calculator users are clamoring for and are receiving desk-top devices that *look like* calculators but are in effect, full capability computers. Most are still somewhat expensive as is noted in chapters ahead. Without doubt, however, the more expensive capabilities of these peripheral units will soon filter down at much lower cost into the hand-held units. The question then arises, "Will the greatly enhanced hand-held units with *full computer* capabilities continue to hold their low $300 to $400 prices." We think yes.

Even in mid-1976 many of the experts and respected industry observers agreed that this transition would indeed occur . . . "within the next several years." Within the hand-held advanced programmable calculator environment, the introduction of the very capable Texas Instruments SR-52 to compete with the (then) only other fully hand-held programmable, the HP-65, was a significant breakthrough in price/performance. This was especially true because the *normal* discount price of the SR-52 was far less than half the cost of the HP-65. Within 10 months, Hewlett-Packard brought out its strongly competitive HP-67 with about twice the capability of its predecessor, the HP-65 (at $795), for less than half the (normal discount) price, or under $400. The TI SR-52 discount price fell to under $200, placing a very capable, card programmable unit within the economic reach of a majority of college students. Because of the enormous success of the HP-67/97, TI quickly offered their exceptional value TI-57, 58, 59 units. Other competition was certain to quickly follow. (Casio, Commodore, and other competing programmables are compared elsewhere.) But, few calculator users and industry observers were prepared for the tremendous capability and low price of the new TI competitors — the ROM-loaded TI-59 particularly. Most experts consider this unit the first of a *third generation* of calculators. The very exceptional model has been labeled as the true **transitional** device — the arrival of a fully capable *calculator-like* **hand-held computer.**

While the *flashy,* increasingly popular microcomputer capabilities and low-cost peripheral devices enticed many enthusiasts to buy them for home computers, the old bugaboos of languages, software, unproven input-output devices, etc. make them still quite inconvenient for mass use. Not so with the extremely convenient, easy input-output, expandable interior and exterior memories of the Texas Instruments TI-59. While the HP-67 and SR-52 offer 224 and 100 program steps respectively, the TI-59, using factory-recorded programs in library cartridges as subroutines to the program in the mainframe memory, brings the total program step capacity to 960.

This is computer size, computer talk, computer capability. The *fact* of preprogrammed plug-in ROM acting as integral parts of the main system simply overpowers all hand-held competition. It is expected that the TI models will soon have non-volatile program memory. With the power turned off, the unit retains data and program, a major computer-like advantage. Instead of multiple sets of blank magnetic cards on which users of the 67 and 52 store their own specific (or factory-supplied) programs, new models will offer user-alterable (and/or factory-preprogrammed) plug-in file cartridges containing two 1,024 bit nonvolatile RAMs, capable of retaining data for years — and each equal to from 20 to 40 program cards of the other two units . . . thus making programs less costly and significantly more convenient to store, use, load, and alter. The versatility of the plug-in ROMs and RAMs permits true customization and/or important expansion of the capabilities of these units. Soon, low prices will include many file cartridges (RAMs), library cartridges for $10 or so.

The TI-59 will be analyzed and compared with the competing units on pages ahead. The objective at this point is to suggest the future uses and impacts of this type calculator—on the calculator markets, the computer markets, and the citizens of an increasingly computerized society. Cost, complexity, and nonproximity to the computer itself have prevented the use of computer capability by the masses. Computer power to the people has long been a cry of activists, hobbyists, and several million students. The TI-59 does really offer true computer power; it is not complex — no more difficult to operate and control than the other major hand-held advanced programmables. And it certainly is not expensive — the discounters and some major mass retailers offer it at below $250. Most significant, however, is the final *personal, individual* control and very wide use — eventually by *the masses* of this and other similar *pocket computers*.

Microcomputer kits and prepackaged control devices are being designed and sold for home computer applications. These will quickly merge with TI-59-type computer capability calculators into common hardware and software for more school and job **personal-use** hand-held computer applications. A third force — product group — has emerged to make the movement a three-pronged drive of computer power for people: the calculator keyboard/preprogrammed *intelligent* (and programmable) terminal. Of the three criteria mentioned above, these have generally been *easy to use* and immediately accessible to users. However, they have been horribly expensive — and the great majority *terminal-only* were *true* remote computer system terminals. They were *dumb* — they only spilled out what the expensive, complex remote computer processed. Nothing else! And the rules, protocols, and limitations to the input capability were fierce. The new microprocessor-controlled TV-like terminals being marketed today, like the advanced calculators — provide for simplified input and immediate response output. They are often very friendly *standalone* computers as well as preprocessing or postprocessing terminals with a central or *host* mini or microcomputer to tie a system together, simplify, and control communication and/or data base complexities. Indeed, many calculator manufacturers have already adapted several types of multi-line displays with desk-top calculators as terminals. And it seems to be a bit of a contest as to whether the calculator-controlled terminal system or the microcomputer-controlled terminal system will predominate. It seems to be a question of expense, ease-of-use, and software availability. On all three counts, the calculator wins — cheaper; more people more familiar; endless *existing* software. Also, low-cost always-available models work very well and many new memory-input devices are excellent.

Perhaps one of the first *prototypes* of the personal calculator terminal is the one pictured and described below. The *Figure Phone* as described and currently produced and the deluxe Systems 1 model, with many added conveniences (programs) is one of the forerunners of low-cost calculator-keyboard (abundant software) personal/computing/communications devices. People are very reluctant to use complex, excessively constrained computer terminal keyboards. They should not be disinclined to use the simple combined calculator-phone number/other-special-function keyboards like the one on the *Figure Phone*.

**FIGURE PHONE is a pushbutton phone with an 8-digit calculator &
a digital clock with a daily calendar. The user can phone and calculate at the same time with no interference in conversation. When
users wish to make a phone call, they are in the 'time' mode. During
the conversation, they may push the CAL button, which puts them in
the 'calculator' mode. The CCE key turns the calculator on for its
operation anytime. The System 1 Deluxe Figure Phone adds: A printout of the accumulated long distance time record; speaker phone and
intercom; radio snooze alarm; calculator with memory, percentage &
constant key; music on hold, etc.**

Certainly the manufacturers of *Figure Phone* and the competitors to follow will
add more capabilities to the current 4-function + built-in calculator in existing models. While keeping the cost down is primary to small business, professional and mass consumer use, it is obvious that scores of additional utility
keys, plug-in ROMs or other software can be integrated at relatively minor
additional costs. (Why not incorporate the TI-59 into the phone and add some
multi-line display capability.)

While these type units do not transmit the data over phone lines, but act
as a convenience in calculating (computing with micro units enclosed) while
phoning, it is not a difficult task to move from this simple capability into
facsimile units, graphic output, etc. for business and scientific company utilization. Indeed, AT&T, with its 15-year-old **Picture Phone**™ and RCA with its
TV-like transmitting **Videovoice,** have demonstrated these capabilities. The
mass use of these two (and other German, Dutch and British similar devices)
has been held back by high production and marketing costs. One suspects that
the engineering hierarchies of these giant corporations have established that
the complexities of these *older* devices absolutely ensure high costs and consequent marketing difficulties. Perhaps it really does take the smaller companies with persistent drives for absolute lowest cost items, using existing
technology (calculator chips and software), to develop the better approach . . . for mass sales of personal computing/communicating power. Indeed, it seems that only the impetus of the growing thousands of computer

hobbyists could move the terminal manufacturers to bring costs down below $500 from minimum $3000 costs for units with far less capability just a year or two previous to mid-1976. Now *independents* with the low-cost terminals have broken the market wide open. The next chapter opens the analysis of the fundamental products which lead the way to *personal computing for consumers*. The foundation is the amazing cost/performance miracles of today's **advanced programmable calculators.**

Selected Calculator Operations Definitions*

ac adapter/charger — Battery pack recharge or direct operation from standard voltage outlets is easily accomplished with the accompanying AC adapter/charger. Most units cannot be overcharged and can be operated indefinitely with the adapter/charger connected.

activate key — Same as initiate button. A primary switch on various keyboard panels which when pressed or initiated will cause the first part or step of a program cycle or a procedure to begin. Same as start key, button or switch.

address — A location in program memory — designated by either an absolute address (a number from 0 through ?) or a label assigned in a program.

addressable memory registers — Addressable memory registers make data manipulations much simpler. The user can store data in any register, retrieve data from any register, or even do register arithmetic, using or modifying data in any register.

addressable registers, hand-held programmables — On some units, registers $R_1, R_2, \ldots, R_9$ constitute the addressable registers. Their respective contents are referred to as $r_1, r_2, \ldots, r_9$. Operations refer to them by number. The registers are typically used to accumulate sums or to store constants or intermediate results. Users can store the value of the stack's X-register in any addressable register, or they can recall the value in any addressable register to the X-register. Additionally, they can store in any register an arithmetic sum, difference, product, or quotient of the contents of the given register and the X-register. For example, if R_5 contains 100 and if X contains 70, users can store the difference $(100 - 70 = 30)$ in R_5.

algebraic operating system (AOS) — Allows sequences to be entered in the same order that they are algebraically stated, provides step function improvement in ease of use with familiar algebraic operation.

algorithm — A prescribed set of well-defined rules or processes for the solution of a problem in a finite number of steps, for example, a full statement of an arithmetic procedure for evaluating sin × to a stated precision. Contrast with heuristic.

alphanumerical — A coding system capable of representing alphabetical characters and other symbols as well as numbers.

analog — The representation of quantities by means of continuous physical signals.

angle change key — If the DEG/RAD switch is set for degrees, pressing the D/R key instructs the calculator to convert the displayed angle from radians to degrees. If the switch is set for radians, pressing this key instructs the calculator to convert the displayed angle from degrees to radians. (some units)

angular modes — The three options, grads, degrees or radians, in which angles are to be expressed. Usually selected by slide switch on upper left of keyboard.

analog-to-digital (A/D) conversion — Production of a digital output, indicating the value of an analog input quantity.

arc key — When pressed as prefix to sin, cos, or tan key, tells calculator to determine the inverse trig function.

arithmetic shift — 1. A shift that does not affect the sign position. 2. A shift that is equivalent to the multiplication of a number by a positive or negative integral power of the radix.

ASCII — An abbreviation for USA Standard Code for Information Interchange.

asynchronous device — A unit which has an operating speed not related to any particular frequency of the system to which it is connected.

automatic clearing — Many calculators automatically clear themselves. When the = key is pressed to complete the evaluation of an expression, all pending calculations are completed, the answer is displayed, and the calculator is prepared for the start of a new problem. It is not necessary to press the 'CLR' key between such calculations. (some units)

automatic constant — Provides for repetitive addition, subtraction, multiplication and division of a number by a constant.

automatic memory stack — In HP units, users perform only one operation at a time, and they see the results as they calculate. The automatic memory stack stores up to four intermediate results in-

*Most definitions above are excerpted from "Calculator Users Guide and Dictionary" by Charles J. Sippl (Matrix Publishers Inc., 430 pp., 1976).

side the unit until the user needs them, then inserts them into the calculation.

balancing error — A specific error which in effect balances or offsets another error, i.e., two offsetting errors of equal values or same numbers of opposite signs could exist and would be most difficult to detect or correct because the various check totals would agree or compare favorably.

base — The radix, or quantity of characters employed in a numbering system; e.g. 2-binary; 8-octal; 10-decimal; 16-hexadecimal.

battery life indicator — Refers to a meter or warning light that indicates the status of the battery life within an electronic calculator.

binary — A characteristic, property, or condition in which there are but two possible alternatives, e.g., the binary number system using 2 as its base and using only the digits zero (0) and one (1).

binary-coded character — Can refer to an alphabetic letter, a decimal digit, a punctuation mark, etc., as represented by a fixed number of consecutive binary digits.

binary-coded decimal (BCD) representation — A system of representing decimal numbers. Each decimal digit is represented by a combination of four binary digits (bits).

binary digit (bit) — A numeral in the binary scale of notation. This digit may be zero (0), or one (1). It may be equivalent to an on or off condition, a yes, or a no. Often abbreviated to (bit).

bit/slice — Refers to microcomputer chip that is a quarter or an eighth of an entire processor. When a cpu is too complex or would dissipate too much heat to be put on a single chip, it is sliced into two-or four-bit chunks which are then wired together on circuit cards.

bit string — A one-dimensional array of bits ordered by reference to the relations between adjacent numbers.

black box — A generic term which can describe any unspecified device performing a special function where the inputs produce specific outputs.

blinking display, hand-held programmable — The display blinks when any of several improper operations are attempted. Depressing any key stops the blinking without otherwise performing the key function. CLX is the recommended blink stopper.

board — An electrical panel which can be altered with the addition or deletion of external wiring. Also known as a plugboard, panel, or wire board.

BPS — Bits per second. In serial transmission, the instantaneous bit speed with which a device or channel transmits a character.

branch — 1. Concerns the capability and procedure of a program instruction designed to modify the function or program sequence. The actual modification is an immediate change in direction, meaning or substance of intent of the programmer.

bug — 1. A program defect or error. Also refers to any circuit fault due to improper design or construction. 2. A mistake or malfunction. 3. An integrated circuit.

bus — A path over which information is transferred, from any of several sources to any of several destinations.

calculate mode — Users manually solve each problem by direct keystroke; entering numbers, performing mathematical operations, computing functions and storing or recalling data from the data memory registers. When a solution sequence exists to solve a repetitive problem, users simply place the calculator in the 'Learn' mode. (some units)

chain calculations — Refers to the operating features of some calculators that include performance of chaining calculations with basic functions by simply pressing the desired function key to use any result in the next problem. Repeated addition and subtraction occurs without re-entering the number. Number entries are cleared with the CE key. A # key (non-add) prints reference numbers on some units.

chain/constant switch — The Chain/Const switch permits normal chain calculations or multiplication and division by a constant without reentering numbers on various units.

chain discount key — Refers to the capability to compute chain or serial discounts without reentry, as well as complementary percentages or meaningful intermediate results. Users enter the exact amount of each discount and the chain discount key computes and prints the percentage. At completion of the problem an (=) key provides the final net . . . on some units.

change sign key — Reverses negative entries or results to their positive equivalents or the reverse without re-entry or manipulation with a single key depression.

chip — Refers to the tiny piece of silicon on which integrated circuits are built. The circuits are mass-produced on circular sheets of silicon called wafers which are then cut into dozens of individual chips. Chips are square or rectangular in shape and range in size from under a tenth of an inch on a side to over a quarter an inch.

CHS change sign key — To key in a negative number, on some units, the user presses the 'chs' key. The number, preceded by a minus sign, will appear in the display.

circuit — 1. A communications link between two or more points. Also channel. 2. The conductor or system of conductors through which an electric current is intended to flow.

circuit, integrated (IC) — Refers to one of several logic circuits, gates, flip-flops which are etched on single crystals, ceramics or other semiconductor materials and designed to use geometric etching and conductive ink or chemical deposition techniques all within a hermetically sealed chip. Some chips with many resistors and transistors are extremely tiny, others are in effect "sandwiches" of individual chips.

clear — An activity to place one or more storage locations into a prescribed state, usually zero or the space character. Contrast with set.

clear entry key — The Clear Entry key generally clears last entry made with 0 through 9 keys. Also stops flashing display without affecting displayed number. The Clear Key clears display and calculation in progress; does not affect contents of memory registers, flags, counters, program memory, or fixed decimal, on most systems. The Clear Memories Key clears all memory registers.

clear error key — On most units the error can be stopped from flashing by pressing 'CE' to remove all internal conditions indicating that an error is present. Whether the calculation can proceed after an error has occurred depends on the type of error, the error itself, the problem, and quantities saved in memory.

clearing — On some units, users clear any numbers that are in the display by pressing 'clx' (clear X). This key erases

the number in the display and replaces it with 0.00.

clear key — A function key to delete an entry, or an entire series of entries from a calculator. The key may be titled (C-), (C), (CE), (CA) or (AC). Some electronic calculators have only a (C) key which may, at first depression, clear the last keyboard entry, and, at second depression, clear everything. It generally has no entry capability.

clear X key, small calculator — CLX prepares the displayed X-register for a new number by replacing any number in the display with zero. Any new number then writes over the zero in X. For example, to press CLX to change the stack.

clock — A device which generates periodic synchronization signals.

conditional key — Each value is tested in X-register against that in Y-register or 0 as indicated. If true, calculator executes instruction in next program memory step. If false, calculator skips next step.

constant — A fixed value or an item of datum that does not vary.

constant, calculator — Allows repetitive calculations using the same number without having to reenter that number for each calculation.

constant-factor storage key — Automatically stores a constant for use in percentage computations, factor equivalent conversions, fractional equivalent conversions or mark up. One key does it all.

constant key — This latching key allows the use of the first factor in multiplication or the second factor in division as a constant for future operations.

constant storage — A part of storage designated to store the invariable quantities required for processing.

control — Those parts of a calculator which carry out instructions in proper sequence, interpret instructions, and apply proper signals.

control register — Also called instruction register, the control register stores the current instruction governing the operation of the calculator for a cycle.

conventions — Concerns various standard and accepted procedures in programs and systems analysis and the abbreviations, symbols, and their meanings as developed for particular systems and programs.

conversion key — Converts amounts to the proper decimal value on a per factor basis (per C, per M, per dozen, etc.) also performs metric conversions.

conversions, calculator — Most scientific calculators allow users to convert from polar coordinates to rectangular coordinates and vice versa. They also enable users to convert to or from several English and metric units.

conversions, degrees/radians key — (2nd D/R) The degrees/radians key instructs the calculator to interpret the displayed number as an angle expressed in decimal degrees and to convert it to radians. Pressing 'INV' '2nd' 'DIR' instructs the calculator to interpret the displayed number as an angle expressed in radians and to convert to degrees. Operation of the degrees/radians key is not dependent on the position of the D/R switch. (T)

coordinate transformation — Conversion from polar coordinates to rectangular coordinates or vice versa, an operation provided by the '2nd' 'P/R' keys or their inverse. (some units)

cosine key — Instructs the calculator to determine the cosine of the displayed angle. Pressing 'INV' 'COS' instructs the calculator to interpret the displayed argument as the cosine of an angle and to calculate the angle.

crd (display) — Indicates side one of card has been read and prompts user to insert side two, face up, into the card reader slot for reading.

cycle — An interval of space or time in which one set of events or phenomena is completed. In alternating current, the time for a change of state from a value through a positive and negative maximum, back to the same value.

data — 1. A representation with characters or analog quantities to which meaning is assigned that expresses facts, concepts, or instructions in a formalized manner suitable for communication, interpretation, or processing by automatic or human means. 2. Information which can be produced or processed, by a calculator, computer or control system.

data base management — A systematic approach to storing, updating, and retrieval of information stored as data items, usually in the form of records in a file, where many users, or even many remote installations, will use common data banks.

data bus — Most calculators communicate externally through the use of a data bus. Most are bidirectional, e.g., capable of transferring data to and from the cpu, storage and peripheral devices.

data format — Rules and procedures describe the way data is held in a file or record, whether in character form, as binary numbers, etc.

data processor — A device capable of performing operations on data, such as a digital computer, analog computer, or a calculator.

data record — A collection of facts, numbers, letters, symbols, etc., that a program can process or produce.

data station — A multipurpose remote-terminal calculator can be used for a broad range of communications applications, as well as for off-line jobs.

dc — An abbreviation for: direct current, direct coupled, digital computer, direction cycle, direct cycle, display console, decimal classification, data conversion, design change and detail condition.

debug — An instruction, program, or action designed in calculator software to search for, correct, and/or eliminate sources of errors in programming routines. There are many types of 'bugs' or 'glitches' that can be located by single step testing, specifically designed programs, or operational procedures.

decimal, binary coded (BCD) — Describing a decimal notation in which the individual decimal digits are represented by a pattern of ones and zeros, e.g., in the 8-4-2-1 coded decimal notation, the number twelve is represented as 00010010 for 1 and 2, respectively, whereas in pure or straight binary notation it is represented as 1100. Related to binary.

decimal, fixed — Restricts the number of decimals to that preselected.

decimal, floating — Refers to the absence of restrictions on the position of the decimal point.

decision — Most often concerns a comparison to determine a verification concerning the existence or non existence of a given condition as a result of developing an alternative action.

decimal selector switch — Positions decimal at full floating or presets at two places.

decrement — A programming device or instruction designed to decrease the contents of a storage location.

dedicated — Generally refers to machines, programs, or procedures that are designed or set apart for special or continued use.

default functions — On some HP units, the five functions above the A, B, C, D, and E keys are known as the default functions. When the user first turns on the calculator, these default functions are present in the unit, and the user can select any one of them by simply pressing the appropriate key, A through E. As soon as the user begins keying in a program, the default functions are lost, and the top row keys, A through E, are used to select programs or routines within programs. To restore the default functions to the unit, the user clears the calculator of all programs.

DEG/RAD keys — Refers to angular mode selection — users flip a switch to perform trig operations in either of two angular modes: degrees or radians. Users can also convert angles from one mode to the other push-button fast.

DEG/RAD switch — Interprets displayed angle in degrees or in radians.

DEL — The delete character.

degrees, minutes, seconds/decimal degrees key — 2nd D.MS — This key instructs the calculator to interpret the displayed number as an angle expressed in degrees, minutes and seconds and to convert it to its decimal equivalent. Pressing 'INV' '2nd' 'D.MS' instructs the calculator to interpret the displayed number as an angle expressed in decimal degrees and to convert it to its degrees, minutes and seconds equivalent.

delete key — The delete key removes displayed instruction and automatically shifts following instructions up when in the learn mode. (some units)

delta — The Greek letter delta (Δ) represents any quantity which is much smaller than any other quantity of the same unit appearing in the same problem. Also refers to a magnetic cell, the difference between the partial-select outputs of the same cell in a one state and in a zero state.

diagnostic — Refers to the detection, discovery, and further isolation of a malfunction and/or mistake.

digital — Pertaining to the utilization of discrete integral numbers in a given base to represent all the quantities that occur in a problem or a calculation. It is possible to express in digital form all information stored, transferred, or processed by a dual-state condition; e.g., on-off, open-closed, and true-false.

digital/analog converter (DAC) — Converts digital signals into a continuous electrical signal suitable for input to an analog computer.

diode — A device having two terminals which conducts electricity more easily in one direction than in the other.

direct memory register addressing — On some units the direct register addressing instruction: 5 STO 10, means to store 5 directly in register 10, as shown in some sketches. Indirect addressing, on the other hand, increases the versatility of all memory registers and allows users to store the address of another memory register for future use.

direct memory register addressing keys — The Store Key stores a displayed number into one of many addressable memory registers. The Recall Key displays data stored in a selected register. The Exchange Key exchanges contents of a selected register with the displayed number.

direct register arithmetic — Users can store a displayed number at any time during a calculation without affecting the calculation in any way. Additionally, they can add the current display register value x to the content of any memory register — subtract, multiply, divide the content of any memory by x. Such modified value then occupies that memory register and x remains unchanged in the display register. (some units)

discrete units — Distinct units of a digital nature as opposed to a continuous information flow, which is analog.

disc storage — A computer memory device capable of storing information magnetically on a disc similar in appearance to a phonograph record.

display, blurring (small calculators) — During execution of a stored program, the display continuously changes and is purposely illegible to indicate that the program is running. When the program stops, the display is steady.

display control keys — An example on the HP-67, there are four keys, 'FIX,' 'SCI,' 'ENG,' and 'DSP' that allow users to control the manner in which numbers appear in the display. 'DSP' followed by a number key changes the number of displayed digits without changing the format. 'FIX' displays numbers in fixed decimal point format; 'SCI' permits users to see numbers in scientific notation. 'ENG'

displays numbers in engineering notation, with exponents of 10 shown in multiples of three (e.g. 10^3, 10^6, 10^{15}).

display functions — These develop power-on and numerical information. They
also provide indications of a negative
number, decimal point, overflow, underflow and error and displays 10-digit man-
tissas and 2-digit exponents, on most
units.

display, hand-held programmable —
On some units, the display is used to show
results, operational errors, low battery
conditions, programs in execution, and
program steps. Additionally, in some
units, W/PRGM mode, the display allows
users to "see" each step of a program in
memory.

display register — The register which
contains the quantity most recently computed, recalled from memory or entered
from the keyboard.

display switching, automatic — Some
units automatically switch the display
from fixed point to full scientific notation whenever the number is too large
or too small to be seen with a fixed decimal point. This feature keeps users from
missing unexpectedly large or small numbers.

double precision — Pertaining to a
quantity having twice as many digits as
are normally carried; e.g., a double-pre-
cision number requires two machine
words in a fixed-word machine.

D/R key — Users slide to D if angle entered is to be expressed in degrees; to R if
it is to be expressed in radians.

DSP (Display) key — The DSP key followed by a number specifies the number
of digits that the unit will display, instead of the normal two digits, capacity is
9 digits after the decimal point. (HP-67)

dump — A small program that outputs
the contents of memory onto hard copy
which may be listings, tape or punched
cards.

dynamic — Pertaining to a quantity that
is affected by time, energy or power, and
therefore indicates a relatively transient
or unstable condition.

dynamic dump — A dump that is performed periodically during the execution
of a program.

edit — To modify a calculator program, or
alter stored data prior to output.

**edit and debug functions, hand-held
units** — These functions allow trial-run

programs to move through a program a
step at a time, forward or backward, to
add more steps, delete, or write over steps,
then record.

editing capability, built-in — Under
program control, data in a program can be
inserted, deleted or changed on existing
programs. The user can back step or forward step and review the last and the current instruction step at the same time on
display.

EIA standard code — A code or coding
system conforming to any one of the standards established by the Electronic Industries Association.

electronic — Any system or device in
which electrons flow through a vacuum,
gas, or semiconductor. Also pertains to devices, circuits, or systems using the principle of electron flow through a conductor.

emulate — A procedure designed to imitate one system with another such that
the imitating system accepts the same data, executes the same programs, and
achieves the same results as the imitated
system. Contrast with simulate.

engineering notation — Special to some
pocket calculators is engineering notation, which allows all numbers to be
shown in a modified scientific notation
with exponents of 10 that are multiples of
three (e.g., 10^3, 10^6, 10^{12}). Whichever notation is selected, the user always maintains the complete 10-digit number internally. Also, the unit switches the display
automatically from fixed point notation to
full scientific notation whenever a number is too large or too small to be seen in
fixed point notation.

error (card reading) — If after a pass of
a card through the card reader, the display shows 'error' that side of the card did
not read properly. Users then press 'clx',
then insert that side of the card into the
slot and let it pass through again.

error conditions — A variety of situations which arise when the calculation encounters ill-defined quantities, illegal operations, or numbers beyond the capacity
of the unit.

**error control, step forward — step
back** — On some units when there is an
error in programming, it's easy to examine the program, by pressing step forward or step back to debug the program.
The printer will list the program steps in
English. Once users detect the error, they
can insert, delete or overwrite a step. If

necessary, the machine automatically renumbers the subsequent program steps.

e to the x power key — Raises e to the power of the displayed number.

exchange — The operation in which the content of the display register is exchanged with that of a specified addressable register.

exchange key — Tells calculator to exchange the x and y quantities in y^x or $^x\sqrt{y}$ before the function is processed. Operands in times ($\times$) and divide ($\div$) can also be changed with this key. (some units)

execute mode (programs) — Users press 'RST' to reset the calculator to the beginning of the program and are then ready to run the program in the execute mode. After entering $\times$, for example, they press 'R/S' and the answer appears in the display. (some units)

execution — The phase during which the unit is running under program control (the run mode). The controlling program is said to be in the process of execution.

execution trace — A trace of instruction execution can be obtained with the optional printer by placing the TRACE switch on the printer in the ON position and stepping through the program using the 'SST' key. At each step, the numeric key code and the contents of the display will be printed. Operative in the calculate and run modes on some units.

exponent — A number placed at the right and above a symbol in typography to indicate the number of times that symbol is a factor, e.g., 10 to the 4 equals $10 \times 10 \times 10 \times 10$, or 10,000.

exponentiation — A built-in two-variable function for raising y to the xth power. Effected by the 'y^x' key.

factorial key — Calculates the factorial (!) of the number displayed — where $0 \leq x \leq 69$, and x is an integer.

fetch — The particular portion of a calculator cycle during which the location of the next instruction is determined. The instruction is taken from memory and modified if necessary. It is then entered into the register.

finite — A quantity that has a limit or boundary, in contrast to infinite, that has no limit.

firmware — A term usually related to microprogramming and those specific software instructions that have been more or

less permanently burned into a ROM control block.

firmware, calculator — Many manufacturers sell read-only memories (ROMs) for special routines, generally called "firmware." Several manufacturers sell basic firmware in the form of separately marketed, preprogrammed ROMs (PROMs), which the user selects to fit his unique requirements and plugs into special slots in the mainframe.

fixed point — A notation or system of arithmetic in which all numeric quantities are expressed by a predetermined number of digits with the point implicitly located at some predetermined position; contrasted with floating point.

fixed point key — Followed by a number from 0 to 9 sets a corresponding number of digits to be displayed after the decimal point. The right-hand digit is rounded up if the digit to the right of it is 5 or more. The original number of digits is retained in the display register to maintain accuracy. Several key sequences are available to take the display out of fixed-point.

flag — Refers to a bit (or bits) used to store one bit of information. A flag has two stable states and is the software analogy of a flip-flop.

flag decisions — Some units offer the availability of up to four flags for tests in programs. Besides tests for zero and conditionals, flags, actually memory devices, can be either SET (true) or CLEAR (false). A running program can then test the flag later in the program and make a decision, depending upon whether the flag was set or clear. (H)

flag operations, calculator — Flags are signals. Some units have five. Each is set or reset by users manually from the keyboard, or as part of a stored program. The flag's condition can be tested by the IF FG transfer instruction. Users can manually control program options directly from the keyboard before execution with flags.

flag signals — Flag signals, flags set, cleared, tested etc. include data entry, error detection, and error override. Change flag without stopping program execution is an added feature on some systems.

flashing display, small calculators — On some units the display flashes when any of several improper operations are attempted. Pressing any key stops the flashing without performing the key function.

flip-flop — A device capable of assuming

one of two stable states, in which interconnected symbols are used to represent operations, data, flow, and equipment.

floating point arithmetic — Arithmetic used in a calculator where the calculator keeps track of the decimal point (contrasted with fixed point arithmetic).

flow chart — Usually a programmers tool for determining a sequence of operations as charted using sets of symbols, directional marks, and other representations to indicate stepped procedures of calculating operation.

format — The arrangement of data according to a fixed plan or design.

four-key memory — This lets users add to, subtract from, recall or clear the memory without affecting the numbers in the display.

function — One quantity (A) is said to be a function of another quantity (B) when no change can be made in B without producing a corresponding change in A and vice versa. Thus, in the equation $y^2 = R^2 - X^2$, Y is a function of X, and Y is also a function.

function key — Pressing the function key, x^2, $1/x$, etc., causes immediate performance of the function.

fuse — A protective device, usually a short piece of wire or chemical compound, constructed to melt and break a circuit when the current exceeds its rated capacity.

garbage — A slang computer term for unwanted and meaningless information carried in memory or storage. Also referred to as hash.

gas discharge displays — Gas discharge displays are devices that use the glow produced by ionized neon gas to form alphanumeric characters. For calculator applications these characters are usually in the form of a 5-by-7 or 7-by-9 dot matrix.

general register — A register used for operations such as binary addition, subtraction, multiplication, and division. General registers are used primarily to compute and modify addresses in a program.

generic — 1. Of, applied to, or referring to a kind, class or group. 2. Inclusive or generally opposed to specific and special.

giga — A prefix signifying one billion, or 10^9.

GIGO (Garbage in-Garbage Out) — A specially coined term used to describe the data into and out of a computer system —

that is, if the input data is bad (garbage in) then the output data will also be bad (garbage out).

GO TO key, small calculators — Followed by a two-digit number, causes calculator to execute the instruction at the specified step number next, and continue program execution sequentially from there.

Go to Key 'GTO' yyy or Label — The go-to key followed by a 3-digit number or label causes the program counter to be set at the called address or label. If the go-to key is used to call a program manually from the keyboard, press 'RUN' to execute program.

grad — A unit of angular measurement in which a right angle equals 100 grads. See angular modes.

handshaking — A descriptive term often used interchangeably with buffering or interfacing, implying a direct connection or matching of specific units or programs.

hang-up — 1. A condition in which the central processor of a calculator is attempting to perform an illegal or forbidden operation or in which it is continually repeating the same routine. 2. An unplanned calculator stop or delay in problem solution, e.g., caused by the inability to escape from a loop.

hang-up prevention — The calculator logic must be designed or modified so that no sequence of valid or invalid instructions can cause the calculator to come to a halt or to go into a nonterminating uninterruptible state. Examples of this latter case are infinitely nested executions or non-terminating indirect addressing.

hard copy — Typewritten or printed characters on paper produced by a calculator at the same time the information is copied or converted into machine language that is not easily read by a human.

hardware — Refers to the metalic or 'hard' components of a calculator system in contrast to the 'soft' or programming components. The components of circuits may be active, passive, or both.

hard-wired logic — Refers to logic designs for control of problem solutions that require interconnection of numerous integrated circuits formed or wired for specific purposes and relatively unalterable. A hard-wired diode matrix is hard-wired logic whereas a RAM, ROM, or CPU can be reprogrammed with little difficulty to change the purpose of operation.

hash total — A summation for checking purposes of one or more corresponding fields of a file that would ordinarily not be summed.

head-cleaning — An occasional maintenance process to ensure proper operation of the magnetic card read/write mechanism.

hertz — A unit of frequency equal to one cycle per second.

heuristic — Pertaining to exploratory methods of problem solving in which solutions are discovered by evaluation of the progress made toward the final result. Contrast with algorithm.

hexadecimal — Refers to whole numbers in positional notation with 16 as the base. Hexadecimal uses 0 through 15, with the first ten represented by 0 through 9 and the last six digits represented by A,B,C, D,E, and F.

high level language comparisons — 1. Such languages are usually problem-oriented or procedure-oriented programming languages as distinguished from machine-oriented and/or mnemonic languages. Machine languages are the final target languages, after compiling, while high level languages are source languages for many programmers and users. Examples of high level languages are: COBOL, BASIC, FORTRAN, ALGOL, etc.

histogram key — Calculates complete histogram on data set. Resulting printout includes cell number, lower bound of cell, number of occurrences in cell, relative percent frequency of cell. (some units)

hit — 1. Refers to momentary electrical disturbance on a circuit. 2. A successful comparison of two items of data. Contrast with match.

human engineering — The science and art of developing machines for human use, giving consideration to the abilities, limitations, habits and preferences of the human operator.

human factors — Refers to the designated application of psychology and related social sciences to systems involving humans and human behavior.

hyperbolic function key — Instructs the calculator to determine the hyperbolic function of the displayed value when pressed as a prefix to the sin, cos, or tan key.

idle light — On some calculators an idle light flashes to indicate an illegal operation has been performed. For example,

dividing by zero, square root of a negative number, log of zero or negative number, entry or result of more than the capacity of the display, raising a number to zero or negative power, depressing two keys simultaneously, depressing keys too quickly in sequence.

IEEE — Institute of Electrical and Electronics Engineers.

illegal — The status of a program which has attempted to perform a non-existent instruction, or to violate the program area reservation check.

illegal operation sequences — Various sequences of keystrokes are meaningless and result in an error condition. Specifically, these include sequences with missing operands such as +, =, ×, etc. For example, sequences with) or = immediately following an arithmetic operator or with two consecutive operators not separated by an operand are illegal. The display flashes the current display-register value. (some units)

indirect address — An address specifying a storage location, which in turn contains either a direct or another indirect address.

indirect address key — This is used as a prefix to a branching or memory instruction to permit indirect addressing. The direct addressing key may be used with many functions — both memory and program. (some units)

indirect instruction — Any instruction which uses the contents of a specified register as a pointer to the actual data register or program address.

information — The meaning that a human assigns to data by means of the known conventions used in their representation.

initialize — To set an instruction, counter, switch, or address to a specified starting condition at a specified time in a program.

input — 1. An adjective referring to a device or collective set of devices used for bringing data into another device. 2. A channel for impressing a state on a device or logic element.

input area — The internal storage area in a calculator or computer into which data from external storage is transferred.

input/output — 1. Commonly called I/O. A general term for equipment used to communicate with a computer. 2. The data involved in such communication. 3.

The media carrying the data for input/output.

insert key — The insert key moves the current and all following instructions down one location when in the learn mode, in some units.

insert key — 'INS' — In the learn mode, pressing this key causes the current instruction and following ones to be moved down one location and causes a zero instruction to be inserted at the current program location. (some units)

instruction set — 1. The set of instructions that a calculating, computing or data-processing system is capable of performing. 2. The set of instructions that an automatic coding system assembles.

instrumentation — The application of devices for the measuring, recording and/or controlling of physical properties and movements.

integer — A whole number as distinguished from a fraction; this is, a number that contains the unit (one) an exact number of times.

integrated circuit (IC) — A combination of interconnected passive and active circuit elements incorporated on a continuous substrate.

intelligence — The developed capability of a device to perform functions that are normally associated with human intelligence, such as reasoning, learning, and self-improvement. (Related to machine learning.)

intelligent terminal — A terminal with some level of programmable "intelligence" for performing pre-processing or post-processing operations.

interactive terminals — Interactive terminals are generally equipped with a display, a keyboard and an incremental printer. Optionally they also include a tape subsystem. Such terminals support interactive, conversational, demand, inquiry, and transaction oriented applications.

interface — 1. Refers to instruments, devices or a concept of a common boundary or matching of adjacent components, circuits, equipment, or system elements. An interface enables devices to yield and/or acquire information from one device or program to another. Although the terms adapter, handshake, buffer have similar meaning, interface is more distinctly a connection to complete an operation. 2. A common boundary — for example, physi-cal connection between two systems or two devices. 3. Specifications of the interconnection between two systems or units.

interface, hand calculators — The hand calculator is an attractive input device since it is built with storage and display room for at least eight digits. It is designed for minimum size, cost and power consumption. And it has a calculating capability frequently useful prior to storage. In addition, a simple eight-digit interface turns hand calculators into input devices for many accessories such as digital recorders, etc.

internal processing registers — The several registers which, along with the display register, are used to evaluate expressions with pending operations without affecting the user's data registers.

interrupt device — External interrupts are caused by an external device requiring attention (such as a signal from a communications device), console switching, by the timer going to zero, and by other procedures.

interrupt function, priority — Priority interrupt functions usually include distinguishing the highest priority interrupt active, remembering lower priority interrupts which are active, selectively enabling or disabling priority interrupts, executing a jump instruction to a specific memory location, and storing the program counter register in a specific location.

INT key — Leaves only integer portion of number in displayed register by truncating fractional portion.

inverse key — This key is used to find the inverse of many functions as sin, cos, tan, sum, etc. An inverse instruction may be cancelled by pressing 'INV' a second time if no other keys have been pressed.

inverse operation — Those operations which result when an operation is prefixed by 'INV' which reverses the effect of the operation.

invert — Refers to various steps to place in a contrary order. To invert the terms of a fraction is to put the numerator in place of the denominator, and vice versa.

I/O (input-output) — Refers to devices, programs, or procedures for accepting or outputting information. As regards microprocessors specifically, package pins are tied directly to the internal bus network to enable I/O to interface the instrument with the associated equipment or programs.

item — 1. A set of one or more fields containing related information. 2. A unit of correlated information relating to a single person or object. 3. The contents of a single message.

iterative — Refers to a procedure or process which repeatedly executes a series of operations until some condition is satisfied. An iterative procedure can be implemented by a loop in a routine.

jacks, pocket calculators — The introduction of pocket calculators featuring internal access connectors or jacks has been recent. Considering the overall capabilities of pocket calculators, the addition of I/O (input/output) connectors has greatly increased their versatility. Such jacks permit their use as counters, for example, or permit data to be recorded on accessory equipment. In addition, an output jack permits a pocket calculator to be used as a portable control unit for various types of electronic instruments or as an input device for computers and microprocessors.

jump — The jump instruction or operation, like the branch instruction, is designed to control the transfer of operations from one point to another point in a control or applications program.

junk — A slang expression that refers to garbled or otherwise unintelligible sequence of signals or other data, especially as received from a communications channel, i.e., hash or garbage.

K — 1. Commonly used to describe the amount of addressable storage units of computer systems. K in computer terminology equals 1,024. For example, 64K signifies 65,536 storage units. 2. Symbol for cathode or dielectric. 3. Abbreviation for Kelvin or kilo.

keyboard — 1. A device for the encoding of data by key depression which causes the generation of the selected code element. 2. Keyboards fall into three basic types — alphanumeric, numeric only and mixed. Alphanumeric keyboards are used for word processing, text processing, data processing and teleprocessing. Numeric only keyboards are used on touchtone telephones, accounting machines and calculators. The touch-tone telephone has come into significant use as a calculator and data input and voice output device.

keyboard-language, calculators — Programmable calculators are ready to use right out of the shipping carton. On keyboard-language calculators a complete operation — such as add, subtract or multiply — is normally defined by a single key. When the key is pressed in the operate mode the operation takes place immediately. Many functions that need several operations — such as storage, search, printing and many user-defined specials — can often be done with at most two key strokes.

keyboard, live — On some units this lets users interact with the system while a program is running to examine or change program variables — or even perform keyboard calculations.

keyboard, multi-function — On some units, each key on the keyboard can perform as many as four different functions. One function is indicated on the flat plane of the key face, while another is printed in black on the slanted face of the key. A third and a fourth function may be indicated by printed symbols in gold and blue, respectively, below the key.

keyboard programming — Programming a keyboard-language calculator is done by switching it to its learn-program mode and pressing the keys in the same sequence that users would to make calculations directly. Thereafter the calculator can repeat a complex sequence automatically, stopping only to wait for new data at selected points or to take prestored data from the memory or registers.
Keyboard-language calculators are easy to master. With almost no experience in programming, users can operate a unit with fair efficiency almost immediately and program effectively in days. The keyboard calculator is powerful. The simpler unit can execute sequentially about 500 programmed steps, and more advanced machines can handle several thousand.

keycodes — In some units keycodes (for register identification, etc.) are read first, the row, then the number of the key in the row, from the top down and from left to right. Digit keys are represented by keycodes 00 through 09. Keycodes for functions then are selected by first pressing a prefix key and then a digit key and referenced by the keycode matrix address, not by 00 through 09. (See manuals for detail.)

key-driven — Any device for translating information into machine-sensible form, which requires an operator to depress a key for each character, is said to be key-driven.

keying — The forming of signals, such as those employed in keyboard transmission, by the interruption of a direct current or modulation of a carrier between discrete values of some characteristics.

keying programs — On some systems, to key in a program, users switch to PRGM mode. They should see 00 in the display. They then key in the listed keys. They are not executed but instead stored in program memory for later execution. The first key is ENTER ↑. When users key it in, the display changes to: 01.41. The number 01 designates the first line of the program. The number 41 designates the key stored in that line. Users can tell what key it is by simply counting down four rows to find the first key. They should arrive at the ENTER ↑ key. The codes are simply the number of rows down and the number of keys across. The digit keys are the exception. Their codes are 00 thru 09 depending on the key. The second key is 3 and the display changes to: 02.03. If there had been a previous program in memory, it would not make any difference. Each key overwrites one line in memory. Users never have to clear program memory before keying in a new program. (some units)

key phrase programming, calculator — The real power of some calculators is easy programming. One type programming is based on key phrases rather than keystrokes. A key phrase is simply a sequence of keystrokes that together perform one function or operation. For example, both f SIN and STO + 5 are key phrases, but they contain two and three keystrokes, respectively. The program memory contains numbered locations for 49 key phrases. When the user writes a program, one type calculator merges keystrokes into key phrases and stores the instructions in program memory.

kickstand, calculator — A kickstand elevates the calculator at an angle to make the display easier to read. On some models it doubles as a carrying handle. Some can be fastened to a desk and the calculator locked in place to prevent theft.

kilo — A prefix meaning one thousand. Its abbreviation is K; e.g. 1K = 1024 and 8K means 8192. In computer use refers to the power of two closest to a number; e.g. 4K word memory is actually 4096 words.

kludge — A computer mimic or humorous term indicating the black box or computer. A kludge is slang for, or representation of, an endearment of the pet computer; i.e., "our kludge".

label — A name assigned to a particular point in a program which can be referenced by a transfer instruction or by program initialization.

labeling, calculators — On some units any part of a program may be labeled by using LABEL and another key for the symbol. This part of the program is then executed by pressing EXECUTE and the appropriate symbol. Labeling provides branch points for "if" conditions or can be used to denote the beginning of separate, independent programs. Users may also use labeling to create subroutines. Usually a subroutine is called from a main program. Upon completion of the subroutine the calculator returns to the main program at the proper location. To accomplish this on some units the RETURN ADDRESS, GO TO DISPLAY sequence is programmed at the end of the subroutine.

label key — While in the learn mode of operation, this key instructs the unit to save the next pressed key as a nonexecutable. Storing a label requires two program locations. The contents of the program counter are associated with the label in later branch operations. Users manuals indicate the keys that may and may not be used as labels.

language — A set of symbols, rules, and conventions utilized for representing and communicating information or data between people, or between people and machines.

LAST X, calculator — In addition to the four stack registers that automatically store intermediate results, some units also contain a separate automatic register, the LAST X register. This register preserves the value that was in the displayed X-register before the performance of a function. To place the contents of the LAST X register into the display again, users press hLAST X. (HP-67)

LCDs-liquid crystal displays — Refers to displays that are sandwiches of two glass plates, spaced typically about .0005" apart with a nematic liquid crystal solution between them and hermetically sealed at the perimeters.

learn mode — In some units the LEARN mode switch allows a program to be keyed into calculator memory. The visual display shows the operator the program step number, and the program code of the next step. A program counter automatically increments each new program step.

learn and print — In this mode each program step learned into memory is automatically printed out on the optional printer. Once a program has been learned into memory, it can be executed by switching to the RUN mode. The program can also be recorded onto the magnetic tape cassette for future use, whereby the program can be automatically reloaded into memory from the tape cassette. (some units)[21]

learn key — LRN — Pressing this key once puts the calculator in the learn mode of operation. This allows the user to begin writing a program into memory. The display is partitioned into two fields: a 3-digit program counter to the left and a 2-digit numeric key code to the right. A key code chart is located in the back of some manuals to correlate keys to key codes and vice versa. Pressing 'LRN' again takes the calculator out of the learn mode and restores the display to its original state. The learn key may not be used as a label or stored in a program. (some units)

learn mode — The calculator can automatically determine various solutions on keyboard programmables, for example, because the entire sequence for calculating can be stored in the program memory. Users first press 'CP' to clear program memory. They then press 'LRN' and 00 00 should appear in the display indicating that the user is in the learn mode. The user carefully keys in the solution sequence, and can turn off the calculator, and then on again if mistakes are made. Other ways of correcting mistakes are also possible. (some units)

LED (light emitting diode) display — LED displays as used in calculators have eight or more digits and are commonly monolithic devices with common cathodes. With character heights of about 0.1 inch, the current requirement for red is about 5 mA per segment but this may rise to 80 mA under short-pulse time sharing conditions.

levels of parentheses — The number of operations made pending by means of open (left) parentheses.

levels of routines — The number of program segments, either active or suspended, and awaiting return of control in a program.

linearity — The relationship between two quantities when a change in a second quantity is directly proportionate to a change in the first quantity.

liquid crystal displays, calculator — Liquid crystals have unusual properties that enable them to be employed in numeric display panels. They belong to a class of chemicals which flow like liquids yet have molecules that form chains like crystals. Normally transparent, they turn opaque when subjected to an ac or dc electric field. Liquid crystals are sandwiched between glass plates, masked to form numeric segments. When a voltage is applied to electrodes across the transparent material, the material composition changes so that it no longer transmits light.

list — To effect a step-by-step printed record of the instructions of a program. (Can be used only with various optional printing units.)

list key — 2nd list — The list key instructs the calculator to engage the printer (when in the printing unit) and lists the stored program starting at the current program location.

load key — A control key, or similar manual device, which is used to input data or instructions into a calculator or control system. The instructions are usually made up of specific routines.

load module — Any portion of a partitioned program which resides (in its entirety) in program memory at some given time.

logarithm — The logarithm of a number is the exponent indicating the power to which it is necessary to raise a given number, called the base, to produce the original number.

logarithm characteristic — The non-negative decimal part of a logarithm is called the mantissa, and the integral part is called the characteristic of a logarithm. For example, in the log 1830 = 0.2625 + 3. 0.2625 is the mantissa and 3 is the characteristic, or 1 less than the number of integers. See any math text for use and rules of logarithms.

logarithm key, common — Calculates the common logarithm (base 10) of the displayed number, x > 0. Pressing 'INV' '2nd' 'log' instructs the calculator to find the antilogarithm (10^x) of the displayed number. (some units)

logarithm key, natural — Calculates

the natural logarithm (base e) of the displayed number, x > 0. Pressing 'INV' 'lnx' instructs the calculator to find the value of e^x, where x is the displayed number. (some units)

logical tests — Those tests performed as a part of conditional transfer instructions.

logic, algebraic (calculator) — Separate plus, minus, and equals keys are found on machines with algebraic logic, and all calculations may be performed in the familiar hand-written sequence. This system has been adopted by many of the better grade portable calculators, including the scientific types. A typical unit, for example, allows a problem such as the sum of products — $(2 \times 3) + (4 \times 5)$ — to be solved by direct keyboard entry of all numbers and instructions in a left-to-right order. The sum of products capability puts calculator memory to a common but very useful purpose.

logic, arithmetic (calculator) — Calculators built with arithmetic logic are quickly spotted from two unique dual-function keys, plus-equals $(+ =)$ and minus-equals $(- =)$. These keys must be pressed after the last number to be added (or subtracted) as well as between each entry (thus, five-plus-three-equals-eight is $5 += 3 += 8$; and five-minus-three-equals-two is $5 + = 3 - = 2$). Multiplication and division keys are used just as when figuring with pencil and paper. This is the arrangement common to most mechanical calculators.

logic, Reverse Polish Notation (RPN) — Provides a 4-level rollable stack and unambiguous, parentheses-free calculations. RPN lets users work through complex problems naturally, cutting them down to size rather than making them more complicated. Intermediate results are displayed as they are calculated, so there are no "hidden" calculations. Intermediate results are "stored" in the stack, so they don't have to be written down.

logical relation — Relates to programming. A logical term in which two expressions are separated by a relational operator. The relational operators are EQ, GE, GT, LE, LT, and NE. See also arithmetic relation.

logic notation systems — There are three basic subdivisions of system organization used inside the present crop of personal calculators: arithmetic logic, algebraic logic, and reverse Polish notation. For the user, this means several schemes exist for entering data into the various brands of electronic calculators. No one method provides serious learning problems, but some shoppers may find their choice of machine strongly influenced by past experiences with mechanical desktop calculators or computers.

logic, RPN (calculator) — Reverse Polish notation, (RPN) a part of all modern computer compilers for languages such as FORTRAN and ALGOL, is favored by Hewlett-Packard for personal calculators (HP-45, -67, -97 and others). Combined with a stack arrangement of memory registers, this system is said to be the most efficient way known for evaluating mathematical expressions and packing considerable calculating power into a small space. The stack memory is particularly useful for handling long, complex problems involving chain calculations.

Operation is based on the fact that arbitrary expressions can be specified unambiguously without parentheses by placing operators immediately before or after their operands. Thus, the expression $(a - b) \times (c - d)$ may be specified as $\times + ab - cd$ (Polish) or $ab + cd - \times$ (reverse Polish). With the help of a stack (last-in-first-out) memory, the reverse Polish expression is evaluated as follows:

Stack memory location							
T							
Z						a + b	
Y		a		a + b	c	a + b	
X	a	b	a + b	c	d	c − d	$(a + b) \cdot (c - d)$
↑	Enter a	Enter b	+	Enter c	Enter d	−	
	Keyboard operation ⟶						

Though straightforward, note that the order of data entry is considerably different from a typical pencil and paper calculation.

Several brands of four-function consumer calculators also use reverse Polish notation. In all cases, this logic system is immediately revealed by the keyboard, which lacks any type of equals function.

logic systems — A logic system is the "language" used to communicate with a calculator — the way in which users key in problems and the way the calculator is designed to handle the problems. One logic system may require users to restructure an equation to conform to the system; another may not. The two most common types of logic systems used in professional pocket calculators are algebraic and RPN logic. Users may wish to check out both systems, and determine which is the easiest to use (especially important when solving complex problems) . . . which is the least confusing (so they can have confidence in answers) . . . and which is the best to use for solving the kinds of problems they face regularly.

loops — Program structures in which an instruction sequence repeats a number of times before exiting to other portions of the program.

loop, closed — Concerns a signal path in a control system represented as a group of units connected in such a manner that a signal started at any point follows a closed path and can be traced back to that point.

low power display — Some units include a red lamp inside the display which will glow to provide a warning when the battery is close to discharge.

LSI — Large-scale integration refers to a component density of more than 500 per chip.

LSI microprocessor — An LSI microprocessor is essentially a complete system on one chip, or at most a few chips. It can be called a microcomputer, if the system normally consists of a CPU, a RAM, an I/O, and a ROM. The ROM is predesigned and can be customized by programing. In examining the semantics of microprocessing, it should be pointed out that the CPU was introduced first. Most people call the combination of CPU with a ROM and a RAM a microprocessor. Some LSI microprocessor systems are complete sets with no interfacing circuitry needed, and they contain a variety of LSI I/O circuits.

Therefore, some industry people now call a completed system a microcomputer — a set of system-designed LSI circuits which have been programmed in the ROM to perform unique functions. All microcomputers contain a small memory which is satisfactory for any manual input, such as a keyboard.

mantissa — The number in scientific notation which is to be multiplied by a given power of ten to equal the quantity desired.

mantissa format — Any given convention for selecting the number of significant digits to be displayed for the mantissa part of a number in scientific notation or for the number displayed when scientific notation is absent.

mantissa, scientific notation — In scientific notation, the term mantissa refers to that part of the number which precedes the exponent. For example, the mantissa in the number $1.234E+2\emptyset\emptyset$ is 1.234.

man/trace/norm switch — On the HP-97 printer, when inserting a card for a run, the switch should be set to *man,* for manual mode.

mark up key — Computes mark up on the selling price automatically printing both the amount of the mark up and selling price. Can also be used with constant mark up percentages to eliminate re-entry. (some units)

matrix printing — The printing of alphanumerical characters by means of the appropriate selection of pins contained in a rectangular array on the printing head.

mega — Prefix denoting 10^6 (one million) Abbreviated M.

memory — One of the three basic CPU components, main memory stores information for future use. Storage and memory are interchangeable expressions. Memories accept and held binary numbers or images.

memory address keys, indirect — These include: Indirect Store. Indirect Recall. Indirect Exchange. Indirect Add. Indirect Subtract. Indirect Multiply. Indirect Divide. Example: the indirect address instruction: 5 IND STO 10 means to store 5, not in register 10, but in the register whose address is found in register 10. Thus, if 15 were previously stored in register 10, then 5 IND STO 10 would mean store in PROD register 15. Register 15 has been indirectly addressed by the given instruction. (some units)

memory, backing — Considered to be

the same as auxiliary storage, i.e., those units whose capacity is relatively larger than working (scratchpad or internal) storage but of longer access time, and which transfer capability is usually in blocks between storage units.

memory bus — The CPU communicates with memory and I/O devices over a memory bus. In different calculators this bus has various names, including I/O bus, data bus or one of a host of proprietary names.

memory, calculator (simple) — A 'constant' or a 'memory' facility is used when a problem requires the repeated use of a single constant. Users key this in only once and then multiply, divide, add, or subtract with this constant by simply pressing the constant key.

memory cassette, calculator example — Some advanced calculators feature a built-in cassette for program, data, or special function key storage.

memory equals + key — On some units this key operates in the same manner as the equals key when multiplication or division has been conditioned and adds the answer to the memory contents. If multiplication or division has not been conditioned, this key will add to memory the contents of the input register.

memory functions — In many machines, each of the memory function keys with the exception of 'CMs' must be followed by a 2-digit decimal number 00-19 to indicate which of the 20 memory registers (or more) is to be affected. Some memory registers are reserved in some units.

memory, "LAST x" — Some units have nine or more addressable memories and a special "LAST x" memory that automatically stores the last number users key in for easy error correction and multiple operations on the same number.

memory light — A light which indicates there is a number in the memory.

memory power — Each pocket calculator should have at least one addressable memory — to store constants or other numbers used more than once in a calculation. The more memories a calculator has, the less writing down of numbers that users have to do. With certain calculators having addressable memories, users can do register arithmetic directly: add to, subtract from, divide into or multiply the contents of a register. This makes data manipulation exceptionally

easy, even when working problems involving three simultaneous linear equations (or other 3×3 matrix inversions). Besides addressable memories, certain pocket calculators have an automatic memory (also called an operational stack, a four-memory stack, etc.). Entries and intermediate answers are stored automatically, then re-entered into the calculation at the appropriate time. Obviously, this eliminates the need to write down and re-enter numbers, which could lead to errors, and it speeds the work.

memory, read-only (ROM) — Refers to memory that cannot be altered in normal use of the calculator. Usually a relatively small memory that contains often-used instructions such as microprograms or system software as firmware.

memory recall — A key which allows the current contents of the memory to be displayed.

memory register — A register in which the contents can be added to or subtracted from. The contents are available until the register is cleared.

memory registers, addressable — These can be used for storage and retrieval of data, or to perform register arithmetic. A 10th ("Last X") register lets users recall last input argument for error correction or for multiple functions of same argument. (some units) (see registers)

memory save — Provides battery-powered carryover through power outages up to 10 minutes to prevent loss of program storage. This is powered-down non-operational mode. (some units)

memory stack, calculator — On some units data areas for programs are organized in main memory as stacks. A stack is a storage allocation method where the last item added is the first item removed. The CPU has registers that automatically keep track of the last area allocated in a stack. The use of the stack means that data areas for a procedure's private variables are allocated dynamically (when the procedure is called into execution), keeping the amount of memory space required by a program to a dynamic minimum The stack also provides the mechanism for passing parameters to procedures and saving and restoring the calling environment (this applies to calling both an application's own procedures and operating system procedures). (some units) merged key phrase codes, Hewlett-Packard (HP-25) — The HP-25 (among others) merges keystrokes into key phrases using a microcoded finite state machine. The machine carefully checks for undefined key sequences. When a valid key phrase is completed, an eight-bit code is fabricated. If the calculator is in run mode, the code is immediately decoded and executed. In program mode, the code is copied into the program memory and then decoded to generate the row-column display. The data registers used for program storage are 56 bits long. Each register can contain seven key phrase codes. Seven such registers comprise the program memory, so all together there are 49 key phrase locations. The HP-25 contains a data storage integrated circuit with sixteen registers of 56 bits each (14 BCD digits). Seven registers are for user programming, eight are for user data, and one is used for the LAST × function.

microcomputer — A general term referring to a complete tiny computing system, consisting of hardware and software, that usually sells for less than $500 and whose main processing blocks are made of semiconductor integrated circuits. In function and structure it is somewhat similar to a minicomputer, with the main difference being price, size, speed of execution, and computing power. The hardware of a microcomputer consists of the microprocessing unit (MPU) which is usually assembled on a PC board with memory, I/O, and auxiliary circuits. Power supplies, control console, and cabinet are separate.

microcomputer CPU — In general aspects, the CPU consists of the following: program counter (PC), instruction register (IR), instruction execution logic, a memory-address register (MAR), a general-purpose register (GPR) file, and an arithmetic and logic unit (ALU).

microprocessing unit (MPU) — The main constituent of the hardware of the microcomputer. It consists of the microprocessor, the main memory (composed of read/write and read-only memory), the input/output interface devices and the clock circuit, in addition to buffer, driver circuits and passive circuit elements. The MPU does not contain power supplies, cabinet and control console and is normally understood to be an assembled printed-circuit board. The level of sophistication of the MPU is that of the named microcomputer.

microprocessor (calculator) — Usually a large scale integrated (LSI) logic circuit that supervises and controls the interconnection, sequencing, timing, measurement, input and output, and other functions of a calculator.

microprogram, calculator chip — A typical calculator chip is merely a microprocessor that has a built-in microprogram to solve arithmetic functions. So, for simple numerical calculations, many designers do not seek trouble with more versatile microprocessors. They take advantage of a calculator's powerful arithmetic internal instruction set. The software is already written.

microprogram control — A ROM and counter form the basis for execution control logic. To select and generate a timing sequence, users set the counter to the start value and increment it for each step. The ROM decodes each counter value to activate appropriate ROM-output lines. This technique is called microprogram control, since the contents of the ROM control the sequence of operations.

minicartridge — The minicartridge looks like a cassette, but works like a 6″ by 4″ cartridge. The unit is smaller in length than a cassette (3″ to 4″), and also not as wide (2½″ to 2¼″). The maximum storage capacity is also smaller by 54%: 140′ of .15″ tape is used on the cartridge, while some cassettes have 300′ of .15″ tape. Actual storage, however, is dependent upon the encoding density and number of tracks, which means that the potential of the cartridge will depend upon the drives developed for it. The H-P (Hewlett Packard) minicartridge drive records on only one track at 800 bpi for storage of 115K bytes. H-P estimates their (and 3M's) minicartridge will last six to seven times longer than the cassette.

minus indicator (negative indicator) — A visual indicator, generally a minus sign (−) light to indicate a negative entry or answer. In many electronic calculators, the (−) occupies one of the display positions, reducing a negative number to a maximum of seven digits (for eight digit electronic calculators).

mixed calculations — The ability of an electronic calculator to perform multiple kinds of calculations within the same problem without continuously having to depress the (=) key.

MKS system — With recommendations accepted by the IEEE and many other engineering groups and organizations, the MKS (meter-kilogram-second) system is used in preference to the CGS (centimeter-gram-second) version of the metric system. The metric system uses a series of multipliers, all powers of ten, which, together with Greek and Latin terminology, indicate the actual size of its units. A kilogram, for example, is 10^3 or 1000 grams.

mnemonic — Assisting or intended to assist, memory; of or pertaining to memory; mnemonics is the art of improving the efficiency of the memory (in computer storage) i.e., MPY equals multiply. See also label.

MOS circuits — Refers to Metal-Oxide Semiconductors. These are semiconductors using a technology which offers very low power dissipation and hence can be made into circuits which jam transistors close together before a critical heat problem arises. Most monolithic memories, calculators and electronic watches use this technology.

MPU — Microprocessor unit.

mu — Greek letter used as symbol for amplification factor; micro-; micron; permeability.

natural logarithm key — Determines logarithm to the base e of the displayed number.

nesting — Operations placed inside of like operations. A nested subroutine is a subroutine found within another subroutine. A nested parentheses set is one found within another set of parentheses.

nesting storage types — As data is transferred into storage, each word in turn enters the top register and is then "pushed down" the column from register to register to make room for the subsequent words as they are assigned. When a word is transferred out of the storage, again only from the top register, other data in the storage moves back up the column from register to register to fill the space left empty. This is accomplished either through programs or the equipment itself.

nesting, two-level — Some programmable calculators which follow the algebraic rules of equation solving for keyboard entry permit two-level nesting. By a single keystroke 28 or more mathematical and statistical functions can be provided. These units offer optional user-definable keys which allow the user to address up to three programs or subroutines by one key depression. Some units provide 512 program steps with additional steps as an option in increments of 512 steps up to a total of 4096. Also, symbolic addressing and indirect addressing techniques make two routines immediately available to users on each designed key.

NiCd — NiCd (nickel Cadmium) batteries are the power supply for most electronic calculators with rechargeable batteries.

nickel-cadmium batteries — Nickel-cadmium batteries are becoming ever more popular in cordless consumer products and electronics building. Although initial cost may seem to be high, nickel-cadmium cells can be recharged so often that their per-unit-of-use performance actually makes them less expensive than almost any other type of battery in the long run. Aside from rechargeability and reasonable cost, these batteries can often directly replace ordinary disposable carbon-zinc cells.

no operation key — In the learn mode on some units, entry of this key is used to delete an unwanted instruction or to provide spacing between program parts for later additions. Program execution simply performs no operation; use of this key does not interfere or alter any key or execution sequence.

non-add key — A key which allows numbers, symbols, etc. to be printed by the electronic calculator but not entered into the calculations.

non-add print key — On some units this key prints the figure entered on the keyboard along with the (#) symbol, discards the figure, and clears the input register.

non-data operation — Any use of an input/output device that does not involve the transfer of data.

nondestructive read — A reading of the information in a register without changing that information.

non-volatile memory — 1. A memory type which holds data even if power has been disconnected. They can store data for years without power. 2. They're nondestructive and immune to external power interruptions.

one-number functions — To use any one-number function key, the user keys in the number and presses the function key or presses the prefix key, then the function key.

operand — A number or numerical expression in a mathematical operation.

overflow — A condition that exists when an entry or an answer is too large for the capacity of the machine. The working register has been exceeded and the excess digits "overflow". The rightmost digits, the least significant ones, are not displayed.

overflow and underflow examples, small calculators — In many systems, program execution halts when any register overflows (numbers with a magnitude greater than $9.999999999 \times 10^{-99}$). If the overflow appears in the X-register, it is easy to determine the operation that caused the overflow by switching to PRGM mode and identifying the code in the display. Occasionally, however, the overflow will occur in one of the data storage registers and occasionally in the Y-register. If a program seems to have stopped arbitrarily and users are sure that they did not press any keys, they should check these other registers.

overflow indication — When more than nine consecutive digits are entered, one type calculator prints ENT OVF to indicate entry overflow. The CE or T key will clear this overflow condition. If a multiplication or division result contains more than nine digits to the left of the decimal, RES OVF is printed and the overflow condition is automatically cleared. The calculator is automatically cleared when ADD OVF is printed, indicating addition overflow.

overwrite — Refers to the activity of placing information in a location and destroying the information previously contained there.

paper advance key — 2nd pap — The paper advance key allows manually advancing the paper in the printer. It advances the paper one line per key stroke.

parameter — 1. Variable which, for a particular purpose, combines other variables in computers. 2. Arbitrary constant, which has a particular value in specified circumstances in physics. 3. Variable which can take the place of one or more other variables in mathematics.

parentheses ( ) — Devices used to set off expressions as in algebra, to ensure they will be evaluated properly before being combined with other expressions.

parentheses, algebraic hierarchy —

Using left-to-right entry. One enters calculations exactly as he writes them. A user combines a 3-level algebraic hierarchy with 9 levels of parentheses. This lets user enter problems containing up to 10 pending operations. This means users don't have to presolve the problem or search for the most appropriate, efficient order of execution. The unit does this automatically. (some units)

parentheses keys — These are used to alter the order of processing according to standard algebraic rules. Pressing = will supply all right parentheses which are missing in order to complete a calculation. Some units are capable of holding up to ten pending operations and numbers with up to nine pending parentheses. The normal order of processing, omitting parentheses or within parenthetical expressions, is as follows: (1) powers and roots (excluding square and square root); (2) multiplication and division; (3) addition and subtraction. (some systems)

pause and compare, calculator — On some pocket units eight comparisons allow the program to react depending on the data in the calculation stack. Together with the GTO (GO TO step number) operation, programs can branch and loop based on numeric results. A function that is new to pocket calculators is PAUSE. When encountered in a program, the calculator stops for a second, displays the most recent result, and then continues the program. This is useful when programming iterative functions because one can watch the function converge or diverge.

pause feature — A valuable feature on some units is the "PAUSE" key. One can use it to momentarily interrupt (about one second per Pause command) the program execution and display the contents of the X register. This gives the opportunity to review or write down intermediate results.

pause key — On specific units when encountered during program execution, *pause* causes the current value of the display register to be displayed for approximately ½ second. When held down on the keyboard during program execution, it inserts approximately ¼ second delay between the execution of each step. (T)

pending operations — Those operations which cannot immediately be completed — pending evaluation of expressions opened by parentheses, or because of the algebraic hierarchy.

percent change key — Automatically compares any two factors, or printing the actual numeric difference between them and the percentage of difference as well.

% CH key — Computes percent of change from number in Y-register to number in displayed X-register. (some units)

percent function example — This function presents answers to multiplication and division in percent form and offers signed results on display. Results are printed in red (negative) or black (positive) and some units offer the discount feature. After execution of a multiplication problem by the percent key, the answer can be added or subtracted from the first factor by pressing the + or − key. Solution time is 290 ms max at 100kHz with display only on some units.

percent key — On some units this key allows entry of factors in percent form. If multiplication or division has been conditioned, this key will execute the problem as for equals with the displayed and printed answer as a percentage. Conditions the machine for the discount (add-on) sequence, on some units.

percent minus key — Reduces any number by any percentage or simple discount, printing both the amount of discount and net. ALL in one operation.

percent operation — Calculations requiring percentage add-ons or discounts are solved with the % key . . . audit symbols "A" or "D" are printed beside the respective result. Some models will also print the ratio of two numbers as a percentage when the numbers are entered as a division problem and completed with the % key.

percent plus key — Adds a tax or percentage increase to any value. Computes and prints both the amount of increase and gross with a single key.

performance evaluation — The analysis in terms of initial objectives and estimates, and usually made on-site, of a data processing system's productivity and capabilities, to provide information on operating experience and to identify corrective actions required if any.

peripheral — Usually input/output equipment used to make hard copies or to read in data from various media (typewriter, punch, tape reader, line printer, etc.).

pointer — A number which resides in data memory but which is used to specify a program address or another addressable register.

pointer, stack — In nested storage types (pushdown), the address of the location at the top of the column is often called the stack pointer and is held in a preassigned register.

polar coordinates — A mathematical system of coordinates for locating a point in a plane by the length of its radius vector and the angle this vector makes with a fixed line.

polar-rectangular conversion — This is used to convert from polar coordinates which describe any point by a radius r and an angle theta θ to rectangular coordinates which describe any point by two distances x and y measured at right angles to each other.

polar/rectangular key — 2nd P/R — The polar-to-rectangular key is used in conjunction with memory register 00 (R_{00}). To convert polar coordinates to rectangular coordinates, the magnitude r of the vector is stored in R_{00}, and the angle θ is entered into the display. Set D/R switch to D when θ is entered or desired in degrees, or set to R when working in radians. By pressing '2nd' 'P/R' the rectangular conversion is made with the y coordinate on some units, and the x coordinate stored in R_{00}. (T)

powers and roots keys y^x, $^x\sqrt{y}$ — These functions first complete pending operations of like kind since the last (and then instruct the calculator to hold the entered function as a pending operation. Note $y \geq 0$. (T)

prefix keys — The HP 67 and some other models offer three prefix keys, f, g, and h. Users press f prefix key before pressing the function key printed in gold on the keyboard above the function key; g to select function printed in blue on slanted face of function key, and h is pressed before function key and selects black function printed on slanted key face.

prefix multipliers — Prefixes which designate a greater or smaller unit than the original, by the factor indicated. These prefixes are:

Prefix	Symbol	Factor
tera	T	10^{12}
giga	G	10^9
mega	M	10^6
kilo	k	10^3
hecto	h	10^2
deka	da	10

deci	d	10^1
centi	c	10^{-2}
milli	m	10^{-3}
micro	u	10^{-6}
nano	n	10^{-9}
pico	p	10^{-12}
femto	f	10^{-15}
atto	a	10^{-18}

pre-programmed calculators — A typical preprogrammed scientific unit offers 72 preprogrammed functions and operations plus eight addressable memories. Users can do register arithmetic on all of them. Because the unit is programmable, the user enters the keystrokes necessary to solve repetitive problems only once. Thereafter, they enter the variables and press the RUN/STOP key for an almost instant answer. Users can add, change, or skip steps and can program the units to perform direct branches or conditional tests. They can display answers in fixed decimal, scientific or engineering notation.

pre-programmed functions, calculator — Many units are pre-programmed to perform all these functions Angle (_) Conv. Degrees/Minutes/Seconds, $+$, $-$, $\times$, $\div$, $1/x$, y^x, x^2, $\sqrt{x}$, LN, LOG, e^x, 10^x, %, Δ%, SINE, ASN, COS, ACS, TAN, ATN, N!, MEAN, STANDARD DEVIATION, TO POLAR/RECTANGULAR, RECTANGULAR/TO POLAR . . . and many more.

pre-programmed functions, hand-held programmables — Typical trigonometric (all in decimal degrees, radians, or grads) are: Sin x; Arc Sin x; Cos x; Arc Cos x; Tan x; Arc Tan x; logarithmic: Log x; Ln x; e^x; 10; others are: y^x; $\sqrt{x}$; $1/x$; π; x^2; n!; conversions between decimal angle (degrees, radians, or grads) and degrees/minutes/seconds; rectangular/polar coordinate conversion; decimal/octal integer conversion; degrees (hours)/minutes/seconds arithmetic; integer/fraction truncation; absolute value; full register arithmetic.

pre-programmed operations — To save program memory and make calculations easier, some mid-size desk calculators permit the storage of over 100 pre-programmed operations for logarithms, trigonometry, statistics and 24 metric conversions as hard-wired capability. For example, users can perform trigonometric functions with a keystroke, determine the standard deviation of a sample of grouped or ungrouped data, and convert kilograms per square centimeter to pounds per square inch.

preprogrammed special functions — On many units, a special class of functions are marked in blue. These are preprogrammed and are accessed by the prefix 2nd f (n). An example, to find the mean, once the sample data has been entered, users press 2nd f (n) mean.

PRGM mode, small calculator — The PRGM (program) mode for some small calculators provides for the recording in a part of the calculator called program memory, for later execution. All operations on the keyboard except three can be recorded for later execution with the PRGM-RUN switch set to PRGM. The three operations that cannot be recorded on some systems are SST, BST, and f PRGM. These three operations work in the PRGM mode to help users write and record their programs.

PRGM-RUN switch — Function keys are recorded in program memory. Display, on some systems, shows program memory step number and the keycode (keyboard row and location in row) of the function key. Function keys may be executed as part of a recorded program or individually by pressing from the keyboard. Input numbers and answers are displayed, except where indicated.

prices, implicit — Same as marginal values, shadow prices, dual-variable levels, etc. — that is, numbers giving the incremental worth of a relaxation of one unit in the right-hand side of a constraint.

primary store — 1. The main store built into a calculator, not necessarily the fast access store. 2. Relatively small immediate or very rapid access store incorporated in some calculators for which the main memory is a slower secondary store.

primitive — The most basic or fundamental unit of data, i.e., a single letter digit, element, or machine code as primitive when related to the ultra-sophisticated codes or languages now available. Also refers to first or second generation computer equipment.

print cradle, calculator — The print cradle permits the hand-held programmable calculator to become a desk-top printing calculator. When the calculator is locked into the cradle, the user is able to print anything shown in the display or print the step-by-step execution of a program. Print and paper advance controls permit the user to handle these functions on the printer as well as on the calculator, and a "trace" key allows monitoring of all functions as they happen on some units. One unit has a thermal printer which prints 5 × 7 dot-matrix characters on a 2.5-in. tape. It prints 20 characters per line.

printed circuit — 1. A circuit in which inter-connecting wires have been replaced by conductive strips printed, etched, etc., onto an insulating board. It may also include similarly formed components on the baseboard. 2. Refers to resistors, capacitors, diodes, transistors and other circuit elements which are mounted on cards and inter-connected by conductor deposits. These special cards are treated with light sensitive emulsion and exposed. The light thus fixes the areas to be retained and an acid bath eats away those portions which are designed to be destroyed. The base is usually a copper clad card.

printer, calculator — Refers to an alphanumeric output-only unit featuring fast speed, quiet operation, and low cost. One 5 × 7 dot matrix print head contains 35 heating elements which generate a 56-character set. The desired character is produced prior to contact with the heat-sensitive paper rather than on impact. It prints a maximum 80-character line at a rate of 30 characters per second.

printer, hand-held — Some units can be affixed to an optional printing unit to permanently record calculations in either calculate or execute mode. In the calculate mode, the printer can selectively print any or all desired intermediate results or provide a complete listing of a stored program. In the run mode, print instructions encountered in the program cause automatic printing of the quantity in the display. Trace mode printing prints all steps performed and corresponding results.

print key — 2nd prt — The key instructs the printer to print the contents of the display.

print-out, memory — A listing of the contents of a storage device, or selected parts of it. (Synonymous with memory dump and core dump.)

print x — On the HP-97 printer, the intermediate results need not be printed. Users can slide the Print Mode switch to NORM to preserve a record of the calculations, and then press 'print x' to print the final answer.

problem — A set of circumstances, situations, or states which develop when some unknown information is to be discovered, i.e., a solution is sought from some known information and a procedure is understood to acquire the unknown.

problem, check — A problem chosen to determine whether the calculator or a program is operating correctly.

problem-solver libraries, financial (calculator) — To assist users in performing financial analyses, some problem solver libraries provide routines for:
- Return on investment
- Discounted cash flow
- Multiple loan analysis
- Single loan analysis
- Leave vs. purchase
- Make vs. buy
- Break-even under certainty
- Break-even under uncertainty
- Depreciation
- Growth rate
- Moving average
- Seasonal analysis
- Cyclical analysis
- Auto covariance/autocorrelation
- Crosscovariance/crosscorrelation
- Exponential smoothing
- Simple regression
- Histogram

problem, test A problem chosen to determine whether the calculator or a program is operating correctly.

process — 1. A course of events occurring according to an intended purpose or effect. 2. A systematic sequence of operations to produce a specified result. 3. To perform operations on data.

processor — A central control unit or set of compiler programs which provide translating, assembling, and related software functions for a given programming language.

product area — Some calculators have an area in main storage to store results of multiplication operations specifically.

product-to-memory-key — 'PROD nn' — The product-to-memory key is used to add the displayed quantity to the specified memory. When 'INV' '2nd' 'PROD' 'nn' is pressed, the number of the specified memory is divided by the displayed number and the results are stored in the same memory.

program — 1. A set of instructions arranged in a proper sequence for directing advanced calculators in performing a desired operation or operations (e.g., the solution of a mathematical problem or the collation of a set of data). 2. To prepare a program (as contrasted with "to code").

program advantages, low cost calculators — Programs are written to save time on repetitive calculations. Once users have written the keystroke procedure for solving a particular problem and recorded it in the calculator, they need no longer devote attention to the individual keystrokes that make up the procedure. They can let the calculator solve each problem for them. And because users can easily check the procedure in their program, they have more confidence in the final answer since they don't have to worry each time about whether or not they have pressed an incorrect key. The calculator performs the drudgery, leaving user's minds free for more creative work.

program, applications — A program written to accomplish a specific user task (such as payroll) as opposed to a supervisory, general purpose, or utility program.

programs, calculating — By using prerecorded magnetic cards (like those supplied in the packages shipped with many calculators) users can do highly complex calculations with minimal effort or study of the calculator itself. Users load a card into the calculator and let the stored program handle the busy part of the calculation. Typically, they just key in the data and start the program running. The program stops when it needs more data or when it displays a result.

program, calculator (low cost) — For small units a program is nothing more than a sequence of manual keystrokes that is remembered by the calculator. Users can then execute the program as often as they like with less chance of error. The answer displayed at the end of execution is the same one users would have obtained by pressing the keys one at a time manually. No prior programming experience is necessary for most small calculator programming.

program chaining — Situations may arise where programs are too long for computer memory. A convenient technique to use if this problem arises is to break the programs into segments and store these segments on tape cassettes. The segments are then loaded into the memory one segment at a time and executed. This procedure is termed "PRO-GRAM CHAINING".

program coding — To write down the step-by-step instructions of a program. Program code results from that program design process.

program counter — The internal counter which controls program execution by sequencing through program memory.

programmable — Capable of being set to operate in a specified manner, or of accepting remote set-points or other commands.

programming keys, calculator — The Programming Keys allow users to write and edit programs, plus they double as special function keys which can be defined to execute a program or a part of a program at the touch of a single key, as components of advanced programmable calculators.

program operation, learn mode — With the calculator in the learn mode, users can construct a program using any of the control, data entry, function and data memory keys and the program control and user-defined keys. On some units, up to 224 entries may be programmed in the learn mode.

program read-card — Insert card, printed side up, into the card reader slot on the right side of the calculator. When the card is partially into the slot, a motor engages and passes the card through the calculator and out a similar slot on the left side of the calculator.

program register — 1. Register in the control unit that stores the current instruction of the program and controls calculator operation during the execution of the program. 2. A temporary storage device or area which retains the instruction code of the instruction being executed.

program saving, calculator — To save the program, users pass a blank card through the calculator, switch to W/PRGM. They write the new definitions of keys A, . . . , E on the magnetic card together with the program title. They then fill out the User Instruction Form to remind how to run the program at a later time. They can write their instructions on the Pocket Instruction Card and carry the magnetic program card with them. There are many possible ways to write programs which give users the required answers. Doubtless many can think of other ways. Some may wish to build variable entry capability into the program instead of storing them manually. Others may wish to have programs calculate differently, etc. (some units)

PROM — 1. Programmable Read-Only Memory is generally any type which is not recorded during its fabrication but which requires a physical operation to program it. Some PROMs can be erased and reprogrammed through special physical processes. 2. A semiconductor diode array which is programmed by fusing or burning out diode junctions.

PROM calculator chip advantages — A calculator chip, when controlled by a PROM and with the help of several mux/demux circuits, can handle arithmetic computation more efficiently than a microprocessor, and the calculator needs no complex compiler software.

protection key — An indicator designed to allow the program access to sections of memory which the program may use, and a denial of access to all other parts of memory, i.e., a memory-protection device with a key which is numbered by the calculator. Usually such keys are for most locations in memory, and when a storage key differs from the program protection key, the program can be interrupted and taken over by a supervisory program to handle the problem which arises.

queue — Refers to waiting lines resulting from temporary delays in providing service.

RAM (Random Access Memory) — This type memory is random because it provides access to any storage location point in the memory immediately by means of vertical and horizontal coordinates. Information may be 'written' in or 'read' out in the same very fast procedure.

random access memory — A memory whose information media are organized into discrete locations, sectors, etc., each uniquely identified by an address. Data may be obtained from such a memory by specifying the data address(es) to the memory, i.e., core, drum, disk.

R↓ and R↑ keys — Rolls down and up the contents of the stack for viewing in displayed X-register.

reading — The process of loading a program from a magnetic card into the program memory.

read only memory (ROM). — A medium scale integrated circuit storage device containing instructions preprogrammed at the manufacturer. The system can obtain program instructions from the ROM but cannot alter the data in the ROM except by ultra violet erasure, in most cases.

readouts, pocket calculator — Readouts for portable and pocket-sized calculator products are available in four different varieties; light-emitting diodes (LEDs), gas discharge, fluorescent, and liquid crystal. By far, red LEDs are the most widely used, usually for practical rather than esthetic reasons.

recall key — Used to recall intermediate statistical quantities stored inside the units for example, sums of squares, sums of cross products, cell contents, etc. (some units)

recall memory key — Automatically recalls an amount from independent memory for use as a factor in any operation.

recharger — A device used to recharge the NiCd batteries found in many smaller calculators.

RCL key — Recall. Followed by address key, this recalls number from primary storage register (R_0 through R_9, R_A through R_E, 1) to zero. (some units)

RCL nn — Recall key. The recall key is used to recall the contents of the specified memory to the display.

record — Refers to a collection of fields; the information relating to one area of activity in a data processing activity. i.e., all information on one inventory item. Sometimes called item.

record program keys — (1) Read/Write. Reads a program from a card into program memory. (2) Inverse Read/Write. Writes (records) a program on the magnetic card from program memory.

recoverable error — Refers to an error condition that allows continued execution of a program.

rectangular coordinates key — The key converts polar magnitude and angle in X- and Y-registers to rectangular x and y coordinates.

recursion — 1. The continued repeating of the same operation or group of operations. 2. Any procedure A, which, while being executed, either calls itself or calls a procedure, B, which in turn calls procedure A.

recursive — Pertaining to a process that is inherently repetitive. The result of each repetition.

redundancy check — Refers to an automatic or programmed check based on the systematic insertion in a message of bits or characters that are used for error-checking purposes; they are redundant, as they can be eliminated without the loss of essential information. Parity checking is a form of redundancy checking.

register — A generic term for any calculator storage unit which may be used to hold a numerical value. See internal processing registers, addressable register, similar to subroutine level counter.

register, accumulator — Refers to that part of the arithmetic unit in which the results of an operation remains, and into which numbers are brought to and from storage.

register arithmetic, calculator — This means the calculator has several memories into which users can store constants or other numbers used more than once in a problem and they can call any one of these back at will so that they have to do very little writing down of numbers. Users can directly add to, subtract from, divide into, or multiply the contents of a memory register. This is handy in solving three simultaneous linear equations or doing similar problems. In addition, certain pocket calculators have a memory called an operational stack. With these, entries and intermediate answers are stored automatically and then re-entered into the calculation at the appropriate time. The vertical stack arrangement is an essential part of RPN-Reverse Polish notation.

register operation, hand-programmable calculator — Efficient evaluation of mathematical expressions is achieved on some units by using four temporary memory registers arranged in a stack in combination with reverse Polish (Lukaiewicz) notation. The operational stack consists of X, Y, Z, and T registers. Intermediate results stored in this stack can be automatically recalled when they are required for further processing by the calculator, eliminating the need for scratch notes or manual re-entry.

Numbers enter the stack from the bottom on a first-in, last-out basis. As a number is keyed in, it goes into the X register and is displayed; when SAVE is pressed, the number is repeated in the Y register, and any number in Y moves up to Z, any number in Z moves up to T, and T is lost. When an operation is performed on data in X and Y, the answer automatically appears on the display and the entire stack drops. (some units)

relational symbols —

Symbol	Sample Relation	Explanation
=	A = B	A is equal to B
<	A < B	A is less than B
< =	A < = B	A is less than or equal to B
>	A > B	A is greater than B
> =	A > = B	A is greater than or equal to B
< >	A < > B	A is not equal to B

repeat add key — On some units this adds the input number to the accumulator. The total contents of the accumulator are displayed while the individual entrys are printed (aligned to the decimal switch) and truncated. "Repeat add" feature also refers to a key that will also execute a previously conditioned multiplication or division. It also executes the percent add-on sequence.

reset — To restore to zero; especially to restore a flag to zero. Also, the instruction which resets all flags, resets the return-pointer registers, and positions the program counter to 000.

reset flag keys, calculator — Reset Flag keys lower or clear specified flag. If Flag. tests to see if specified flag is set. If it is, then transfer occurs to the location or label. If flag is reset, no transfer occurs. For example, 2nd if flg 3011 means if flag is set, transfer to program location 011. Or, 2nd if flg 3 A means if flag 3 is set, transfer to that segment of the program labeled A. Test Flag tests to see if specified flag is set. If it is not, then transfer occurs to the location or label. If it is, no transfer. For example, INV 2nd if flg 3 A means transfer to A if flag 3 is reset. (some units)

reset key, error — Refers to a push button that when pushed acknowledges an error and resets the error detection mechanism indicated by the check light. This is required to restart a program after an error has been discovered in batch mode.

reset program key — This instructs the calculator to reset the program counter, all user flags (0-4) and the subroutine return-pointer register to zero.

"return" key — In many calculators, the "Return" key enables the user to start at the beginning of his program again. If this key is used as part of a stored program, it stops execution of the program and returns control to the keyboard for manual operation.

return key, subroutine — The return key stops execution of a subroutine and branches back to the instruction following the last subroutine branch. Program will halt on a return instruction if there is no address in the subroutine return-pointer register, or if the subroutine was called manually from the keyboard.

return pointer — An indicator showing where to return control in a program after the processing sequence has been diverted to a subroutine.

return pointer registers — The two registers which internally provide the return pointers for up to two subroutines. (T)

reverse Polish notation (RPN) — A type of logic in calculators which allows the user to enter every problem from left to right exactly as it is written. There is no need to be concerned about operational hierarchy as the logic system handles it all automatically. This type of logic is distinguishable because the electronic calculator has no equals key. It has an enter key instead. (See RPN definitions.)

RND key — Rounds mantissa of 10-digit number in X-register to actual value seen in the display.

robot — Refers to a specific device equipped with sensing instruments for detecting input signals or environmental conditions but with a reacting or guidance mechanism, which can perform sensing, calculations, etc., and with stored programs for resultant actions, i.e., a machine running itself.

ROM (read only memory) — 1. A blank ROM can be considered to be a mosaic of undifferentiated cells. Many types of ROMs exist. A basic type of ROM is one programmed by a mask pattern as part of the final manufacturing stage. PROMs are 'programmable' ROMs. ROMs are relatively permanent although they can be erased with the aid of an ultraviolet irradiation instrument. Others can be electrically erased and are called EPROMs. 2. Information is stored permanently or semi-permanently and is read out, but not altered in operation.

root — A number which produces a given number when taken as a factor an indicated number of times, i.e., 2 is the 4th root of 16.

RO (Receive Only) — A receive only printer.

round — To adjust the least significant digits retained in truncation to partially reflect the dropped portion; e.g., when rounded to the digits, the decimal number 2.7561 becomes 2.76.

round down (TRUNCATE, CUTOFF) — The ability to ignore and drop any digits beyond a certain decimal position.

round equals key — On some units this key will execute a previously conditioned operation and will print and display the answer aligned and rounded as required. In the case of addition or subtraction, the accumulator will be printed and displayed and cleared.

rounding — Often less important or less significant digits are dropped for development of increased accuracy by adding the more significant digits that are retained. The rounding rule of adding 5 in the left-most position to be dropped would then round 2.3456 to 2.346 for rounding to three decimals.

rounding error — The error that results when the less significant digits of a number are dropped and the most significant digits are then adjusted.

round up — Similar to round off except that in examining the extra position, if that digit is a one or greater, it increases the previous digit by one.

routine — A set of calculator instructions arranged in a correct sequence and used to direct a calculator.

RPN keying order — Some systems can save a number in each of the four registers. Most problems can be solved by keying in the numbers in the same order as they appear in the original expression, that is, from left-to-right. To work a problem, users key in the first number. If there is an operation they can perform at this point, they do it. If there is not, they press ENTER↑. Now they key in the next number. They perform any operation that can be done (+, −, ×, ÷, etc.). If there is no operation they can perform, they ENTER↑ this number and repeat the procedure, keying in the next number.

RPN method — The RPN method does take some getting used to. But, once users learn it, they can use the RPN method to solve almost any mathematical expression — confidently, consistently. Proponents suggest these four easy-to-follow steps:

1. Starting at the left side of the problem, key in the first or next number.
2. Determine if any operations can be

performed. If so, do all operations possible.

3. If not, press ENTER↑ to save the number for future use.

4. Repeat steps 1 through 3 until the calculation is completed.

run — 1. One routine or several routines automatically linked so that they form an operating unit, during which manual interruptions are not normally required to be made by the calculator operator. 2. One performance of a routine on a calculator involving loading, reading, processing and writing. 3. The execution of one or more programs that are linked to form one operating program.

run, calculate, and learn modes — With some calculator systems, the run mode allows users to quickly solve complex problems with programs from prerecorded magnetic cards. The calculate mode lets them use hand-held units as powerful calculators to solve problems manually. And with the learn mode, users of these units teach the calculator unique calculating methods. In one specific line all modes can use nine levels of parentheses, 20 independent memory registers and 224 program locations. When users combine this capability with prerecorded programs, or programs they originate, they have a valuable computational resource.

run key — RUN — Instructs calculator to execute a program, beginning with present location of program counter.

run/stop — R/S key — This had the effect of reversing the status of processing. If a program is running it will be stopped; if it is stopped, 'R/S' will restart processing at the current position of the program counter. When 'R/S' is encountered within a program, processing is halted until 'R/S' is pressed again. This allows for data entry or a look at intermediate results before the end of processing.

run switch — The W/PRGM-RUN switch on some units is set to run when a program is being read and to W/PRGM to write a program on a card.

scientific notation — The number is entered or a result is displayed in terms of a power of 10. For example, the number 1234 is entered as $1.234 \times 10^{+3}$ and the number 0.001234 would appear as 1.234×10^{-3}.

scientific pocket calculators A scientific calculator performs all arithmetic,

log and trig calculations, including rectangular/polar conversions and common antilog evaluations. And it lets users do their trig functions in either radians or degrees. Users just flip a switch. They also generally offer full display formatting, so users can choose between fixed decimal and scientific notation.

scientific professional calculators — A professional scientific calculator should provide the standard log and trig functions, so users don't have to refer to tables or interpolate from those tables. These "full scientific" calculators also provide exponential, square root and reciprocal functions. For handling more advanced types of scientific, engineering, mathematical or statistical problems, an "advanced scientific" calculator is necessary with the built-in functions found in the full scientific machines, plus a variety of others, depending upon which model is selected. These may include: mean, standard deviation, linear regression (trend line), and U.S./metric conversions. Advanced models also offer more memory power, more sophisticated trig functions, such as rectangular coordinate/polar coordinate conversion, selectable modes (degrees, radians and, possibly grads), conversion between decimal angle and angle in degrees/minutes/seconds . . . and others. This added capability facilitates the handling of complex problems and can drastically reduce the time and effort necessary to solve them. For example, polar/rectangular coordinate conversions lets users add or subtract vector components in seconds, simply by pressing a few keys. The most proficient type of professional scientific pocket calculators is the programmable. When solving complex, repetitive or iterative problems, programming can be invaluable. Users enter a problem-solving sequence of keystrokes just once. . . . then, with just one keystroke initiate the entire sequence — as often as desired. Whatever scientific calculator is chosen, the more functions and features it has, the more capability it has to solve more types of problems — problems that are most complex — faster and easier, reducing work, and the chance for error.

second function accessing — Many calculator keys have dual (or more) functions. To execute a function shown on the key, users simply press that key. On many units the first function is printed on the key and the second function command is executed by pressing '2nd' then pressing the key immediately below the desired second function. When '2nd' is pressed twice in succession, the calculator returns to first-function operation.

second function, calculator — The second function on most systems provides a second use for nearly every key, increasing the power of the calculator without increasing its size.

semantics — Refers to the relationships between symbols and their intended meanings independent of their interpretation devices.

semiconductor — 1. A material with an electrical conductivity between that of a metal and an insulator. Its electrical conductivity, which is generally very sensitive to the presence of impurities and some structural faults, will increase as the temperature does. This is in contrast with a metal, in which conductivity decreases as its temperature rises. 2. A material whose resistivity is between that of conductors and insulators, and whose resistivity can sometimes be changed by light, an electric field or a magnetic field.

sensor — Refers to a transducer or other device whose input is a quantitative measure of some external physical phenomenon and whose output can be read by a computer or calculator.

sequence memory, calculator — Some low-priced calculators contain a programmable sequence memory. For example, one model remembers a sequence of function-key operations up to a total of 10. This includes any sequence of plus-equals (+ =); minus-equals (− =; multiply (×); divide (÷); percent (%); add to memory (M+); subtract from memory (M−); and recall memory (RM). Clear memory (CM) cannot be used in a program, but this function is programmed by depressing recall-memory twice. Thus, the user can store a program and repeat it without having to remember the particular key operations initially required.

set flag key — The set-flag key, followed by a 1-digit number (0-4) indicates which of the five available flags is to be set. A special key sequence will reset the specified flag to zero. (some units)

SF Set flag — Followed by flag designator (0, 1, 2, or 3) sets flag true.

short circuit — 1. Also called a short. 2.

An abnormal connection of relatively low resistance between two points of a circuit. The result is a flow of excess (often damaging) current between these points.

sigma (Σ, accumulate) — A key or switch that will automatically total the results of a series of calculations. This key or switch identifies an automatic register.

sign — 1. A symbol which distinguishes negative from positive quantities. 2. A symbol which indicates whether a quantity is greater or less than zero.

signal — 1. A visable, audible, or other conveyor of information. 2. The intelligence, message, or effect to be conveyed over a communication system.

significant digit — A digit that contributes to the precision of a numeral. The number of significant digits is counted beginning with the digit contributing the most value, called the most significant digit, and ending with the one contributing the least value, called the least significant digit.

significant figures (overflow sign) — This is the result displayed after automatic machine runoff. For example, when an eight-digit calculator computes 45689 × 98754, it will display 45115603, although the actual result is 4511560305. The last two digits, 0 and 5, are not displayed, since the machine is limited to eight digits; only the most significant ones are displayed. The symbol to the left of the result indicates that the number is larger than the display can handle (i.e., overflow sign). (some units)

sine key — Instruct the calculator to determine the sine of the displayed angle. Pressing 'INV' 'sin' instructs the calculator to interpret the displayed argument as the sine of an angle and to calculate the angle. (some units)

single step — Pertaining to a method of operating a calculator in which each step is performed in response to a single manual operation.

single step debug — One innovative feature of some units is the behavior of the SST (Single Step) key in run mode. This key was designed to help the user debug programs. It allows the user to execute his program one key phrase at a time. When the SST key is held down, the display shows the line number and the key phrase that is to be executed next. Releasing the SST key executes just that key phrase, and the numerical results appear in the display. This feature makes debugging programs quite easy because the user can tiptoe through his programs, seeing both the key phrases and their results, one phrase at a time. The display when the SST key is held down includes the step number, so checking program flow and branching is easy.

single step key — SST — Causes the program counter to be incremented by one. In the learn mode, pressing this key causes the next storage location to be displayed. When not in the learn mode, pressing this key causes the program to be executed one step at a time. The single step key may not be used as a label or stored in a program. (some units)

single-step key, small systems — Displays step number and keycode of current program memory step when pressed; executes instruction, displays result, and moves to next step when released.

single-step operation — A method of operating an automatic calculator manually, in which a single instruction or part of an instruction is performed in response to a single operation of a manual control. This method is generally used for detecting mistakes.

single-variable functions — These are the simplest operations and operate only on the display register and do not interact with the full algebraic hierarchy. Thus, they may be used at any point in a calculation. Examples are: Square key, Reciprocal key, common log key. (T)

skip instruction — An instruction having no effect other than directing the processor to proceed to another instruction designated in the storage portion.

sliderule calculations — Most such operations are interpreted to be: roots, squares, powers, reciprocals, factorials, common and natural logarithms and their inverses, trigonometric (sin, cos, tan) and hyperbolic (sinh, cosh, tanh) functions and their inverses, etc.

software — 1. The term software was invented to contrast with the "iron" or hardware of a computer system. Software items are programs, languages, and procedures of a computer system. Software libraries for microprocessors are being built and assembled in heavy competition among suppliers, both manufacturers and distributors. 2. The internal programs or routines are prepared professionally to simplify programming and computer operations. Uses permit the programmer to use his own language (English) or mathematics (algebra) in communicating with the calculator. 3. Various programming aids are frequently supplied by the manufacturers to facilitate the purchaser's efficient operation of the equipment. Such software items include various assemblers, generators, subroutine libraries, compilers, operating systems, and industry-application programs.

space character — Relates to a special operating and graphic character designed to prevent a print. (SP)

special function keys, calculator — There are ten special function keys in the upper-left keyboard area of some models. Each key can have two functions or programs assigned to it for a maximum of twenty. The special function keys can be used effectively in 3 different ways.

1. To represent text where text is used as a typing aid.
2. To represent functions. The functions can be single or multi-line functions and different parameters can be passed to the function from the mainline program or between functions.
3. To represent an entire program.

Programming and editing rules for the special function keys are the same as those for normal programming.

special function keys (SFK) — Special function keys (hence SFK) reduce complex calculations to a few simple entries. From these hardwired keys, users can order groups of four or six. The result is a calculator that users virtually design themselves for their own applications. The potential applications are virtually endless. Some of the special function keys are: depreciation, mark-up, amortization, loan payment, power (for integer exponents), per cent change, mean, standard deviation, store in, store out, etc. The result — complex problems become simple enough for even untrained operators.

special routine keys, calculators — Some types of molded, high-rise keys give users error-free instant access to up to 32 hard-wired Special Routines and up to 32 of their own programmed routines. Each register or program is clearly labeled with color-coded interchangeable routine strips, on some units.

square root key — Automatically computes the square root of any positive entry or result.

SST key — When one unit is in the "WRITE PROGRAM" mode, this "SINGLE STEP" key lets users step through each program instruction in the program memory, as the display shows a number for each step. This number represents the location (row and column) of the key corresponding to that particular instruction. For example, "34" refers to the key in row 3, column 4 — "RCL." (Exception: digit keys are represented by the numbers 00 to 09.) If the "SST" key is used with this unit the "RUN" mode users can execute a program one step at a time.

stack advantages — A pushdown stack is essentially a Last-in-First-Out (LIFO) buffer. As data are added, the stack moves down, with the last item added taking the top position. Stack height varies with the number of stored items, increasing or decreasing with the entering or retrieving of data. The words "push" (move down) and "pop" (retrieve the most recently stored item) are used to describe its operation. In actual practice, a hardware-implemented pushdown stack is a collection of registers with a counter which serves as a "pointer" to indicate the most recently loaded register. Registers are unloaded in the reverse of the sequence in which they were loaded. The principal benefit of the pushdown stack is an aid to compiling. By reducing the use of registers necessary for temporary storage, stack architecture can greatly decrease the number of steps required in a program, thereby reducing costs.

stack, automatic memory — Automatic storage is made possible on some units as registers inside the calculator are positioned to form the automatic memory stack. These registers are labelled X, Y, Z, and T. The displayed X register is the only visible one and is *stacked* on the bottom. The four registers are cleared to zero when the unit is switched ON. (some units)

stack lift enable/disable, hand-held programmables — On some specific units, when users key in a new number after a calculation, the calculated result is automatically lifted in the stack, relieving users of the need to save the result (by pressing ENTER↑) before keying in the number. The same lifting action occurs if users recall a value to X from a storage register, from the Last X register, or if users recall the permanently stored value of π. Users may have observed that certain other operations also enable the

Stack Lift while CLX and ENTER↑ disable the lift (after CLX and ENTER↑ are pressed). Users will generally be quite unaware of the lift status because the operation is so natural for most calculations. However, many operations have no effect on the Stack Lift.

stack manipulation — The R↓ (roll down), R↑ (roll up) and x⇌y (x exchange y) keys allow users to review the stack contents or to shift data within the stack for computation at any time. The contents of the registers only are shifted; the actual registers themselves maintain their positions. The $h\downarrow R$ and $h\uparrow R$ keys roll the stack contents up or down one to four times. The h $x\rightleftharpoons y$ exchanges contents of the X and Y registers.

stack review — Users can quickly review the contents of the stack at any time using the g STK operation. When they press these keys, the contents of the stack are shifted, one register at a time, into the X-register and displayed for about a half-second each. The order of display is T, Z, Y, and the X-register contents again. While a g STK operation is being performed, the decimal point blinks twice during the display of the contents of each register, to identify this function as a pause during a running program. The program has not stopped. Pressing and holding any key while the calculator is executing a stack review, freezes the contents of the stack in the display, permitting the user to write down or examine the number. Upon release, the contents of the next stack register to be displayed is shown.

stack rotating, small calculators — The R↓ (roll down) key lets users review the entire stack contents at any time. To see how this key works, load the stack with the numbers 1 through 4 by pressing:

4 ENTER↑ 3 ENTER↑ 2 ENTER↑ 1

If users then press R↓, the stack contents are rotated.

standard deviation key — The standard deviation (a measure of dispersion around the mean) is calculated using data in the applicable storage registers and the s (standard deviation) key. Pressing fs uses the data in registers R_3 (n), R_6 (Σx^2), and R_7 (Σx) to calculate the standard deviation according to the formula:

$$s_x = \sqrt{\dfrac{\sum x^2 - \dfrac{(\sum x)^2}{n}}{n-1}}$$

as used in some units.

STEP and LIST keys — On some units STEP and LIST keys are used for debugging and program documentation. Editing is also available in these units. The register arithmetic keys help eliminate keystrokes in the program and are useful in statistical applications. Indirect addressing of data registers is possible in the simplest manner and shortens the number of program steps users need to do for successive operations on a number of pieces of data.

STK key — Automatic stack review. Flashes contents of stack in order T, Z, Y, X, with blinking decimal point operating.

sto — store key — Followed by a number key, it stores displayed number in storage registers specified. Followed by arithmetic operator key, it performs storage register arithmetic. (some units)

STO nn — **store key** — The store key is used to store the displayed number in the specified memory.

stop key A push button on the control panel which can halt the processing. This often happens only after the completion of an instruction being executed at a given moment.

storage — 1. The act of storing information (also see store). 2. Sometimes called a memory. Any device in which information can be stored. 3. A calculator section used primarily for storing information in electrostatic, ferroelectric, magnetic, acoustic, optical, chemical, electronic, electrical, mechanical, etc., form. Such a section is sometimes called a memory, or a store, in British terminology. 4. Pertaining to a device into which data can be entered, in which they can be held, and from which they can be retrieved at a later time.

storage, nonvolatile — Storage media that retains information in the absence of power and which may be made available upon restoration of power, e.g., magnetic tapes, drums, or cores.

storage register — A register is used for storing numbers. Unlike the memory register, no addition or subtraction in this register is possible. It is a place to put a number until needed later in the calculations. For example, when utilizing a constant, that number is placed into storage and recalled at the point in calculating when it is needed.

storage stack — A group of storage elements connected together in some fashion,

i.e., a stack of data could be operated on a first-in, first-out basis.

storage types, nesting — As data is transferred into storage, each word in turn enters the top register and is then "pushed down" the column from register to register to make room for the subsequent words as they are assigned. When a word is transferred out of the storage, again only from the top register, other data in the storage moves back up the column from register to register to fill the space left empty. This is accomplished either through programs or the equipment itself.

store — 1. To transfer an element of information to a device from which the unaltered information can be obtained at a later time. 2. To retain data in a device from which it can be obtained at a later time.

store memory key — Automatically stores an entry or result in an independent memory.

storing and recalling data, hand-held programmables — To store a number appearing in the display (whether the result of a calculation or keystroke entry), on some systems:

1. Press STO.
2. Press a number key 1 through 9 to specify in which of the nine registers the number is to be stored.

If the selected storage register already has a number in it, the old number will be overwritten by the new one. The value in X will remain unchanged. To recall a number previously stored in one of the nine addressable memory registers; on the same system:

1. Press RCL.
2. Press a number key (1 through 9) to specify which of the nine registers the number is to be recalled from.

Recalling a number does not remove it from the storage register. Rather, a copy of the stored number is transferred to the display — the original remains in the storage register until either: (1) a new number is stored in the same register, (2) the calculator is turned off, or (3) all nine registers are cleared by pressing.

storing and recalling numbers, nonstack — Although the stack automatically holds intermediate results in some units occasionally users will find the need to set aside some number or group of numbers to be used in calculations much later.

For this purpose, some units provide users with 20 or more storage locations in addition to the stack.

subroutine — An isolated program segment used primarily for repetitive calculations. It returns to the calling routine (either the main or another subroutine) upon completion of its task.

subroutine key — SBR yyy or Label — The subroutine key must be followed by a label or a 3-digit address indicating the subroutine the program is to execute next. Some calculators are capable of two levels of surboutines. A return (rtn) instruction in a subroutine will automatically return the program to the program address immediately following SBR yyy or Label. (T)

subroutine level counter — An indicator showing where to return control in a program after the processing sequence has been diverted to a subroutine.

subtotal key — On some units this key will print the accumulator contents without alignment on truncation and without altering machine status.

sum and store key — Adds the displayed number algebraically to the number in the memory.

summations key — Summation calculations use the $\Sigma +$ (Sigma plus) key to total numbers for use in other calculations. These summations are particularly useful when working with vectors and statistics.

SUM nn — sum-to-memory key — This is used to add the displayed quantity to the specified memory. When INV SUM nn is pressed, the displayed number is subtracted from the specified memory.

sum + key ($\Sigma +$) — Instant conversion from polar to rectangular coordinates . . . or vice-versa. And vector calculations are available when users also use the $\Sigma +$ key to simultaneously accumulate two coordinates on some units. Statistical analysis is easier . . . because the $\Sigma +$ key provides a running total when summing numbers, keeps track of the number of entries, and automatically computes the sum of the squares. The $\bar{x},s$ key calculates the arithmetic mean and the standard deviation.

systems approach — Looking at the over-all situation rather than the narrow implications of the task at hand; particularly, looking for interrelationships between the task at hand and other functions which relate to it.

tangent key — tan — Instructs the calculator to determine the tangent of the displayed angle. Pressing 'INV' 'tan' instructs the calculator to interpret the displayed arguments as the tangent of an angle and to calculate the angle. (T)

test data — Refers to a set of data developed specifically to test the adequacy of a calculator run or system. The data may be actual data that have been taken from previous operations, or artificial data created for this purpose. (some units)

test flag key — The Test Flag key tests to see if a specified flag is set. If it is not, then transfer occurs to the location or label. If it is, no transfer. For example, INV 2nd if flg 3 A means transfer to A if flag 3 is reset.

test flags keys condition — The condition of the flags can be tested automatically at any point in user programs by using these "TEST FLAG 1" and "TEST FLAG 2" keys to include an appropriate test flag instruction. The program will either advance sequentially or skip over the next steps, depending on the condition of the tested flag. These keys allow users to compare the values in the X and Y registers. If the test condition is not met, the program skips over the next two steps. If the test condition is met, the program continues with the next step. This allows the users to perform conditional branches based on the results of the test. (some units)

test register — On some units this is the register to which the display is compared for conditional branches, or checking intermediate results for possible pass along to subroutine operations.

thermal printer, calculator — For high quality, hard-copy output one type Thermal Printer provides 260 lines/minute speed equivalent to 3,600 words/minute. It produces page-width, fully-formatted, alphanumeric text, tables, or simple plots.

throughput — 1. Relates to the speed with which problems, programs, or segments are performed. Throughput can vary from application as well as from one piece of equipment to another although they are the same brand, and even model. 2. The total useful information processed or communicated during a specified time period.

time-sharing — 1. A computing technique by which more than one terminal device can use the input, processing and output facilities of a central computer simultaneously. 2. A specific method of operation in which a computer facility is shared by several users for different purposes at (apparently) the same time. Although the computer actually services each user in sequence, the high speed of the computer makes it appear that the users are all handled simultaneously.

top-down — The approach whereby a problem is solved in the large before details are filled in.

trace — A printer capability for automatically recording each step executed and its result.

trace mode — The trace mode is a valuable tool in debugging programs. Users can either select it from the keyboard or program it to examine part of a program's activity, then cancel it with a normal statement following the suspected part of the program, on some systems. The trace mode is obtained with the TRACE key. In this mode, during program execution the printer lists the number of each line and any quantities it stores. This allows users to verify intermediate results and detect logic errors. (some units)

trace operation — The trace mode for some units is a print function which is commanded from the printer rather than from the calculator. It is particularly useful in tracing manual computations, providing hard copy of the results, and in debugging programs.

trace switch — On the HP-97, the best way to see how simple functions operate is with the Print Mode switch set to *trace* to give a complete record of inputs, functions, and answers.

transcendental functions — Transcendental functions are those such as sines, cosines, logarithms, etc.: and polar/rectangular coordinate conversions for handling vectors and complex arithmetic.

transducers devices — Refers to specific elements or devices which have the capability of receiving information in the form of one physical quantity and converting it to information in the form of the same or other physical quantities. This particularly relates to specific cases of devices such as primary elements, signal transducers and various transmitters.

transfer instructions — Those instructions which can cause the program counter to be repositioned to a point other than that which would be reached by normal incrementing. There are several types of transfers on some units:

If Positive. Tests display register for positive or zero. If it is, transfer occurs to a location or label. If the test fails, transfer does not occur. If zero. Tests display register for zero. If it is, transfer occurs to a location or label. If not, no transfer. If Error. Tests for an error condition (flashing display). If it is, transfer occurs to a location or label. If not, no transfer. Decrement and Skip on Zero. Decrements the contents of memory register 00, then tests these contents for zero. If it is not zero, transfer occurs to a location or label. If it is, no transfer.

t-register — Special test register separate from other storage areas. For conditional branching tests and special functions.

trigonometric functions — Trigonometric and inverse trigonometric functions use the D/R switch mode selected when accepting an argument or returning a result. The domain of the inverse sine or cosine function is defined for $-1 \le y \le 1$.

truncation — 1. Ending of a computational procedure in accordance with some program rule as soon as a specified accuracy has been reached. 2. Rejection of final digits in a number, thus lessening precision (but not necessarily accuracy).

two-number functions — Two-number functions require two numbers to be present in order for the operation to be successful. Plus, minus, divide, and multiply are examples. The operation occurs when the function key is pressed; both numbers must be in the calculator BEFORE the function key is pressed. (some units)

unconditional transfers — Unconditional transfers *always* reposition the program counter to some out-of-sequence location. **Conditional transfers,** or branching instructions, make a test and either transfer or not (fall through) depending upon the outcome of the test.

underflow — When the calculator's capacity is exceeded, some of the least significant digits are discarded and the resulting display is sometimes zero.

underflow (continue), small calculators — If a result develops that is too small in magnitude to be carried in a register ($< 10^{-99}$), the register is set to zero; a running program would continue execution.

underflow indicator — 0.0000000 appears in the display and a warning light is possibly activated. In many electronic calculators that number is lost, but some provide a capability to retrieve the number.

user definable keys, advanced calculator — A special feature that aids the advanced calculator's role as a terminal is a set of up to 20 user-definable keys, called special function keys, that are available to store often-used sequences like telephone numbers or user sign-on codes. Only a single keystroke is needed to dial a telephone number, to send a user code, or to perform an entire sign-on sequence including dialing.

user-definable keys, preprogrammed — On some units, 13 or more keys can be preprogrammed to execute specific functions by automatically jumping to specific locations within the unit's memory.

user-definable key tag (optional on some units) — On some units (mainly desk-top) eight or more user-definable keys can be converted to user-definable operation. In the CALC (some units), each key initiates a search for a specific tag in the program memory. The keys are labeled with the customer's description for the functions, helping to eliminate operator errors.

user defined keys — 'A' through 'E' '2nd' 'A" through '2nd' 'E". These keys instruct the calculator to perform a transfer to the subroutine associated with the key (when previously defined as a label) and automatically begin execution. (some units)

variable — 1. Any factor or condition which can be measured, altered, or controlled (e.g., temperature, pressure, flow, liquid level, humidity, weight, chemical composition, color, etc.). 2. A quantity that can assume any of a given set of values.

vector arithmetic — Many calculators are ideal for vector arithmetic problems. Once the sums of the x and y coordinates of all vectors are accumulated, they can be converted back to the equivalent polar form using the rectangular to polar function.

video terminal — A computer terminal that incorporates a cathode-ray tube (CRT) for displaying information on a screen. Some terminals are designed for data entry as well as display, and feature built-in microcomputers or minicomputers, both edit and format input, and operate as stand-alone data processing systems.

volatile — A characteristic of becoming lost or erased when power is removed, i.e., the loss of data where it is not returned or recovered when power is restored. Some such units, as tape units, are in a volatile condition if such a power loss occurs.

volt — MKSA unit of p.d. or e.m.f., such that the p.d. across a conductor is 1 volt when 1 amp in it dissipates 1 W of power. This is 1 J/s, or 10^7 erg/s, a mechanical unit.

watt — Abbreviated W. A unit of the electric power required to do work at the rate of 1 joule per second. It is the power expended when 1 ampere of direct current flows through a resistance of 1 ohm.

word — A set of characters that occupies one storage location and is treated by the computer circuits as a unit and transported as such. Ordinarily a word is treated by the control unit as an instruction.

write — In a computer: 1. To copy, usually from internal to external storage. 2. To transfer elements of information to an output medium. 3. To record information in a register, location, or other storage device or medium.

write key — A code in the program status double-word that is used in conjunction with a memory lock to determine whether or not a program may write into a specific page of actual addresses.

writing — The process of recording a program on a magnetic card.

W/PRGM switch — To load keystrokes into a program on H-P calculators, the W/PRGM-RUN switch should be set to W/PRGM, and the 'f' and 'clx' should be pressed to clear the calculator.

x exchange t key — This exchanges the display register value x with the T-register value t. This key is used for data entry with coordinate conversions and certain conditional tests described in manuals.

-x- Flash X — Pauses to display contents of X-register for 5 seconds. Used to write down answers or to interface programs with HP 67 to 97.

y to the x power key — Raises a number to a power.

CHAPTER 4

PROGRAMMABLE CALCULATORS — HAND-HELD UNITS: OPERATIONS AND APPLICATIONS

Computing Capability Without Computer Complexities

One of the prime purposes for developing this text was to emphasize the significant superiority of **programmable** calculators over *fixed capability* machines. For very narrow ranges of *on the job* operations, it is obvious that highly specialized preprogrammed machines, such as those specifically designed for statisticians, bankers, surveyors, etc. *might be* a good choice for these precisely limited uses. However, programmable units, as the pages ahead will attest, can be, and often are, highly preprogrammed for statistics, business functions, etc. and **additionally** contain programmable capability. And it can be strongly argued that practically every *on the job* user will many times in his career find the need for very specific self-developed programs that are *just right* for many slightly or solidly different tasks, procedures, or formulas he or she is required to use quite often. And the programmability feature then pays for itself many times. Many observers believe that, for the few extra dollars they might cost, programmables are practically always the best choice — and this is especially true for students at any level of their educational progress.

Most students are at first tempted to explore, as a curiosity, the unusual capabilities of calculators. Few of them want to be *locked in* to just those capabilities that are available as special function keys or as preprogrammed capabilities. Even for the *under $30* programmable units noted ahead, students find very wide ranges of adventure as they develop *their own* simple but personally valuable programs. They then can use them regularly, consistently, and very rapidly for particular problems and solutions. From a teacher's standpoint, the extra versatility offered by programmable units, even those with only 100 or so program step capability, provides the student with far greater ranges of opportunity for learning more combinations, more techniques, and neater procedures for solving both complex as well as the most elementary formula problems. The challenges, the wider range of opportunity, the pragmatic utilization of a great many specific formulas and techniques through programmability of calculating instruments practically assure an election of these types of machines for classroom and current or future *on the job* purchases. The several thousand members of the many calculator clubs, especially the HP-Users and TI Users Clubs, certainly realize and strongly profess the exciting capabilities of their programmables. And most *voting* students will *elect* programmables over *fixed function* machines.

Unfortunately many calculator buyers, especially those who are not mathematics-oriented, upon reading about the capabilities, capacities and procedures of various programmable units, become frightened with and about such words as: stacks, labels, subroutines, flags, branching, etc. But, with just a day or so of practice, with at least the simpler programmables, they find that using these handy program control *tools* is really quite easy. The first few pages of this chapter attempt to demonstrate this by beginning with the most elementary key-programmables, Sinclair's Cambridge and the Litronix 2290. The reader is first introduced to some simple four-function operations and is then lead very slowly into the Learn and Execute modes of elementary 10-step programs. Several sample programs are presented that relate specifically to both models before discussions of comparisons and contrasts are developed that are related to the next step-up units, the Sinclair Scientific Key-programmables, the National Semiconductor Key-programmable units, and the low-cost Canon units. Other key-programmables, similar to these, are available in the same price ranges. The very popular Hewlett-Packard model 25 and model 55 are analyzed, and they are comparable to the Texas Instruments' under $100 SR-56. A slightly different key-programmable, the Casio PRO 101 is discussed, and several programmed problem examples are displayed throughout the chapter to show some unique features of these low-cost key-programmable types.

Following this, in the next chapter some of the Monroe tape-programmable models are shown and described. There are many models of desk-top key-programmables, but the discussion of these is also left to the introductory section of the following chapter on Programmable Calculator Systems. The middle section of Chapter 5 is devoted to the hand-held *fully* or exterior programmable units. These are the exceptionally high-capability units that are, in effect, true hand-held computers. They include the Card-programmable TI 59 and HP-67/97 and others. Various other new machines are operable with file cartridges and tapes, and RAMs and ROMs. Although the attributes of these type machines will be compared and contrasted, the programming capabilities will be treated descriptively instead of tutorially. Programming manuals available with purchase from the manufacturers are very adequate to start users on their way. And the several User Club newsletters are very adept and thorough in providing explanations of the more exotic and special features of the expandable programming techniques of these units.

The Need for Sophisticated Capabilities from Simple, Easy-to-Use Products

Discussions were developed in the first sections of this book which related the use of calculators as being built within telephones, pens, watches, etc. Some companies incorporate them within leather-bound notebooks, 3-ring binders, desk-set memo-calendar sets, and scores of other convenient business and school appliances or aids. Because of today's very low prices for small calculator units, these novelty items can contain scientific and even programmable units — and with some very simple sensing and interfacing circuits, they can also control many appliances. A calculator's external appearance reveals very little about its true computer-like capability. And most calculators can now easily be equipped to supply more functions than log, trig, exponential, etc. plus memory and interrupt. And most include logic systems that are simple, consistent and practical to use.

The most important characteristics of these machines that develop a continuing attraction to businessmen, scientists, students, researchers, teachers, etc. are their very personal use. The user is in the midst of and has control of the calculating loop — he or she is not *outside* waiting for someone else to do the program, to address the terminal, or establish rules of how, when, and where to make computations. The computer-like power is immediately at hand — on the user's desk, at work or at home, and he or she can try alternative approaches, play hunches, try *what if* solutions. Programmable users can try their own routines. They do not rely only on existing programs, and if some of the absolute non-programmers do, there are tens of thousands of tested and proven programs from which they can choose. This permits users to make best use of their time resources by eliminating a great deal of manual calculating work and/or avoiding the delays inherent in working with a large computer system. With improved computing speed and accuracy these instruments save time in planning projects, developing prototype products, designing cost models, materials lists, inventory control, personnel records and payroll programs for many small financial, service, or manufacturing enterprises.

Conscientious users can learn to operate their programmable units in a few hours and can become truly expert programmers in just a few weeks of diligent study and practice. Editing and modifying programs is not too difficult, and new peripherals are being used and announced almost weekly. Many of the new input, memory, output, and control peripherals are described on pages in chapters ahead. Markets for portable, personal computing power and peripherals have been substantially broadened because customers have been provided with simpler products, services and versatile machines that they can personally *train* to operate as their needs require. Any two- to ten-person shop can now afford either personally-used hand-held programmable calculators or the very capable, but still low-cost, programmable desk-top units. These include the TI SR-60 *user-prompting* machine and the HP-97, the former somewhat more than $1000 and the latter considerably less. These two are outstanding among many other computing low-cost programmable calculator models.

Computer service bureaus offering remote computer terminal service have not been successful in speedy, direct, simple and low-cost service. Owned and personally operated calculator systems have performed much more effectively on all ranges of cost/performance bases. With computer systems, in-house or by using remote service company terminals, customers were usually required to learn completely new procedures, systems, and even languages. The current and potential mass users of calculator systems are not computer professionals. They are instead regular departmental or small business users whose managers have neither time nor desire to learn some complicated programming scheme that **eventually** might prove helpful. In developing any new market, product simplicity and ready usefulness are the keys. **Product** simplicity implies overall **service** simplicity including: programming, presentation of results, potential communication with other products, etc. Continuing the tradition of older computer product or service sales of forcing the customer to learn computer jargon, change business methods, train new people, etc. simply won't do anymore. Efficient, low-cost calculators with simple programming versatility are most appealing to the huge potential of *small shop* markets.

English-language programming is now the rule. Simpler products with readily-available application programs (or easily-written custom ones) that can be used in many ranges of businesses, industries, and professions are winning over very rapidly. These businesses and professions are sophisticated markets, but the devices must be designed for use by nonsophisticated people. Data residing in calculator systems are also far more **secure** (software and memory) than they are with the services from remote computers. Other key advantages of calculator systems are fast, personal response, greater reliability, low-cost back-up availability, personal responsibility for errors or foulups, etc. But product simplicity with all its implications is the key factor. The users of these simpler programming products can best begin by owning and diligently exploring the capabilities of hand-held units first, then move up to desktops.

Consumer-Oriented Programmable Calculators — Everybody's a Programmer . . .

Do you know any 9-year-old programmers? They are around — and many of them have learned on *consumer type* Litronix, HP, TI, or National Semi programmables. It's fun for them to work out a simple chained problem with addition, subtraction, and division — in the Learn mode — and after that simply insert the numbers to get new answers from the same formula. Automobile, insurance, and real estate salesmen use them, after only an hour of practice, to *formula-calculate* some very large deals. And many of these people forgot "everything they ever learned" about algebra in high school. Several years ago some very large calculator suppliers realized that too many machines were being designed only for engineers by engineers. Practically none of the calculator designers were consumer-oriented, and until recently, none of them were advised to consider the general public as users of programmable machines. After some initial successes and especially due to demands by a great many elementary and secondary school teachers, many models of low-cost programmables are now being produced and marketed to housewives, students, etc. in mass quantities. Even the quite sophisticated key-programmables, the SR-56, the NS 4615, and the HP-25 are selling around or below $100, the HP-25 about $25 or so above the $100 mark. It is therefore easy to understand why many teachers elect to use them as *first use* calculators as they teach their operations in classes. The MOS-LSI chips designed as programmable types are only a slight amount higher in original cost than the lowest cost 4-6 function circuits — and the advertising appeal and customer satisfaction have continued to encourage new market entry of other programmables by more suppliers such as Casio, Commodore, and Canon.

The ever-alert calculator manufacturers, most of the largest — Texas Instruments, Hewlett-Packard, National Semiconductor, others — also make terminals, computer peripherals, etc. They realize that these instruments are a fundamental part of the microprocessor-use training ground. A microprocessor in a box with a Cathode Ray Tube (CRT) becomes an intelligent terminal; a microprocessor in a box with a calibrated *scope* suddenly becomes a complete diagnostic test center, and a microprocessor in a calculator case, when connected to a few peripherals, becomes a de facto computer system. We will note ahead a considerable variety of microprocessors within boxes have special function keyboards and interfaces to transducers that sense signals from a great many devices and control them. These then become excellent programmable calculator *computing* or control systems.

Users Discover Programmables Can be Immensely Useful — and Convenient

Programmable calculators (PC) prove exceptionally valuable because users are able to make increasingly better decisions more quickly and more comfortably. Programmables are especially helpful if calculations must be iterated many times. The programmable can do in minutes what would take perhaps a half hour to do tediously by hand. It can iterate 10, 20, or as many times as the users wants; generally, the more one iterates, the better the accuracy. Programmables are a great help in designing. Users input the process parameters and the operating points. The programmable calculates the dimensions. And they very often are used in the lab to evaluate prototypes. If one of the components is not up to spec, users can check the numbers and make an on-the-spot evaluation of the design.

Tax accounting clerks, for example, need only put in sales dollars. The PC then computes: local tax, state tax, total tax. This often saves as much as 80% of the time it normally takes to complete this task. One user reported that it formerly took a good eight hours without any interruptions, but with a PC only an hour-and-a-half was required for sales tax accounting. PCs permit instant turn-around allowing for examining different alternatives very rapidly . . . replacing intuition with insight and facts. Many users claim they are able to examine more alternatives in a few hours than they would have been able to do in a week's time considering the delayed queues and waiting necessary with strict computer procedures. The results are better understanding of many more factors that influence specific problems. Other PC users can track complex equations and can work with numbers instead of going to models or mockups, which are expensive.

Writing and using calculator programs cuts down turn-around time. Since users don't need to go through computer schedules, costs are reduced dramatically without cutting back on quality. PCs permit yield improvements because users can spot what's causing the problem quicker. Production engineers are constantly running data reductions, evaluating yield and related process parameters. PCs are handier, always available, quicker. Statisticians can do correlations in hours where they formerly required all day. Many users find them intriguing for constant experimentation, and they use them in such hobbies as amateur radio, photography . . . and many types of games, puzzles, and learning experiences.

Low-cost programmables are certainly more significant advances to businessmen and managers than were sliderule calculators introduced just a short time ago. Now, individual users of hand-held calculators have gained a many-step functional increase in personal computing capability. There are millions of non-math-oriented leaders in this world that quite absolutely will not learn the procedures and nuances of computers. But a great majority of these individuals have no reluctance whatever of using the simple English-type programming languages of calculators which are truly not *languages* at all but standard procedures of simple math or other types of straightforward problem-solving. These men and women now have gained *painlessly* much of that same more complex computer capability but now with the simple use of the keys of their programmables. They use them for: projections, forecasts, optimization, data reduction, *what if* matrices (game theory), loops and iterations, risk analysis, probability, mathematical modeling, worst-case analysis, and an endless array of other sophisticated computing and analyses. And, they aren't required to wait in line for access to the computer, learn complex languages, or settle for something less — like depending upon a junior assistant to *help* them compute or actually do their *processing* job.

How do personal programmables help owners to use far more insight, cope more successfully with many more operations, handle more data to make better decisions? Why are these decisions now chosen from more options, from better data bases . . . made more quickly and definitely more accurately? The special function keys (SFKs) on calculators are fine, but they're only a minor part of these successes. Programmability is the real magic. Programming is really not much more than straightforward logical thinking, since every problem has a logical flow. It is not difficult to inject the constants and variables to develop ranges of solutions and to make the necessary evaluations among options. Problems are stated mathematically, using equations to determine what is to be done and in the proper sequence. Generally this is followed by keying in an example and testing accuracy and reasonableness of answers. The program is then *in*. The user can step backward or forward through the program to edit it.

The program is then tested and corrected, if necessary; its structure is accepted. This is followed by the numbers — variables, constants, the operators $(+, -, \times, \div)$ and the relational statements, if branching is part of the program or model — such as, "Is the answer less than, equal to, or greater than "x", then GO TO, etc. There is no need to key in the program again. It is either stored internally (on key-programmables) or is permanently stored on and enterable from the program card, strip, tape, cartridge, ROM, etc. After one solution, many users explore other options with their own unique *what if* procedures. It's fast, easy, and productive. This results in *personalized* optimization, or loops that provide wide ranges of potential or *certain* results.

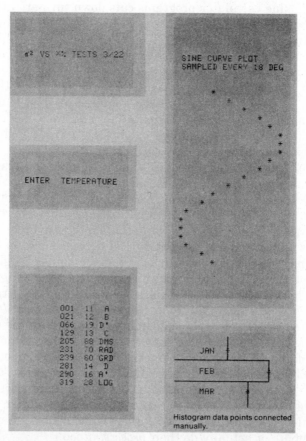

r² VS x% TESTS 3/22

SINE CURVE PLOT
SAMPLED EVERY 18 DEG

ENTER   TEMPERATURE

001	11	A
021	12	B
066	19	D'
129	13	C
205	88	DMS
231	70	RAD
239	80	GRD
281	14	D
290	16	A'
319	28	LOG

JAN

FEB

MAR

Histogram data points connected manually.

At left, top to bottom, key features of the PC-100-A include program heading capability, user prompting messages and program label and location listings. Also, the printer can also plot curves or histograms as shown at right.

In many cases the results can be recorded permanently on output many varieties of media — print, tape, cartridges, etc. or flashed to Cathode Ray Tube (CRT) or other visual display. And data can be graphed or plotted with the use of small, convenient plotters that are now low-cost accessories to many programmable calculator systems. And now, even many hand-held programmables have printing options, such as Texas Instruments (TI) PC-100, shown above. Or, the printers are parts of the units themselves, as shown in the photographs of the popular Hewlett-Packard programmable HP-97 or the TI SR-60 programmable *prompting* unit in Chapter 5. These units, and other models with printers, permit hard copy printing of intermediate results, ranges of answers, detail alphanumeric print-outs of entire programs, all data used, memory contents, unit conversions, etc.

Programs are also low cost, readily available from tens of thousands of dealers. An example of some optional libraries of prerecorded programs for the hand-held TI 52, 59 are listed below, with suggested retail price of $29.95 (often heavily discounted by 30% to 50% at many stores) — and more libraries were in preparation, in 1977, including: Navigation, Surveying, Aviation, etc.

Math Library. Hyperbolic functions, quadratic and cubic equations, simultaneous equations, interpolation, numerical integration, differential equations, matrix operations, base conversions, triangle solutions, complex functions, and more. 34 program cards.

Electrical Engineering Library. Active filters, resonant circuits, T-π networks and transformations, transmission lines, phase-locked loops, transistor amplifiers, Fourier series, coils, power transformers, controlled rectifier and power supply circuits, and more. 25 programs.

Statistics Library. Means, moments, standard deviations, random numbers, permutations and combinations, t-statistics, analysis of variance, regression analysis (linear, power curve, exponential, logarithmic, quadratic), multiple regression, histograms, 12 distributions (normal, chi squared, Poisson, Weibull, hypergeometric, etc.). 29 programs.

Finance Library. Ordinary annuities, compound interest, accrued interest, sinking fund, annuity due, bond yield and value, days between dates, annuities with balloon payments, interest rate conversions, add-on rate installment loans, loan amortization, interest rebate, depreciation (SL, DB, and SOYD) and crossover, variable cash flows, internal rate of return, capital budgeting, and more. 32 programs.

The Continuing Price Reductions for Products and Programs

Almost from the outset of the introduction of **consumer** calculators, it has been a buyer's market. Although demand grew rapidly, the calculator industry, based principally in the U.S., Japan, Hong Kong, Indonesia and on a minor basis in England, was only able to keep millions of units in full supply. Sales and discounts became so common that users seldom paid the original list price for their units. This was true for consumer units as well as professional and advanced programmable units, at least after HP caught up with the demand for its HP-65. The HP-67 was such a significant improvement over the HP-65 and at a slashing competition-forced new price discounted below $400, generally, that the delivery schedule was backlogged at first. The same was true with the TI 57, 58, 59. But the heavy and effective promotions and the huge 30,000 outlet distribution network established by Texas Instruments kept all those who wanted low-cost, full capability, ROM-type advanced programmables quite satisfied.

Since the buyer is still in full command, product choice is not constrained by material shortages, quality-breakdown problems, or strictly-held factory-suggested list prices. The mass retailers took the lead with price-cutting using massive national campaigns, multi-million multi-color brochure mailings, multi-colored mass-media display ads, strong TV campaigns, etc. The campus book stores, electronics shops, department and office supply stores, and the multiplying specialized *Computer Shops* such as the Byte, MITS, and Computer Shack chains, and others, including some with several thousand members stores, generally followed the price-cutting patterns. This *competition at its best* forced manufacturers to mastermind new technology and production efficiencies — and they were up to the task. The result is a new and very widespread computing capability and power at prices completely unimaginable a year or two previous. The impact is also being felt in the *home* computer markets and the sudden almost tripling of production of low-cost computer terminal units. How many users of low-cost simple or programmable calculators will step up to the more advanced units — and how quickly? The answers to these questions might evolve as more calculator users are trained in and graduate from the school systems — elementary, secondary and the 2-year, 4-year and grad schools of the colleges and universities. How fast do users move up? Quite fast, as we shall see. But, first — let's *keep it simple!* The low-cost key-programmables explain a lot.

The features of the $29.95 Sinclair Cambridge Programmable

The Cambridge Programmable is genuinely pocketable. A mere 4½" × 2", it weighs about 2 oz., a palm of the hand size. The Cambridge Programmable is both *a scientific calculator* with a memory, algebraic logic and brackets (which means enter a calculation exactly as you write it), and a *programmable calculator* which offers simple, flexible through-the-keyboard program entry and operation. The Cambridge Programmable has a 36-step program memory, and features conditional and unconditional branch instructions *(go to* and *go if negative)*.

There is also a step facility, which allows users to step through the program to check that it has been entered correctly. If there is any programming error, the learn key allows users to correct single steps without destroying any of the remainder of the program. To achieve this, each program key-stroke has an identifying code, or 'check symbol'. (The symbols for the digit keys are the digits themselves, while the symbols for the operator keys are letters printed beside the keys.)

Use the 294-program library to tailor the machine to your own specialty

The Sinclair Cambridge Programmable can be programmed to handle calculations concerned with *any* specialty. The unit has 19 multifunction keys. Once it's programmed, it can even be given to an operator who doesn't understand the program! To save time, and to help inexperienced programmers, Sinclair have produced a library of 294 programs ready to be entered straight into the calculator. Using these standard programs, the Cambridge Programmable solves problems from quadratic equations (where the program gives both real and imaginary roots) to twin-T filter design, and from linear regression to bond yields. It even plays a lunar landing game! To realise the full power of the Cambridge Programmable, the Program Library is a must. (The calculator is supplied with 12 sample programs, and full instructions for entering user's own programs. The four books in the program library are available at $4 each, or $10 for the complete set.)

One of the reasons for the many models of programmables — from the under $30 Cambridge to the $8000-$10,000 multi-terminal calculator systems — is that the designers of these devices and systems can react far more quickly to advances in the circuitry and new discoveries than their computer-oriented counterparts. The turnaround from design idea to testable product has become shorter and shorter as prices continue to fall for sophisticated large scale calculator-type integrated circuits, keyboard variety, and heavily-competing display technologies. Capability and versatility have shot up while costs and design times have severely decreased. Many new vendors have entered the microcomputer markets, and their products have come to look more and more like expanded programmable calculator systems. They discover new computing, controlling and communicating capabilities for systems of devices and design them into more and more calculator-like devices. Why? Because people are not scared of these devices as they are of computer-looking devices. The new microprocessor control devices are powerful, well-designed, proved-reliable, reasonably-priced, and easily-operated devices. Innovations and improvements will probably never cease.

Friendliness for the human interface makes programmable calculators the most satisfactory *climb* up to home computers. People enjoy, have fun using, programmable calculators, — in effect using computer power with emphasis on ease of use. These are personal, immediate use, *intelligent* machines that humans can quickly change, correct and improve . . . by themselves — without interpreters and tough rules. It won't be long before users will operate **hand-held** programmables with the *easy and fun* computer language, BASIC, as they do with several desk-top models already. This is alphanumeric, full computer, control. Voice output from calculators is already *old hat,* and large data bases accessible by hand-held units is no longer just a *trick.* No sooner had several major manufacturers made major announcements of the nonvolatility (non-disappearing memory with power off) for their hand-held programmables, than HP announced that capability for its model 25 and 29C. Other firms announced it for several of their units. In these and an increasing number of units, storing programs in inexpensive hand-held calculators for days, months, or years after the battery power has been switched off is a big marketing *plus*. But, let us start at the bottom of the line of programmables — the move-up is easy and fun.

Programmability for the Very Low-Cost Units is the ability to store instructions and to automatically execute them with a very few *triggering* keystrokes. The ability to store (record) strings of keystrokes means that entire difficult formulas can be *set inside* the unit and then produced by the touch of, in most cases, a single key. Most formulas then execute automatically, sequentially, precisely and very rapidly the steps keyed-in and output the results on display, on print, or both. Programmability assists most effectively the user-needed characteristics of visibility, verifiability, and modifiability.

Keyboard-programmables, or key-programmable, units are the lowest cost and simplest, of the five classes of programmables as noted on the chart. Without the need to build in a magnetic card reader to accept program strips, etc., the programmability function is neither expensive nor difficult to design into a calculator. It is expected that most calculators of the future will contain this capability, providing more power, usability, and versatility. Such calculators provide the means of exploring, and for better understanding, the mathematical concepts of the scientific world and the "scientific method" problem-solving procedures of the business and industrial world. Those young students using programmable calculators have been known to very quickly come to grips with math, and often with real enthusiasm and zeal, while without them, they remained confused, irritated, and uncomfortable with most aspects of it. Grade school teachers should be most anxious to introduce them early, to utilize the true value of calculators in the *fun and learn* processes to stimulate the interest and progress made by these youngsters when they discover the drudgery is out of math — and the machine seeks and searches for the answers if they themselves can discover and understand the problem.

PROGRAMMABLE CALCULATOR FOR CONSUMERS

Designed For Use In: Retailing, Accounting, Forecasting and Budgeting — A simple programmable **consumer** calculator — it lists for $29.95 — can store and execute a sequence of 10 program steps. The 2290 and/or Sinclair Cambridge simplifies calculations wherever a repetitive sequence of steps is involved, such as in figuring markups or discounts on store inventory or in calculating the prices and total of a string of purchases with the sales tax included. It is also suitable for solving math problems such as the sum of squares and the value of a string of parallel resistances. The calculator remembers a sequence of function-key operations up to a total of 10. This includes any sequence of plus-equals (+ =); minus-equals (− =); multiply (×); divide (÷); percent (%); add to memory (M +); subtract from memory (M −); and recall memory (RM). Clear memory (CM) cannot be used in a program, but this function is programmed by depressing recall-memory twice.

The $29.95 calculator (Cambridge and 2990 are very similar) does not have exotic programming and branching as the high-priced programmable scientific machines do. To insert a program in the 2290, the display and memory are first cleared. To instruct the machine to store the program, a "learn" (L) key is pressed. The sequence of data and function keys is then pressed in the proper order until the program sequence is finished, at which point a "Stop" or S key is pushed. To execute a program, the numerical data are entered and an "execute" key (E) is operated in the proper sequence.

For example, the program to calculate the prices of a number of items, including a 6% sales tax on each, involves the following:

	Key Pressed	Display
Clear display	C/ON	0.
Clear memory	CM	0.
Enter tax (%)	6	6
Add to memory	M+	6.
Learn program	L	6.
Enter item price ($)	10	10
Multiply	×	10.
Recall tax from memory	RM	6.
Times percent	%	.6
Answer ($)	+ =	10.6
Stop earning sequence	S	10.6

Now sales tax computations can be made by entering the price and depressing Enter. For example, the price of $11, $12 and $13 items, with tax, and calculated by:

	Key Depressed	Display
Enter price	11	11
Press enter	E	11.66
Enter price	12	12
Press enter	E	12.72

Enter price	13	13
Press enter	E	13.78

There is no need to press any of the program or function keys again.

From this point, on sales tax computations are made simply by entering any article price and pressing the execute (E) key, which then displays the price-plus-sales-tax total.

While no square root key appears, the internal "chip" has been designed to give that function in a nonorthodox manner. For example, to obtain a square root, the number is entered followed by depressing the divide-by and plus-equal keys.

The LED display on the 2290 is unusually bright because each digit draws 150 mA instead of the usual 100. Battery life with alkaline dry cells is 18 hours.

The 2290 also has standard four-function Litronix consumer-calculator features with a four-key accumulating memory, and the usual constant K. A significant battery-saving feature of the line is that the calculator automatically turns itself off after 12 minutes without an entry. (See the $50 programmable by Sinclair Radionics, Inc. and the low-cost units by National Semiconductor Corp, (Norvus), Hewlett-Packard and Texas Instruments.)

OPERATING INSTRUCTIONS AND FUNCTIONS

The following is a summary of functions performed by individual keys. Users refer to these functions once they have learned how to use the calculator. Various examples follow in order to show the simplicity of use of the calculator.

C/ON Initial power on clears calculator, including memory. If last entry was a number, one press clears last entry. If display indicates overflow, one press clears overflow conditions. Two presses will clear calculator, but not program or data saved in memory.

OFF Turns calculator off. Once off, all data is erased from calculator, including that which was saved in memory and program.

CM Clear memory. Sets the value of memory to 0.

RM One press of key recalls data saved in memory to the display. Two presses of key clears data saved in memory.

M − Subtracts the display from data saved in memory. Repetitive subtractions of the display from data saved in memory can be done by pressing this key the specified number of times.

M + Adds the display to data saved in memory. Repetitive addition of the display to data saved in memory can be done by pressing this key the specified number of times.

0 — 9 Number entry keys.

• Enters decimal point.

% Used in conjunction with ×, the % is used to find the percentage of a given number. Used in conjunction with + =, the % of a base number is added to that base in the display. Used with − =, the % of a base number is discounted from that base in the display

When used in conjunction with ÷, the % function can be used for yield calculations.

+ = Directs calculator to add display to previous number when used in addition operation. If depressed twice or more in succession, the calculator remembers the original display and adds it to the current value of the display. If a previous multiplication or division has been entered, this key will complete the operation.

− = Directs calculator to subtract display from previous number when used in subtraction operation. If depressed twice or more in succession, the calculator remembers the original display and subtracts it from the current value of the display. If a previous multiplication or division has been entered, this key reverses the sign of the display, and then completes the operation.

× Directs calculator to multiply display by the following number. To multiply by a negative number, press ×, then the multiplier, then − = to complete the operation. If the preceding operation was a multiply or divide, it directs the calculator to complete that operation, display the results, and then multiply that display by the following number.

÷ Directs calculator to divide display by the following number. To divide by a negative number, press ÷, then the divisor then − = to complete the operation. If the preceding operation was a multiply or divide, it directs the calculator to complete that operation, display the results, and then divide that display by the following number.

SPECIAL COMBINATIONS

×, + = When these two keys are pressed consecutively, the calculator squares the number in the display.

÷, + = When these two keys are pressed consecutively, the calculator takes the square root of the number in the display.

PROGRAMMING KEYS

L Begins Learning Sequence and erases the previous program. Turns the learn light on and readies the calculator to accept program steps.

S Stops Learning Sequence and Starts Program Sequence. Turns off the learn light and readies the calculator to start accepting numbers at the beginning of the program.

E Enters the current value of display in the next data position in the program and continues running the program until the next data position.

DISPLAY

Error Signal — When an improper sequence of functions is entered into the calculator, the word "Error" will flash in the display. A single press of C/ON restores display.

Program Learn Indicator — A program learn indicator light appears at the left side of the display window when the L key is pressed and will go out once the S or E key is pressed.

Minus Sign — Appears immediately to left of the displayed number to indicate a negative number.

Decimal Point — Calculator automatically positions decimal point to maintain full eight digit accuracy.

Overflow Indication — A square around the decimal point . will appear in the display when calculation has gone beyond capacity and refuses to permit further entries until C/ON has been pressed.

Battery Saving Display Flasher — After approximately 50 seconds of non-use, display will begin flashing on and off and continue to do this until approximately 12 minutes of non-use have passed at which time it will automatically turn itself completely off.

What is a Program?

A calculator *program* is simply a series of keyboard operations that must be done in a particular sequence to yield a correct answer — add, multiply, subtract, divide or other functions. Often this identical series of steps must be performed again and again — for example, to solve a recurring problem where only the *numbers* change but not the way they must be manipulated. With its ability to be programmed, the 2290 *learns* these program sequences and can repeat them automatically, saving the user time and button pressing, and reducing the chance of error.

How to Write a Program

Users program their Litronix calculator by example. They press the L key; and the calculator clears any previous program it had remembered, and gets ready to learn a new program. The calculator will remember the sequence in which users enter numbers and save the function keys; each function key represents one program step. Learn mode lasts until users depress the S key, or until they have entered 10 program steps.

For example, consider computation of sales tax, to give total sales price. To teach their calculator to do sales tax calculations they do the following:

	Key Depressed	Displayed
Clear display	C/ON	0.
Clear memory	CM	0.
Begin learning	L	9.●
Enter price	10	10.●
Press multiply	×	10.●
Enter sales tax rate	6	6.●
Press per cent	%	0.6.●
Press plus equals	+ =	10.6.●
Stop learning	S	10.6

The calculator has now learned how to compute add on tax. The price of a $10 object with 6% sales tax is $10.60. Now as an example, execute the program to calculate the total price of a $11 item with 6% sales tax.

How To Execute a Program

To execute a program, press the E key, after entering numbers, but not function keys, in the same sequence that was used when the L key was depressed. The calculator will sequentially substitute the numbers entered, one by one, into the learned program.

	Key Depressed	Display
Enter price	11	11
Press Enter	E	11.
Enter sales tax rate	6	6
Press Enter	E	11.66

Note that the price was entered first, and sales tax rate second as in the learning sequence. This is what happens if users enter sales tax rate first and price second.

Incorrect Use of Program

	Key Depressed	Display
Enter sales tax rate	6	6
Press Enter	E	6.
Enter Price	11	11
Press Enter	E	6.66

A completely meaningless answer results. Note that if the sales tax is constant, this program can be simplified so that only the price need be entered.

The sales tax rate can be saved in the memory, and the RM key used in the program.

OPERATING EXAMPLES WITHOUT PROGRAMMING

Addition of Whole Numbers
Add 40 and 47

Clear display	C/ON	0.
Enter first number	40	40
Press plus equals	+ =	40.
Enter second number	47	47
Press plus equals	+ =	87.

Addition of Number (Dollars) with Decimal (Cents)
Add $10.13, $6.00, $5.70

Clear display	C/ON	0.
Enter first number	10.13	10.13
Press plus equals		
Enter second number	6.00	6.00
Press plus equals	+ =	16.13
Enter third number	5.70	5.70
Enter plus equals	+ =	21.83

Subtracting Whole Numbers
Subtract 16 from 17

Enter number to be subtracted from	17	17
Press plus equals	+ =	17.
Enter number to subtract	16	16
Press minus equals	− =	1.

Subtracting Numbers with Decimal
Subtract 4.2 and 6 from 3

Enter number to be subtracted from	3	3
Press plus equals	+ =	3.
Enter first number to subtract	4.2	4.2
Press minus equals	− =	− 1.2
Enter second number to subtract	6	6
Press minus equals	− =	− 7.2

Chained Addition Subtraction and 'Repeat'
Add 5, 6.2, 6.2, then subtract 41.1, then
   add 12.8 and 12.8

Clear display	C/ON	0.
Enter first number	5	5
Press plus equals	+ =	5.
Enter second number	6.2	6.2
Press plus equals	+ =	11.2
Press plus equals	+ =	17.4

Note that users do not have to enter the third number (6.2) since it is the same as the second, and Litronix calculator has a repeat operation function for addition and subtraction.

Enter fourth number	41.1	41.1
Press minus equals	− =	− 23.7
Enter fifth number	12.8	12.8
Press plus equals	+ =	− 10.9
Press plus equals	+ =	1.9

Multiplication of Whole Numbers
Multiply 21 by 15

Enter first number	21	21
Press multiply	×	21.

Enter second number	15	15
Press plus equals	+ =	315.

Multiplication of Numbers with Decimals
Multiply 10.2 gallons by 57.9¢

Enter first number	10.2	10.2
Press multiply	×	10.2
Enter second number	.579	.579
Press plus equals	+ =	5.9058

Chained Multiplication
Multiply 5 feet by 2 feet by 3½ feet

Enter first number	5	5
Press multiply	×	5.
Enter second number	2	2
Press multiply	×	10.
Enter third number	3.5	3.5
Press plus equals	+ =	35.

Division, Including Decimal Values
Compute ⅝

Enter number to be divided	5	5
Press divide	÷	5.
Enter number to divide with	8	8
Press plus equals	+ =	0.625

Calculating Per Cent (%)

The percent key has 3 uses.
(1) x is what % of y?
(2) What is x% of y?
(3) Compute what x% of y and then
      add or subtract that number to y.

(1) 3 is what % of 4?

Enter first number	3	3
Press divide	÷	3.
Enter second number	4	4
Press per cent	%	75.

   3 is 75% of 4

(2) What is 11.1% of 43?

Enter first number	43	43
Press multiply	×	43.
Enter second number	11.1	11.1
Press per cent	%	4.773

   4.773 is 11.1% of 43

(3) What is the new value of a $14
item if it is marked up 8%

Enter first number	14	14
Press multiply	×	14.
Enter second number	8	8
Press per cent	%	1.12
Press plus equals	+ =	15.12

   The price of the item is $15.12

Joice Black has a problem. She can buy 7 oz. of Brand X detergent for 59¢ or she can buy the economy size which is 16 oz. for $1.89. Which is the better value? To answer this question one computes the price per ounce. The smaller price per ounce is the better value.

7 oz. 59¢

	Keys Depressed	Display
Clear display	C/ON	0.
Enter price	.59	0.59
	÷	0.59

Enter quantity		7	7
		+ =	.08428571

16 oz. for $1.89

	Keys Depressed	Display
Clear display	C/ON	0.
Enter price	1.89	1.89
	÷	1.89
Enter quantity	16	16
	+ =	0.118125

At a little over 8¢ per ounce, the 7 oz. size is more economical than the 11¢ per ounce (16 oz.) container.

Mary Garcia wants to balance her budget. She will take her income and subtract her fixed expenses to arrive at the amount of money she is free to spend. Mary is paid $195 per week. She pays $140 a month for rent, $45 a week for food, $125 a month on her car, $10 a week for gas and oil, $40 monthly for her insurance bills, and $15 monthly for her utility bills. To calculate,

	Key Depressed	Display
Clear display	C/ON	0.
Clear memory	CM	0.
Enter weekly income	195	195
	×	195.
Enter number of weeks in month	4.3	4.3
	+ =	838.5
Store this value in memory	M+	838.5
Enter rent payments	140	140
Subtract from memory	M−	140.
Enter weekly food bill	45	45
	×	45.
Enter weeks in month	4.3	4.3
	+ =	193.5
Subtract from memory	M−	193.5
Enter monthly car payment	125	125
Subtract from memory	M−	125.
Enter weekly gas and oil bill	10	10
	×	10.
Enter weeks in month	4.3	4.3
	+ =	43.
Subtract from memory	M−	43.
Enter monthly insurance	40	40
Subtract from memory	M−	40.
Enter monthly utility bill	15	15
Subtract from memory	M −	15.

Mary now presses RM to recall memory and sees that she has $282 discretionary monthly income.

WITH PROGRAMMING

Jim Fournier, a small businessman, wants to discount his line of toasters. Before he finalizes this decision, however, he needs the new price of each toaster and the updated value of his inventory. To do this he teaches his Litronix calculator the following sequence.

	Key Depressed	Display
Clear display	C/ON	0.
Clear memory	CM	0.
Begin learning sequence	L	0..
Enter price of toaster (top of line — the New Yorker)	49.95	49.95..
	×	49..
Enter discount rate	10	10.
Compute discount	%	4.995.
Discounted price	− =	44.995.
	×	44.995.

At this point, the display indicates what the cost of Jim's top of the line toaster would be with a 10% discount. Jim now enters the number of New Yorkers in stock.

	3	3.
	+ =	134.865.
Save updated value of inventory in memory.	M+	134.865.
Stop learning sequence	S	134.865

Memory now contains the new inventory value of Jim's 3 New Yorker toasters. Since Jim has 15 Angeleno toasters, he wishes to discount them 12% so that they will start moving. He does the following steps.

Enter price of toaster	39.95	39.95
	E	39.95
Enter discount rate	12	12
	E	35.156

The display now indicates what the new price of the Angelenos would be.

Enter number of toasters	15	15
	E	527.34

Using his program, Jim calculates the discount price for the rest of his toasters and generates this new table.

TOASTER	CURRENT PRICE	DISCOUNT RATE	NO. IN STOCK	NEW PRICE	NEW INVEN- TORY VALUE
New Yorker	49.95	10	3	44.955	134.865
Angeleno	39.95	12	15	35.156	527.34
Foridian	33.33	10	5	29.997	149.985
Franciscan	25.25	10	5	22.725	113.625
Bostonian	19.99	8	8	18.3908	147.1264
					1072.9414

Esther Edwards wishes to buy a new car. There are three dealers in town who offer the model she is interested in, the new California Motors compact, the Flash. The three dealers, Fred's Auto, Hiram's Motors, and Ron's Auto, are each offering a different 'deal.' Esther wants to determine which would be the best deal on a price basis, and what her monthly payments would be. These are the deals:

	Base Price	Yearly Add-On Interest Rate	Length Of Loan
Fred's	3500	7	3 Years
Hiram's	3750	6.5	3 Years
Ron's	4000	6	3 Years

Esther figures which is the best deal on her Litronix calculator. She teaches her calculator the following steps:

	Key Depressed	Display
Begin Learning sequence	L	0.
Enter price	3500	3500.
	×	3500..
Enter rate of interest	7	7.
	%	245..
	+ =	3745..
	+ =	3990..
	+ =	4235..
	÷	4235..

The display now indicates the total price of the car. To find her monthly payments and to complete the learning sequence, Esther follows with:

Enter number of months	36	36.
Depress plus equals	+ =	117.63888.
Stop learning sequence	S	

The price of Fred's car was $4235. The monthly payments will be $117.64. To calculate Hiram's total price, Esther does the following:

Enter price of car	3750	3750
	E	3750.
Enter rate of interest	6.5	6.5
	E	4481.25
Enter number of months	36	36
	E	124.47916

Hiram's car will cost $4481.25 and will have monthly payments of $124.48. The price of Ron's car will be calculated in the same manner.

Enter price of car	4000	4000
	E	4000.
Enter rate of interest	6	6
	E	4720.
Enter number of months	36	36
	E	131.11111

On the basis of price and monthly payments it is clear that Fred is offering Esther the best "deal."

Sinclair's Scientific Programmable is not an ordinary calculator. It has only 19 keys — and, for a programmable, a very low price — but its problem-solving capability exceeds that of any ordinary scientific calculator. The big plus is programmability — the ability to remember a calculation sequence of up to 24 steps entered directly from the keyboard. Once stored in the program memory, a calculation sequence can be recalled at the touch of a single key, and applied to new numbers to produce new results. For users who carry out repetitive calculations, the Scientific Programmable will save many key strokes and lots of time. It will also save users from errors, since the calculation sequence will be recalled exactly as originally entered, over and over again.

A distinct engineering achievement lies behind the capability and low price of this calculator. The Sinclair Scientific Programmable was one of the first among many programmable calculators to use a single integrated circuit. The entire logic, data storage and program storage of this calculator are contained

The Sinclair Scientific Programmable for under $50 . . .

in a single chip — a chip developed by Sinclair engineers. Others quickly followed, and one-chip machines are becoming standard.

Programmable characteristics

Entering a calculation sequence into the program memory is quite easy. Users press the BE key to tell the calculator to remember a sequence. They key in the calculation almost exactly as they normally would. They use VAR at the points where they'll want the program to stop, so that they can enter new numbers or display partial results. During entry the number of steps is displayed, so they won't exceed the program memory's capacity. When they've finished they press BE again to tell the calculator that the sequence is complete. The program is now available until they overwrite it with another program or until they switch the calculator off. To enter new numbers, they press EXEC, and get new results. The Scientific Programmable can be used as an ordinary scientific calculator. Even half-way through the execution of a program, users can stop, carry out a calculation from the keyboard, then press EXEC to continue execution of the program when they're ready. Once users have entered a program it is available at the touch of a key until they overwrite it with another program or switch off. But the program doesn't interfere with the calculator's normal operation in any way; it is stored in a separate program memory area and is available only when needed.

With the Sinclair Program Library users don't have to be programmers. For easier use of the Scientific Programmable's full problem-solving capability, each calculator comes with a fully documented library of hundreds of programs to solve standard problems, and complete instructions on how to use them. Typical programs and costs are shown below. As regards applications, the Scientific Programmable has many applications in areas of computation other than repetitive calculations. It can be used for the analysis of experimental data, the evaluation of integer functions, and with a variety of methods for the iterative solution of equations. They are dealt with in detail in the instruction book and Program Library. And, although the Scientific Programmable is no toy, it does play games — and wins! The display is a 5 digit mantissa with 2 digit exponent. Number entry is floating decimal point and/or scientific notation; results are in scientific notation. It uses Reverse Polish Notation logic. Its preprogrammed functions are sine, cosine arctangent (radians), log, alog (base 10), square root, reciprocal, change sign, clear/clear entry. It has memory to store, recall and exchange.

The Scientific Programmable is small enough to hold in one's hand and big enough to use on one's desk. It measures 6" × 2⅞" × 1¼", has non-slip rubber feet and a big green display. It uses small, inexpensive 9v battery or the Sinclair A adapter.

Sinclair Offers Free Custom Programming Service — If users have an application for the Sinclair Scientific Programmable which is not covered by the Program Library, Sinclair's software support team will devise a custom program to solve the problem. Users must write to Sinclair clearly explaining the problem and they will send a program that can be used with Scientific Programmable to solve it. There is no charge for this service.

Which Low-Cost Calculator Is Best For Students and Engineers? — Prospective users who go about attempting to select the right calculator generally ask themselves two basic questions: 1. What types of problems will the calculator usually be used to solve? 2. What are the most difficult types of problems the calculator may be called upon to solve? If users can obtain a calculator with enough functions to satisfy both types of problem-solving situations at a satisfactory price, they should buy it. However many might make mistakes if they forego the more advanced capability — they will discover costs are so very low.

Most simple and compound arithmetical calculations can be done on four-function units. Engineers, however, would most likely want to add specialized functions such as reciprocal, squaring, and square-root calculation. In more advanced applications — such as in preparing mechanical drawings, doing geometric and navigation problems, trigonometric functions are needed. Rectangular-to-polar coordinate conversion keys are desirable because they minimize keystrokes and, therefore, shorten calculating time. For many purposes and especially in the designing of electrical and electronic circuits the engineer uses logarithmic functions — common log, common antilog, natural log, natural antilog — and exponential functions, square roots, and nth roots. When working with statistics — such as those used in quality control and time analysis problems — the engineer should look for logarithmic, exponential, and factorial functions as well as mean and standard deviation capabilities.

The Standard and Programmable Statisticians — Low cost units from Novus (National Semiconductor Corp.) The Novus 6030 is a fully-featured pocket calculator priced within the means of all serious users, professionals and students alike. Especially dedicated to statistical problems, the Novus Statistician features pre-programmed, single-key calculations of most common statistical formulas. Countless hours can be saved in performing statistical calculations. And more important, the chances for calculating or entry errors are virtually eliminated. As an extremely accurate scientific tool, Novus 6030 is a valuable business machine that offers four-function performance (addition, subtraction, multiplication, division) as well as some important extras. Like automatic square roots, a live % key with automatic add-on or discount and net, a separate accumulating memory, standard deviation, coefficient of correlation, and regression line. Its handy business/commercial logic lets users perform addition and subtraction arithmetically (as on an adding machine) and multiplication and division algebraically.

Performance features are:

- Single-key summation of x, x^2 and n.
- Single-key calculation of a mean and standard deviation.
- Single-key summation of x and y values for linear correlation and regression.
- Single-key calculation of linear correlation coefficient and slope of curve.
- Single-key calculation of y-axis intercept or any point of y-axis.
- Separate keys to remove incorrect x and y values.
- Single key to enter frequency for standard deviation of grouped data.
- Mean and standard deviation calculated without destroying summations, enabling additions or deletions.
- Single key to clear all statistical summations.
- Square, square root and change sign functions.
- Automatic constant in multiplication and division.
- Automatic repeat addition and subtraction.
- Full accumulating memory with memory-plus and equals-plus.
- Floating entries and intermediate answers.
- "Live" % key with automatic add-on or discount and net.
- Indicator light for low battery condition.
- MOS/LSI solid-state circuitry for durability and dependability.
- Bright, eight-digit LED display.

Many important statistical formulas have been pre-programmed into the Novus 6030 to assure absolute accuracy. The possibility of entry errors is greatly reduced since most of the Statistician's special function keys require only single entries.

Call Clears all statistical summations.

r [reg] Linear correlation and regression.

y val y-intercept.

x [σ] Mean and standard deviation.

Σ Y Summation of y values.

del Y Delete a y value.

Novus 6030 Statistician and 6035 Programmable Statistician at about $35 and $90 respectively.

The Novus 6035 adds Programmability Power — Added keys on the Programmable Statician (6035) are:

del X Delete an x value.
Σ X Summation of x values.
CHS Change sign.
M+ Adds displayed number to contents of memory.
√ Square root. Automatically determines square root of displayed number.
Freq Enters frequency of grouped data.
= + Adds results of calculation to contents of memory.
[MR]/MC Memory recall displays contents of separate accumulating memory. Memory clear function erases contents of memory.
% Percent key.

The addition of learn-mode programming to the already powerful Novus Statistician creates a truly innovative combination of calculating power, convenience and affordability. The Statistician's programming capability means users can virtually eliminate the possibility of errors in performing repetitious calculations. Its unique programming features include:

- Simplified programming. Users engage a Learn Switch and perform a problem in normal manner. The Novus 4525 records the formula and lets users debug the program as it's written.
- The learn-mode capacity totals 100 separate steps.
- Several different programs can be contained at the same time.
- Constant factors can be entered as program steps.
- Delete feature lets users correct programs while they are writing them.
- Skip key permits skipping over entire programs to access additional programs within 100-step capacity.
- Programs remain intact until new programs are written over or until the Statistician is turned off.
- Users have total freedom to select keyboard entries as variables or constants.

Novus 4520 Scientist/4525 Programmable Scientist

- Automatic warning signal in display lets users know when they exceed programming capacity.
- The Novus Programmable Statistician is rechargeable and comes complete with nickel cadmium batteries, charger and attractive vinyl carrying case.

Competing with the Sinclair Scientific Programmable is the Novus 4515 Programmable Mathematician above (right) at about $50.00.

The Novus Low-Cost Programmables — Novus, the National Semiconductor Co. line of programmables, represent currently three models, The Scientist, the Statistician, and the Financier. They are available as non-programmables also, at about $40 to $50 less cost.

The Novus 4525 Programmable Scientist offers all the features found on the basic Scientist. Its programming features include:

- Simplified programming. Users engage a Learn Switch and perform a problem in normal manner. The Novus 4525 records the formula and lets users debug the program as it's written.
- The learn-mode capacity totals 100 separate steps.
- Several different programs can be contained at the same time.
- Delete feature lets users correct programs while writing them.
- Skip key permits skipping over entire programs to access additional programs within 100-step capacity.
- Programs remain intact until new programs are written over or until the Scientist is turned off.
- Users have total freedom to select keyboard entries as variables or constants.

The Novus 6025 Financier is specifically dedicated to solving the kinds of problems that create the biggest problems for users. Time and money problems. The kind users work with every day in business and financial professions such as banking, real estate, insurance or accounting. The Financier has been pre-programmed to solve hundreds of these problems and more. Yet the Financier is as easy to operate as any basic adding machine. And it's priced, in many markets, somewhat lower than many comparable calculators on the market.

Novus 6020 Financier/6025 Programmable Financier

The performance features of the Novus 6025 enable users to solve complicated problems such as present and future value, loan payments, depreciation, amortization, annuities, annual percentage rate conversions, sum-of-digits depreciation.

Professional engineers and scientists are offered the 4525 Novus Scientist priced within the means of most serious users, professionals and students alike. In addition to numerous pre-programmed arithmetic, trigonometric, and logarithmic functions, the Novus Scientists feature a rollable 4-level stack, coupled with RPN (Reverse Polish Notation), for efficient evaluation of all mathematical expressions and are key-programmable.

Especially dedicated to statistical problems, the Novus 6035 Statistician features pre-programmed, single-key calculations of most common statistical formulas. What this means to most users is that countless hours can be saved in performing statistical calculations. Also, the chances for calculating or entry errors are virtually eliminated. The 6035 is a business machine that offers four-function performance (addition, subtraction, multiplication, division) as well as some important extras. Like automatic square roots, a live % key with automatic add-on or discount and net, and a separate accumulating memory and the unit is key programmable.

Because the difference between key-programmables and card-programmables is so distinct, little further discussion is needed here. The examples of product immediately ahead attest to the range of capability, but it might be best at this stage to introduce the concepts, now becoming very popular and wide-ranging, of dual and multicolor keys to expand the range of keyboard pre-programming and programmability. When using the National Semiconductor 4615 Programmable for example, the key legend explains that this below $100 calculator uses three-stack RPN logic. Several of 36 keys do double duty by using a gold-colored shift key. When this is pressed, the function printed in gold beneath the key is brought into play instead of the one in silver above it. The programmable feature is controlled by four blue keys arranged vertically along the left side of the keyboard and labelled from top to bottom: DEL, SKIP, HALT, and START; plus a three-position slide switch at the top labelled: LOAD, STEP, RUN.

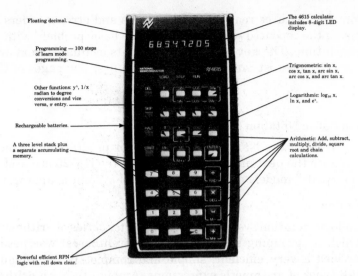

Floating decimal.

Programming — 100 steps of learn mode programming.

Other functions: y^x, $1/x$ radian to degree conversions and vice versa, π entry.

Rechargeable batteries.

A three level stack plus a separate accumulating memory.

Powerful efficient RPN logic with roll down clear.

The 4615 calculator includes 8-digit LED display.

Trigonometric: sin x, cos x, tan x, arc sin x, arc cos x, and arc tan x.

Logarithmic: $\log_{10}$ x, ln x, and e^x.

Arithmetic: Add, subtract, multiply, divide, square root and chain calculations.

The National Semiconductor 4615 sliderule calculator is a 100-step, keyboard programmable calculator with arithmetic, log and trig functions and features RPN (reverse Polish notation), three-level register stack and accumulating memory. 4615 offers Simple Operation: users simply engage the "load" switch and perform a problem in the normal manner. The 4615 records the formula for later use with other variables. Because users can use one set of variables to solve a problem while the calculator is in the learn mode, they can check and debug their program while it is being written. 100 Step Programming Capacity: Several different programs can be contained at the same time. Delete Feature: Lets users correct programs while they write them. Skip Key: Lets users select the program they want to use from within the 100 step capacity. All programs remain intact within the memory until new programs are written over them or until the calculator is turned off. Users have total control over whether entries are keyed in as variables or formula constants. Automatic signal in display warns users when they exceed programming capacity.

Learn-mode programming begins with the slide switch at LOAD. Users press START and then key in a sequence of steps to solve a problem. Users press HALT each time before they insert a variable. The calculator 'remembers' exactly, and when users put the slide switch at RUN and press START, it will go through the same sequence of steps automatically, only stopping at any HALT for users to insert a new variable, and with the new answer displayed at the end of the sequence. This unit and others have 100 steps of programming available at one time so users can program these units with one large program or as many small programs as will fit into 100 steps. Pressing SKIP in the LOAD position terminates one program and marks the beginning of another. In the RUN position, the SKIP key is used as a kind of tab key to skip over unwanted programs to reach the one users want. The DEL key is used to erase, or delete, erroneous steps. With the switch in STEP position, users can go through a program or programs a step at a time by repeatedly pressing the START KEY.

Programmable features really are time-savers and error-avoiders in situations requiring the repeated working of the same basic problem with different data used each time. The key-programmable units evaluated next are a step-up from the very low-cost units discussed in the first few pages of this chapter.

The Reverse Polish Notation (RPN) System

Because several of the National Semiconductor programmable models use RPN and because the next model to be evaluated, the HP-25 is one of the most popular "no equals" models a review of the RPN system is appropriate here.

Calculating Power

In 1949, a logic notation system was developed for series of arithmetic operations in which no grouping symbol (such as parentheses) was needed. This system provided a very efficient, simple and completely unambiguous language for all types of arithmetic expressions. Ambiguity in an arithmetic expression occurs when there is some questions as to the order in which the operations are to be performed; since different operation orders many times produce different answers. For example, does the expression $2 + 3 \div 4$ really mean $(2 + 3) \div 4$ or $2 + (3 \div 4)$?

Hewlett-Packard selected this system for their calculators after evaluating other languages available; i.e., various forms of algebraic notation and some computer languages. The advantages of HP's logic system to the user are best viewed in light of the user being able to "work" the calculator with total consistency. Each problem is approached the same way, no matter how simple or complex, regardless of length. Each function on the calculator always works the same way, computing the answer immediately. There is no delay or waiting for an equal key or some other operation key to be pushed.

The basis for the logic system HP uses is that before an operation can be performed, the *number* or *numbers* needed for that operation must be available (somewhere in the calculator). Then, when the desired operation key is pushed, that operation takes place immediately! A short discussion may help here. There are only two types of basic arithmetic operations; one (1) number operations and two (2) number operations. The one (1) number operations (such as $1/x, \sqrt{x}, x^2$, SIN, COS, TAN, log, ln, etc.) require only one (1) memory location (the display) for the number to occupy until the operation is performed. The two (2) number operations (such as $+, -, \times, \div, y^x$, etc.) require two (2) memory locations (the display plus one other) for the two numbers to occupy until the operation is performed. The importance of these two types of basic operations is overwhelming. No matter how large or complex an equation is, it can always be broken down into a series of one and two number operations; much the same way people would do a large complex equation with pencil and paper. Starting with one and two number sets whose operations can be performed — doing these computations — combining these intermediate results with other numbers and operations — doing further computations until there is but a single number left — the answer. This is exactly the way Hewlett-Packard calculators work. In fact, Hewlett-Packard's system also displays every intermediate result. This allows the users to follow all substeps of a calculation and reassures them that the final result is correct. Likewise, there are many instances when the user wants to record intermediate answers for future use.

Therefore, a calculator with only two (2) memory locations, (say X, Y as illustrated below) is needed to solve all basic kinds of arithmetic operations.

Location Y   0.00
Location X   0.00
(Display)

Using the HP logic system one number operations are very simple. The user keys in the number and then pushes the desired operation key — the answer is immediately computed and displayed. For two number operations, using HP's system, the user keys in the first number, presses the ENTER↑ key, keys in the second number and then pushes the desired operation key. The ENTER↑ key signals the calculator that the first number is entered and at the same time copies the first number into the second memory location Y.

No "=" key is needed — If you will look at the keyboard of any HP calculator shown in this catalog, you will see that none has an "=" key. Nor are there any keys for parentheses. None are needed.

Instead, all HP calculators have a key like this: ENTER ↑

Thanks to this key, and RPN logic, you get four major advantages you don't get with most other calculators:

1. You work with only two numbers at a time, just as if you were solving the problem with paper and pencil. (Only incredibly faster.)

Even the most complex problems are broken down into a series of easily-handled two-number problems, which you can solve in any order that's convenient — left to right, right to left, or from the middle of the equation outwards.

No matter what kind of problem it is, there's no restructuring to do . . . no rearranging of the equation as is so often necessary with other calculators, to conform to algebraic logic.

So there's less confusion and less chance for error.

2. The function is immediately calculated.

With the HP calculator, pressing the function key initiates the desired action, so you get your answer immediately.

For example, to find the square root of 16, simply press three keys . . . 1 6 √x . . . and your answer immediately appears on the display . . . 4.00

And it's just as fast and easy to calculate squares, cosines, factorials or other functions.

3. The intermediate answer is displayed.

This enables you to check your calculation every step of the way . . . so you can do something about if it it doesn't look "right."

4. The intermediate answer is automatically stored.

So there's no need to store it manually, by keying in each digit, if the number is needed in the next calculation.

Obviously, this saves keystrokes and helps prevent errors. And you can easily recall the intermediate answer if need be.

Four major advantages — to give you *confidence in your computations.*

Just four simple steps — To use any Hewlett-Packard pocket calculator, just follow these four simple steps . . .

1. Key in the first number.
2. Enter it into the stack (press the "ENTER↑" key).
3. Key in the second number.
4. Press the function key.

And if your numbers are already stored in the calculator as intermediate answers, all you have to do is hit the function key.

Could anything be easier . . . or faster?

Here's an example — Let's take a simple problem — 2.5 × 4 — and solve it with an HP calculator, using the four steps shown above . . .

1. Key in the first number: 2 · 5
2. Enter it into the stack: ENTER↑
3. Key in the second number: 4
4. Press the function key: ×

Your answer appears on the display: 10.00

Now let's try a slightly more difficult problem: $(2 + 6) \times (9 - 3.5)$.

Working from left to right, press . . . 2 ENTER↑ 6 +

The display shows the intermediate answer: 8.00

To solve for $(9 - 3.5)$, press . . . 9 ENTER↑ 3 · 5 −

The display shows: 5.50

To multiply the two intermediate answers (which have been automatically stored), press . . . ×

And the displays shows: 44.00

Even if your problem were as complex as converting indicated air speed to the true mach number . . .

$$\sqrt{5\left(\left[\left[\left(\frac{400}{661.5}\right)^2 .2 + 1\right]^{\frac{1.4}{.4}} - 1\right)\frac{29.96}{15} + 1\right]^{.286} - 1\right)}$$

. . . you would still be able to solve it quickly, easily and without confusion if you used an HP calculator.

Under the structure shown in the previous diagram (the two memory location calculator), all intermediate answers would have to be stored away in some independent memory location (if available) or written down on a piece of paper. Watch out for those 9 and 10 digit intermediate results! Hewlett-Packard has solved this problem and wedded its logic system to 4 memory locations, by just adding two more memory locations (Z and T) to the two already discussed; as shown below:

Location T	0.00
Location Z	0.00
Location Y	0.00
Location X (Display)	0.00

All calculations are done the same way previously described except now there are two extra locations to hold the intermediate results, the Hewlett-Packard has designed this system to automatically save and retrieve these intermediate results as needed. An additional advantage of HP's logic system is for multiple operations on the same number. By pressing the ENTER↑ key twice after keying in a number, the user can often avoid the need to key a number in again or manually store and recall it from a storage register. Hewlett-Packard also provided the ability to look through all 4 memory locations to see what numbers are there and be able to switch the contents of the X-location with the Y-location. An example is probably the easiest way to see how the whole system works together.

Find the monthly payment on a 30 year (360 payment), $30,000 loan having an annual interest of 6% (.005/month).

$$\text{Monthly Payment} = \frac{\text{Principal} \times \text{Monthly Interest Rate}}{1 - [1/(1 + \text{Monthly Interest Rate})^{\text{Payments}}]}$$

$$= \frac{30,000 \times .005}{1 - [1/(1.005)^{360}]}$$

	1	2
T	0.00	0.00
Z	0.00	0.00
Y	0.00	30000.00
X	30000.00	30000.00
Key	**30000**	**ENTER ↑**

	3	4
T	0.00	0.00
Z	0.00	0.00
Y	30000.00	0.00
X	.005	150.00
Key	**.005**	**×**

	5	6
T	0.00	0.00
Z	0.00	150.00
Y	150.00	1.00
X	1.00	1.00
Key	**1**	**ENTER ↑**

	7	8
T	0.00	150.00
Z	150.00	1.00
Y	1.00	1.005
X	1.005	1.005
Key	**1.005**	**ENTER ↑**

	9	10
T	150.00	150.00
Z	1.00	150.00
Y	1.005	1.00
X	360.00	6.0225
Key	**360**	y^x

	11	12
T	150.00	150.00
Z	150.00	150.00
Y	1.00	150.00
X	.16604	.83396
Key	$1/x$	**−**

	13	14
T	150.00	
Z	150.00	
Y	150.00	RESULT
X	179.87	$179.87
Key	÷	**Monthly Payment**

SCIENTIFIC NOTATION

Scientific notation is very important to the pocket calculator user. It is the most convenient and economical way of expressing large and small numbers; and at the same time, it gives additional computation accuracy over non-scientific notation calculators. A number written in scientific notation has the general form of $A \times 10^b$ where A (the mantissa) is a number between 1 and 10, and b (the exponent) is a positive or negative integer. Some examples of numbers written in scientific notation are:

a. 3.219×10^{26}
    where   A =   3.219   b =   26

b. $-4.32618596 \times 10^{-10}$
where   A $= -4.32618596$ b $= -10$

c. -9.12619831×10^9
where   A $= -9.12619831$ b $=$ 9

d. 6.889×10^{-15}
where   A $=$ 6.889   b $= -15$

In non-scientific notation (fixed or floating point notation) these numbers would be represented as:

a. 321900000000000000000000000000.00
b. $-$.000000000432618596
c. $-9126198310.$
d.   .000000000000006889

Unfortunately, pocket calculators do not have enough digits in the display to handle these large and small numbers (if they did, they wouldn't be pocket calculators). In fact, most calculators have, at the maximum, 8 or 10 digit displays and many have even less. If, for example, the above 4 numbers were answers to problems solved on a calculator with a 10 digit display (without scientific notation) they would be displayed as:

a.   c.
   0000000000. $-9126198310.$
b.   d.
   .0000000004   .0000000000

Actually, a. would indicate an overflow, b. is partially correct, c. is correct and d. would indicate an underflow.

A 10 digit calculator without scientific notation can only handle numbers in the range:

9,999,999,999. to .0000000001

which are really not particularly large or small in any area of science and many areas of business (where accuracy is needed down to the penny).

Hewlett-Packard has scientific notation on all of its calculators (its calculators work in fixed/floating point notation also). HP-21 and HP-25 calculators display 8 significant digits in the mantissa, plus the exponent. Other HP calculators display 10 digits plus the exponent. Thus, the previous 4 numbers would be displayed on most HP calculators as:

a.   c.
   3.219   26 -9.12619831 09
b.   d.
   -4.32618596 -10 6.889 -15

In fact, Hewlett-Packard calculators will handle numbers as large as $9.999999999 \times 10^{99}$ (that is 10 followed by 99 0's) and numbers as small as $1.000000000 \times 10^{-99}$ (that is 1 preceded by 99 0's then the decimal point.) Thus, the user's calculating range has increased from 20 digits to 200 digits.

The second, and equally important area of concern for scientific notation, is that of additional accuracy of the numbers during a long calculation. Without scientific notation, numbers larger than 8 or 10 digits overflow the display; and this fact is usually signalled to the user (overflow light lights up; or display blinks, etc.) and that ends that particular problem solution. However, small numbers are a more serious problem. Without scientific notation, very small numbers show up as zero, or some part of the original number. Some typical examples of computed small numbers could be:

actual number   .00000000004423
                                displayed as   .0000000000
actual number   .0000000008612
                                displayed as   .0000000009
actual number   .0000000003497
                                displayed as   .0000000003
actual number   .000000012456
                                displayed as   .0000000125

Thus, the displayed answer incurs from close to 0% up to 100% error (i.e., 100% error is a completely wrong answer). And this error compounds itself if the number is used in further computations.

Hewlett-Packard calculators, whether showing a number in fixed/floating point notation or scientific notation, always internally maintain the number in scientific notation with full display digit accuracy. Some examples of this are shown below:

	Fixed Point Notation Display A	Scientific Notation Internal Number B
$\dfrac{56}{1.2 \times 10^{10}}$	.0000000047	4.666666667 − 09
$\dfrac{21}{3.1 \times 10^{10}}$	.0000000007	6.774193548 − 11
$\dfrac{14}{2.9 \times 10^{20}}$	.0000000000	4.827586207 − 30
$\dfrac{98}{1.32 \times 10^{6}}$	.0000742424	7.424242424 − 05

Even if the display on a Hewlett-Packard calculator shows the number in column A, the number in column B (the more accurate number) would be used internally for further computations. This internal number representation guarantees the user the additional accuracy available with scientific notation.

As noted, with a stack arrangement of memory registers, this system is said to be quite an efficient way for evaluating mathematical expressions and packing considerable calculating power into a small space. The stack memory is particularly useful for handling long, complex problems involving chain calculations.

Operation is based on the fact that arbitrary expressions can be specified unambiguously without parentheses by placing operators immediately before or after their operands. Thus, the expression $(a - b) \times (c - d)$ may be specified as $\times + ab - cd$ (Polish) or $ab + cd - \times$ (reverse Polish). With the help of a stack (last-in-first-out) memory, the reverse Polish expression is evaluated as follows:

T							
Z					a + b		
Y		a		a + b	c	a + b	
X	a	b	a + b	c	d	c − d	(a + b) · (c − d)
↑	Enter a	Enter b	+	Enter c	Enter d	−	

Stack memory location

Keyboard operation ⟶

Though straightforward, note that the order of data entry is considerably different from a typical pencil and paper calculation.

Several brands of four-function consumer calculators also use reverse Polish notation. In all cases, this logic system is immediately revealed by the keyboard, which lacks any type of equals function.

The HP-25 and the HP-25C With Nonvolatile Memory

The HP-25 is considered a prime competitor for students to use as they learn the intricacies of advanced programmable calculators. Hewlett-Packard evidently considered it important enough to decide that it would be their first hand-held model to have nonvolatile memory. The HP-25C saves a program for instant reuse without lost time for programming.

The continuous memory capability of the HP-25C can provide tremendous values in time-saving and convenience to any scientist, engineer or student who uses a few long programs repeatedly — for example, if twenty percent of a user's programs will solve most of their problems.

The HP-25C retains a program — no matter how often switched on and off — by means of sophisticated complementary metal oxide silicon circuitry (C-MOS). The last program stored is saved, ready for use, until users clear it or enters a new program. As a result users can program a frequently-needed calculation once, and then perform it as often as necessary — hour after hour, day after day — without the bother or lost time caused by reentering their program. Users may add special functions not on the keyboard.

Continuous memory makes it possible to add specialized functions to those already preprogrammed into the HP-25C. For example, if one anticipates extensive work with hyperbolics, he or she can program them into the HP-25C where they will be retained by the continuous memory for repeated calculations at the touch of a key. Many specialized functions can be programmed into the HP-25C for fast keystroke calculations, including conversions such as decimal degree/radian, octal/decimal; statistical functions; pricing analysis functions; real estate functions; business functions and many others.

The HP-25C remembers data collected for later use. The HP-25C with continuous memory not only retains all information in its 49-step program memory, it also retains all data in the 8 addressable registers and the LAST-X register. (See below.)

The capability permits the use of the HP-25C as a notebook to save data from previous problems for later use or to keep the sum of statistical data entries while taking samples in the field. For example, surveyors doing traverses in the field can keep intermediate results even while the calculator is turned off between readings. The power economy greatly extends battery operating time.

Since the HP-25C may be switched off between calculations without losing programs or data, battery operating time can be significantly extended. Even when changing batteries, the HP-25C will retain programs and data. When batteries are removed a capacitor temporarily furnishes power to the continuous memory circuits. Depending on the charge of the battery being replaced, time available for the exchange is between 5 seconds and 2 minutes. The extended battery operating time made possible by C-MOS circuitry makes the HP-25C ideal for many uses in the field where time between data collections is prolonged; for example, navigation, surveying, and many other applications.

The HP-25C has all the capabilities of the HP-25 — plus continuous memory. Two data storage chips in the calculator use CMOS (complementary metal oxide semiconductor) technology to achieve continuous memory. Typically, the two chips require about 5 μW steady power drain to preserve the information. This figure represents about 1/80,000 of the 400 mW normally used when the machine is on. The model 25C is priced at $200, but it is often discounted.

PROGRAMMABLE HP-25 HAS BUILT-IN POWER TO SOLVE TECHNICAL PROBLEMS

Programmed to solve 72 scientific, engineering and mathematical functions, the HP-25 saves users time solving difficult technical problems. In addition, it has 8 addressable memories, each capable of register arithmetic. The HP-25's programming power includes a 49-step memory. Each step in this memory can accommodate multi-keystroke functions, because the keycodes of all pre-fixed functions — including the register arithmetic functions — merge. Thus, users gain extra capacity. With the HP-25, users enter the keystrokes necessary to solve representative problems only once. Thereafter, they enter the variables and press the Run/Stop key for an almost instant answer. Users can add, change or skip steps and can program the HP-25 to perform direct branches of conditional tests. And the hand-held unit offers not only fixed and scientific but also engineering notation (i.e., exponent displayed as a multiple of $10^{\pm 3}$ as in giga and nano). The RPN logic system with 4-register stack allows users to evaluate any expression without copying parenthesis or worrying about hierarchies or restructuring before entering. Preprogrammed functions of the HP-25 include log and trigonometric functions, the latter in degrees, radians or grads; rectangular/polar and decimal hours/hours-minutes-seconds conversions; mean and standard deviation; and summations.

The calculator's 49 steps of program memory are coupled with merged key-codes that conserve steps to effectively expand memory capacity. An "Integer/Function" key permits storage of two numbers in a single memory and an "Absolute Value" key adds to the storage capacity and flexibility of the HP-25's programming. Users may perform full register arithmetic on the data in each of the eight addressable memories.

Keystroke programmability is the four-step answer to repetitive problem. Users:

1. Turn the HP-25 on and switch to PRGM;
2. Enter the keystrokes necessary to solve the problem and switch to RUN;
3. Key in a set of variables and press the R/S (Run/Stop) key;
4. Repeat step three for each iteration.

Users save time, gain precision and flexibility because they can verify formulas or test alternate approaches with near complete programmability. Users can add, check, or change program steps at will. They use the SST (Single-STep) or BST (Back-STep) key and Display to locate the steps they want to check or change, then enter their changes. The HP-25 displays all program steps, so they can always tell at a glance where they are in their routine. The HP-25 has a PAUSE key that lets users write one-second interrupts into their programs, in case they want to pick up intermediate results or verify the progress of a calculation. Thus the HP-25 is a complete keystroke programmable calculator.

With branching and conditional test capability users can program the HP-25 to perform direct branches or conditional tests based on eight different logic comparisons. A program, in this case, is a sequence of keystrokes used to solve a problem. The HP-25 can retain and repeat a program up to 49 steps in length. So users don't have to press the same keys again and again when the same problem is worked with different data.

PRGM — RUN

Users set the HP-25 to PROGRAM mode by flipping a switch. They press the keys they'd normally press to solve the problem. (But don't enter the data.) Their program is retained in the HP-25's program memory.

To solve the problem, they switch to RUN mode and enter the data. They then press the "Run/Stop" key to run their program. Seconds later, the answer appears on the HP-25 display. To solve other problems using the same program, they enter the new data and press the "Run/Stop" key again. Because their program does the calculation automatically — users just sit back and watch it — there's less chance for error than if they had to repeat the keystroke sequence themselves step by step. Also it takes but a fraction of the time.

The HP-25 can be programmed to make decisions because it can do conditional branching, using eight relational tests. Users can program it to test the relationship between two values, by means of these tests:

$$x < y \quad x \geq y \quad x \neq y \quad x = y \text{ or}$$
$$x < 0 \quad x \geq 0 \quad x \neq 0 \quad x = 0$$

Depending on the outcome of the tests, the HP-25 will automatically skip a step of the program . . . or it will continue through the program in sequence. Or, by the means of the "Go TO" key, users can program the HP-25 to branch directly to a specified step, and then continue executing the program.

Both types of branching — conditional and direct — are useful in solving a variety of programming problems.

Here are the other extras: engineering notation, RPN logic, and integer/fraction truncation key, absolute value key. The application manual supplied helps users to realize the full potential of their new scientific calculator. 54 programs are included from the varied areas of algebra, number theory, trig, analytical geometry, numerical methods, statistics, finance, surveying, navigation and even games.

Hewlett-Packard's Low-Cost HP-25 Programmable Scientific Pocket Calculator Aids

Programming Power Available in HP-25 Scientific Key-Programmable Pocket Calculator

The PRGM-RUN switch is on the top right. Users simply set the HP-25C to PROGRAM mode by flipping a switch. They then press the keys they normally press to solve the problem. (But don't enter the data.) The program is retained in the HP-25C's program memory. The R/S Key is used to solve the problem. Users switch to RUN mode and enter the data. Then press the "Run/Stop" key to run the program. Seconds later, the answer appears on the HP-25C display. To solve other problems using the same program enter the new data and press the "Run/Stop" key again. Because the program does the calculation automatically — there's less chance for error. Every step and function is clearly explained — with illustrated, step-by-step directions — in the HP-25C Owner's Handbook. An example of a typical problem from the HP-25C Applications Programs Book is in the following box. The program memory uses a simple numeric code, based on the position of each key on the keyboard. For example, "31" means "3 rows down, 1st key" — the "ENTER" key. Some key codes will appear as two or three pairs of numbers. To conserve steps, each prefixed function (e.g., "f", "x") takes only one program memory step. When users single-step through a program, the code numbers are visible on the HP-25C display. This system lets them know where they are in the program memory and what the program looks like step-by-step. Testing and editing programs — to make sure complex solutions are correct — is thus greatly simplified.

The "Back STep" and "Single STep" keys allows review of the entire memory one step at a time, in either direction. Or users can press the "Go TO" key, along with the number of the step they want. Users can change their program, they simply stop at the appropriate step and key in a new entry, which will overwrite the previous one. To test program a step at a time, they switch to RUN and press "SST" repeatedly. They can see the numeric code when they press the key and the intermediate solution when they release the key.

The HP-25C Decision Branching

Like a computer, the HP-25C can be programmed to make decisions, because it can do conditional branching. Users can program it to test the relationship between two values, by means of these tests:

$$x < y \quad x \geq y \quad x \neq y \quad x = y$$

Depending on the outcome of the tests, the HP-25C will *automatically* skip a step of the program . . . or it will continue through the program in sequence. or, by means of the "Go TO" key, users can program the HP-25C to branch directly to a specified step, and then continue executing the program. Both types of branching — conditional and direct — are useful in solving a variety of programming problems . . . and make most work easier. And users can also program the HP-25C to PAUSE during the running of their program.

The "PAUSE" is used to momentarily interrupt (about one second per Pause command) the program execution and display the contents of the X register. This gives users the opportunity to review or write down intermediate results, data, the value of a counter of other output. The example below shows one use. The ABSolute value function allows users to get the absolute value, or magnitude, of a number within a programmed calculation. The INTeger/FRACtion truncation function allows users to keep only the integer or fractional portion of a number. This is especially useful in base conversion, random number generation and other specialized routines. In addition, users can integer-fractionalize their data and double the number of data points they can save in the registers.

The HP-25C Preprogrammed Keyboard Functions

In addition to its programming power, the HP-25C provides preprogrammed functions most used by scientists and engineers, including: Extra trigonometric capabilities, rectangular/polar coordinate conversions, angle (time) conversions, logarithmic functions, extra statistical capability, and summa-

Here's an example of keystroke programming

Suppose you were asked to plot the trajectory of a stone which is hurled into the air with an initial velocity V at an angle to the horizontal of θ.

Neglecting drag due to friction with the atmosphere, the following equations describe the stone's x- and y- coordinates as functions of the time t;

$x = vt \cos \theta$

$y = vt \sin \theta - \frac{1}{2} gt^2$

Where x = the horizontal
distance the
stone has
traveled

y = height of the
stone

g = acceleration
due to gravity
(9.8 m/s² or
32 ft/s²)

Using a page from the HP-25C *Applications Programs Book* as a guide, here's how you would program the solution on the HP-25C:

KEY ENTRY	DISPLAY LINE	CODE	COMMENTS
	00		
f → R	01	14 09	Use polar-to-rectangular for
STO 2	02	23 02	$v_x = v \cos \theta$-horix. vel.
x ≷ y	03	21	
STO 3	04	23 03	$v_y = v \sin \theta$ = vert. vel.
0	05	00	
STO 4	06	23 04	Initialize: t = 0
RCL 0	07	24 00	Start of loop
STO +4	08	23 51 04	Next time interval:
RCL 4	09	24 04	$t \leftarrow t + \Delta t$
g x²	10	15 02	
RCL 1	11	24 01	
x	12	61	
2	13	02	
÷	14	71	
CHS	15	32	
RCL 4	16	24 04	
RCL 3	17	24 03	
x	18	61	
+	19	51	$y = v_y t - \frac{1}{2} gt^2$
RCL 4	20	24 04	
RCL 2	21	24 02	
x	22	61	$x = v_x t$
RCL 4	23	24 04	
f PAUSE	24	14 74	Pause to display t
R↓	25	22	
R/S	26	74	Halt and display x
x ≷ y	27	21	
R/S	28	74	Halt and display y
GTO	29	13 07	Branch back for next t
	30		

STEP	INSTRUCTIONS	INPUT DATA/UNITS	KEYS		OUTPUT DATA/UNITS
1	Key in program				
2	Store time interval	Δt	STO	0	
3	Store gravitational constant	g	STO	1	
4	Input angle and initial speed	θ	ENTER		
		v	f	PRGM	
5	Perform steps 5 and 6 any				
	number of times: Display time		R/S		(t)
	and horizontal distance				x
6	Display height		R/S		y
7	To change θ or v, go to step 4.				
	To change Δt or g, go to				
	appropriate step, store new				
	value, then go to step 4.				

Problem:

Plot the trajectory of a stone cast upwards with a velocity of 20 m/s at an angle of 30° to the horizontal. Use intervals of ¼ second between points plotted. Let g = 9.8 m/s².

Solution:

0.25 STO O 9.8 STO 1 30 ↑ 20 f PRGM R/S ————————————————→ 0.25 (t₁)

→ 0.25 (t_1)

4.33 (x_1)

R/S ————————————————————————————————————→ 2.19 (y_1)

R/S ————————————————————————————————————→ 0.50 (t_2)

8.66 (x_2)

R/S ————————————————————————————————————→ 3.78 (y_2)

R/S ————————————————————————————————————→ 0.75 (t_3)

12.99 (x_3)

R/S ————————————————————————————————————→ 4.74 (y_3)

Continue until y becomes negative.

The table of these results is shown below:

t	0.25	0.50	0.75	1.00	1.25	1.50	1.75	2.00	2.25
x	4.33	8.66	12.99	17.32	21.65	25.98	30.31	34.64	38.97
y	2.19	3.78	4.74	5.10	4.84	3.98	2.49	0.40	−2.31

tions. The "Σ +" key automatically calculates n, Σ x, Σ x², Σ y, Σ xy for statistical and vector calculations. Data may be deleted via the "Σ −" key.

The HP-25C calculates the mean and standard deviation and offers a choice of display formats: FIX SCI ENG When users first turn on the HP-25C, the display "wakes up" in fixed point notation, with the display rounded to two decimal places. By pressing "f", "FIX " and a number key (0 to 9), users can specify the number of decimal places. Or they can select scientific notation, by pressing "f", "SCI" and a number key to specify the number of decimal places (up to seven digits after the decimal point). − 14641278 − 12

Engineering notation on HP pocket calculators allows all numbers to be shown in a modified scientific notation with exponents of 10 that are multiples of three (*e.g.*, 10^3, 10^6, 10^{12}). This is particularly useful in scientific and engineering calculations, where units of measure are often specified in multiples of 10^3. When the HP-25C is in engineering notation, the first three digits are always present but users can display up to 8 total digits. Whichever notation is selected, the HP-25C always maintains the complete 10-digit number internally. Also, the HP-25C switches the display automatically from fixed point notation to full scientific notation whenever a number is too large or too small to be seen in fixed point notation.

HP-25C Memory Power

In addition to the 49-step program memory the HP-25C has 8 addressable registers

R_0 Instead of writing down and re-entering numbers manually, users can
R_1 simply store them in any or all of the eight addressable memory registers,
R_2 and recall them when needed. The registers may also be used for register
R_3 arithmetic — directly adding to, subtracting from, dividing into or multi-
R_4 plying the register contents. Eight addressable registers and register
R_5 arithmetic make data manipulation easy, especially with programmed
R_6 problem-solving.
R_7

HP-25 Applications Programs Book to Help Get the Most Out of the HP-25

These HP-25 Applications Programs — 54 in 1976 — have been drawn from the varied areas of algebra and number theory, trigonometry and analytical geometry, numerical methods, statistics, finance, surveying, navigation, and games. Each program is furnished with a full explanation which includes a description of the problem, and pertinent equations, a list of keystrokes to be entered into program memory, a set of instructions for running the program, and an example or two, with solutions. To use these programs does not require any proficiency in programming. The first program in each chapter contains, in addition to the usual explanations, a more detailed description of the problem, a commented list of the program keystrokes with a step-by-step tracing of the contents of the stack registers, and a list of the keystrokes required to solve the example problem. Whenever an interesting programming technique is used in one of these programs, it is described in a short section headed "Programming Remarks."

The Battle of Key-Programmables — A Strong Competitor: TI's SR-56

Competing strongly against the NS key-programmables and the HP-25 (and others, see below), the SR-56, offers several strong criteria for student purchase. One of the strongest is its capability for use with the TI printer; another is its low price. But, it also offers more. A brief analysis is presented, followed by some comparisons. (The SR-56 was superceded in 1977 by the TI-57.)

The key programmable SR-56 is a 100 step, 10 memory calculator with an Algebraic Operating System (AOS) featuring left to right entry and 9 levels of parentheses. Like TI's SR-52 hand-held card programmable, the SR-56 is compatible with the PC-100 print cradle, which allows complete tracing and print-out of any calculator operation. Over 25 scientific and statistical operations are possible from the keyboard, and 2 looping capabilities and 4 levels of subroutines allow sophisticated programming approaches which are new to the general run available key programmable units.

The SR-56 is very suitable for students and professionals who frequently need to solve repetitive problems, or explore multiple options within single problems. Its ease-of-use, however, makes the SR-56 a desirable tool for businessmen or financiers who make forecasting and estimating decisions on the basis of extended calculations. With twenty-five (25) preprogrammed arithmetic and transcendental functions, the SR-56 is capable of handling quite difficult computational problems. Logs, trigs and coordinate-conversions are just a few of the transcendental functions. The SR-56's ten (10) user memories have full register arithmetic to facilitate their use and increase the calculator functionality.

A key programmable calculator, the SR-56 can "remember" up to 100 program steps. And with an extensive repertoire of conditional and unconditional branches, it is capable of solving problems previously solvable only on large-scale computers. There are three unconditional branches and six conditional branches which include four levels of subroutines and two loop control instructions. Two more features are unique to most hand-held programmables: (1) An independent test register permits comparison with the value in display at any point in a calculation without interfering with the processing in progress; (2) A dual function pause key allows the display to be viable during program execution for ½ second or provides for automatic single step program operation. Selected editing functions permit easy entry and correction of user programs. With single step and back step keys, the users can quickly sequence through its program memory to locate a program error. With the write-over capability of the calculator design, erroneous key pushes can be replaced with the proper key push while extra keypushes can be negated by using the NOP key. A 10 + 2 digit VLED display has full floating point with Scientific Notation format. Moreover, format is controllable via the fixed point option. The unit is fully rechargeable and comes complete with a standard charger. A 56-program applications booklet is included with the SR-56, with programs for Mathematics, Electrical Engineering, Statistics, Finance, Surveying and other disciplines.

Printers for TI Portable — The PC-100 print cradle permits TI's SR-52 and SR-56 hand-held programmable calculators to become desk-top printing calculators. When the calculator is locked into the cradle, the user is able to print anything shown in the display or print the step-by-step execution of a program. Print and paper advance controls permit the user to handle these functions on the PC-100 as well as on the calculator, and a "trace" key allows monitoring of all functions as they happen. The PC-100 has a thermal printer which prints 5 × 7 dot-matrix characters on a 2.5-in. tape. It prints 20 characters per line and sold for $295 in 1976. In 1977, some stores sold the upgraded PC 100A for less than $150. (The SR-52 has been enhanced and is now the TI-59.)

This SR-56 is a 100-step, 10 memory Key programmable calculator with Algebraic Operating System and looping. It was superceded in 1977 by the 150-step TI-57. The SR-52 is now the TI-59.

TI Programmables Use AOS — Algebraic Operating System

With the introduction of the SR-50 slide rule calculator a few years ago, Texas Instruments had a choice: algebraic entry or Reverse Polish Notation (RPN). TI chose algebraic entry because they felt it was the most natural and easiest to use. Their views continue to gain more strength with the SR-60, TI 57, 58 and 59 programmable calculators. TI confirmed their major decision for the power and ease of use when its unique Algebraic Operating System was internationally publicized. For many, the system is easier to use than to explain. AOS is more than just algebraic entry. It's a *full* algebraic hierarchy coupled with multiple levels of parentheses. This means more pending operations, as well as easy left-to-right entry of expressions — both numbers *and* functions. It is, in effect, algebraic hierarchy.

This is the universally recognized order of performing calculations. Functions first. Powers and roots. Multiplication or division. Then addition or subtraction. AOS performs calculations in this order. But users have the option to change the order whenever they wish by using the parenthesis keys.

More Pending Operations Are Important

With AOS, users can compute complex equations directly. For example, a seemingly simple calculation like this:

$$1 + 3 \times \left[4 + \frac{5}{\left(7 - \frac{2}{9}\right)} \right] = \, ?$$

It contains *six* pending operations as it's written. An SR-52 or SR-56 programmable calculator with full AOS easily handles it just as it's stated, left-to-right. Users don't have to rearrange the equation, or remember what's in the stack as with RPN. A calculator with "full" AOS *remembers* both the numbers and functions in its register stack. And performs them according to algebraic hierarchy. As more operations become pending, the stack fills up (as shown in the diagram). Finally, when the equals key is pressed, the operations in the register stack are performed to give the answer (15.21311475), automatically.

Here's How AOS Stacks Up

AOS remembers both numbers and operations, so users key-in their equation left-to-right. RPN only remembers numbers, users have to remember operations and the order.

Register No. in Stack	SR-52 Numbers	Oper.	SR-56 Numbers	Oper.	RPN Calculators
11	0				
10	0				
9	0		Numbers	Oper.	
8	0		0		
7	1	+	1	+	
6	3	× (	3	× (	
5	4	+	4	+	Numbers
4	5	÷ (	5	÷ (	5
3	7	−	7	−	7
2	2	÷	2	÷	2
1	9		9		9

9 levels of parentheses	9 levels of parentheses	4-register stack including
10 pending operations	7 pending operations	the display
11-register stack, including the display	8-register stack, including the display	

The SR-56: Programmability for Decision-Making

The SR-56 branches like a computer. Just as with the SR-52, program steps are usually processed as they're entered. But sometimes program steps need to be handled out of sequential order. This change is called branching. The SR-56 is capable of direct addressing which means users specify the instruction they wish it to go to. The SR-56 has three unconditional branches which include: Go to; Reset; Subroutine (4 levels). And six conditional branches, which include two for loop control and four test register comparisons.

A unique independent test register lets users compare the value in the display with the value in the test register — without interfering with the processes in progress. If test conditions are met, then a conditional branch is made. Otherwise the sequence continues. This sketch shows a conditional branch to instruction 27. If the t-register had contained an eight, then no branch would be made. The program would go on to location 12. There are four types of tests which users can monitor at the display: Greater than or equal; Less than; Equal; Not equal.

Program Memory Location	Key		t Register reg.	value
08	7		t	6
09	x ≥ t			
10	2			
11	7			

26	=
27	R/S
28	RST

Extra Memories Help With Tough Problems

With 10 user memories, users can store and recall data and add, subtract, multiply or divide directly within a memory register, without affecting the calculation in progress. The machine also has a unique pause key that works two ways. To illustrate: This program sums consecutive integers: $\sum_0^N$ k. RCL 0 recalls the integer k from data memory 0 (5, in this case). This is summed (+) and the result displayed by the pause instruction in location 03. Decrement-and-skip-on-zero (DSZ) instructs the SR-56 to reduce the integer by one, loop back to location 00 and repeat the summation with the next integer. The loop continues until data memory 0 has been decremented to zero which completes the program. Meanwhile, the display shows each step in the summation: $5 + 4 + 3 + 2 + 1$.

Program Memory Location	Key		Data Memory	Value		
00	RCL		0	5		5.
01	0					
02	+					9.
03	Pause					
04	dsz					12.
05	0					
06	0					14.
07	0					
08	=					
09	R/S					15.

Or, users may hold the pause key down and they'll see the result of every step in their program (½-second a step).

Programming the SR-56 — Using Algebraic Operating System (AOS)

Programming is basically logical thinking. Every problem has a logical flow, from beginning to end. There may be a few constants that must be injected and several variables to be put in which might change the course. Users must learn to compensate for these. The same is true of programming.

Following are steps through the procedure.

Ten Basic Programming Steps

1. **State your problem mathematically.** Gather the equations and determine how you want the program to solve them.
2. **Key in your procedure.** List the keystrokes required to do the problem manually. Use the convenient Coding Form that comes with programmable as a guide. Key them in and the calculator will remember.
3. **Try an example.** Before you start doing a real problem, be sure you have a good program. An easy way is to try an example. So try one with an answer you know is correct.
4. **Key in your numbers.** Let the calculator try it in the way you told it. It will make the calculations which were keyed in back in Step 2 and give you an answer.
5. **Is this the answer you expected?** Yes or No. If No, then you'll want to re-examine what you keyed-in and . . .
6. **Make changes.** Step forward or backward through the program as necessary. Make insertions, deletions, or changes. Then go back and try your example again. This time when you reach Step 5 your answer looks good.
7. **Now do a real problem.** Your program is structured and tested — ready for your numbers. No need to key-in the program again, only the variables. The calculator will do the work, and give you the answer.
8. **Do you have more numbers?** Here you can explore options: Ask what-if. Optimize. Sensitivity test your assumptions. Or, determine what happens under worst-case conditions. Take the Yes path.
9. **Loop.** Here's the real value of a true programmable calculator. Because your work is done. From here on you get answers — many answers, and all automatically.

Editing

Single-step and back-step keys let you quickly sequence through program memory to detect errors or examine what you've done. If you push a key you didn't mean to, you can write-over it with the NOP key.

Clarifying Programming Jargon

The entire description of the programming process was done using programming symbols and terminology. The list of keystrokes which you entered in Step 2 is the *program*. The calculator remembered it in its internal *program memory*. Any time you wished, you were able to *run the program*. That is, you commanded the calculator to perform every step you keyed-in. In the diagram you made *decisions*(diamonds) based on *conditions* (a good or bad answer). In a true programmable, you can instruct the calculator to make decisions for you. Decisions based on conditions that you've determined: Positive or negative. Zero or otherwise. An error condition. All are *conditional branching* examples.

After you made changes, *edited* the program, you went back for another crack at the example. Here you made an *unconditional branch* — does not depend on a Yes/No decision. Meanwhile, the calculator remembers the changes. The procedure of keying in the numbers and running the program to get an answer was done in several places. When a procedure can stand alone it is called a *subroutine*. Going to a subroutine is a *call*. When completed, it goes back to where the call was made — a *return*.

A *loop* is no more than running through the same series of keystrokes for as many numbers or variables as you need. So you can generate tables, curves or matrices.

As you can see, the jargon describes rather simple concepts. And that's all users need to begin building programs. Your roadmap is the *flow chart* — the logical, step-by-step, graphical representation of your problem/solution.

A Sample Problem to Try

Here's one that occurs in analysis of a digital or analog electronic circuit. Structural vibration. A servomechanism. A shock absorber. Even a sociological or economic model: Determine the overshoot of the step response of an underdamped second-order system as a function of the damping factor, a.

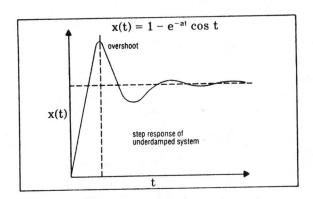

$$x(t) = 1 - e^{-at} \cos t$$

overshoot

x(t)

step response of underdamped system

t

This could be solved analytically. But with an SR-52 or SR-56 users can quickly get numerical answers, which is what they need.

Users program the calculator to compute the value of x (t) for a specific t, and compare that value to the previously determined peak value. If the answer is less than the previous peak, they go on and compute x (t) for the next value of t. If this answer is greater than the previous peak, they make it the new peak value and continue for the next value of t, until maximum t is reached.

Now they may want this procedure repeated for several values of "a": 0.5 to 0.1 in increments of 0.1. In the SR-52 and SR-56, users can define the entire procedure as a *subroutine* and write a new, smaller program which uses this subroutine procedure in a loop. The top subroutine can be added to the end of this small program — and be *called* from it.

Notice how programs are built-up. From simple blocks into increasingly complex programs.

And It's a Powerful Slide Rule

With 74 preprogrammed functions and operations, the SR-56 can handle your problems quickly: from logarithms and trigonometry (degrees, radians or grads), to more advanced statistical problems, and polar/rectangular conversions.

An Applications Library is Available

SR-56 applications library. A 192-page collection of programs are all pre-written. Users select a program and follow the listing (putting in their own data, of course). And, they immediately begin using the SR-56's computing power to solve their own problems.

The program in the Applications Library were chosen specifically on the basis of occupational demands. Each program contains a thorough description of how it works and the conditions under which it operates. There are also extensive examples of each program in typical problem solving situations.
• Math (10 programs) • Statistics (12 programs) • Finance (11 programs) • Electrical Engineering (11 programs) • Navigation (7 programs) • Miscellaneous and games (5 programs)

Procedure to Solve a Problem on the SR-56 and Print Answers on the PC-100

Location in program memory	Your keystrokes	Comments
00	5	
01	STO	
02	0	
03	RCL	
04	0	
05	×	
06	•	Calculates values for "a": 0.5, 0.4, 0.3, 0.2, 0.1
07	1	
08	=	
09	STO	
10	2	
11	subr	
12	1	Call the subroutine which calculates the overshoot.
13	8	
14	dsz	
15	0	Subroutine returns here. Now Loop for five values of "a"
16	3	
17	R/S	
18	0	
19	STO	Calculate the overshoot.
20		
98	prt pause	Display or print overshoot.
99	rtn	Now return to location 14.

Here is the Overshoot Problem

Let's start at the top, program memory location 00. First we're going to calculate the overshoot for an "a" of 0.5. We enter the integer 5 and store it in data memory 0. At location 03 we recall (RCL) the integer from data memory 0 and multiply it by 0.1 to get 0.5. Then store the result in data memory 2 (STO 2) for later use. Next we call the subroutine (SUBR) in location 18. This is the procedure (not shown in full) for finding the overshoot. When it's finished, it will display (or print on the PC-100) the overshoot, then return to the location following the subroutine call (location 14). Here the calculator decrements (or reduces) the integer value in memory 0 (5) by one. Then it loops back to location 03 again. Looping continues until a zero appears in data memory 0. The calculator then skips to program memory location 17 and stops (R/S). Thus calculating and printing overshoot for five values of "a".

The PC-100 Thermal Printer for the SR-56 and SR-52

There is considerable convenience of getting a hard copy print out of: Data; Intermediate results; Answers. And there is efficiency of listing an entire program at the push of a key. Or, printing the calculator's *entire* data memory contents with a simple program. And users can see *every* step of their program as it's executed — both the number and the function. TI's exclusive PC-100 printer is ready to print long ballistic trajectories or short unit conversions; or, from complex tax analyses to simple cost/price margins.

For technology: Users plot the frequency response of an amplifier or filter circuit. Explore transient response of a complex control system. List component values in design. Or, multiple statistics: Mean; Standard deviation; Correlation coefficients. They can follow the convergence of their iterative solution to a transcendental equation.

For business and finance: Users print streams of cash flows and their discounted present values. Generate a complete loan amortization schedule. List sales results with trend line data. Create tables of effective yields. Investigate learning curve numbers. Compare depreciation schedules using alternate methods. (The PC 100A model is designed for the TI 57, 58 and 59 models.)

The Printer Simplifies Program Editing

Users can get listings fast. They push the list key and the PC-100 prints out the SR-52's entire 224-step program memory in about 80 seconds, or less than half that time for the SR-56's 100-step memory. It identifies program code, and its position in program memory — on the tape. Editing is easier and faster, when users can have the whole program in front of them. Users may also see each program step executed. They push the trace key. Then every calculation that's performed in their program is printed. The full number and the operation. Store prints out STO. Logarithms prints out LOG. Errors are a question mark (?). Users can follow subroutine calls and returns. Conditional, and unconditional branches and loops and conversions and register operations. In fact, everything their SR-52 and SR-56 can do in a program. Thus they can be sure it is doing what they want it to. A real help when users are developing new programs. Because users can get inside a program, see it, operate on it, and edit it, they're sure it's running right and giving the answers they need.

Specific Print Out Results

With the keys on the PC-100, or on the calculator keyboard, users put the PC-100 under program control and they can generate data for graphs and tables without having to look at the calculator's display.

List Your Program

With two keypushes on the SR-52 or SR-56, you can list your entire program. The list shows the memory locations as well as the memory's contents.

Here's the listing of the overshoot program that was done on the SR-56 (page 194). The column on the left is the program memory location. And the right column is the two-digit key code for each instruction — its position on the keyboard (row and column). For example, 34 means third row, fourth column (RCL key).

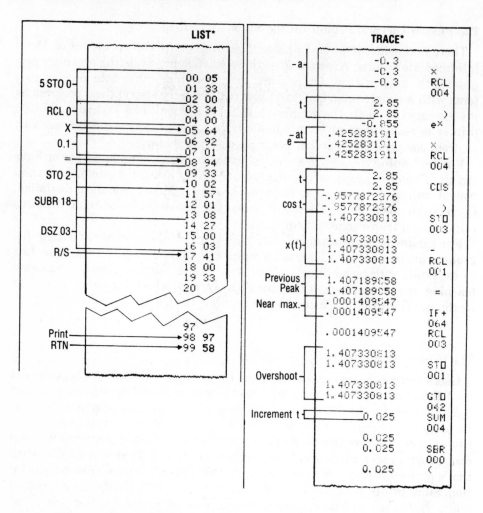

Trace Program Execution Step-By-Step

Using the TRACE key you can *see* every number that's in the calculator's display register. And the instruction as it's being performed. All right on the tape — automatically. The perfect way to debug your programs.

This tape is a trace print out of the subroutine which found the peak value in the overshoot problem (page 000). It was done on an SR-52.

Convenient to Use. And Key-Lock Security, Too

Simply remove the SR-52's or SR-56's battery pack. Press the calculator down on the connectors, turn the key, and you're ready to print. You can leave your programmable locked on the PC-100 and take the key with you.

The Casio Key-Programmable PRO-101 Features Include

- **Simple programming** — Programming is done by simply following the steps of the formula, there is no necessity for a special program language.
- **256 program steps and up to 15 divisions** — Casio has managed to give the PRO-101 as many as 256 program steps — a remarkable capacity for the small size of the machine. These steps can be divided freely for a maximum of 15 programs at one time.

CASIO PRO-101 ELECTRONIC CALCULATOR

- **Calculating capacity boosted by jump functions** — With judgment of value size $(x > y, x = y, x < y)$ real jump functions are available. For example, conditional jump (IF), optional unconditional jump to designated addresses (GOTO), manual jump (MJ), etc. Sub-programs are also easy.
- **15 memories for increased data programming** — With fifteen memories, each of ten digits, built into the PRO-101 there's plenty of capacity for data storage, totaling and complex calculations.
- **Easy handling of subroutines** — Subroutines can be formed in the execution of the main program and freely used any number of times.
- **Convenient indirect address designation** — During execution of a program, addresses can be indirectly designated to the 15 data memories for easy control even without direct designation.
- **Automatic program check** — In the event of a programming error the MISS lamp will light and the input lock.
- **Immediate program confirmation, revision and erasing** — Use of the CHECK key confirms the number of steps and the commands of a program. It is also a straightforward operation to partially revise, erase or interrupt a program with a new program.
- **Easiest possible operation** — Any manual calculation follows the same sequence as the written formula and calculations can be performed during the execution of a program calculation. When using a program, simply input the data and press the ENT key. During a program calculation the computer indicates which is the input data and which is the answer.
- **Up to one year program storage** — 3 long-lasting silver oxide batteries are used for program storage with up to 12 months retention of data, if the power source is turned off, providing new programs are not entered.
- **Multiple manual calculation functions** — With 10 digits, an independent memory and such functions as $\sqrt{\ }$, %, a^n, $+/-$, round-off/cut-off, automatic constants for $+/-/x/a^n$, etc, a whole spectrum of complex calculations can be performed without even using the program function.

Programming is Performed in Accordance with the Formula. Program Writing and Operations are Done on the "Conversational Format"

- **Program example**

At a yearly compounded interest rate of 6.5%, find the total principal and interest, and the return.

The total principal and interest is cut off to the nearest dollar.

Principal	Period	Total principal and interest	Return
$4,000 $3,000 $3,500	3 years 15 years 9 years	($4,831) ($7,715) ($6,168)	(6.92%) (10.47%) (8.46%)

---

(1) Formula

- Total principal and interest = principal $\times$ (1 + interest rate)^{period}
- Return $= \dfrac{\text{total principal and interest} - \text{principal}}{\text{principal} \times \text{period}} \times 100$

---

(2) Programming

a. Use program numbers 1 ~ 15 for programs.
   PR# 1: (PR# 1: is program No. 1.)
   * A max. of 15 programs can be carried out with each program designated by a number.

b. Each item of the program calculation formula will correspond to a data memory number 1 ~ 15.
   When principal is put in memory①, period in②, total principal and interest in③, and return in④, total principal and interest = principal $\times$ (1 + interest rate)^{period}.
   Or,③=①$\times$ (1 + interest rate)②

   Return $= \dfrac{\text{Total principal and interest} - \text{principal}}{\text{principal} \times \text{period}} \times 100.$

   Or,④(=)③$-$①$\div$①$\div$②$\times$ K100
   Consequently, the program will be written:
   $3 = \underline{\text{K}1.065}\, a^n\, 2 \times 1:$
     $\downarrow$
     Constant 1.065

   $\underline{\text{Total principal and interest}} = (1 + 0.065)^{\underline{period}} \times \underline{\text{principal}}$
      $\downarrow$ $\downarrow$ $\downarrow$
     (Memory 3)   (Memory 2)   (Memory 1)

   $4 \underline{(=)} 3 - 1 \div 1 \div 2 \times \underline{\text{K}100};$
     $\downarrow$ $\downarrow$
   To obtain answer in   Constant 100
   floating decimal mode

   Return $= \dfrac{\text{Total principal and interest} - \text{principal}}{\text{Principal} \times \text{period}} \times 100$
     $\downarrow$
   (Memory 4)

c. The data to be input into the formula is the principal and period, therefore:
   ENT 1: 2: [Input is①(principal) and②(period).] is written.
     $\downarrow$
   ENT Message

d. Which is the answer to the calculation?
   The answer is the total principal and interest, and the return, therefore:
   ANS 3: 4: [The answer is③(total principal and interest)
     $\downarrow$ and④(return).] is written.
   ANS Message

e. Always write END at the completion of any program.

* The basic programming sequence is:
1. PR# designation
2. ENT message
3. Calculation formula
4. ANS message
5. END

To correct program the completed programs we proceed as follows:

PR# 1:
ENT 1: 2:
$3 = K1.065\ a^n\ 2 \times 1$:
$4 (=) 3 - 1 \div 1 \div 2 \times K100$:
ANS 3: 4:
END

(3) Writing the Program

Set the program switch at the "W" position and press the keys in the same sequence as the programming.

OPERATION	READ-OUT		REMARK
PR#	256	P	display of the remaining number of
1	256	P1	steps.
:	1	P1	Step No. 1.
ENT	2	−03−	Step No. 2, ENT code displayed.
1	3	1	Step No. 3, memory No. 1 displayed
:	4	−14−	Step No. 4, : code displayed.
2	5	2	Step No. 5, memory No. 2 displayed.
:	6	−14−	Step No. 6, : code displayed.
3	7	3	Step No. 7, memory No. 3 displayed.
=	8	−01−	Step No. 8, = code displayed.
K	9	0 k	Step No. 9, "K" lamp lights.
1 · 0 6 5	14	1.065 k	Step No. 14, constant 1.065 displayed.
a^n	15	−12−	Step No. 15, a^n code displayed.
2	16	2	Step No. 16, memory No. 2 displayed.
×	17	−06−	Step No. 17, × code displayed.

(Below omitted)

*Program confirmation is easy as the number of steps and code number are always displayed. If there is a programming error during operation, the calculator detects it, the MISS lamp lights and input is locked automatically.

(4) Program Calculation

1) Set the program switch at the "Comp" position.
2) Set the decimal mode and place selectors at the "CUT", "0" positions respectively so that the total principal and interest is cut off to the nearest dollar.
3) Assign the program number.

OPERATION	READ-OUT	
PR# 1 :	ENT 1	0.

↳ Input of the memory 1 (principal) and depress ENT.

4 0 0 0 EXT	ENT 2	0.
(Principal)		

↳ Input of the memory 2 (period) and depress ENT.

3 ENT	ANS 3	4831.
(Period)		

↳ Answer of memory 3 (total principal and interest) and depress ANS.

ANS	ANS 4	6.925

↳ Answer of memory 4 (return) and depress ANS.

ANS	END 0.	

↳ Program is completed. Depress END. Depress RETURN to repeat the calculation.

RETURN   ENT 1   0.
  ↳ Input of the memory 1 (principal) and depress ENT.
Proceed with the operation according to the indication appearing in the left side of the read-out. Finally, depress END.
END   0.

SUMMARY: WHAT CALCULATOR USERS WANT — CALCULATOR DESIGNERS PROVIDE

What do calculator users want in the future? What users want imaginative designers provide—and the markets are so huge that mass production demand means large risk design and promotion budgets get approved. What users want is already provided by the technology and being delivered by the manufacturers. The typical serious calculator user is a problem solver, and usually a multi-discipline problem solver. Users expected more capability, more memory, more input-output ease, and they are getting it. All in the same package and at much lower cost than expected. The alphanumeric calculator is already here in several desk-top models; efficient printers are available in hand-held models. Obviously the hand-held alphanumeric printing calculator with large additive memories and high-level language programmability is only a year or two away. This poses several questions, only a few of which might be asked at this point.

Calculator users are growing in sophistication. As the user reaches a skill level and has mastered his present machine, he wants more capability, more memory, faster execution speeds, and more complex firmware. Many thousands of users experiment with their machines, try to solve other problems, etc. They like to share *discoveries* and techniques. Almost any calculator owner who becomes aware of applications information directly applicable to his calculator, will want to acquire that information. Calculator users sophistication increases rapidly among professionals. Will the calculator's levels of complexity and capability exceed man's technical and mathematical limits? Have some of today's pocket calculators already reached a complexity level that only a relatively few *experts* can use them? The opposite is true.

Today every college campus has a large percentage of students using *slide rule* calculators like any other tool. The next step was programmability. Today there are 100-step+ scratch-pad programmable machines that cost less than $100. In early 1972 the four-function calculator broke the $100 price barrier. Successful users of scratch-pad programmable machines already want to move up to machines with editing and conditional branching capability. The manufacturers of these machines have provided applications information to attract customers. Most transcend the scratch-pad programmable storage and many are fully programmable (looping and editing) machines. Once a user *plays with* a fully programmable he or she realizes how important it is to have mass memory with tapes, cassettes, cartridges, ROM, etc. They want pause capability, prompting messages on displays, audio (if only tones), loops, nonvolatility, etc. plus timing capabilities, and the list goes on. The technology is here for all this.

Most users already apply their calculators to personal and business affairs. Data handling capability is already enough that the machine takes on such tasks as record keeping and measurement. Complex analysis of data is possible because of the extensive firmware functions built into the machine. The capability of many machines is so great that many are calculating most of the time. The longer run times of programs upsets some owners, and a keyboard interrupt capability has become a necessary feature. This allows a short, quick keyboard, time or register inspection operation to be performed while the previously executing program waits. Our complex, high technology society now has users applying calculators not only to time and money problems, but to such problems as optimizing the routes, asset use investments, etc. Measurement and numbers now continually take on a greater meaning for people. The hardware and firmware are ready, but will the users applications information and proper education catch up?

How do most designers feel about this? One anonymous H-P designer stated: "Ten years from now we will be able to create a product that will set on your thumbnail and solve the problems that you would encounter in almost any environment, except for problems of astronomical size or those requiring vast data bases. The problem right now isn't in the electronics. It's more in deciding who your customers are going to be, what their requirements are. Maybe it's because electronics is my business, but I think the electronics is the easier part. So a lot of work will be going into finding a solution for a particular environment, but one that doesn't extend too far beyond it."

One of the most exciting areas, and something that is a lot of fun, is the use of calculator games. They spurred the demand for electronic games using micro-computers. All are already going fantastically well! Many observers can recall target, pong and one that lets users fly an airplane through an obstacle course. Many of us have noted that often there are long lines of people waiting to play! A year or so ago the user probably needed a quarter. Now millions of users can hook them up to their TV and have lots of fun. Most see more fun there than in pure mathematics, but that's what all these games use — in their fundamental algorithms. And the calculator started all this, too.

In this text we are more interested, and especially at this point, in what people are doing with calculators in the present era. We have already become aware of some of the variety of users. We have noted, for example, that many systems are sold to the following wide range of people:

GENERAL BUSINESS DATA PROCESSING from accounts receivable to inventory reports are easily handled on the system	ADVANCED MATHEMATICS & STATISTICS are handled easily on calculators saving users the cost of more expensive computers or time sharing.	ENGINEERS use calculators to solve complex problems easily and quickly. The "Basic" language feature allows them to develop their own programs	LARGE VISUAL DISPLAY is an extra on many calculators. It lets users see steps of their programming before it is entered or results before final printing.
AUTO DEALERS use calculators to instantly figure customers' deals. Contract is instantly produced at the touch of a button.	SURVEYORS & CIVIL ENGINEERS use a whole "family" of calculators, printers and flat bed plotters to produce final reports and drawings.	GOVERNMENT & MUNICIPAL BOND TRADERS and financial managers use special calculators to instantly calculate sophisticated financial transactions.	ENGINEERS, MATHEMATICIANS AND STATISTICIANS use Programmable Calculators to save hours of calculating time and print final results in any format.

Calculators as Computers?

Most people are well aware that computers can store programs and data, can move from one program to another to perform complex processing and control functions; they can receive automatic input, display and print out solutions to complex problems. **Calculators can't do these things. NOT SO!** In 1973 a revolution in calculators occurred. They became *computer-effective* without using that *scare* word. One typical *computing* calculator, for example, is owned by a container manufacturer. It is used for cost estimating payroll, labor distribution, production statistics — accumulated, stored, and output on command and for preparing invoices. Fifteen *programmables,* with *pro-*

grams jointly developed with the supplier, write and record new systems on magnetic cards and cassettes for either internal or external storage of data and records — for re-entry or production of *processed* documents.

MOST OF THE ABOVE ARE **COMPUTER** FUNCTIONS. A box company with 200 employees doing $10,000,000 in sales, uses its *programmables* with prerecorded manufacturing formulas, costs, and selling prices to determine *twice-a-day profitability* of its products. Data and programs are input with tape cassettes while other variable input follows *code charts* used by operators. Output is accessible only by management who know the programs. "With our programmables we can give our salesmen price and inventory quotations in less than five minutes, instead of days. . . ." TEK model 31 and other programmable calculators provide user-definable keys which can be customized to perform any sequence of math operation. With an overlay, the customized keys can be labelled in the user's language, allowing an operator to solve multistep problems without necessarily being aware of the math involved. They have 35 or more math functions on their keyboards, readers for programmed entry—magnetic cards, ROMs, or special tape cartridges, and can be equipped with various printers, optional expanded memories, etc. THESE ARE COMPUTER TERMS AND COMPUTER FUNCTIONS. COMPUTER CAPABILITIES ARE QUICK *FRONT* DOOR ENTRY TO FULL *SYSTEMS.* (See Chapters 6 and 7 for machine and capability descriptions.)

Millions of such programmable calculators are expected to be in use during the late 1970's and more and more of them with even greater storage, retrieval, computing, and *processing* sophistication—most with wide ranges of commercial, scientific, and educational programs. And now prices have reached down well below $500. Thus, personal computers plus programming with informational storage and retrieval—and complex problem-solving capabilities have indeed reached the common man and the masses. The lines of definition between programmable calculators, microcomputers, minicomputers, and computer systems have become somewhat obscured. Most calculator types can become more than special purpose. Most are general purpose to accept variable programs. Practically all new desk-top types of programmables accept or can be converted to use many types of input, output, memory, or communication devices . . . and all are *personal* computers, for faster, more accurate solutions to problems and information manipulation.

We will analyze in a degree of detail in chapters ahead that many desk-top calculators have **real** computer power. They are programmed to perform cost analysis, billing, inventory and production control. They are often programmed for problems which are unique to specific companies. Many use the computer language BASIC which can be learned in a week, and there is practically no limit to the number of programs that can be used as long as they are not too long or complex. They avoid the need for *in-house* programmers or the long wait to *get on* the large company computers. Costs range in the $200-$300 per month areas for *full systems.*

We will also note in chapters ahead that many programmable calculator users quickly step up to units with visual display screens and larger *memories.* They become in effect *intelligent* computer terminals or true mini computers in the form of terminals. Accountants and managers are able to *view* stored information and problem solutions in seconds. Such computing *calculators* are able to control wide ranges of peripheral equipment, such items as: plotters, CRT *face* copiers, printers, key-punched or *ball point* pen input devices. And they can be accessed remotely over normal telephone lines. This opens calculator users to a whole new world of "Data Communications."

CHAPTER 5
THE STEP-UP TO ADVANCED HAND-HELD PRODUCTS: CAPABILITIES AND PROCEDURES

INTRODUCTION: THE NEW GENERATION: CALCULATORS, CALCULATOR-WATCHES AND HOME COMPUTERS

During the otherwise slow and somewhat dull summer of 1977 several technological explosions occurred resulting in a barrage of new microelectronics products. The marketing people in a half dozen separate industries felt the earth beneath them shake, so reverberating were the impacts. Rumors of *new generations* of calculators, computing games, calculator watches, home computers, video tape recorders (VTRs), video disk players heard in the recent past suddenly became machines and devices on retail and distributor shelves. Although we are primarily concerned with calculators in this book, we cannot avoid discussion of alternative calculating/computing instruments. Thus, to realize perspective, to picture specific units as part of the total scene, and to interpret the convergence of many *information processing* devices and to note particularly their competitive relationships, the discussion must expand somewhat for the next few pages.

The 'new generation' of hand-held calculators is by far the true miracle of cost-performance, among all the processing machines. All three major American calculator manufacturers, Texas Instrument (TI), Hewlett-Packard (HP), and National Semiconductor (NS) proudly promoted their *intelligence engines*. This is perhaps a better connotation for this generation of calculators, because alphanumeric hard copy output has become a dominant characteristic of some of the units, and *solution of systems problems* rather than the mere calculation of numbers is the new direction of tiny calculators, though such capabilities cost less than $250 in high quality programmables. The second qualification for labeling these machines *new generation* is the tremendous increase in storage capability through the use of Read Only Memory (ROM) chips initially used in the TI products. The TI-58 and TI-59 hand-held units and other desktops offer plug-in *exterior* mass memory in wide ranges of versatility, as noted ahead. And, both NS and HP have excellent **pragmatic-prestige** calculator-watches on the market, as has Hughes and several others. Because several electronic games manufacturers use microprocessors for control and capability ranges, as well as calculator-like, input-output devices and offer calculating capabilities output for tv viewing, these products must be compared, if only briefly here, with the new calculators. Most of these products were introduced during the Western Home Computer Faire in San Francisco, the Consumer Electronics Show in Chicago, and the National Computer Conference in Dallas in June and July of 1977, and one of the biggest *surprises* of all three shows was the PET Home and Business microcomputer built within a CRT (Cathode Ray Tube) terminal integrating an excellent keyboard and cassette input-output controller . . . all for under $600. This is severe competition for many high-end calculators, but drew immediate and wide competition itself from the Heath (kit) home and business computers, the Apple II home computer and a dozen others, as discussed ahead.

How do video cassette and video disk players fit into this picture? At least a dozen brands of video cassette recorders that play through practically any tv set are now available from Japanese and American companies, including Beta-max, RCA, Zenith, Panasonic, Sanyo, Sylvania, and so on. And this has pushed the competing video disk machines onto the frenzied market, first in Germany and Japan, and now in the U.S. The German machines were the first to be sold here, but were quickly followed by the Philips-MCA (N.V. Philips, the huge Dutch electronics conglomerate and Music Corporation of America, the American film, music giant) video disk player. The magic for calculator and computer people is that the video disk storage technique is binary, or digital. Thus, while the video disk player may be purchased for entertainment only, it is just what's needed for a computer or calculator user. The video disk system coupled with microprocessors (the heart of microcomputers and calculators) and keyboards develop incredibly powerful *audio/visual/computational/educational/recreational* devices. According to Philips-MCA, the entire Encyclopaedia Britannica, with all its supplements, could easily be stored on a single disk. The storage capability of one video disk is 10^{11} bits of information. Philips spokesmen have announced that the disk measures 30 centimeters in diameter and, in its 40,000 tracks, can hold 10 billion bits, that the error rate of 1 in 10 billion is attainable, i.e., the equivalent to a one bit error per disk. (Space does not permit further discussion of these video products or the programmable *intelligent* games in this book. The reader is referred to: "Personal and Home Electronics Buyers Guide" (Prentice Hall, 1978 by the same authors.)

For too long calculator manufacturers have neglected the businessman in their development of hand-held or low-cost preprogrammed and programmable machines. This important marketing error was resolved somewhat with the mid-1977 offering of products from both TI and HP. As we will note ahead, the TI hand-held programmable MBA is a significant business math and statistical capability advancement over its *Business Analyst* in that the MBA, at $65 to $80, has a *Learn* key that allows the MBA machine to remember a sequence of up to 32 keystrokes, any one of which may include multi-step programmed financial functions to provide exceptional power. And the recently introduced HP-92 Investor is a medium-priced ($550 to $625) desktop preprogrammed portable printing calculator combining full financial evaluation and computation capabilities with mathematical and statistical functions. HP also began marketing its latest scientific pocket calculator that features 98 fully merged program steps, that typically hold 175 separate operations, with full program editing functions and continuous memory. It's called the HP-29C, which sells for less than $200, while the same unit as a hand-held printer, the 19C, retails for about $300 from many discount dealers.

Of great significance to business and scientific calculator users and all other types as well, was the availability "before Christmas 1977" (according to published reports of quotations by company spokesmen) of the NS 7100. The 'below $400' calculator has algebraic hierarchy, is fully merged and works smoothly because users can access all the registers easily. It has two 32,768-bit ROMs offering 240 merged program steps, 32 addressable data-storage registers, and a line of factory-programmed plug-in library cartridges. Use of the cartridges as subroutines brings step capacity to 4,240. Potential buyers are advised that the NS 7100 exclusive input-output port will provide big future payoff. But, National Semiconductor cancelled plans for marketing the unit. It was offered to other manufacturers who expressed interest. Because it may still become available to consumers, we will use it for comparative purposes in this text.

These products resulted in the demise of the popular SR-52 from TI, succeeded by the twice as powerful $260-300 TI-59, and the SR-56 now succeeded by the $65-$80 TI-57 with significantly more power and versatility, and for those who step up to the $100-$125 TI-58, big advantages with the use of the plug-in ROMs, called by TI, "Solid State Software." The $165-$200 HP-29C pushes its now $120-$150 HP-25C a bit out of the limelight (reducing its price by more than $50, at least) and offers potential users even more capability and printing as well in the $300-$345 19C model.

The first section of this chapter is devoted to a listing and comparison of the features of this new generation of calculators with particular emphasis to insertable ROM, partitioning, and other versatility attributes, particularly the TI and NS products. The 19-C from HP is an important breakthrough because of its small size, printing capability and range of power, but for its price many will compare it to the combination of the TI-58 and PC-100A printer for $260-$300 total, offering the user alphanumerics and some plotting capability as well. But, all of these units, and the many games noted above, plus the home computers, have one thing in common and that is the need for programming knowledge and experience. And users of calculators and home computers can easily and quickly learn first, the most basic calculator fundamentals — and then go as far as they want, such as, into BASIC, FORTRAN, and other higher level languages. Many heavy users of calculators predict that a hand-held calculator with a BASIC interpreter within it is coming very soon, and when combined with interior or exterior printers, the line between advanced calculators and home computers will blur into practical disappearance. The specific aspects of programming, however, are most important. And these can be most conveniently learned on the simple programmables with procedures such as those covered in previous chapters, or those noted ahead for the TI MBA model, and the very straightforward TI-57 and HP-19C or 29C. From those very low cost machines it is a practice and experience step to the more advanced TI-58, TI-59 and HP-67 or HP-97. As noted many times throughout this book, the authors suggest that for the few extra dollars involved, potential users should always buy that extra power and versatility that they might expect to need in the future. And they should remember, the cheapest thing around, barring practically nothing, is information processing with electronics. The best examples, by far, are programmable calculators. Soon, very few of us will be without them in much of our daily activity.

The Calculator-Watch Competition — Two of the Leading Products from HP and NS

The Hewlett-Packard CMOS LED wristwatch-calculator is a hybrid six-chip design using a trickle charge from the battery to retain information when the calculator is turned off. The watch contains 38,000 LSI transistors. One of the original models, the Pulsar, used an 8-to-10 chip hybrid combination. The

The NS calculator-watch is the leader in calculating capability and offers a more readable Liquid Crystal Display than the LED types. The unit has a list price of $350 but will probably be discounted well below the $300 mark. It has 19 dual function keys, dual night viewing, scientific notation, uses two batteries.

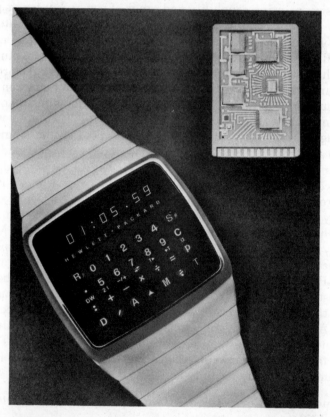

The Hewlett-Packard Model 01 Calculator-Watch is an alarm time-keeping intermix of functions with calculating capability. It is a jewelry store item priced from $650 up. It uses a LED display, powered by three batteries and is an attractive pragmatic-prestige item.

Hughes modules, shown in earlier pages, are based on a three-chip design — two for calculator functions, and one for timing. National uses a two-chip CMOS design with 16K of ROM and 384 bits of RAM and a liquid crystal display. The HP 01 model feeds watch time directly into its computations; it features interaction between timekeeping and calculation circuits. Calculator functions, fewer than the NS model, include add, subtract, multiply, divide, percentage, net amount, chain, and repeat operation on previous results or new information. While only seven rounded digits are displayed, the calculator has 11-digit internal accuracy. The unit also has stopwatch features, two ways to set its audible alarms, four memory registers, and a 200-year calendar implemented in its program-controlled processor, which contains 4K 10-bit words of ROM. Its 28 tiny aluminum keys (6 finger-operated, 22 stylus-operated) transmit motion through a thin rubber membrane, to move a conductive foil layer into contact with the gold connection on the hybrid substrate. The first model, at least, is being sold "solely through fine jewelry shops" for a list price of $650 in stainless steel and $750 in gold-filled cases. Power is supplied by three .08-oz electric watch batteries, with a life of 3 to 6-months for the two display batteries and 6 months to a year for the processor battery.

The NS model is a fully scientific calculator that displays the six most significant digits without any buttons being pressed. The remaining two can be shown by pressing a button. The calculator has a memory in which eight digits can be stored. It can process natural and common logarithms and their antilogs, compute angular and inverse functions of sine, cosine and tangent. It is preprogrammed to perform square-root reciprocal and pi functions and to change signs, and it can use scientific notation, the keyboard being activated by a stylus or ball point pen. Of the 20 keys, the calculator uses 19, eighteen of which are dual-function, the 20th being the *function* key for use in accessing a second function for the other keys. Operating any of the calculator keys instantly puts the watch in the calculate mode; remaining there until a *watch* key is depressed, to return to the timekeeping mode. The watch displays hours, minutes, seconds, the day of the week, and the date using an automatic calendar. While the calculator is processing the figures, an indicator blinks. The watch uses two batteries, and two backlights make the display readable at night. The suggested retail price is $350. With this capability, it should prove very popular at this price. However, some discounters in mid-1977 were already marketing calculator watches as low as $150, but not with this quite exceptional capacity for problem-solving nor of this quality.

There will obviously be many such products which, in addition to timekeeping, will perform manipulations such as storing dates, calculating past dates, converting days, hours, minutes, seconds, into increments down to nanoseconds — and 20 to 25-function watch/calculator combinations are in planning and design stages — financial calculations, metric conversions, and so on. One type, the CompuChron adds in the convenience of stored telephone numbers to its eight-digit LED calculator and time unit.

Some Breaks for Businessmen and Financial Analysts

Before moving into the luxury of "Solid State Software" or insertable (plug-in) ROM machines, some important notes should be made concerning the first programmable strictly business (and statistical) capability hand-held machine, the MBA by TI, and the first portable (though desktop type) business printer machine, the HP-92 Investor from HP. The $65-$80 MBA features a surprising number of preprogrammed business and financial calculations and includes the important 32-stroke programmability feature. The preprogrammed functions allow users to obtain fast answers to complex math, statistical and financial questions with a small number of keystrokes. Computations such as net present value for variable cash flows, internal rate of return, trendline analysis, mean, variance, and standard deviation, accumulated interest and remaining loan balance, and annuity calculations may be determined rapidly with the MBA. In addition, basic time value of money problems involving simple and compound interest, and present and future value calculations, are readily solved directly on the keyboard.

The "Learn" key feature, as previously noted with other easy operation programmables, allows a sequence of up to 32 keystrokes to be programmed into the calculator memory. That entire sequence, as customized by the user for highly particular tasks, can then be repeated with a push of a single key. When used in conjunction with other preprogrammed functions, such as compound interest, this feature provides a great capability for many types of individualistic financial problems. Combining programming with multi-function single key use, programs can actually be developed that contain up to 100 steps and more. It is an especially useful machine for business administrators, advanced students, real estate managers, accountants, financial analysts, and planners, controllers, bank and credit loan officers, investment analysts, stock

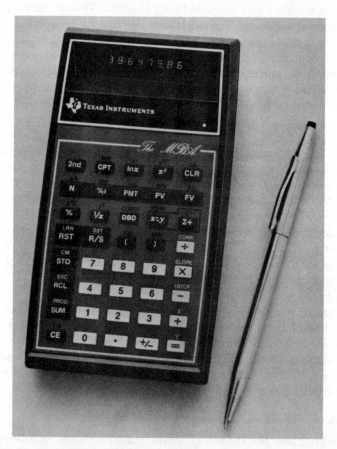

The Texas Instruments MBA Calculator is a 32-step key programmable machine with many preprogrammed functions (single-press) for statistical and financial analysis. These multi-function capabilities may be combined with the user's own specific programs for single-key instant repeatability with new variables, storable in 12 data memories.

brokers, bond traders, and budget and cost analysts. The unit has 12 data memories and numbers can be stored, recalled or summed in each of them. It uses the TI algebraic operating system (AOS) allowing, as do other TI units, complex math expressions to be entered the way they are stated, from left to right. For only a few dollars more it is a big step-up from the TI Business Analyst, and TI Money Manager. Fifteen sets of parentheses are available at each of 4 processing levels to interpret mathematical sequences.

The HP-92 is bound to be a very popular calculator because of the neat package — a compact 2½ pound 9″ × 8″ × 2.5″ briefcase-size unit — with a great number of preprogrammed capabilities. Because of the price, from $550 from discounters, to the $625 list price, and the nonprogrammability, many potential users might hold back from purchase, however. It is obviously a high quality machine with wide-ranging capabilities relating to annuities, bonds, depreciation schedules, and so on. The HP-92's ability to calculate five variable financial problems is the result of their new financial algorithm (the sequence of operations programmed into the integrated circuit chip of the unit) that makes it more adaptable to frequently encountered investment problems. The statistical characteristics include six registers and the two basic operations of standard deviation and linear regression & linear estimate. Additional math functions enable the user to perform curve linear regression. In conjunction with the calculator's amortization function, the printer produces permanent, formatted and labeled amortization schedules, and this is a big capability plus. The HP-92's thirty storage registers allow the user to perform multiple financial and statistical calculations on the same data without the need to re-enter that data or the fear of losing it during the course of the calculations. Many

The HP-92, a new portable, printing calculator, combines full financial evaluation and computation capabilities with mathematical and statistical functions. Designed for professional investment analysts, bond investors, mortgage bankers, real estate investors and lessors, the calculator features such important functions as annuity with five variables, amortization scheduling, bond price and yield, and straight-line sum of the year's digits and declining balance depreciation.

POCKET PRINTER: The HP-10, first of a new family of pocket-sized Hewlett-Packard printing calculators, is a simple, easy-to-use calculator for retail and office business applications, everyday personal calculations and schoolwork. The calculator features a quiet thermal printer, buffered keyboard, and percentage, constant and memory keys.

The HP-29C, a new keystroke pocket-sized programmable scientific calculator, features 98 fully merged program steps, full editing functions and continuous memory. Designed for engineers, scientists, technician, surveyors and students, the HP-29C offers a full range of advanced scientific functions.

users will find this capability attractive because they can quickly evaluate different aspects of a problem to achieve the best possible solution. Some users who might want to key in their own programs and still have the printer capability will compare the combination of the TI-58 and TI-59 with the TI printer, the PC-100A, which offers ROM snap-in 25- to 40-program units and alphanumeric plus plotting capability. Others, partial to HP, will consider the key programmable hand-held HP-19C, which is a powerful hand-held lower cost printer. A photo of the type of printer and case can be noted from the HP-10 shown, while the other photo shows the HP-29C. This type printer is contained in the 19C version of the 29C.

The HP-29C being sold from $160 to $195 is an upgrade of the HP-25C, has 98 fully merged program steps, typically holding 175 separate operations, with full program editing functions and continuous memory. It has 3 subroutine levels, 10 addressable labels, indirect addressing, and insert/delete editing. The unit also is equipped with the standard programming functions of back-step, single step, pause, and a total of 10 decision tests. Data can be retained in 16 of the data storage registers.

The fully merged programming allows as many as four keystrokes to be combined into a single step of memory, meaning that true memory size is typically 175 keystrokes. Programming is further simplified by the 30 storage registers. And, CMOS memory chips used in the construction of the machine allow programs and data to be retained in memory for long periods after the calculator has been turned off, with little battery drain. As an added convenience, characters and formats on the display are saved in the continuous memory. RPN, a favorite of many users, is the 'language' of the 29C, and all of the HP scientific capabilities are available on the machine.

The "Solid State Software" Breakthroughs of the TI-58 and TI-59 Machines

Some of the first users of the TI-59 were most amused when it was used to combine with the PC-100A printer to give instructions in hard copy on how to operate the units, and they were well pleased with the presentation of the answers to problems in charts and graphs. Both the TI-58 and TI-59 feature 5,000 step electronic libraries in the form of "half-matchbook-sized" snap-in ROMs in the small square slot in the lower back of the machines. These miracle ROMs offer the choice of any one of dozens of programs to be called into either machine by pressing one or two keys, instead of feeding "gum-stick" sized cards into the readers of the former hot product, the SR-52, and now its successor the TI-59. The TI-59 is widely touted to have twice the power of the SR-52 at just above half the price. An article in the *Wall Street Journal,* emphasized as one of the most important features the partitioning capabilities, as follows: "This feature makes it possible to handle short problems with many numbers — such as budgets or statistical calculations — by using as many as 100 memories in the machine, or long problems with many operations but little data — such as stock option or astronomical calculations — by using almost all of the program steps but few memories." The article further stated that with lower prices, many professionals were turning to calculators to solve problems they once worked through timesharing on large, central computers. Concerning the NS 7100 the article quoted the capacity of 4,096 program steps for this machine and its projected use as the central processor in a computing system to control or get data from such peripheral machines as a magnetic tape drive, a printer, a plotter, or a tv display. Security analysts were quoted as stating that these machines are "heavy stuff" threatening to cut the desk-top market with these "little" fully capable units. (The NS 7100 was cancelled in late 1977.)

The plastic plug-in ROMs (program libraries) contain 40,000 bits and measure ⅝ by ¾ by ¼ inches and can be addressed from the calculator's keyboard or inserted as subroutines in other programs developed by the user, making applications far simpler than running several to many magnetic strips through the printer, and often jamming them. Although this capability still remains (and has been enhanced) on the TI-59, many users prefer the ROMs, although

PROGRAM STEPS				480	
			400		10
		320	20		
	240*	30*			
160	40				
80	50				
60	MEMORIES				

*Calculator in this configuration when turned on.
May be changed from the keyboard or in a program.

With the TI Programmable 58, program steps and memory registers can be varied by the user. The calculator has a 240-program step and 30-memory configuration when turned on, and this may be changed from the keyboard or in a program.

PROGRAM STEPS				960	
			880		10
		800		20	
	720	30			
640	40				
560	50				
480*	60*				
400	70				
320	80				
240	90				
160	100	MEMORIES			

*Calculator is in this configuration when turned on.
May be changed from the keyboard or in a program.

With the TI Programmable 59, program steps and memory registers can be varied by the user. The calculator has a 480-program step and 60-memory configuration when turned on, and this may be changed from the keyboard or in a program.

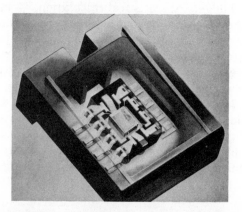

The Solid State Software module for the new TI Programmable 58 and TI Programmable 59 calculators is a product of TI's micro-memory technology. It contains prewritten programs that once occupied almost two dozen magnetic cards which are now encapsulated in a tiny plastic module small enough to sit on your fingernail.

they cannot be altered while the mag strips can. The TI-58 and TI-59 are sold with a master library program **cube** (ROM) that contains programs to solve problems such as matrix inversion, simultaneous equations, and other very basic functions. Other program libraries available for about $25 to $40 include statistics, real estate, investments, marine navigation, surveying, and many more.

The Comparisons and Extra Capabilities of the TI Units Coupled with the PC 100-A Printer

It seemed a major strategic move for TI to break the $80 barrier for scientific programmable units and to thus achieve perhaps the dominant calculator for the mass-use high school and junior college first user market. The TI-57 being sold around nationally by discounters for about $65 is a strong competitor for not only HP and NS, but for the Japanese and other Far East machines and the British units as well. It very adequately replaces the former 'about $100' SR-56 and remains at about half the price of the competing, high quality and well-received HP-25. The TI-57 is a single chip microprocessor with the equivalent capacity of nearly 30,000 transistors, a very powerful calculator chip. The machine has the capability to store up to 150 keystrokes in 50 multi-step program locations. The TI product manager for programmable calculators was quoted as saying, "During 1976, nearly 400,000 people joined the ranks of these who discovered the benefits of using these (programmable) machines both on and off the job. By 1979, TI expects over three million people a year will be buying programmables." With the low price of the TI-57, they evidently expect this to be the lead machine. The machine has 8 addressable multi-use memories, comes with an easy learning *step-by-step* programming guide called, "Making Tracks Into Programming," uses popular AOS programming system features for editing, single-step and back-step to review programs and insert and delete keys for adding and removing instructions at any time. It has six conditional and three unconditional branches, 10 labels for selective repetitive problem solving and two levels of subroutines for more efficient use of program memory.

The TI-58, which sells for about $100 (list $124.95), is a very low priced unit to use the prerecorded program libraries (up to 5,000 steps), but does not have the magnetic card memory capability that the TI-59 has. The TI-59 has a list price of $299.95 but sells nationally for $240 to $270 from discount stores. Two mag-strip cards add 960 more program steps. Basically the two calculators then differ only in storage capability. Users can partition the TI-58 with up to 480 program steps or up to 60 memory registers. They can do the same for the TI-59 with up to 960 steps or up to 100 memory registers. For every increase or decrease by 10 memories, 80 program steps are added or taken away in storage. Changing program steps affect the amount of memory in an opposite way. When all 100 memory registers are used with the TI-59, however, 160 program steps remain available to users. Programs in the insertable ROM can be addressed repeatedly from the calculator keyboard or be inserted as subroutines. Both machines permit program data and listings to be printed on the PC-100A printer; the master library included with either unit covers 25 prewritten programs in engineering, mathematics, statistics and finance. Both units have up to 10 registers available for looping, increment and decrement — and the same number of user flags for set, reset and test. Up to six levels of subroutines are available and four types of display testing with an independent test register. Addressing with the calculators is easily flexible, with absolute, indirect and label modes for addressing program steps, and direct and indirect for data registers. All editing capabilities are quick and sure.

The PC-100A TI thermal printer produces hard copy records and headings, prompting messages, and program codes as well as plotter data. Many stores were offering the combination TI-58 and PC 100A printer for less than $250 providing excellent desk-top calculator capability for a very low price. Some users see the combination as a replacement of batch processing and timesharing on computers thereby eliminating the wait to *get on* the computer and the expense of computer time, but still having practically equivalent processing and hard copy capability. For example, all TI engineers, whether veterans or new employees are given free TI-59s and several computers have already been replaced. A flag at the beginning of the program, on the TI-59, allows normal operation, but prevents the program from being listed on paper tape, a dictate for some military applications.

Features of the PC-100A Printer and Plotter

The PC100A printer from Texas Instruments now has alphabetic and special character printing and plotting capabilities which are implemented by features in two TI programmable calculators introduced recently. Any TI handheld, programmable calculator except the TI Programmable 57 can be attached to the PC-100A print cradle to become a desktop printing calculator. New features of the printer are possible with the introduction of the TI Programmable 58 and TI Programmable 59 calculators and the added features work only with those two models. Formerly limited to numeric characters, the new capability to print letters allows users to include headings on program lists, label their outputs or program-in prompting messages. Special symbols can also be printed like squares, square roots, and punctuation marks. With the prompting capability, professionals can include instructions in a program to guide assistants and secretaries through required program steps. Each character is entered by means of a two-digit code directly from the calculator keyboard or in data memories. Characters from a program are entered automatically. Capability is provided for 64 characters, including blank spaces on 2.5 inch wide thermal paper. Maximum line length is 20 characters and more than three lines and 60 characters a second can be printed. Plot curves or histograms can be made from the calculator keyboard or directly from a program. A new listing format shows key symbols and codes as well as the contents of all memory registers and all program labels and their location. The new model, like its predecessor, will also print, list or trace program steps for easy editing and debugging of program listings. It has a suggested retail price of $199.95. The PC-100A can also be used with SR-52 and SR-56 programmable calculators, although the new alphabetic and plotting features are only possible with the TI Programmable 58 and 59 models.

Perhaps, the reader can be most enlightened with the comparative capabilities of the new machines with each other and the older, but big selling SR-52, by reading the interpretation put forth in the June, 1977 Newsletter "52-Notes," the cooperative news-sharing organ of the SR-52 Users Club (with a name change in the offing). The publisher, Richard C. Vanderburgh (9459 Taylorsville Road, Dayton, OH 45424) writes as follows:

The New TI PPCs

The speculation is over (for awhile) following TI's announcement the last week in May of the New TI Programmable 57, 58, and 59 calculators. The 57 looks like even tougher HP-25 competition than the SR-56, with 10 labels and an $80 list price; the 58 and 59 are something else, packing some fascinating new features that it is hard to believe can be squeezed into a slightly smaller

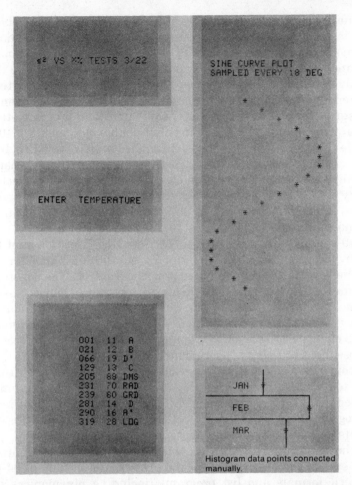

At left, top to bottom, new features of the PC-100-A include program heading capability, user prompting messages and program label and location listings. Also, the printer can now plot curves or histograms as shown at right.

New alphabetic and special character printing capability are available now along with the numeric printing output of the Texas Instruments PC-100-A printer, as shown at left. The program listing at right shows a new third column of alphanumeric printing which now identifies the key codes in the second column.

package than the 52, and at list prices of $125 and $300 respectively. Both use the same instruction set, accept 5000-step plug-in read-only-memory (ROM) program modules, and plug into the PC-100A printer; the 58 has half the 59's memory, and no card reader. The discussion that follows applies to the 59, but is generally applicable to the 58 except for the differences just noted.

120 general purpose memory registers are partitionable between data and program storage use: 1 data register is equivalent to 8 program steps from a 0/960 data/program mix to 100/160 in partitionable increments of 10 registers (11 possible configurations). Once a partition has been established, boundaries cannot be crossed (as with the 52). Partitioning/repartitioning can be done from the keyboard or under program control, except when a protected (in the proprietary sense) card has been read, in which case the user cannot get into LRN mode, single step, or recall as data, or copy on to another card the program memory contents.

The 5000-step ROM modules (which TI calls CROM for Constant ROM) are accessed by program number, and run by subroutine name for execution through the keyboard or under user-program control. The Master Library (which comes with each machine) holds 25 programs from a 52-step D.MS add/subtract/scaling routine to an 898-step matrix determinant/inverse/simultaneous equations leviathan that will handle up to a 9×9 matrix, or a system of 8 equations. Once a CROM program has been accessed from the keyboard, subsequent pressing of user-defined keys (A-E') refer to the CROM program subroutines, but a CROM program must be accessed each time a subroutine is to be called under user-program control. CROM programs may be down-loaded into user-program memory for inspection and/or editing, and run as user programs, but not the reverse. Configuring new CROMS is an expensive manufacturing process, and is not a practical user capability.

One of the most powerful of the new features is a set of 39 Control Operations that enable the user to control the printer in a variety of 64-character alphanumeric formats and list programs (including mnemonics), data, and labels; calculate a few special statistical functions; control and announce partitioning; configure error-state processing; and control increment/decrement of the first ten data registers. Control operations are executable manually and under program (user or CROM) control.

The 59's mag cards are slightly smaller than the 52's, and so cannot be used interchangeably. Each card reads/writes 2 of four memory banks, irrespective of partitioning. Each bank holds 30 data registers or 240 program steps, or equivalent mixes of each. Data registers number from the last of bank 4 up through the last third of bank 1 (2-digit addressing does not reach past Reg 99); program steps start at the beginning of bank 1, with step 959 ending bank 4. As examples: program steps 160-167 are equivalent to data register 99; steps 472-479/Reg 60; and 952-959/Reg 00. Partitioning is specified by data registers. For example, the sequence: 2 *Op 17 produces a 20/800 data/program-step mix. But since program protection is by bank, a bank that contains any data registers cannot be protected, and steps 720-791 in this example could not be protected.

The 59 keyboard is the 52's 5 × 9 matrix with some rearrangement, renaming, and the following changes: x!, D/R, inferr, ifpos, ifzro, and xrty have been eliminated, and CP, Pgm, xEt, Eng, Int, abs, Pause, x = t, Nop, Op, xGEt, sigma +, x bar, Rad, and Grad added. Most key codes follow the usual quasi-x,y addressing, with a few exceptions to handle merged Ind functions. 8 of the possible 100 op-codes are unused, and are the 59's pseudos. Cursory investigation reveals that of the 8 (op-codes: 21, 26, 31, 41, 46, 51, 56, and 82), p82 is the most interesting: no matter what is displayed, it always causes the next step to be skipped; if zero (or in some cases a small number) is displayed, when the skipped step is R/S, Nop, or INVSBR (the 59's rtn), execution of the p82 sets an error condition. P21, p26, p31, and p41 (SST) appear to behave as they do for the 52. So it seems that there will be some challenge to exploring the 59's pseudos, if not so much as for the 52. Incidently, the 59's pseudos are easier to create because of a register-address merging feature: in LRN mode, any 2-digits following a keyed register command (i.e. STO, RCL, etc) are merged into a single step, and the STO, RCL, . . . can be deleted later. (You can do the same thing with GTO). But when you're editing a register sequence you have to rewrite the command as well as the address. For example, if you wanted to change STO 73 to STO 74, starting at the step containing the 74 would produce the 2 steps: 07 04 instead of the desired 74, so instead, beginning at the STO step: STO 74 would give you the desired sequence.

Other non-52 or 56 features include: 6-level subroutine calls; 10 flags; indirect flag, Pgm, Op, fix addressing; Dsz of Reg 00-09; SBR n from the keyboard initiates execution (true for the 57 also); 13-digit display arithmetic; and a manually initiated R/S during program execution will not halt execution in the middle of connected sequences.

On the negative side, varying in degree of severity and subjective importance: Only 8 mantissa digits are displayed when in Sci or Eng format (like the HP-25), although 13 digits can be carried in the display register unless EE is executed, in which case rounding is to 8 places; there is no built-in factorial function, and although Pgm 16 (combinations, permutations, factorials) will calculate a factorial, 3 subroutine calls are required, and Reg 01-04 are used; polar/rectangular functions and character-print buffers use 4 stack registers; there is no manual D/R switch or other equivalent to the 52's interrupt processing capability; there is apparently no user access to the stack registers, and thus no fractured digits; the same 52/56 trig and log function anomalies prevail (V1N2p3 and V2N2p1); the same code-transfer rules apply (V1N2p2); there is no INV or Ind viability through subroutine calls; and a timing comparison of a short Dsz loop showed that the 59 took twice as long as the 52 (varying display format appeared to have no effect). This longer Dsz execution time is probably due to the addressing of a particular register (which neither the 52 nor 56 have to do).

The following features will probably be viewed by some users as plus and by others as minus: Program execution halts when an undefined label is encountered; mag cards cannot be protected from accidental over-write (although since read is automatic there should be little need for the black tab type of protection); there appears to be no special 0 divide error state (V1N1p2); and there are no "crashes" except for the p21 sin sequence.

One of the powerful features of the 59/PC-100A combination is that they can be programmed to operate like an interactive computer terminal. The following program illustrates this capability. Press A, and you're off on a graded course in arithmetic!

TI-59 Program: Interactive Arithmetic Teacher

Program Listing:

```
000:  *Lbl B STO 0 *Lbl E RCL*Ind 0 *Op 1 *Op 20 RCL*Ind 0 *Op 2 *Op 20
018:  RCL*Ind 0 *Op 3 *Op 20 RCL*Ind 0 *Op 4 *Op 20 *Op 5 INVSBR
033:  *Lbl C *CP *B' X RCL 79 = *Int *x=t C STO 75 *Lbl 3' *B' X RCL 79
052:  = *Int *x=t 3' xEt RCL 75 INVSBR *Lbl D *Pause xEt *Pause INVSBR
066:  *Lbl A 1 B E E E E E *Adv E *Adv *Lbl 9' 10 STO 79 0 STO 77 STO 78
089:  *Lbl 1' 29 B O R/S *Cp *x=t 2' C + D STO 76 = xEt 47 *Op 4
110:  *Lbl 6' CLR R/S STO 74 *x=t 4' *A' 313237 *Op 4 xEt *Op 06 453241
136:  *Op 4 RCL 74 *Op 06 53 B *Adv GTO *1' *Lbl *2' E O R/S *CP *x=t
155:  *5' C + xEt = STO 75 - D STO 76 = xEt 20 *Op 4 GTO *6' *Lbl *5'
176:  E O R/S *CP *x=t *7' C X D STO 76 = xEt 50 *Op 4 GTO *6' *Lbl *7'
197:  E O R/S *CP *x=t *8' C X xEt = STO 75 div D STO 76 = xEt 72
217:  *Op 4 GTO *6' *Lbl *8' *Adv 57 B 3221 *Op 4 *RCL 77 *Op 6 RCL 78
239:  *Prt E E O R/S *CP INV *x=t *9' E *Adv *Adv *Adv CLR R/S *Lbl *4'
256:  1 SUM 77 *A' 3632 *Op 4 xEt *Op 06 45 B E O R/S *CP *x=t *1' 10
280:  *Prd 79 GTO *1' *Lbl *A' 1 SUM 78 RCL 75 *Op 06 64 *Op 4 RCL 76
299:  *Op 6 INVSBR *Lbl *B' *pi X RCL 73 = INV *Int STO 73 INVSBR
```

Pre-stored Data:

```
01:  2324572465 3000223224 3122003732 37173637 4532413500 1335243723
07:  3017372415 0 1314242724 3745401331 3643173500 3441173620 3724323136
14:  2002132 3500451736 5700010000 2132350031 140273232 2600213235
20:  16243620 3327134520 3313413617 1600323317 3513311636 2617450013
26:  3136431735 5737231731 35413140 4313313700 3732001316 1671000000
32:  0 4313313700 3732003641 1437351315 3771000000 4313313700 3732003041
39:  2737243327 4571000000 4313313700 3732001624 4224161771 0 4532410043
46:  1735170035 2422233773 43133137 2313351617 3500333532 1427173036
52:  7100000000 1424351620 1435132431 1716001641 3115177300 4532413500
58:  3615323517 24360000 0 3335321427 1730364043 1331370037 3200373545
65:  2132350013 14173737 1735003615 3235177100 2313421700 1300312415
71:  1700161345 4014451740 .1415926536 0 0 0 0 0 0
```

National Semiconductor (NS) 7100 Hand-held Programmable
Calculator Offers Permanent-storage
(Availability and changes unknown at press time)

The latest competition in *fully* (exterior) programmables for the HP-67/97 and TI 58-59 offers powerful capabilities. The all-semiconductor-memory model 7100 if and when offered uses three different types of memory to achieve nonvolatility. This is an important advantage, in many cases, that HP uses and TI has announced for some lower-priced calculator models and can be expected to include in new versions of the TI-59 and HP 67/97. A distinct difference of the 7100 is the factory-programmed plug-in *library* cartridges instead of preprogrammed magnetic cards used by the two competitors. These cartridges contain 16,384-bit mask-programmable memory. And instead of another set of blank magnetic cards on which the user can permanently store his own specifically-developed programs, the 7100 system offers user-alterable plug-in file cartridges containing two 1,024-bit nonvolatile metal-nitride-oxide-semiconductor RAMs capable of retaining data for years without power. The NS cartridges are physically different from TI's CROMs.

The heart of the below $400 fully programmable unit is a 1.5-2.5 inch printed circuit board containing 11 chips including processor, RAM, PROM, and interfaces. A key design difference is that the preprogrammed plug-in ROM acts as an integral part of the system, making it unnecessary to *dump* it into working registers. This frees the internal memory and gives users of the 7100 a number of capabilities that the competing units do not possess. For example, the NS 7100 uses pending operations, 240 merged-program steps and

The competitive National Semiconductor (NS) 7100 with 4,240 program step capacity also has several improvements not usually found in hand-held units: besides the indirect addressing, direct and indirect register arithmetic, page-referenced addressing a nonvolatile memory, relative addressing and input/output instructions complement the power of the machine. The I/O port will interface to many devices. (Picture made prior to cancellation by National Semiconductor Corp.)

32 user-available data storage registers compared with the significantly lesser capabilities of the HP 67/97. Of greater significance, use of the factory-recorded programs in the library cartridges as subroutines to the program in the mainframe memory brings the total program step capacity to 4,240. In effect, if the user develops a program that is larger than 240 merged steps in the internal memory, another 240 steps can be stored on the file cartridge and used as a subroutine. By comparison, to store 4,240 steps in the SR-52 would require 21 cards and a similar number in the HP-67/97. The 7100 has four subroutine levels and eight program flags, versus 4 for the HP-67/97. The 7100 uses straight algebraic logic and has only 3 levels of parentheses versus nine for the TI-59. The low cost of the 7100 is developed because it has no motor-driven card reader and is made from standard chips. Supplied with the calculator are two file cartridges, a library cartridge with a 75-program math pac, battery, case, charger, etc.

An Operations Comparative Analysis Critique of TI, HP, and NS Hand-Held Machines

Although the specific operations characteristics of these machines are covered in the next chapter, the reader might, at this point, desire a preview of how each stands when compared and mildly critiqued against each of its competitors — and down to the keystroke level.

The Hewlett-Packard 67 and 97 offers 5 data registers (A-E) that can be used for general purpose storage. There are 10 additional *primary* registers (0-9) all of which have corresponding *secondary* registers. The 15 primary memories can be written into and read from with the **sto** and **rcl** keys as usual, but the secondary registers cannot be accessed so easily. A **p⇄s** key (primary exchange secondary) key is offered which swaps the contents of the 10 primary memories with the 10 secondary memories. Once in the primary storage the data can be handled as usual, and swapped back if desired. Notice that all of the memories have a one-keystroke address. Other desirable traits of this seemingly cumbersome duality are:

— **f clreg** key clears only primary registers, secondaries are protected (useful in programming)

— statistical function keys load into only secondary registers, protecting the more frequently used data in the primaries

Only the primary registers 0-9 can accept memory arithmetic directly (such as **sto** + **3**), but all primary and secondary memories have addresses (numbered 0-24) and can be manipulated through indirection using the I register.

The I register on the 67 and 97 serves many functions, perhaps too many. It can hold the address of a memory register that is being manipulated indirectly, or the address of a memory register that contains the address of a location in program memory where control of a running program is to branch. It is also used as the counter for the **dsz** (decrement and skip if zero) instruction, which is used for iterative looping through program segments. HP is too conscious of the user-environment to allow critical overuse of the I register, so they also supply a **dsz (i)** key to allow any memory to be used as the loop counter through indirection. Unfortunately, the I register must once again be used for this indirection. If indirection or indexing are not needed the I register can be used as a convenient general register with one-keystroke storage **x⇄I**.

The 67 and 97 also include the 4 stack registers used by the RPN logic system, but which are also available for very short-term storage though use of multiple **enter** strokes and the **r↓** (roll down) key. the **last x** register is on these machines and is useful. Another one of the many thoughtful *human engineering* features which HP is known for, is the *Automatic Register Review* **h reg,** which steps through all of the machines addressable memories, displaying first the memory's address and then its contents. Texas Instruments did not put so much thoughtful design effort into their memory allocation. Their low-end programmable, TI 57 has only 8 data registers, and all of them serve both the user and the machine. This overuse of the user's registers gives stored data very little security and will easily give the novice programming problems. Since this machine was designed for the novice this is particularly unfortunate.

Multiple Use of Data Registers in the TI 57

Reg	Uses
0	dsz index; n for summation key (stats)
1	summation of y values (stats)
2	summation of y squared values (stats)
3	summation of x values (stats)
4	summation of x squared values (stats)
5	summation of xy values (stats); storage of 3rd pending value when parenthesis nesting goes that deeply
6	4th pending value of parenthesis nesting
7	t register; last value of x, plus one, used in trend line analysis as x co-ordinate

The 57 does not allow indirection but does have many other advanced programming features:

— 50 program steps

— 2 levels of subroutine nesting

— subroutine and program labels (0-9)

— x ≥ t and x = t, and their inverses, for conditional branching

Huge program capacity is afforded the 58 and 59 through *solid-state software* modules that plug into the back of the calculators. The modules contain 5000 programming steps. They must be programmed at the factory, however, and cannot be altered by the user. The programs in the modules can be run from the keyboard or used as subroutines in programs written in the program user space. This is possible because the TI machines now will treat **inv sbr** as a return from a subroutine only if a subroutine call is pending, otherwise it will be treated as a run-stop.

National Semiconductor model 7100 also incorporates huge capacity pre-programmed *library cartridges* (4000 steps). There are 240 steps programmable from the keyboard which can be edited in the same fashion as the TI and HP program space. These 240 steps can be recorded into a second detachable module called a file cartridge and saved for later use. The file cartridge needs to be re-recorded once a year to refresh its memory circuits. The file cartridge can also be used as run-able program memory space when it is attached to the machine, giving the 7100 a total of 480 user-alterable program steps. By keying and recording 240 steps at a time the total 480 step program memory space can be recorded. The fact that the 7100 users semiconductor cartridges for its alterable external storage eliminates the need for the card reader and all of the problems associated with any mechanical device.

All of the program, data, and special-purpose registers of the HP and TI calculators *volatile*. When the calculator is turned off all storage is lost. Not only are the 240 steps recorded in the 7100's file cartridge safely externally stored, but the 240 steps that remain in the calculator are *non-volatile;* they remain even if the calculator is turned off and on again. Thirty-two of the machines 37 data registers are also *non-volatile*. All of the *non-volatile* registers survive on the batteries *trickle-current,* which does not discharge the battery significantly faster than spontaneous discharge of the battery alone.

All of the calculators, except the TI 57, have programming flags (TI 58 and 59 have 10, HP 67 and 97 have 3, and NS 7100 has 8). Programming flags, as noted, are memory registers that don't remember numbers but instead remember one of two possible *states*. A flag is either *set* (true) or *clear* (false). It is useful only in programs where branching is needed. A test of a flag can be put at a point in the program where the question "should I branch or continue" is asked. A flag test can often be used instead of data register comparisons.

In the HP machines the flags are numbered 0-3. Flags 0 and 1 are *command-clear* flags in that they must always be set and cleared manually from the keyboard or an explicit program step, as opposed to *test-cleared* flags, 2 and 3, which are automatically cleared whenever they are tested (or they can also be cleared manually). Flag 3 is also the *data entry flag*. It is set true whenever data is keyed into the calculator. This is useful in many circumstances, notably in conjunction with the *pause* function. The *pause* lasts for only one second but an additional second is added for each key depressed during a pause. A loop of pauses can be programmed to continue until flag 3 is set. In this way a flashing display will *prompt* the user to enter data and the program will continue automatically when the user is finished entering the number. This will work fine as long as the user doesn't take longer than one second per keystroke.

In the TI 58 and 59 the flags 7, 8 and 9 take on special functions also. Pressing **2nd op nn** (where nn is 00-39) executes one of the 40 *special control functions*. **2nd op 18** instructs the calculator to set flag 7 if no error condition exists, **2nd op 19** sets flag 7 if an error condition does exist. If flag 8 is set, a running program will halt when an error condition occurs. (The NS 7100 has a specific keyboard-labeled function that tests for an error condition.) Flag 9 controls the trace function when the PC-100A printer is attached.

All of these programmable calculators have the basic mathematical, scientific, and statistical functions that users have come to expect from the more sophisticated machines. These functions include:

— per cent and percent change keys
— absolute value, integer part, fractional part
— display control functions
   fixed point, scientific notation, engineering notation
— n!, $1/x$, x^2, $\sqrt{x}$, y^x
— polar/rectangular co-ordinate conversion
— statistics
   $\Sigma+$, $\Sigma-$, $\bar{x}$, s
— trigonometry
   sin, cos, tan, arcsin, arccos, arctan
   degrees/radian conversion, hours-minutes-seconds/decimal-hour conversion
   degrees, rads, grads modes
— logarithmic functions
   10^x, e^x, log, ln

There are many small differences between the machines with regard to these functions. For example, TI machines also have linear regression functions available from the keyboard. HP offers a **rnd** function which rounds the number carried internally to the number of digits shown in the display. Since the conditional branch operators use the internal form of the displayed number in their comparisons this is useful to minimize the bad effects of round-off error inherent in all digital calculating devices.

Overall, Hewlett-Packard is known for the effort it puts into its *human engineering*. Many functions that need three keystrokes on TI machines need two on HP machines. Hewlett-Packard keyboards are always colorfully labeled and organized for maximum user convenience which often make programs clearer and shorter. Many of TI's keystrokes are now triple-merged into one programming step, but HP's programming steps have always been as dense as possible. The HP machines test a total of eight conditionals (four relations between x and 0 and four relations between x and y registers), TI tests four ($x \geq t$, $x = t$ and their inverses), and NS tests four ($x < 0$ $x > 0$, $x = 0$ and **error**).

Furthermore, the HP documentation (user handbooks, programming guides, explanations of programs contained in program library packages) is always well-written and easy for the novice to follow.

Users clubs exist for the TI and HP machines and the companies themselves offer facilities for acquiring new software. Some of the card programmable libraries include:

— management and finance
— statistics
— mathematics and numerical analysis
— navigation
— engineering

Each company will undoubtedly offer an extensive variety of pre-programmed cartridges.

The printing device associated with the HP 97 prints letters as well as numbers when it is listing programs but only numbers when programs are running. Through manipulation of the number of digits shown in the display one can devise programs that print a series of numbers of varying lengths. These lengths can be made to vary with the magnitude of a dependent variable that the program is continually evaluating; thus the output, when turned on its side, will be a graph of the function being traced. (See alphanumeric capabilities, Ch. 6.)

The PC-100A ($149.95 to $199.95) from TI is far superior in these capacities. Like the HP printing device this printer can list programs and trace program execution (very useful for debugging programs) but it can also print numbers, letters, and many special characters while under program control. This feature can be used to print out headings, prompting messages, and has formating control (through the printing of blanks) that allows graphs to be plotted cleanly, as shown on previous pages.

In conclusion, the following dollar-value comparison is offered. Even though the TI 57 has some serious shortcomings, for $65 to $79.95, the purchaser is getting unprecedented power per dollar. When comparing the TI 58 and 59 against the HP machines the main consideration certainly has to be the price. Even though HP machines are traditionally of high quality, as mentioned, the TI products offer more data memory, program memory, printer capability and above all, massive 5000 step program libraries that just pop in, all for less money.

However, National Semiconductor if offered is a machine with abilities comparable to the TI line which is priced to compete with them. The calculator from NS has a competitive design and functional ability as well as the ability to quickly attach massive read-only program modules. Further, since NS's machine uses semiconductor external storage instead of magnetic cards, the weight and problems of the card reader are eliminated. Much of the 7100's user memories are *non-volatile,* which is often a convenience. Finally, the one thing NS is offering that none of the others are is an input/output port on the calculator. The intentions for this port are uncertain but the possibilities are very powerful ideas. Almost certainly a printing device will attach here and perhaps a cassette tape recorder to allow reading and writing of data under program control. (The machine was designed to allow programs in the read-only memory module to redefine the functions of the keys on the keyboard, to, in effect, change the operating system of the calculator. A printer-compatible cartridge could easily contain the factory-written program to change two of the keys to read and write keys.) The ultimate potential of this port is to allow the calculator to connect, through an interface, directly to a higher level computer, thus converting the calculator to an inexpensive computer terminal with the special features of detachability and independent processing power.

To Move Forward Into Programming — A Review of Fundamentals and Flowcharts

For many new calculator users, with little or no mathematics background, it is best to start with the most fundamental, straightforward concepts of programming. Thus, in this brief introductory essay, the wide range of topics of programming procedures will be covered simply and loosely principally to demonstrate direction and scope. After this opening, the reader will be taken back *to start over* but, the second time more detail, procedural steps analysis and examples will be used to establish emphasis and solidify program basics. Programming means planning, first—preferrably with the use of flowcharts. Then it concerns the writing of definite steps for a procedure that can be performed automatically by a calculating or computing device to achieve the desired goal. The result, answer, or achievement sought must be clearly defined. Also, before the programming begins, the user should be very familiar with the calculating capabilities, capacities, and techniques of the specific machine to be used. The operations manuals of the various machines will provide the precise but sometimes difficult to follow details for programming each model.

Data have been generally considered to be facts or meaningful information that is expressed in numeric form. The processing of this data refers to the application of various operations or actions on the data so that the result can be used for further processing (analysis for meaning) or for the formation of intermediate conclusions or for making final judgements from the answers achieved. The *answers* may be more data for a scientist conducting experiments, charts for a production manager planning schedules, specific totals for an accountant completing an audit, or calculations for a homeowner analyzing his costs, projections, etc. Processing develops and demonstrates the significance of data, gives the data or the information it represents increased meaning and value. Rational analysis and decisions are based on solutions to particular problems, the problems first being expressed in the form of a series of steps developed into a program. The program is the first basis for all processing. Most leaders in business, industry, and scientific enterprise today realize that survival and prosperity are strongly related to the efficiency with which information is managed. Budgets are based on the cost/effectiveness of programs and machines that function to input, process, and output data on an accurate and timely basis. Problems must be structured, solved, and analyzed, and programs are the input/output answer.

The Basic Data Processing System—A Simplified Cycle

Identifiable parts and functions of an operation or business are first examined and organized on a time- or step-flow basis. The simplest procedure is to assign numeric designators or magnitudes to things and activities; then, the relationships of these numbers can become the data or information to be processed. The numbers are then put through the input, processing, output cycle. Input on programmable calculators can be from the keyboard, typewriter peripheral, tape or disk, sensing or counting device, magnetic cards, and in some cases punched or mark-sense cards or other media, from testing or measuring instruments, or simply from electronic pulses. Processing means doing 'something' to the data—usually mathematically, such as: sequencing, comparing, or manipulating in some fashion. Processing follows the planned sequencing of programmed steps, and it relates to every movement of data within the system and every change or operation applied. Although most processing operations require several or a great many steps, they may be invisible to a machine operator because they are internally programmed by: (a) fixed logic (immutable design) (b) programmed into ROM (or Electrically Alterable ROM—EAROM), or (c) microprogrammed by using the original CPU instruction set (firmware). Wide use is made of the latter two devices for utilizing User Definable Keys, as will be noted in pages ahead.

Output refers to the act of sending the processed data outside of the machine either in machine-readable form (cards, tapes, etc.) for further processing or in human intelligence form, such as in print, visual display, plots or other graphics, or in audible sound, such as with alarms, voice-answerback, etc. All of the three-cycle activities require previous programs for direction, limits, etc.; the programs are the planned series of activities. The programs had to be initially designed, written and tested—and debugged. Flowcharts or other graphic representations are prepared first to display direction, ordering, etc. of program steps as well as to establish the decision points. Each activity is broken down into individual instructions or commands; some call for comparisons, the result of which will determine varying paths of future direction or branches to totally new programs. Instructions indicate at each given instant what the next action will be. Programs should be clear enough so that other people, unfamiliar with the activity, can also use them without excessive study or delay. Good documentation is essential.

The programmer may use foresight, judgment, and many 'humches' as he or she develops a program. But, once it is input to the calculator, the program does not posess these human traits. It will perform exactly and rigorously as the instructions are written unless and until a human being or another program alters it. Thus the programmable calculator can be made to operate under automatic (programmed) control, operator control or a combination of both. Many of the desk-top calculators analyzed have up to and beyond a 5000 step program capability. Thus, a program this long could be performed repeatedly, automatically for a thousand or more separate tests or as a payroll program for 1000 or more employees. Or that same size program could give yes or no (go-no go) responses to a thousand different signals. The CPU or central processing unit *(chip)* of a calculator handles control (starting, stopping, changing, etc.) arithmetic operation, and memory transfers. Calculators must also contain a counter device or system. The counter is usually a register. A register is simply a device or *place* capable of containing a certain amount of data in bit form, i.e., a 0 or a 1, as coded. Some registers contain 6 bits, 8 or 12, and these **groups of bits** (usually 8) are called bytes. In the standard binary-coded-decimal (BCD) machines, 8 bits can represent two numerals or one character. If a machine has 100 instructions, numbered 1 to 100, the program counter (register) could register 50, indicating the next instruction to be performed would be the 50th instruction.

Memory: Storing Data and Instructions

The calculator user first encounters memory when he notes he can store intermediate results and when he can store constants what will be used in repeated calculations, thus avoiding entering a same number each time the calculation is used. In a payroll problem (program) for example, all relevant data (employee social security number, dependents, pay rate, hours worked, etc.) are input into the memory portion of the calculating device. When the payroll program is performed, this data would be retrieved from memory for arithmetic manipulation. The data retrieved from memory continues as the program progresses. Some of the intermediate results (running totals, etc.) continue to be stored until the final output is printed.

All the desktop models analyzed previously and ahead have exterior memory (storage) devices, such as magnetic tape, cards, disks, etc. Tapes and cards are serial; each single instruction or piece of listed data follows another. Rewinds are necessary to get to data that are at the beginning of the tape or card. Disks, however, are random access devices; a disk head can go (read or write) directly to a piece of data on a track without going first to the beginning or end. (Because minidisks are now appearing—5.25 inch sizes for less than $250 in quantities, users may look forward to these exterior or interior mass storage devices—See Olivetti P6060, and others ahead.) Memory sizes and capacities vary considerably as do their access speeds. Each memory location has an address by which it may be designated or called. In most machines with say, 100 memory locations, numbered 0 to 100, if a user specifies that data are to be stored at address 16, he means the 17th location in memory. Most programmable calculators divide memory into two areas (though some of the latest permit intermix use), data storage and program memory. For example, the instruction to multiply two numbers could be placed in program memory, and the numbers to be multiplied would be placed in data storage.

One very basic differentiating characteristic between programmable calculators and nonprogrammable units is the ability of the former to store instructions in a coded form so that they may be executed later; the fully programmable units have the ability to store data and instructions on **external** devices, such as cards, cassettes, ROM, disks, etc. and read data and instructions from these devices or media. With instructions and data stored in memory, the machine can be operated automatically, once the program is set in motion by an operator, stopping only when the appropriate command is given or when the program is completed. Instructions are executed sequentially or as branched by program control; the answers are automatically displayed or output in one of several other ways. The I/O devices are the peripherals. The storage of data and instructions capabilities and capacities relate to registers. Recall that an address is a place and an identification such as a name, label, or number (code) for a location in memory. A register is a location capable of storing a specified amount of data or an instruction; they are usually temporary storage *residences*. Computers and calculators have many different types of registers including, address registers, instruction registers, shift registers, index registers, etc. An instruction register is very important because it is used to hold an instruction that is to be executed. An address register is used to hold an address and is important in indirect addressing, as noted ahead. Using a shift register, the stored data can be moved to the left or right; an index register is used to alter, test, or manipulate addresses or instructions. These are important concepts for all programmers and are the bases for addressing, register arithmetic, and scores of other calculator operations. It should be noted also that different sizes of registers and locations in memory are the rule; a register might contain 16 digits of data, 32 digits, etc. In this discussion the term character refers to a numeric, alphabetic or other type symbol while the term digit is synonymous with a numeric character. It is common practice to store numbers using exponential notation. The form is $a \times 10^b$ where a is a mixed decimal number between 1 and 10 and the exponent b is a whole number (integer). For example, the number 258,400 would be expressed as 2.584×10^5.

Registers: Purpose and Operations

To use the number of registers as a measure of calculator capability, the engineer must first understand their purpose and the sizes they come in. In general, a register is a memory circuit that is big enough to store a 12-digit or longer floating-point number, its sign and a two-digit exponent with its sign. This is equivalent to four, 16-bit words. Therefore a common calculator with 100 registers has the equivalent of about 400, 16-bit words of memory. In some calculators all registers can be used interchangeably for either program or data storage. Other calculators have registers set aside for data only, while different registers hold program information only. When used for program storage, a register holds from eight to 16 steps in keyboard machines, and about eight characters of program in an algebraic machine. In judging calculator capability the number of registers alone is insufficient information. The size and allowed flexibility in using the registers must also be considered. To use total program steps as an effective measure of calculator capability, a user must know how much calculating is done with each step. In most keyboard machines, arithmetic operations use one or at most two steps. Storage and recall operations and indirect arithmetic operations call for from two to six steps. Conditional transfer operations require two to five steps. And special functions, like trig or square root, usually need only one step. A comparison of step-capacity numbers only, can be quite misleading. The types of problems that the user will be solving have a great effect on the meaning of this capacity number.

Indirect register addressing

Many calculators provide certain keys dedicated to special registers whose contents are then used to address other registers. This feature is called indirect addressing. The data contents of these special registers can be automatically changed as directed by the program. Indirect addressing is particularly useful in loop portions of a program. An instruction in the loop may designate such a special register each time the loop makes its sequence. The contents of the special register can be changed before the start of a succeeding loop sequence. This provides considerable flexibility in programming complex sequences as other registers, indirectly addressed by each circuit of the loop, call up new data, of programming routines. (See loops ahead.)

Ordinary Addressing Methods

We have noted that data or program memory can be designed with storage locations having almost any number of characters. One hypothetical type would require each machine language instruction to have three digits. In this case the memory is designed with three characters per storage location. Hypothetically again, with a memory possessing a total of 1000 storage locations (000 through 999), a section of memory would appear to the users as:

$$\boxed{1\,|\,2\,|\,6\,|\,5\,|\,8\,|\,1\,|\,1\,|\,3\,|\,3\,|\,2\,|\,6\,|\,4}$$

Memory Locations:　323　　324　　325　　326

The four quite standard methods of addressing most commonly used to address memory locations are: direct addressing, indirect addressing, symbolic addressing and indexed addressing. Direct addressing is the simplest because the programmer straightforwardly specifies the numeric address of the location of the data or instruction that is to be stored or retrieved. Example: Store the number 31.6 in location 538. Indirect addressing involves one step beyond, but a very important one. Using indirect addressing, the programmer gives an address that specifies a storage location that contains either a direct address or another indirect address. Thus, in operation, on the TI SR-52, for example, the indirect instruction is formed by preceding the normal direct instruction by 2nd IND. The effect of the indirect instruction 2nd IND RCL 04 would be to recall the value not in data register 04 but rather the value in the data register named by the contents of register 04 (R_{04}). If the value stored in R_{04} were 11 then the instruction would recall the value stored in R_{11}. And, in continuing our example, an instruction used in indirect addressing might be, "Store the number 32.6 at the address specified by the contents of location 538." An indirect execution example is shown below: "Execute the instruction to be found at the address contained in location 412." It can be seen that location 412 refers to location 886, where the instruction 123 is found.

Location 412　　　　　　　　　　　Location 886

Very wide use is made of indirect addressing in looping, in register arithmetic, and in branching. Potential purchasers should always be sure that their machine has this capability if any type of sophisticated calculating is to be attempted.

Symbolic addressing is simply the representation by a symbol convenient to the programmer. For example, an instruction could state in effect: "Store the number 32.5 at the address represented by the symbol #. The # is the symbol elected. To use this capability the machine must be able to handle keeping tract of a number of symbols and the numeric addresses they represent. The symbol could also be a numeric or alphabetic character or a group of numeric or alphabetic characters. An example would be, "Execute the program that begins in the address corresponding to the symbol 234.

The concept of indexed addressing is a bit more complex. Index usually means an ordered reference list of items of data or symbols. In indexed addressing, the address given is modified by the contents of an index register to obtain the actual address of the desired instruction or item of data. If a programmer desires to execute a sequence of instructions that are referenced by addresses ranging from 6 to 85, but that sequence of instructions must be moved so that it begins in location 260, the following instruction using indexed addressing accomplishes that. "Execute the program beginning at the address of 6 plus the contents of the index register. Earlier, 254 would have been placed in the index register to accomplish this. Indexed addressing makes it possible to relocate programs easily without having to change the addresses in all the instructions. Another example follows: "Obtain the instruction stored at address 225 plus the contents of the index register."

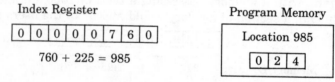

Index Register

| 0 | 0 | 0 | 0 | 0 | 7 | 6 | 0 |

760 + 225 = 985

Program Memory

Location 985

| 0 | 2 | 4 |

Thus, instruction 024 would be obtained. Other uses for Indexed Registers will be noted ahead, most of which relate to sequences of control. Most sequence of control systems are the normal numerical step execution. These systems execute instructions stored in locations 1, 2, 3, 4, 5, etc. or 100, 101, 102, etc. The counter keeps track of the location in program memory; when a program is being executed the counter contains the address of the next instruction and is incremented by one on each execution. This changes when **jump** or **transfer** are used.

Jumps, Flags, and Branches

Continuing explanations of programming techniques in an elementary vein, the jump or transfer instruction performs a departure from the normal sequence of instruction execution. A jump or transfer is itself an instruction. It might cause, for example, after normal execution of instruction 1, 2, 3, 4, 5, and 6, a jump instruction to instruction 13. The typical jump instruction specifies the address to which the program is to return to continue its execution. The program counter, instead of simply incrementing from 6 to 7, would have the value 13 inserted and the counter would then continue to increment from address 13. Jumps are often necessary when programs must be broken into specific segments to fit into a section of a program memory where other porgrams might already be stored. More often the jump is used when a programmer desires to transfer control to some specific point in the program. An example of a jump instruction is shown below. Location 234 contains a Jump instruction that transfers control to 716.

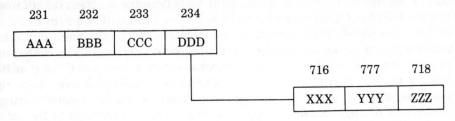

Tests of sensing devices, tests of calculations, and scores of other yes or no, on or off, zero or not zero are used to cause sequences of instructions to be executed only when preplanned results of these tests are actually achieved. Thus, some instructions designed by a programmer will execute only if a certain calculated result is zero and another sequence of instructions will execute if the resultant number is not zero. It is essential for a great many calculator operations to be able to test for the existance of certain conditions. One very common device that is used is a **flag.** Most flags are variables with two possible values, i.e., set or not set or off or on, and these can be set by the program. The flag condition is used to indicate the presence or absence of some condition. For example, if A is calculated to be greater than B, a flag can be set to the 'on' position, and such a flag setting can be used to cause a jump or it may be tested later to execute an instruction or cause some other action. On some systems, **sense switches** can be manually set on various devices, the calculator mainframe itself, for example, and a program can test to see if the sense switch is on or off. Generally, if it is on, a jump is made to another part of a program or sequence of instructions in memory. If the program is instructed to continue if the sense switch is off, that is also part of a sense switch result. Thus, a decision point is a location in the program where one of two, or in some instances, several possible choices of the execution of sequences of instructions can begin or be halted.

A **branch** is the activity resulting from a test or of a selection of an instruction or sequence of instructions out of the normal order. A branch is similar to a jump, but the branch is a transfer that usually occurs as a result of a decision or test, i.e., a specific part of the program or sequence of instructions will execute only if certain conditions are met. The machine must save the address of the next instruction after the Branch instruction if the programmer wants the program to return to the original sequence of instructions after the branch instruction has been executed. Generally, the programmer will plan for the return after the alternate sequence of instructions has been completed by branching. The address of the next instruction in the original sequence can be inserted back in the program counter, as noted, and the program will continue execution from that point.

Branches are especially important in looping. A **loop** is an instruction sequence that is repeated continually until some final condition is met. The procedure is very different for different models of calculators. (See looping below.) Loops are generally controlled by **subroutines.** A standard definition of a routine is a program or set of instructions designed to perform some specific action upon data. A **subroutine** is generally considered to be a routine or program that is dependent upon or subordinate to a main program or routine. It might also be an independent routine used by a main program. An example might concern a chemistry lab experiment that has a program that requires repeated calculation of a mathematical function. The function evaluation is done by means of a complicated series of formula steps. It would be a waste to rewrite that series of instructions each time the function calculation is required. Instead a subroutine is written and will compute the values of the function on demand. The subroutine then can be used by the main program whenever it is required or branched to. **Open subroutines** can be inserted in a program at each point in the program where it is to be used. **Closed subroutines,** on the other hand, appear once and are entered whenever they are needed, usually by means of a branch. When subroutines are entered during program execution, the address following the branch instruction to the subroutine is saved; when completed the main program resumes. Programmers who use closed subroutines generally save space in program memory for them. All programmers should use flowcharts—and simply make changes in the chart, then in the program itself for the various devices.

Subroutines on the TEK 31 calculator system can be called from the keyboard in addition to their normal program execution. This keyboard calling makes it easy to write conveniently used modular programs. This type of program construction permits fast changes in configuration. Consequently, debugging is also simplified. For future reference any subroutine, no matter what its function, is easily stored on a magnetic tape. The recorder is built right into the 31. This way when new applications present themselves users won't need to invest their time rekeying.

There is no problem getting there and back. To use the subroutine in a program, a method of getting to it as well as back again must be provided. It depends on the program and machine configuration as to which of several alternative linking techniques are used. Linking refers to getting at a subroutine. One simple method is to put the subroutine at the beginning of the memory, which requires only a stroke on the "start" key for execution. Another method is to place the subroutine at a specified spot in the calculator and use the "go to" command to bring it into use. Users could also store its location in a register and later recall to display and simply touch the "go to display" key to program the execution of this task. Probably the most convenient way of linking is the labeling technique. Users simply put in a label key and any symbol (a symbol is nearly any key in the calculator) as the first two sequences of the subroutine. That symbol is then used with the label key.

The Importance of Flowcharts: A Decision Map to Prevent Errors, Save Time

A flowchart is a procedural listing, an outline, of the sequence of how a program solves a problem. This helps the programmer to avoid getting lost, to avoid breaks, to serve as shorthand notation for program segmentation. Some flowcharts are very simple; others are complex, and fully documented so that they may be reused or checked by other programmers or users. Flow charts may be exact duplicates of the procedures, using several *blocks* to demonstrate the keys pressed, the decision results, etc. while others may consist of a single block showing a simple (but complete) linear step-use of the flow of the program. It is essential that programmers use the flowchart symbols that are accepted as standards throughout the calculator industry, i.e., the conventions of meaning for circles, dots, squares, diamonds, etc. After the flowchart is drawn, the symbols properly (sequentially) connected, the programmer substitutes groups of instructions for each element of the flowchart. Use of flowcharts is universal in all calculator users' manuals to help all owners understand not only programming but how to create, edit, eliminate errors, document, addend many types of instructions, subroutines, and other techniques as loops, etc. The user must be continually reminded that if he did not program the sequence of instructions correctly, the result will not be correct. Similarly, the instructions themselves must be correct ones that the machine is capable of accepting. The six basic steps to follow in developing a program are: Define the Problem; Solve the Problem Manually; Flowchart and Write the Program; Key the Instructions into Memory; Test the Program, and Edit and Retest Until Correct. (The flowcharts, programs and procedures of conditioned testing, labels and program stepping for a hypothetical problem and machine are shown on the following pages.)

Procedural Steps to Programming

Problem definition requires a delineation of information on hand, the result desired, and an organized approach to program development. The next procedure is to convert the information and solution procedures to an algorithm, a step-wise mathematical expression of the components and the relationships between them. The next step is to solve the problem manually, using simple numbers if necessary to check the sequencing and reasonableness. The preparation of the flowchart follows, and from this base, the program can be written. The flowchart illustrates the operation of the completed program as it is to be executed on the calculator. Writing the program will require the close use of the owners' manuals to be certain all keystroke, memory, and transfer instruction rules are followed. The aid of a notepad is usually necessary. Here also the differences between RPN and Algebraic systems become most important.

Several pages have been devoted to these distinctions and more will be used to demonstrate these important differences. About a dozen machines mentioned with some depth in this book relate to RPN programming—the National 4000 Hand-Held Series; the HP 25, 67, 97, and 9815. They are all big selling highly praised machines, used throughout the world. The *enter vs equals* dichotomy arises but discussion of the argument is not appropriate at this point. While keying in the program the specific rules of each language must be used, and the same set of circumstances is true if BASIC language machines are used. Also, many different types of rules relate to card, tape, cartridge, ROM, and Disk program development and entry to the calculator system. In general, the program or learn modes are used to develop programs. The fifth step is to test and run the program for accurate results using sample or the actual variables of the problem itself. If the program develops an incorrect answer, the next steps are flawed. Editing and retesting are almost always a necessary procedure to verify answers and procedures. There are many crosschecks and other techniques recommended by the various manufacturers.

Editing relates to advancing the calculator through the program one step at a time. The display will show the step number on better machines, and those with print capability will be of very important assistance for diagnostic inspection of procedure and specific steps. The most advanced machines have diagnostic cards, *prompting* and other aids to assist in editing programs. If there is too much *busywork* indicated, it is *back to the flowchart* to check for broken rules, sequences, or improper procedure, as can most easily be noted in the documentation of the flowcharted program. As users accumulate personal or specific company libraries of programs, they quickly discover the true value of flowcharts and documentation—to demonstrate the procedures to others, to amend or addend various programs, and to provide a history of program development by specific people. This suggests that each programmer has a definite style; this is often a unique but a continuous accumulation of techniques and tricks, of shorthand efficiency, and of a display of expertise of talented people. Users who belong to the various calculator clubs will discover that the heaviest contributors of programs are true stylists, and all can learn much from them.

Decisions and a Conditional Testing — Example

In this example, one often wishes to jump to another program or program segment or branch to a subroutine only if some condition is satisfied. The hypothetical machine is capable of testing the number in the Entry register to see if it satisfies a particular condition, and, if the condition is satisfied, performing the required jump or branch. You can test the number in the Entry register for the following conditions:

> Greater than zero (>0)
> Less than zero (<0)
> Equal to zero ($=0$)
> Greater than or equal to zero (≥ 0)
> Less than or equal to zero (≤ 0)
> Not equal to zero ($\neq 0$)

The machine can also test whether an entry has been made from the keyboard.

A conditional test always asks a question. If the answer is yes, the program jumps or branches to the label that you specify. If the answer is *no*, the calculator continues to execute the program steps that follow the test.

Flowchart Symbols for Testing

At this point, we will add another symbol to our "vocabulary" of flowchart symbols. A diamond-shaped box is used to indicate a test for some condition.

Symbol

Meaning

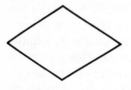

Test. A test is made for the condition indicated by the words in the diamond. One flowline enters the diamond. Two or three flowlines exit from the diamond-shaped box. The exit flow lines are usually labelled "yes" or "no" (if there are two exits).

Example:

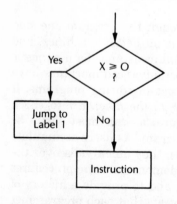

In the portion of a flowchart shown, a number X is tested to determine if it is greater than or equal to zero. If the answer is "yes", a Jump is made to a program segment labelled 1; if the answer is "no", the program continues in sequence.

Conditional Jump

The key sequences, instruction codes and meanings for the *Conditional Jump* instructions are given in the following table. The label to which the Jump is to be made must be specified immediately after the Conditional Jump instruction.

Key Sequence	Instruction Code	Meaning
JUMP +	351	Jump, if the number in the E-register is positive, to the label specified in the following memory step.
JUMP −	352	Jump, if the number in the E-register is negative.
JUMP + −	353	Jump if the number in the E-register is positive or negative, but not zero.
JUMP =	354	Jump if the number in the E-register is zero.
JUMP + =	355	Jump if the number in the E-register is greater than or equal to zero.
JUMP − =	356	Jump if the number in the E-register is less than or equal to zero.
JUMP + − =	357	Jump if an entry has been made from the keyboard.

Example:

The key sequence JUMP + = 2 means "Jump to label 2 if the number in the E-register is greater than or equal to zero."

Conditional Branch

The key sequences, instruction codes and meanings for the *Conditional Branch* instruction are given in the following table. The label to which the branch is to be made must be specified immediately following the Conditional Branch instruction on our hypothetical machine.

Key Sequence	Instruction Code	Meaning
f BRANCH +	361	Branch, if the number in the E-register is positive, to the label specified in the following memory step.
f BRANCH −	362	Branch, if the number in the E-register is negative.
f BRANCH + −	363	Branch, if the number in the E-register is positive or negative, but not zero.
f BRANCH =	364	Branch, if the number in the E-register is equal to zero.
f BRANCH + =	365	Branch, if the number in the E-register is greater than or equal to zero.
f BRANCH − =	366	Branch, if the number in the E-register is less than or equal to zero.
f BRANCH + − =	367	Branch, if an entry has been made from the keyboard.

Example:

The key sequence f BRANCH − 3 means "Branch to label 3 if the number in the E-register is negative."

Sample Program Using a Conditional Jump

A Conditional Jump instruction is used in the following program that calculates the sum of the first 17 integers $(1 + 2 \cdots + 16 + 17)$. As shown in the flowchart, the number in register 0 is tested to see if it equals 17. If it equals 17, a jump is made; if it doesn't equal 17, the program continues to the next memory step in sequence.

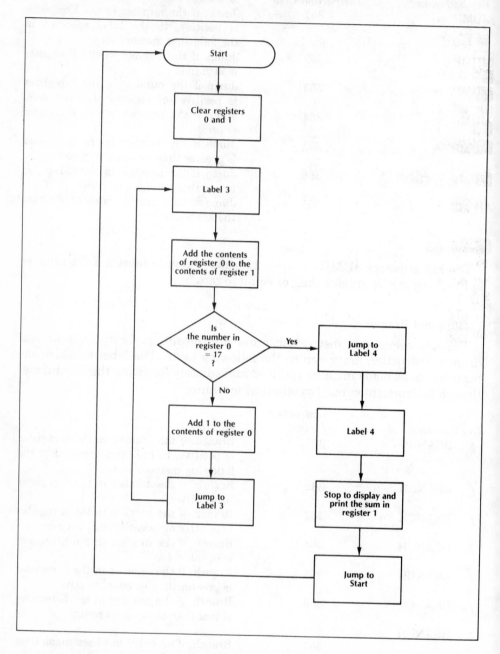

The program is loaded as follows:

Do This	See This	Comments
JUMP START/STOP RUN STEP/LOAD	. 001	
CLEAR		
STₙ 0 0		
STₙ 0 1	001 .006	Clear registers 0 and 1.
▮ ▮ 3 LABEL	203 .007	Label 3.
RCLₙ 0 0		
STₙ + 0 1	001 .011	Add the number in register 0 to the number in register 1.
▮ 1 7 =	020 .015	Subtract 17 from the number in the E-register.
JUMP = 4	004 .017	If the number in the Entry register equals 0, jump to label 4. Otherwise continue.
1		
STₙ + 0 0	000 .020	Increment Register 0.
JUMP 3	003 .022	Jump to Label 3.
▮ ▮ LABEL 4	204 .023	Label 4 is at step 023.
RCLₙ 0 1		
PRINT START/STOP	033 .027	Print and Stop to display the sum in register 1.
JUMP START/STOP	033 .029	Return to the start of the program.
▮ RUN STEP/LOAD	0 . 0000	Switch to Run mode to prepare for program execution.

•001	037	CL	
•002	300	ST	
•003	000		
•003	000		
•004	300	ST	
•004	300	ST	
•001	037	CL	
•002	300	ST	
•003	000		
•003	000		
•004	300	ST	
•005	000		
•005	001		
•006	100	F	
•006	200	L	
•006	203	L	3
•007	310	RC	
•008	000		
•008	000		
•009	300	ST	
•009	301	+	
•010	000		
•010	001		
•011	022	−	
•012	001		1
•013	007		7
•014	020	=	
•015	350	J	
•015	354	=	
•016	004		4
•017	001		1
•018	300	ST	
•018	301	+	
•019	000		
•019	000		
•020	350	J	
•021	003		3
•022	100	F	
•022	200	L	
•022	204	L	4
•023	310	RC	
•024	000		
•024	001		
•025	034	PT	
•026	033	S	S
•027	350	J	
•028	033	S	S

To run the program:

Do This

[START STOP]

See This

$\boxed{\qquad 153.0000 \qquad}$

153·0000

The sum of the first 17 integers is 153.

Sample Program that Tests whether an Entry Has Been Made

In this program we wish to calculate

$$y = a^{2.7}$$

for a number of values of a. The Identifier 1 is used to indicate that a new value is to be entered. If *an entry has been made*, the program jumps to Label 2 and performs the calculation. If no entry has been made (indicating all calculations have been done) the Identifier 8 is displayed and the program is terminated.

The flowchart for this program is shown on p. 237.

To load the program

Do This	See This	Comments
[JUMP] [START STOP] [Run Step Load]	$\boxed{\qquad .001}$	
[1]	$\boxed{001 \quad .002}$	Enter 1.
[IDENT]	$\boxed{032 \quad .003}$	Identifier.
[START STOP]	$\boxed{033 \quad .004}$	Stop to enter value of a
[JUMP] [+] [−] [=]	$\boxed{357 \quad .005}$	Jump if an entry has been made to Label 2.
[2]	$\boxed{002 \quad .006}$	
[8]	$\boxed{010 \quad .007}$	Enter 8.
[IDENT] [PRINT]	$\boxed{034 \quad .009}$	Display and print the Identifier.
[START STOP]	$\boxed{033 \quad .010}$	End of program.
(Press [FWD] 10 times)	$\boxed{\qquad .020}$	Move to step 020.
[LABEL] [2]	$\boxed{202 \quad .021}$	Label 2 is arbitrarily placed at step 020.
[PRINT]	$\boxed{034 \quad .022}$	Print the value of a entered.
[aˣ]	$\boxed{025 \quad .023}$	aˣ function.
[2] [·] [7]	$\boxed{007 \quad .026}$	Enter exponent.
[=]	$\boxed{020 \quad .027}$	Calculate y.
[PRINT] [START STOP]	$\boxed{033 \quad .029}$	Display and print y.
[·] [JUMP] [START STOP] [Run Step Load]	$\boxed{033 \quad .032}$	Print a dotted line and return to step 001.
	$\boxed{\qquad 0.0000}$	Switch to Run mode.

•001	001		⅃
•002	032	I D	
•003	033	S S	
•004	350	J	
•004	351	+	
•004	353	−	
•004	357	=	
•005	002		2
•006	010		8
•007	032	I D	
•008	034	P T	
•009	033	S S	
•010			
•011			
•012			
•013			
•014			
•015			
•016			
•017			
•018			
•019			
•020	100	F	
•020	200	L	
•020	202	L 2	
•021	034	P T	
•022	025	&	
•023	002		2
•024	012		d
•025	007		7
•026	020	=	
•027	034	P T	
•028	033	S S	
•029	100	F	
•029	112	D T	
•030	350	J	
•031	033	S S	

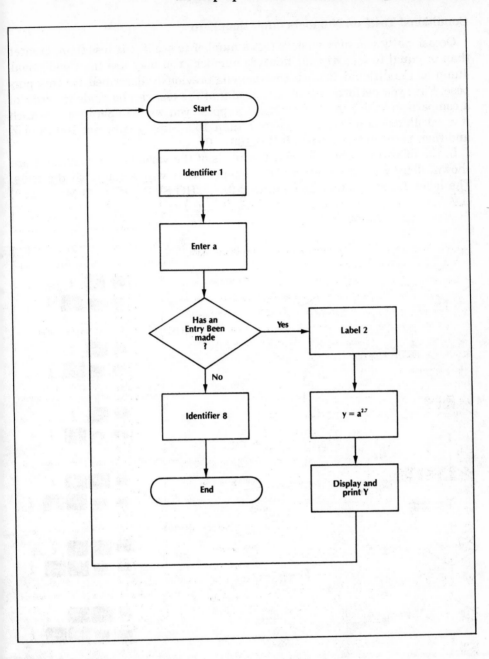

To run the program for values of a = 2, 3 and 4:

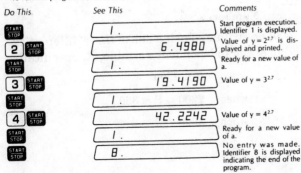

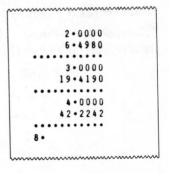

Notice how the dotted line formats the printed tape, making it easier to read.

Conditional Tests on Numbers other than Zero

Occasionally you may wish to test a number to see if it is less than, greater than or equal to a particular nonzero number. You may use the Conditional Jump or Conditional Branch instructions previously described for this purpose. First you perform a subtraction so that the test can be made in terms of a comparison with zero. For example, suppose you want to perform a Branch if a calculated number, Z, is greater than 100. Simply subtract 100 from Z and then perform the Branch if $Z - 100 > 0$.

In the following table, flowchart symbols of the various test conditions are shown along with the instruction sequences that will accomplish the tests. The label, l, may assume the values 0-9, ·, CHG SIGN, EXP, D/M/S, (or).

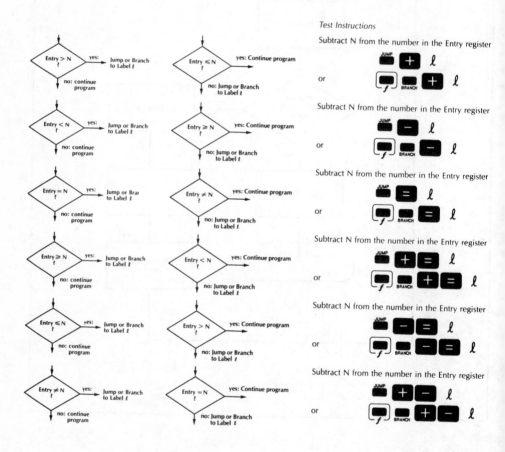

Sample Program: Testing Nonzero Numbers

Suppose that a function, F, is to be evaluated using one of three different expressions depending on the value of the independent variable, R. Specifically,

$$F = 10^{(1.78 - \log R)} \qquad \text{when} \quad R \le 2200$$

$$F = 10^{(-3.7 + 0.65 \log R)} \qquad \text{when} \quad 2200 < R \le 3600$$

$$F = 10^{(-0.5 - 0.25 \log R)} \qquad \text{when} \quad 3600 < R$$

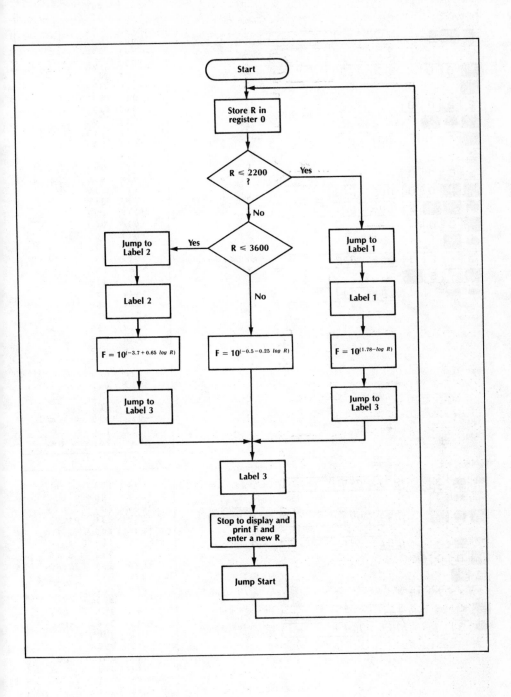

The flowchart for this program is shown on p. 239 and includes two Conditional Jumps depending on whether $R \leq 2200$ and $R \leq 3600$. The value of R is assumed to be in the Entry register at the start of the program.

To load the program

Do This	See This	Comments
JUMP START/STOP RUN STEP LOAD	.001	Load program starting at step 001.
PRINT	034 .002	Print R.
ST_n 0 0	000 .004	Store R in Register 0.
−		
2 2 0 0		
= JUMP −		
= 1	001 .012	Test for $R \leq 2200$. If true, jump to label 1.
CHG SIGN		
3 6 0 0		
RCL_A + 0 0	000 .019	
JUMP − = 2	002 .021	Test for $R \leq 3600$. If true, jump to label 2.
RCL_A 0 0		
LOG ×		
CHG SIGN . 2 5	005 .029	If R is not True for the above test, then $R > 3600$ and $F = 10^{(-0.5 - 0.25 \log R)}$
− . 5 =		
10^x	161 .034	

Do This	See This	Comments
LABEL 3	203 .035	Label 3 is at step 033.
PRINT .		Stop to display F, print a line of dots and enter a new R. Then jump to step 001.
START/STOP JUMP START/STOP	033 .040	
LABEL 1	201 .041	Label 1 is at step 037.
RCL_A 0 0 LOG		
CHG SIGN +		
1 . 7 8		
= 10^x	161 .052	If $R \leq 2200$, then $F = 10^{(1.78 - \log R)}$
JUMP 3	003 .054	Jump to label 3 to display value of F.

•001	034	rT	
•002	300	ST	
•003	000		
•003	000		
•004	022	−	
•005	002		2
•006	002		2
•007	000		0
•008	000		0
•009	020	=	
•010	350	J	
•010	352	−	
•010	356	=	
•011	001		1
•012	013	S	
•013	003		3
•014	006		6
•015	000		0
•016	000		0
•017	310	RC	
•017	311	+	
•018	000		
•018	000		
•019	350	J	
•019	352	−	
•019	356	=	
•020	002		2
•021	310	RC	
•022	000		
•022	000		
•023	061	LG	
•024	023	×	
•025	013	S	
•026	012	d	
•027	002		2
•028	005		5
•029	022	−	
•030	012	d	
•031	005		5
•032	020	=	
•033	100	F	
•033	161	L−₁	

•034	100	F	
•034	200	L	
•034	203	L ₃	
•035	034	PT	
•036	100	F	
•036	112	D T	
•037	033	S S	
•038	350	J	
•039	033	S S	
•040	100	F	
•040	200	L	
•040	201	L ₁	
•041	310	RC	
•042	000		
•042	000		
•043	061	LG	
•044	013	S	
•045	021	+	
•046	001		1
•047	012	d	
•048	007		7
•049	010		8
•050	020	=	
•051	100	F	
•051	161	L−₁	
•052	350	J	
•053	003		3

Do This	See This	Comments
[■] [■] [2] LABEL	202 .055	Label 2 is at step 051.
RCL_n [0] [0] LOG		
[×] [.] [6] [5]	005 .062	If $2200 < R \le 3600$, then $F = 10^{(-3.7 + 0.65 \log R)}$
[−] [3] [.] [7]		
[=] [■] [■] 10^x	161 .068	
JUMP [3]	003 .070	Jump to label 3 to display value of F.
RUN STEP LOAD	0.0000	Switch to Run mode in preparation for program execution.

```
•054   100      F
•054   200      L
•054   202      L  2
•055   310      RC
•056   000
•056   000
•057   061      LG
•058   023        ×
•059   012        d
•060   006          6
•061   005          5
•062   022       −
•063   003          3
•064   012        d
•065   007          7
•066   020       =
•067   100      F
•067   161      L−1
•068   350   J
•069   003          3
```

To run the program for values of R = 600, 3000 and 8000

Do This	See This	Comments
[6] [0] [0]	600.0000	Enter R = 600.
START STOP	0.1004	Value of F for R = 600.
[3] [0] [0] [0]	3,000.0000	Enter R = 3000.
START STOP	0.0363	Value of F for R = 3000.
[8] [0] [0] [0]	8,000.0000	Enter R = 8000.
START STOP	0.0334	Value of F for R = 8000.

```
600•0000
   0•1004
•••••••••••
3,000•0000
    0•0363
•••••••••••
8,000•0000
    0•0334
•••••••••••
```

Stepping Through a Program

The hypothetical machine permits you to execute a program one step at a time. Using this feature, you may observe program execution closely. This is particularly useful in determining what modifications a program may require. To step through a program, first set the RUN/STEP/LOAD switch to RUN/STEP/LOAD, and place the PRINTER switch in the OFF position.

When in Step mode, each time you press START/STOP the following things happen:

- The display shows program information for about one second. The current memory step, its code and the previous and next code are also shown, in the Load format previously described.
- The instruction at the current location is executed and the result of the instruction is displayed. (Multi-step instructions like RCL_n 0 0 are executed together as one instruction.)
- After the instruction is executed, the program stops with the current contents of the Entry register in the display. You must press START/STOP again to continue stepping through the program.

If you move the RUN/STEP/LOAD switch from RUN/STEP/LOAD to RUN/STEP/LOAD, pressing START/STOP will cause program execution from the current step in memory.

If you follow the above procedure with the PRINTER switch ON, the step number, instruction code, and printer symbol are printed each time an instruction is executed, calculation results are printed after calculations and the display shows only the contents of the E-register after each instruction. (Other printers, the HP-97, PC 100-A, etc. will function differently, scrutinized for proper operation.)

The Rise of Home Computers as Competitors to Calculators

It is fitting that we close this chapter with a few pertinent notes concerning a rapidly accelerating movement of intelligent games and home computers as used first by hobbyists and engineers and now by professional people, students, and wide ranges of business people as well. The home microcomputer really has its origin from calculator chip development. The original microprocessor was an unplanned development by large scale integrated circuit designers (from Intel Corp. with an order from a Japanese firm) faced with designing a calculator chip with changing requirements. Unintentionally, they backed into the microprocessor (and by adding memory, control and Input-Output, into the microcomputer) by designing a universal calculator chip that could be programmed like a computer for various functions. Now, microcomputers use high level languages, control industrial equipment and consumer appliances and toys, and are incorporated into thousands of communications and automation items. When keyboards, printers, video displays, floppy disks, and other peripherals are connected to or integrated with the various microcomputers, they become complete computing systems. The discussion below of four such microcomputers attests to this, and the accompanying photographs show the range of capability and easy interface to all types of individuals . . . as they learn, play and profit.

Nearly all microprocessor families can be purchased mounted on chips or boards interfaced easily to peripheral and memory boards and usable with standard programs and code conversions through ROM or other easily programmed media. The video games by Bally, RCA, Fairchild, National Semiconductor and others are often advertised as computers because they have a computer-like memory. Thus, with the home tv as an output device, the games' calculator-type terminals as input devices, and the microprocessors in the games for control, selection, decision-making, and calculating, the *game-type* home computer will *back into* personal use rapidly. And, once used *as a computer* people will want more versatility. Many feel the home computer will then come to affect us more drastically than television did; the possible applications are unlimited. Scores of brands are available, a dozen or more personal computer periodicals have subscriber totals reaching from 35,000 to well over 100,000. Although this is a calculator book, intelligent readers will desire to be aware of some of the latest microcomputer products, and in a limited space, we shall discuss four models as being representative of the deluge soon to come.

The Heath Company Products and Competition from Apple II and Commodore's PET, a Display-Integrated System

Most *micro*computers are 8-bit types; the larger *mini*computers are often 16-bit types for larger word efficiency. The Heath Co. of Benton Harbor, MI. introduced one of each in late summer, 1977. The Heath Company was the first major corporation to enter the Home Computer market. All of the major semiconductor manufacturers had previously introduced board and chip systems, but they were the *bare bones* types to be designed into other products by original equipment manufacturers (OEMs), although National Semi-Conductor Corp. sold many thousands of SC/MP boards and calculator-like terminals for $95 each as *learner* microcomputer systems. Scores of small *assembler* firms bought chips and other gear and sold complete systems to computer stores and by display ads in magazines and direct mail. The Heath company is a division of Schlumberger, Ltd. which is listed on the New York Stock Exchange. The Heath Company alone does about $100 million in sales of Heathkits for ama-

Heathkit H8 Digital Computer

Heathkit H9 CRT Terminal

teur radio, hi-fi and stereo components, electronic devices test instruments, auto and marine accessories, and so on. When the Heath people entered the home computer market with the products pictured and described here, they met head-on with all the smaller fabricator firms and Commodore, a large international firm that recently purchased an American semiconductor manufacturer, MOS Technology Inc., maker of the popular 6502 microprocessor chip. This chip is used in the popular KIM microcomputers, the PET (see below) and the Apple II, also pictured on these pages.

The Heath Company very wisely bought their microprocessor, the LSI-11 chip, from Digital Equipment Corp., (DEC) the largest minicomputer manufacturer, with more than 80,000 of their minicomputer models in use. Thus, thousands of programs have been written and are readily available for the DEC computers . . . and a good portion of these programs will work, some with minor adjustments, with the new Heath H-11 systems. This answers the very frequent question. "What can you do with a home computer?" The Heath response: with the proper programs, thousands of things . . . from accounting, device and appliance control, information processing and retrieval, and the lists would fill many pages. The other minicomputer manufacturers and semiconductor companies were not silent long. Data General Corp., the second largest mini maker (35,000+ systems out) announced they would have a MicroNova (Nova is their best selling mini) in a home version for about $2000 very soon, and rumors were rampant that National Semiconductor, Texas Instruments, and others had their units in near-production stages.

Heath's 50 retail stores and multi-million catalog mailings offer the new home computer line. They have combined with large magazine display ads and other widespread media campaigns the DEC and Heath reputations for excellent service and documentation (and education) to offer users at least 1000 *tried and true* programs from the Digital Equipment Computer Users Society (DECUS) library. A great many of these have been developed for, or can run on, the LSI-11 microcomputer, and thus the Heath model H-11 which uses it as its primary component, i.e, same instruction set as several models of DEC minis. The price of this system is a competitive $1295, and peripherals available include: 4K memory, parallel interface, serial/cassette interface, video terminal, paper tape reader/punch (both pictured), and others. Many manuals and teaching items are offered for the complete amateur. The lower cost system, the H-8 8-bit system uses the popular Intel 8080A microprocessor chip — and at least a thousand programs are also available for this instruction set, and the price is a very low $375. Though the Heath products are in kit form, they are modular and very easy to assemble. The H-11 includes an editor, PAL-11 assembler, linker, on-line debugging package, I/O executive, BASIC and FOCAL interpreters — all are important for immediate or *turnkey* use of the systems. The terminal available for $530 (kit) is a 12-inch CRT with a 67-key ASCII keyboard with a 12-line, 80-character format. The unit can be formatted in four columns of 12 lines, 20 characters wide, and has a cursor control. Users can format on the screen, and when satisfied, batch into their system. Heath has its own revolving charge credit plan to get customers into microcomputer systems easily. Heath expects 20% of their revenue to be derived from computers in the future and is fully committed to continuing education of customers, increasing software development . . . and many more products. But, they're in the battle with giants — watch out for TI, NS, Fairchild, and others.

Heathkit H10 Papertape Reader/Punch

Heathkit H11 Digital Computer

The Apple II and the PET Take Side Glances at the "Dynabook"

The Apple II is representative of the keenly inventive small company product lines. "Ready for use the moment it's unpacked . . . fully assembled and pre-tested, the Apple II can be connected to any standard television set using an inexpensive RF modulator . . . your tv screen becomes Apple II's output, displaying full alphanumeric characters and video graphics in 15 colors. Input to the unit is simple — an alphanumeric keyboard is built into the Apple II's compact molded case." And that's the way the appealing line goes. A single printed-circuit board contains the microprocessor, system memory (up to 12K bytes ROM and 48K bytes RAM) and all other electronic components and interfaces" . . . and users don't need to know a RAM from a ROM to use the system . . . it has BASIC, the English-like programming language built-in." The system can use an audio cassette recorder/player (for storing and loading programs), an Apple's GAME I/O connector (for paddles and other interactive game controls), a speaker and connectors for up to 8 peripheral boards . . . are just a few sidelights. For example, users can write their own video action games, and the company claims most beginners can start writing their own BASIC programs within an afternoon . . . because Apple II's BASIC is an integer BASIC that contains numerous unique extensions, designed particularly for personal computing applications. COLOR, PLOT, HLIN (draw horizontal line), VLIN (draw vertical line), SCRN (x,y) (reads screen color) and PDL (game paddle read function) are a few examples.

The design people at Apple Computer Inc., Cupertino, CA. realize that most people are swept fast by color and offer on the display 24 lines of 40 characters and color graphics (40 wide × 48 high resolution — 15 colors) or high resolution graphics (280 wide × 192 high — 4 colors — black, white, violet, green). In both modes, 4 lines of text may optionally be displayed at the bottom of the screen to allow users to give game instructions, label graphics, or have the computer ask the user questions. All display modes are software selectable using standard BASIC commands; switching to two previously stored screen images is fast from two memory blocks. Because this system is designed for many games, with sound, color, photon torpedos. Klingons, and so on, it could become very popular as a teaching device, as a budget tracker, bookkeeping device, and so on. It is expandable into music synthesis systems, and the 1001 things other computer enthusiasts do with their systems . . . and with a price of $1298 assembled or $598 in board form (without case, keyboard, power supply or accessories), it should attract hobbyists with limited budgets. But,

A PERSONAL COMPUTER THAT'S FUN AND FUNCTIONAL. This compact APPLE II serves the needs of today's computer hobbyist, providing a complete home computer center. With capabilities that go far beyond advanced calculators and video games, APPLE II uses the family color TV set for graphic display. APPLE II, recently announced, sells for $1295.

"OPEN THE GARAGE DOOR, HAL!" Game paddles or built-in-keyboard talk to Apple II, the home table-top computer that connects to a color television set. Write your own action games, draw dazzling 15-color displays, solve engineering problems, or use it as the heart of an automation system of your own design.

as it was distributed in summer of 1977, it had rough competition from PET buyers and *waiters* — because of tremendous interest in the $600 — all in one package system.

Commodore International Ltd, the parent company of Commodore Business Machines, Inc. (Palo Alto, CA.) offers a $595 cassette-programmable "Personal Electronic Transactor" or Pet home and business microcomputer using the same microprocessor chip as the Apple II. But through some miraculous tooling, the design combines it with a 9-inch black and white CRT, a 73-key keyboard, and 4K bits of RAM operating with BASIC program language for a very neat, versatile system. The marketing people see its use in schools, business (for inventory keeping, accounting, and so on), and home use since it weighs only 44 pounds and interfaces to plotters, recorders, floppy-disk memories, and many more. The all-in-one unit contains a video display to show 40 columns by 25 lines from among 64 standard ASCII characters or 64 graphics-related characters. It has a winking cursor with full motion control for editing and screen control functions; future versions are expected to be able to use more games, have two cassettes for program load, and an upper-and lower-case graphic set. From the reception the unit received at three electronics-computer shows and conferences, the unit can indeed sell up to the "several hundred thousand" the company expects it can market. The KIM-I and KIM-II board microcomputers have sold tens of thousands to satisfied customers, and this marketing is handled by the same people — its sales were begun by the components company Commodore acquired, and rumors are that Sears and other mass merchandisers are interested in these products. The Pet's memory includes 12K bytes of ROM, 4K bytes of RAM and 8K bytes for use of the BASIC interpreter; the user RAM is expandable to 32K bytes. The keyboard is very functional and eye-appealing because of its colors and clean arrangement. But, though Sears, Penneys and Montgomery-Ward may be interested, the giant Radio Shack chain of electronics stores (estimated at 5000+ outlets) has announced that they will soon offer their own versions of home and small business computers. This is all very interesting, but some strange things are going on over at Xerox . . . and that's another story.

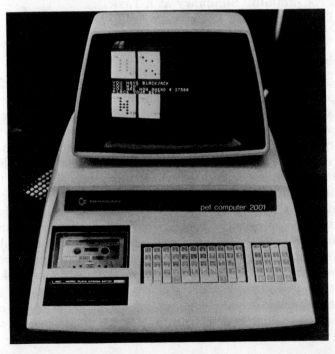

Most intriguing, though no longer mysterious, is the "Dynabook" that is said to be able to display printed pages on its screen: black on white, white on black, red on green, etc. in many styles, typefaces, small or large, and things can be personally written on them. Many types of digitizers and *touch screens* are available using light pens, ball point pens, and so on to *write* physically on screens (circling and moving words around, etc.) But most users still prefer to control from the keyboard. The device is not yet quite down to the size of a book, but it is a general purpose computer with the ability to do parallel processing on eight different levels, according to several articles about the machine, i.e. the way humans think — about several things simultaneously. The machine is the computer dream of Alan Kay — and though reports are that it can store vast quantities of information, index and systemize, keep records and do many "creative" things, simulate, animate, and so on with a screen that can be written on, painted on, offer musical output, complete experiments with words and sounds, and on and on, no one from Xerox suggests that the product is anywhere near a marketing stage. But, such capabilities are in the minds of many designers besides those at Xerox. Just as we will note ahead, give calculators to talented, creative people and they will get them to perform tasks that only *garage-bench* geniuses would even dream about . . . such as bringing out alphanumerics from the numeric only HP-67 and HP-97, and do graphics with them besides. HP engineers didn't think of that, but calculator club members have built the programs and devices to do this and many more *great things*. The Dynabook may be a leading edge of the new personal electronics technology, but it is only one of thousands that will carry many dreams to reality. The combination of calculators and computers with the deep investigation and wierd and unsupervised experimentation — by several hundreds of thousands of *better mousetrap* kinds of minds will lead us into strange new worlds, jobs, products, procedures. And it has all just begun . . . with prices of electronics capabilities continuing to fall . . . opening personal calculating and computing devices to any and every curious mind and adventurous spirit.

Programming Summary as a Task . . . Then as Fun . . . Then as an Art . . .

Programming and People

The programming process has been the subject of thousands of articles in trade and professional journals and hundreds of books. Obviously there is no single or 'best' way to complete a program or to solve a complex problem. It is quite rare when two programs for detailed problem solutions written by two different programmers turn out to be identical. The order, instruction selection, and techniques very often reflect the programmer's individual personality or background. As each programmer gains experience on the various type of machines he or she owns or uses, new personal styles evolve. One programmer may develop very distinctive craftiness to develop highly optimized (fewest instruction) programs. Another may use particular ingenuity in the development of a blend of practically all the instructions available. Others will be most conservative using only the specified, straightforward coding, i.e., the most basic procedures and codes. This generally consumes more time and space than is necessary, but the clarity of purpose and the sureness of documentation become great assets. A quick inspection of "good" code by another user will immediately demonstrate the scope and purpose of the project.

Thus, each type of programming technique will have advantages and short-comings. The style developed by most programmers is the one that most adequately fulfills his or her needs. At first, most users will avoid branching, indirect addressing, loops and subroutines. But once used successfully, these same programmers will swear by their developed keystroke convenience and time-saving effectiveness. Indeed, a great number of calculator users become enthused almost to the addictive stage as they revel in each stage of programming successes. The calculator users' clubs are loaded with members who have become completely involved with the utility and power of their machines first, then the idiosyncracies and intricacies of that power and versatility. It is not unusual to find calculator users, whether they are doctors, accountants, engineers, students, or housewives, who have used their personal control of computing calculators to advance in their jobs, to reach higher levels of personal confidence and to enjoy fuller lives with changed objectives for their futures.

Low-Cost Calculator Systems for Small Business

Excessive amounts of repetitive calculations frequently performed by under-qualified personnel, more often than not, lead to rushed through work, greatly increasing the instance of errors in final management reports. Important recommendations or decisions that are based on incorrect calculation results. To avoid such mistakes many firms spend costly supervisory time to audit and correct calculating errors. When mistakes go uncorrected, negative reaction occurs from customers, as well as from suppliers and employees. But this work can be automated and made practically *goof proof.*

Once a standard procedure (routine) is established [payroll, cost estimating, account distribution] and it is programmed into a calculator system, it becomes virtually impossible to create wrong answers. Only the correct variable information need be entered by the operator. The complex computational routines are automatically performed by the programmable calculator system. Clear alpha print-outs let the system actually instruct the user what to enter at each step along the way. This also means that managers can train personnel in a much shorter time to use the system. And they can use unskilled personnel with confidence. (See: HP-97, SR60A and others ahead.)

Also, excessive computation workloads, besides causing errors, oftentimes result in jobs not getting done on time. In consequence, late recommendations or decisions lessen management effectiveness. Delayed decisions also can have a negative effect on many important business activities, e.g. retarding cash flow or resulting in frequent inventory stock outs. And to avoid such problems, managers may be forced into costly overtime or may try to put the job on the computer at eventually greater cost and delay, if these systems are complex.

Increased speed, along with assured accuracy, is what makes advanced calculator systems superior. Advanced calculators easily substitute for computers over a wide range of repetitive and complex applications. Users merely load a prerecorded program from a magnetic card (or ROM) into the programmable's memory. Low salaried operators enter only variables in a given application. This eliminates long, tedious manual calculations and operator decision-making, thus speeding up the entire calculating process.

Every type and size business today is confronted almost daily with the need to generate more and more information with greater speed and accuracy. Information is the daily lifeblood of every business—payroll, sales analysis, job cost estimating, account distribution and a host of other applications. This information is often too urgent or time consuming to be processed by the big computers, especially for businesses with less than 200 employees. TI, HP, Olivetti, Victor and others offer a practical solution—automating business calculations with powerful and advanced programmable business systems. These practical programmables bridge the gap between conventional calculators and expensive data processing systems or services. And they are simple to operate because the alpha printout and changeable key top labels actually instruct the operator how to run through any application. These programmables are ideal for both the small businessman or almost any operating department in large corporations, wherever there is a need to cut back errors while automating for faster results.

We have often mentioned the great value of software, and in a brief review some types are noted below.

Software for Programmable Calculators

We have previously noted that perhaps the biggest surprise to *computer people* regarding the competing programmable calculators was the speed with which the suppliers quickly produced combined hardware and software versatility for their units. The competence of many amateur programmable calculator users depends on software—the range and capability of the programs that they use. Calculator user's clubs, program exchanges and supplier firms are offering an abundance of very pragmatic programs. It's much easier now to use cartridges, cassettes, cards, RAMs and ROMs on a calculator and start operating them as computers than to spend a day or two on actual computers doing testing, etc. For those times when users may want to do their very specific programming, it's nice to have many types of machines which program easily and quickly. And particularly ones that do not demand special languages like FORTRAN or COBOL. Hundreds of models of calculators can now be programmed through their keyboards with relative ease and speed by pressing the appropriate keys in straight-forward easy-to-learn sequence. As an example, as early as 1974 complete turn-key (ready-to-go) very pragmatic systems were available for the following applications for several types of calculators, and more were added rapidly by users and members of clubs and Users Groups. Among them were:

Civil engineering	Auto dealer contracts
Surveying	Real estate
Bond trading	Extended mathematics
General statistical & miscellaneous mathematics	Education package
	Investment analysis
Bond package for billing and paying	Extended surveying
Distribution functions & test stations	Gear package
Analysis of variance & regression analysis	Plotter utility package
Extended analysis of variance & regression analysis	Life insurance
	Heating, ventilation & air conditioning
Geodetic surveying	Government bond trading
Clinical pathology	Installment loans
Regression analysis with plotting	Petro-chemistry
Bond billing (Corporate & municipal)	Medical histories

Some typical Victor 4900 applications are: Installment Loans; Leasing Contracts; Financial Analysis; Sales Analysis; Distribution; Media Analysis; Mortgage Closings; IRA Account Projections; Budgeting; Statistical Analysis; Retail Store End-of-Day Balancing; Tax Computations; Inventory Control and a myriad of other applications in business, industry, education and government.

Practically all programmables now have a software commitment for prepared, prepackaged program libraries in both general and specific areas. This capability, following the example of Wang, allows a programmable calculator to serve several different needs for engineers or professional individuals (i.e., a manager who performs statistical analysis, financial accounting, and personal financing in the course of a typical day). These library programs can provide a wider range of complicated functions with a high level of sophistication for a lower price than a comparable dedicated calculator. Many programmable claculators will be enhanced, like the HP-25C, with the advent of nonvolatile memory and program areas which will allow the user to turn the calculator off and on and not lose its contents for a later session. The ability to read and write both memory and program areas on magnetic strips has become commonplace. In order to aid the owner in the use of more sophisticated calculators, many printers are now being offered. It will be entirely possible to connect many pocket calculators to inexpensive printing devices to obtain audit trails for both calculation and program executions. This provides a listing of a stored program which is now practically a requirement as memory sizes increase. Enhanced operation can be expected with the development of alphanumeric display capability on pocket calculators. This can allow an interactive mode between the user and a program which he or someone else has written.

Improved performance will be through the use of distributed logic and parallel operations, both of which were beyond the capability of early calculator chips and many current designs. Programmable models have now become commonplace. The demand to perform longer and more involved calculations now also requires reduction in current execution time. The NS 7100 hand-held unit now has available a peripheral interface and may also serve as remote I/O terminals in computer systems. The calculator will assume more of a role in understanding the user so the user is freed to work his problem, not the pocket calculator. The increased programming capability available in many machines now allow many calculators to "talk" a more natural user language. An example of this is the use of a full algebraic hierarchy (ALG or AOS) with multiple levels of parentheses. These and other programming techniques are the bases for discussion of these chapters.

To facilitate the discussion of programming techniques and capabilities, three specific machines are used as bases that have not been mentioned to this stage. Thus, besides using excerpts from the Owner's Manuals of the HP-92, 97 and 9371, specific programming applications will relate to: the Texas Instruments SR-60A, the Olivetti P6060, and the Victor 4900. Thus the reader will become familiar not only with hand-held units but desk-tops as well. The programming power of these and others allows extremely complicated programming procedures. For versatile problem solving the designers of these units wanted users to have the ability to make a permanent record of programs and then rerecord them into the calculator whenever they wished. Thus, they have built-in ROM and card read/write ability. Programs can be read from or written into program memory by inserting magnetic cards or ROM's into the slots of the calculators.

To give the programmer flexibility the best machines are equipped with a complete set of program control instructions including:

1) User definable keys (UDKs)
2) A subroutine capability
3) Numeric conditionals

    4) Flags
    5) Branching
    6) Program interrupts
    7) An automatic counter for looping
    8) Indirect addressing
    9) Expandable memory
  10) Versatile I/O
  11) Editing
  12) Conversions capability
  13) Statistics and math functions
  14) Memory arithmetic

These instructions extend the programming power to applications which require looping or iteration and also allow efficient utilization of program memory when areas or programs are duplicated.

High volume and technical progress have resulted in decreasing prices and ever increasing volume for low-end calculators. An impressive improvement from a technical standpoint has been the increase in function capability per unit area of silicon available from new LSI designs. New algorithms and logic techniques, important circuit innovations, improvements in masking and overall tighter manufacturing tolerances have reduced die sizes by over 50% for comparable functionality in the last few years. The reader might be interested in a very quick review of MOS and LSI. It might help with the better understanding of the hardware features and software capabilities discussions that lie ahead.

MOS CHIPS—HOW THEY'RE MADE
The LSI Process

Metal, oxide and silicon, or "MOS", are the three key materials used in manufacturing large scale integrated (LSI) circuits. Typically built-up on a chip of silicon less than ¼ inch square, one circuit may contain more than 16,000 transistors. The steps generally include:

1) design engineers check a drawing 500 times larger than the finished circuit . . .
2) . . . which is built up in layers, each layer requiring its own drawing that when combined, represent all of the elements that control the functions and flow of current throughout the circuit.
3) Each drawing is reduced photographically and with great precision, to its final size. It becomes a photographic negative called a mask, containing many minute duplicates of the circuit design. In proper sequence, the masks are contact printed on the surface of a silicon wafer coated with a photosensitive material.
4) Between each printing the wafer is further processed. Oxides are deposited to protect the surface of the circuit. "Windows" etched through the oxide allow the introduction of impurities to form transistors. Vaporized metal is deposited in a pattern that will conduct the current throughout the device.
5) When the processed wafer is finally sliced into individual chips the result is a number of minute slivers of silicon, on each of which every function of the circuit has been reproduced.
6) The chip is then mounted in its package and sealed . . .
7) . . . and the finished product plugged into a printed circuit board, ready to operate in the product for which it was designed.

Circuits that Remember—LSI Memory

These are LSI devices in which "bits" of information can be stored and retrieved in a digital form, that is, a combination of 1's and 0's which are transmitted electronically by a series of "on" or "off" signals. Many firms make three types of memory circuits. The RAM (Random Access Memory) stores digital data that can be continually changed and randomly retrieved. The ROM (Read Only Memory) stores fixed information, such as a logarithm table (some latest types hold 32,768 bits). The EPROM (Electrically Programmable ROM) also stores fixed information that can be later erased with ultraviolet light and new data entered. These circuits are used in great volume in the memory banks of all types of computers, in computer terminals (where data is entered and retrieved), and in advanced business and scientific calculators. (EAROMs are electrically alterable ROMs.)

Circuits that Think—Then Act

The smallest member of the computer family is the microcomputer. Its major components are contained on as few as one, or at most several large scale integrated circuits called microprocessors. Many firms make whole families of microprocessor and related chips that can be combined in many different ways depending how the microcomputer is to be used. Traffic controllers, supermarket checkout terminals, machine tool controllers, airline reservation terminals, automotive systems controllers, are just a few of the hundreds of applications in which the microcomputer is playing a critical role. To function, the microcomputer must be programmed for its specific application. Several companies provide Microcomputer Development Centers for just that purpose.

Custom LSI circuits, designed or manufactured to the precise and generally proprietary specifications of a particular customer, are a large part of the various components companys' business. The largest designers and producers of MOS/LSI custom circuits, concentrate primarily in three areas, the industrial, consumer, and communications markets. Digital TV and HiFi controllers, electronic games, oven, range and dryer controls, auto fuel injection systems, CB radios and sewing machines, are just a few of the consumer products controlled by these devices. In the communications market, these companies provide or design products for the largest telephone equipment manufacturers in the free world, and thousands of smaller modern, terminal and other equipment suppliers. And calculator circuits led the way to all this . . . and more.

Calculating/Computing Products

We have noted that various series of programmable electronic calculators are sold primarily as systems in which calculators are combined with peripheral equipment and application software. These systems are sold to commercial, scientific, engineering, medical and educational users. Systems range generally from $500 to $45,000 depending on the model, peripheral equipment and software chosen by the customer. Many powerful calculating systems provide small computer capability by using BASIC computer language and offer a line of twenty to thirty peripheral devices. These systems can handle small-scale data processing for business and accounting applications as well as problem solving for statistical, scientific and engineering users. Memories can be expanded from 4,096 or 8,192 (in increments of 4,096 or 8,192) to 32,768 or 65,636 steps (or bytes) and more. Peripheral equipment available for these BASIC systems include: output typewriters, high-speed printers, input, keyboards, CRT console displays, magnetic tape cassette reader/recorders, digital and analog plotters, disk memory storage devices, card readers and telecommunication options. Libraries of BASIC programs and subroutines covering mathematical, engineering and commercial applications are available to users in ever-expanding numbers and ranges of capabilities. Many companies also offer *hardwired* (ROM) programmed memory modules for standard applications, such as advanced statistics and surveying. Applications examples of many areas are noted in the last two chapters on pages ahead. An Appendix is offered at the end of this text to assist the reader with the characteristics and capabilities of many program examples.

A Footnote: The "Power Expansion" of the PCs Brings Wide Response

Programmable calculators (PCs) obviously are having tremendous impact on the engineer's everyday working techniques. Many magazines are receiving an increasing amount of mail that is heavily weighted toward calculator tips and novel programs. Several have published a number of calculator-related features over the years. The arrival on the scene of new, powerful programmable calculators has opened up some new possibilities. Some have found themselves with a backlog of intriguing and worthwhile calculator programs, as readers submit them for sharing with other engineers. **Electronics Magazine** and **Calculator/Computer Magazine** offer a regular calculator forum. So, if readers have worked up interesting programs or have noteworthy operating tips, they can send them in so that they can be passed on to other calculator users. Some tips from various readers were printed in other periodicals and club newsletters.

CHAPTER 6
PROGRAMMABLE CALCULATOR
SYSTEMS: PRODUCT AND
PROGRAMMING CAPABILITIES

INTRODUCTION: CALCULATORS ARE NOW TRUE
SYSTEMS — WITH EXPANSIVE CAPACITY
AND HARD COPY GRAPHICS

In its simplest form, a program for a calculator is a series of keystrokes which will perform automatically from memory and in sequence some predesigned calculation or problem solution technique. It can be compared to an automatic dishwasher, which upon activating the first button will perform a series of wash cycles and drying procedures. In a calculator, whether that designated series of commands (instructions) is keystroked into memory or is already recorded on a card, tape, ROM, or disk, each keystroke (represented internally as a numerical code) will perform automatically, in sequence as each of the previously stored codes is recalled, interpreted and executed. We will be concerned on pages ahead with writing, listing, running, tracing, recording various types of instructions and programs. Programs free users from the need to remember equations, constants, numerical algorithms, and mechanical processes of obtaining an answer to a well formulated problem. Calculator users do not require prior programming experience to create their own programs in a manner equivalent to practically any mathematical sequence that can be stated.

For example, the Texas Instruments TI-59 has 960 program storage locations. When a user places the calculator in the learn mode, it will remember up to 960 calculation steps and numbers that can be repeated on command, i.e., as per each instruction. Also the TI-59 permits the use of 72 labels that quickly identify or can assist in a transfer to any program segment. Using any of the 100 addressable memory registers on the TI-59, storage and recall of data can be performed by direct register arithmetic. This means that addition, subtraction, multiplication or division can be performed with any memory register without affecting the calculation in progress. Ten internal processing registers are used to hold operands (an argument, constant, parameter, answer, etc.) for calculations in progress. Also, ten logical decision functions permit users to program their calculator to make repetitive decisions and branch to appropriate program segments automatically without interruption. To assist in these procedures, ten program flags are available to be set, reset, and tested under program control. Six subroutine levels may be defined, which when called by the main program or another subroutine, will execute and then automatically return control to the calling routine. (A subroutine is a subsidiary or supplementary program part.) Up to 240 program steps can be stored on a single magnetic card, and an optional printing unit (the PC-100A) permits users to obtain a permanent record of calculations, programs, and internal processing. The TI-59 operates in the calculate mode (manual operation as a general-purpose calculator), in the run mode, using a prerecorded program or one developed by the user to perform the designed sequential steps, or in the learn mode during which the user keys in steps directly into the program memory for immediate use in the run mode. Users may step through program memory, displaying the instructions for editing purposes, i.e., to discover and correct mistakes. Once users have corrected mis-keyed or misordered series of instructions and are content the program is right, it is no longer necessary to key in these steps again. Users should consult and become thoroughly familiar with the operation or owners' manuals to understand and then practice keyboard techniques, such as, the use of doubly labeled keys, triply labeled ones—and on the HP-67 (as noted) the four distinct functions represented by the face, underside of the keys or the two symbols (in colors) beneath the keys. These manuals indicate the necessary prefix keys required to be pressed first to achieve the second, third, or fourth function. It is absolutely vital that many hours of keyboard and 'sample' problem-solving practice precede programming.

Again using the TI-59 as an example, creating a program involves entering the predesigned instructions directly into program memory using the learn mode by pressing the LRN key. After entering the instructions, using the halt instruction (HLT) to substitute for the variable data to be entered later in these places, the user again presses the LRN key to transfer out of the learn mode. The program is then in memory and, if desired, can be recorded on a magnetic card. This is the easy part, and the various owners' manuals again provide the special rules and nuances particular to each model or type of calculator, such as how to 'clear' (turn the calculator off and on again, on some units), how to store, label, etc. Many of these capabilities will be explained on pages ahead. We have moved a bit fast and need to step back a bit.

Programming is *logical* thinking. Using the programming manual with the handy coding form and user instruction tablet, users can write programs in just a few hours. More than likely they won't be able to write **optimum** programs straight-off. These programs are ones that run the fastest and use the fewest steps. However, they can begin writing programs that work very well and fast. They press LRN to store each keystroke and press it again, and the machine has learned the program. It's ready to run. New users can record any program on a blank magnetic card, and make it part of their personal library to use again and again. As their programming knowledge develops they discover how this skill magnifies their professional capability.

After a few weeks of practice, experience and experimentation, many users become deeply involved with optimization, mathematical modeling, data reductions, *what if* matrices, risk analyses, forecasts, probability, worst case analysis — and the only tool necessary is the calculator, a very effective device. Personal programmables help users to cope with large amounts of complex data, to explore problems and procedures with insight and adventure — to assist in making better decisions based on more and highly accurate data, from broader data bases and through the use of more options. For example, users report handling long calculations in determining optimum locations in a warehousing system, copying cards and sending them to clients for use on their calculators. Others pre-processing and post-processing data get it in more usable form. Others gain great confidence by using the TI-59 and a PC-100A printer to screen entries, check for errors, program completeness, etc. When the calculator is locked into the desk-top printer cradle, the user is able to print anything shown in the display or print the step-by-step execution of a program. The silent electronic printer has a 2.5 inch thermal tape allowing for 20 characters per line; each character is printed in a 5×7 dot matrix, and the printer is fully controllable from the calculator keyboard or card program. Such printers became available in early 1976. The easy to use, easy to program units save many users from the extra time and bother they formerly required when they were forced to use a larger computer system and a complex, expensive terminal.

What the User Programmers Cooperatively Contribute to Make Programmables More Valuable

Although the manufacturers are developing software for customers at a rapid pace, it is the users themselves as members of clubs and contributors to users groups, as noted below, who are helping most to make personal calculators more valuable to all. The interesting list below attests to this excellent progress.

EXAMPLES OF USER-SUBMITTED PROGRAMS
(Extracted from some 5000 available programs)

BUSINESS
  Experience Curve for Manufacturing Cost
  Summation of Ledger Columns
  Amortization Schedule
  New Product Growth Factor—Gompertz Method
  Multi-Family Land Use Evaluation
  Manufacturing Learning Curve—Unit and Cumulative Cost
  Pert Estimating
  Universal Rate of Return
  Multivariate Corporate Failure Prediction Model
MATHEMATICS
  4×4 Determinant and Simultaneous Equations
  Complex Arithmetic
  Complex Functions
  Radar Range-height Calculation
  Function and Derivatives
  Maxima and Minima
  La Grange Polynomial Interpolation
  Numerical Integration
  Differential Equations
ENGINEERING
  Phase Shift Oscillator Design
  Rectangular Waveguide Calculations
  Transmittal Laser Pulse Energy
  Aircraft Flyby Look — Angles and Rates
  Bode of Transfer Function with Eighth Order Polynominal
  Phase Locked Loop Design, Acoustic Horn Evaluation
  Ballistic Missile, Range, Elevation Angle

Biomechanics
Two-Instrument Radial Survey
COMPUTER SCIENCE
Binary Coded Decimal with Parity to Decimal Conversion
Control Data Computer Octal Dump Decoding
Decimal to IBM 370 Floating Point Hexadecimal Conversion
Octal Debug Aid
Optimum Disk File Blocking
Timesharing Wait Model
Sentential Logic
PROBABILITY AND STATISTICS
Moments, Skewness and Kurtosis
Permutations and Combinations
Two-State Markov Chain Matrix
Five Variable Regression Analysis
Chi Square Proportion Difference
Biserial Correlation Coefficient
The Cochran Q Test
QUALITY ASSURANCE/RELIABILITY
Redundant System Reliability
Aerhenius Chemical Reaction Rate
X Bar and R Control Charts
Correlation: Reliability and Validity
NATURAL SCIENCES
Environmental Noise Levels
Acid-base Balance
Creatinine Clearance
Enzyme Kinetics
ECG Data Optimization
Blood Acid-Base Status
Fick Cardiac Output
Oxygen Saturation and Content
Tumor Growth
Absorption Spectroscopy Calibration
Orbital Mechanics
GAMES
Casino Game Model for Study of Behavior
Simulation Wargame
Combat Odds
Space Ship Landing Simulator
Underwater Submarine Hunt
Biorhythms
Space Battle
Space Docking
AIR NAVIGATION
Flight Plan and Verification
Predict Freezing Level
Dead Reckoning
Rhumbline Navigation
Great Circle Flying
Position and Navigation by One VOR
Weight and Balance
Moon Sight Reduction

MARINE NAVIGATION
Course Made Good from Three Bearings
Map Initialization
Running Fix from One Object
Planet Location
Sextant Correction
Storm Avoidance
Distance and Bearing to the Mark Sun Sight Reduction

Hewlett-Packard's Latest Fully Programmable Portable Calculators

The HP-67 and HP-97 printer model are the most powerful personal calculators Hewlett-Packard had built to 1978. Both can handle programs of up to 224 steps. As noted ahead, there's a lot more to program capacity than just the number of steps available.

For example, all prefix functions and operations are merged — conserving steps — allowing users to store two or three keystrokes as a single program instruction.

Also, users can directly record the contents of all 26 data storage registers on a separate magnetic card for easy reloading later. The result is a substantial saving in program steps since constants and other numerical data don't have to be incorporated in programs. Some of the power features built into the HP-67 and HP-97 are:
   3 Levels of Subroutines
   10 User Definable Functions
   10 Conditional/Decision Functions
   4 Flags
   3 Types of Addressing
      Label Addressing
      Relative Addressing
      Indirect Addressing
Thus, the TI-59 and HP-67 and HP-97 are real competitors.

Breakthrough Number Two: Ease of Use

With the HP-67 and HP-97, and TI-59 card readers *automatically* record the display modes and flag status separately from programs. What's more, the HP-67 prompts users — via a "Crd" display — when there's additional information on the card that must be loaded into the machine. It's virtually impossible to improperly load programs or data from the cards. Also the HP-67/97 "smart" card readers enable users to automatically expand the capacity of either calculator *beyond* 224 steps. Here's how: At the appropriate point in a program — and under program control — the card reader can automatically turn on and read another card. This new card can be used to load either selected portions of program memory or selected data registers.

For ease of editing, the line number and all keycodes of every instruction are displayed. Users can insert, delete or change functions at any point in their program. And, they can check or execute their programs step-by-step in order to locate programming errors. The HP-67 and HP-97 offer easy to use: RPN logic and four-register automatic-memory-stack.

With the TI-58-9, a separate printer is used. The HP-67 and HP-97 are identical in both versatility and capability. All programs written and recorded on the HP-67 can be loaded and run on the HP-97 (and vice-versa). The HP-67 gives shirt-pocket portability. The battery-powered HP-97 gives attaché case compactness plus a quiet, built-in thermal printer. Programming, debugging and editing are much faster and easier with a printer. The printer provides hard copy not only of routine calculations but also of programs, listed by stepnumber, key mnemonic and keycode. Or users can TRACE a running program and have the stepnumber, function, and result printed for each step as it is executed. And users can also list the contents of the automatic memory stack or the contents of the data storage registers. With a clear record of programs or data, users don't have to remember what they've done and what remains to be done.

Hewlett-Packard's Program of Product/Owner Support

With either the $450 HP-67 or the $750 HP-97 users get all of the following: A detailed Owner's Handbook and Programming Guide, Standard Application Pac (with 15 programs of broad appeal), and a free one-year subscription to a Newsletter that provides programming assistance and keeps users informed about new Application Pacs. Optional Application Pacs of up to 24 prerecorded programs are available in a variety of disciplines such as statistics, mathematics, finance, electrical engineering, surveying, mechanical engineering, and medicine. In addition, Hewlett-Packard maintains a User's Library of programs contributed by owners, as does TI, and NS has one planned.

The Top Hand-Held Calculator Products — More Capacity, Better and Easier Programming

This chapter investigates the usefulness of the various card programmable

The HP-67 pocket-sized calculator and the HP-97 (above) printing calculator both perform the same functions, and programs recorded on tiny magnetic cards on either machine will work on the other. HP-97 provides printed record of calculations, operations, memory and program registers.

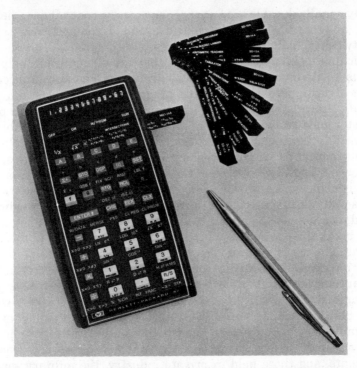

The Hewlett-Packard HP-67 With Program Cards. The fully programmable personal calculator that has as much as three times the program memory capacity as predecessor, the HP-65.

hand-held calculators, principally the TI-58 and TI-59, the HP-67 and HP-97 and the NS 7100. Many aspects of calculator functions, programming and programmability are discussed with particular emphasis on managerial use, engineering problem-solving, and general educational use. The conclusion recurring throughout is that these machines provide significant advantages in learning and using mathematical concepts; that these various calculators simplify and enhance; and that these machines are pragmatically important management tools for any type of business supervisor and industrial leader from foreman to top executive. We have noted that in June of 1977, the TI-59 replaced the SR-52 by offering 960 user programmable steps plus a 5000 step library cartridge demonstrating a very rapid evolution in hand-held calculators. Also, in 1977, the high consumer demand and intense market competition produced the National Semiconductor 7100 with an input-output port and the most computer-like of the hand-held units.* These machines provided challenges to the then current market leadership of the HP-67 and its companion printer unit, the HP-97. The minor but still intense competitive battles for the key-programmable units persisted, with the HP-57 supplanting the HP-56, and the HP-29C overtaking the HP-25C, while inroads were occurring with some Casio, National Semiconductor, Sinclair, Commodore and other key-programmables. The key-programmable TI MBA model was the first inroad to the massive business management market, and one might expect it to soon have a companion unit that contains a printer, as the HP-19C is the hand-held printer model companion to the HP-29C. And, as previously noted, many expect a BASIC language calculator to be out soon to thus blur quite completely the line between programmable calculators and small size home computers. The hand-held units, whatever their type, are specifically advantageous because they are

*The MS 7100 was **not** marketed in 1977 by National Semiconductor Corp.

relatively small, durable and inexpensive, very controllable, flexible, and portable, and they are easy to learn, to use, and to step-up to faster and higher-capability units, such as home computers.

As teaching tools to educational aids, they are of significant help in providing the user with much needed help in learning mathematical concepts, understanding algorithms, flowcharts, and programming concepts and principles. Specifically, calculator users in a learning environment are able to compute much faster and to solve many more problems, and are therefore able to devote more time to other important matters. Practically all users develop a desire, some an urgency, to learn more about the machine's capabilities, the art of programming, and the development of new problem solutions. For those students and business personnel who have shied away from mathematics-oriented problems and solution attempts, calculators have a way of providing new insight and intuition for them as they write simple programs, and in many cases serve to 'break the ice', so to speak, in developing confidence in these, to them, new areas. The use of programs on cards, on ROM devices, and in the case of the NS 7100, from other media, increases the power, versatility and range of system automation far beyond what most calculator users have previously even imagined. The use of printers, especially the TI PC 100-A with alpha-numeric plotting and prompting capabilities, increases the advantages even more significantly. The first few "calculator courses" in high schools, junior colleges, and universities have had exceptionally good responses from teachers and students, and those held in private industry, the military services, and elsewhere have received praise from practically all sources. A major role of educational procedures is to spend a greater portion of class time to teach new calculator users when and how to select and use a particular algorithm or program to solve particular problems instead of the 'wastage' of many hours of time in the pure mechanics of arithmetical and mathematical calculations, formerly tediously completed over long hours 'by hand.' The more important aspects of problem-solving can be stressed, e.g., how to recognize a problem environment and detail, how to break it down into components and relationships, how to analyze each component, value, and relational significance, and how to efficiently accomplish the task of proceeding toward a variety of solutions, for 'what if' types of comparisons. The process of 'number crunching' is treated appropriately as of minor significance to the above techniques. Thus, those students that are traditionally slower manipulators of numbers but good problem analysts finally can establish their equality or superiority of 'brain' work despite their lack of skill in mechanical 'figure' work. Calculators in this sense are great equalizers because formulas do NOT have to be memorized, adeptness at pure calculation is not primary as before, but knowing what to do with numbers becomes the greater skill.

As each learner's ability to use his machine improves, he or she discovers that analytical powers are very fundamental, that flowcharting procedures, personally developed, enable each of them to see the problem in graphic form and that redefinition of programs improves efficiency. Students begin to recognize their thinking processes, to organize their thinking concerning specific tasks, to graphically display, with the proper programs, the steps necessary to complete the task or problem solution, and to understand the advantages of being able to make logical comparisons and distinctions between facts, hypotheses, and procedures. Certainly educators should have no fear of these machines, of the student's use of them, or of their increasing capabilities. Certainly too, all students should be taught the use of calculators during their school years to increase the range of their problem solving capability, to learn to better understand problem solution development and solution versatility, and specifically to be prepared to use them in 'the outside world' in which they will work and live. To be unprepared in calculator use capability is to be unprepared to meet life as it exists today in a world of ever-increasing information manipulation.

Programmability — the Capabilities and Techniques Are Primary to Efficient Calculator Use

Programmability in essence concerns putting an algorithm in proper form so that a specific machine can accept and resolve it. It involves the use of a type of machine language, generally AOS or RPN, plus the merging of keystrokes into program steps and is based on the type and number of program steps available and the design of the machine to ease the process throughout. Individual machines are judged by their simplicity, speed, power, range of capabilities, and convenience of use, all in relation to original cost. We have already established the relative costs and capabilities of the machines, but in this chapter, we will add some specific programmability characteristics to close the discussion of hand-held machines before progressing into the variety of desk-top units and then the description and analysis of a wide range of applications. We have also already covered the use of AOS and RPN but will offer ahead a few more examples. Generally, with AOS, users enter the problem into the machine as it is normally written down while with RPN, users enter the problem into the machine as it is normally calculated. With RPN the user must remember to ALWAYS enter the operator after the variable; the AOS user must remember where the implied symbols go.

Basic calculator programming concepts have been introduced in previous chapters. In-depth discussion of exotic intermediate and advanced programming are not provided in this book because such discussion is readily available in manufacturer's handbooks, special literature available concerning specific programs and processes, and from the several user club publications. A discussion of some of the major capabilities of the three best-selling fully programmable machines in the hand-held class, the HP-67, TI-59, and NS 7100 will be offered in an attempt to denote major or significant differences which the reader might consider if he owns one or two of the above or prior to their purchase. However, the discussion in no way is meant as a substitute for the excellent user manuals provided by the three competing companies. HP has always been justifiably proud of their manuals, and the new TI educational products are highly recommended, particularly the "Personal Programming" manual for the TI-58 and TI-59. Much of the discussion will relate to the differences between the AOS and RPN systems, perhaps a boring subject to those familiar to either or both systems. The discussion will be unbiased, management oriented, but quite basic. The unusual tricks, special hobbyist applications, and very personal programming 'modifications' will be mentioned only in passing and quite unextensively. The discussion of the NS 7100 will be left to the latter portion of this chapter.

Color Coding, Special Function Keys, Key Abbreviations

Practically all manufacturers use most keys for at least two purposes to avoid adding too many keys to the keyboard. Generally, the primary function is centered in one color upon the flat upper surface of the key itself. The secondary functions are listed in a different color above, below, or upon an angled face of the key. Thus, a specific key may have associated functions listed in one, two, three, or four different colors and the primary colors of the keys themselves vary according to purpose. For example, the TI-59 is equipped with numerous functions designed to save time and increase the accuracy of calculations. The first function is printed right on the key; the second function is printed above the key. Users will push the 2nd key followed by the key immediately below the function shown. The inverse key, INV, also provides additional calculator functions without increasing the number of keys on the TI-59. When users press the INV key before a particular function or key, the purpose of that function or key is reversed. The INV key works together with quite a few keys on the calculator to provide extra functions, or to reverse an operation. The 2nd and INV keys allow 108 different keyboard operations to be performed using only 45 keys. More about this later. The HP-67 has three colors, (yellow: f), (blue: g), (black: h), the notation corresponding indirectly by using standard symbols for mathematical functions (f,g,h) such that the user can easily modify the thought process to: "Use the function of the key (f or key, g of key, h of key) by first pressing the color matched and appropriately labeled second function key (f,g,h)." The reader can note that the color coding greatly simplifies actual usage and complicates only the reading of documented programs by novice users, e.g., a novice user would tend to look at the keyboard, see what color a desired function is and then push appropriate keys to execute the function without difficulty. The novice is not required to memorize that $\sqrt{x}$ is always preceded by 2nd of f since the color coding, in actual usage, readily prompts appropriate action. The documentation of programs normally includes all keys which must be pressed, such that $\sqrt{x}$ becomes 2nd $\sqrt{x}$ or *$\sqrt{x}$ or f$\sqrt{x}$, which may seem a bit strange at first. But, the often-heard cry of amateurs and novices that documented programs are "difficult to read" appears a bit unfounded. Although the prefix key notations do clutter the thought process somewhat, they are vital when one uses a machine since the machine is at hand and there is no real choice but to use prefix keys. New or different does not necessarily equate to difficult, and this can be said of most 'somewhat strange' calculator procedures. On the TI-59, when 2nd is pressed twice in succession or if the key that does not have a second function is pressed after 2nd, the calculator returns to the first function operation.

With the TI-59, each time the user turns on the machine there are 60 data registers available (30 for the TI-58), and these are variable with the amount of program memory, as previously noted. These registers store numbers needed for later use. Users indicate which register they want to use by specifying its two-digit number XX, for example, STO 08. The CE and CLR keys do not affect what is in the memories; however, pressing 2nd CMs clears all data registers simultaneously (places 0 in all registers). The STORE, RECALL, AND MEMORY EXCHANGE keys and sequences are simple operations, as are MEMORY SUM and MEMORY PRODUCT, and the display and notation keys have been covered. Algebraic functions, square, roots, reciprocals, powers, and so on are direct, and natural log and common log are developed simply, the latter using INV and 2nd function keys, with the TI-58-59. And most users have little difficulty with modes and conversions, such as angular/polar, and so on or with the statistical function keys as mean, variance, and standard deviation, or even regressions on the 58 and 59.

However, some words are necessary concerning the program libraries of these two machines. The programming information (software) for the TI-58 and TI-59 is contained in a tiny solid-state "chip" of silicon, similar to the actual CPU chip of the control center of the calculator. The tiny 'cube' that slips into the slot on the lower back center of the machine is a powerhouse of program steps all accessible from the keyboard anytime, and these are available in an increasing variety of capability. A 'library' as TI markets it, is a library module (cube or CROM), a manual explaining in detail the use of each program in that library, a storage case and a set of program label cards. TI urges that users be sure their body is free of static electricity before handling any module, especially when the charger is connected because this grounds the calculator. Users may simply touch any metal object to electrically discharge their bodies. The contents of a module can be severely damaged by static discharges. Loading and unloading the modules should be done only when the calculator is OFF. The module is inserted notched-end first with the labeled side up into the small compartment; it slips in effortlessly, and the cover panel secures the module against the contacts for immediate operation. Calling a particular program is done by requesting it by its number since each program in a library has its own number. The required sequence is 2nd Pgm mm, where mm is the two-digit number assigned to the program itself. The nonmagnetic program label card included for each program specifies the user-defined key assignments and can be fitted into the window above these keys once it is separated from the sheet of labels. When a program is used, processing actually enters the module and performs its task. To gain access to the library program users can bring it into program memory. Then all the calculator's programming tools can be used to analyze the individual steps and alter the program to their particular needs if necessary. Actually, only a copy of a program is brought into program memory, the module contents can never be changed. The procedure to download a program is as follows: Verify that there is sufficient program memory space available for the incoming program; then, press 2nd Pgm mm to designate which program to download, and press 2nd Op 09 to download the program. The user cannot place an altered program back into the library module. To preserve a "new" program, users can write down each step on a coding form, record it onto a magnetic card (or cards) if the user has a TI-59, or list it if the user has a printing unit. A request to download one of these programs flashes the display.

Programming Procedures in Some Specific Areas

Personal programming is being performed by people of practically all ages, training, and occupation. The calculating power is there for everyone to try, test, and enjoy. The language is simply the means by which users communicate with their machines. Fear of learning a "new language" to operate card-programmable units is really not justified. It is not difficult at all to supply implied parentheses or equality signs as with AOS or be required to always enter the operator after the mathematical variables (RPN) and be required to become familiar with a long list of abbreviations — but, this does not constitute the requirement to "learn a new language." Calculator language is heavily weighted with common sense and the familiar use of arithmetic and basic mathematics. Like computer programs, calculator programs follow precisely the steps designed unwaveringly, whether the user wants it that way or not. Once the user has learned to recognize the abbreviations, he or she is ready to operate or to program. And, it is not difficult to first learn one system, such as AOS, and because many abbreviations are the same, to quickly master RPN, as well. Handbooks provide complete listings for each function and abbreviation. Users will quickly note that many functions require sequenced keystrokes, but the abbreviation OU, can mean other use, and User Club members are very familiar with many extra powers of their favorite machine. Some examples below indicate the almost phonetic designations of the codes and abbreviations. The key code systems used by both systems closely correspond to the location of each key in an imaginary superimposed second quadrant xy matrix. The y-value is read first, neglecting the minus sign, i.e., row, column. Thus the primary function of the key at topmost, leftmost (the A key) is coded 11, the primary function of the key at fourth row down, third column to the right is 43, etc. As one exception to this pattern, on both type machines, numeric keys are directly coded 00, 01, . . ., 09. This exception causes no confusion both because it is direct and because there is no "zero row" of keys.

The procedure generally, is to first define the problem very clearly and carefully in order to develop a proper solution method (algorithm) best done, of course, with the use of a flow diagram. With this base a data register assignment schedule is designed after which the translation of the flow diagram into keystrokes begins. The program is then entered, tested, errors corrected, and the editing begins. The program is then retested and recorded followed by the documentation, e.g., the development of written step-by-step instructions describing how to use the program. Users err importantly if they do not write proper documentation because it is very easy to forget how to use various programs without these written aids. Forms are available to fill out providing detail information required to run the program. In finer detail for the TI-58 and TI-59, users press 2nd CP to position the program pointer at location 000 and clear all of program memory. This replaces the need to turn the calculator OFF and then ON again. Users press LRN to place the calculator in this important mode, and then key in the program, not forgetting any necessary 2nd prefixes. It is necessary to make sure the program does not exceed the program memory size — and to run test problems to correct or edit the program according to the procedures outlined in the "Editing Programs" sections of the specific machine workbook. The editing instructions relate to storing in any program location, replacing an instruction with another, deleting an instruction and closing up the hole, creating spaces for additional instructions and single-stepping forward or backward through program memory without disturbing its contents. These features allow users to inspect, correct and modify a program without having to reenter correct instructions.

User Definable Keys and Labels — Recording on Cards

A series of keys at the top of the keyboard on the AOS machines and the HP-67, 97 are most significant. Labeling a segment of a user program with one of these keys allows users to press that key in the calculate mode and have that program segment accessed instantly. Users actually define the function of that key so that it acts like the other functions on the keyboard. The sequence may completely fill program memory or can be as short as necessary to fit a particular problem-solving segment. Each of the user-defined keys can be assigned to a program sequence and executed at will whether it is encountered while running a program or from the keyboard. Relocation is made to the area of the program labeled with that user-defined key and processing is performed. Common labels, transfer instructions, subroutines, and so on are features discussed in future paragraphs.

The sequence for recording or reading magnetic cards is relatively simple. After keying in a program to memory, the program is permanently stored on the card by passing the card through the card reader. Initializing the card reader to record requires the proper setting of a switch on the HP-67 or several keystrokes on the TI-59. Data from storage registers can also be permanently stored on cards. Initializing the card reader for data requires the setting of a switch and two keystrokes on the HP-67; a special program card must be used together with a blank data card on the TI-59, using two keystrokes with each card. Stored programs or data remains on the cards until the information is intentionally altered by the user, i.e., the cards are reusable or can be permanently filed for dedicated use. Several techniques are used on different calculators to prevent accidental altering of cards, or to abort protections used to prevent accidental destruction of card information in order to reuse "permanent" cards. All of these systems work well, hence, these differences are of significance for specific military or high priority corporate programs or data. The TI products have specific 'non print' lockout features. Program execution normally stops only when a "HLT" or "R/S" instruction is encountered, or when an error condition is created (such as dividing by zero or branching to a non-existent label) or when the RTN instruction is encountered in the primary routine being executed. Conversely, levels function only to identify the starting point of a called subroutine. Thus, encountering an uncalled label during program execution has no effect at all; the label is merely ignored. For this reason, labels can sometimes be nested such that the same single step number ends every subroutine in the nest.

Some Basic Differences of Elementary Procedures Between RPN and Algebraic Machines

RPN machines have the following start and stop program procedures. One or two program control keys begin execution of a program, such as: START, RUN, R/S (Run/Stop). Execution of a program stops with the following keys, HALT, HLT, R/S. The RTN (Return) key stops program execution and returns the calculator to the beginning of program memory. Some of these units allow users to execute a program by pressing a user-definable key, such as A B C D or E. These keys can be used, as well as others, to identify a particular program or program segment by preceding the keystrokes one would use to manually solve the problem with the *label* sequence: Press *label* key, then any user-definable key, then key in the program. This labels the program enabling the user to execute it by pressing the appropriate user-definable key. Users can store the label and also store several separate or interactive programs in their machine simultaneously and thereafter select any of them by pressing the appropriate user-definable key. Labels are further discussed on pages ahead showing other uses.

RPN machines have versatile editing features permitting users to change instructions, delete mistakes and in effect, debug a program quite quickly. The SST key permits single stepping; and in RUN mode, some units execute the program one step at a time as SST is depressed, permitting a review of intermediate results. The BST key backsteps the program one step at a time. The GO TO key directs the machine to proceed in any specified program or program step, i.e. GTO B or GTO 025. The DEL or delete key handles the deletion of any specified instruction from program memory, moving all subsequent instructions up one step. By assigning addresses to various steps or segments of a program, the units can use the line number of each step in a program as an address, as noted above, with the labelling notation. Program writing is simpler and has more versatility (power) when users don't need to keep track of address changes each time a program is revised. Program transfers can be executed either unconditionally or as a result of a test, flag, etc. Unconditional transfers are easiest with the GO TO procedure with a specified program step or label. GO TO procedures are also used as parts of the program for automatic transfer, for cycling sections several times. Conditional transfers are great for decision-making. Ten or more conditional transfer instructions are available and in various combinations on these machines. These are relational tests such as, "Is the condition (answer) zero or not zero, etc. Usually if *yes,* the calculator proceeds with normal program execution, and usually if *no,* the program will skip or jump (branch) one or more steps and then continue normal execution. These transfers (tests) provide the capability for the program to respond automatically to a wide variety of environmental or circumstantial conditions, which arise from results of other system components or are specifically planned and designed to fulfill the general scheme or solution procedure.

Flags, Counters, Subroutines and Miscellaneous Transfer Capabilities

Continuing with RPN type machines, the use of flags (status signals) which can be set or not set or cleared by users or the calculators, in effect, ask the program whether or not that flag is set. Generally, if true, the program continues sequentially; if not, the program generally skips one or more steps. The keys are SF or ST FLG to set the flags; CF to clear the flag, and F? or if FLG to ask, "Is the flag set?" Counters, as noted elsewhere in this chapter, cycle the machine through a segment of program steps a specific number of times, decrementing or incrementing one from the number stored in a particular memory register. In some cases, when the value in a memory register is NOT zero, program execution continues sequentially. And if the value in the register reaches zero, the program can skip one or more steps to then resume execution. RPN keys for these two functions are: ISZ for Increment and Skip on Zero and DSZ for Decrement and Skip on Zero. (See Box for HP-67/97 control key designations)

HP67/97 Control Key Designations

10 User-Definable Keys.

There are ten user-definable keys you can use for any special function you may require—such as defining portions of your program for subroutines or branches. They may be executed from the keyboard or from within a program. In addition, there are ten numerical labels (LBL 0 thru LBL 9). These user-definable keys and labels may be executed from the keyboard or from within a program.

Pause

If you need to key in data or load a card in the middle of your program or to see an intermediate answer—no problem. The PAUSE function initially interrupts program execution and displays current results for about 1 second. At that time, you can optionally enter data from the keyboard or load magnetic cards. The interruption is extended for as long as necessary. If you want the program stopped indefinitely, you can use the R/S (RUN/ STOP) function.

Direct Branching

Though program steps are executed sequentially in many programs, you have the power to transfer (branch) program execution to any part of program memory you desire.

GTO Go To.

When followed by a label designator (A through E, f A through f E, or 0 through 9) GTO directly branches program execution to the specified label.

Subroutines

When a series of instructions is executed several times in a program, you can save program memory by executing that series as a subroutine.

GSB Go Subroutine.

A GSB instruction followed by a label designator (A through E, f A through f E, 0 through 9) branches program execution to the label specified just as a GTO instruction does. But, using the GSB instruction, program execution is then "returned" automatically to the step following the GSB instruction when the next RTN (Return) instruction is executed (see following illustration).

A GSB instruction can also be used within a subroutine to a depth of three levels.

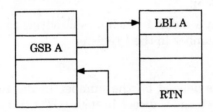

After a GSB instruction, RTN transfers program execution to the program step following the GSB.

Conditional Branching.

$x \neq y$, $x = y$, $x \leq y$, $x > y$
$x \neq 0$, $x = 0$, $x < 0$, $x > 0$

These keys allow your program to make decisions for you by testing the values in the X- and Y-registers or by testing the value in the X-register against zero as indicated. If the data test is true, the calculator will "do" the next instruction in program memory. (Remember "Do If True.") If the data test is false, program execution branches around the next instruction.

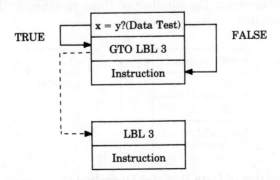

The next step is executed if $x = y$. Program execution branches around one step if x does not equal y.

Flags.

You can use the four flags in the calculator for tests in your programs. They can be set, cleared, or tested. When a flag is tested, the calculator executes the next step if the flag is set ("Do If True" again). The calculator branches around the next step if the flag is clear. Flags F0 and F1 are command-cleared flags. Once they have been set, they remain set until cleared using a CLF (Clear Flag) instruction. Flags F2 and F3 are test-cleared flags. They are cleared automatically following a test instruction and remain cleared until they are set again. Flag F3 is also a data-entry flag—that is, as soon as you enter a number from the keyboard or from a magnetic card, flag F3 is set.

Indirect Control.

The (i) key combined with certain other functions uses the number stored in the specially-defined I-register to control those functions. This indirect control gives you the power and versatility you need to complement the extra large program capacity and data capacity.

Indirect Addressing.

You can perform a direct branch or subroutine to a label specified by the current number in the I-register.

GTO (i) GSB (i)

These operations depend on the number in the I-register. If it is positive they perform a direct branch (GTO (i)) or a subroutine (GSB (i)) to the label specified.

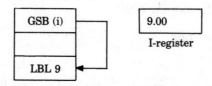

Relative Addressing.

GTO (i) GSB (i)

When the number in the I-register is a negative number these instructions perform a direct branch (GTO (i)) or a subroutine (GSB (i)) backward the number of steps specified by the current negative number in the I-register.

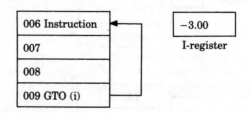

Indirect Control of Data Register Operations.

You can also use the I-register to specify the address of a storage register.

STO (i)

This instruction stores the displayed number in the storage register specified by the value in the I-register.

RCL (i)

This instruction recalls the contents of the storage register specified by the value in the I-register.

STO + (i), STO − (i)
STO × (i), STO ÷ (i)

These four instructions perform storage register arithmetic upon the contents of the storage register specified by the value in the I-register.

ISZ (i) DSZ (i)

You can also increment (ISZ (i)) or decrement (DSZ (i)) the contents of the storage register specified by the value in the I-register and then test against zero. If the contents equal zero, program execution branches around the next step in program memory.

A significant operational improvement of the HP-67/97 is the "smart" card reader. In addition to data recording and reading, the card reader serves as a prompter for proper operation. It automatically checks and retains the display mode, angular mode setting and status of the four flags. It also detects whether information on the card consists of data for the storage registers or program steps. Users find it virtually impossible to improperly load programs or data from the cards.

Subroutines as used in calculators are much like the same program segments used in computers. They are used to repeat specific sets of instructions that are used frequently in various programs or procedures. In essence, it is much more efficient to program the repeated sections once and as separate subprograms (subroutines) than it is to repeat the programming each time the sequence is necessary or desired. Using RPN and other machines, a subroutine assigned with a label of a user-definable key will execute and divert to the subroutine whenever the appropriate label is encountered. A special instruction key RTN is placed at the end of a subroutine to return program execution to the main program after the execution of the subroutine.

The Way Calculators 'Crumble'—The Transition from the HP-65 to the HP-67

The HP-65 was and is an excellent machine; most owners love 'em. Thousands of purchasers fully agree they were worth their price of $795. However, after a bit more than two years for most owners, their resale value dropped to about 1/5 their cost. The reason was the introduction of the HP-67—"three times the power at half the cost." An article by Sam Davis (Electronic Engineering Times, July 5, 1956) is reprinted here to give the full details.

"Calculators Updated With Smart Card-Reader"

Using mutually interchangeable programs, both Hewlett-Packard's new programmable HP-97 printing calculator at $750 and the

HP-67 hand-held (soft-copy) unit at $450 exceed the performance of the pioneering $795 HP-65.

"We asked HP-65 users what they wanted in an improved programmable calculator," product manager Glenn Theodore says. "They wanted better programming capability, so we expanded the programming steps for the two new calculators to 224 from the 100 in the HP-65. Also, in the HP-65 every keystroke requires one location in the program memory; with the 67 and 97, only one location is required regardless of whether one, two or three keystrokes are used. As a result, both the HP-67 and 97 provide about three times the programming capability of the HP-65—and at a lower cost."

Programming cards for the 67 and 97 are similar in appearance to the 65, but are configured differently. In the HP-65, data is stored on only one side of the magnetic card and a single pass through the card-reader enters a program. With the HP-67/97 programming cards, 112 program steps are stored on each side and two passes enter the program into the calculator.

"More programming assistance was also requested by HP-65 users," Theodore notes. "To satisfy this, we almost tripled the documentation for the 67 and 97 compared to the 65. We sorted out about a dozen things people asked for and described them in detail in the new manual. One example is a more comprehensive explanation of flags, another, a more extensive presentation of flow charts."

Flexible Registers

Another improvement requested by users was added flexibility for the data registers, which are used for temporary storage of numeric, decimally coded data. The HP-65's nine data registers were increased to 26 in the HP-67/97. Also, the 67/97 offers the capability to store the contents of the data registers onto the programming cards and vice versa, a feature not provided with the HP-65. However, program memory storage is provided in all three calculators.

Additional improvements in the 67 and 97 over the 65 include eight conditional tests instead of four, three types of addressing schemes instead of one, automatic review of storage register contents, and 14 conditional execution functions, including four flags. Also, the number of user-definable keys in the HP-67 is doubled through use of an additional shift key.

One difference between the hand-held HP-67 and the HP-97 printing calculator, other than size and the printer, is the number of keys. The HP-67 has 35 of them including three shift keys, whereas the HP-97 has 56 with only one shift key. Another difference is the HP-97 LEDs, which are about twice the height of the HP-67's.

Intelligent Reader

Theodore feels the most significant operational improvement of the HP-67/97 over the HP-65 is utilization of a "smart" card-reader. While transferring programs from the magnetic cards to the calculator, the card-reader automatically checks and retains the display mode, angular mode setting and status of the four flags. It also detects whether information on the card consists of data for the storage registers or program steps. After a program card is inserted into the calculator, the card-reader signals the calculator to prompt the user by displaying "Crd" on the LED readouts if there's information on the other side that must be read. Theodore believes that adding intelligence to the card-reader simplifies calculator operation by eliminating the need to keep track of which side programs are stored.

An enhancement in the 67/97 card-reader is the use of **a 28-bit checksum for error detection.** The HP-65 has no such error detection; it merely counts the bits as they come in, and when it gets the right number it assumes the information to be correct.

Peter Dickinson, project manager for both the 67 and 97, says conventional PMOS technology is used throughout. "We did come up with a unique chip, called a DataROM," he explains. "It consists of 1k of RAM and 10k of ROM in a single 8-pin package. One reason we were able to reduce the price of the HP-67 from the HP-65 (which is housed in the same size case) is this new chip. **Besides the processing circuits, the HP-65 has two 16-pin ICs and a hybrid circuit mounted on a four-layer PC board.** It is outperformed by the HP-67 using the same processing circuits, the DataROM, a two-sided board and no hybrid circuits. Needless to say, the maintainability of the HP-67 is superior to that of the HP-65. The 8-pin Data-ROM has positive, negative and ground pins, two clock pins, a sync, address and an output pin. Serial input data is converted to a parallel format and addresses the memory whose parallel data is converted to a serial output."

Looping

Perhaps one of the most powerful decision making tools of the calculator programmer is his proper use of looping. The technique involves the repeated use of part of the program's calculation to continue to repeat (loop) until a specified point, answer, or other criteria is met. The tests for this criteria and the subsequent stop or movement from the loop develops the key decision making power. Looping mechanically involves a program within a program. One program performs the calculations while the other instructs the calculator how many times to loop, i.e., how many times the calculation or process is to be continued as controlled by the instruction ending or branching from the loop. The technique of looping for decision making concerns the procedure for following a fixed program pattern. At the outset a decision is made whether to continue executing the program. The decision is consumated by essentially comparing one number with another. If the result of the comparison meets the preset criteria, generally the program will require a stop of the loop, and one or two programming steps are then skipped, the latter case prevails for most H-P machines. As an example, if a zero appears in register 9, the decision is made (as programmed) to stop and subsequently to skip the steps GTO and 2. The instruction RTN is then executed which stops the execution of the total program. In RPN machines looping can be stopped with an R/S function with the g DSZ function.

Looping requiring decision making usually consists of a program that has a subroutine that performs the calculation and an instruction (or several) that controls the subroutine. Most calculator decision making procedures, like loops, involve **relational tests.** Some others involve the counter or the decrement (or implement) of numerals until a zero, for example, is reached in a register. Most relational tests concern the 'greater than, equal to, or less than' comparisons of stated or computed numerals. The relational test occurs in most cases after some computation is made with the 'answer' as the primary comparison numeral. The results of relational tests become the 'trigger' for the program to stop, branch, or execute. Flags when used within a program, rather than those set manually, are similar in principal to relational tests because the criteria is generally 'yes or no', i.e., set or not set. All decision capabilities are powerful program steps.

At this point one of the most important characteristics of RPN machines should be analyzed. Some notes from the HP-67 owners manual outline the famous stack:

The Automatic Memory Stack and Last X

The Stack

Automatic storage of intermediate results is the reason that the HP-67 slides so easily through the most complex equations. And automatic storage is made possible by the Hewlett-Packard automatic memory stack.

Initial Display

When you first switch the calculator ON, the display shows 0.00 in RUN mode. This represents the contents of the display or "X-register."

Set the W/PRGM-RUN switch W/PRGM RUN to RUN.

Switch the HP-67 OFF, then ON.

Basically, numbers are stored and manipulated in the machine "registers." Each number, no matter how few digits (e.g., 0, 1, or 5) or how many (e.g., 3.141592654, −23.28362, or $2.87148907 \times 10^{27}$), occupies one entire register.

The displayed X-register, which is the only visible register, is one of four registers inside the calculator that are positioned to form the automatic memory stack. We label these registers X, Y, Z, and T. They are "stacked" one on top of the other with the displayed X-register on the bottom. When the calculator is switched ON, these four registers are cleared to zero.

Name	Register	
T	0.00	
Z	0.00	
Y	0.00	
X	0.00	Always displayed

Clearing the Display

When you press CLx *(clear x)*, the displayed X-register is cleared to zero. No other register is affected when you press CLx.

Press CLx now, and the stack contents are changed . . .

	... from this ...				... to this.	
T	4.00			T	4.00	
Z	3.00			Z	3.00	
Y	1.00			Y	1.00	
X	2.00	Display.		X	0.00	Display.

Although it may be comforting, *it is never necessary to clear the displayed X-register when starting a new calculation.* This will become obvious when you see how old results in the stack are automatically lifted by new entries.

The ENTER↑ KEY

When you key a number into the calculator, its contents are written into the displayed X-register. For example, if you key in the number 314.32 now, you can see that the display contents are altered.

When you key in 314.32 with the stack contents intact from previous examples the contents of the stack registers are changed . . .

	. . . from this . . .	
T	4.00	
Z	3.00	
Y	1.00	
X	0.00	Display.

	. . . to this.	
T	4.00	
Z	3.00	
Y	1.00	
X	314.32	Display.

In order to key in another number at this point, you must first terminate digit entry—i.e., you must indicate to the calculator that you have completed keying in the first number and that any new digits you key in are part of a new number.

Use the ENTER↑ key to separate the digits of the first number from the digits of the second.

When you press the ENTER↑ key, the contents of the stack registers are changed . . .

	. . . from this . . .	
T	4.00	
Z	3.00	
Y	1.00	
X	314.32	Display.

	. . . to this.	
T	3.00	
Z	1.00	
Y	314.32	
X	314.32	Display.

As you can see, the number in the displayed X-register is copied into Y. The numbers in Y and Z have also been transferred to Z and T, respectively, and the number in T has been lost off the top of the stack.

Immediately after pressing ENTER↑, the X-register is prepared for a new number, and that new number writes over the number in X. For example, key in the number 543.28 and the contents of the stack registers change . . .

	. . . from this . . .	
T	3.00	
Z	1.00	
Y	314.32	
X	314.32	Display.

	. . . to this.	
T	3.00	
Z	1.00	
Y	314.32	
X	543.28	Display.

CLx replaces any number in the display with zero. Any new number then writes over the zero in X.

For example, if you had meant to key in 689.4 instead of 543.28, you would press CLx now to change the stack . . .

	. . . from this . . .	
T	3.00	
Z	1.00	
Y	314.32	
X	543.28	Display.

	. . . to this.	
T	3.00	
Z	1.00	
Y	314.32	
X	0.00	Display

and then key in 689.4 to change the stack . . .

	. . . from this . . .	
T	3.00	
Z	1.00	
Y	314.32	
X	0.00	Display.

	. . . to this.	
T	3.00	
Z	1.00	
Y	314.32	
X	689.4	Display.

Notice that numbers in the stack do not move when a new number is keyed in immediately after you press ENTER↑, CLx, or g STK. However, numbers in the stack *do* lift upward when a new number is keyed in immediately after you press most other functions, including h R↑, h R↓, and h x≤y. (If you follow a regular function like R↓ or x² with g STK, then key in a number, the stack will lift.)

One-Number Functions and the Stack

One-number functions execute upon the number in the X-register only, and the contents of the Y-, Z-, and T-registers are unaffected when a one-number function key is pressed.

For example, with numbers positioned in the stack as in the earlier example, pressing f √x changes the stack contents . . .

. . . from this . . .   . . . to this.

T	3.00		T	3.00	
Z	1.00		Z	1.00	
Y	314.32		Y	314.32	
X	689.4	Display.	X	26.26	Display.

The one-number function executes upon only the number in the displayed X-register, and the answer writes over the number that was in the X-register. No other stack register is affected by a one-number function.

Two-Number Functions and the Stack

Hewlett-Packard calculators do arithmetic by positioning the numbers in the stack the same way you would on paper. For instance, if you wanted to add 34 and 21 you would write 34 on a piece of paper and then write 21 underneath it, like this:

$$\begin{array}{r} 34 \\ 21 \end{array}$$

and then you would add, like this:

$$\begin{array}{r} 34 \\ +21 \\ \hline 55 \end{array}$$

Numbers are positioned the same way in the HP-97. Here's how it is done. (As you know, it is not necessary to remove earlier results from the stack before beginning a new calculation, but for clarity, the following example is shown with the stack cleared to all zeros initially. If you want the contents of your stack registers to match the ones here, first clear the stack by using the CLx and ENTER↑ keys to fill the stack with zeros.)

Press	Display	
CLx	0.00	
ENTER↑	0.00	
ENTER↑	0.00	
ENTER↑	0.00	Stack cleared to zeros initially.
34	34.	34 is keyed into X.
ENTER↑	34.00	34 is copied into Y.
21	21.	21 writes over the 34 in X.

Now 34 and 21 are sitting vertically in the stack as shown below, so we can add.

T	0.00	
Z	0.00	
Y	34.00	
X	21.	Display.

Press	Display	
+	55.00	The answer.

The simple old-fashioned math notation helps explain how to use your calculator. Both numbers are always positioned in the stack in the natural order first, then the operation is executed when the function key is pressed. *There are no exceptions to this rule.* Subtraction, multiplication, and division work the same way. In each case, the data must be in the proper position before the operation can be performed.

Chain Arithmetic

You've already learned how to key numbers into the calculator and perform calculations with them. In each case you first needed to position the numbers in the stack manually using the ENTER↑ key. However, the stack also performs many movements automatically. These automatic movements add to its computing efficiency and ease of use, and it is these movements that automatically store intermediate results. The stack automatically "lifts" every calculated number in the stack when a new number is keyed in because it knows that after it completes a calculation, any new digits you key in are a part of a new number. Also, the stack automatically "drops" when you perform a two'number operation.

To see how it works, let's solve

$$16 + 30 + 11 + 17 = ?$$

If you press CLx first, you will begin with zeros in all the stack registers, as in the example below, but of course, you can also do the calculation without first clearing the stack.

Remember, too, that you can always monitor the contents of the stack at any time by using the g STK operation.

Press	Stack Contents		
16	T	0.00	16 is keyed into the displayed X-register.
	Z	0.00	
	Y	0.00	
	X	16.	
ENTER↑	T	0.00	16 is copied into Y.
	Z	0.00	
	Y	16.00	
	X	16.00	
30	T	0.00	30 writes over the 16 in X.
	Z	0.00	
	Y	16.00	
	X	30.	
+	T	0.00	16 and 30 are added together. The answer 46, is displayed.
	Z	0.00	
	Y	0.00	
	X	46.00	
11	T	0.00	11 is keyed into the displayed X-register. The 46 in the stack is automatically raised.
	Z	0.00	
	Y	46.00	
	X	11.	
+	T	0.00	46 and 11 are added together. The answer, 57, is displayed.
	Z	0.00	
	Y	0.00	
	X	57.00	

17	T	0.00	17 is keyed into the X-register. 57 is automatically entered into Y.
	Z	0.00	
	Y	57.00	
	X	17.	

+	T	0.00	57 and 17 are added together for the final answer.
	Z	0.00	
	Y	0.00	
	X	74.00	

After any calculation or number manipulation, the stack automatically lifts when a new number is keyed in. Because operations are performed when the operations are pressed, the length of such chain problems is unlimited unless a number in one of the stack registers exceeds the range of the calculator (up to $9.999999999 \times 10^{99}$).

In addition to the automatic stack lift after a calculation, the stack automatically drops during calculations involving both X- and Y-registers. It happened in the above example, but let's do the problem differently to see this feature more clearly, For clarity, first press CLx to clear the X-register. Now, again solve 16 + 30 + 11 + 17 = ?

Press		Stack Contents	
16	T	0.00	16 is keyed into the displayed X-register.
	Z	0.00	
	Y	0.00	
	X	16.	

ENTER↑	T	0.00	16 is copied into Y.
	Z	0.00	
	Y	16.00	
	X	16.00	

30	T	0.00	30 is written over the 16 in X.
	Z	0.00	
	Y	16.00	
	X	30.	

ENTER↑	T	0.00	30 is entered into Y. 16 is lifted up to Z.
	Z	16.00	
	Y	30.00	
	X	30.00	

11	T	0.00	11 is keyed into the displayed register.
	X	16.00	
	Y	30.00	
	X	11.	

ENTER↑	T	16.00	11 is copied into Y. 16 and 30 are lifted up to T and Z respectively.
	Z	30.00	
	Y	11.00	
	X	11.00	

17	T	16.00	17 is written over the 11 in X.
	Z	30.00	
	Y	11.00	
	X	17.	

+	T	16.00
	Z	16.00
	Y	30.00
	X	28.00

17 and 11 are added together and the rest of the stack drops. 16 drops to Z and is also duplicated in T. 30 and 28 are ready to be added.

+	T	16.00
	Z	16.00
	Y	16.00
	X	58.00

30 and 28 are added together and the stack drops again. Now 16 and 58 are ready to be added.

+	T	16.00
	Z	16.00
	Y	16.00
	X	74.00

16 and 58 are added together for the final answer and the stack continues to drop.

The same dropping action also occurs with −, × and ÷. The number in T is duplicated in T and drops to Z, the number in Z drops to Y, and the numbers in the Y and X combine to give the answer, which is visible in the X-register.

This automatic lift and drop of the stack give you tremendous computing power, since you can retain and position intermediate results in long calculations without the necessity of reentering the numbers.

Order of Execution

When you see a problem like this one:

$$5 \times [(3 \div 4) - (5 \div 2) + (4 \times 3)] \div (3 \times .213),$$

you must decide where to begin before you ever press a key.

Experienced HP calculator users have determined that by starting every problem at its innermost number of parentheses and working outward, just as you would with paper and pencil, you maximize the efficiency and power of your HP calculator. Of course, with the HP-67 you have tremendous versatility in the order of execution.

For example, you could work the problem above by beginning at the left side of the equation and simply working through it in left-to-right order. All problems cannot be solved using left-to-right order, however, and the best order for solving any problem is to begin with the innermost parentheses and work outward. So, to solve the problem above:

Press	Display	
3	3.	
ENTER↑	3.00	
4	4.	
÷	0.75	Intermediate answer for $(3 \div 4)$.
5	5.	
ENTER↑	5.00	
2	2.	
÷	2.50	Intermediate answer for $(5 \div 2)$.
−	−1.75	Intermediate answer for $(3 \div 4) - (5 \div 2)$.
4	4.	
ENTER↑	4.00	
3	3.	

×	12.00	Intermediate answer for (4 × 3).
+	10.25	Intermediate answer for (3 ÷ 4) − (5 ÷ 2) + (4 × 3).
3	3.	
ENTER↑	3.00	
.213	2.13	
×	0.64	Intermediate answer for (3 × .213).
÷	16.04	
5	5.	The first number is keyed in.
×	80.20	The final answer.

LAST X

In addition to the four stack registers that automatically store intermediate results, the HP-67 also contains a separate automatic register, the LAST X register. This register preserves the value that was in the displayed X-register before the performance of a function. To place the contents of the LAST X register into the display again, press h LSTx.

Recovering from Mistakes

LSTx makes it easy to recover from keystroke mistakes, such as pressing the wrong function key or keying in the wrong number.

Example: Divide 12 by 2.157 after you have mistakenly divided by 3.157.

Press	Display	
12	12.	
ENTER↑	12.00	
3.157 ÷	3.80	Oops! You made a mistake.
h LSTx	3.16	Retrieves that last entry (3.157).
×	12.00	You're back at the beginning.
2.157 ÷	5.56	The correct answer.

In the above example, when the first ÷ is pressed, followed by h LSTx, the contents of the stack and LAST X registers are changed . . .

. . . from this . . .		. . . to this . . .		. . . to this.
T	0.00	T	0.00	T	0.00
Z	0.00	Z	0.00	Z	0.00
Y	12.00	Y	0.00	Y	3.80
X	3.157	X	3.80	X	3.16

÷ ····· ► LAST X   3.157 ····· h LSTx

This makes possible the correction illustrated in the example above.

Recovering a Number for Calculation

The LAST X register is useful in calculations where a number occurs more than once. By recovering a number using LSTx, you do not have to key that number into the calculator again.

Example: Calculate

$$\frac{7.32 + 3.650112331}{3.650112331}$$

Press	Display
7.32	7.32
ENTER↑	7.32

3.650112331	3.650112331	
+	10.97	Intermediate answer.
h LSTx	3.65	Recalls 3.650112331 to X-register.
÷	3.01	The answer.

Constant Arithmetic

You may have noticed that whenever the stack drops because of a two-number operation (not because of R↓), the number in the T-register is reproduced there. This stack operation can be used to insert a constant into a problem.

Example: A bacteriologist tests a certain strain whose population typically increases by 15% each day. If he starts a sample culture of 1000, what will be the bacteria population at the end of each day for six consecutive days?

Method: Put the growth factor (1.15) in the Y-, Z-, and T-registers and put the original population (1000) in the X-register. Thereafter, you get the new population whenever you press ×.

Manipulating Stack Contents

The R↓ (roll down), R↑ (roll up), and x≤y (x exchange y) keys allow you to review the stack contents or to shift data within the stack for computation at any time.

Reviewing the Stack

To see how the R↓ key works, first load the stack with numbers 1 through 4 by pressing:

4 ENTER↑ 3 ENTER↑ 2 ENTER↑ 1

The numbers that you keyed in are now loaded into the stack, and its contents look like this:

T	4.00	
Z	3.00	
Y	2.00	
X	1.	Display.

When you press h R↓, the stack contents shift downward one register. So the last number that you have keyed in will be rotated around to the T-register when you press h R↓. When you press h R↓ again, the stack contents again roll downward one register.

When you press h R↓, the stack contents are rotated . . .

. . . from this . . .   . . . to this.

T	4.00		T	1.00	
Z	3.00		Z	4.00	
Y	2.00		Y	3.00	
X	1.	Display.	X	2.00	Display.

Notice that the *contents* of the registers are shifted. The actual registers themselves maintain their positions. The contents of the X-register are always displayed, so 2.00 is now visible.

Press h R↓ again and the stack contents are shifted . . .

. . . from this . . .   . . . to this.

T	1.00		T	2.00	
Z	4.00		Z	1.00	
Y	3.00		Y	4.00	
X	2.00	Display.	X	3.00	Display.

Press h R↓ twice more . . . and the stack shifts . . .

... through this ...   ... back to the start again.

T		3.00			T		4.00	
Z		2.00			Z		3.00	
Y		1.00			Y		2.00	
X		4.00	Display.		X		1.00	Display.

Once again the number 1.00 is in the displayed X-register. Four presses of h R↓ roll the stack down four times, returning the contents of the stack to their original registers.

You can also manipulate the stack contents using h R↑ *(roll up)*. This key rolls the stack contents *up* instead of down, but it otherwise operates in the same manner as h R↓.

Exchanging x and y

The x≤y *(x exchange y)* key exchanges the contents of the X- and the Y-registers without affecting the Z- and T-registers, If you press h x≤y with data intact from the previous example, the numbers in the X- and Y-registers will be changed . . .

... from this ...   ... to this.

	T	4.00		T	4.00	
	Z	3.00		Z	3.00	
	Y	2.00		Y	1.00	
Display.	X	1.00		X	2.00	Display.

Similarly, pressing h x≤y again will restore the numbers in the X- and Y-registers to their original places. This function can be used to position numbers in the stack, whether operating manually or from a program, or simply to bring the contents of the Y-register into the X-register for display.

Notice that whenever you move numbers in the stack using one of the data manipulation keys, the actual stack registers maintain their positions. Only the *contents* of the registers are shifted. The contents of the X-register are always displayed.

Automatic Stack Review

If you wish to quickly review the contents of the stack at any time, use the g STK operation. When you press g STK, the contents of the stack are shifted, one register at a time, into the X-register and displayed for about a half-second each. The order of display is T, Z, Y, and finally the X-register contents again. Press g STK now and see the contents of the entire stack displayed. (If the stack contents in your calculator remain intact from the previous example, your displays should match the ones shown below):

Press	Display
g STK	4.00
	3.00
	1.00
	2.00

g STK operates exactly as four presses of h R↑. You can see that after displaying the contents of the entire stack, the original contents of the X-register are returned there and displayed.

While a g STK operation is being performed, the decimal point blinks twice during the display of the contents of each register. This is to identify this function as a program pause during a running program, so that you will not think the program has stopped.

When operating the HP-67 manually from the keyboard, you can slow down or speed up the review of the stack contents by pressing R/S or any other key on the keyboard while the calculator is executing a g STK stack review. As long as you hold the key depressed, the contents of the stack register currently being displayed will remain "frozen" in the display, permitting you to write down or examine the number. As soon as you release the key you are holding depressed, the contents of the next stack register to be displayed are shown.

Note: If the g STK stack review is being executed as part of a running program, depressing a key to "freeze" a stack register display will cause the program to halt execution after the f STK has been executed.

Some HP-97 Printer Characteristics

Before discussing some of the more esoteric capabilities of the HP-67/97, as developed by some dedicated and superenthused experts of the HP-65 Users Club, a simpler notation of some of the capabilities is necessary for beginners. These HP instruments permit users to write programs of up to 224 steps. However, every function (one, two, or three keystrokes) is merged to take only one step of program memory. Very handy also are the 26 data storage registers providing memory needed for problem solutions. Users can record or load the contents of program memory or the data storage registers on their magnetic cards, using, when necessary, the three levels of subroutines, ten user-definable keys, ten conditional/decision functions, four flags, direct addressing to labels, relative addressing and indirect addressing. The preprogrammed functions cover the usual trig, exponential, log, statistical and angular conversions including sines, cosines, tangents and their inverses in three angular modes; natural and common logs and anti-logs; pi; related arithmetic functions; coordinate conversions; angle conversions; angle addition. Two variable summations (n, Σx, Σx^2, Σy, Σy^2, Σxy) are stored for easy access.

Users can adjust or correct input data without having to repeat an entire calculation. With data keyed in, they can calculate the mean and standard deviation or use the summations to compute other statistical functions.

The useful editing features are also included enabling easy review of programs, forward or backward, and jumping to any step in the program — or inserting or deleting steps, as desired.

On the HP-97, users may list a program (stepnumber, key mnemonic and, optionally, the keycode), contents of the automatic memory stack, or the contents of the data storage registers. And you have three printing modes to choose from. With the printer switch set to MANUAL, the printer will operate only when the Print X key or a list function is executed from the keyboard or from within a program. With the switch set to NORMAL, the printer will record all entered data and functions. With the switch set to TRACE, the printer will list the stepnumber, function and result of each step of an executing program or the operation and results of a manual calculation.

The printer is a valuable aid in editing programs or long calculations. Users don't have to remember what they've done or what remains to be done. They see everything at once, clearly, on tape. The HP-97 and HP-67 print and display in fixed decimal and scientific notation, common in many scientific calculators. They also print and display in engineering notation, where values are displayed with exponents that are multiples of three. This is useful in working with many units of measure, such as kilo (10^3), nano (10^{-9}), etc.

Printed tape simplifies checking programs or calculations

With the HP-97 you have the additional advantage of a printed tape to help you with your editing. You can list your programs, as shown below, and easily check them for mistakes.

Ø26	*LBLA		21	11
Ø27	FØ?	16	23	.ØØ
Ø28	SPC		16	−11
Ø29	RCLE		36	15
Ø30	1			Ø1
Ø31	+			−55
Ø32	FØ?	16	23	ØØ
Ø33	PRTX			−14
Ø34	X ⇄ Y			−41
Ø35	FØ?	16	23	ØØ
Ø36	PRTX			−14

Card Reader Capabilities Listing

Record/Load all data registers; Load selected data registers; Record/Load entire program memory; Merge program subsections; Angular mode, flag settings, and display status are recorded with program recording and reset with program loading; User is prompted for proper operation when loading; Card reader operations can be initiated manually or under program control (except program recording).

The HP-67 Operational Capability—Some 'Special' Notes from HP-65 Users Club Members

Perhaps the first, tightest and best explanation of the HP-67 as it was introduced was written by one of the top calculator experts, Richard J. Nelson, founder and head of the HP-65 Users Club. It is excerpted with his permission from "65 Notes", the club's newsletter, Vol. 3, No. 5, page 3, June, 1976, and proceeds as follows:

HP-67 Firmware

The HP-67 has a total of 26 data registers, 4 stack registers and a LSTx register. Sixteen of the 26 are called primary registers and are identified 0 thru 9, A thru E, and I. The remaining 10 registers are secondary, or secure registers. These registers are addressable by exchanging (all 10 at once) with the registers 0 thru 9. The I register is the index register for sophisticated programs using indirect addressing, etc. It will be a very busy register indeed. All 26 registers are indirectly addressable through the single index register. Not being able to use any register as an index register may appear disappointing at first, but considering the unique flexibility of the I register and all codes merged, this should not be a serious drawback. The use of only one I register facilitates triple merged codes and reduces keyboard business.

Two PAUSE functions are possible on the HP-67. A five-second pause, key -x- is the same as a print instruction for the HP-97. The second pause, a standard one-second pause, is extended whenever a key is pressed to allow entering data while a program is executing. A card can also be read during the pause.

A STACK REVIEW function automatically displays the stack in T, Z, Y, X order. This function is programmable and to distinguish between stack review and pause, the decimal point blinks twice for each register displayed. Another function new to pocket calculators is the REGISTER REVIEW. Pressing h, 3 will cause the registers to be displayed one at a time with a 1-second pause for each. A number in the exponent field tells which register is coming up next.

The addition of indirect addressing, fully merged codes, and line numbers makes the HP-67 a powerful machine for the programmer. With the exception of indirect addressing, anyone who has used an HP-25, 55 or 65 will readily adapt to the HP-67. Ten labels, A-E and a-e, are the user defined keys. With three levels of subroutines, a new key GSB, GO SUB, is added. LBL is a pre-fixed key, f, LBL. The index register, I, needs explanation. This will only be a partial description due to the many different ways it may be used:

Indirect addressing on the HP-67 is performed using the I register which may contain any number between -999 to +25. If an indirect recall of a register is performed, the register found in the I register (#0 to 25) will be recalled. STO, RCL, GTO and DSP may be done indirectly. The DSZ function, which uses R8 on the HP-65, has a companion function, ISZ. ISZ is increment skip on zero, which adds 1 to a negative number, in the register designated by the I register. Using the I register any or all of the 26 registers may be designated as a DSZ or ISZ register. The 340 page owners handbook gives numerous examples using the I register.

Program editing and debugging is accomplished with the GTO, DEL, SST, and BST keys. The BST and SST keys operate like the HP-25 keys. Press down SST and the step is shown in the display. Release the key and the step is executed. The GTO is different, however, and performs differently in RUN than in W/PRGM. In run mode the calculator will go to a line number if in the format GTO, .nnn. This does not work while executing a program. Any line (relative addressing) can be branched to if a negative number is in the I register. The instruction GTO, (I) then causes the program pointer to "back up" the number of steps in the I register. Any number from -1 to -999 will work. A line forward in the program can also be reached. For example, if the program came to GTO, (I) at step 98 and you wanted to skip ahead to step 102 (4 steps forward), the number -220 must be in the I register at that time.

The registers are identified as primary registers 0 - 9, A - E (20-25) and I (26), and secondary registers S0 - S9 (10-19). The ten secondary registers are protected registers and data storage is accomplished by the P $\rightleftarrows$ S key (primary secondary exchange). All ten secondary and primary registers are exchanged at the same time. The secondary registers are also used by the Σ^+ and Σ^- keys. The registers are: S4-Σx, S5-Σx^2, S6-Σy, S7-Σy^2, S8-Σxy and S9-n.

Four flags are available on the HP-67. They are flags 0 thru 3. Flags 0 and 1 are the same as the HP-65. Flags 2 and 3 are cleared when they are tested. Flag 3 is unique, and intended for data entry use. The flag is set for data entry and cleared after the program resumes after data entry.

Three levels of subroutines are possible, i.e., three addresses are stored for the program pointer to be able to return. Any number of levels may be called, but the pointer can only return back up three levels.

Smart Card Reader

The term "smart card reader" has been suggested to describe the many "smart" things that the card reader records and reads from a card. A program card will have the following automatically recorded by the card reader: (a) the fact that the card is a program card, (b) the card is side 1 or side 2, (c) if two passes are required, (d) status of all flags, (e) angular mode, (f) display mode, and (g) a check sum.

The calculator can also record all 26 data registers onto a card (all or partially). The primary registers, all 16, on side 1 and the secondary registers on side 2. A data card will have the following automatically recorded by the card reader: (a) the fact that the card is a data card, (b) the card is side 1 or side 2, (c) if two passes are required, and (d) a check sum.

When reading a program card the display, angular mode and flags will automatically be set. If the card is a data card, the registers will be filled when reading. One half of the card can be program and the other half data. Automatic card reading is possible under program control and instructions being read from a card can be overlaid into memory starting at any step if desired using the MERGE key.

The HP-97 uses the new high accuracy algorithms which have an accuracy of ±1 count in the 10th decimal for all functions. Four Pacs are available immediately with four more to be available soon. A 67/97 library and newsletter will be announced. Conflicting information doesn't permit details. Members who have seen the owners manual have been impressed with its color and humor. The Standard Pac contains 14 programs:

1. Moving Average Follows Trends and Data.
2. Tabulator.
3. Curve Plotting.
4. Calendar Functions.
5. Annuities and Compound Amounts.
6. Follow Me - Programmable Program.
7. Triangle Solutions.
8. Vectors.
9. Polynomial Evaluation.
10. Matrix Operations.
11. Calculus and Roots of f(x).
12. Metric Conversions (20).
13. Arithmetic Teacher.
14. Lunar Lander Game.

Mr. Richard J. Nelson continues his evaluations in the July issue of "65 Notes" (Vol. 3, No. 6, page 4) specifically pertaining to the HP-97, as follows: ". . . the HP-67 and HP-97 have interchangeable software; i.e., programs recorded on magnetic cards from one machine may be loaded and run on the other machine. Data cards are also interchangeable between the two calculators. All functions and switches operate alike on the two calculators, with the exception of the printing functions on the HP-97 and the automatic list functions of the HP-67.

The major difference between the HP-97 and the HP-67 calculators (aside from price: $750 vs $450, respectively, and size) is the fact that the HP-97 also incorporates a built-in printer, similar in many ways with that of the HP-91. Since the HP-97 has a built-in printer which can not only print results of calculations, stack contents, and register contents, but also a listing of the program currently in the program memory, it is a very significant contribution to the state of the art of pocket programmable calculators.

On the HP-97, when you press the f PRINT PRGM keys, the calculator immediately begins printing the contents of the program memory beginning with the step to which the calculator is set. This feature allows the user to list a complete program at any time, whether you are loading it, single-stepping through it, or because you simply wish to know the contents of the program memory. The calculator will print the contents of the program memory until it encounters two R/S instructions in succeeding steps (unlike the HP-65, both the HP-67 and HP-97 fill the contents of program memory with R/S instructions when the f PRGM command is given, instead of NOP instructions), until you press R/S (or any key) from the keyboard, or until step 224 is printed. This is a very powerful feature for editing and documentation of programs written for the 67/97."

This is followed by 4 more excellent articles from the same issue by, respectively, Mr. Richard J. Nelson, Santa Ana, CA., Mr. Hal Brown, King of Prussia, PA., and David Kemper, Northridge, CA., as follows:

The HP-67, Let Me Demonstrate

Programs which demonstrate the new features of the HP-67 are handy for the dealer and new owner alike. One of the most impressive, yet easily understood, programs is the Triangle solutions (SD-07A) program in the Standard PAC. A good example to use is the well known 3, 4, 5 right triangle. After loading the program, key 3 enter 90 enter 4 "D" and let the machine do its work. The complete 'solution' to the triangle will be displayed using the -X- 'pause'. The side, angle, side, angle, etc., answers will be displayed in succession going clockwise from the 3 side. As a final touch the area is displayed. Without exception, this program has impressed all who have seen it demonstrated.

Another program which is handy to demonstrate and illustrates the use of indirect addressing, and automatic merged data reading of a card. Let's call it a "Telephone Number Scratch Pad Demonstrator". The program below is recorded on Side 2 of a blank card. Be sure to set display to DSP 4 before recording. Side 1 is used for data. The program has notations to explain its operation so the reader can try to follow the execution step by step. The purpose of the program is to demonstrate how the data registers of the HP-67 can be recorded on a card and how the HP-67 can automatically read a card and display the register contents.

User Instructions. Starting with R_0 key in telephone numbers. Suggestion: use format nnn.nnnn. Remember last register used. This program only uses the first ten registers which is more than enough to demonstrate. The last register used is keyed in later so only those that were used are displayed. Press f, w/DATA and pass side 1 of the Demo program through the calculator. Turn machine off and on again. Recall several registers used, to demonstrate that they are all zero due to the machine being turned off. Load program from side 2. Observe that the display changes from 0.00 to 0.0000 when the card was read. This shows the 'smart' card reader. Key last register used and press A. The program will loop for about ten seconds. While the program is decrementing (to give you time) insert side 1 into the card reader. Just slip the card in a very short distance. With the end of your finger gently push the card in (while the machine is running) until it stops and the card bows slightly. That is far enough. Wait. In a few seconds the machine will stop looping, read the card and start displaying the register contents decrementing from the register that was keyed in when 'A' was pressed. This program demonstrates or illustrates the following features:

- Smart card reader—sets display format automatically.
- Ability to record program and data on same card.
- Ability to read card under program control.
- Ability to merge data from card into registers (i.e., only those registers used).

- Use of DSZ and ISZ.
- Use of indirect addressing for sequential data output.
- Use of pause.

The program follows. Many alternate methods could be used to accomplish the same task. The register review feature was not used because it shows all the registers which is time wasting during a demo. Two -X- instructions could be used for steps 3 thru 8 for a delay to allow placing the card into the card reader. Alternately a pause countdown could be used to provide a delay. The register number could be displayed prior to its contents by using RCI if that feature is desired.

1. f LBL A	31 25 11	START	12. h PAUSE	35 72		
2. STO E	33 15	STORE R_{max}	13. RCL E	34 15	USE R_{max}	
3. 3	03	DECREMENT	14. CHS	42	TO START RECALL	
4. 0	00	I REGISTER	15. h ST I	35 33	LOOP R_{max} TO R_0	
5. h ST I	35 33	30 times for	16. f LBL 1	31 25 01		
6. f LBL 0	31 25 00	10 second	17. RCL (i)	34 24	R_{max} TO R_1	
7. f DSZ	31 33	delay	18. h PAUSE	35 72	RECALL WITH	
8. GTO 0	22 00		19. f ISZ	31 34	PAUSE LOOP	
9. RCL E	34 15	RECALL R_{max}	20. GTO 1	22 01		
10. h ST I	35 33	READ CARD	21. RCL 0	34 00	RECALL R_0	
11. g MERGE	32 41	R_0 TO R_{max}	22. R/S	84	STOP	

A handy data card to have to demonstrate the use of the register review feature — and other features — contains numbers to be stored in each side of the decimal point, i.e., R_0-0, R_1-1.1, R_2-2.2; ... R_{25}-25.25. Using this method, whenever a number comes up in the display, you know where it came from. To make up a 'Register Test Data' card, key as follows:

Turn machine on: key — 10.10, STO 0, 11.11, ST 1, 12.12, STO 2, etc., to 19.19, STO 9. Next, key f, P⇄S. Now key 1.1, STO 1, 2.2, STO 2, 3.3, STO 3, etc., to 9.9, STO.9. Continue with: 20.20, STO A, 21.21, STO B, 22.22, STO C, 23.23, STO D, 24.24, STO E, 25.25, h, ST I. Now all the registers (R_0 thru R_{25}) have data. Verify by keying h, REG. Check the secondary registers R_{10} thru R_{19} by: f, P⇄S, h, REG. Now key f, P⇄S again to get data back into proper registers. Key f, W/DATA. The display shows Crd. Stick in side 1, then side 2. The registers are now recorded onto the card. Turn machine off, then on. Insert card. Display shows Crd, so read other side. Key h, REG. Verify contents. Verify secondary registers by f, P⇄S, h, REG. If all is OK, clip corners of card. This should be done because the data card can become garbage (bad data) during a demonstration and confuse you and the person to whom you are demonstrating if a mistake is made.

The MERGE feature can be demonstrated easily using the 'Register Test Data' card. Turn on machine. This demonstration will show only R_0 thru R_5 will have test data taken from the 'Register Test Data Card'. Recall several registers or press h, REG to be convinced that the registers all contain zero. Key 5, h, ST I. This stores 5 in the I register which will only allow data up to and including R_5 to be stored if g, MERGE is keyed prior to inserting the Register Test Data Card. Key: g, MERGE and insert the card. Observe that Crd comes up in the display. If you had inserted side 1, that is all that was required. Crd in the display means "read the other side also". (The card reader is smart, not brilliant.) Read the other side. Now key h, REG to prove that only R_0 thru R_5 contains data. Check R_{10}-R_{19} by f, P⇄S, h, REG. Pretty slick! The HP-67 has many features to demonstrate, but those described above include most of the highlights and only take about 5-10 minutes, depending upon the 'audience'.

Users Review

The HP-67 is another calculator with a strong HP personality. One year in development, and a second thought after the HP-97, the HP-67 is a little short of the polished near-perfection of past machines. Many reasons may help explain this, with competition, and a big move to Oregon being near, if not at the top of the list. Along with the 97/67 comes a new era of user attitude, communication, and interest. This can be seen by the outstanding documentation associated with the machines. The Standard PAC, for example, actually has programming techniques in separate sections associated with most programs. The "Owners Handbook and Programming Guide" is very well written and illustrated. Even though it is a bit wordy in spots, the newcomer will welcome the added help in getting into programming.

The HP-67 has a different character than the HP-65. The HP-67 is more mature and disciplined. Obvious care was taken to avoid certain "problem areas" that HP-65 users discovered on the HP-65. The instructions are well defined, and it almost appears that the machine was designed to reject any operations not specifically defined or allowed. The triple merged codes that HP-25 users found so powerful make the HP-67 almost awesome with 224 steps. The ability to record 600 plus keystrokes into memory must represent the upper limit for a calculator without printing capability.

Many members have commented on the location and nomenclature of the keyboard, but like anything new, it takes a little time. One problem becomes immediately apparent for users of other HP machines. The placement of function designations on the keyboard **below** the keys takes some getting used to. There must be some *human* reason for this rather than a conservative basis for such a major change. If the user remembers: TO INSURE YOURSELF THAT YOU ARE PRESSING THE RIGHT KEY. COVER THE KEY NOMENCLATURE WITH YOUR FINGER SO YOU CAN'T SEE IT.

Aside from some disappointments some users may have had because they expected more, the HP-67 will be another winner. The -X- pause, register and stack review, fully flexible I register, write and merge data, flags, and an excellent choice of pre-programmed functions will inspire the user to a new level of program writing accomplishment. Just as the 100-step limit of the HP-65 was its greatest asset, the single I register of the HP-67 will be its greatest asset in inspiring the user to high levels of programming efficiency.

Some users will miss the clear stack. For debug purposes it is convenient to be able to **know** that the stack was in a known status; i.e., zero. Also, programmers who initialize LAST X for its use as a constant, etc., will miss a clear stack. HP-65 users will have strong feelings about the HP-67 and its instruction set, but after a few days programming the HP-67, the true power of the machine will begin to sink in. All those programs that required so much work to get 'into' the HP-65 will be more likely to be accommodated by the HP-67. Regardless of how you feel about the HP-67 now, a few hours at the keyboard, and the excitement, fascination, challenge, and HP flavor will start all over again just like it was the HP-65.

As noted previously in 65 NOTES, some of the firmware algorithms have been improved — mostly to produce higher accuracy (e.g., Sin 3600000030° = 5.000000000-01). But more significant, in my opinion, is improvement in the Y^x firmware such that it works with negative Y if X is an integer. With the exception of the HP-91, which also has this capability, to my knowledge no other portable calculator with a Y^x key can handle negative Y. This feature should prove valuable for controlling the sign of expressions; for example, a $(-1)^x$ factor can be used to produce sign change on alternate terms of an alternating-sign series.

Ten of the 26 storage registers in the HP-67/97 are called secondary or 'protected'. In general they are not directly accessible. At first thought this seems to be a significant shortcoming, but in practice isn't. At most only two program steps are required to access any of the secondary registers: P⇄S, followed by a store or recall command. Any one of the secondary registers can be indirectly addressed via the I register, and registers R14 & R16 can be accessed via Σ+ (this point is not made in the manual, but the values in Rx & Ry are summed into R14/R16 with Σ+ and recalled from R14/R16 with RCL Σ+). The latter is intended for statistical analysis of a group of values, but there is no reason it can't be used to store and recall single values.

There is no NOP key per se, although the SPACE key performs the same function on the HP-67. On the HP-97 this key produces a blank line on the paper tape. Actually there is little need for a no-operation key on the HP-67. Since conditional branch test failures cause skip of only one program step, the NOP is not needed as fill-in when only a single-step operation or command is to be skipped. The only use I have thought of for a no-operation key is to fill-in directly below a DSZ/ISZ when increment/decrement is desired without skip-on-zero.

Considering the large number of programs already written for the HP-65/55/25, there will be interest in their potential use on the HP-67/97. A large percentage will run as written, or with only minor modification. Cards written on the HP-65 cannot be read into the HP-67/97, but the programs can be keyed in. Other than noting the changed key designations on inverse functions (they are now directly identified rather than inversely identified by the f^{-1} key), only a few problem areas need attention. **Watch for conditional branch tests (the X/Y compares and DSZ) that are followed by two single-step operations. They will not run as written on the HP-67/97.** The Lampman split-logic will also not run as written.

Not required, but possibly desirable, is adding letter labels at the beginning of programs that don't have them. Unlike the HP-65, the HP-67/97 will not return to step 000 and run when an undefined user-definable key is pressed.

Programs written for the HP-25 and HP-55 will run as written after replacing line addresses with label addresses and inserting labels at the required places.

Many programs written for other models could run more efficiently on the HP-67/97 if rewritten to take advantage of the new features, but until that is done it is nice to know most will run with little or no modification.

The new features of the HP-67/97 are mind boggling. In the few days exposure I have had it was possible only to recognize the potential. Indirect addressing is a powerful tool for handling arrays of values. Used with ISZ or DSZ it permits store and recall of array values one at a time by means of a very simple loop. Also extremely valuable will be the ability to record and read data on/from a card.

For very sophisticated and long programs the MERGE key will be handy. It permits modifying part of a program without affecting other parts by reading a card (under 'hands off' program control if desired). This is especially valuable when a main control program, stored on one card, may be used with a number of different sub-program cards. An example is the calculus and Roots of f(s) program provided with the Standard PAC. Sub-programs containing f(s), stored on other cards, can be read-in and merged with the main program. Also, in principle, the MERGE command can be used to increase the number of available program steps indefinitely if the operator is willing to feed cards in as required. 336 steps can be run 'hands off' following start of the run and partial insertion of the second card. 'Hands off' is limited to 336 steps since the machine can't flip the card over and read the second side. For kicks I wrote a dummy 336 step program — most steps were skipped during program run. It worked like a charm, reading the second card under program control then proceeding through the new instructions.

The comments above apply to both the HP-67 and HP-97. The HP-97, of course, has a printer as well as more and larger keys, plus a larger display. The printer, in addition to its obvious advantage in providing hard-copy results of computations, is extremely valuable for debugging and editing a program. In TRACE mode it prints out all commands plus the numerical results at each step. One can quickly spot the place where a program produced unexpected results. This feature is also available on the HP-67 by single-stepping through in RUN mode, but of course, the steps are not printed and the error is not as readily spotted.

A nice feature is the commonality of card recording/reading in the HP-67 and HP-97. Even though the keyboards are different the same information is recorded or read identically on the two machines. Thus, the owner of an HP-67 who knows a willing friend with an HP-97 can get listings and/or traces of his programs. Keycodes printed by the 97 will not be correct for the 67, but the alpha-numeric step listing will be.

Many more things could be said about these new models, but probably by the time this is read you will have had personal experience with them. It's my guess the full potential of these machines will not be known for several years.

(Hal Brown (362) King of Prussia, PA)

Efficient 67/97 Conditional Branching

Part 1: x register comparisons:

1. if $(x \leq 0)$ step: f x < 0
f x = 0
step

2. if $(x \geq 0)$ step: f x < 0
f x = 0
step

3. if $(x \geq 0)$ step: g x ≤ y
g x = y
step

4. if $(x < y)$ step: g x = y
GTO 0   (note: LBL 0 may be used as often as neces-
g x ≤ y   sary)
step
f LBL 0

5. if $(y = x)$ step: ≅ $(x = y)$: g x = y
6. if $(y \neq x)$ step: ≅ $(x \neq y)$: g x ≠ y
7. if $(y > x)$ step: ≅ $(x < y)$ (see #4 above)
8. if $(y = x)$ step: ≅ $(x \leq y)$: g x ≤ y
9. if $(y < x)$ step: ≅ $(x > y)$: g x > y
10. if $(y \leq x)$ step: ≅ $(x \geq y)$ (see #3 above)

Part 2: flags

1. if (flag n is set) step: hF?n
step

2. if (flag n is clear) step: (except a GSBj)

hF?n
GTO 0
Step
f LBL 0

3. if (flag n is clear) fGSBj (slightly more efficient)

f GSB j   f LBL j
hF?n
hRTN
•
•
•
hRTN

4. flip flag 2 or flag 3 to opposite state   hF?n

GTO 0
hSFn
f LBL 0

5. flip flag 0 or 1 to opposite state hF?n

GTO 0
hSFn
GTO 1
f LBL 0
hCFn
f LBL 1

6. if (flag n is set) f GSB j else f GSB k

```
hF?n        f LBL j      f LBL k
f GSB j      (hSFn)*      hF?n
f GSB k        •          hRTN
               •           •
               •           •
         hRTN              •
                         hRTN
```

*if flag is 2 or 3

7. if (flag n is set) f GSB j else f GSB k: special case where flag is 2 or 3 and **not** to be automatically cleared

```
hF?n        f LBL j      f LBL k
GTO 0        hSFn          •
f GSB k       •            •
GTO 1         •            •
f LBL 0       •          h RTN
f GSB j      hRTN
f LBL 1
```

(Lee H. Skinner (256) Albuquerque, N.M.)

The Product and Operations Analysis of the National Semiconductor Model 7100*

The first note about the NS 7100 appeared in the June, 1976 HP-65 Users Club Newsletter. It is quoted below. This was followed by two articles in **Electronics** magazine ("National's Scientific Calculator Has Long-Term Semiconductor Memory," June 10, 1976, page 29-30), and "National's Belated Programmable Ready," June 9, 1977, page 41-2.)

May 14, 1976. Bob Johnson, Product Manager of Advanced Consumer Products, of the Consumer Products Division of National Semiconductor (NS), described a new (significantly different) calculator. The 7100 will be the first high end calculator in the same class as the HP-67 and SR-52. The 7100 will be

*In October 1977, National Semiconductor Corp. decided **not** to market the MS 7100. The information offered above is for comparison purposes. Also, another firm might purchase the rights to market this machine.

billed as an all silicon calculator with no moving parts (i.e., card reader). The following features were mentioned:

- 480 merged steps
- 32 memories (pseudo nonvolatile)
- 5 volatile memories
- CMOS RAMS
- 64 labels
- 8 flags
- 9 levels parenthesis
- 12 metric conversions
- All angular conversions
- 3 angular modes: Deg., Rad., Grad.; Deg., Min., Sec.
- Variety of display modes
- EROM file cartridge

- 1 DSZ
- $400 price class
- 3 modes: Load, Edit, Run
- (1 second) wait
- 10 digits
- 2 exponent
- 2 guard digits
- Any angular measure to any other
- $\sqrt{\ }, Y^x$
- %, CHS
- $X \rightleftarrows Y, X \rightleftarrows$ Memory
- π, e
- Library cartridge

The concept is quite valid, but the practicality of plugging in and handling the various ROMS is unknown. The file cartridge will cost approximately $20, which is 100 times the equivalent memory cost on a magnetic card. The internal 240-step memory is read into the file cartridge. The special design process of paging for memory labels allows either memory to be accessed during program execution for a total of 480 steps of a user-programmed program. The unique feature of the 7100 is the Library Cartridge of 4,000 steps with 256 subprograms possible. A complete library of programs is in the calculator at the same time. The calculator will have two file cartridges and one library cartridge supplied with the calculator. A plastic card provides memory codes for the various programs in the Library Cartridge. The file cartridge is good for a year (no battery) before it requires a refresh (read and rewrite). The internal memory is maintained by the battery and will hold its program (same for data registers) as long as the battery lasts ($<1\mu$a current drain which is about the same as the battery self-discharge rate).

It seems obvious that the calculator is designed for handshaking with the outside world. There will most likely be additional input/output devices in the future.

The *data sheet* promotional handout from the company is a bit more definitive especially as regards decision-making, debugging, decrement and branch on zero, preprogrammed functions.

NS 7100 General Features

National Semiconductor applies complete semiconductor technology to the programmable calculator.

The new National Semiconductor (NS) Model 7100 incorporates 3 different types of semiconductor program memory:

1. **A 240 step non-volatile program memory.** Turn power off, calculator retains data and program. This mainframe program memory operates independently from file or library cartridge.

2. **File cartridge.** Semiconductors housed in a tiny cartridge — insert the file cartridge into the calculator, depress a key and record the 240 step mainframe program onto the cartridge for use at a later date. . .

or

Insert file cartridge on which you previously stored a 240 step program and use it as a subroutine for a second 240 step program in the mainframe program memory

= A total program step capability of **480**

3. **Library cartridge.** A factory programmed semiconductor cartridge inserted into the calculator puts **4,000** steps of programming at your command instantaneously. Use these factory recorded programs as subroutines to the 240 step program in the mainframe program memory

= A total program step capacity of **4,240**

Programming Features

Decision Making: Conditional and unconditional branching. Test display contents for four "if" conditions: x = 0, x > 0, x> 0, *Error*.

Eight Flags: Set or reset flags manually or through programming.

Symbolic Labeling: For efficient program design, identify branch points using a label so that during program modification no time is wasted, no errors made related to changing absolute address branch points.

32 Non-volatile Data Storage Memories: Fully addressable with register arithmetic which allows arithmetic operations to be performed directly in memory — saves keystrokes and program steps, and adds five more volatile but equally accessible memories.

NS 7100 Decision Making

IF = 0   These keys are used in conjunction with a go to GTO, go to label
              GTLB, or GET command and cause those commands to be executed
IF < 0   only if one of the following conditions are met:
                 If display register contains zero
IF ≥ 0   If display register contains a number less than zero
                 If display register contains a number greater than zero

8 FLAGS

TF   The "test flag" TF, "set flag" SF and "reset flag" RF keys used in
SF   conjunction with a go to GTO, go to label GTLB or GET command
RF   cause those commands to be executed depending on the position of
        the flag.

        It is possible to set and reset flags manually or through programming
        and therein lies the advantage of this computer capability.

DSZ   The "decrement and skip on zero" key is another feature designed
        to simplify programming and minimize program steps. For those
        often encountered situations which require a branch to occur after
        a fixed number of data points have been entered or after a certain
        number of subroutine iterations are complete; for example, the
        DSZ key writes a program instruction which causes memory register
        22 to be decremented by one (1) with each iteration. The contents of
        memory 22 are scanned at each interval and when contents are zero,
        a branch occurs.

Debugging Features

BSP   The "backspace" BSP key causes the program pointer to move one
        instruction backwards into the mainframe program memory.

000	∿∿	Top of memory
001	∿∿	
002	∿∿	←¬
003	∿∿	--⌐ BSP moves program
		pointer back one instruction

INS   The "insert" INS key permits the insertion of program steps at any
        position in the mainframe program memory.

SST   The "single step" SST key allows you to step through the mainframe program memory one step at a time while viewing the step number code representing each program instruction for the purpose of finding incorrect instructions. Also SST Execute in any program page.

Decrement and Skip on Zero: Another feature to simplify programming and minimize steps. The contents of the special memory are scanned at intervals specified in the program in order that an automatic branch occurs when this register contains zero.

Debugging Features: Complete computer-like features for the final construction of programs you write yourself: backspace, insert, single-step, delete and pack features

Keyboard functions: 66 Keyboard functions and 23 key functions for programming.
Including 9 levels of parentheses
Trig and Log functions
Statistical functions
Metric conversions
Indirect register addressing from any register
Memory subscripting

7100 Preprogrammed functions

Left justified entry
Trig and log functions and their inverses
Degree/radian/grad and DMS modes
Integer/fraction isolation
Statistical summations, standard deviation, mean
Factorial
Memory register arithmetic MS + (−, ×, ÷) key sequence
DMS conversion
Polar/rectangular conversion
Square root, nth root, Y^x, X^2, $1/X$
%, Delta %
Change sign
X-Y and X-M register exchange
PI, e
Parenthesis, 9 levels
Clear second function key depression by pressing it again
Clear entry/clear function
Clear All clears calculator registers and memories
12 metric conversions including:
   kilograms to pounds mass
   Newtons to pounds force; — CM ↔ in.; °C ↔ °F; GAL ↔ LIT
   joules to Foot pounds force
Scientific, engineering, fixed and floating point notation

National Semiconductor Model 7100 Summary

- Programmable calculator with external storage provided by semiconductor cartridge
- Algebraic logic 9-level parentheses
- Standard engineering keyboard functions **plus** many convenience features
- Rechargeable battery pack
- New case and styling
- Double shot, tactile keyboard

- Standard equipment:
  - 2 files cartridges
  - 1 library cartridge, math package — over 170 programs
  - Battery pack
  - Carrying case
  - Charger
- Instructions: (1) Basic (user's manual)
  - (2) Library cartridge

NS 7100 Functional Description

The 7100 is an algebraic machine with true hierarchy. The only compromise to the pure algebra concept is that the single variable functions (trig functions, exponentials, logs, conversions) operate as soon as the keys are depressed (eg., to take sin of 30°, depress 30, sin).

I. Hierarchy

The Hierarchy is the standard math hierarchy and the same one used in most computer programming languages like Fortran and Algol. The hierarchy of functions, in descending order is:

1.	Y^x,	$X\sqrt{Y}$	– Highest Order
2.	X,	÷	– Intermediate Order
3.	+,	–	– Lowest Order

This means, simply, that in any expression, the exponential function is performed first, followed by multiply or divide with addition or subtraction performed last. Thus the expression:

$$A + B \times C \ Y^x \ D \equiv A + (B \times (C^D)) \equiv A + B \cdot C^D$$
$$\text{Key Stroke Sequence} \equiv \text{Mathematical Equation}$$

In calculations, the functions are performed, and results appear in the display, whenever functions of the same or lower level are indicated — or whenever an = key is depressed. In the preceding example, the result would be displayed only when the = key is depressed. The following should make this clearer:

Expression: $A \times B \times C + D \ Y^x \ E \times F \div G - H =$

Key	Display
A	A
+	A
B	B
×	$A \cdot B$
C	C
+	$(A \cdot B \cdot C)$
D	D
Y^x	D
E	E
×	D^E
F	F
÷	$(D^E \cdot F)$
G	G
–	$(D^E \cdot F \div G) + (A \cdot B \cdot C)$
H	H
=	$A \cdot B \cdot C + (D^E \cdot F \div G) - H$

Basically, the 7100 pushes the current calculated result, along with the pending function code, into a nine level stack whenever a left parenthesis or a higher order function is entered. The stack is pushed down, and the pending operation evaluated, on depression of the right parenthesis or lower order function keys. In that context, the 7100 has nine levels of parenthesis or a nine level hierarchy stack, or any combination of the two adding up to nine registers of pending operations.

II. **Registers**
   A. There are 37 user addressable registers, or memories, in the 7100. Addressing is done by a form of subscripting; each register has been assigned a two digit code and can be addressed using the keyboard memory instruction keys or through the indirect addressing features of the machine.
   B. Allocation of Registers:
   1. M_{00} through M_{21}: Memories unused in any way by internal programming.
   2. M_{34} through M_{36}: Memories which are also used to store the following statistical terms during statistical calculations:

$$\Sigma x \rightarrow m_{34}$$
$$\Sigma x_2 \rightarrow M_{35}$$
$$n \rightarrow M_{36}$$

   3. M_{22} is the Decrement and Skip on Zero register and is controlled in this mode by the "DSZ" key instruction.
   4. M_{23} through M_{31}: Registers constituting the nine level parenthesis and hierarchy stack. Register M_{31} is the first, or lowest, level and M_{23} the ninth. M_{32} through M_{36} are volatile and their contents are lost when the on-off switch is in the off position. M_{00} through M_{31} are non-volatile as long as the battery pack is charged, so data is stored in them independent of the on-off switch.
   5. M_{32} is the working or Y-Register. It can be addressed by the memory instruction keys or the "x $\leftrightarrow$ y" exchange key or through indirect addressing. It is a volatile register.
   6. M_{33} is the display, or X-Register. It can also be addressed by the memory function keys and by indirect addressing. It is also volatile.

III. **Basic Machine Operations**
   A. Power On
   Clears machine but leaves memories and program information intact. The stack is cleared; however, if the user had entered data into any of the top six levels of the stack before turning the calculator off, the value will be preserved. The stack is always cleared on power on.

   B. Arithmetic Keyboard Operations
   These are by and large self explanatory and they will not be dwelt upon here, except for those a little out of the ordinary. The 7100 is a six function machine with a full complement of scientific and conversion functions.
   1. **The " = " Key:** In a machine with hierarchy, the = key must be used with discretion. It collapses the stack completely by completing all pending operations and terminates the operation.
   2. **" $\rightarrow$ P", " $\rightarrow$ R", and "Δ%" Keys:** The rectangular to polar, polar to rectangular and delta percent keys are two-variable functions that require values in the x and y registers. It is not important how these values are entered into x and y as these functions do not alter

the status of pending operations; however, for clarity, it is recommended that the x ↔ y exchange function be used (or the x → y transfer (→ M, 35)).

Thus a recommended sequence is: A, "x ↔ y", B followed by the appropriate two-variable function keys: "→ P", "→ R", or "Δ%". The two variables in the result are also stored in x and y. "Δ%" returns percent difference ($\frac{y_0 - x_0}{x_0} \div 100$) in x and the difference $(y_0 - x_0)$ in y. "→ P" returns the angle in x and the magnitude in y; "→ R" places x in x and y in y.

3. **"Conv" Key:** This function is for the conversion of the displayed number from one angular dimension to another angular dimension without changing the machine angular mode. The sequence is:

"L", "Conv", "Deg", "Rad"

This tells the 7100 that the number in the display is assumed to be in degrees and converts it to radians.

4. **Angular Modes:** The 7100 has four angular modes: Degrees, Radians, Grads, and DMS.

5. **Decimal Point Format Modes:** There are three decimal format modes set by using the appropriate mode key in conjunction with the digit select key, "DS". The "DS" Key defines the total number of digits to be displayed in the mantissa. Let:

   n = Number of digits displayed to right of the decimal point in the mantissa. 5/4 round off automatically takes place in the n + 1 digit.

   I = Number of digits displayed to the left of the decimal point in the mantissa.

   M = Total number of digits to be displayed in the mantissa. M = I + n. The mantissa is represented as:

$$\pm \underbrace{xxxx}_{I} \cdot \underbrace{xxx}_{n}$$

The number of digits to be displayed in the mantissa is defined by the key sequence: "L", "DS", "m"; where $1 \le m \le 10$.

m = 10 at power-on.

The four decimal format modes are:

a. Fixed Point. The number of positions to the right of the dp is selected by the sequence: "L", "Fix", "n", where:

$$0 \le n \le 9 \text{ and } 1 + n \le 10.$$

If $10^{-n} \le 1 + n < 10^{10}$, the display mode automatically coverts to Scientific Notation.

b. Scientific Notation: The "SCI" key sets the mode to display all numbers in the form:

$$\pm I. \underbrace{xxx}_{n} \quad \underbrace{yy}_{exp}, \text{ where } I \ne 0$$

c. Engineering: All entries and results are displayed in a modified scientific notation with all exponents a multiple of 3.

d. Floating Point: Floating Point notation is automatically set at power-on or the key sequence: "L", "Fix", ".".

6. **Clear Functions:** There are four clearing modes in the 7100:

a. "C" Key, Depressed once — the display register, M_{36}, is cleared; clear entry function.

b. "C" Key, Depressed twice in succession — Registers M_{26} through M_{36} are cleared.

c. "U", "CPGM" — Internal program storage is cleared. All registers, flags, and modes are undisturbed.

d. "L", "CA" — Clear all. All registers and flags are cleared. Modes are returned to Power-On condition.

7. **Keyboard Error Corrections — Multiple Function Keys:** If the incorrect function key is depressed, the 7100 allows a form of recovery by permitting the second function key (or successive function key) to over-ride the preceding key or function. The last function key hit is the one remembered. This produces some interesting (and potentially useful) characteristics with respect to the hierarchy, as the following examples illustrate. (Note, in these examples "+" and "−" are interchangeable; "x" and "÷" are interchangeable; and "y^x" and "$\sqrt[x]{y}$" are interchangeable because each pair is at the same level of hierarchy.)

Key Sequence		Functional Sequence
A + B + −	equivalent to	A + B −
A + B + − + − +	" "	A + B +
A + B + X	" "	(A + B) X
A + B + X +	" "	A + B +
A + B Y^x +	" "	A + B +
A × B × +	" "	(A · B) +
A × B × Y^x	" "	(A · B) Y^x
A × B × X	" "	A · B ·
Etc.		

8. **Function Key followed by "=" Key**

Key Sequence		Function
A × =	equivalent to	A^2
A ÷ =	" "	1
A + =	" "	2A
A − =	" "	0
A Y^x =	" "	A^A
A $\sqrt[x]{Y}$ =	" "	$\sqrt[A]{A}$

9. **% Key Operation**

The % key does **not** contain an implied equals except during add on/subtract problems. It changes the displayed number to a percent by dividing by 100. There is one special sequence with the % key: $A \pm B \%$

This is the same as: $A \pm \dfrac{B}{100} \cdot A \to A \left(1 \pm \dfrac{B}{100}\right)$

This is for add-on, discount problems.

IV. **Keyboard Register Instructions**

A. Memory Operations

Key Sequence	Memory Operation
$\to M_i$, nn	The value of x is copied into Register M_{nn}, where nn has the range: $00 \leq nn \leq 36$.
M_i, nn	The value of Register M_{nn} is copied into X.
$X \leftrightarrow M_i$, nn	The values of X and Register M_{nn} are exchanged.
$\to M_i$, +, nn	The value of X is added to the value of m_{nn} and the result is stored in M_{nn}.
$\to M^i$, −, nn	The value of X is subtracted from the value of M^{nn}, and the result is stored in M_{nn}.

$\to M_i, \times, nn$	The value of X is multiplied by the value of M_{nn} and the product is stored in M_{nn}.
$\to M_i, \div, nn$	The value of M_{nn} is divided by the value of X and the quotient is stored in M_{nn}.

B. Working Register Instructions — Special Cases

Registers M_{35} and M_{36} (Y and X) are working registers. The following describes their operations:

Key Sequence	Register Operation
$\to M_i, 35$	$X \to Y$
$M_i, 35$	$Y \to X$
$X \leftrightarrow M_i, 35$ or "X $\leftrightarrow$ Y" Key $\Big\}$	$X \leftrightarrow Y$
$\to M_i, 36$	X rounded to DS $\to$ X
$M_i, 36$	N ∅ P
$X \leftrightarrow M_i, 36$	n ∅ P
$\to M_i, +, 35$	$X + Y \to Y$
$\to M_i, -, 35$	$Y - X \to Y$
$\to M_i, \times, 35$	$Y \cdot X \to Y$
$\to M_i, \div, 35$	$Y \div X \to Y$
$\to M_i, +, 36$	$X + Y \to X$
$\to M_i, -, 36$	$0 \to X$
$\to M_i, \times, 36$	$X^2 \to X$
$\to M_i, \div, 36$	$1 \to X$

V. Indirect Addressing

All the addressable registers may be used for indirect addressing. The sequences are as follows:

Key Sequence	Register Operation
$\to M_i, M_i, nn$	Store X (display) to register specified by contents of Register M_{nn} (integer part specifies Memory #)
M_i, M_i, nn	Recall to X (display) register specified by Register M_{nn}.
$X \leftrightarrow M_i, M_i, nn$	Exchange X with register specified by Register M_{nn}.
$\to M_i, +, M_i, nn$	Add X to Register specified by contents of Register
$\to M_i, M_i, +, nn$	M_{nn} — similarly for other memory operations.

VI. Indirect Addressing — GTØ and GTO LBL

Normal GTO Sequence:	GTØ nnn ← three digit address GTØ LBL nnn ↖ three digit label
Indirect Address Sequence:	GTØ, M_i, nn – Go to address specified by Memory nn GTØ, LBL, M_i, nn – Go to label specified by Memory nn.

VII. Error Modes

The 7100 makes attempts to provide the user with error information. If the user attempts to write to the stack when there is data for the hierarchy there, a warning will be given in the form: Error nn, where nn = error code. The user can then decide whether or not to heed the warning by use of the "If ERR" function key and a repeat of the intended sequence. Similarly, if the stack attempts to go into areas where data is stored, an error code is displayed. In no case, however, will the stack be permitted to exceed nine levels.

Where possible, the 7100 will generate results for error calculations; the user, by means of the "If ERR" key, can choose to use those results or abort. Only two functions are permitted after Error: "CE" and "If ERR", all others are ignored.

Some Notes From a True Calculator Design Pioneer

(R. Panholzer, EE Dept., Naval Postgrad School (NPS), Monterey, California 93940, one of the developers of the original algorithms of the 7100 offers: "some thoughts on the topic of calculators")

"It is unfortunate that most pocket calculators on the market today were shaped either by the "dollar sign" or by computer-oriented people.

Technology has, however, long since advanced to the point where calculator designs should be carried out with the user first and foremost in mind!

Typical pocket calculator users are high school and college students, technicians, engineers, and scientists, as well as a host of "non science" professional people. Users of the less sophisticated pocket calculators can be found in practically all walks of life.

The first exposure to a mathematical "language" everyone receives is in grade school, and later on in high school. The language algebra. We learn that $1 + 2 \times 3 = 7$, and not 9. We become familiar with the sequence in which two-variable operations in a more involved expression are carried out, in short, the concept of a mathematical hierarchy.

With millions of people all around the world being educated this way, it is surprising to see that even today other "languages" are found on calculators intended for the ordinary mortal; other languages such as Reverse Polish, Arithmetic, Psuedo-Algebraic. Let us not pollute the world of mathematics any further by adding more such languages!

The Ideal Calculator

One thing, the ideal calculator is **not** a computer. Its inner workings may (and usually do) resemble a computer structure, but the user should not have to concern himself with computer concepts like registers, stacks, etc.

What, then, are the features of our IDEAL calculator:

(1) The language: fully algebraic

A computation like $1 + 2 \times 3^4$ must have a keying sequence exactly like we write and show the correct result when we press = (correct result: 163)

(2) The "storing" and "recalling" of numbers should be viewed in mathematical terms. If we want to use a number in later computations, we would simply "give it a name" or a symbol mathematically. We would write $12 \rightarrow M$, which simply means we have assigned the symbol M to the number 12. Since we usually need many symbols, we distinguish them by the use of subscripts. To allow two-dimensional arrays of numbers (such as found in Matrix Algebra) we select a double-subscript notation. The statement $12 \rightarrow M_{23}$ would now mean that the number 12 was given the symbol M_{23}. Now we can write our formulas in truly algebraic form on the keyboard of our calculator

$$M_{23} + M_{13} \times M_{16}{}^{M_{17}} =$$

This concept is easily expandable: a payoff of "clean (mathematical) living." Let's try the following

$$\pi \rightarrow M_{12}$$
$$12 \rightarrow M_{23}$$

and now we write

$$M_{M_{23}}$$

We have used M_{23} as a subscript! Pressing the key sequence MM23 means I want M_{12} (which we assigned the value π) and π will appear in the display. This introduces the concept of "indirect addressing" as it is called by computer people in a purely mathematical fashion.

This points out another desirable property of our ideal calculator:

(3) The unsophisticated user should not be confused by features used only by the more advanced person. The indirect subscripting feature does **not** add another key, and becomes hidden to the uninitiated.

(4) Our calculator should be "forgiving." Any mistake in keying-in problems should be resolved if it can be done uniquely: forgetting to close a parenthesis before pressing = writing hyper-arc-sine or arc-by per-sin should be the same, etc.

(5) Ideally there should be only 1 switch: the ON-OFF switch. However, as programmability is added, an additional switch is acceptable. There should be **no** switch for setting DEGR. — RADS — GRADS, or for setting the format of the display. Why? The fewer switches the less a user will be confused. And, since a switch cannot be flipped by a program, the answer displayed could be in RADIANS, while the switch points to DEGR.

(6) Our ideal calculator should have no moving parts, which automatically makes it more reliable. This requirement is hard to meet with our present-day keyboard philosophy — users mount some tactile feedback on the keys. For programmable calculators, however, this means no motors to pull magnetic cards or tapes, for recording or reading programs.

Some Thoughts about the Ideal *Programmable* Calculator

(1) As technology moves on, the number of available program steps will be plentiful. The preoccupation with "saving progr. steps" by either selecting a step-conserving programming language or by resorting to "clever" programming tricks will finally become obsolete. What **is** important is the clarity of a program.

(2) We should be able to write a program from left to right: one "mathematical sentence" following another when comprising the solution to problem. Later, for documentation, any format that is convenient will do.

(3) Apart from the usual programming commands which allow unconditional and conditional branching, nesting of subroutines, etc. a sufficient number of flags and labels should be provided.

(4) Editing should be made as convenient as possible! Step by step viewing of a program forward and backward, insertion and deletion of steps, single step execution of the program, are all necessary features.

(5) Merged program steps (whenever feasible) should be provided to "package" key-stroke sequences that belong together.

Notes on the "7100" Qualities

The following points of the previous discussion of the "IDEAL" calculator are met by the 7100:

(1) Language

(2) The Key M_i and $\rightarrow M_i$ satisfy the math concept for "storing" and "recalling;" the 7100 has complete indirect subscripting capabilities!

(3) The layout of the 7100 satisfies this point to a large degree

(4) Can't answer in detail, but seems O.K.

(5) Satisfies the minimum number $ of switch requirements

(6) This is where the 7100 really stands out. Nobody else has that capability yet.

* * * * * *

Other features of interest:
— 10 pending operations possible
— Direct **and indirect** memory arithmetic with all registers
— All registers accessable (including the ones for the math. hierarchy)
— Direct **and indirect** addressing of program locations (steps), absolute and labeled. (This is a "mind-blower!")
— Automatic change of display format when mode switch is changed.

Advanced PPC Applications — HP-67/97 Alphanumerics

The Personal Programmable Calculator, PPC, is a microprocessor that has been ROM, read only memory, programmed to handle numbers in BCD, binary coded decimal, rather than binary as most computers do. The instruction set on the top of the line models is capable of handling an amazing array of complex and difficult problems. The programmability of these machines allows the user to be creative in program writing and most models on the market today have thousands of talented users developing programs.

Advanced applications of PPC's, however, involve more than the hardware, machine, or the software, programs. Applications of the PPC involve those uses of the calculator that go beyond the defined, designed, and intended use of the machine. A simple example to contrast applications with software is the use of the calculator to compute postage in a mail room. The postage rate tables are in the program and the user simply keys the weight and class of mail to get the postage. Another application of the machine would be to use the machine to check the calibration of the rate scale because it weighs exactly 9 ounces. Applications include software, but go beyond the normal restrictions of the defined instruction set. The following examples illustrate a few advanced applications of Hewlett-Packard calculators.

Making the HP-67 "talk". The HP-67 has two English *words* programmed into the machine to act as display prompts to tell the user something important. The first is ERROR, which appears whenever an improper operation is performed. The second is Crd which tells the user that the second half of a magnetic card should also be read and is a feature of the calculators *smart* card reader. The question that advanced HP-67 users ask is: Can the letters r, C, o, d, e, be made to appear in the display in any order and mixed with the digits 0-9 to make words? The answer is yes — with the right techniques. The addition of a quasi-alphanumeric display to programs adds a powerful new dimension to using the HP-67 and its printer companion, the HP-97. Questions and responses add life to programs. The moon rocket lander program, for example, is modified to show *ready* in the display when the *pilot* should key in his rocket BURN. A variation would be *I is ready*. Only a brief description of the technique is possible here.

The word or phrase is actually a special number that is stored in a data register and is recalled to the display. The special number is entered into the machine from a magnetic card that loads data into the machine's registers. The secret of the whole word/phrase concept lies in the generation of the special numbers which are best described as non-BCD numbers, or non-normalized-numbers, NNN's. The study and use of NNN's has been a favorite pastime for calculator enthusiasts ever since the first PPC, the HP-65, was introduced in January 1974. Hewlett-Packard does not discuss NNN's in their owners manual and won't provide information on them.

To produce the required NNN's that display the word/phrase users want, requires a knowledge of the internal codes used by the calculator to record program steps on magnetic cards. Through a long process of analysis using magna-see™ to *develop* the magnetic fields, and a magnifying glass, these codes have been broken. See *65 Notes,* January 1977, and following issues for full details. The technique used is to determine the codes that make each position of the display appear blank, 0-9, or r, C, o, d, E, press the calculator keys that place these codes — usually a nonsense sequence of keys, — into program memory, record these steps on a magnetic card, and read the card into the machine to place the program steps into data registers. The trick is to fool the calculator into reading program steps as data. This is done by keying write data, and reading the card with the special instructions on it. When the card is halfway through the machine, turn it off. Turn on again to finish reading the card. The display will show ERROR. The card, if you were lucky, had a data loader recorded on it followed by program steps. Reading the card a second time will cause the machine to load the special program sequence into the data registers. The display will show ERROR again, but the steps will be in the machine because of a design oversight of not clearing the data registers under this error condition.

The NNN's are now in the machine, and can be recalled to see if the "spelling" is right, etc. Arrange them in the registers as desired and record them for future use as regular data. Thousands of such words have been generated and recorded, 32 to a magnetic card — primary registers both sides of the card. Because the process of assembling the codes required, and converting them into keystrokes, and finally getting them into the machine is complex and time consuming users swap cards of words for use in programs.

Several coding forms, and decoding programs have been written to make the task easier and the whole process involves application, not just software.

The word/phrases that added excitement and wonder to HP-67 and HP-97 displays caused an interesting problem. HP-97 thermal printers turned on and not off when printing certain NNN's and literally went up in smoke. It is actually possible to write a program, load it into an HP-97, and have the machine self-destruct by the first person to come along and press the keys.

Programs like the HP poem which reads:

35 45 65 55	so raise a
Classics	glass boys
alas alas	ere ye
all are	also are
discarded.	recalled
Good	released
Soldiers	recycled or
dead early	obsolesced.

or the ticker tape display that comes across the display character by character from the right to read coca-cola or the HP commercial that says an HP-67 or 97 is a good deal. One program even presents a puppet show, which when viewed with the scenerio being read is startling in its dramatic portrayal of a large creature chasing a smaller one, devouring him and smiling, saying "is so good." One particularly good program converts the HP-67 into an interactive terminal that answers questions and performs 13 special functions. The machine is given one of three personalities, Gerold, Ida or Ella, by reading the respective data card. The program uses another applications technique, the Rausch keyboard overlay which associates three letters with each number and allows fast, convenient entering of English words to be processed by a program. An interesting story is told by the user who was demonstrating the Gerold & Ida program to a secretary who was told to ask the machine a question. A phone call called the HP-67 owner away for a moment and when he returned he found the girl red faced and astounded. What happened, he asked. She said that she had keyed in climax, and she showed him the calculator which had responded with "yes baby."

HP-97 Graphics. The HP-97 printer burn-out problem was soon isolated to a problem with a certain character, the E. Additionally, the discovery that the letters r, C, o, d, E would print ., −, +, *, blank, and blank, opened the door to another series of advanced applications that are called HP-97 special graphics. Using the proper NNN's allow any combination of the digits and special symbols.

The first use of the now acceptable displays intended for printing on HP-97 printers was horizontal 1″ high banners that printed messages from magnetic cards mailed to friends.

All kinds of vertical and horizontal alphabets, special symbols, etc. have been developed. Histograms and 12 level curve plotting is possible.

The Black Box. The process of making the NNN's required for the advanced applications described above is greatly simplified by using the HP-67 black box. This home-made box is simply a variable resistor short circuited by a push button switch. The box is plugged into the HP-67 and the button pressed to add the resistance in series with the battery to provide a momentary drop in voltage. If the resistance is adjusted properly, the calculator display will show many strange combinations of letters, numbers, and decrementing counters — another use of NNN's. With the HP-67 in w/PRGM mode the button is pressed until 000 84 appears in the display. This special mode allows the user to key the special codes directly into the secondary registers. Word/phrase/ graphics NNN's may be keyed into the machine and recorded on magnetic cards by the thousands. The Black Box is easy to build, costs less than $10 and cannot hurt the calculator. See *65 Notes,* June 1977, V4N5 for details.

"Black Box" for the HP-67/97 Alphanumerics

The above examples illustrate the activities of advanced users of PPC's. All machines have their "hidden capabilities" that are unknown to all but members of calculator clubs that exist for all PPC's. The development of these applications represent the collective work of many club members but the basic work in HP-67 word/phrases was done by Lou Cargile of Texarkana, AK based partially on work done by David Kemper of Northridge, CA. Major HP-97 graphics studies were done by Mark Snitily of Seattle, WA, based in part on Lou Cargile's work withNNN's. The Council of Personal Programmable Calculator Users Organizations lists the following clubs.

Council of Personal Programmable Calculator Users Organizations (CPPCUO)

Member Organizations

Organization:	HP-65 Users Club.
Membership:	1200
Machines supported:	HP-25, 25C, 55, 67, 97.
Publication:	65 NOTES
Editor:	Richard J. Nelson (714) 639-7810
Published:	Monthly since June 1974
Address:	2541 W. Camden Place
	Santa Ana, CA 92704
	U.S.A.

Organization:	MICAC (Mikro-Taschen-computer Anwender-club).
Membership:	800
Machines supported:	HP-25, 25C, 65, 67, 97; SR-52, 56, TI-57, 58, 59.
Publication:	display
Editor:	Heinrich Schnepf (0221) 502676
Published:	Bi-monthly since June 1975
Address:	Buchenweg 24
	D 5000 Koeln 40
	West Germany

Organization:	SR-52 Users Club.
Membership:	700
Machines supported:	SR-52, 56
Publication:	52-NOTES
Editor:	Richard C. Vanderburgh (513) 255-6502
Published:	Monthly since June 1976
Address:	9459 Taylorsville Road
	Dayton, OH 45424
	U.S.A.

Organization:	The National 7100 Users Club.
Membership:	Organizational
Machines supported:	7100
Publication:	The National News-letter
Editor:	Dean Lampman (513) 793-7000
Published:	First issue: November 1976*
Address:	5440 Cooper Road
	Cincinnati, OH 45242
	U.S.A.

Address for the Council is: CPPCUO 2220 S. Anne Street, Santa Ana, CA 92704

Summary: . . . And the Move Forward

Advanced Programmable Calculators: What Software and Peripherals Can Do

The programmable calculator has proven to be the ideal choice for many types of engineering systems. The magnitude of possible applications, especially when the portability of the systems are considered, makes the market for software development for every application conceivable a gigantic one. Most standard software is provided to users for general data acquisition and also for the more common calculations. But many end users want to tailor the software for their own requirements. Thus, the ease-of-programming characteristic of most calculators is almost mandatory for all types of systems. In addition, the user-definable key design procedures allow the users to essentially customize the systems with great software variety. Many full processing systems maintain the economic advantages associated with calculators by providing this flexibility for less than $300 and $700. Thus the era of reasonably priced programmable systems has just begun. More capability for the same price or less cost is the direction and dimension of these systems. These new systems of computer power and versatility in today's programmable calculators clearly show that the microcomputer-based products have grown up and out, all over the world. The micro is the heart and brain of these advanced systems. And the input (keys) and output (display and printer) and case provide the means to hold and carry the hardware to wherever an information system task may be.

The latter portion of this chapter shows that the latest calculators have *real* commercial computer power. They are programmed to perform cost analysis, billing, inventory and production control. They are often programmed for problems which are unique to specific companies. Printer hand units will soon use the computer language BASIC which can be learned in a week, and there is practically no limit to the number of programs that can be used as long as they are not too long or complex. They avoid the need for *inhouse* programmers or the long wait to *get on* the large company computers. Costs range in the $200 — $300 per month areas even for very sophisticated systems, but we will note ahead that some desk-top products cost only $1800 to $3000.

Many advanced programmable calculator users will quickly step up to units with larger visual display screens and larger *memories*. These become in effect *intelligent* computer terminals or true minicomputers in the form of terminals. Accountants and managers are then able to *view* stored information and problem solutions in seconds. Most computing *calculators* are able to control wide ranges of peripheral equipment, such items as: plotters, CRT *face* copiers, printers, "key-prompting" or *ball point* pen input devices. And they can be accessed remotely over normal telephone lines.

Programmables as Primary Tools for All Engineers

No longer must all engineers confront themselves with company machine-language computer programming. Today's advanced calculators feature languages oriented to ease of usage and structured to reduce the cost of learning. Engineers typically find the BASIC language or close derivatives not only easy to learn and master, but also pleasantly conversational. Contrasted with slower methods using paper annotations and repetitive manipulations with less powerful tools, many examples ahead demonstrate the tremendous power of advanced calculators. Most show the time savings possible when solving complex calculations and, of course, there are attendant increases in numerical accuracy.

Programming calculators also possess considerable learning capacity that results in increased flexibility of use. In contrast with preprogrammed calculators, programmable machines are characterized by operator-generated software, most often consisting of many variables, looping statements and testing functions. On some of the desktop calculator systems noted ahead, the design engineer applications provide good examples. Interacting with the calculator, the design engineer typically generates his program via the keyboard, or he loads a canned software program from magnetic cards, mag tape, cassette, or even by calling up a program from a peripheral high-speed disk memory. The designer can interact with a calculator by observing peripheral outputs of plotters or by modifying circuit parameters upon displayed program requests. Should he be confronted with a big number-crunching problem, calculators are now available with memory capacities of up to 64k bytes of read/write memory (R/W) and several 32k byte segments of read-only memory (ROM).

Expandable Fingertip Problem-Solving Power

The calculators in the various desk-top series ahead are ready to take on very tough problems — no matter what math form those problems may take. Most users think of them as personal computing systems. Most of the companies offer a variety of peripherals and options which let users custom-tailor systems to fit specific needs. If users need a lot of storage, they add a random access disk, on some units, with 32,768 storage registers. For on-line work, many systems offer various interfaces which let users tie calculators directly to 90% of all scientific instruments on the market.

Like a computer, advanced calculators operate with lightning speed. Like a computer, most can execute highly sophisticated programs involving looping, branching, and multi-level subroutines. Unlike a computer, these systems offer instantaneous turnaround, ease of operation, and low initial cost which can be rapidly amortized. These *systems* will fit on top of a desk and can be operated without special programming experience.

For practically any small operation, a less than $2500 unit can be a smart and economical alternative to a computer. If firms are computer users or owners, advanced calculators still make a lot of sense: users can slash their terminal time and streamline their work flow by turning over many of the computer's chores to the instantly accessible calculators.

Power to Meet Increasing Needs

To insure maximum value to the user, a programmable calculator should offer maximum expandability. Although users buy calculators to meet their present needs, they still have an eye on the future. Therefore, their calculators should have room for internal and external expandability sufficient to keep pace with increasing demands. This expandability is not only practical, but economical as well; it lets users buy the power they need at the time they need it. Expandability is a strong characteristic of advanced systems, and all desired modifications can usually be made without sending the unit back to the factory. Constructed with highly reliable integrated circuits, these systems offer many desirable features:

- Easily programmed via keyboard
- Programs stored on magnetic tape cassettes for speed and convenience
- Many special function keys which may be custom-programmed by the user to execute operations which are frequently used. These keys may also be used to address storage registers, subroutines, etc.

To facilitate customizing, the various desk-top systems are divided into two major classes: those whose memories can be expanded both externally and internally, and those whose capabilities can be expanded with communications and the BASIC language.

Many users start with the basic units, then add power. An output writer will enable users to put results in practically any format they want: company forms, contracts-ledger sheets, etc. When there are mountains of data to be analyzed, users appreciate various high-speed printers which list answers as fast as they can be calculated. Whatever peripherals users choose, they are generally assured of high standards of design and service. And with many wide ranges of peripherals, the capability of these systems is practically unlimited in meeting not only users present needs, but also most foreseeable future needs.

The next section of the book marks a distinct division and new orientation because the material to follow, with but a few exceptions, relates specifically to calculator systems and not calculating units. Each analysis of the main calculator products is also concerned with its main unit but as part of an actual or potential system that offers hard copy or exterior input and/or output. The phrase *hard copy* is used because this type of output can be and usually is paper or some printed or magnetized media. Such media as input or output is optional but the capability is present and available. Oftentimes, however, the user may not elect to use it, if a record is not needed or desirable. We will note that many of the desk top calculator systems to be reviewed have input and output as magnetic tape cassettes or cartridges, that practically all these main calculating units can be programmed (instructed) to develop printouts using either line or matrix printers, and that many of them can direct or control typewriters, display terminals (such as Cathode Ray Tubes — CRTs), plotters, voice-answer-back, disks and other peripheral devices. Thus, these type calculators are, in essense, the primary parts of programmable calculating systems or true computing systems.

Oftentimes when students or new users of calculator systems are concerned about possible difficulties related to mastry of these devices they require a bit of a push — or better, some pragmatic motivation. Most students, businessmen, industrialists, and professionals well realize that the world is rapidly turning into *fields of automated information retrieval* that must be controlled by individuals. And most also realize that sooner or later they must become involved with these systems — not as witnesses or bystanders but as personal controllers of the devices and operations. A great many of the more than 100 million calculator users already perceive that programs — or software — will be the top priority use item. The users of advanced hand-held programmable calculators are already well aware of the tricks of simple programming — the use of flags, registers, memories, subroutines, etc. But, as the reader has noted in the latter sections of this chapter, it is obvious that the really great capabilities of the newer units, the National 7100, for example, are related to peripherals and exterior memories. These are in the form of ROMs, PROMs, file and memory cartridges, tape cassettes, etc. To be really informed and ready users must be aware of and able to intelligently purchase, purposefully utilize and readily expand his or her personal capabilities with these devices. Because much of the versatility of these *ready-made* or easy-to-prepare media devices relate to memory or program control, they are called alternately either software or *firmware,* depending upon the ease of alterability.

Firmware products more distinctly relate to some types of programming built into ROM, e.g., fixed logic as a part of control sections of calculators or computers, or various other microprogrammable circuitry systems that can be added to or removed from calculators, microcomputers, minis or standard computing systems. In this book, firmware, as related to calculators will be concerned with ROM that generally becomes either an integral part of or an extension of programming capability or specific control appendages to various calculating units. With firmware, users can tailor calculators to their specific application. Firmware changes or adds to customizing the capability of calculator systems. It makes software (media programs) adaptable and more efficient; and processing faster and more useful. Firmware is like hardware; it becomes part of a calculator, makes it different from others. Its form can develop near-absolute protection for proprietary software because routines are made *hard*. It has the flexibility of software with the advantages of hardware, but no new hardware need be bought. More about ROM — plug-in control and programmable ROM, on pages ahead. . .

A General Statement on Software Variety — for Small Systems

System Software: An office executive coordinates the staff. A computer needs an executive to coordinate all the equipment in its system. It's called an Operating System (OS), Executive, or System Software. In nearly all small computers — and many large ones — control is accomplished by programs stored in the main memory. The drawbacks are that a substantial part of expensive memory is taken up with routine, non-productive functions. The executive software in the machine automatically does the execution and controls the tape drive, typewriter, printer, card reader, and so forth. Software for special equipment, such as the Plotter, or Modem, is often contained in the pre-programmed, plug-in ROM's described earlier.

Applications Software: To make sure a system starts to work the moment it lands on a desk, suppliers can provide users with packaged solutions for a host of problems. They generally have packages for Finance, Structural Engineering, Statistics, Electronic Engineering, Mathematics, Education, and many more. Depending on needs, users can buy one program to solve one particular problem. Or they can get an entire library that will take care of most of the problems in their business.

Specialty Software: Most enterprises will have problems that are unique to their particular operation. With the simplified programming and operation of calculators, users can most probably develop their own programs — or modify existing programs — to take care of their needs.

If, however, the do-it-yourself approach would require an inordinate allocation of resources, suppliers offer three alternatives:

First, the supplier **Software Team.** They have a problem-solving background in many disciplines and, in most cases, they can take care of problems for a modest charge. Field Engineers dig into users problems and help find the best solution.

Second, members of **User Groups** become part of a big family. A family with interests ranging from putting men on the moon to putting dollars on the bottom line. Chances are good they've encountered problems similar to most. They get together, through newsletters, magazines, and club meetings, for an exchange of ideas.

Finally are services and programs available from **Commercial Software** houses and from universities. Users can purchase programs, usually for nominal fees, from their libraries.

CHAPTER 7

THE STEP-UP TO DESK-TOP
COMPUTING CALCULATOR SYSTEMS

PROLOGUE

We now cover two of the least complicated and lowest cost advanced desk-top calculators, the Victor 4900 and the Texas Instruments SR-60A, power step-ups from hand-held units. As will be noted on pages ahead, some of the calculator manufacturers have moved quite rapidly into the small business computer areas, leaving the *pure* calculator markets for the others. The Tektronix 4051 system employs an 11-inch diagonal CRT storage tube with graphics and alphanumerics but keeps the highly advantageous calculator-like keyboard. The Wang 2200S is a similar *terminal-based* calculator upgrade with practical total computer capability while retaining ease of use calculator characteristics. Many microcomputers now imitate the Olivetti P6060, HP 9825 and 9830, the Sharp PC-2600 and others that now routinely use disks and/or exterior ROMs. And most of these either already have BASIC language capabilities or will soon be so equipped, usually with some redesign and a BASIC interpreter in ROM. It becomes quickly obvious to observers that disk-expandable memory, BASIC language capabilities, interface utilization of terminals, typewriters, plotters, and other I/O devices, sensors, and instruments are essential characteristics of truly competitive advanced calculator systems.

It is equally true that these *computing* calculator systems are built on microcomputer *chip* technology. The strategy seems to be, and it appears to be a strong and successful one, to stay with what customers desire most — simplicity of operation. This means the use of *comfortable* calculator keyboard system design; calculator operational languages (with the *addition* of BASIC for those who want it), and the fulfillment of customer demand for the add-on availability of *snap-in* extra memory *segments* using low-cost tape and disk media or ROM/RAM/PROM devices. And, as noted several times in these pages, microcomputer suppliers seeking sales directly to end users have now quickly turned to calculator-type keyboards, and in several cases, the use of calculators themselves as entry devices for speed and procedure simplicity. The 100 million *plus* calculators now in the hands of users throughout the world have lead and continue to *push and pull* all types of engineers, businessmen, professionals, students and teachers into the *computer* world as they trade up from their first-used four-function machines, then simple programmables, to the ultimate personal use *computing* calculator — hand-held or desk-top — *system*.

Tektronix, Inc. was one of the first to note that users are indeed replacing minicomputers with their Model 31 programmable calculator. Many began using their 31/53 calculator instrumentation system. Many other users began ordering the 31/10 graphic calculator that uses the 4010 graphics terminal; the 4661 digital plotter and the 4922 flexible disk memory. Tektronix didn't wait long to offer even more capability.

The Price Comparison — Cost Effectiveness Analysis Problems

Price comparisons are most difficult because of varying discounts, product quality, manufacturer warranties and service reputations, peripherals availability and costs, and differing applications needs. Adding more problems for evaluations by potential purchasers are the sudden changes in basic unit prices. The TI SR-60A has quite obviously taken over price leadership at $1995 (late 1977), and its performance, and expandability features are highly commendable. But, with extra cost extended memory, how does it compare to the Victor 4900 at about $2300, or the HP 9815A at $2900, or the Tek E31 at about $2500, and it goes on. By the same most difficult dollar function reasoning or comparative *performance* evaluating, the Olivetti P6060 with disk, at about $6000 to $8000 vs. several disk-based micro systems at *under $10,000* must compare to HP's 9825A at $5900 (without disk option) or Tektronix 4051 (BASIC for graphics) at less than $7000; and all these prices are extremely volatile. In mid-1976, for example, HP cut its price for the 9830A by 30%, and with the consistently falling component (especially memory) prices and increased capability of microcomputer chips, price unpredictability is the only rule. How much more value is obtained from Tektronix's big screen 4051 system over the more expensive 5-inch screen of IBM's 5100 *personal computer* system? How much extra does the HP9825A's *live* keyboard provide? It allows the user to perform simple calculations, examine and change variables, and list programs while the calculator is performing other operations.

For some users, the addition of BASIC language capability is very fundamental, expanding future owner-developed software capability far beyond what non-BASIC calculators offer. But, other smaller system users simply do not need this capability, and they dislike or will refuse to pay for a capability they do not want or will not use. How important is *super* speed to some calculator users? It is of minor value to some but of major significance to others. Thus, it behooves each potential calculator purchaser to make deep and *our best use* evaluations of all products available. Only then will they be able to make the best decision as regards individual use and specific pragmatic criteria. The pages ahead are designed to be of some assistance not only to make proper evaluations but to establish the differences between models and brands and to designate some of the operating characteristics and procedures associated with most of the highly competitive systems. Advice: be wary of extravagant claims; be thorough and objective in analyses.

The Hardware of Two Typical Low Cost Advanced Programmable Systems: The Victor 4900 and the TI SR-60.

Victor Electronic Programmable Printing Calculators* — Basically, three programmable models of Programmable Electronic Printing Calculators head the Victor line of modern machines. They are all similar in their design and function, but vary in numbers of registers and programs steps (see chart).

---

* Much of the discussion following represents excerpts and summaries of material in the Victor program and system manuals, with permission from Victor Comptometer Corp., Chicago, Illinois.

Programing data storage ranges from 128 to as many as 1792 steps. This allows economical purchasing by fitting the specific calculator to the needs of the job. We are concerned with the Victor 4900.

The Victor 4900 is a programmable desk-top calculator with the capabilities of: 14 digit accuracy; alphanumeric printing; programming either from the keyboard or with an internal card reader of up to 1792 steps; easy insertion and deletion of program steps; program listing; automatic and single step tracing; three working registers, two accumulating registers, alphanumeric buffer register, and up to 200 data storage registers; up to 100 program codes (tags); indirect addressing of registers; full complement of arithmetic, calendar, and mathematical functions, and 10 user definable keys.

Calculator Operation

Capacity and range: 14 digits (plus algebraic sign and decimal point); 1×10^{-13} to $9.9999999999999 \times 10^{13}$; overflow indication.

Numerical entry: $0 - 9$, ·, change sign, clear entry.

Arithmetic functions: Add, subtract, subtotal, total, multiply, divide, percent, square root; constant operation

Decimal system: Floating point; decimal set and round off controls.

Keyboard registers: Entry (K), accumulating (A), product (W), memory one (M1) and memory two (M2).

Memory arithmetic functions: Add, subtract, accumulate products, store, recall and clear.

Printer controls: Print/non-add, paper feed.

Hardwired functions: Calendar (200 year range): Days between dates, resulting date.

Logarithmic: Natural log, common log, antilog (base e), raise to a power, and reciprocal.

Trigonometric: Sin, cos, tan, arcsin, arccos, arctan, and enter Pi.

Manipulative: Shift decimal point, integer/fraction split, absolute value and truncate.

Adding Machine Operation

Active functions: Add, subtract, subtotal, total, clear entry (all other keys electronically locked out).

Decimal system: Automatic insertion of decimal point during numeral entry.

Physical dimensions: 15½ in. × 12⅜ in. × 6⅝ in. (39.7 cm × 31.7 cm × 17.0 cm). Weight: 25 lbs. (11.3 kg.).

Input (Keyboard)

Standard 10 key pad designed for touch operation; raised execute (I/ +) key; alternate execute (II/ −) key; negative entry (change sign) key; 10 User Definable Keys (with removable application label).

Output (Printer)

Line length: 30 characters (10 characters/in.).
Printing rate: 90-200 lines per minute.
Line spacing: 6 lines per inch.
Character set: A-Z, 0-9, −, /, ;, „ blank,), !, @, #, $, %, ¢, &, *, (, +, ?, ", :, =, ÷, ‖, ⦀.
Character format: 5 × 7 dot matrix; 0. 1 inch high.
Multiple copies: 4 maximum (form thickness not to exceed .006 in.).
Maximum duty cycle: 1000 full lines (30 characters) over any 30 minute period at 25° C (77° F).
Ribbon: 2 color (red/black is standard).
Standard paper roll: 3⁷/₁₆ in. (max.) wide by 175 feet (approx.) long.

Internal Program Data Storage

A total of 1792 bytes of semiconductor memory can be organized (by the programmer) into desired allocations of program steps and data registers. One data register is equivalent to 8 program steps:
Minimum program steps: 192
Maximum program steps: 1792
Minimum data registers: 0
Maximum data registers: 200 (14 digits, algebraic sign and decimal point.)

Typical Memory Allocations:

Program steps	1792	1392	992	592	192
Data registers	0	50	100	150	200

External Program Data Storage

A built-in manually loaded, magnetic recording device permits reproduction, and subsequent reading, of any part of the internal program/data memory. The external storage medium is a magnetic card. The magnetic card size is approximately 2 in. × 5 in. and contains one magnetic surface and one writable surface for identification:

Capacity: 512 bytes per magnetic card (each magnetic card can store 2 separate blocks of information; a single block can store either 256 bytes of program memory or the contents of up to 32 data registers).

Cycle speed: Reading requires approximately 1½ seconds per block; recording requires approximately 3 seconds per block.

Safeguards: In order to achieve reliable operation, the following features are designed into the system:

- automatic verification of program or data when reading and recording magnetic cards.
- ERROR indication after 3 automatic attempts to read or record a block of information.
- ERROR indication if magnetic card is not properly seated for accurate reading or recording.

• Permanent protection against inadvertent destruction or alteration of programs/data stored on magnetic cards.

Programable Instruction Set

In addition to all of the calculator functions, there is a powerful repertoire of computer-like instructions that can be assembled in the program memory:

direct register arithmetic — all memory arithmetic functions can be performed by any data register. In addition, there are instructions for incrementing (+ 1) and decrementing (− 1) any data register.

indirect register addressing — using any data register as an "index" register, all memory arithmetic functions can be performed in another register, the specific address of which is specified by the contents of the "index" register.

direct program addressing — any location in the program memory can be addressed by directly specifying the program memory location.

symbolic program addressing — utilizing up to 99 different "tags", program addresses can be indirectly specified by the program memory locations of the various "tags".

unconditional jumping — by utilizing either direct or indirect addressing schemes, the normal program flow can be altered with jump instructions.

conditional jumping and skipping — the normal flow can be altered with a set of conditional jumping (to a specified program memory address or tag location) and skipping (past the next instruction) instructions. The algebraic state of the active register (K or A), the mathematical relationship between the K and A registers, and whether or not the *EX* key is depressed can be tested.

Subroutines

In order to reuse certain common sections of a program, sequencing of instructions can be constructed such that the system automatically does the housekeeping that is required to keep track of program flow. Utilizing either the direct or the symbolic addressing schemes, all unconditional and conditional jump instructions have counterpart "subroutine jump" instructions. Upon execution of the subroutine jump instructions, the system remembers the program memory location at which the program flow should resume when a "return" instruction terminates the subroutine.

Subroutines may be nested up to 5 levels. The 5 return addresses are remembered in a first-in/last out memory stack. An additional instruction that enables the most recent address to be discarded is available. When it is desired to "skip" the instruction location at a return address, this can be done using an appropriate instruction.

Read/Write Data

Up to 32 data registers can be recorded on a magnetic card by specifying the address of the first register to be recorded, as well as the exact number of registers to be recorded. Similarly, a read instruction may be programmed.

Printing Instructions

Numeric data can be printed, according to the decimal setting, under the following formats: "ENT" symbol, "%" symbol "Pnn" symbol (00 ≤ nn ≤ 99), date (M/DD/YYYY), "$" symbol, and left justified.

Alphanumeric messages can be loaded from the program memory into a 30 character print buffer which can be printed either by itself or with the contents of the keyboard register.

Program Editing

Programmed instructions can be changed; instructions can be inserted and deleted with automatic renumbering of all instructions; the program/data memory can be dumped in the form of a sequential listing of instructions or the contents of all non-zero data registers; selective listing of the locations of all print, halt and program jumping instructions.

Application Programs

Victor maintains a library from which application programs can be ordered. Also, custom programming service is available on a contract basis.

Operating Characteristics of Model 4900

Keyboard, Accumulating and Working Registers: proper operation of the Model 4900 requires insight into the type of registers available for working with numbers. Also, the interaction between these registers should be understood by the operator in order to make efficient use of the many time saving features designed into the Model 4900.

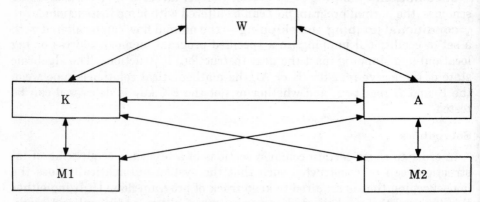

The diagram above indicates the interaction of the Keyboard, Accumulating and Working Registers in the Model 4900. All entries made with the numeral entry keys are contained in the KEYBOARD register (or K-register). In addition, most calculated results are contained in the K-register.

The ACCUMULATING register (or A-register) contains the accumulated results of addition and subtraction calculations.

Multiplication and division calculations use the WORKING register (or W-register).

Active Register: the interaction of the K, A and W registers is based on a unique principle which employs the concept of an "active" register. For many common applications, your understanding of the register "activity" will save you valuable time and reduce your chance of error. This understanding will come after you closely study many of the examples in this manual.

Register Capacity: all of the registers in the Model 4900 have the same capacity. You can work with numbers having up to 14 digits without exceeding the register capacity. In the event an entry or calculated result does exceed the 14 digit capacity, this "overflow" condition will be indicated by the ERROR lamp.

Each register maintains the proper decimal point location, as well as the algebraic sign of the number it contains.

Keyboard Memory Registers: in addition to the K, A and W registers, the Model 4900 has 2 accumulating memories which you can use to save time in many applications. These registers are referred to as MEMORY ONE (or M1) and MEMORY TWO (or M2). Whenever either of these memories are "in use," the appropriate indicator lamps will be lit.

Data Memory Registers: up to 200 additional data registers are available. You can store and recall numbers from the keyboard whenever applications require their use. The contents of the data memory registers can be stored on magnetic cards using the magnetic card reader/recorder.

Power-On Conditions: when the Model 4900 is turned ON, all registers are cleared to zero, and the decimal control will automatically be set at 2. The printer will signify that power has been restored to the unit by printing 0.00 CC on the paper tape.

In the event that power is accidentally removed, or if the required line voltage falls below minimum, the contents of all registers will be lost. When power is restored, the printing of 0.00 CC will indicate the establishment of the power-ON condition.

Decimal and Roundoff Controls: the Model 4900's decimal system provides floating point results in most calculations. When it is necessary to secure results which have been rounded off (or truncated), the rounding (or truncation) will occur at whatever decimal setting you have selected. The number of decimal digits (digits occurring to the right of the decimal point) can be selected from the keyboard.

The following flowchart describes what happens at each step of a typical program:

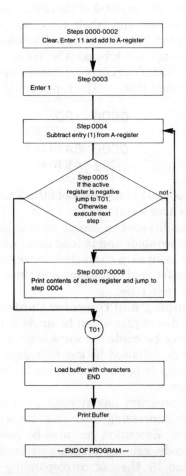

Remembering that the lefthand column printed during a trace execution is always the contents of the active register and that if the active register is negative the entire line will print in red, one may run a trace by setting mode selector to TRC and depressing 0 +/I. The last part of the trace in red should look like this:

```
1- 0004   -
1- 0005*J- T01
1- 0011    T01
1- 0012 AST
1- 0013 #E
1- 0014 #N
1- 0015 #D
1- 0016 ATM
1- 0017*PBB
```
END
```
1- 0019  RT9
```

This is the first time during the execution of the program that the active register has been negative when the jump to tag if minus instruction was executed at step 0005. Whereas before the program flow continued with step 0007, this time it continued with step 0011 identified by T01. It would be very instructive if you would compare the trace to the flow chart step by step.

Other Special Capabilities of the Victor 4900

Alphanumeric Labeling

An outstanding feature of the 4900 is its ability to be programed to print written operating instructions and labels for inputs and outputs. Let's start by rewriting the program so that the halts are labeled: ENTER A, ENTER B and ENTER C; and the output is labeled ANSWER:.

Set MODE selector to PRG. Depress 0 +/I followed by C/ALL. So far it is the same as before. Now depress P/# · . The tape should look like this:

```
0000  PG

0000 CA
0001 AST
```

The AST to the right of 0001 is the symbol for the alpha start instruction, a single step instruction whose keystrokes are P/# · . When this instruction is executed, the 4900 is conditioned to accept succeeding instructions as codes for letters, numbers, and symbols and to load them into the buffer register for subsequent printing. Up to 30 such characters representing a full line of printing can be held in the buffer register at any one time. Each alpha instruction is a numerical two-keystroke code.

Subroutine Direct Jumping and Operator Controlled Branching

Just as unconditional direct jumps can be made both to step locations and tags, subroutine jumps can be made the same way. The keystrokes for a subroutine direct jump are S_D followed by the four digits representing the step number to which the jump is being made. This instruction always occupies two steps of program memory.

When execution of a program has stopped at a halt instruction, execution can be resumed by depressing +/I. This causes execution to start at the very next instruction. Execution can also be resumed by depressing J_T followed by a two digit code, causing program execution to start at the point in the program identified by the tag corresponding to the two digit code.

If there is no such tag in program memory, the ERROR indicator will light.
Subroutine Nesting

Actually up to five step numbers for RTO instructions can be stored at any one time. These step numbers are used on a last in-first out basis—the most recent one being the one used and erased by the execution of an RTO instruction.

This means that up to five subroutines—but no more—can be "nested"—one within another. The RTO instruction for a UDK subroutine counts as a subroutine return for nesting purposes.

Two Memory Application — Average Markup

Many applications require the use of both keyboard memories (M1 and M2). The MEMORY TWO key enables you to perform all of the memory functions (MRC, MR, M+, M−, =, + and = −) in Memory 2. When you want to perform an operation in Memory 2, press the MEMORY TWO key followed by the desired memory function key. The selection of Memory 2 for the next memory function is indicated by the green M2 SEL lamp which lights when the MEMORY TWO key is pressed. Upon the execution of the desired memory function the M2 SEL lamp will turn off, indicating that subsequent memory functions will apply to Memory 1. If the M2 SEL light is on, pressing the MEMORY TWO key will turn it off without executing a memory operation.

Qty.	Price Ea.	Cost Ea.	Price Amt.	Cost Amt.
2	$3.55	$1.75	$ 7.10	$ 3.50
4	1.85	.98	7.40	3.92
12	4.95	2.90	59.40	34.80
			73.90	42.22

$$\text{Average markup} = \frac{73.90 - 42.22}{73.90} \times 100\% = 42.87\%$$

	Display			K	A	W	M1	M2
SET·C ALL	0.00 CA	.2		0.00	0.00	0.00	0.00	0.00
	2 X		×	2	0.00	2	0.00	0.00
	3.55 =+ 7.10		=+	7.10	0.00	2	7.10	0.00
	1.75 =+ 3.50	2	M2 =+	3.50	0.00	2	7.10	3.50
	4 X ·		×	4	0.00	4	7.10	3.50
	1.85 =+ 7.40		=+	7.40	0.00	4	14.50	3.50
	0.98 =+ 3.92	2	M2 =+	3.92	0.00	4	14.50	7.42
	12 X		×	12	0.00	12	14.50	7.42
	4.95 =+ 59.40		=+	59.40	0.00	12	73.90	7.42
	2.90 =+ 34.80	2	M2 =+	34.80	0.00	12	73.90	42.22
MRC	73.90 MC			73.90	0.00	12	0.00	42.22
÷	73.90 ÷			73.90	0.00	73.90	0.00	42.22
+	73.90 +			73.90	73.90	73.90	0.00	42.22
M2 MRC	42.22 MC2			42.22	73.90	73.90	0.00	0.00
−	42.22 −			42.22	31.68	73.90	0.00	0.00
EX	31.68 EX			73.90	0.00	31.68	0.00	0.00
%	73.90 % 42.87			42.87	73.90	73.90	0.00	0.00

Applications Using Data Memory Registers

The Model 4900 has 200 independent data memory registers which can be used to store numbers such as constants or intermediate results. At any time during a calculation you can recall the contents of any data memory register into the K-register for further processing.

The data memory registers have 3 digit addresses numbered from 000 to 199. When you want to store the contents of the active register (K or A) in a specific data memory register, press the DATA STORE key DS; then, using the numeral entry keys, enter the 3 digits of the register address.

You can recall the contents of any one of the 200 data memory registers into the K-register by pressing the DATA RECALL key DR followed by entering the 3 digits that specify the desired register's address.

If you attempt to specify a register address greater than 199, the ERROR lamp will light indicating an illegal operation. In the event you started a data storage or recall operation and wish to cancel it prior to entering the last digit of the register address, pressing the CLEAR key will cause the previous keystrokes to be ignored; however, the active register will not be cleared.

If a program has been stored in the Model 4900 memory, you should exercise caution when using data memory registers. Consult the user documentation supplied with the program to determine which registers are available. In general, use the lowest address possible when attempting to store numbers in data memory registers.

Application Using Data Memory Registers — Cost Estimating

Repeated calculation of production lot cost according to a cost equation provides an example of using the data memory registers to store constants to avoid unnecessary keyboard entries.

Example
Cost = 3.72 + .57 (quantity) + .71 (mat'l. thickness)

Keys	Display		K	A	W	M1	M2
SET	.2						
C AlI	0.00 CA		0.00	0.00	0.00	0.00	
	3.72 S001	DS 0 0 1	3.72	0.00	0.00	0.00	
	0.57 S002	DS 0 0 2	.57	0.00	0.00	0.00	
	0.71 S003	DS 0 0 3	.71	0.00	0.00	0.00	
Lot A quan. = 12 mat'l. thickness = ¼" Cost = $10.74							
DR 0 0 1	3.72 R001		3.72	0.00	0.00	0.00	
M+	3.72 M+		3.72	0.00	0.00	3.72	
DR 0 0 2	0.57 R002		.57	0.00	0.00	3.72	
X	0.57 X		.57	0.00	.57	3.72	
	12 =+	=+					
	6.84		6.84	0.00	.57	10.56	
DR 0 0 3	0.71 R003		.71	0.00	.57	10.56	
X	0.71 X		.71	0.00	.71	10.56	
	0.25 =+	=+					
	0.18		.18	0.00	.71	10.74	
MC	10.74 MC		10.74	0.00	.71	0.00	

NOT USED

Lot B quan. = 28   mat'l. thickness = ⅜"   Cost = $19.95

Keys	Display					
DR 0 0 1	3.72 R001		3.72	0.00	0.00	0.00
M+	3.72 M+		3.72	0.00	0.00	3.72
DR 0 0 2	0.57 R002		.57	0.00	0.00	3.72
X	0.57 X		.57	0.00	.57	3.72
	28 =+	=+				
	15.96		15.96	0.00	.57	19.68
DR 0 0 3	0.71 R003		.71	0.00	.57	19.68
X	0.71 X		.71	0.00	.71	19.68
	0.375 =+	=+				
	0.27		.27	0.00	.71	19.95
MRC	19.95 MC		19.95	0.00	.71	0.00

Financial Applications

The W-register is not affected by the power raising function allowing the amount, interest factor and number of time periods to be entered in any order.

Compound Amount

$25,000 compounded annually at 7¾% for 20 years.

$(1.0775)^{20} = \$111,246.30$

Keys	Display		K	A	W	M1	M2
SET C ALL	.2						
	0.00 CA		0.00	0.00	0.00		
	25,000 X	X	25000	0.00	25000		
	1.0775 +	+	1.0775	1.0775	25000	N O T U S E D	N O T U S E D
	20 A*K						
	4.4498521012	PRF 9	4.44985...	0.00	25000		
	4.4498521012 =						
=	111,246.30253		111246.30253	0.00	25000		
n	111,246.30 R0		111246.30	0.00			

Present Value

End of Year	Amount
2	$(78,000)
4	196,000

Present Value = $51,666

Keys	Display		K	A	W	M1	M2
SET C ALL	.2						
	0.00 CA		0.00	0.00	0.00	0.00	
	78,000 ÷	÷	78000	0.00	78000	0.00	
	1.155 +	+	1.155	1.155	78000	0.00	N O T U S E D
	2 A*K						
	1.3340250000	PRF 9	1.334025	0.00	78000	0.00	
	1.3340250000 =-						
=-	58,469.67		-58469.67	0.00	1.334025	-58469.67	
	196,000 ÷	÷	196000	0.00	196000	-58469.67	
	1.155 +	+	1.155	1.155	196000	-58469.67	
	4 A*K						
	1.7796227006	PRF 9	1.7796227006	0.00	196000	-58469.67	
	1.7796227006 =+						
=+	110,135.70		110135.70	0.00	1.7796227	51666.03	
MR0	51,666.03 MC		51666.03	0.00	1.7796227	0.00	

Financial Applications

Discount Note
Simple interest rate = 8.25%   term = 180 days   principal = $12,000
interest = 488.22   proceeds of loan = $11,511.78
date borrowed: 7/04/76
date due: 12/31/76

Display		K	A	W	M1	M2
	.2					
0.00	CA	0.00	0.00	0.00	0.00	
0.0825	÷	.0825	0.00	.0825	0.00	
365	X	.000226..	0.00	.000226..	0.00	
180	X	.040684..	0.00	.040684..	0.00	
12,000	M+	12000	0.00	.040684..	12000	
12,000	=–	488.22	0.00	.040684..	11511.78	N
488.22		11511.78	0.00	.040684..	0.00	O
11,511.78	MC					T
704.1976	+	704.1976	704.1976	.040684..	0.00	U S E D
180	DAT	1231.1976	0.00	.040684..	0.00	
1,231.1976						

Early Payoff
Actual Payoff Date: 11/6/76
Amount Due: $11,362.60

Display		K	A	W	M1	M2
0.00	CA	0.00	0.00	0.00	0.00	
1,106.1976	+	1106.1976	0.00	1106.1976	0.00	
1,231.1976	DAY	55	0.00	0.00	0.00	
55						
55	÷	55	0.00	55	0.00	N
180	X	.305555..	0.00	.305555..	0.00	O T
488.22	=–	149.18	0.00	.305555..	–149.18	U S E D
149.18						
11,511.78	M+	11511.78	0.00	.305555..	11362.60	
11,362.60	MC	11362.60	0.00	.305555..	0.00	

Preprogrammed Functions — Financial

Although there are several preprogrammed (or hardwired) mathematical functions available for use on the Model 4900, you will find the following 3 to be especially useful for financial applications involving the time value of money:

Example
PRF 9
Raise a number (A) to a power (K) $(1.05)^{20} = 2.6532977052$

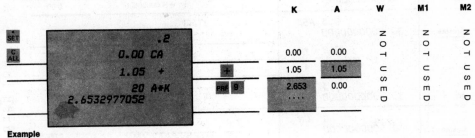

	K	A	W	M1	M2
	0.00	0.00	NOT USED	NOT USED	NOT USED
	1.05	1.05			
	2.653	0.00			
	....				

Example
PRF M+
Days between 2 dates
7/4/1976*
   to
7/4/2076
days = 27,635
*Dates must be entered as MMDD.YYYY

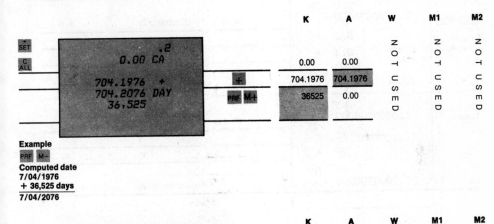

	K	A	W	M1	M2
	0.00	0.00	NOT USED	NOT USED	NOT USED
	704.1976	704.1976			
	36525	0.00			

Example
PRF M−
Computed date
7/04/1976
+ 36,525 days
7/04/2076

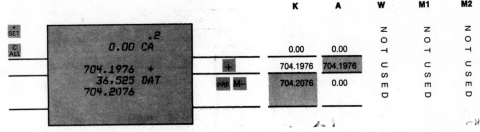

	K	A	W	M1	M2
	0.00	0.00	NOT USED	NOT USED	NOT USED
	704.1976	704.1976			
	704.2076	0.00			

Preprogrammed Functions — Mathematical and Others

Sine

		K	A	W
	30 SN 0.5000000000			
		PRF 0	0.5000000000	0.00
	10 +		10	10
	20 +		20	30
PRF 0	30 SN 0.5000000000			
			0.5000000000	0.00

Arcsine

		K	A	W
	0.5 ASN 30.0000000000			
		PRF 1	30.0000000	0.00
	0.2 +		0.2	0.2
	0.3 +		0.3	0.5
PRF 1	0.5 ASN 30.0000000000			
			30.0000000000	0.00

Cosine

		K	A	W
	60 CN 0.5000000000			
		PRF 2	0.5000000000	0.00
	20 +		20	20
	40 +		40	60
PRF 2	60 CN 0.5000000000			
			0.5000000000	0.00

Arccosine

		K	A	W
	0.5 ACN 60.0000000000			
		PRF 3	60.0000000000	0.00
	0.2 +		0.2	0.2
	0.3 +		0.3	0.5
PRF 3	0.5 ACN 60.0000000000			
			60.0000000000	0.00

Tangent

		K	A	W
	45 TN 1.0000000000			
		PRF 4	1.0000000000	0.00
	15 +		15	15
	30 +		30	45
PRF 4	45 TN 1.0000000000			
			1.0000000000	0.00

NOT USED

Preprogrammed Functions — Mathematical and Others

Arctangent

Display / Operation	PRF	K	A	W
1 ATN 44.9999999999	PRF 5	1	0.00	
0.4 +	+	.4	4	
0.6 +	+	.6	1.0	
PRF 5 — 1.0 ATN 44.9999999999		44.9999999999	0.00	

Natural logarithm

Display / Operation	PRF	K	A	W
2.7182818285 LN 1.0000000000	PRF 6	1.0000000000	0.00	
1 +	+		1	
1.7182818285 +	+	1.7182818285	2.7182818285	
PRF 6 — 2.7182818285 LN 1.0000000000		1.0000000000	0.00	

e^x

Display / Operation	PRF	K	A	W
1 ALN 2.7182818285	PRF 7	2.7182818285	0.00	
0.4 +	+	.4	.4	
0.6 +	+	.6	1.0	
PRF 7 — 1.0 ALN 2.7182818285		2.7182818285	0.00	

Common logarithm

Display / Operation	PRF	K	A	W
10 LG 1.0000000000	PRF 8	1.0000000000	0.00	
4 +	+	4	4	
6 +	+	6	10	
PRF 8 — 10 LG 1.0000000000		1.0000000000	0.00	

a^k

Display / Operation	PRF	K	A	W
3 +	+	3	3	
PRF 9 — 4 A*K 81.0000000003	PRF 9	81.0000000003	0.00	

NOT USED

Preprogrammed Functions — Mathematical and Others

reciprocal

			K	A	W
	3 1/X 0.3333333333333	PRF MRC	0.3333333333333	0.00	
	1 +	+	1	1	
	2 +	+	2	3	
PRF MRC	3 1/X 0.3333333333333	.	0.3333333333333	0.00	
pi (π)					
PRF MR	3.1415926535898 PI		3.1415926535898	0.00	
integer fraction	1,234,567.5555555 #	P/#	1234567.5555555	0.00	
PRF %	1,234,567.0000000 IF 0.5555555		0.5555555	1234567.0000000	
T	1,234,567.00 T		1234567.00	0.00	
	1,234,567 +	+	1234567	1234567	
	0.5555555 +	+	0.5555555	1234567.555555	
PRF %	1,234,567.0000000 IF 0.5555555		0.5555555	1234567.0000000	
shift decimal point right	1.25 #	P/#	1.25	00	
PRF × 3	1,250 X3		1250	0.00	
	1.225 +	+	1.225	1.225	
PRF × 3	1,225 X3		1225	0.00	
shift decimal point left	1.25 #	P/#	1.25	0.00	
PRF ÷ 3	0.00125 ÷3		.00125	0.00	
	1.25 +	+	1.25	1.25	
PRF ÷ 3	0.00125 ÷3		0.00125	0.00	
PRF MR	0.0000000000001 #		0.0000000000001	0.00	
PRF ÷ 1	0.0000000000001 ÷1 ERROR		.		

Error condition caused by loss of non-zero digit due to shifting decimal point left.

NOT USED (W column)

Preprogrammed Functions — Mathematical and Others

Label	Instruction	Key	K	A	W
Rotate A	1 X	×	1	0.00	1
	2 +	+	2	2	1
	3 #	P/#	3	2	1
PRF T	1.00 RA		1.00	3.00	2.00
PRF T	2.00 RA		2.00	1.00	3.00
PRF T	3.00 RA		3.00	2.00	1.00
Rotate W	1 X	×	1	0.00	1
	2 +	+	2	2	1
	3 #	P/#	3	2	1
PRF S	2.00 RW		2.00	1.00	3.00
PRF S	1.00 RW		1.00	3.00	2.00
PRF S	3.00 RW		3.00	2.00	1.00
Truncate	1.999 #	P/#	1.999	0.00	0.00
PRF ⌐	1.99 TR		1.99	0.00	0.00
	1.999 +	+	1.999	1.999	0.00
PRF ⌐	1.99 TR		1.999	1.99	0.00
PRF T	0.00 RA		0.00	1.999	1.99
P/#	1.999 #		0.00	1.999	1.99
Absolute value	2-CS	CS	−2	0.00	0.00
PRF CS	2 AV		2	0.00	0.00
	2-CS	CS	−2	0.00	0.00
+	2- +		−2	−2	0.00
PRF CS	2 AV		−2	2	0.00
PRF T	0.00 RA		0.00	−2	2
P/#	2.00- T		0.00	−2	2

A Typical Company Payroll Problem and Solution

A few years ago, a construction company had a problem. Figuring the payroll, job costing and profit and losses was getting to be a time-consuming tedious operation. Depending on the situations, anywhere from 30 to 50 electricians, office and shop people were working at 10 different wage scales, and the amount of new jobs kept mounting. The problem was solved with a Victor 4900 programable printing calculator.

With information stored on small magnetic cards, it was just a matter of inserting a card and entering a few variables. The programs tell the calculator when to stop for the indexing of these figures. The calculator automatically figures up and prints out the amount to be paid and each deduction for income tax, Social Security, union dues and benefits. It automatically computes the hours times the pay with separate figures for overtime and the total. It subtracts the deductions and prints monthly, quarterly and yearly totals. Even the taxes are figured automatically. The clerk was happy to be relieved of looking through federal forms and figuring all the different percentages.

In figuring the costs of a job, it is necessary to calculate overhead percentages based on labor, benefits, taxes and expenses. The clerk enters the card and a few figures, and the calculator prints out profits and losses for the month and year to date. All multiplying and subtracting is automatic. The programmable calculator also doubles as an adding machine for miscellaneous figuring during the day. Because it is so easy to learn the operation of the programmable, another office employee could step in and run the programs in case of illness or vacation.

Tracing the Program

Automatic tracing is initiated either by entering the beginning step number followed by +/I or by J_T followed by a tag number. Tracing can be halted by depressing INT.

Single-step tracing is initiated when in TRC mode (idle) by depressing PR/F P/#. Then either a step number followed by +/I or J_T followed by a tag number will start the single step-trace at the specified location. Thereafter, each depression of +/I will cause the execution of the next instruction. Single-step tracing can be discontinued by depressing INT.

When in single-step trace mode depressing P/# will cause the printing of all stored subroutine return addresses labeled by S, in addition to the contents of the K, A, W, M1 and M2 registers in that order. The arithmetic operations are not affected by this operation.

In addition, the contents of any storage register can be printed without affecting the arithmetic operations. This is done by depressing DR followed by the desired register number. (Excerpts are from Victor's Instruction Manual.)

Texas Instruments Offers the SR-60A to Challenge All Others in Price/Performance*

A Prompting, Programmable, Printing Calculator with an Alphanumeric Display that Communicates with the User — Strongly value-packed but after costs of some units is Texas Instrument's SR-60A. Its business capability ranges from solving intricate financial analyses and long-range forecasting, to simpler operations like payroll and amortization. For technology there are 46 scientific functions on the keyboard and 480 program steps for complex programming. This capacity can be expanded to 1,920 steps and 100 data memories with its optional module. It can be set for anything between 2640 program steps and 10 registers to 80 program steps and 330 registers. Programming: The SR-60A's unique 20-character display lets the user run alphanumeric programs which "ask" for information at successive stages of the problem. The SR-60A then waits for a user response before continuing. This dialogue allows even a novice to work with complicated problems immediately.

Programming is easy and straightforward yet flexible for the user with: 78 labels, 10 flags, 10 branches 4 levels of subroutines, and 2 modes of indirect operation, and quite complete program editing capability. It can store and manipulate one character at a time or groups of five characters using 2ⁿᵈ STO, 2ⁿᵈ RCL and 2ⁿᵈ EKC. And, by using the printer users can list and trace the actual program execution. Programs are written and recorded on magnetic cards. When programs are listed, alpha fields are printed as letters not as instruction steps. If the user wants to clear his program 2ⁿᵈ CMS clears only program memory. With alphanumeric prompting, the cards can be used by assistants or secretaries. A person generally needs a minimum amount of instruction and a general concept of what's to be solved to have answers in seconds.

---

*Much of the following discussion represents excerpts, summaries, and paraphrasing of various SR-60A manuals, with permission of Texas Instruments, Inc. It is an attempt to highlight the capabilities and characteristics of this low cost calculating system. For full details and descriptions, the reader is invited to contact a local TI dealer or distributor.

Ten prerecorded cards are included in the SR-60A's Basic Library: power transformer and filter design; add-on rate installment loans and compound interest; polynomial evaluation, cubic and quadratic equations; basic statistics; and random number generator and diagnostics, etc. Well over 100 optional additional programs are available, including many on business. Printing: The SR-60A's quiet printer provides a scaled replica of what appears on the alphanumeric display on 2½-inch thermal paper. Users can get a hard copy of any keyboard calculation that appears on the display, a complete program list of the contents of the data registers, whether entered from the keyboard or run from a program card.

Additional cards, designed for specific technical and business applications, are available priced from $95 each. TI was able to hold down the SR-60A's manufacturing cost (and its price) by making almost everything in the unit, including the case. Two diagnostic programs are also supplied to test the SR-60A's internal operation. Users also get a Basic Library Manual which details each program, contains sample problems, user-instructions and program listings.

The SR-60A Basic Library offers a basic variety of mathematical programs that will add to user problem-solving capability. Six libraries containing well over 100 different programs are available. Finance, with 21 programs and Electrical Engineering with 16 programs were available first. The others: Math I, 20 programs; Math II, 18 programs; Statistics, 19 programs; and Sur veying, 7 programs.

Special features of the SR-60A are as follows:

- Decrement and skip on zero (2nd GO TO)
- Dual labels, for total of 152 labels (LBL 2nd X^2)
- Subroutine levels are twelve deep
- The SR-60A plus MEM OPT 2 has a suggested retail price of $2595.00. Normal partition line is 3840 program steps and 310 data registers. The memory can range from 6240 program steps and 10 registers to 80 program steps and 780 registers.
- The SR-60A plus MEM OPT 2 and MEM OPT 3 has a suggested retail price of $2995.00. Normal partition line is 5760 program steps and 430 registers. The memory can range from 7920 program steps and 160 registers to 1280 program steps and 990 registers.
- RS-232-C Module
- Single or dual cassette interface

Here is a sampling of the kinds of problems the SR-60A can be programmed to handle:

Business — Profit and loss statements, Balance sheets, Payroll, Trend lines, Economical ordering, Depreciation schedules, Crossover between straight line and declining balance, Loan amortization, Discounted cash flow, Simple and compound interest, Rule of 78's, Annuities, Days between dates, Date conversion, Bond yield.

Technology/Science—Evaluate complex functions, Evaluate polynomials with complex coefficients, Find real and complex roots of cubic and quadratic equations, Solve transcendental equations, Approximate integrals, Find approximate solutions of differential equations, Assist in power transformer design, Assist in filter design, Performance of many statistical calculations.

SR-60A Prompting — The alphanumeric prompting feature used in conjunction with programming, displays letters, numbers and special symbols that let users make words and phrases that will later "ask" for entries or decisions to solve the problem. The SR-60A's large (1¼ by 9¼-inch) 20-character light emitting diode display (5 by 7 dot matrix) "asks" users for their input, in terms they understand, at each stage of the problem — then waits for their keyed in response before it continues. So users really interact or "talk through" a problem — users providing raw data, the SR-60A giving back complete answers. This rapid dialogue lets users solve a problem using different inputs, letting them explore multiple options. And, should the dialogue be interrupted, users leave the SR-60A on and its display will tell them where they are when they return.

The SR-60A's prompting features help users to know the problem by keeping track of steps and eliminating demands on their mental organization. As long as the user gives the appropriate input to each question, he doesn't need to know how to "solve" the problem — the SR-60A does it automatically.

Any program can be recorded on blank magnetic cards for continued use. Algebraic operating systems (AOS) with 9 levels of parentheses solves problems with up to 10 pending operations. Entry is left-to-right just as the problem is written. Results are displayed up to 10 digits, plus two more for power of 10 exponents. The SR-60A's trace mode key automatically begins recording all calculations whether entered from the keyboard of run with a program. So users can see how the program is being executed. This is very useful for editing and debugging a program. It conveniently lets users verify that instructions are keyed in correctly and get a quick check on hastily constructed programs, or programs not carefully documented. Users verify that program results are based on correctly formulated problems.

SR-60A Keys and Programming Procedure — Programming is really no more than taking small problems and integrating them to solve bigger problems. On the SR-60A programming is merely listing the keystrokes necessary to carry the problem through to its solution. Some may still feel that programming is too complex for the untrained person to master. A view that probably is helped along by the vocabulary associated with programming. Words like direct and indirect addressing, conditional and unconditional branching, labels, and flags sound esoteric and abstract. Yet these words are just a shorthand use to describe manipluations almost anyone can grasp. In fact, they're not even mathematical.

Even though the SR-60A has many functions, no one can anticipate all their needs. Fifteen user-defined keys are provided to make them any function users may need. The Label key tells the SR-60A that the next key pressed will be a label. There are 77 keys, including the user-defined keys, that can be used as labels. If Positive, If Zero, and If Error are keys that test the contents of the display. Branching occurs if the conditions: positive, zero, or flashing display are true. Branching occurs if the conditions are not true when these keys are prefixed by the 2nd key.

Alternate calculating paths can be defined by the Set Flag key followed by a number from 0 through 9 then the Test Flag key tests the state of the flag — set or reset. The SR-60A branches if the specified flag is set, or continues sequentially if the flag is not set. 2nd, Test Flag reverses the sense of the test. The indirect addressing (IND) key is used with unconditional, conditional and data memory keys. An example: IND, TFLG, 2,05. means that SR-60A tests flag number 2, and looks at the contents of the data memory register 05 to find the program address to which to branch if flag 2 is set. The Que key halts the SR-60A's operation and waits for a response from these keys: Yes, No, Not Known, Not Apply, Enter. Press Yes and the SR-60A branches to the first label which follows Que. Pressing No causes it to branch to the second label, and so on. These five label keys are equivalent to a five-way branch. The alphabetical letters and symbols on keys are activated by the Alpha key to enter prompting messages for display or print. The convenient Pause key permits a message or result to be displayed for about ½ second.

The SR-60A's editing and debugging keys let users go through a program one set at a time. Or single-step backward through a program. The Insert key moves the current and all following instructions down one location so that a change can be made at any place within a program without rewriting it. Users remove the displayed instruction and move all following instructions up with the Delete key. The SR-60A can also print a trace, or a record, of all functions, numbers and calculations.

Two Prompting/Programming Examples That Show How Easy the SR-60A Operates

Compound Interest
(Solve for Present Value)

Step Prompting Message/ Printout	Your Response
1. Enter present value	Not known
2. Enter interest %	9
3. Enter no. periods	24
4. Enter future value	5000
5. Present value (Printed)	

Payroll Calculation*

Step Prompting Message/ Printout	Your Response
1. Enter employee card	Feed card into SR-60A
2. Employee SSN (Printed)	
3. Company number (Printed)	
4. Regular hours	Enter straight time hours
5. Overtime rate 1	Enter time and one-half hours
6. Overtime rate 2	Enter double time hours.
7. Miscellaneous pay	Enter miscellaneous pay
8. Gross wages (Printed)	
9. Federal withholding tax (Printed)	
10. State withholding tax (Printed)	
11. Local withholding tax (Printed)	
13. FICA deduction (Printed)	
13. Voluntary deductions (Printed)	
13. Voluntary deductions (Printed)	
14. Total voluntary deduction (Printed)	
15. Net wages due (Printed)	
16. Year to date totals for each of above (Printed)	
17. Enter employee card for update	Feed card into SR-60A (records all year to date totals on employee card)

*Requires optional expansion module.

The SR-60A and the Competition

The unit has 95 keys, including 40 for mathematical functions, 46 for scientific functions, and the rest mostly for instructions. It should be noted the 480 program memory locations and 40 data memories are expandable to 1,920 program locations and 100 data memories with a $700 optional module, making the total suggested price $2395. Some users suggest that the TI calculator is generally comparable in performance to Hewlett-Packard Co.'s 9815A

($2,900), Canon Inc.'s SX310 introduced in June '75 ($2,895), Sharp Electronic Corp's. recently introduced Model 2610 ($3,200), Tek31 (about $3000), Victor 4900 ($2300). These and others are analyzed in pages ahead. If Texas Instruments follows past and current marketing strategies, it will reduce the SR-60A main unit price to make it the strong price/performance leader to thereby capture a major share of the desk-top advanced calculator market. Other aspects of the SR-60A suggest that Texas Instruments can and intends to fight some major marketing and price wars to achieve their goals. The SR-60A is being retailed in major department stores and is serviced locally. The company uses calculator chips that are in its mass production line for several calculator models. All components except the power transformer and a few switches are built in-house by TI. The SR-60A is designed for both business and technical operations. For future development, the unit is essential as a 'building block' for a major system of calculator 'computing' power. At the outset, users were told to expect numerous add-on peripherals — both memory and input-output, to expand its capability in data storage and versatility of utilization. Staying true to form in September, 1976, Texas Instruments announced further memory expansion for up to 5,760 steps and up to 480 data registers. This was most significant to users and provoked competitors. But, to be up in the big leagues, the SR-60A would need more. And, it wasn't long before it got it. In December, 1976, TI announced typewriter and plotter interfaces for the SR-60A and the availability of typewriters and plotters to work with the SR-60A to substantially expand the range of output for this low-cost advanced desk-top calculator. To reach further up into mass memory storage and data input and better 'system' capability, TI announced that in the first half of 1977 magnetic tape cassette input and storage capabilities would be available and that communications interfaces would permit the use of the SR-60A as a terminal and as a base for true 'system' operation.

The HP-97 Fully-Programmable Printing Calculator combines programming power and the usefulness of a quiet thermal printer. The HP-97 operates on batteries as well as AC—so users can have a printed record whenever and wherever they need it.

The SR-60A is a multi-purpose desk-top programmable calculator from Texas Instruments Incorporated.

Texas Instruments Inc. conducted many surveys and market analyses to determine the various desirable design features and saturation distribution activities. Some of the data are summarized below. It is interesting to note that an encouragingly significant segment of the market lies in business (34.4%) and 'at home' users (10%) categories. As greater numbers of calculator users turn to programmables—the several HP, TI, and National Semiconductor models—and now the Casio, Canon, Litronix, and others, also—more people are becoming capable of very efficiently operating advanced desk-tops such as the SR-60A. It seems that TI is especially anxious to gear up for this market . . . as they also spearhead drives for the financial, banking, laboratory, engineering, governmental and other markets. And the TI drives for educational use lead other competitors.

SR-60A CUSTOMER PROFILE BY PROFESSION

Business	34.4%
Engineering/Physics	41.0%
Statistics & Probability	5.3%
Medical Sciences	4.5%
Social & Natural Sciencies	75.%
Math & Numerical Analysis	1.5%
Other	5.9%
	100.0%

PROFILE OF SR-60A END USER

- Uses the calculator 4 hours per day, 5 days a week.
- 10% use the SR-60A at home.
- 78% use of SR-60A at the office.
- 12% use the SR-60A at the lab.
- 22% of the owners are individuals
- 78% of the owners are companies
- 14% of the owners purchased their calculator from a sub dealer.

EARLY TYPICAL SR-60A APPLICATIONS

Accounting
  General Ledger
  Invoicing
  Payroll
  Inventory Control
  Income Tax Preparation
  Personal Tax Planning
  Auditing (Statistical Sampling)
Securities & Financial
  Bond Value & Yields
  Call Option Valuation
  Optimum Spreads & Hedges
Credit Life Calculations
Banking
APR Declaration
Real Estate Investment Analysis
Life Insurance
Sales Forecasting
Auto Insurance Premiums
Econometric Modeling
Statistics
  Quality Control
  Reliability
  Sociology/Psychology
Education
Medical
  Clinical Diagnosis
  Pathology
  Opthalmic Surgery
  Optometry
  Biochemistry
  Pulmonary Functions
  Radiology
  Electrocardiograms
Chemistry/Materials/Processes
  Soldering
  Solution Concentrations
  Organic Laboratory
  Analytical Chemistry
  Coatings

Physics
Optics
Geology
Seismology
Mining
Personnel (Retirement Benefits)
Personnel (Compensation)
Facilities Management/
  Engineering
Bidding/Estimates
Engineering Project Management
Lighting
Computer Architecture
Calculator Algorithin Testing
Agriculture
Forestry
Cattle Feeding
Cotton Warehousing
Mechanical Engineering
  Heat Transfer
  Heating/Ventilating/AC
  Vibrations
  Gas Turbines
  Refrigeration
Aerodynamics
Acoustics
  Architecture
  Surveying
  Highway Design
Construction Job Estimation
  Ellipsometer
  Civil Engineering
  Stress Analysis
  Fluid Flow
  Structures
Electrical Engineering
  Circuit Design
  Process Control
  Communication Systems
  Radar
  Lasers
  Control Systems
  Semiconductors
  Power Control
  Dynamic Programming

**A Typical Small Business Program Available from TI for the SR-60A:
The Finance 9-A Program**

Depreciation—Straight Line and Sum of Digits

This program prints a depreciation schedule for an asset using either the straight-line or sum-of-years-digits method. The schedule for each year includes year, depreciation for that year, and the remaining value at the end of the year.

With the straight line method the same amount of depreciation occurs each year according to the following equation.

$$DEP = (C - S)/L$$

where DEP = depreciation per year
C = cost of asset
S = estimated salvage value
L = life of asset in years

With the sum-of-years-digits method more depreciation occurs in the first year than the second, more in the second than the third, etc. as determined by the following equation.

$$DEP_K = \frac{L + 1 - K}{SOYD} (C - S)$$

Where DEP_K = depreciation in Kth year
$SOYD = \frac{1}{2}[INT(L) + 1][INT(L) + 2FRAC(L)]$
$INT(L)$ = Integer years of life
$FRAC(L)$ = Fractional years of life

Fractional years life are permitted. The fractional year is assumed to be at the end of the asset's life.

USER INSTRUCTIONS

Step	Display	Instruction	Press	Go to
1		Load card 9 side A		
2	Straight line?	a. For straight line depreciation	Yes	4
		b. For sum of digits	No	
3	Sum of digits?	a. For sum of digits depreciation	Yes	
		b. For straight line	No	2
4	Enter cost	Key in cost of asset	Enter	
5	Enter life (years)	Key in life in years	Enter	
6	Enter salvage value	Key in salvage value estimate	Enter	
7		Depreciation schedule is printed		
8		To restart	Que	2

Example
Determine the sum of digits schedule for an asset costing $4000 with a 4½ year life and an estimated salvage value of $925.

Display	Press	Print
		**DEPRECIATION
STRAIGHT LINE?	NO	
SUM OF DIGITS?	YES	SUM OF DIGITS
ENTER COST	4000 ENTER	COST
		4000.00
ENTER LIFE (YEARS)	4.5 Enter	LIFE (YEARS)
		4.5
ENTER SALVAGE VALUE	925 ENTER	SALVAGE VALUE
		925.00

Display continued on next page.

```
                              ***
                              YEAR
                              DEPRECIATION
                              REMAINING VALUE
                                        1.
                              1107.00
                              2893.00
                                        2.
                               861.00
                              2032.00
                                        3.
                               615.00
                              1417.00
                                        4.
                               369.00
                              1048.00
                                       4.5
                               123.00
                               925.00
```

Example of Three Available SR-60A Libraries: Statistics, Electrical Engineering, and Finance

Statistics Library

Statpak-60

Basic Statistics for One or Two Variables. The mean, standard deviation and standard error are found for a set of observations on a variable. The observations may be entered either as grouped or ungrouped data. For a set of observations on two variables these measures are found for each. The covariance and correlation coefficient relating the two are also found.

Means and Moments. For grouped or ungrouped data the arithmetic, geometric, and harmonic means are calculated. Also, the second, third, and fourth moments about the mean and the coefficients of skewness and kurtosis are computed.

Random Number Generator. Uniformly distributed random numbers for the interval (0,1) are found using a linear congruential method. Normally distributed random numbers for specified mean and standard deviation are found with the direct method.

One-Way Analysis of Variance. A one-way analysis of variance is performed on treatment groups of observations. The mean and variance are calculated for each treatment group and for the overall set of observations. The total, treatment, and error sum of squares are calculated and used to find an F statistic to test the differences between population means of the treatment groups.

Two-Way Analysis of Variance. For an array of values representing random samples from a normal population a two-way analysis of variance is performed. The mean and variance for the overall table are found. Total column, and row sum of squares are calculated and used to find F statistics to test significance of row and column effects on the observations.

Contingency Table Analysis. A contingency table is analyzed using the chi-square statistic to test the independence between row and column classifications. The total, column, and row sums are computed and used to find the expected frequency in each cell of the table.

t Statistic Evaluation. The t statistic is evaluated for either paired observations or independent random samples from two normal populations. For paired observations the average difference is used to evaluate the t statistic to test the hypothesis that the means of the populations are equal. For independent random samples of the statistic tests the hypothesis that the means are separated by a specified difference.

Rank Sum Tests. The Wilcox rank sum and the Mann-Whitney test statistics are evaluated for two samples. The samples are ordered and their ranks used to calculate the statistics. A normal deviate is compared with rank mean and variance to test the hypothesis that both samples come from populations with the same cumulative distribution function.

Linear Regression. A straight line is fit by linear regression to a set of observations on variables x and y. The line is $y = ax + b$. The coefficient of determination, the standard error of y on x, and the standard error for the coefficients a and b are computed.

Exponential, Power, Logarithmic Curve Fits. The curves $y = ae^{bx}$, $y = ax^b$, and $y = a + b \ln x$ are fit by the least squares method to a set of observations on the variables x and y. The coefficient of determination is found for each case.

Multiple Linear Regression. An equation of the form $Z = a_0 + a_1 x + a_2 y$ is fit to sets of observations on x, y, and z. A coefficient to test "goodness of fit" and means and variances for each variable are also computed.

Polynomial Regression. An equation of the form $y = a_0 + a_1 x + a_2 x^2 + \ldots + a_n x^n$ is fit to sets of observations on the variables x and y. The maximum value of n is determined by the relation $n^2 + 3n + 12 \leq$ # regs.

Histogram Construction. A histogram with a specified number of cells is constructed to fit sets of observations on two variables. The cell width and a data offset are entered and information about each cell is calculated together with the mean and variance of the input data.

Normal Distribution. The values of f(x) and P(x) are found for a given x or the value of x is found for a given P(x). A normal distribution is assumed in the calculations.

Chi-square and t Distributions. The values of f(x) and P(x) are found for a given x. Either Chi-square or t distributions may be assumed in the calculations.

F Distribution. The value of P(x) is computed for given x and degrees of freedom. An F distribution is assumed in the calculations.

Bivariate and Logarithmic Normal Distributions. The value of f(x) is found for a given x assuming a logarithmic normal distribution of specified mean and variance. The value of f(x,y) is found for given x and y assuming a bivariate normal distribution of specified means, variances, and correlation coefficient.

Weibull and Poisson Distributions. The values of f(x) and P(x) are found for x assuming a Weibull distribution. The values of f(x) and P(x) are found for x assuming a Poisson distribution.

Binomial and Negative Binomial Distributions. The values of f(x) and P(x) are found for given x assuming either a binomial or negative binomial distribution with specified parameters.

Geometric and Hypergeometric Distributions. The values of f(x) and P(x) are found for a given x assuming either a geometric or hypergeometric distribution with specified parameters.

Electrical Engineering Library

EE PAK-60

Active High and Low Pass Filter Design. High and low pass active filters are designed for given center frequency, gain, and Q. Values for the resistors and capacitors in the infinite-gain, multiple-feedback circuits are calculated.

Active Bandpass Filter Design. Second-order active bandpass filters are designed using a multiple-feedback network. Both high-Q and low-Q circuits may be realized. Standard values may be selected to minimize implementation problems.

Chebyshev and Butterworth Filter Design. Chebyshev and Butterworth low-pass filters are designed for specified filter order, termination resistance and corner frequency. For the Chebyshev filter, allowable ripple may be specified.

Passive Bandpass Filter Design. Passive bandpass filters are realized for specified filter order, center frequency, termination resistance, 3-dB bandwidth, and passband ripple. Either a Chebyshev or Butterworth filter type may be selected.

Resonant Circuits. The impedance and resonant frequency are calculated for series or parallel resonant circuits whose component values are specified.

Attenuators. Component values for T and π impedance matching circuits are found for specified input and output impedances and desired loss. Minimum loss pad matching may be performed for given impedances.

T to π Transformations. T (p) networks are transformed to π (T) networks having the same characteristics. The impedances for each part of the network are specified.

Ladder Network Analysis. The input impedance for a ladder network is calculated. The network may be composed of any combination of resistors, capacitors, and inductors in shunt or series additions.

Coil Properties. The inductance or number of turns for a single or multilayer coil may be found given wire diameter and dimensions of coil.

Power Transformer Design. Core weight is calculated for specified power requirements. Then for a specified core area, flux density and frequency, the number of primary and secondary turns is found.

Rectifier Circuits. Full-wave of half-wave rectifier circuits are evaluated for given component values, input voltage and frequency. The dc output voltage and peak-to-peak ripple are calculated.

Transmission Line Impedance. The impedance of seven types of transmission lines may be calculated. The types are coaxial, 2-wire, single conductor near ground, balanced shielded line, parallel near ground 4-wire, and 5-wire.

S and Y Parameter Transformation. A set of S (Y) parameters expressed as magnitudes and angles is transformed to a set of Y (S) parameters.

Phase Locked Loops. Natural frequency, damping factor, and loop noise bandwidth are found for either passive or active phase locked loops. Loop gain and component values for the circuits are required as inputs.

Transistor Amplifier Design. Collector current and sensitivity factors are computed for transistor circuits with specified current gain, supply voltage, and resistor values.

Fourier Series. Fourier coefficients are computed for discrete values of a periodic function. Sine and cosine coefficients are found and may be used to calculate new values of the function.

Finance Library
FIN PAK-60

Compound Interest. Calculates any one of the four variables (PV, FV, I, N) in the compound interest equation, given the other three as inputs.

Rate Conversion. Computes either nominal or effective annual interest rate, given the other. Either continuous compounding or a specified number of periods may be used.

Accrued Interest. Calculates interest earned, but not collected, for a given loan amount.

Days Between Dates. Calculates the number of days between two dates. Either the actual number or the number based on a 30 day month, 360 day per year may be found.

Ordinary Annuity. Solves for any one of the four variables (PV, I, PMT, I) in the ordinary annuity equations, given the other three. An ordinary annuity is a series of equal payments to be paid at the end of successive periods of equal length.

Sinking Fund. This routine differs from the ordinary annuity routine in that the FV equations are used rather than the PV equations.

Annuity With Balloon Payment. A variation of the ordinary annuity calculations to allow for premature payment of a loan balance (balloon payment) coincident with some regularly scheduled payment.

Annuity Due With Future Value. Calculates annuity due values for cases involving payment at the beginning of the compounding period (such as savings plans) rather than at the end of the compounding period as in ordinary annuity.

Annuity Due With Present Value. Calculates values from the annuity due equation using present value and assuming payment is at the beginning of the compounding period.

Annuity Due With Present Value and Balloon Payment. A variation of the annuity due with present value calculations to allow for a balloon payment payoff prior to final payment. Such a calculation occurs with conversion of a leasing agreement to a purchase agreement (lease with option to buy).

Amortized Loan Schedule. Prints a complete schedule of payments showing the principal and interest portions of each payment, the accumulated interest and principal at each payment, and the remaining principal balance.

Constant Payment To Principal Loan Schedule. Prints a complete schedule of payments showing the interest portion and total of each payment, the accumulated interest and principal at each payment, and the remaining principal balance.

Add-On Rate Installment Loan. Calculates the payment amount and annual percentage rate for an installment loan.

Interest Rebate—Rule of 78's. Calculates the interest rebate and remaining principal balance due for an add-on rate installment loan using the rule of 78's.

Linear Regression Analysis. Calculates the linear least squares fit to a set of input data points $(y = mx + b)$, standard deviation of x and y data, correlation coefficient, and standard error.

Total, Average, Percent Contribution. Calculates the total, average, and percent contribution of a series of values.

Depreciation—Straight-Line And Sum-Of-Digits. Computes a depreciation schedule using either straight-line or sum-of-years-digits method.

Declining Balance Depreciation With Crossover Point. Computes depreciation using the declining balance method and finds the crossover point with straight-line depreciation.

Internal Rate Of Return. Calculates the rate of return which equates the present value of investments and cash flows (positive and negative).

Net Present Value. Calculates the net present value of time distributed cash flows for a given discount rate. Also determines the profitability index.

Bond Yield And Present Value. Solves for the discount rate which equates the present value of future interest and principal payments with the current bond market price, or this routine calculates the present value of all future interest and principal payments of a bond.

The SR-60A comes equipped with customized software: A 72-page Operating Manual details all keystrokes and operations. A 96-page Programming Manual provides comprehensive, detailed information and numerous examples on how to program. A Basic Library Manual shows how to use the 8 prerecorded programs and the 2 diagnostic tests that are contained on the 5 prerecorded magnetic cards. Three blank cards and a head cleaner to remove oxides and foreign particles from the read/write head are also included. All cards can be conveniently stored in the handy magnetic-card holder. There's a 50-sheet tablet of Coding Forms and User Instructions to help users write their own programs. And finally, a dust cover and a 3-wire 120-volt power cord which plugs into a standard 115-volt outlet complete the package. (Note: The SR-60A can also be operated by 220 volts by placing its voltage switch in the 220 position and changing the power cord.)

Using Prerecorded Programs on the SR-60A

Those persons who desire may use the SR-60A to run prerecorded programs without learning the mathematical and programming details of the calculator. While no prior programming or calculator experience is required, the users should know something about the program, the calculator, and "what happens when" in order to respond to the questions and statements presented during the program. The program, as an accumulation of instructions or keystrokes which solves a specific problem, whether it is recorded on cards, tapes, or if other media is read and remembered by the calculator. The program is also developed so that it will automatically run the machine (perform and execute the keystrokes) and to solve the problem without stopping except to remind the operator to make pertinent decisions or press keys representing new variables or other needed data. The characteristic of 'prompting' as related to the SR-60A stems from the ability of the machine to display and print up to 20 characters and numbers which allows the operator to respond to the displayed message with YES, NO, NOT APPLY, NOT KNOWN, or ENTER keys. Therefore, when a program is running and some unknown quantity is needed to complete the problem solution, such as ENTER INTEREST (%), the calculator will stop and issue (display) that 'prompting.' At this point the operator simply keys in the interest rate, presses the ENTER key and the program continues. In other cases, the operator is permitted to use NOT APPLY or NOT KNOWN, as the case may be. As related to decisions to be made by the operator, the calculator might prompt with a question, such as NEW VALUE OF X? When this occurs, the operator has the option of two answer keys, YES or NO. PROMPTING DESIRED? is the most frequent message, which is turned on whenever the power switch is first used or the CLEAR ALL key is pressed. If the operator answers with a NO key, the display goes to zero and the calculator is ready for manual calculations. If the answer is with the YES key, this indicates the user wishes to run a program. The display then prompts the operator with the instructions, PUSH YES, LOAD CARD. As the YES key is pressed again, the magnetic card-reading unit begins running allowing the prerecorded program to be read. These messages are standard, but many more can be developed from the prerecorded programs. Thus, the originator of the program is responsible for the programmed messages after they have been made to fit within the 20-character allotment.

To run a prerecorded program, two items in addition to the calculator are needed. Users must have the prerecorded magnetic card containing the program, and the user instructions for the program should be available for reference. User instructions are just what the name implies, a set of instructions to tell (the user) in as few words as possible, how to use the program. The chart below illustrates a completed User Instructions form developed for the SR-60A. This User Instructions form is for the Compound Interest program from the Basic Library provided with the calculator.

Referring to the chart, notice there are five columns: STEP, DISPLAY, INSTRUCTION, PRESS and GO TO. The STEP column simply provides a sequential reference for the major events of the program. The DISPLAY column shows the prompting messages to be displayed by the calculator during the program. The INSTRUCTION column provides itemized instructions on the decision or response required for the message in the DISPLAY column. The PRESS column shows the key to be pressed that corresponds to the selected instruction. If the program does not advance sequentially from one step to the next, the GO TO column shows the step number the program proceeds to if the key in the adjacent PRESS column is pressed.

STEP	DISPLAY	INSTRUCTION	PRESS	GO TO
1		Load card 2 side B		
2	ENTER PRESENT VALUE	a. If present value is known, key it in	ENTER	
		b. If unknown	NOT KNOWN	
3	ENTER FUTURE VALUE	a. If future value is known, key it in	ENTER	
		b. If unknown	NOT KNOWN	
4	ENTER INTEREST (%)	a. If interest rate per period is known, key it in	ENTER	
		b. If unknown	NOT KNOWN	
5	ENTER NO. PERIODS	a. If number of periods is known, key it in	ENTER	
		b. If unknown	NOT KNOWN	
6		Value of the unknown variable is computed and printed.		2

Note: Interest is entered and printed as a percentage. For example, 9% is entered as 9. [From SR-60A Operating Manual.]

Now consider running the COMPOUND INTEREST program. For explanation purposes, assume the problem to be solved is that you wish to find the future value of a $500 deposit into a savings account after five years if the interest rate is 6%, compounded annually.

The first step of the user instructions shown in the chart is to Load Card 2 Side B. This is a blanket instruction used for each program and is described in the front of the Program Manual of each library.

1. Set input power switch on or press CLEAR ALL key. Display shows PROMPTING DESIRED?
2. To run a program press YES key. Display shows PRESS YES, LOAD CARD.
3. Press YES key. Display goes blank and card-reader motor begins running.
4. Insert the end of the magnetic card into the card-reader slot with the arrow corresponding to the desired program title pointing toward the slot. Users gently feed the card into the slot until it is pulled through the cal-

culator by the motor. They should not hold or restrict card travel while engaged by the motor.

5. If one is running a program which uses only one side of a card, he or she proceeds to step 6. Otherwise, they continue with this step. After the motor stops, the display will show PRESS YES, LOAD CARD. A user will locate the next card in the sequence, press YES, repeat step 4 and then repeat the procedure until all cards are entered. Users DO NOT USE THE **CLEAR ALL** KEY UNLESS IT IS NECESSARY TO RESTART THE LOADING PROCEDURE.

6. After the motor stops, a user removes the card and returns it to holder. The printer* should print the title of the program. Users proceed to the second step of the user instructions. If after the motor stops, a flashing question mark appears on the display, the user restarts this loading procedure with step 1. If difficulty persists, the user refers to *In Case of Difficulty* in the Maintenance and Service section of the manual.

With step 1 of the user instructions completed, the display shows ENTER PRESENT VALUE, indicating the program is at step 2. To minimize confusion, the user instructions do not show the printout of a program. The printout below represents the tape of the present problem with the result of each step indicated by number.

By observing the response choices in the INSTRUCTION column, the correct action is to key in the present value (500) and press the **ENTER** key. The calculator now displays ENTER FUTURE VALUE which indicates the program is at step 3. Since future value is an unknown quantity, the only response is to press the **NOT KNOWN** key. The printer does not respond for this operation. The display now shows ENTER INTEREST (%) as indicated by step 4. Since this is a known value, users key in the interest rate (6) and press the **ENTER** key. The display now shows ENTER NO. PERIODS, indicating step 5. The last response is to key in the number of years (5), press the **ENTER** key and step 6 is automatically completed with the printout of the future value. The only entry in the GO TO column is following step 6, which indicates the program automatically returns to step 2 for users to begin another problem.

There are a few variations in the basic display format not illustrated by the previous problem which are used in other programs. One other method to display the message ENTER PRESENT VALUE is PRESENT VALUE =. The

---

**COMPOUND INTEREST

PRESENT VALUE =
500.00
INTEREST (%) =
6.
NO. PERIODS =
5.

FUTURE VALUE
669.11

***
Typical Program Printout

---

*Some programs do not automatically engage the printer. Users proceed to the second step of the user instructions for normal display indication.

equals sign implies that a number should be keyed in and followed by the **ENTER** key. Another form of message commonly displayed is a word or words followed by a question mark. The response to a question should be either **YES** or **NO**.

Tips for Running Programs on the SR-60A

As in using any machine or calculator, it is reasonable to expect that some errors will be made when first using prerecorded programs. By reading the instructions carefully, users should soon be able to run a program with confidence. Reading the following hints will help solve most of the common difficulties. A good practice is to **first solve a known problem** i.e., to run a program the first time with a problem which has a known answer. At least one example problem is included with each program in the Basic Library. As regards **entry errors,** an erroneous entry may be corrected before the **ENTER** key is pressed by pressing the **CE** key. Entry errors discovered after the **ENTER** key has been pressed cannot normally be corrected. Users press the **QUE** key to restart the program. Some programs are specially written to ask for deletions or corrections. The user instructions should be consulted in these cases.

As regards **intermediate calculations,** the Basic Library programs allow users to perform manual calculations after they stop with a prompting message. The appropriate response key must then be pressed to continue running the program. A simple test can be made to determine if intermediate calculations will affect the program. When the prompting message appears and intermediate calculations are desired before continuing the program, users press the **CE** key and observe the displayed number. They next press the equals key. If the displayed number does not change, intermediate calculations are possible. Otherwise, they press **QUE** to restart program. The following keys should not be used in an intermediate calculation: The 30 programming keys on the right side, **CLEAR MEM, CLEAR ALL,** and **TRACE, DEG MODE** or **LIMITED PRECISION** unless status lights are observed and restored to

Loading a magnetic card.

same status before continuing program, and the **STORE, EXCH, PROD** and **SUM** keys without first checking for registers used by the program. As regards **wrong answers or flashing display,** the typical reasons are: Entries which force the calculator into overflow, underflow, or an error condition—users should check for limits in program description. Pressing the **ENTER** key without making a number entry. Incorrect number entry. For program errors—users refer to *In Case of Difficulty* in Maintenance and Service section of the manual.

PROGRAM PROMPTING FUNCTIONS CONTINUED

Consider the difficulty in remembering key entries, etc., for a program which requires many entries in a specific order. A detailed procedure would be needed until memorized. Now consider how simple it would be to run a program where the calculator is able to display messages and questions pertaining to the exact entry it needs to continue the program. And in addition, a detailed printout identifies entries and results by name. The prompting functions of the SR-60A permit this type of program operation. A prompting operation frees you from memorizing lengthy procedures because the SR-60A can display messages or questions in plain English (or any other language using the same alphabet) and effectively lead you step-by-step through complex calculations. This section provides a description of the calculator functions directly related to prompting.

Alphanumeric Operations

Prompting messages are generated by using the **ALPHA** key. The key sequence to generate a message is the same whether used in a program or manually on the keyboard.

Alphanumeric Key [ALPHA/$\overline{\text{ALPHA}}$]—Used to start and end an alphanumeric field. The first and succeeding alternate strokes of this key cause key entries to be placed in the alpha-display register in a left-to-right order. The second and alternate strokes of this key terminate the alphanumeric field and restore normal keyboard operation. **ALPHA** key entries must always be used in pairs for proper operation. A pair is as follows:

Normal Operation ALPHA/ALPHA Alphanumeric Entries
ALPHA/ALPHA Normal Operation

There are several important aspects related to alphanumeric entries. Keep the following points in mind when making alphanumeric entries:

1. A maximum of 20 characters (including spaces) can be entered into an alphanumeric field. Any entries resulting in more than 20 characters are lost.
2. Attempts to enter more than 23 characters will automatically terminate the alphanumeric field, cause a flashing display, and execute the normal function of the key entry causing the flashing display.
3. The **CLEAR ALL** or **CLEAR** key may not be used within an alphanumeric field. The clear key will terminate an alphanumeric field. However, it produces an unmatched alpha instruction in a program and will cause improper operation.
4. An erroneous entry made while making alphanumeric entries can only be corrected by terminating the alphanumeric field and starting over.
5. Program steps that make up an alphanumeric field in a program may be edited (note item 4) like any other part of the program unless it is necessary to enter the letters U, V, W, X, or Z (control keys). The complete alphanumeric field concerned will have to be reentered if any of the control keys are to be entered.

Each key entry in an alphanumeric field produces one, two, or three characters representing the key. The single-character alphabet entries are made by the programming keys on the right side of the calculator. The upper half of each key is marked with the letter or symbol produced in an alphanumeric field. Numbers are produced by the numerical keys, and the decimal point (period), (,), X, ÷, +, − (dash) and = keys also produce single-digit characters as marked. The figure below illustrates the alphanumeric representation of the other keys when used in an alphanumeric field. The **DEG MODE, PRINT, TRACE, PAPER ADV** and **LIMITED PRECISION** keys produce special symbols and punctuation marks that are not represented on the keys. Notice in the figure that the identification for each key takes one or three character locations in the display. A space will always appear following a key that is represented by two characters.

Example: Key in the alphanumeric message SR-60A CALCULATOR.

Key Sequence

ALPHA/ALPHA S/RTN R/SUBR − 6 0 SPACE/RUN C/e_3 A/e_1 L/LIST
C/e_3 U/STEP L/LIST A/e_1 T/QUE 0/IF O R/SUBR ALPHA/ALPHA

The alphanumeric message remains in the display after the second **ALPHA** key is pressed until another key is pressed and the display reverts to the numeric-display register. The only exception is the **PAPER ADV** key, which does not affect the display. When a mathematical function key is pressed while a message is displayed, the function is performed on the contents of the numeric-display register and the result is then displayed.

When executed as part of a program, the **PAUSE, HALT** and **RTN** instructions may be executed one time without losing the displayed alphanumeric message. The one-time execution limit has only one possible exception and that is the **QUE** instruction as described in following paragraphs. The result is that if two **PAUSE** instructions are executed following an alphanumeric message, the first pause will display the message and the second will display the numeric-display register contents. The same sequence using **PRINT** instruction will behave the same way and has some advantages.

Key	Display	Key	Display	Key	Display
DEG MODE	°	2nd	II	Δ%	Δ%__†
PRINT	/	Lnx	LNX	STORE	STO
TRACE	*	LOG	LOG	RECALL	RCL
PAPER ADV	, (Comma)	x!	X!__†	SUM	Σ
LIMITED PRECISION	' (Apostrophe)	x^2	X²__†	%	%
e_6/D/R	D/R	x≥K	x≥K	YES	YES
e_7/ARC	ARC	e^x	e$_x$__†	NO	NO__†
e_8/HYP	HYP	10^x	10^x	NOT APPLY	N/A
e_9/D.MS	DMS	1/x	1/X	NOT KNOWN	UNK
e_{10}/x≥R	x≥R	$\sqrt{x}$	√X__†	ENTER	ENT
e_{11}/SIN	SIN	CLEAR MEM	CMS	CE	CE__†
e_{12}/COS	COS	EXCH	XM__†	FIX	FIX
e_{13}/TAN	TAN	PROD	II	EE	EE__†
e_{14}/π	π	Int x	INT	y^x	Y^x__†
e_{15}/P/R	P/R			x√Y	x√Y

†The open underline indicates an automatic character space.

Alphanumeric Key Identification

Example: Construct a simple program to solve the X + 5% with the input value of X, the equation and result printed.

Location	Key Code
0000	LBL
0001	e1
0002	ALF
0003	DEL (x)
0004	=
0005	ALF
0006	PRT
0007	PRT
0008	+
0009	5
0010	%
0011	=

Location	Key Code
0012	ALF
0013	DEL (x)
0014	+
0015	5
0016	%
0017	=
0018	ALF
0019	PRT
0020	PRT
0021	RTN

Enter	Press
100	A/e₁

Print
X =
X + 5% = 100.
            105.

In this example, the double PRT instruction is used in two places. The first alphanumeric message (X =) is printed at location 0006 and the entered value of X is printed at location 0007. Then the actual result is calculated by locations 0008 through 0011 followed by the second message and two PRT instructions. The program would have operated just as well if the calculation in locations 0008 through 0011 were moved to a position between the two print instructions at 0019 and 0020. Both ways have some advantages. The double print instruction prevents attracting user attention to the printer when the numerical result may not be printed until some time later. On the other hand, placing the alphanumeric field and print instruction before a long calculation will cause the message to flicker in the display while the calculation is in progress. The choice really depends on personal preference.

Another thing to note from the previous example is that a number in the display (display register) prior to generating an alphanumeric message is easily recovered following the message.

Prompting Control (QUE) and Responses

In addition to the keys related to generating alphanumeric messages, there are six keys which directly control the calculator prompting operations: **QUE, YES, NO, NOT APPLY, NOT KNOWN** and **ENTER.** Basically the **QUE** key is the control function and the others are designated as response keys.

Queue KEY [QUE]—When executed in a program, the program stops with the contents of the alpha display register in the display. The **QUE** instruction must be followed by four labels which correlate with program segments to be executed depending upon which response key is pressed.

QUE, label 1, label 2, label 3, label 4, Normal instructions

Yes   NO   NOT APPLY   NOT KNOWN   ENTER

When **YES** is pressed program operation transfers to label 1, **NO** to label 2, etc. The **ENTER** key simply causes the program to resume with the fifth location after the **QUE.**

The transfer control of the QUE instruction can be limited to one label if response is required of only one of the response keys.

Response Key, **QUE**, Label, Normal instructions

In this case, a response key (**YES, NO, NOT APPLY, NOT KNOWN** or **ENTER**) stored immediately before the QUE instruction will enable a transfer to the label when that particular response key is pressed. All other response keys cause the program to continue with the next instruction following the QUE and label instructions.

Response Keys [YES, NO, NOT APPLY, NOT KNOWN, ENTER]— These keys are used to manually respond to a message or question displayed following execution of a QUE instruction. Refer to *Guidelines for Prompting* in the manual for a description of the ways the response may be used.

The figure below illustrates the two program versions of the QUE instruction. The first form with four labels is the most versatile but the second form can save program space when only a yes or no response is required. Note that while the alphanumeric message is shown in the program immediately before the QUE instruction, the QUE instruction will cause the last entered alphanumeric message in the alpha-display register to appear without regard to when it was entered. For example, you can enter a message from the keyboard, then run a program which has a QUE instruction without a stored alpha field and the keyboard message will appear again.

Example: What is the procedure which allows an alphanumeric message entered from the keyboard to be displayed and printed more than one time without reentering the message?

Key Code
LBL
e1
QUE

When stored in program memory, this simple three-step program will cause the last stored alphanumeric message to reappear. This operation does not allow using the response keys unless more instructions are added as shown in the figure. Also note that if the alpha-display register is empty (after using **CLEAR ALL** or pressing **ALPHA** twice in succession), the display will be blank if e_1 is pressed to execute the QUE instruction. Simply press another key such as **CE** or = to restore the numeric display-register contents to the display.

Guidelines for Prompting

There are many ways to set up a prompting program. The versatility of the QUE instruction and the alphanumeric messages make it necessary to establish general guidelines for messages used in programs. The following guidelines have been developed for standardization of the prerecorded library programs in the Basic Library and the optional libraries.

Program Title

When required, program titles should print automatically when the card is loaded. The title should be preceded by a paper advance and should be set off from other messages by beginning with two asterisks.

Examples: **COMPOUND INTEREST
**STATISTICS

Response Key	Key Code	Comments
	.	
	.	
	.	
	ALF	

```
                              .
                              .
                      Alphanumeric
                      Message
                              .
                      ALF
                      Que                   Program stops
                                            and displays message
YES ............... ➤ e4 ➤ ........... Transfer to label e4
NO ............... ➤ D/R ➤ ........... Transfer to label D/R
NOT APPLY ..... ➤ D/R ➤ ........... Transfer to label D/R
NOT KNOWN ... ➤ 10ˣ ➤ ........... Transfer to label 10ˣ
ENTER ........... ⌐   +              Execute + and continue
                    ↓ 2              program
                      =
                              .
                              .
                      ALF
                              .
                              .
                      Alphanumeric
                      Message
                              .
                              .
                      ALF                 Presets QUE to transfer
                      YES                 only on a Yes response
                                          Program stops and
                      QUE                 displays message
YES ................. e4 ................ Transfer to label e4
NO ............... ⌐       +            All other responses execute +
NOT APPLY ...     }  •  2            and continue program
NOT KNOWN ..  ⌐          =
ENTER ...............
```

$$10^x$$

QUE Instruction Format

Questions

Questions of the yes/no variety appear as written in general usage. A question mark terminates the question word or phrase and the response should be with the **YES** or **NO** key. Questions are not usually printed.

                Examples: DELETIONS?
                            MARRIED?

Data Entry

Data entry is prompted using two methods. The first method is used whenever program space permits separate messages for prompting and printout. Beginning a message with the word ENTER implies the program needs additional data and the **ENTER** key is to be pressed after keying in the data. In some cases the response could be **NOT KNOWN** or **NOT APPLY** which means the value called by the message is to be solved for or ignored by the program.

                Examples: ENTER INTEREST (%)
                            ENTER VALUE OF X

A second method to ask for data is designed to be used as a printout and a message to enter data. An equals sign is used with a message to indicate data entry is expected. The same message can be printed to identify the entered data.

Examples: INTEREST (%) =
VALUE OF X =

Results

Results are printed with an appropriate alphanumeric name.

Examples: FUTURE VALUE
NET PAY

It is good practice to indicate when a program completes all calculations. The common identifier for the end of a program is to print three asterisks after the final result.

Location	Key Code	Location	Key Code	Location	Key Code
0000	PA	0020	ALF	0038	ALF
0001	ALF	0021	INS (W)	0039	e1 (A)
0002	LST (L)	0022	SF (I)	0040	SBR (R)
0003	e5 (E)	0023	e4 (D)	0041	e5 (E)
0004	IF+ (N)	0024	QUE (T)	0042	e1 (A)
0005	WRT (G)	0025	AUX (H)	0043	ALF
0006	QUE (T)	0026	= (=)	0044	PA
0007	AUX (H)	0027	ALF	0045	PRT
0008	= (=)	0028	PRT	0046	RCL
0009	ALF	0029	LBL	0047	PRT
0010	PRT	0030	LOG	0048	ALF
0011	LBL	0031	QUE	0049	TRC (*)
0012	LNX	0032	LOG	0050	TRC (*)
0013	QUE	0033	LOG	0051	TRC (*)
0014	LNX	0034	LOG	0052	ALF
0015	LNX	0035	LOG	0053	PRT
0016	LNX	0036	II	0054	RTN
0017	LNX	0037	PRT		
0018	STO				
0019	PRT				

To enable the program to start by using the **QUE** key, instructions start at location 0000. The first instruction is paper advance (PA). Paper advance at the start of the program takes slack out of the printer drive system which may result from tearing the paper off. If the drive system has slack, the characters in the first line printed may appear with flat tops or even as dashes.

Locations 0001 through 0010 enter and print the first prompting message LENGTH=. The QUE instruction at 0013 halts the program and displays the same message. In this case, the only response desired is a numerical key entry followed by the **ENTER** key. Since there must be labels in the first four locations following the **QUE** key, the ideal situation is to have labels such that if any response key other than **ENTER** is pressed, the program is not affected. Preceding the QUE with LBL, LNX and following QUE with LNX in the four label positions permits such operation. If **YES** is pressed, the program simply executes the QUE instruction again and waits for another response. When the value for the length is keyed in and **ENTER** is pressed, it is stored in R_{00} at 0018 and printed at 0019.

In similar manner, the width is asked for by locations 0020 through 0035. In this case, label LOG is used with the QUE instruction to control improper responses. As with any transfer instruction, if the QUE instruction is followed by a label that is not identified in program memory with the label key, a question mark will flash in the display.

The width value is multiplied times the height in R_{00} by the product instruction at 0036. The width is then printed at 0037. Locations 0038 through 0045 enter and print the message AREA to identify the result. The paper advance instruction was used to set the result apart from the entered values. The area result is recalled and printed at locations 0046 and 0047. The remaining instructions cause three asterisks to be printed to indicate end of program.

It should be noted before further analysis of the SR-60A that it is considered by many observers to be the forerunner to an onrush of 'prompting' desk-top programmables because of its low price, versatility, simplicity of operation, and expandability. The basic SR-60A has a 480-step program memory and 40 data registers. Optional memory expansion, to a 1920-step program memory and 100 data registers, is available to increase the programming power of the SR-60A. Also, an interface connector is provided at the back of the calculator to allow auxiliary equipment to be easily added. The AUX key on the keyboard is reserved to control the auxiliary operations. The interfaces available are for use with typewriters, tapes, extra memory, and communications devices. TI is one of the largest suppliers in the field and is expected to conduct strong marketing programs to attempt to replace millions of electro-mechanical machines that have now become almost totally obsoleted for all major use. The maintainability of the SR-60A is as straightforward as running a program. Five plug-in modules comprise the inner workings. In the event that a module malfunctions, a service representative can often isolate and replace the module in minutes. Also, the keys are individually replaceable so that down time for many reasons is an absolute minimum.

The SR-60A Operating Manual explains the format and keyboarding characteristics of the machine very adequately. Fixed-Point Format, Scientific-Notation Format, Mixing Numbers from the Two Formats, Clearing and Entering Numbers and the functions of all the keys are clearly portrayed on the pages together with examples outlined. The calculator hierarchy, use of parentheses, handling of function entry errors, calculations with constants, display indications and control, fix-decimal key, rounding, fraction, and precision control and handling of error conditions are all matter of fact items for user study and mastery.

Basic Printer Operations with the SR-60A

The basic difficulty for office use of most hand-held units is the lack of hard copy printout. One of the most basic selling advantages of the low-cost Texas Instruments' hand-held programmables, the SR-56 and SR-52 is that they are usable with the PC-100 optional printer. For many accountants, laboratory workers, and scores of other calculator users the immediate 'hard copy check' is very fundamental. For them and others there is nothing so comfortable as a quick, very positive check of input accuracy from hard copy. For others, it is most important to use the printouts as diagnostic aids and to have a more workable 'paper document' to use in constant 'what-if' analyses. The SR-60A printer is a sturdy but simple one for these purposes.

The printer is built into the SR-60A to provide users with a permanent record of calculations. When running prerecorded programs, the printout tape is the primary source of data and results while the display normally presents prompting messages and instructions. The paper used by the printer is a heat-sensitive type paper (thermal paper). The only mechanical part of the printer is a precision stepper motor which turns the rubber roller to move the paper past the stationary electronic printheads. When printing, the paper is driven past the printheads in tiny steps. Between each step, small semiconductor elements are heated very quickly by electronic circuits to produce color spots on the thermal paper. After several steps, these spots form the numbers, letters and symbols you can read on the thermal paper.

Since the printer is basically an electronic device, using metal probes or other sharp objects may damage the printheads. Users should refer to the Maintenance and Service section of the operating manual for paper replacement instructions and for instructions about proper care of the printer.

The Paper Advance Key [**PAPER ADV**] advances the printer paper without printing. If the key is pressed quickly, a single unwritten line is advanced. If the key is held down, the paper will continue to advance. The paper advance instruction is a programmable instruction. **Print Key** [**PRINT**] causes the current contents of the display to be printed. If the content of the display is an alphanumeric message, it will be cleared from the display after printing. **Trace Key** [**TRACE**] causes the calculator to enter the trace mode. In this mode every new function or result is automatically printed. Number entry keys do not cause a line to be printed. A number entry followed by a function will cause a line to be printed. When the trace key is pressed, an indicator comes on above the key and remains on until the key is pressed again. When in the trace mode of operation, the printer provides a detailed record of numbers, function entries and results. Since the calculator must devote some amount of time to the printing process, it will ignore keyboard entries during the short printing periods following function entries. Users should **be careful not to make entries while the printer is operating.** The trace operation may also be controlled by flat 9 in a program.

Preprogrammed Functions of the SR-60A

There are 22 preprogrammed key functions which are first-level type operations (except $\Delta\%$). This means that none of these operations will affect a pending operation. The $\Delta\%$ key is an exception, because it can complete another $\Delta\%$ operation and is designated a second-level operation. The 16 keys used for these functions operate on the contents of the display register except the D.MS function which operates only on the displayed number.

These 'special' functions include: Square key (x^2), Square Root Key, Reciprocal, Factorial, Log and Antilog, Power Key, Trig Functions, Degree Mode Key, Sine Key, Arc Sine Key, etc. Hyperbolics, Conversions, (Polar/Rectangular, etc.) and others.

Entering and Printing Reference Data on the SR-60A

The alphanumeric capabilities of the SR-60A can be used to print out reference data along with the normal numbers and results of a calculation. The block of keys on the right side of the circulator are basically programming keys. However, users note that the top half of all but one have alphabetical letters, symbols, etc. This is all that is needed to be concerned with as regards printing reference data. The programming functions are described in the Programming Manual. But, the reader might be interested in some of the methodology.

The **ALPHA** key in the lower right-hand corner is the control key for enabling the alphabetical functions of the other keys. The operation of the **ALPHA** key is very simple. Users press it once, the alpha mode is then enabled and all mathematical and programming key functions are locked out. Pressing the **ALPHA** key again takes the calculator out of alpha mode and returns keys to their normal functions. Entering and exiting the alpha mode does not affect the number in the numeric display register or any pending operations. This is possible because when in the alpha mode, all entries are routed to the alpha display register without affecting the numeric display register. The **CLEAR** key may be used to exit the alpha mode and simultaneously clear the numeric display and processing registers.

For a simple example of the alpha mode, users press the **ALPHA** key one time and press the **A, B, C, D** and **E** keys. They note that the **A** key caused an A to appear in the left-most digit of the display, the **B** key placed a B in the second digit, etc. They continue by pressing keys, **F, G, H, I, J, K, L, M, N, O, P, Q, R, S** and **T**. The display shows 20 letters which is the maximum number of characters which may be entered at a time. They then press the **ALPHA** key again and the calculator is out of the alpha mode even though the contents of the alpha display register are still displayed. Pressing the **PRINT** key will print the letters in the display and the display automatically switches back to the contents of the numeric display register. All other keys (except **CLEAR** and **CLEAR ALL**) produce letters or a symbol representative of the key function when in the alpha mode. The **DEG MODE, PRINT, TRACE, PAPER ADV** and **LIMITED PRECISION** keys are assigned special symbols and punctuation marks in the alpha mode. **DEG MODE** produces a degree symbol, **PRINT** produces a slash mark, **TRACE** produces an asterisk, **PAPER ADV** produces a comma, and **LIMITED PRECISION** produces an apostrophe. The key marked **SPACE** produces one blank digit each time it is pressed.

If an error is made while in the alpha mode, users press **ALPHA** to exit the alpha mode and start over. When operating the printer in the trace mode, the alpha message will be automatically printed when the **ALPHA** key is pressed to exit the alpha mode. If users desire to return the display to the numeric display register without printing or without affecting the contents of the numeric register, they press a non-mathematical function key. A detailed description of alphanumeric functions is included in the PROGRAM PROMPTING FUNCTIONS section of the Programming Manual.

INTRODUCTION TO PROGRAMMING OF THE SR-60A

The programmability of the SR-60A makes it a powerful and versatile calculator. With the unique prompting feature for simple operation, an alphanumeric display and printer, a typewriter interface and permanent storage capability on tapes, plotters or magnetic cards, the communicating SR-60A represents a technological breakthrough in desktop calculators. If various users professions involve numbers, and they frequently need to solve a series of simple math problems or even complex expressions, the SR-60A can save valuable time. An important fact about the simplicity of programming of the SR-60A is that users are not limited to using prerecorded programs on fixed key functions prepared by someone else. Regardless of their office use or profession, if users can solve their problems on a standard calculator, they can also usually learn to program the SR-60A to solve their problems without becoming a professional programmer.

A program is a list of precise instructions in specific order to be executed faithfully in a literal way. A language is merely the means by which users can communicate with their calculator. Applied to programming, a language is a necessary means to communicate a program to a calculator. Most calculator languages are heavily weighted toward arithmetic functions. If users have experience in carrying out arithmetic calculations, on any calculator, they know much of the SR-60A programming language. The functions presented in the Operating Manual for keyboard operation can be used in virtually the same way in stored programs.

Advanced calculators, like all computers, perform with literal faithfulness only those instructions presented to it. For new users this characteristic makes working with these machines a mixed experience. The result is that the user must be extra careful to program the calculator very precisely. A calculator will do exactly what it is instructed to do, regardless of whether the user wants it done that way or not. Simple programs may be entered, checked and run with little effort, or difficulty. Even though the SR-60A language is very arithmetic and algebraic in structure and use, a complex program requires forethought and planning. A well structured program will enable the various parts of the program to work efficiently and effectively together. If a new user has done very little programming, he or she will find the following ideas useful. If a user is familiar with programming concepts, the ideas will serve as a review and orientation toward calculator programming. One thing to remember is that a calculator is not a computer. Those who have computer programming experience should not assume the SR-60A program language to be the same as any other computer language, all functions are designed to correlate with calculator functions as closely as possible.

Users should interpret the following list of TI's suggestions in order to help develop their own programming style.

1. **Define the problem very clearly and carefully.** Identify the formulas, variables and desired results. What is known? What is to be determined? How are the known and the unknown related?
2. **Develop an algorithm or method of solution.** The calculating and programming capabilities of the calculator must be considered here. Remember, strictly speaking, calculators do not solve problems. They carry out your solutions precisely the way users program them.
3. **Develop a flow diagram.** Here it is essential to develop interactions between various parts of the solution.
4. **Translate the flow diagram into keystrokes.** Users enter the keystroke sequence on the coding form. It is useful to list all labels, memory registers, and flags used, in the space indicated on the coding form.
5. **Enter program.** Press **RESET, LEARN** and key in the complete program from the coding form. When entry is complete, press **LEARN** to remove the calculator from the learn mode.
6. **Edit program.** Press **RESET, LIST** to obtain a hard copy listing of a program. Notice that when the calculator reaches a blank space, it will halt in the learn mode. Return calculator to keyboard mode by pressing **LEARN** and **RESET**. Compare hard copy with coding form.
7. **Document user instructions.** Fill out a User Instructions form, detailing information required to run the program.
8. **Run or store program.** Run the program according to the user instructions and/or store the program on a magnetic card or tape cassette for future use.

Program construction can be aided by noticing that every program consists of smaller building blocks. There are four elementary structures upon which most calculator programs can be built.

1. Sequential operations with no choice of order
2. Sequential operations with a choice of order
3. Branches
4. Loops

These and other aspects of the SR-60A will be discussed on pages ahead.

Functions of a Label on the SR-60A

From the flow diagrams in the first part of this section, you can easily see that it is necessary to have reference points within a program. This is particularly true for branching and looping. Since every instruction has a specific address in program memory and since the instruction counter can be arbitrarily set to any address, instruction addresses can be used as reference points. The use of a numerical address, however, is not always convenient. The calculator provides a way to handle addressing without using the absolute numerical address. This method is by using labels.

Labels

There are two types of labels in the SR-60A, program labels and user defined key labels. There are 77 labels possible on the calculator as noted below. Notice that certain specific keys may not be used as labels under normal circumstances.

Label Key [LABEL]—When in the learn mode of operation, this key instructs the calculator to save the next key entry as a non-executable label. The non-executable label and the next address are saved in the internal label-file register. A key may only be identified as a label (prefixed with **LABEL**) one time in the program memory. However, a label may be called or transferred to as many times as desired. The **LABEL** key should not be used as a label.

Using labels in a program is similar to using tabs in a notebook. A label is a key that has been identified as a marker for a particular segment of a program (sometimes identified as a subroutine) or even a complete program. When a label is called in a program or from the keyboard (**GO TO X^2**, etc.), the calculator will find the label in the label-file register and set the instruction counter to the corresponding address. There are two major advantages in using labels. One is that labels may be used in place of the three- or four-digit addresses required for conditional and unconditional program transfers. The second is that exclusive use of labels in a program permits inserting or deleting program steps without worrying about the changing addresses of other instructions.

Any of the 77 possible label keys can be used as program labels. However, it is normally desirable to reserve the 15 keys identified with e_1 through e_{15} as user defined key labels. The main difference between the two label types is the ways they are used. Program labels are used internally in a program to identify required transfer points for subroutines, if-conditions, etc. User defined key labels are used when easy access to specific parts of a program is needed from the keyboard. See *User Defined Keys* description in the various manuals.

As the program is entered, the calculator develops a label file. The address of the first executable instruction in a labeled sequence is saved in the label file. For example, consider the following program segment:

Location	Key
0101	LABEL
0102	X^2
0103	2
0104	+
0105	2
0106	=

The non-executable sequence **LABEL, X^2** alerts the calculator to save the address 0103 in the label file as being associated with the label X^2. Consequently, when an introduction such as **GO TO X^2** is encountered, the instruction counter is set to 0103.

Even though X^2 has been used as a label, this will not prohibit its being used elsewhere in the program in its normal role. By using the label file, the calculator is able to determine from context which usage is intended.

User Defined Keys

There are five keys, e_1 through e_5, which are specifically designated as user defined keys, and ten more (e_6 through e_{15}) which have the option of being designated as user defined keys. When any of the first five keys are prefixed with the **LABEL** key in a program and the same key is pressed on the keyboard, the calculator will retrieve the address at the label from the label file and automatically begin program execution starting at that address. The other ten keys will behave in the same manner if they are prefixed with the **2nd** key.

It is important to note that the e_6 through e_{15} identifiers never appear in the program memory or on a program listing. The actual label for e_6 is D/R, e_7 is ARC, etc. Even though you desire to use e_6 as a user defined label, you need only to store LABEL, D/R in the program. The **2nd** key prefix when calling the label is what makes it function as a user defined key.

Another unique feature of the user defined keys is that when stored in a program, the calculator will treat the stored instruction the same as when you manually press the key, with one addition. When a user defined key is stored alone in a program (not prefixed with **GO TO,** etc.), the program segment is treated as a subroutine and operates with the same rules set up when actually using the **SUBR** key. The description of *Subroutine Transfers* further illustrates this function.

To illustrate user defined keys and types of labels, consider a program to cube a number and add the result to 27. That is, calculate $y^3 + 27$ for various values of y. Three versions of the program are shown to compare definition and usage: using + as a label, e_1 as a label and e_6 as a label.

Location	Key	Comments
0000	LABEL	
0001	+	Label
0002	y^x	These two instructions cause whatever is in the display to be cubed
0003	3	
0004	+	This is the normal usage +
0005	2⎫	
0006	7⎬	27
0007	=	
0008	RTN	Either a HALT or RTN can be used here

It is probably better to use **RTN** if this segment of code is ever to be used as part of another program. If the program is a stand-alone program, **RTN** acts like **HALT.**

To enter the program into program memory, press **RESET, LEARN,** then enter in sequence the above segment of code. To take the calculator out of learn mode, press **LEARN** again. To execute the program just entered, press **RESET,** key in a value for y and then press **GO TO,** +, **RUN** and the answer will be displayed.

Example:

Enter	Press	Display	Comments
	Y/RESET CLEAR MEM	0	
3	$/GO TO + SPACE/RUN	54.	RUN tells the calculator to start the calculation

Now modify the already stored program in the following way. Press **RESET, LEARN,** the display will read 0000 LBL. Press **STEP** (the single-step key). The display now reads 0001+. Now press e_1. The + which was at location 0001 has now been replaced by e_1. To see this, press **BSTEP** and the display reads 0001 e1. Press **LEARN** to return to calculate mode.

Enter	Press		Display	Comments
3	A/e_1		54.	e_1 behaves like a function key such as e^x or ln x, etc.

Notice that there is no need to press **RESET** or **GO TO** before e_1, nor is there any need to press **RUN**. By way of comparison perform the following.

Enter	Press	Display	Comments
3	$/GO TO A/e_1	3	Only the instruction counter is set to e_1.
	SPACE/RUN	54.	Program is executed.

In the same way as before, press **RESET, LEARN, STEP** the display shows 0001 e1. Replace e_1 in this instruction by e_6. This is done by pressing **D/R**. When there is no danger of confusion, this will be denoted simply by e_6. Now press **BSTEP**. The display reads 0001 D/R. The designation D/R is the label name for e_6. Return the calculator to calculate mode by pressing **LEARN**.

Enter	Press	Display	Comments
3	2nd e_6/D/R	54.	Thus to execute the program, the second function of D/R is needed.

Of course, the same principles are followed for e_7 through e_{15}.

Editing on the SR-60A

In the previous examples, two keys were used to assist in altering or editing the program, **STEP** and **BSTEP**. There are four of these editing keys. They affect program storage or the instruction counter; they may not be written into a program. The two keys already considered allow stepping forward and backward through the storage locations to verify or change program steps.

Step Key [STEP]—Causes the instruction counter to be incremented by one. In the learn mode, this causes the next storage location to be displayed. While not in the learn mode, pressing this key causes the program to be executed one step at a time except an alphanumeric field will run automatically and the **STEP** key must be held down to stop the program at the end of the field.

Back Step Key [BSTEP]—Causes the instruction counter to be decremented by one. In the learn mode, this causes the previous instruction and address to be displayed. While not in the learn mode, pressing this key has no effect.

Insert Key [INSRT]—In the learn mode, this key causes the instruction at the displayed address and all following instructions to shift to the next higher address. A null instruction is inserted at the displayed address. A program instruction in location 479 (1919 in the expanded calculator) is lost when the insert key is pressed.

Delete Key [DLETE]—In the learn mode, this key causes the instruction at the displayed address to be deleted and shifts all the following instructions to the next lower address. A null instruction is placed in the last program memory location.

As users quickly see, program storage may be examined by pressing **RESET** and **LEARN** and then stepping through a program using the **STEP** key. The instruction counter has an associated alphanumeric key code which may be used to verify the stored program. A stored key instruction can be replaced by pressing another key when the unwanted key code is displayed. The change may be verified using the **BSTEP** key. The **INSRT** key permits adding a new key instruction at any point in a program without affecting existing instructions.

A Very Simple Program and the Use of the TRACE Mode from the SR-60A Operations Workbook

The Problem: If you have $8000 now and invest it at 5% ... compounded yearly ... what will you have 12 years in the *future?* And so you are looking for Future Value. To work this on the keyboard, we'd do it like this ... 8000 × $(1 + .05)^{12}$ = Future Value. Or as a general expression, we could say Present Value × (1 + interest)$^{\text{No. of compounding periods}}$ = Future Value (or more concisely) $FV = PV (1 + i)^n$. Now, it is with this general expression we actually do the instructing of the calculator, because we want it to be able to solve the problem in the same general way for *any* set of numbers we enter.

So, really, all you are doing differently when you program is leaving "holes" into which you will later put variable numbers. With the SR-60A, the main way to leave holes is to put labels there. And that is why $PV \times (1 + i)^n$ = is programmed with "holes".

$$\Box \times (1 + \Box\%)^\Box = FV$$

What you see above is exactly what the calculator does: it stores the framework of a problem and lets you fill the holes. And to keep things straight, it labels the holes:

$$\overset{e_1}{\Box} \times (1 + \overset{e_2}{\Box}\%) \overset{e_3}{\Box} = FV$$

So all you have to do, once you have the framework, or program, is fill those holes. (To do that, remember, just press the numbers on the keyboard, and press the label key where you want those numbers entered, and the SR-60A does the rest ... as many times as you want it to.)

So let's see the list of program steps and what is actually happening in them.

LRN	(to tell the SR-60A it's going to "learn" now)
LABEL	(to tell the SR-60A it has a "hole" here)
e_1	(to label the "hole")
×	
(	
1	
+	
HLT	(Here you say, "Hold everything. I've got another hole".)
LABEL	
e_2	
%	
)	
y^x	(This tells the SR-60A what function it will perform with the number in the next "hole" ...)
HLT	
LABEL	
e_3	
=	
HLT	
LRN	(This gets you back to the calculating mode, where you need to be to insert variables and solve the problem.)

Now, if you've keyed all the steps in properly, you can solve the same problem you saw on the screen simply by entering 8000 ... then press e_1 ... 5 ... e_2 ... and 12 ... e_3 ... and your answer should be 14366.85061.

Now you should remember that if you want to compound *monthly*, you would have to divide that 5 by 12 and make the number of compounding periods 144 (for the total number of months in 12 years). To do that, you might include another label after percent . . . to show how many parts of the year that percent is divided into . . . and another label to multiply the e_3 box by the number of parts per year.

See if you can go back to the program we just wrote out and modify it to deal with monthly or even daily compounding. To be kind, we'll put a correct set of program steps for this modification at the end of this section. (Hint: you'll need to use labels e_4 and e_5).

The basic SR-60A has 40 data registers. Not only can users store numbers in those 40 registers, but they can use them for an assortment of other functions.

1. You can use them to add, subtract, multiply, or divide without bothering the mainstream of calculations.
2. In programming, they can use them as information "banks" and as branches for the calculator to use for side calculations
3. Users can use them for INDIRECT ADDRESSING in programs . . . This is like sending a letter to someone in New York asking that it be forwarded to Chicago . . . Users instruct the program to go to a memory . . . where it gets forwarded to another memory . . . or a program address. People who program a lot do this to save steps.

This workbook example concentrates on Number 1.

Press

7
STO   This stores the number in data register 13
13

5
SUM   This adds the number 5 to whatever is in data register 13
13

RCL   If you did good work, the recall of data register 13 should
13   show *12*

4
2nd   Here you are *dividing* the number 12, which is still in data
PROD   register 13, by 4. You use 2nd PROD because that tells the
13   SR-60A to do the *reverse* of multiplication, or division

RCL   If you did good work, your display should now read 3
13

Data registers can thus live their own lives apart from your keyboard calculations.

Trace Debugging

The function of TRACE in debugging a program . . . in this example problem . . . shows that a user put in × instead of plus before the e_2 label. Obviously, the program would get the wrong answer, but how easily could one find out *why?*

With the TRACE feature, users can print-out a faulty program which is attempting to execute, and see just where things are going wrong. Here's what the tape would look like if a user had put in that ×.

```
        0
              e1
8000.    ×
8000.    (
   1.    ×      (One can see that the program went wrong here)
   1.    HLT
```

1.		
	e2	
5.	%	
0.05		
0.05	)	
0.05		
0.05	Yˣ	
0.05	HLT	
0.05		
	e3	
12.	=	
1.953125-12		
1.953125-12	HLT	(And got this very wrong answer)
1.953125-12		

There are certainly errors *more* drastic than the one shown, but with this small example, a user can see how the TRACE feature of the SR-60A can help immensely in writing a workable program.

Try a Programmable Calculator Instead of a Computer

We have reviewed in this chapter the types of programs and languages, special keyboard and algebraic capabilities, and the users' wide choice of programming techniques. We have also noted: most of the peripherals available to computers can be used, including card readers, tape readers and punches, X-Y plotters, output printers, digitizing devices and general-purpose interfaces; keyboards are used not only for entering data for on-the-spot calculations but also for entering programs, and separate keyboard sections are available for special functions. Most of the program language appears right on the keyboard. Displays show calculated results, input data and programs, and they range from a simple numerical presentation to a complete alphanumeric, real-time output. Often there's a built-in prompting, a hard-copy printer, and usually there is a magnetic-card or cassette unit for storing and reading data and programs.

Programmable calculators, once rarely used in business but heavily used by engineers, are rapidly becoming one of the most valuable tools that all types of businessmen and managers share. Calculators can serve managers and engineers both at their desks and in the laboratories. At their desks, the machines provide rapid, easy solution of problems that otherwise wouldn't be attempted or that would require a small computer to solve. In offices or laboratories, the calculator can make speedy calculations between measurements or may act as a central processing unit and controls an automated test system or word processing operation.

Programmable calculators are getting both smaller and larger. Even hand-held machines are starting to intrude on the realm of the business computer. Larger programmable calculators — with a full array of peripherals, such as printers, plotters, digitizers, expandable memory, etc. — are being used as substitutes for computers over a wide range of applications.

Engineers sometimes ask: "For my job, do I need a programmable calculator, a minicomputer or a time-shared terminal?" The answer comes from a thorough understanding of the capabilities and limitations of each. Many articles have been written about the capabilities and limitations of minicomputers and time-sharing. Not much has been said about programmable calculators. All ranges of managers need this information. This book is designed to assist in the analysis of the capabilities of the programmable calculator and possible applications. The first section gives a broad overview, explaining functional capability, simple programming and calculator structure in a general way. There is also a discussion of the use of a calculator as a system component.

The second section considers the programming features of the calculators and their limitations. And the third section discusses the expansion of a calculator system with peripherals and the applications they control.

Software Costs can be Problems

Until recently only computer-based systems had the power and capacity to manipulate the large amounts of data generated by automatic test and measurement systems. And application software costs were — and still are — high. But sophisticated electronic calculators, with interfaces tailored to various kinds of instruments and peripherals, are also available now from manufacturers like Hewlett-Packard, Monroe, Tektronix, Texas Instruments, Wang and many others.

These calculators are, in increasing numbers, taking over tasks formerly performed by minicomputers because they are much simpler and less costly to program. And, as we have noted, they have added computing power, gained through the use of peripherals normally associated with computers, including disc files, printers and terminals.

On some systems too much time is required to program and to load previously written programs. Much time can be cut in constructing and checking out programs. And users can load directly with the keyboard or they can use off-line methods, like cards or paper tape. Restrictions on program input vary with the calculator but many new features apply to data input. Features such as trace mode allow faster program debugging and more efficient editing.

Permanent program storage avoids the problems of power loss. Cassette tapes and PROMs are among the most convenient of these; magnetic cards are among the least convenient because of the greater possibility of misloading, the longer loading time, and the limited capacity.

Checked-out software can be changed to firmware for permanent storage — an attractive feature for a production-line, calculator-controlled, system (Tektronix, for one, offers such a PROM programming service, also Hewlett-Packard and National Semiconductor).

Examples of ROM Identity

The H P-9825A desk-top advanced calculator offers ROM capability that is bound to be imitated by competitors. A brief discussion is warranted here.

The 9825 is designed to easily connect to peripherals and instruments without extensive hardware setup procedures or complex and time-consuming programming tasks. Three fundamental capabilities within the General I/O ROM allows users to control and communicate with most peripherals.

Formatted read/write capabilities are the heart of the General I/O ROM. Users can send completely formatted data to such peripherals as tape punches and printers and receive data from paper tape readers, digitizers, and card readers without any special knowledge of interfacing procedures. Single character read/write capabilities of the General I/O ROM allow the 9825 to send and receive non-ASCII control characters as well as data words of up to 16 bits in length. Status/control capabilities of the ROM monitor peripheral devices for error conditions or their operating status.

The Extended I/O ROM gives sophisticated interfacing capabilities by offering these features: interrupt permits the system to branch to a subroutine from anywhere in the program to service a request from an external device. This is accomplished by four simple statements. Additional ROM's are available to extend the language capabilities of the calculator for those who want to expand performance. Here's a sample: string ROM provides strings and string arrays whose lengths are limited only by available memory. A full set of string functions and operators allows you to easily manipulate your alphanumeric data. Advanced programming ROM provides for next looping, split and integer number packing, parameter-passing functions and sub-routines with local variables, and a variable cross-reference command. Matrix ROM adds standard matrix operators such as inversion and multiplication, plus a large number of multidimensional array operators.

Advanced calculators versus minis is a debate. Often minicomputer approaches to control systems are not the most desirable. Also, the problems of interfacing and software are often difficult, time consuming and unpredictable. The high-level languages available in minicomputers generally call for a large memory. Many also may not be applicable to some machine control uses. Assembly or machine-language programs of microcomputers are often unwieldy and are generally unsuitable for many industrial uses. Tasks such as data gathering and reduction, monitoring processing data, controlling numerical-input equipment, operating test equipment and providing terminal services are ideal for advanced calculators.

Computer-like performance — at a low price is what this book is all about. Although much capability is now inexpensive, many calculator supplier specifications can be confusing. Various vendors' products use their own high-level languages so that the age-old computer problems of "how much memory" and "which benchmark programs" can also bother users with calculator systems.

Aids in specifications include the following factors: peripherals capabilities; system speed; programming languages; storage requirements; and data input and output media. Other important factors include documentation, vendor support, program security, facilities and environmental requirements, maintenance and, of course, total system cost. Typical calculator-controlled systems measure circuit parameters, perform calculations and plot curves. Peripherals include external cassette tape units, digital plotters, nine-track, write-only tape transports, thermal line printers, etc.

Besides cassette storage for further processing, the calculators use paper tape; disk storage; and modems with buffers add capacity to systems. Data to the calculator are entered when the program requests it, or when users interrupt processing to change a variable. Or data enter automatically under program control. Various calculators offer an external interrupt capability through the keyboard or by program interrogation. Halting a program with the keyboard can disrupt the sequence of operation, however. Depending on the input device, either numerics or alphanumerics can be entered. There may be restrictions on the destination of the input, however.

The hardware cost and software expense is much lower than that of a comparable minicomputer or difficult to input and program microcomputer. Calculators which use BASIC are easier to program, because in several the BASIC interpreter is resident in ROM; so users don't have the problem of loading interpreters. There is a strong trend toward use of BASIC in calculators for on-line operations. Users find that these applications are becoming so sophisticated that unless they have a very low-cost system for the simplest applications, the use of BASIC is a real requirement. (See Appendix.)

Users must be concerned with interfaces. A line of HP instruments, including frequency synthesizers, signal generators, counters, microwave oscillators, a digital multimeter, a word generator and a 40-channel scanner are all compatible with the HP-IB bus, which is Hewlett-Packard's implementation of the

IEEE Standard 488-1975 digital interface for programmable instruments. Preassembled HP-IB systems include those for data acquisition, spectrum analysis and network analysis.

The Tektronix 31/53 calculator can interface directly as plug-ins with that company-s volt-meters, frequency counters, and a/d converter and a 16-channel scanner. Tektronix also has a general-purpose BCD interface — the 152 — which provides a full input and output for most of the commonly available instruments in the electronic design field today. With the 152, users can take data directly into the calculator memory by direct memory access — a feature normally found only on a minicomputer — at upwards of 15 k readings per second. For those instruments that normally communicate with a Teletype using bit-serial data, Tektronix has a bit-serial interface, the 154. The bus structure in the Tek 31 calculator is unique to that machine, but Tektronix also offers instruments using the IEEE interface.

Tektronix and Hewlett-Packard both provide calculator-driven instruments and systems that can use their own, as well as other manufacturers', instruments. HP offers the 9825 calculator, which has high level language programmability; the 9830, which incorporates BASIC in its programs; but the low cost 9815 desk-top uses reverse-Polish notation and is programmed like the HP programmable pocket calculators. Both the HP 9825 and 9830 have cartridges and cassettes for program storage, and they both also have room for several ROMs besides those supplied with the machines. A magnetic tape cartridge in the Tektronix 31-53 and other calculators provides automatic data acquisition, logging and statistical routines for interchangeable plug-in modules.

Because the big desk-top systems made efficient and cost/effective use of ROM and RAM or Read/Write insertable memory, it was logical to expect these attributes of calculator systems would soon be available in hand-held units. The National Semiconductor 7100 offers much of this utility. The reader can expect that some of the capabilities of *complete systems* such as those available of the HP 9830 A and B will be on the way for lower cost systems due to the rapidly decreasing price of such semiconductor memory devices. A brief analysis of the 9830 *systems* will serve as *coming attractions* for mass sale at very low prices. Some of these systems are defined by HP as follows: *A consulting engineering system* could include the 9830 with big memory, Matrix ROM, Page Printer, and Plotter. Versatility is the word here. Not only will the System 30 handle complex structural problems — steel and concrete column design, concrete beam design, pre-stress beam design, shear-and-moment plotting — but it'll handle business problems as well. **A research lab system** would conceivably consist of a Model 30 with big memory, Matrix ROM, Page Printer, High-speed Tape Reader, and Plotter. At this level, a Fourier Analysis or a Two-Way Analysis of Variance would be finished almost instantly. A 20 x 20 matrix inversion might take the better part of a minute.

Business system for small manufacturing concerns might consist of the Model 30 with small memory, String Variable ROM, Peripheral Tape Cassette, Hopper Card Reader, and Typewriter. With this configuration users could automate nearly every number-crunching task in their shop: payroll, billing, loan contracts, inventory control. What's more they'll get vital management information to help make astute decisions for cutting costs, bidding jobs, planning investments, and the like. As an added bonus, System 30 could maintain a list of important customers, periodically mailing them "personal" letters describing important new products or services.

A Model 30 Educational System would conceivably include a Model 30

with small memory, String Variable ROM, Marked Card Reader, Page Print-er, and Plotter. In this configuration, it's a most versatile educational tool —
equally at home in the science, mathematics, business, or computer science
class room. The Model 30 raises scientific education out of the tedium of rou-tine calculation and into the challenging arena of abstract concepts. A process
that's enhanced by a complete package of educational programs and teaching
materials. HP educational software is considered some of the finest and most
advanced in the U.S. and it's available on all levels — from elementary
through university.

With the Model 30, users can choose one or more of three types of memory to
enhance the power of the system. Depending on the application, users can add
to the mainframe (Read/Write) memory for extra-large problems. Or they can
select one or more pre-programmed Read-Only-Memories that increase the
language and system flexibility of the Model 30. Or, they can add Tape Cas-settes for added file capability. Engineers, for instance, need lots of Read/Write
memory, and a very sophisticated language to solve their sophisticated prob-lems. Statisticians will need lots of mass storage to manage a data base. While
those in Scientific Research might need both, since problems in this area are
often very complex — and have lots of data. The choice, of course, depends on
the price/performance trade-off's. These price/performance trade-off decisions
become happier ones for users as prices continue to fall with technological ad-vances, lower cost mass production techniques and mass-market competition
from many strong dependable manufacturers.

CHAPTER 8

THE STEP-UP TO DESK-TOP COMPUTING CALCULATOR SYSTEMS CONTINUED

Prologue

The Bookkeeper Clerks Are Suddenly *Computing* Payroll, Inventory Control . . . Searching Data Bases

The primary factor and perhaps the chief advantage of advanced programmable calculators over mini and microcomputers per se, is the *friendliness* of the input, the output and the operations language . . . *entering problems as you would say them.* The *familiar* keyboard is the easy *human interface* to these computing systems, and the immediacy of response is the personal and direct control that entices advanced calculator use and purchase in preference to computers or their *protocol-bogged* remote terminals. *Power on* means "go" for calculator users; mistakes cost nothing — in time, perplexed exasperation, or *tell me why* embarrassment. Users of calculators do not need to confess their errors to a systems analyst or seek advice from a distant employee of a time-sharing computer company. Calculator users easily move up from a *key per function* machine to a simple programmable device to advanced machines, as long as most calculator manufacturers stay with that familiar keyboard and that easy-use language, whether it be RPN or Algebraic, or even simple to learn, BASIC. It is important to note that BASIC is the essential *simple* language if dual-disk mass storage is added to the various calculator systems. Such disk calculator systems can quite neatly perform as batch or time-sharing terminals, handling remote job entry, numerical tape preparation, payroll, inventory control, structural design, etc.

Although calculators were not originally developed to replace minicomputers or *outside* time-sharing terminals, they certainly are doing just that. Of greater significance, however, they are bringing new millions of non-expert people into a new wide world of computer control. Just a year or two ago, calculators did not threaten minicomputers. Few experts predicted that they would be sold in hundreds of millions. And, fewer still envisioned advanced programmable calculators with disks, CRT terminals, several languages, and full alphanumeric capability. Regular bookkeeping clerks are now handling complex payroll and inventory control on $2000 *prompting* calculators. They learn the technique in a *few minutes* to type the word GET and the name of the program wanted, to enter data and to push a button labeled EXECUTE. The calculator is equipped with these special function keys. For example, it might have an ADD PARTS key, which the clerk would push after keying the number of parts to be added to inventory. Using a calculator as a terminal means the data and information is back quickly without red tape, protocol errors, or hangups. As noted ahead, plug-in *blocks* (ROMs or PROMs) assist the *clerk* in *computer* sorting, interfacing with plotters, disks, searching data bases, and an endless array of new and special capabilities. And TI's SR-60A *prompting* assistance particularly, has forced competitors to offer the same capability.

Growing Up

The programmable calculator system is a powerful way to do many things. Use it as an independent processor or manage large, complex systems. They can include graphic terminals, digital plotters, teleprinters, typewriter terminals, magnetic tape, paper tape/punch readers.

In fact, the programmable calculator can be the brain of most any system wanted. And it is often self-contained.

The Tektronix Tek-31 Basic Systems
Offer Graphics Displays

Tek-31 Programmable Calculator Computer Power, Calculator Ease — the Tek-31 is capable of dealing with complex problems, sophisticated programs and controlling systems. There are 35 math functions at user fingertips. Because the 31 follows natural math hierarchy to work problems users can enter data in a free format: ordinary floating, scientific floating or mixed decimal. Exponents, trig and hyperbolic functions are often solved on the keyboard. There is a full set of alpha characters. When users work this with the user-definable overlay, they get easy interaction between man and machine for versatility. Many users customize with overlays. The overlays let them define 24 keys to specialize in many problem areas by changing the math function keys to a users own subroutines. They combine several functions they use often into one key and label it. When they need that complete operation, they press the customized key and get complex patterns resolved with one key stroke.

Alphanumeric Printer — The alphanumeric printer and keyboard work together to make operation quite easy. Besides giving hard copy printout of results, the printer aids programming. While users write a program, the printer copies it. This makes it easy to check for errors. Then it's simple to edit with the proper keys. The conversational ability of the 31 is especially useful for systems work. Users can set up a program and turn over the operation to practically anyone. The calculator will print instructions, telling the user when to input data on the keyboard or when to press a key to sample from a system component and when to turn on or off another instrument.

Tektronix 31/53 Calculator Instrumentation System — Tektronix' 31/53 system complete with plug ins, is ready for immediate data acquisition and analysis. It measures time, frequency, temperature, count, voltage, current, resistance and can compute displacement, volume or pressure. It processes, evaluates, documents and records.

Programming uses an alphanumeric keyboard with user definable overlay or magnetic tape cartridge.

Standard Software:
- Data Logging on alphanumeric printer with sampling rate and numbers; single or dual source.

- Data Reduction. Statistical summaries of variables and frequency distribution.
- Data Acquisition. Stores data internally and generates least squares curve fits for a line, expotential or power function.
- Magnetic tape cartridge. Stores programs or data.

Principal Hardware Characteristics

Alphanumerics with user-definable keys. Stores data, computes, outputs to printer, display terminal or X-Y plotter. Memory steps, 512 expandable to 8,192; Data registers, 74 expandable to 1,010.

Digital Display. 7 Segment Gas Discharge. 10 digit plus two exponents.

Data Acquisition. 153 Instrumentation Interface enables calculator to read instruments; supplies power to plug ins.

Optional Plug Ins. Users choose from four TM 500 modular test and measurement instruments. Up to 20 plug ins can be operated with additional interface units.

Direct Inputs. Any electrical signal — voltage, current, resistance, temperature, time, and frequency.

X-Y Plotter. Optional 4661 Digital Plotter gives fast, accurate graphic representations of data.

Graphic Terminal. Optional 4010 displays alphanumeric and graphic expression of calculator output. The 4010-1 is hard copy compatible.

PROM. A user's own program up to 1,024 steps permanently reside in the calculator, without reducing MOS memory. Instant-on; more efficient operation.

Calculator System in Quality Control, An Example — A core memory manufacturer tests and matches magnetic characteristics of 50,000 cores from weekly production of eighty million. The former data acquisition system gave printouts of a 17-cell frequency distribution of each tested component. This meant manual processing of 30,000 printouts to produce closely-matched sets. The 31 calculator and 153 interface automated the system. Now, the calculator initiates tests, collects, processes and stores data. Then, compares data with acceptable test limits. Finally, it retrieves individual lot data, compares and matches similar components. The result is a saving of 34 manhours weekly and a production boost. Also, the calculator handles engineering and accounting work on the side.

Special Low-Cost Tektronix E-31 — With inherent capabilities identical to those of the 31, the E31 is exclusively a stand-alone processor. It is designed without add-on I/O capacity to offer significant savings to those not looking to expand their calculator into graphic, instrumentation or other systems. The E31 has a natural math keyboard and English-type programming. Its 35 built-in math functions and 24 user-definable keys permit short-cuts and shorthand calculations. The 512-step, 74-register memory is standard on the E31, expandable up to many times that capacity. In addition, there's magnetic tape storage to make programming power virtually unlimited.

There are many more convenience features that figure into the E31, like complete alphanumerics; total editing ability; flashing display for illegal or overrange math operations; and an optional silent alphanumeric printer.

Silent Alphanumeric Thermal Printer Option — Some E31 Printer Features: The E31 Calculator Printer operates in alpha and numeric characters which makes it invaluable for two reasons. First, program listing. The printer, using English mnemonics, lists each program step in sequence. The second advantage is interactive programs. When prompted by the program, the printer can ask the user for specific data input. Also, titled solutions are easily produced the same way. Thus, the printer not only provides for convenient execution but provides a printed copy of the program and each of its steps. Other E-31 Printer features include: a print display that results in the printing of the alpha information with whatever numerical data that is on the display. The printer can also be operated exclusively of any program. It has an automatic indication of overrange or illegal operations, and the thermal printing paper has a capacity of 18,000 lines per roll.

The standard E31 programmable calculator from Tektronix, Inc., has 512 program steps and 74 data registers. Memory expansion packs are available as options for expanding program steps and data registers. The unit has English-like programming keys and a simple keyboard that performs mathematical calculations the way users write them. It has more than 30 built-in math functions.

30/10 Graphic Calculator — Rapid and interactive graphics and alphanumerics offer vivid descriptions of math concepts drawn on the 31/10 personal graphic calculator system. It's a good combination of mathematician and designer. The 31 programmable calculator has computational power and the 4010-1 Graphic Terminal is a big display system. With both machines sitting at users' desks, they have two keyboards to work with. The math keyboard of the calculator and the teletype keyboard of the terminal let users concentrate on ideas instead of mechanics, and their concepts take form on the bright screen because the system is fast. For example they tap the calculator's remote key to send these commands to the terminal: Erase screen. Accept X-Y coordinate data. Enable graphics. Start or start alpha. Print alpha. Make hard copies with optional hard copy unit. The big screen capacity of the 4010-1 terminal puts up 2590 characters. There are 35 lines of 74 upper case alpha and numeric characters per line.

The Tek-31 Interactive Calculator System shown with various interface boards

As for graphics, it's fast with fineline draftsmanship. Drawing time is 2.6 ms. with 1024 by 1024 addressable points and 1024 on X by 780 on Y viewable points. Software lets users go to work immediately. They plug in a tape cartridge and get: automatic scaling, data plotting, X-Y coordinate value scaling, labelling and statistical operations. The 31/10 has capacity to meet many needs. Mathematical capacity via the 31 calculator with 35 math functions. Program and data storage memory — 74 data registers and 512 program steps. Both can grow with options. Users store the results on tape cartridge or print it on the 31 alphanumeric printer. The hard copy unit takes only 18 seconds to knock out the first copy and 10 seconds for extras.

User-Definable Overlays, An Example — There's a user-definable overlay which makes the calculator more approachable, yet still maintains the machine's basic math capability. Users custom label keys in their own language. For example, they might label a key standard deviation. Then, with a single keystroke, that function is executed. This feature allows even the inexperienced operator to use the machine, freeing the engineer from time spent entering data. The alphanumerics of the Tek 31 make interaction between users and the machine even easier.

With its alpha capability, the calculator can communicate with some other operator. It will ask for input instructions and label the results on the alphanumeric printer. An Example: Operators can —

Use the definable overlay and 24 keys to deal with special interests; set up a subroutine for each of these 24 keys and then label the overlay. An operator need only punch a key for the results desired. For example you could label keys magnitude, phase, real and imaginary to handle complex numbers.

Or for statistical work label them mean, variance, standard deviation and linear regression. A single keystroke does it.

There are other features which make programming simple: conditional and unconditional branching, editing, symbolic addressing and subroutine nesting.

Return addresses can be sequentially stored and recalled to permit nesting of subroutines, or can be used to compute a new starting point.

The growing trend of using programmable calculators as system processor-controllers makes good sense. They are flexible, easily programmed, adaptable, expandable — and extremely cost effective.

The calculator itself is a system. Users develop functional block diagrams utilizing data input via keyboard or magnetic tape; data processing through tape input; data manipulation and analysis by internal mathematical functions; storage in machine memory, mag-tape, and disc; and data output through the alphanumeric printer.

Users expand on that with interfaces and a wide range of instrumentation and they can see the calculator as the processor-manager of any system. Here is another specific example:

Interactive calculator replaces manual plotting of radioimmunoassay techniques which measure hormone and drug levels in the human body. Previously, it took half an hour of manual plotting to get test results after the radioactive complexes were counted. Now, tape cartridge programs ask for information as the operator inputs data into the 31 keyboard. In five minutes, the calculator prints an alphanumeric plot of hormone concentrations.

Two peripherals make the system more useful and faster. Since the radioactive complex count comes from a TTY printer, a tape reader inputs data automatically into the calculator. And a 4661 digital plotter gives a graphic comparison to a standard curve.

Tek-31 Programming Procedure, an Example — In addition to conditional and unconditional branching, on the Tek 31 users have full editing capability, they can symbolically address and nest subroutines, and alphanumerics are as simple as typing one's name. With these features and the ease of programming, the computational power of a computer is available at user fingertips. And in a language they already understand.

Decision making within a user program is a simple matter with the "if" condition keys (conditional branching). The number in the display may be tested for less than zero, equal to zero, or greater than or equal to zero. In addition, users can test the condition of a programmable flag and test to see if the calculator has overranged or attempted an illegal math operation (indicated by a flashing display). If the conditions are not met, the sequential program execution is interrupted and program control branches to the appropriate point in the program. In addition to these conditional branches, four types of unconditional branches are available.

If there is an error in programming, it's easy to examine the program by → ← pressing step forward or step back to debug the program. The printer will list the program steps in English for users. Once users detect the error, they can insert, delete or overwrite a step. If necessary, the machine automatically renumbers the subsequent program steps. Symbolically labeling a subroutine allows users to call a subroutine by its name rather than by its location in memory. The calculator will remember the subroutine location. All users have to do is tell the calculator which subroutine they want. The calculator finds the subroutine, executes it and automatically returns.

In order to return to the proper point in the program after branching to a subroutine, the calculator automatically remembers the return address. This return address may be sequentially stored and recalled to permit nesting of subroutines, or modified to alter the return address.

With the alpha capability in the Tek 31, the calculator actually communicates with the operator. Because the calculator can print instructions, ask for input and label results, an experienced operator is no longer a necessity. Any one who can press the start key can get the right answers.

Output — Reading the operations and results is easy in the large, bright display. Messages displayed tell users what mode they're in and if an error has been made. When users need hard copy, the silent alphanumeric thermal printer provides it.

The wide variety of input and output peripherals users can interface to the Tek 31 can provide more power. These include the graphic computer terminal and x-y plotter.

Tektronix' 153 Analog to Digital Converter and 16-Channel Scanner

For single or multipoint data acquisition to 50 readings per second the TEKTRONIX 31/53 Calculator Instrumentation System can make proper connections to manual instruments. Two specific Tektronix products make data acquisition go faster and farther. The 153 Analog to Digital Converter Plug-In measures voltage with three to ten times more samplings per second than previously possible with the DM 501 Digital Multimeter. The 16-Channel Scanner Plug-In allows manual or automatically stepped multi-channel switching with adjustable rates and unlimited cascading.

The 153 A/D Converter gives user access to fast changing phenomena, such as is required in digitizing analog outputs of laboratory instruments or in multipoint scanning applications. The A/D Converter has a 2 ms. sampling window to provide accurate tracking of abruptly changing signals, while maintaining full 3½-digit resolution.

On the other hand, the DM 501 Digital Multimeter commands 5 readings per second, and is perfect for all kinds of slow-changing voltage, resistance and current measurements with 4½ digit precision (10 μV resolution for D.C. volts with MOD 718 D). Pressure, temperature, force and displacement transducers are typical sources in calculator-based data acquisition systems using this versatile instrument.

The end result is to push manual strip chart analysis or hand copying of printer output a little closer to extinction.

Quantitative analysis of strip chart data now easily falls within range of the 31/53. Computation of area under each curve, peak heights and time between peaks are all performed by the push of a button on the 31 calculator. The 153 A/D Converter opens up 31/53 applications with chromatographs, infrared or ultraviolet spectrophotometers, X-ray defractometers, and other analytical lab instruments. And at any time, users can pull the Tektronix 31 off-line to perform independent statistical and mathematical computations.

Multipoint monitoring: The scanner steps in. The 153 A/D Converter is connected to individual test points via the Tektronix reed relay 16-Channel Scanner. Sequential scans may be stepped in remotely, via the 153 I/F, or may be advanced manually, via its front panel control STEP button. A rate potentiometer adjusts flash rate signal to the 31 calculator from 10 pulses per second to 1 pulse per 10 seconds.

With the scanner in action, the 31/53 can monitor, log, process, and analyze readings from multiple sources; compare data with acceptable test limits; and signal complications. Any number of scanners may be cascaded together, so they're a time and trouble-saver along even the longest line.

Ready to read, scanner or not. Either the calculator or any external trigger can control the Converter sampling. A jumper strap within the A/D Converter may be set for an "internal" rate of sampling, wherein a REMOTE command from the calculator signals the transfer of a data sample held in the A/D Converter to the 31. Upon completion of the data transfer, a new sample is automatically generated and held. When set for "external," the scanner's pulse generator or other negative-going TTL pulses will trigger the converter to take and hold a sample. This not only permits the most precise time intervals between samples, it enables two plug-ins to update x and y data simultaneously when the external trigger inputs are paralleled. The calculator may thereby address each plug-in separately to log, analyze, compare and store individual data. Users can step the scanner or synchronize an external process directly from the plug-in. Speed is greater than 50 samples per second in direct addressing programs, 18 in indirect.

Tektronix 31/53 Calculator Instrumentation System Summary and Layout

Tektronix' 31/53 system complete with plug ins, is ready for immediate data acquisition and analysis. It measures time, frequency, temperature, count, voltage, current, resistance and can compute displacement, volume or pressure. It processes, evaluates, documents and records.

Programming. By alphanumeric keyboard with user definable overlay or magnetic tape cartridge.

Standard Software:

Data Logging on alphanumeric printer with sampling rate and numbers; single or dual source.

Data Reduction. Statistical summaries of variables and frequency distribution. Data Acquisition. Stores data internally and generates least squares curve fits for a line, exponential or power function.

Magnetic Tape Cartridge. Stores programs or data.

System Processor. 31 Programmable Calculator. Natural math heirarchy. Alphanumerics with user-definable keys. Stores data, computes, outputs to printer, display terminal or X-Y plotter. Memory steps: 512 expandable to 8,192. Data registers: 74 expandable to 1,010.

Digital Display. 7 Segment Gas Discharge. 10 digit plus two exponents.

Data Acquisition. 153 Instrumentation Interface enables calculator to read instruments; supplies power to plug ins.

· **Optional Plug Ins.** Choose from four TM 500 modular test and measurement instruments. Up to 20 plug ins can be operated with additional interface units.

Direct Inputs. Any electrical signal — voltage, current, resistance, temperature, time, and frequency.

X-Y Plotter. Optional 4661 Digital Plotter gives fast, accurate graphic representations of data.

Graphic Terminal. Optional 4010 displays alphanumeric and graphic expression of calculator output. The 4010-1 is hard copy compatible.

PROM. A user's own program with up to 1,024 steps permanently resides in the calculator, without reducing MOS memory. Instant-on; more efficient operation.

Tektronix 154 Calculator RS-232-C Interface

The 154 is self-contained and housed, with its own power supply, in a very compact package. It has two input-output connectors on the front for calculator peripherals, (a plotter, for example). The two-way ASCII connectors are located at the rear. One is the RS-232-C connector. The other is for 20 mA current loop devices. Using the 154, the calculator and the terminal become interactive, either alpha or numeric.

The 154 Interface job is to give users better data control. It does that by putting extra power in the TEKTRONIX 31 Programmable Calculator. The 31 has a great deal of programming and processing competence. Now users can put that competence to work on instrumentation and computer peripherals from a variety of makers. By linking the 31 to the RS-232-C compatible device users can create a very efficient data handling package. The term "data handling" covers a lot of ground. The Calculator-Interface combination does a lot for users.

Through the 154 Interface, the 31 can acquire information from any RS-232-C compatible instrumentation. The calculator will listen to and react to machines quickly. The 31 can also be part of the conversation when disc, card, punched paper and mag tape readers are operating.

Talking to Terminals

The 31, using the 154, can interact to teletype or like terminals to print out quality control reports, financial analyses or tabularized data. By feeding control commands and data through the 31, users can get many keyboard details normally required by an operator. And these things are brought to bear on a very useful full page format. All copy can be duplicated on the 31 printer as well as special steps, listings or operator instructions not normally transmitted to the terminal. Data can be keyed in on the terminal and printed on the 31 or vice versa. The 154 will interface with a wide range of models from a variety of manufacturers such as:

Digital Equipment Corp., Model LA-30 Decwriter (300 baud, current loop).

GTE Information Systems, Model 5741 Communications Terminal (300 baud, RS-232-C).

NCR Model 260-6 ASR Terminal with mag tape cassette (300 baud RS-232-C).

Tektronix Models 4010, 4013, 4023 Display Terminals (1200 baud, RS-232-C).

Teletype Corp. Model 33 ASR with paper tape (110 baud, current loop).

Texas Instruments Model 733 KSR Typewriter Terminal (300 baud, RS-232-C).

Texas Instruments Model 733 ASR Typewriter Terminal with dual magnetic tape cassettes (300 baud, RS-232-C).

The categories above aren't really as distinct as they may appear and in fact may all be part of the same operation. That's especially true when users combine a 31 Calculator, 154 Interface, Teletype, data acquisition equipment and some form of card, tape or disc storage. That makes for an unusually versatile system. All RS-232-C bit serial ASCII devices include most teleprinter terminals, crt terminals, output printers, paper tape punch readers, card punch readers, digital tape cassettes, etc. It also provides a 20 mA current loop operation, for use with a standard Teletype.

Tektronix 152 General Purpose BCD Interface

The 152 Interface links Tektronix Calculators directly to digital peripherals. With the 152 users get input/output calculator control over power supplies, meters, counters and even such things as multi-channel analyzers. This control means manual data entry, with all its limitations, can be overcome. It means the calculator can now acquire data automatically from a wide range of peripherals and instrumentation by using the calculator's output commands. The 152 can translate them into very flexible external control. The commands do the starting, stopping, and execution of certain remote operations. That would naturally involve passing on information about data limits, ranges and frequencies to programmable instruments and signal sources.

The 31 can keep track of what's going on. With convenient logging and listing features, the low-cost 152 puts computer-like power at user disposal providing power and control four ways:

ONE: Direct Memory Access:

If information is coming in a hurry the 152 can transmit data to the calculator memory and perform mathematical operations easily. Either processing or storage is simply a matter of keyboard or program control. The 152 allows the calculator to keep track of up to 1000 samples per second. This way the access can be stopped when a set number of samples have gone by. They come in through the standard 64 inputs which can be doubled and tripled with options.

TWO: Direct to Display:

With the 152, interfaced peripherals may write directly into the calculator display. The calculator then uses the displayed digits as it would any data entry. The information may then be processed, logged and stored at a rate to 20 samples per second. This operation too, may be manual from the keyboard or automatic with program control.

THREE: Peripheral Control:

The 152 Interface features two-way transmission. This means the 31 can actually control programmable, parallel format instruments. D/A converters and multiplexers are examples.

FOUR: Trigger Pulses:

With six built-in triggers, generated by the calculator, external circuitry can be put to work. This allows the calculator, through the 152, to start or stop a process, energize a light or turn on a ramp generator, etc. If necessary, trigger pulse widths may be widened from 300 ns with an easy internal adjustment.

These four operations show that the calculator/interface/peripheral combination forms a powerful system to do whatever is needed done with data acquisition and data control. It's a strong system — a system that transmits, receives, processes, monitors and stores.

Operation:

The 152 is operated by REMOTE commands from the calculator. Executed either from the keyboard or by program control, a REMOTE command is simply the REMOTE keycode followed by two digits. The first digit represents TENS and calls the interface. The second digit stands for UNITS and defines what interaction is to take place. This aspect may be compared with dialing a particular phone number with the conversation or data exchange to follow.

Addressing:

REMOTE ADDRESS SELECTION is an important part of the 152 operation. Separate addresses chosen for the 6 triggers may be labelled REMOTE
81, REMOTE 82 and so on. Three other modes can be used (DIRECT TO DIS-
PLAY, DIRECT MEMORY ACCESS AND PERIPHERAL CONTROL), and
could be addressed REMOTE 87, 88 and 89. The 152 is set to recognize these
addresses as belonging to a particular instrument or operation. If changes in
signal polarity are necessary, strap selectable jumper wires may be switched.

The 152 Will Interface to:

DVM's, counters, scanners, time generators and programmable power supplies. Almost all peripheral devices with Binary Coded Decimal (BCD), full bit
parallel input/output. It will also interface to many devices accepting straight
binary or binary coded octal addressing.

SOME EXAMPLES OF TEKTRONIX SOFTWARE

Tektronix' 31 and E31 Statistics Library, Vol. 1. — Designed in large
part for the 512-step basic memory, the volume includes general statistics,
tests, distributions, and curve fitting programs as enabled by the 31's enhanced memory configuration. Also contains curve fitting programs for expanded 1024-step calculator.

Tektronix' 31 and E31 Statistics Library, Vol. 2. — Coupled with an Option 4 equipped calculator, this volume offers additional programs for one, two
and three-way analyses of variance; randomized complete block/Latin square;
t-tests; Bartlett's test: F-distribution; and t-distribution.

Tektronix' 31 and E31 Statistics Library, Vol. 3. — Programs in this volume require a minimum Option 4 memory configuration (2048 steps). They
include multiple linear regression, and polynomial and linearized regressions.
With the 31, all data and regression equations may be plotted on the 4661
Digital Plotter. Three data correction options are provided.

Tektronix' 1 Mathematics Library. — GEOMETRY AND TRIGONOM-
ETRY. Includes plane triangle and plane closed polygon solutions.

GENERAL FUNCTIONS. Provides for the evaluation of gamma functions
and factorials and number base conversion.

POLYNOMINALS. For solving quadratic and cubic equations, real roots of
functions, and 3rd order interpolation.

Tektronix' 31 and E31 Mathematics Library, Vol. 1. — Designed primarily for the basic 512-step, 64-register memory, Vol. 1 contains all the 21
programs plus more complex calculations involving matrix arithmetic, complex operators, vector magnitudes, and so on.

Tektronix' 31 and E31 Electrical Engineering Library, Vol. 1. — This
volume contains two major programs:

FFT AND ASSOCIATED OPERATIONS. Handles real time, complex time,
and complex frequency waveforms; calculates waveform limits; performs discrete Fourier Transforms or its inverse; calculates convolution/deconvolution
and cross-correlation; plots waveforms on optional graphic terminal or plotter
(for the 31); and allows user to write his own analysis program using subroutines provided.

FOURIER SERIES. Calculates and evaluates Fourier series in terms of sine
and cosine coefficients or in terms of complex coefficients. With the 31 it allows
digital plotting or graphic display.

Tektronix' 31 and E31 Electrical Engineering Library, Vol. 2. —
MICROWAVE CIRCUIT ANALYSIS. An extensive package for circuit analysis that includes parameter conversions; cascade, series, and parallel interconnections; finding lumped matched networks. Parameter printout includes

K, U, G_{max} and other gains, f_{max} and f_T, VSWR's, return losses, and gammas for optimum matching.

Tektronix' 31 Electrical Engineering Library, Vol. 3. — PLOTTING AND MAPPING. Facilitates graphics representation on the 4661 Digital Plotter or 4010 Graphic Terminal of various parameters associated with microwave circuit design using Polar and Smith Chart formats.

4661 Alpha Character Generator Software ROM. — This is a routine stored in a plug-in ROM, for drawing letters, numbers and symbols on the plotter. Characters may be executed from the keyboard or under program control.

Simultaneous equations and matrices. — For solving two and three simultaneous equations; 3rd-order determinants; 3rd-order matrix inversion and eigen-value solutions.

VECTORS. Includes vector addition and subtraction, vector cross products, coordinate transforms, vector scalar product and angle, among others.

COMPLEX OPERATORS. Expert programming for a variety of complex operators, from +, −, ×, ÷, to arctanh Z.

INTEGRATION AND DIFFERENTIAL EQUATIONS. Includes Nth-order differential equations and two simultaneous differential equations.

Systems Software

31/53 Instrumentation System. — DATA REDUCTION PROGRAM. Gathers data from one or two instruments, prints data provided by each sampling, makes statistical computations of variables and frequency distribution, and stores "running totals" in registers. In the case of dual sources, co-variance and correlation coefficients are also calculated.

DATA ACQUISITION PROGRAM. Gathers and stores data in R registers. At the user's option, the program prints data as each sample is taken, or as a comprehensive print-out during execution of statistical parameters program. Curve fitting program generates least squares curve fits for a line, exponential or power function.

31/10 Graphic Calculator System. — STANDARD PLOT PROGRAMS. Includes standard data plots; function plots that enable plotting of any user-defined single variable function; and histogram plots, which allow generating and updating histograms.

OPTIONAL PLOT PROGRAM. As an expansion of the standard plot program, it is designed to run with Option 4 Memory (2048 steps). Accommodates one or two variable data, pie chart and frequency distribution plots, and allows such additional display features as pre-determined size and location of viewing window and axis labeling.

31/4661 Digital Plotter System. — DATA PLOT PROGRAM. Plots data within a user-defined plot area. User defined axes with tic marks are also available.

FUNCTION PLOT PROGRAM. Plots single variable functions. Allows auto-scaling, plus selection of window size and location, axis intersection, horizontal and vertical tic intervals.

HISTOGRAM PLOT PROGRAM. Provides user-selected plot size, data limits, cell width, and an edit feature.

4921/4922 Flexible Disc File Management. OVERLAY MONITOR PROGRAMS. Provide interactive file management capabilities through user-defined overlay.

RUN-TIME ROUTINES. Perform data I/O, data file manipulation, and program file overlaying into memory under program control.

UTILITY PROGRAMS. Perform various housekeeping and miscellaneous functions.

4661 Extended Graphics Program Library. — Contains programs designed for the 31 with memory options 1 and 9, plus the 4661 Digital Plotter. Included are two- and three-dimensional data plots; two- and three-dimensional function plots; polar data plots; and polar function plots.

Customized Software

The Tektronix software library is not the last word in programming. Users can revise these programs to meet their special needs, build new programs from spare parts, or write their own from scratch. With a memory configuration range from 128 steps to a large 8192 steps on the 31's Option 10, plus linking capability and magnetic tape storage, the range is virtually unlimited.

If users find a need for custom software to fit their special application, they may call their Tektronix representative.

The Olivetti P6060 Computing Calculator — A Trend Setter

Observers of the calculator products marketplace have hoped and expected that user demands for more memory, a great deal more, would become available at much greater convenience and lower cost due to advances in many microelectronics areas. Businessmen especially, but engineers, industrialists, educators, and governmental division managers as well, deeply appreciate the ease of use, human factors designs, and absence of the *computer fear* syndrome some advanced programmable desk calculators offer. In more straightforward language, they want to use calculators, and use them extensively INSTEAD OF COMPUTERS, but they want the calculators to perform more computer capabilities — but simply. Data cassettes, insertable RAM and ROM, and other small-size memory add-ons are fine for some purposes, but for the BIG jobs, they are often clumsy, expensive, and inadequate. The answer is memory, as integral parts of the main machines, in the millions of bits — megabit ranges. This means disks, low cost disks, the *floppy* disk types. But, memory of this size means data base entry and retrieval, and that means a data base man-

Olivetti's Compact 'disk included' BASIC Keyboard P6060 Computing Calculator

agement system of some type must also be available. These systems are *old hat* in the computer world. But they are terribly complex, expensive, — and many users justifiably hate them.

Calculator manufacturers, relying for their success on *personalized solutions* to computing problems, sell their systems because they are approachable, conversational, direct people to machine systems that provide keyboard immediate-response action. To properly handle data management **simply and directly** on low-cost calculators, these units require a rather sophisticated operating system — and a *tried and true* easy to learn and use language, besides low cost machine integrated floppies. The most obvious language to use is BASIC. Several advanced calculators have used and continue to have BASIC language capability, but adding *clamping on* disks as exterior peripherals has been awkward and expensive. The Olivetti P6060, released for sale in late 1976, seems to have put it all together — compactly, simply, and very neatly. The disk is incorporated in the very sleek main calculator; it has an alphanumeric and a BASIC keyboard, an exceptional operating system and great peripheral versatility, convenience, and capabilities expandability. The system beckons close analysis. For starters, it is interactive, intelligent — and low cost. Is it adaptable, expandable?

The Typewriter-sized P6060 Computing Calculator: Handy and Powerful

The P6060 on a user's desk is indeed instantly available, instantly approachable . . . communicating immediately through its display and printer. Because the P6060 can be programmed in BASIC (a powerful extension of the language), the simplest language to use, the job doesn't require computer professionals. The efficiency result is that anyone can quickly and confidently create specific programs to solve individual problems.

If work involves standard, clearly defined computing problems corresponding to specific applications that change infrequently but are time consuming nevertheless, then the P6060 personal computer system may make only one demand on time, i.e., the selection of the appropriate program(s) from the Olivetti or other applications libraries already recorded on today's most convenient storage medium — the floppy disk. For example, the P6060 application disk library ranges from numerical and statistical analysis to structural analysis and design. From medicine to surveying. From financial analysis to numerical control.

These and other programs are designed for flexible use; they are modular in design and can be extended and modified as users adapt them to systems to meet specific needs. BASIC is very widely used. Old tried and true programs fit or new programs can be readily obtained from existing libraries or written at any time. Compactness is also important. As a self-contained desktop system programmed in BASIC, the Olivetti P6060 is always on site — a constantly available problem solver.

BASIC Keyboard and Display: Convenient Program Checking

The P6060's BASIC (Ansi and ECMA compatible, provides enhanced facilities, e.g., random file handling, string manipulation, MAT statements, built-in functions. Programs written in BASIC can be entered directly on the keyboard and checked instantly on the display. The alphanumeric keyboard includes 26 statements in BASIC as well as the most frequently used commands on single keys, and provides for user-definable functions. The display guides the user and identifies possible errors of syntax or logic. Programs stored on floppy disks can be easily recalled and modified at any time. Users' own programs can be added to augment Olivetti standard packages.

External Connections for even Greater Power

The power of the P6060 personal minicomputer can be easily expanded beyond the basic desktop system. The more power application needs, the more the P6060 makes available through connection to a wide range of external devices. If an application requires rapid access to large amounts of data, the P6060 can be connected to moving head disk units with up to 10 megabytes (million bytes) of randomly accessable data. Compatible media for storage of large amounts of sequential data can be connected to computer-compatible magnetic tape, magnetic tape cassette units, paper tape readers, and punches, etc. Rapid, large volume printing can be connected to a variety of high speed impact printers for graphics and drawings. The P6060 can be connected to both analog and digital plotters for graphic output; or to digitizers, for generating data from film and drawings.

For automatic analysis of data from Analytical Instruments the P6060 can be connected, through an EIA RS 232 C (CITT V24) interface, to a wide variety of industrial and medical instrumentation.

The communications capabilities of the system also include:
- Transmitting/receiving data to/from remote locations
- Accessing a large computer facility
- Running programs in languages other than BASIC. The P6060 can also function as a terminal in a Time-Sharing environment through the same RS 232 C interface.

Overall System Modularity and Expandability

The architecture of the P6060 personal minicomputer system is modular in concept, design and implementation. Memory modules, for example, allow the internal memory capacity to be increased from 40K to 80K bytes (user memory from 8K to 48K bytes) in 8K increments. One floppy disk alone can store the Operating System, user programs and data files. A second floppy disk can triple user capacity. (See detail below). The integrated printer can provide formatted, hard copy output. Users also have a significant number of alternatives available for personalizing the solution to their computing problems. For example:
- They may choose high speed impact printers in place of the integrated thermal printer;
- They may choose among several large plotters instead of using the plotting functions of the integrated printer; and
- They may choose moving head disk units in place of the second floppy disk unit.

In each case they can minimize their investment while obtaining only the configuration they need with practically no restrictions on future growth.

The Operating System

The Operating System, which controls all functions of the P6060, resides on a system floppy disk, taking up approximately 120K bytes, allowing more than half of the disk for user programs and data storage. This sophisticated system manages not only the BASIC and COMMAND languages, but also provides for extended facilities (such as matrix and string manipulation, peripheral control, plotting function, and terminal emulation.) The extended modules are brought into the internal memory only when specifically required, optimizing total memory utilization. The Operating System is designed with the same modular concept as the P6060 itself, providing flexibility, power and expandability which can adapt to a user's present and future needs.

Typical P6060 configurations will consist of:
CPU/8K/Printer/Single Floppy
CPU/8K/Printer/Dual Floppies
CPU/16K/Printer/Dual Floppies
CPU/24K/Printer/Dual Floppies
CPU/32K/Printer/Dual Floppies
CPU/40K/Printer/Dual Floppies
CPU/48K/Printer/Dual Floppies

THE OLIVETTI INTERACTIVE P 6060 "BASIC" KEYBOARD DISK INCORPORATED SYSTEM DETAIL
General Purpose, Desktop System, Programmable in BASIC

Basic Unit — The basic unit consists of: central memory (RAM); read-only memory (ROM); arithmetic-logic unit; full alphanumeric keyboard; console; alphanumeric display; and floppy disk read/write unit (single drive).

Options — The basic unit options are: central memory extensions; integrated alphanumeric printer; second drive for floppy disk read/write unit; one or two Olivetti Standard (IPSO) interfaces, for connection to compatible peripheral units; DCC 6609 interface, for connection to the moving head disk cartridge unit; and asynchronous line control unit for time-sharing applications and for connection to compatible EIA RS 232 C (CCITT V 24) peripheral units.

Basic Unit

Central memory (RAM — Random Access Memory) — MOS integrated circuit design. Capacity of 40K 8 bit bytes, of which 32 kbytes are reserved for operating system resident on floppy disk, and 8 kbytes are available to the user for program and data storage. Access time: 700 nsec.

Read Only Memory (ROM) — ROM loader consisting of bi-polar LSI circuits for calling the operating system into the reserved area in central memory (32 K). Loading occurs automatically when the system is activated. Access time: 350 nsec.

Arithmetic-Logic Unit — Receives and executes program instructions from central memory.

Input/Output Channels — 16 channels for exchange of information between the central unit and input/output units (both integrated and peripheral). Total overlapping of input/output and processing operations. Mode of operation: multiplexor, for simultaneous management of input/output interfaces; and selector, for high-speed management of one input/output interface. Direct Memory Access (DMA).

Alphanumeric Keyboard — Electronic keyboard, with 80-character buffer: alphanumeric BASIC section, for entering statements, commands, and alphanumeric strings (26 full BASIC words on single keys); editing section; algebraic section, for entering numeric data and algebraic operators; section for user-definable functions under either program or manual control; two end-of-line (EOL) keys; result keys, for recalling four stack registers in calculator mode; and command section, with full commands on single keys.

Console — Consists of: illuminating switches for selection of operating modes; indicator lights to show system status; and decimal wheel to select output precision in calculator mode.

Alphanumeric Display — Plasma display can represent complete set of ISO character (upper and lower case, special characters, etc.). Capacity: 32 characters (5 × 7 matrix); pointer to indicate current operating position; 80-character buffer; pointer can be shifted, and line "moved" left or right when consisting of more than 32 characters (up to maximum of 80 characters). Display shows: keyboard entries; programmed data and messages; system messages; complete program lines; lines of text; results in calculator mode; and error messages.

Floppy Disk Read/Write Unit — For exchange of operating system, program, data and text files between floppy disk and central memory. Exchanges are carried out in blocks of 128 characters. Average access time: 333 msec (including latency and settling time). Nominal transfer speed: 250 kbits/sec.

Options

Central Memory Extensions — Central memory can be expanded to 48, 56, 64, 72 or 80 kbytes (corresponding to 16, 24, 32, 40 or 48 kbytes of user memory).

Integrated Alphanumeric Printer — Thermal serial printer, handling complete set of ISO characters (upper and lower case, special characters, etc.). Printing line: 80 characters (5×7 matrix). Printing speed: 80 char/sec. Two buffers, 80 characters each. Prints program output in specified format. Lists programs or texts. Acts as plotter.

Second Drive for Floppy Disk Read/Write Unit — Enables second floppy disk to be used, increasing storage and file handling capacity (programs, data or text).

Olivetti Standard Peripheral Interface (IPSO) — For data management and exchange between central memory and IPSO peripheral units. System can be supplied with one or two interfaces; each enables up to 4 input, 4 output, or 4 input/output units to be connected simultaneously. Maximum exchange speed: 20,000 cps. Input/output: serial by character, parallel by $8 + 1$ bits.

Moving Head Disk Unit Interface (DCC 6609) — Enables connection of DCU 7292 moving head disk external mass memory unit. Average access time: 50.5 msec (including latency time). Transfer speed: 300 kbytes/sec.

Asynchronous Line Control Unit — For connection to data transmission lines (time-sharing) and compatible EIA RS 232 C (CCITT V 24) peripheral units.

External Connections

IPSO Peripherals — high speed impact printers; punched tape readers; tape punch; punched card reader; cassette tape units; measuring instrument adaptor; plotters; computer compatible magnetic tape unit; input/output typewriter.

Moving Head Disk Unit (DCU 7292) — Random access external mass memory for data, programs and operating systems. Unit consists of two disks, one fixed and one removable (total capacity: 9.8 Mbytes). Average access time: 50.5 msec (including latency time). Transfer speed: 300 kbytes/sec.

Serial Peripheral Units — All compatible EIA RS 232 C (CCITT V 24) serial peripherals.

Time-sharing — The P 6060 can be used as a time-sharing terminal connected to remote computers, through the asynchronous line control unit.

Representation of Variables in Memory

Simple numeric variables, and each element of array numeric variables, are represented in floating point with double or single precision as requested: double precision (8 bytes), with 13 digit mantissa, 2 digit exponent (from -99 to $+99$) and sign; and single precision (4 bytes), with 6 digit mantissa, 2 digit exponent (from −63 to +63) and sign. Simple alphanumeric variables and each element of array alphanumeric variables are represented in 16 bytes. User may request any representation from one byte to a maximum of 1023 bytes.

Programming Language

P 6060 uses extended version of BASIC (Beginners All-purpose Symbolic Instruction Code) compatible with ANSI and ECMA Standards. Main features: input format in fixed point and floating point; output format automatically in integer, fixed or floating point, depending on order of magnitude; output formats selected by program; immediate execution of statements in calculator mode; handles external files of various types (data, program, text) sequential or random data files; simultaneous program access to data files; subroutines and functions (single-line or multi-line; user definable keys; program chaining; strings variables; matrix operations; and plotting functions for integrated printer.

Operating System

Operating system resides on floppy disk, modular in structure, to allow dynamic loading into central memory. Organization: basic system: modules automatically loaded into reserved areas (32 K) in central memory — extended system: modules for logic extension of system (handling strings, matrices, etc.).

Main functions of basic system: interpretation of machine language; compilation of programs; interpretation and execution of system commands (program editing, management of program libraries and data, etc.; compilation of statements in calculator mode; management of integrated input/output units; handling, under program control, of data files resident in external memory; and execution of utility programs (disk copy, file copy, disk reorganization, etc.).

Main functions of extended system: handling strings; matrix manipulation; use of integrated printer for plotting; management of input-output operations with IPSO peripherals; and use of system as terminal.

Accessories

Thermal paper for integrated printer. Available in blue or black. Width: 222 mm (8.74 in.); length: 75 m (246 ft.).

Floppy Disk: capacity of 250 kbytes. Divided into 77 tracks, sub-divided into 26 sectors, of 128 bytes each. Stores: operating system, and Olivetti and user application software.

Sample Applications Segments for the P6060

1. Education	Computer-Assisted-Instruction (CAI) Computer Sciences • School Mathematics of all grades • Biological Modeling • Science and Engineering • Statistical Modeling • Simulation • Structural Geology • Recreational Math • Computer Games
2. Communications and Transportation	Market and Media Research • Routing and Scheduling • Freight Rating • Containerized Cargo • Statistical Modeling • Election Returns • Paramutual Calculations
3. Medicine and Life Sciences	Clinical Chemistry • Pathology • Hematology • Blood Gases • Coagulation • Gastric Analysis • Electrophoresis • Immunochemistry • Urine Chemistry • Isotope Medicine • Lab Statistics • Quality Control • Biomedical Research • Profit Analysis • Liquid Scintillation • Radioimmunoassay • Cardiopulmonary Function • Clinical Workload Recording • Radiotherapy

4. Civil Engineering and Surveying	General Land Surveying • Topography and Stadia • Triangulation • Earthwork • Road Building • Geodetic Surveying • Hydraulics • Sewage Treatment • Backwater Curve • Flow Distribution • Automatic Drawings • Labor Costing
5. Engineering Design and Management	Structural Analysis • Steel, Foundation, Reinforced Concrete, Prestressed Concrete and Bridge Design • Maintenance Inspection of Bridges • Steel Detailing • Pressure Vessel Sizing • Heating, Ventilating and Air Conditioning Design (HVAC) • Estimating • Job Costing • Critical Path (PERT)
6. Manufacturing and Industrial Research	Numerical Control • Industrial Design • Production of working drawings • Production Planning and Control • Shop Planimetry • Job Costing • Quality Control • Metallurgy • Function Evaluation, Curve Fitting • Operations Research • Chemical Engineering
7. Business and Finance	Investment Analysis • Economic and Price Analysis • Sales Forecasting • Distribution • Inventory Control

OLIVETTI P-652 ADVANCED PROGRAMMABLE CALCULATOR SYSTEM

The P 652 consists of:
- a central memory (RAM) of 4K semi-bytes
- standard keyboard functions with microprogrammed sequences for common mathematical routines and peripheral unit control
- an arithmetic-logic unit
- an operating keyboard with 10-key entry pad and function keys
- an integrated 30cps roll printer with 28 print positions
- an integrated unit for reading and recording magnetic cards
- an optional ROM for special mathematical and statistical functions

A serial I/O interface for connection of peripheral units is standard with the basic unit. An interface for the MLU 600 random access tape cartridge unit and DAS 600 Disk Unit is optional.

Central Memory (RAM) — This is a 2μsec random access memory of MOS type integrated circuitry. Capacity is 4K semi-bytes of 4 bits each equivalent to 16,384 bits. It is possible to store 1800 alphanumeric characters (bytes) of 8 bits each; 1200 program instructions (Address and Operation) of 12 bits each. Registers may contain numeric data, alphanumeric data or instructions permitting 100% memory utilization. There are also: 2 operating registers (M and A), each of which may contain a number represented in floating point; 8 Base registers for indirect addressing each of which may contain a 4-digit integer without sign; 4 sense switches, each internally settable and having binary condition on or off; 60 extra bytes available through indirect addressing.

Olivetti P 652 Specific Features — There are 17 microprogrammed routines for the evaluation of:

sin x	e^x
cos x	b^x, to any base
tan x	Ln x
Rectangular to	Log_{10} x
Polar	$\sqrt{x}$
arcsin x	π
arccos x	Polar to
arctan x	Rectangular
arctan x	

For the trigonometric functions angles may be in either degrees or radians and the argument taken from either the M or A Operating register. Keys for these functions appear on the console for both manual operation and program compilations.

Optional ROM — This memory contains 20 microprogrammed routines for special mathematical and statistical functions with error correction procedures. These functions are accessed by the F key and the 10-key numeric keyboard.

Instruction Set — Over 70 generic instructions are available for arithmetic, transfer, logic, standard and optional ROM functions. 24 different conditions for branching to 110 different Labels. Both direct and indirect addressing available. Each 12 bit instruction consists of an address and operation. Peripheral commands use additional bytes for unit and mode identification.

Memory Origins — Dynamic partitioning of central memory is available through 110 different origin definitions, separate from the 110 Labels.

Subroutines — 110 Labels are available for subroutine definition with option of 4 different types of return jumps. Subroutines may be nested to 7 levels.

General Keyboard — Simplified numeric keyboard with 10 keys plus decimal point and algebraic negative sign which can be entered either before or after the number.

E key for entering numbers in scientific notation. Keyboard Clear key for clearing last figure or instruction entered. General Reset key for clearing central memory. Start/Stop key for data entry and program continue.

Operation Keys — Keys for addition, subtraction, multiplication, division, register accumulation, and register clearing. (See Standard Keyboard Functions for other basic mathematical functions.)

Data transfer keys featuring transfers among registers and both operating registers, M and A. Key for peripheral commands and format. Key for Reading a Magnetic Card (Variable Block Length). Key for Writing a Magnetic Card (Variable Block Length).

Special Keys — Key for routine selection. 100 routine labels may be referenced directly or indirectly. An additional 10 may be referenced indirectly. Key for subroutine selection. Key for indirect addressing. Key for addressing the Base Registers. Key for various condition setting and sensing. Key for various command modifications and to define memory partitions (origins).

Switches and Controls — Power supply on/off switch. Switch for Program printing. Single Step Switch for error location. A program may be either printed or executed in single step mode and instructions added or deleted without auxiliary cards. Decimal Wheel for setting 0-15 print decimals in fixed point, either rounded or truncated. Error light (red light) indicating operating error. Correct Operation light (intermittent green light). Read/Write light (yellow light). Program Switch for Setting program options or modes at the console. Switch for compiling programs keyed in through the keyboard.

Recording and Correction of Programs — The instructions are entered into memory through the machine's keyboard. Programs can be printed from memory either automatically, or step by step operator control. This allows accurate location of an error, which can then be corrected without complete re-entry of the program. Long programs may be recorded on a number of cards and executed sequentially.

Magnetic Card Read/Record Unit — This allows the program and data stored in the main memory to be recorded on magnetic cards, and conversely, the contents of a card to be loaded into the Main Memory. Positive Read/Write controls to prevent inadvertent erasure of card or internal memory.

Printing Unit — Serial printing using a revolving drum unit. The unit prints all keyboard entries and partial and final numeric results as required. Program listings may also be obtained. Error message for peripheral error conditions are automatically printed when they occur. General Reset, Read and Write commands all print, allowing an audit trail of operator actions. Capacity: 28 print positions for floating point or fixed point output, (rounded or truncated, with decimal point and sign) register identification and program symbols. Speed: 30 characters per second.

P 652 Systems — The MLU 600 magnetic tape cartridge unit may be connected to the basic unit through an optional interface. This provides a random access file in the form of replaceable magnetic tape cartridges, each equivalent to 22,400 instructions, 4,480 numeric data, or 33,600 alphanumeric characters. It is also possible to connect through the standard interface as many as 4 peripheral units simultaneously, such as: LN20 Paper tape reader, PN20 Paper tape punch, Editor 4/ST Input/output typewriter, XY Plotters. Many instructions such as: Gamma Spectrometers, Multichannel Analyzers, Liquid Scintillation Counters, etc.

The DAS 600 Disk Unit specifications relate the characteristics of this random access memory for use with the P 652 programmable calculator. The P 652 is preset to operate with either the disk unit or tape unit depending upon the I/O ROM and internal interface cable it contains. The DAS is available in 40, 80, 120, or 160 kilobyte memory. The memory is composed of a non-interchangeable magnetic disk containing 32 concentric tracks. Reading and recording occurs through a series of fixed heads organized into groups of eight, with one head corresponding to one track exclusively. Thus, one group of 8 heads can read and/or record 8 tracks of information (40 kbytes) and 4 groups of 8 heads can read the maximum of 32 tracks (160 kbytes).

The P 652 Has Computer Type Architecture — Numeric Data — The P 652 can store up to 240 signed numeric data represented in floating point with 12 digit mantissa and exponent from -99 to $+99$. Numeric data may be entered in natural decimal or scientific notation. Printing is automatic for all input data and may be floating point, fixed-rounded or fixed-truncated for all output data. The contents of each machine register may be printed by a single instruction.

Alphanumeric Data — The P 652 can store up 1860 alphanumeric characters (bytes) using an ASCII character set. Input, processing, and output is available through many different media.

Program Instructions — The P 652 can store a resident program of up to 1200 program instructions. These are true single address computer instructions (address and operation, not merely "steps". Long programs can be chained. Programs can be key-entered into the memory or by a magnetic card on which the program has been previously recorded. Registers may contain numeric data, alphanumeric data, or instructions, permitting 100% memory utilization.

Dynamic Memory Partitioning — 110 memory origins are available, permitting the creation of special "reserved" areas for system software. Memory origin definitions can be made either directly or indirectly.

Subroutines — 110 memory labels are available for subroutine definitions with the option of 4 different types of return jumps. Subroutines may be nested to 7 levels.

Indirect Addressing — 10 Base registers are available for indirect addressing of operands, labels, subroutines, and memory origins.

Easy Program Logic — Users don't have to be a computer professional to program the P 652. Its convenient keyboard language (all the convenience of a mnemonic assembly language) permits compilation of complex programs directly at the keyboard. No keypunching involved. There are 24 different conditions for branching to 110 different labels. Four sense-switches, which can be set internally or externally, and one console "program" switch permit greatly simplified operating procedures for even the most complex program.

Single Step Debugging — Users check and change programs instantly, step-by-step, through the single-stepping facility. Program code may be altered, inserted or deleted directly at the keyboard. Both program printing and execution may be inspected in this manner with complete access to intermediate results at any stage in execution.

Peripherals — It is possible to connect through the standard interface as many as 4 peripheral units simultaneously, such as: LN 20 Paper tape reader; PN 20 Paper tape punch; Editor 4/ST Input/Output typewriter; Instrument controllers for gamma spectrometers, multichannel analyzers, liquid scintillation counters, etc.; XY Plotters. The standard interface permits a 3,000 character per second data transfer rate. The MLU 600 magnetic tape cartridge unit may be connected to the basic unit through an optional interface. This provides a random access file in the form of replaceable magnetic tape cartridges, each equivalent to 22,400 instructions, 4,480 numeric data, or 33,600 alphanumeric characters.

Both Basic and Applications Software — The Olivetti P 652 has one of the largest supporting software libraries in existence for this type of equipment. An extensive series in BASIC Software supplies the user with common (and some not so common) numerical routines and algorithms in the form of programs very much like a FORTRAN math or statistics library — although far more comprehensive. Utility routines for system configurations are also included. These programs stand on their own but the user can also incorporate the techniques into his own programs.

Olivetti BASIC Software consists of routines in: Frequency Distributions • Paired Data Analysis • Regression Analysis • Trend Analysis and Time Series • Statistical Significance • Analysis of Variance • Probability and Sampling Distributions • Stochastic Processes • Combinatorial Analysis • Generation of Functions • Solution of Equations • Linear Algebra • Curve Fitting • Optimization • Numerical Integration • Interpolation and Differentiation • Differential and Integral Equations • Analytic Geometry • Elementary Functions • Higher Mathematical Functions • Non-Book Functions •Magnetic Card Utility Routines • Magnetic Tape Utility Routines. Highlights of the basic software library available for mathematical and statistical routines are: Multiple Linear Regression for 16 or Less, Independent Variables or polynominal fit to 13th degree, Eigenvalues of a Real Matrix of order 9 or less and new methods in general root finding, Revised-Simplex Linear Programming System, Exact probabilities for 2×2 and 2×3 Contingency Tables, Extensive Analysis of Variance software for Two Way, Three Way Layouts, Balanced and Unbalanced designs, Incomplete designs, factorial designs, hierarchical designs, etc.

Above — The Wang Model 600 Operating as the Input-Output and Control of Instrumentation — The Wang 600 is an advanced programmable calculating system with 16 high-rise, finger-molded special function keys that make available 32 subroutine identifiers for dedicated functions. Magnetic tape cassette records long, multi-program blocks; loads programs into memory, and is available for auxiliary storage. Visual display and optional plug-in ROM's (read only memory) are key features.

Magnetic Tape Cassette — Designed for both recording long multi-program blocks onto magnetic tape and loading programs into memory, the Cassette Tape option can also be used for auxiliary storage. A tape can hold up to 12 blocks of 1,848 program steps of 2,772 full storage registers per side. For automatic chaining of programs or data storage and retrieval, the 600 Tape Drive features programmable "READ" and "WRITE" commands . . . under complete program control. VERIFY insures that programs have been loaded and gives manual identification of individual blocks of programs. A parity check with a flashing ERROR INDICATOR LIGHT feature proves data has been entered correctly from the tape. A full line of peripherals is available.

Plug-In ROM's — Optional plug-in ROM's (Read Only Memory) add up to 2,048 more program steps of single keystroke, hard-wired functions. Five low-cost special purpose ROM's are available for statistics, advanced statistics, formula programming (algebraic), extended alpha listing and surveying. Custom ROM's are also available for specialized programs. Once a program has been reproduced on the custom ROM, it cannot be listed, looked at or printed. This feature gives complete privacy and assurance that unauthorized personnel cannot access a listing of programs. Yet with proper instruction, programs can be run with single keystroke operation.

Wang Model 700 Calculator — Another of Wang's Advanced Programmable Calculators combines the easy keyboard operation of manual calculators with the sophistication and power of large programmable calculators, a valuable combination for the scientific and business user. The complete set of fully interfaced peripheral equipment, including an output writer, plotters, a paper tape reader, an on-line interface, a high-speed printer, a disk drive, a dual tape drive, plus various other input and output devices, can provide flexibility for designing the calculating system for every application.

The 700 Series Calculators feature sixteen user-definable special function keys. In a given program these keys are readily assigned specific functions or subroutines which can be executed by a single keystroke. This can allow the user to write specific single-keystroke programs in each application. A magnetic tape cassette drive, records programs for future reference. Programs can be chained together for automatic execution; specific programs can be loaded under program control. Just as with the Wang 600, the 700 calculators are supported by a library of programs, which modify the machine for specific applications. Statistics, engineering, surveying, and medical programs can be entered into calculators with a single keystroke, enabling the evaluation of data entered either manually or automatically from various instruments. Available investment and financing programs compute, and actually type out legal contracts. The system can be further enhanced for automatic letter writing. Wang Laboratories provides software and field support enabling the system to be installed and operating on the day it is delivered.

Education — Wang Laboratories offers periodic programming seminars on the 700, designed to develop and sharpen basic calculator skills. The courses concentrate on manual and programming techniques, with emphasis on the relationship of the calculator to various peripherals in a given calculating system. In addition, the Wang customer organization, SWAP, provides the medium for interchange of programs and programming techniques among Wang users.

The 700 calculating system consists of a calculator and various input and output devices to communicate with the calculator. The 700 calculator is available in two different memory configurations:

700   960 program steps-120 total registers
720 1,948 program steps-248 total registers

If memory requirements expand, the 700 can be field-retrofitted to the larger storage capacity of the 720.

Magnetic Tape Cassette — The magnetic tape cassette drive provides for the storage of approximately 20,000 program steps per cassette, all 20,000 of which can be chained together for automatic execution under program control. A programmable SEARCH capability enables the calculator to automatically SEARCH, LOAD, and EXECUTE specific programs on tape.

Programming — Programs are entered in either the LEARN mode by touching keys in the proper sequence or in the RUN mode by loading instructions from the magnetic tape cassette. In a program, 256 subroutine codes are available to define subroutines. Subroutines can be nested five levels deep. The 700 has full decision-making capability which enables the subsequent path of the program to be determined by the results of calculations. Iterations can thereby be set up which are performed until certain conditions are met. Debugging of programs is facilitated with a TRACE mode of operation. The STEP, INSERT, and DELETE available on the "C" versions of the 700 and 720 also are useful for program debugging.

Peripheral Equipment — The 701 Output Writer types alphabetic and numeric output from the calculator with full format control. In the 702 Plotter, complete digital plotting is combined with the alphanumeric capability of the 701. Plots are therefore easily titled and labeled. With the 703 Paper Tape Reader, raw data is automatically input into the Wang Calculating system providing for an efficient "data reduction" system. Programs and data can be prepared "off-line" and input automatically from the 704 Card Reader. Instrumentation and analytical equipment are interfaced directly to the calculator using the Model 705 Micro Interface. "On-line" data acquisition is therefore facilitated. With the 706 Teletype, input and output of alphanumeric data is readily accomplished in the Wang Calculating system. The 708 Extended Memory provides external storage in increments of 4,096 program steps.

Memory controller — This is an external core memory which is utilized to store from, or recall to, the main memory of the 700, program steps, data, or alphabetic information. The 708-1 can contain as many as eight 708-2 Core Modules and, as a result, has a peak capacity of 32,768 program steps.

Plotting Output Writer — A specially modified electric typewriter with the capability of producing formatted alphanumeric output. It not only plots a graph, but also labels points. (Also available as the 702-p, a portable unit with a separate electronics package.)

Micro Interface — The 705-1 is an interface which may be hooked directly on-line to most available digital voltmeters. It produces a low cost on-line data reduction system.

Teletype Terminal — For remote or local operation, the 707 constitutes a teletype terminal and control device. There are even acoustic coupler stations for remote operation of up to four terminals.

Large programs and sets of data can be stored easily and inexpensively on the 709 or 729 Dual Tape Cassette Drive. Each 150' tape cassette can store a maximum of 90,000 program steps or the contents of 11,250 storage registers. Over 262,000 program steps can be stored and accessed randomly on the 710 Disk. The Model 711 Input/Output Writer provides a convenient means for entering alphabetic information into the calculator as well as the printout capability of the 701 Output Writer. With the 714 Marked Sense Card Reader, data and programs can be entered directly into the system. Since the cards are prepared "off-line" without tying up the calculators, the system is more efficient The 718 Extended Memory provides additional storage capacity in increments of 1,024 program steps. Since the 700 Calculator can address multiple peripherals, more than one 718 can be incorporated into a single system. Hardcopy output is printed at 150 characters per second or up to 200 lines per minute on the 721 High Speed Printer. In the 700 Calculating System, the 722 Input Keyboard enables alphabetic, numeric and formatting instructions to be typed directly into the calculator. The 727 Communications Interface enables two calculators to communicate via voice grade telephone lines.

Digital Flatbed Plotter — The 732 provides continuous line or point plotting of data keyed in via the 700 keyboard. Circles, bar graphs, subdivision plans as well as highway horizontal and vertical alignment plans may be plotted on the 31" × 42" surface. Any type of paper as well as various types of pens may be used.

Dual Removable Flexible Disk — The 740 consists of two disk platters, both removable and easily stored. The storage capacity of each unit is divided between the two platters; 131,072 bytes or 262,144 bytes per platter depending on the model chosen. Data can be recorded on only one side of each platter and is transferred at a rate of 300 ms per 256 bytes.

Dual Magnetic Tape Cassette Reader/Recorder — The 729 contains two separately controlled magnetic tape cassette units for recording from, or reading data into, the main memory of the 700C or 720C Calculators only. Up to 115,200 program steps can be contained on the 729's cassettes.

Fixed/Removable Disk — The 730 adds considerable programming power to the Wang 700: up to 4,915,200 program steps or 614,400 storage registers. Under keyboard control, the 730 offers high-speed random access storage and retrieval of alphanumeric information.

Wang Communications

The WU-7 is probably the first microcomputer ever to team up with a programmable calculator, specifically the Wang 600 and 700 units. Thus equipped, the calculator can communicate with other Wang calculators, with a variety of other devices, or computers at line rates ranging from 110 to 9,600 baud. The WU-7 performs the code translation, formatting, buffering, serializing, and other operations so that the communications task doesn't become too burdensome. Another use for the WU-70 is handling data from instruments and special purpose apparatus. Many manufacturers of these devices offer tty-compatible plugs for printing and connections to minis. The varying code sequences (protocol) are automatically handled by the WU-7. (DIGITAL LABORATORIES, Cambridge, Mass.)

Sales and Service — Wang Systems are sold and serviced from more than 100 offices across the United States and in 47 countries worldwide.

A Wang 2200S Computing System: Computer Power with Calculator Convenience — (see above) Computer power through a powerful, hard-wired BASIC language interpreter, 4k to 32k bytes of user memory, a 16-line CRT, and a most comprehensive line of peripherals describes the 2200S. Calculator convenience is through a typewriter-like keyboard which inputs complete BASIC verbs with a single keystroke each and accesses 32 subroutines in memory.

Instant-on powerful BASIC allows users to converse with the system through the touch of a key, or a glance at the silent screen. Users input program statements with a single keystroke each; renumber a program automatically in increments they determine; alter, insert, delete as they choose; the system will pinpoint and identify syntax errors for the ultimate in ease of programming. It handles a 16×16 matrix inversion with 4k bytes of memory, or a 61×61 matrix inversion with 32k bytes, and uses a MATRIX ROM to speed up the operations. It manipulates bits and bytes with assembler-like statements, such as AND, OR, XOR or ROTATE.

Recently Wang introduced microprocessor-based peripherals and two software packages for multi-user distributed data processing. There are two new computers in the new line. One is the portable computer system (PCS), a 57-pound machine selling for $5,400. It will compete head-on with the IBM 5100. The PCS price includes a new processor in Wang's 2200 series, 8,000 bytes of semiconductor random-access memory, and 42,500 bytes of read-only memory. The PCS includes a 9-inch CRT display, full alphanumeric keyboard, a tape cassette for program loading and storage, and controllers for a new printer and plotter. The random-access memory is expandable to 32,000 bytes.

Sharp CS-4500 Electronic Printing/Display Calculator with Interchangeable Cartridge Keyboards — The CS-4500 calculator offers interchangeable special applications. In addition to functioning as a 14-digit printing calculator, the CS-4500 features a keyboard of 8 special purpose keys that can be used for any number of special applications, merely by inserting a cartridge into the calculator. Cartridge and matching keyboard templates are available for a variety of business, financial, statistical and other applications. This means that a single CS-4500 can be utilized with a selection of cartridges

to fill the needs of several departments within a business. If users want to do some invoicing they insert the Sharpvoicer cartridge, snap the Sharpvoicer template over the keyboard, and they're ready to do invoicing. After the invoicing is done and they want to figure some proration and distribution, they simply replace the invoicing cartridge and template with the Pro-Rater cartridge and template, and they can go. The Sharp users calculator library can have as many application keyboards on hand as they need to give them the benefits of several special purpose calculators without the cost of several calculators. Features of the CS-4501:

- Interchangeable cartridges for specialized applications. Provides calculating capabilities that approximate the level of programs of computers.
- 8 kinds of exclusive calculations with each cartridge.
- Once a calculation is chosen, other exclusive keys are electronically locked.

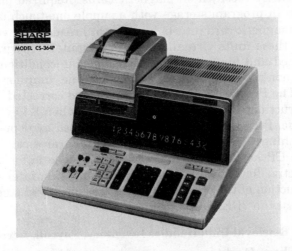

The Stepup: The Sharp CS-364P-II — It can program up to 144 main routine steps into nine groups and 144 subroutine steps with speed and convenience. The answer is printed too, if desired. (See above) Each program is stored on a magnetic card for future reference. Users insert the magnetic card into the slot conveniently located on the upper front below the printer, and the data is instantly printed out. The user's own specially programmed library of calculations is available anytime they need it.

LSI (Large-Scale-Integration) makes the difference. Thousands of parts are eliminated to provide maximum miniaturization. At the same time performance is significantly improved. The unit has 12 memory registers, 3 working registers and program storage. It can carry out the simplest to the most complex calculations up to 16 digits instantly. A special "DEBUG" mode enables logical thinking for mathematical calculations. And each program is easily and quickly checked by the "CHECK" mode operation. A special jump system also enables programs to be repeated, branched and jumped by simply pressing a button. Other extras include zero suppress system, electronic punctuation, rounding up/off/down device and automatic credit card balance systems.

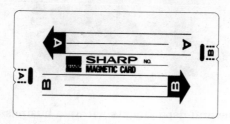

Magnetic Cards for Completely Independent Subroutine — Subroutines are completely independent of main routines and the subroutines alone may be recorded on the magnetic cards. They are also used for manual operation so users can get the answers to various kinds of functions with one-touch key operations. Users can develop external memorization of numerals. Operation DATA, RECORD gives the instruction to record the numbers stored in all the 12 memory registers on the magnetic card and DATA ENTER gives the instruction to transfer the numerals recorded on the magnetic card to memory registers.

Efficient Magnetic Card System — Once the programming is complete, programs are easily recorded on magnetic cards. Required programs are instantly written in program storage with a simple one-touch operation of the keys with the magnetic card inserts into the card reader. Convenient jumping system makes these units virtually a "mini-computer". Programs can be repeated, branched and jumped. The unit includes unconditional jump, negative jump and non-zero jump system and subroutine jump for maximum versatile utility. The Programs are easily checked and corrected. The number of steps and instructions are displayed step by step when S key is depressed in "CHECK" mode. Programs can be optionally jumped by depressing numeral keys after touching → x < 0, x = 0, SUB keys. Programs can be corrected by depressing the CP key. The "DEBUG" function mode is for educational instruction. Effective for logical thinking in mathematics, intermediate results and next instruction of the operation process are displayed step by step when S key is depressed in "DEBUG" mode.

Sharp PC-2600 Retrieval Unit: Handles Inventory, Payroll, Accounts

The newest Sharp **Desktop,** programmable print/display calculator system performs the general computing and retrieval functions of more expensive systems and can be tailored to special needs. System PC-2600 uses a floppy disk with a 19,240 bit memory and more than 246,000 programing steps. Adding a second disk doubles capacity. The central processor is a microcomputer with 16 digits plus decimal point and sign. The discharge printer has an alphanumeric printout speed of 5 to 10 lines per second. An operator can perform simple or complex calculations using 98 memory registers, three working registers, and program storage. A jump system allows programs to be repeated, branched, and easily transferred, and a check mode reviews programs for errors.

The Sharp PC-2600 permits users to program, from the basic machine, up to 1024 main routine steps into 49 groups, as well as 1024 subroutine steps with high speed and convenience. The unit offers 98 memory registers, 3 working registers and expandable program storage.

Sharp PC-2600 with disks and I/O typewriter

Advanced Monroe Calculators Can Communicate with Peripherals, Laboratory and Medical Instrumentation and Over Phone Lines with Accoustic Couplers and Modems — When interfaced with the unique micro-programming of the Model 1800 Series calculators, the software-driven Monroe 395 Interface provides the user greater flexibility in full utilization of total system performance. Numerical data, alpha of variable length, and software program input or output are accepted. Data editing, validating, and output formatting can be readily incorporated into the software programs.

The 1800 Series Calculator with a Model 395 will interface to peripheral devices using 20 mA. current loop. EAI RS-232C or CCITT V. 24. The coding designated character acceptable is ASCII at 110, 150, 300, 600 or 1200 baud (or any two of these), either half or full duplex.

An 1800 Series calculator with a Model 395 Teleprinter Interface can accept or output numerical data, alpha strings of variable lengths or programs. Because the 1800 Series calculators are uniquely micro-programmable, the Interface is software driven. Users have flexibility in optimization of their total system performance. Data editing and validating as well as output formatting may be incorporated in the application software.

Monroe 1800 Series Tape Cassette Calculator Systems — The Monroe 1800 Series calculators are in effect, powerful and versatile microcomputer systems. The "brains" of this system is a user microprogrammable microprocessor, 7 kilobytes of ROM (Read Only Memory) operating system and hi-level instructions, and 1.5 kilobytes of working storage. This microprocessor subsystem is complemented by one of four keyboards for input, a 21 column printer for output and a magnetic card reader/writer for offline program and data storage.

All of these essentials are conveniently packaged in a rugged, desk-top unit with easy access I/O ports for additional system elements. Three of the models are offered with full program editing keyboards including the 1880 with mathematical and scientific ROM's, the 1860 with mathematical and statistical ROM's and the 1830 with 13 user-definable keys and mathematical and business ROM's. The Model 1810 offers additional user-definable keys in place of the programming keys of the 1830 with the same ROM functions.

In addition to the 100 plus instructions available in the keyboard code set, the 1800 Series offer user access to 256 microprogramming instructions for writing the user's own operating system and I/O control. The I/O capability of the 1800 Series ranges from a PIO (Peripheral Input-Output) bit-serial bus, up to 8-bit parallel input, byte or word transfer, Direct Memory Access (DMA) and interrupts. Main memory expansion in 512 byte increments are offered as options.

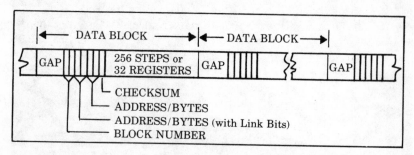

Monroe's Cassette System Characteristics — Monroe's low-cost tape cassette drive systems provide programming and storage expansion capabilities for 1800 series desk-top calculators. With the Monroe 392/1800 Cassette Drive System, 1800 calculator users are not limited in problem solving capacity by the number of program steps that can be stored in the machine at any one time. (See photo) Automatic program control allows users to write more sophisticated programs on preconditioned tapes. Large programs can be divided into a number of blocks, each holding 256 steps. A final command at the end of the block reads the next program into tape memory. This procedure can be repeated (up to 150 blocks) until the program has been completed. The 392/1800 system lets users access over 38,000 programming steps per side of tape. One convenient C30 Phillips type tape cassette is comparable to 150 individual magnetic cards, making reading and writing information more automatic, less time consuming.

The system's powerful interface assembly offers both READ ONLY and READ/WRITE ports, allowing the 1800 calculator user to selectively control the connected tape drive. Reading and writing operations can be done with single or dual tape cassette drives. However, dual drives make updating information easier, more convenient. The 392/1800 Tape Cassette Drive System can be used with any Monroe 1800 series calculator for storage of information, giving expanded capabilities many users require.

Manual or Programmed Tape Operations — Tape drives may be operated manually by touching the appropriate sequence of keys on the 1800 keyboard, or the 1800 may be programmed to operate drives automatically as part of the applications program. Preconditioned tapes are an attractive extra. Preconditioning divides the tape into the number of blocks specified by the operator. Each block is assigned a number in sequence beginning with one.

Automatic Error Checks — The 392/1800 system automatically checks for error conditions which affect operation or data information. Conditions such as: comparing sum of bits read with bits written; whether read/write head is past block requested; attempted read of block with no data; and preconditioning errors.

Add-on capabilities through peripherals expand the system. Peripherals such as the Monroe Model 300 I/O Writer or Model 395 Teleprinter Interface can be used with the 392-1800 system, allowing alphanumeric information to be written on or read from tape.

Basic 392/1800 Drive Functions — Functions which can be accessed manually or under program control. Users can:

- write a block of information on tape as part of multiple block file
- write a block of information on tape as single block file
- read a file of information from tape, using address recorded on tape to determine where in computer memory each block should be stored
- read a file of information from tape into specified address in computer memory (addresses recorded on tape are ignored)
- specify which drive information to be read from under manual or program control

Users can also duplicate tapes; update tapes with new or changed information; use pre-programmed tapes with up to 15 minutes of programmed material per side.

The Monroe Model 1860 Electronic Programmable Printing Calculator combines the features of a scientific/statistical calculator, extensive problem-solving capability and hard-wired keyboard functions with versatile programming commands.

Monroe Model 1880 Survey System — The 1880 is a compact, advanced system that will handle the everyday simple, as well as complex, mathematical problems of the surveyor. The Model 1880 Electronic Programmable Printing Calculator is specifically designed to perform surveying calculations; an optional Input/Output Writer accepts alphanumeric information from the calculator and prints it in standard format.

A hydraulic engineering software package with a wide range of applications using the Monroe 1880 programmable calculator to perform its computations is a software package written in the language of the engineer. It offers a total of sixteen programs to provide the user with information to select the best design for the project.

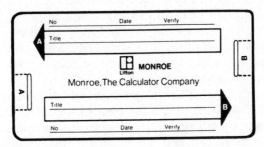

Magnetic Program Card — Capacity per side: 256 instructions or the contents of 32 data registers.

Monroe's structural engineering software package is unique, powerful and yet flexible. With Monroe software, simple beam analysis can now be computed using one program. Frame analysis, which almost always required a computer, can now be done effectively on the calculator. This adaptable package has a wide range of applications which can be used in a variety of standard structural engineering computations. It is divided into 3 sections, encompassing Structural Engineering Programs, Steel Design Programs, and Concrete Design Programs.

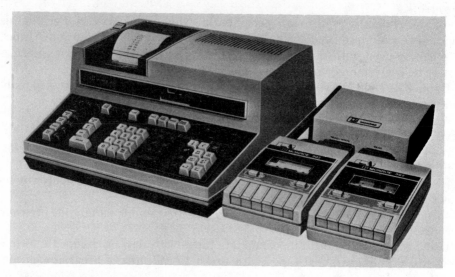

The 392/1800 system permits access of over 38,000 programming steps per side of tape.

The HP Power Calculators: The 9815, 9825, and 9830

The H-P 9815 calculator combines keystroke calculating convenience, dedicated problem solving and an optional two-channel I/O to give users versatility and power in solving problems from the simple to the sophisticated. An AUTO-START capability and high-speed dual-track data cartridge capable of storing 96,384 bytes of data and programs are features that make the 9815A calculator a variable and easily customized choice for virtually any lab. Add optional interface capabilities and users can easily extend powerful 9815 desk-top computing capabilities.

The 13-pound (5.9 kg) calculator features the Hewlett-Packard stack-oriented logic system simplifying keystroke calculations and giving fast answers. The buffered keyboard contains 24 preprogrammed functions, 4 arithmetic keys plus keys for memory-stack manipulation and 15 special function keys. The thermal printer prints up to 16 characters per line at 2.8 lines per second. In addition, there is an easy-to-read numeric display. With the addition of the optional two-channel I/O structure, users can add 9815 Series peripheral; devices, including the 9871 printer/plotter, (see ahead) the 9862 plotter, tape reader or tape punches, or a digitizer.

The 9815 also mates with BCD instruments and devices with 8-bit parallel interfaces. The 9815 accommodates the Hewlett-Packard Interface Bus (HP-IB), allowing users to control, gather, and process data from as many as 14 different HP-IB compatible test and measurement instruments. The 9815 contains computer language functions for programming power and performance. The standard 9815 has 472 steps of program memory and 10 data storage registers. An option is available to expand the calculator's internal memory to 2,008 program steps. Many standard problem solutions are available from the extensive library of pre-recorded programs in statistics, engineering, science and surveying.

Model 9815 Operating Characteristics — A series of keystrokes can be stored in the memory of the 9815 to solve the same problem many times. Then users recall the program any time they wish. They stroke the keys only once, the 9815 does it from then on. The 9815 provides them with a set of keys that lets them control their program. These keys are grouped on the left of the calculator keyboard. They provide appropriate instructions to organize and direct the execution of the program. The keystrokes reference easy-to-remember mnemonics like GO TO or STEP.

The programming language of the 9815 brings together decision making ability and efficient execution. For example, the IF instruction acts as a qualifier for making decisions. Similarly, FOR NEXT loops automatically control repetition of program segments. GO TO, GO TO X, GO SUB X all identify branching instructions that tell the calculator where to execute the next step in computation. SUBROUTINES in 9815 logic can be nested up to seven deep. And FLAGS can be set to identify special program conditions. Users may want to modify or correct their program. The special editing features of the 9815 help them change program steps, update their program addressing, recall any program step, and step through any program sequence with ease and convenience. Simple and direct keystrokes establish a rapid and natural editing technique that is represented in three easy steps. First, users list their program. Program steps and instructions are labeled in language they understand. In most cases, error messages tell precisely what went wrong in concise phrases. Second, users identify the areas of the program they would like to change. They key in that particular address, and make that change. If this step requires that branching addresses in the program be changed, the 9815 takes care of it automatically. The third step in the editing process is simply to run the program to verify the changes.

H-P 9815 Cartridges, Overlays and Programs — A cartridge, key overlay, and AUTO START let users dedicate the 9815 to solve their problem. The cartridge carries the prerecorded program to the 9815. The overlay labels the 15 user-definable keys for single keystroke execution of program steps that define a function special to various professions, unique operations, or commands required for peripherals. When users turn the power on, the AUTO START feature automatically loads File 0 and executes the program. Also Hewlett-Packard has an extensive library of programs for the 9815. This convenience establishes operation of various programs without extensive set-up procedures. Convenient prerecorded programs are available for complex problem solving in electrical engineering, statistics, medicine, and surveying — to name a few.

Changing applications is as easy as changing cartridges. The cartridge itself is small — smaller than the typical cassette, yet it can hold 96,384 bytes of data and programs (roughly 45 programs with 2,008 steps). So anyone can have his own library of programs. Not only can the 9815 easily solve the problems of the engineer, it can also deal effectively with the problems of the statistician, the doctor, the analyst, and the businessman. Anyone who can insert a prerecorded cartridge and turn on the power can solve a problem on the calculator. Secretaries, clerks, and part-time help can operate the 9815 to get the solutions to problems.

Users Can Dedicate the 9815 as a Stand-Alone Calculator or as a Powerful System — Users can dedicate their units in seconds to solve their problems, not just as a stand-alone unit, but as a powerful system as well. Read-only memory built into each cable and into the calculator gives fast response to specific needs. Operation and language features that are built in establish the rapport that only a dedicated system can have. A cartridge. A template. Automatic operation. For example, the printer and the display interact to provide two kinds of immediately available information. The printer gives labeled copy that identifies both what was done and how it was done. The display tells where in the calculation procedure users are and the result of each intermediate calculation. The printer and display are the tools with which the 9815 closes the communication gap between man and machine.

Rapid calculations are standard because the 9815 combines buffered keyboard operations, the logic of an operational stack, and a rational key layout. The entire right half of the keyboard is designed especially for keystroke problem solving. The far right block of keys contain 24 preprogrammed scientific functions. The next group of keys lets users access the operational stack and perform four-function arithmetic. These keys are adjacent to the 10-key numeric pad. Thus, users can pull together the "adding machine" portion and the scientific functions for complex problem solving. The results are a matter of record because they can be printed for permanent reference. Complex scientific problems and four-function calculations can be handled in much the same way. Because many of the scientific functions users may need are preprogrammed, it takes no more keystrokes to find the log or sin of a number than it does to perform any of the math operations with the same number. Intermediate calculations are automatically stored in the four-register operational stack, or users can assign them to any of the 10 permanent storage registers or any of the data registers in calculator memory. This immediately accessible data is easy to manipulate, thus eliminating the need for pencil and paper notations. The 9815 always retains 12 significant digits of the result; and whatever scientific numeric format users choose, the answer is calculated to 12-digit accuracy.

The 9815 reacts to users special requirements — by allocating memory into either program steps and/or data registers. If users want 50 registers instead of the 10 permanent registers, they tell the calculator 5 0 SHIFT STORE. Thus, users can partition the basic memory of the 9815, which is 472 program steps, any way they choose. Optionally users can expand to 2,008 program

The HP-9815-A with Cassette

steps, which increase the basic memory four times — all of which can be partitioned by them. The 9815 extends its memory with the data cartridge. Bi-directional search, coupled with interchangeable data and program storage, gives users power, flexibility, and speed. The tape drive can search at 1524mm per second (60 inches per second). It can read or write data and programs at 254mm per second (10 inches per second). This means that, in the time it takes a user check his watch, the 9815 has loaded, checked, and is running a program 1,500 steps long.

Interfacing with the HP-9815 Series — An optional I/O structure adds another dimension to the 9815. Users can choose whether or not they want the 9815 to be equipped with general interfacing capabilities. The 2-channel configuration in the back of the calculator gives users plug-to-plug compatibility with many HP 9800 Series peripherals. These peripherals allow them to extend the input and output capabilities of the 9815. Another advantage of choosing the I/O configuration is this calculator's easy connection to a wide range of digital voltmeters, counters, or other instruments.

Each peripheral for the 9815 is equipped with an individual interface. Users can plug one to another. Each dedicated peripheral cable contains read-only memory which, when the cable is connected, provides all the special language and unique programming instructions necessary. The HP 9871A Printer is a prime example. The 9871 extends the output capabilities of the 9815 by providing a full-character impact writer with a fixed carriage and a 96-character interchangeable disk. The 9871 fills forms, creates reports, and draws charts and graphs rapidly and easily under program control of the 9815.

The 9815 can control instruments, gather data, and process that data. For this purpose, three general types of interface cards are available: general 8-bit I/O, BCD input, and HP-IB. General 8-bit I/O provides compatability with tape punches, tape readers, instruments . . . The general 8-bit I/O has built-in I/O buffers, recognizes programmable logic levels, and is capable of handling input speeds up to 2,000 bytes per second. The BCD input card operates with digital voltmeters, electronic counters, and BCD measurement systems. It can handle both 9-digit input and 8-bit control output. The 9815 is plug-to-plug compatible with HP-IB instruments. Up to 14 HP-IB instruments can be interconnected to a single HP-IB interface card. With two I/O channels, the 9815 can have up to 15 different instruments distributed between its channels. And the 9815 is fully compatible with all Hewlett-Packard HP-IB instruments. This is a versatile calculator accepting 15 different instruments. The 9815 has some important features that simplify the task even further. Programmable data logic levels give the ability to tell the 9815 what to look for in + or − logic levels. The tape cartridge complements the system with 98,384 bytes of data storage. The cartridge and the AUTO START provide users with the capability for power-fail restart in remote locations when the 9815 is a part of an interfacing system. So no matter where users are, immediate data acquisition and instrumentation control become possible where they were uncomfortable before.

The HP 9871A printer extends the output characteristics of the 9800 series desk-top programmable calculators. This impact printer is a full-character, fixed carriage peripheral that can be used to fill out forms, create reports, draw charts and plot graphs using the bi-directional platen and carrier. It also features programmable horizontal and vertical tabulation. In addition to the standard 96-character, upper/lower case print wheel, optional interchangeable wheels are available for ASCII character sets and European character sets. The 9871 is a versatile printer, accommodating paper up to 15 inches (38 cm)

Hewlett-Packard's 9815 Desk-Top Scientific Calculator and 9871 Output Printer

wide and prints up to 132 columns at 10 characters per inch. Average printing speed is 30 cps. Six-part paper is single-sheet or continuous-feed form may also be used. The HP 9871A was priced at $3400 in 1976.

HP's 9825A Desk-Top Programmable Calculator with 9866B Printer — Hewlett-Packard introduced a new programming language. HPL designed for subroutine nesting and flags and which allows 26 variables and 26 multi-dimensional array variables. The 9825 also features 12 special function keys and shift functions that can allow 24 operations. The company said the live keyboard had never been featured on a desk-top calculator before and allows several additional functions.

The 9825 includes a 32-character LED display and a built-in 16-character thermal printer with upper and lower case alphanumeric readout.

The thermal line printer with upper and lower case and plotting capabilities is called the 9866B. The unit contains a 95-character ASCII set, upper and lower case alphabet and symbols reproduced by a 5 by 7 dot matrix and printer

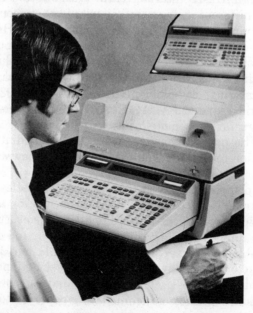

speed of 240 lines per minute, 80 characters per line. The 9866B in early 1976 cost $3,350 and is designed to be used with all H-P 9800 desk-top programmable calculators. Like the 9815, the 9825 calculator includes a dual-track cartridge with storage of 250,000 bytes, a 2,750 byte-per-second transfer rate, a search speed of 90 inches per second and a read/write speed of 22 inches per second.

The 9825 comes with 8,000 bytes of internal read/write memory that can be expanded in 8k increments to 32k bytes. The unit also features four plug-in slots for optional ROMs.

HP Desk-Top Calculator Model 9825-A Capabilities — The powerful medium-priced desk-top programmable calculator with many features previously found on minicomputers became available from Hewlett-Packard in early 1976. The 26-pound model 9825A, then priced at $5,900, is designed primarily for use in engineering, research and statistics. Its speed, interfacing abilities, and computer-like features make it particularly useful as the controller of an instrument system (see photo), for pilot process-control applications, remote data collection and production control. It also can be a powerful stand-alone computing tool.

A "live" keyboard allows users to change program variables, perform complex calculations, call subroutines and record and list programs while the calculator is performing other operations. This and various other significant features incorporated in the 9825A include: interrupt; input/output speeds up to 300,000 bytes per second; direct memory access; high-performance, bidirectional tape drive; multidimensional arrays; automatic memory record and load; extended internal calculation range ($\pm 10^{511}$ to $\pm 10^{-511}$), and optional plug-in read-only memory (ROMs). ROM add-ons include string operations, matrix manipulation, plotter control routines and I/O facilities. Three operational statistics software packages were available in early 1976 with more planned for release.

The 9825A uses a high-level programming language, called HPL, as noted, for controller applications as well as data processing. HPL handles subroutine nesting and flags and allows 26 simple variables and 26 multidimensional-array variables, limited only by the size of the calculator memory. Error locations are identified by a flashing cursor in the 32-character LED display. Fixed- and floating-point formats can be set by the user from the keyboard.

The 9825A's keyboard has 12 special function keys that, with a shift key, can handle 24 different operations. With the live keyboard, the user can perform simple calculations, examine and change program variables, and list programs while the calculator is performing other operations. Although the calculator appears to be doing these tasks simultaneously, the interrupt capability is actually apportioning operations on a priority basis. The speed of 9825A makes it seem as if everything is happening at once. The unit has a 32-character LED display and a thermal printer.

With search and rewind speeds of 90 inches per second and read/write speed of 22 in./s, the 9825A's built-in tape cartridge drive gives an average access time of 6 s. It provides automatic verification during recording.

The 9825A uses what HP calls second-generation n-channel MOS circuitry designed to provide high-speed internal calculation. The N/MOS chips consist of a binary processor chip, an input/output chip, and an extended math chip. There are four bipolar display chips. The 16-bit microprocessor employed in the 9825 has appeared also in H-P's 9871A printer/plotter. The chip, a custom 16-bit N/MOS microprocessor, was built at H-P's semiconductor facility. The 9815 calculator uses a Motorola eight-bit N/MOS microprocessor and was the first of the H-P desk-top calculators to use a microprocessor.

The HP 9825A functions as a systems controller. This means users can tackle sophisticated interfacing jobs without being a computer expert. The powerful and easy-to-use language HPL, high-speed data cartridge, live keyboard, interrupt, multidimensional arrays and high-speed input/output, are just a few of the versatile features that can make this possible. Also available: A choice of I/O methods and speeds: Formatted read/write up to 16k bytes/sec; Burst read/write up to 70k bytes/sec, Direct Memory Access (DMA) up to 400k transfers/sec. The power of 26 multidimensional arrays whose size is limited only by available memory and the flexibility of HPL's formula-oriented problem solving capability gives users easy-to-learn power.

Model 9825 System Performance — The 9825 Computing Calculator is a very versatile, very powerful device for high-speed problem-solving and for interfacing applications. It also offers these performance-oriented features:

- Vectored priority interrupt allows virtually simultaneous processing of multiple jobs. It's easily programmed to suspend processing, gather or send data and messages to instruments and peripherals, then automatically return to the original job.
- Up to 400k transfers per second direct memory access provides minicomputer speeds which allow real-time data acquisition and data transfer with high-speed devices.
- High-speed, 250k byte tape cartridge with 6-second average access time permits rapid processing of data and loading of programs.
- Multidimensional arrays allow users to organize data logically, thus saving program space and execution time. A 20×20 matrix can be inverted in 10 seconds.
- Buffered I/O increases throughout by providing a programmable software buffer between the program and an external device.
- Memory load and record allows users to suspend processing whenever they want and store the complete contents of memory on tape
  — including data and pointers
  — for continuation later on.
- Interfacing to any of eight HP calculator peripherals through three I/O slots, and up to 45 different instruments via HP Interface Buses.
- Simultaneous processing of several diverse jobs. Operators using a 9825 to control an instrument test stand, and acquiring data from it at speeds in excess of 1000 bytes a second; then can print the results on the HP 9866B Thermal Line Printer. At the same time, the same 9825 can also be processing and plotting a statistical problem. And through the 9825's live keyboard, users can check the progress of either programs and can change parameters if they desire.

Floppy Disk System for the HP 9825

Hewlett-Packard recently introduced two flexible disk drives to expand use of its 9825 programmable desktop calculator. The drives, the 9885M master and the 9885S slave, have a memory capacity of up to 468,480 bytes per disk. Flexible disks for the drives are priced at $14.

The drives are aimed at laboratory test, measurement and control and financial applications. Each 9885M can manage the operations of up to three 9885S units simultaneously. The 9825 can direct up to eight 9885M units, for a total of up to 32 separate disks with 14.9 megabytes of user-available memory.

Features of both new models include transfer speeds of up to 23,000 bytes per second, using the calculator's direct memory access feature, and a double density read/write for greater access rate (304 msec. for random access) and storage capacity.

The flexible disk is controlled by an easy-to-use, high level command system employing a directory which keeps track of 320 named files. In addition, both models provide a write-verify mode to ensure that information recorded on the disk is identical to the source information in the calculator memory. Coupled with the interfacing capabilities of the HP 9825 calculator, multiple disk systems lend themselves to laboratory test, measurement and control applications. Large quantities of digital and analog data can be gathered from instruments and stored on the disk for future manipulation. Long programs can be recorded, stored and run easily. In business and commercial applications, the disks allow storage and analysis of large quantities of financial information or use of complex programs for problem solutions.

I/O Expander for the HP-9825A

An input/output (I/O) expander that triples the number of I/O channels on the HP 9825 desktop programmable calculator from three to nine is labeled 9878A I/O expander. It has seven I/O slots, and comes with a six-foot cable with an integral I/O card to plug into one of the three 9825 calculator I/O slots. Two of the new expanders may be plugged into a calculator at once. The 9878 is designed for use in process control applications, research laboratories, engineering instrumentation laboratories, or anywhere the speed and ease-of-use of the 9825 programmable calculator can aid in the control of large instrumentation systems. The 9825 and the expander can accommodate 16-bit parallel cards for general purpose interfacing, BCD cards for BCD devices, or HP-IB cards for use with instruments that conform to IEEE Standard 488-1975. A feature of the expander is a built-in "integrity" light that indicates whether the calculator and expander are both turned on and properly connected.

HP Calculators Control Instruments with Easy Do-It-Yourself Interfacing

Users can easily interface their instruments — scanners, counters, spectrometers, meters, converters and many others — with an HP calculator, thus achieving greater efficiency of the use of their outputs. An automated system giving results and reports faster and easier eliminates manual readings, adjustments and calculations, freeing you for creative project management.

Many users have found that HP 9815 and HP 9825 computing controllers make interfacing practical and inexpensive. Whether the interfacing application is simple data logging, dedicated instrument control, or large system integration, these controllers can save time and money while increasing productivity. Converting the signals from one device into signals the connecting device can use, or vice versa, is now simplified. Users plug the correct interface card into the back of the controller that fits a need. Users connect their instrument to the other end of the I/O card, program their controller with a few simple instructions, and they're ready to put their automated system to work.

Types of interfaces available for the 9815 and 9825 include:

HP-IB — Hewlett-Packard Interface Bus — up to 14 instruments with built-in HP-IB capability can be interconnected to a computing controller via this interface system, HP's implementation of IEEE Standard 488-1975. Bidirectional, asynchronous communication is now possible between many instruments.

BCD — The Instrumentation/Measurement Interface — the majority of instruments produced today output four-bit parallel BCD data.

Bit-Parallel — The General Purpose Interface — Users choose either 8 or 16-bit parallel input bus and an 8 or 16-bit parallel latched output bus combination. They use this interface to connect to HP devices such as plotters, tape readers, printers, or other equipment such as scanners, scanning electron microscopes, etc.

The HP 9815 calculator is an inexpensive alternative to manual monitoring of an instrument or small system. For large complex instrumentation systems, the HP 9825 can interface to as many as 42 measuring instruments through its three I/O slots. The internal processing speed is so fast that transferring data and commands, accepting inputs, analyzing data, and printing or plotting results appear to happen simultaneously.

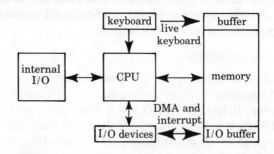

HP Model 9825A Operations Order

Hewlett-Packard Series 9800, Model 30 Calculator With Printer, Plotter and Card Reader

Hewlett Packard's 9830 is a 32-character-display, desk-top calculator providing a standard read/write memory of 4k bytes, expandable to 16k bytes. A built-in language compiler provides an additional 16k bytes of hard-wired memory. Further expansion is possible with read-only-memory (ROM) modules. Among features are: alphanumeric keyboard, built-in tape cassette, and BASIC language plus interface to a range of peripherals (see above).

The HP 9830 Description — The HP 9830 is a general purpose, desk-top calculator with the power and peripherals necessary to solve complex engineering problems, provide reports for accounting services, generate medical diagnoses . . . in other words, compute answers for a wide range of applications.

The 9830A provides users with a standard read/write memory of 4k bytes, expandable to 16k bytes. And it has a built-in BASIC language compiler which provides an additional 16k bytes of hard-wired memory. Users can further expand the computational capacity and peripheral control functions with read-only-memory (ROM) modules. Using the ROM's and expanded memory features, the 9830 becomes a 48K-byte computing calculator.

Complementing the memory is a built-in cassette providing an additional 64k bytes of data or program storage. User programs or data can be entered into the 9830 by cassette or by the typewriter-like keyboard. During calculator programming or program execution, the 32-character LED display gives users crisp, alphanumeric messages or presents results.

The 9830 is designed to allow users to easily configure a system to meet their present needs and still allow for expansion to meet future needs. Users can choose from the tape readers, tape punches, typewriters, line and page printers, digitizers, plotters, data communications interfaces, cassette memories, a 4.8M byte mass memory subsystem, and a selection of general purpose interface cards, plus prerecorded software Pac's.

Features —
- Alphanumeric Keyboard
- 32-Character LED Display
- Built-in Tape Cassette
- Hard-wired BASIC Language
- Add-on ROM Memory
- Expandable Read/Write Memory
- 12 Significant Digits
- Full Trigonometric Capability
- Boolean Algebraic Capability
- Special Functions Keys
- Broad Range of Peripherals
- Instrumentation Control Capability
- Data Communications Interface

Mass Memory Subsystem Description — The HP 9880B Mass Memory Subsystem provides the HP 9830A Calculator with the large data storage capability required for applications such as payroll, account maintenance, inventory control, patient records, credit verification and large banks of data for structural design, statistical analysis and many other scientific, industrial and commercial fields.

The memory media of this peripheral is a permanently installed memory platter and an interchangeable cartridge (HP 12869A), each having a capacity of 2.4 million bytes; this is the equivalent of more than 600,000 total items of data of 12 digits each.

One of the main advantages of this system is data safety and security. Master data can be recorded on the removable cartridge, transferred into the calculator for manipulation, stored temporarily on the fixed memory platter for further use by the calculator's program and verification prior to modifying the master data on the removable cartridge. Also with this system, duplication of data files is easily accomplished. Year to date payroll data, inventory updating, account receivables and payables updating are just a few examples where this dual system offers great safety of the data base and affords the opportunity to verify the results prior to modification of master files. Should an error occur, it is easily corrected by repeating the operation, since the initial data still resides on the removable memory cartridge.

In addition to providing a large amount of data storage, the 9880B Mass Memory Subsystem is fast. A 10×10 array can be transferred to the cartridge in about 1 second and a typical 250 line program of 2000 words can be transferred in less than 2 seconds.

The HP 9880B Mass Memory Subsystem can be expanded in terms of increased data and program handling capacity. Up to two HP 9867B's can be connected to one HP 9830A Calculator through one HP 11305A Controller. The

UNIT command enables the user to address any one of the desired memory platters.

Also, for increased versatility, up to four HP 9830A Calculators can be connected to the Mass Memory through the same Controller; however, only one calculator can be used to access the system at any one time. The HP 11305A Controller will sequentially service any of the four 9830A's requesting access to the mass memory.

Mass Memory Commands — As many as 10 data files can be used in one FILES statement at the same time.

Each file on the mass memory device is identified by a unique name of 1 to 6 characters in length.

Program and special function key files are accessed by using the SAVE, GET, and CHAIN commands.

Data files are created with the OPEN command; the user specifies the number of records to be reserved. The READ and PRINT statements permit both sequential and random data access.

Program and data files are erased from the mass memory by using the KILL command.

The IF END statement makes end of file processing routines easy to write.

The CATALOG command causes information about the files contained on the mass memory devices to be printed.

The UNIT command allows the user to access up to 4 mass memory platters from one calculator.

With the PROTECT command only authorized users, those who know the protection code, can access a data file. Also, protected files cannot be accidentally erased.

Special commands are also provided to allow the user to copy and to rename files and to create backup copies of files either on cassettes or on additional cartridges.

Many other commands and statements correspond to common time-share system commands and statements.

In conjunction with the String Variables ROM, strings can be stored as data, and they also can be used as variables for the access of files by name.

With the Matrix Operations ROM, two additional statements, MAT PRINT and MAT READ are available with the Mass Memory ROM.

Specifications —

Data Capacity Available to User	
Bytes	4,866,048
Bytes per word	2
Words per record	256
Number of records	9,504 (4752/platter)
Maximum number of files	1,536 (768/platter)
Speed	
Average access time	42.5 m sec.
Data transfer time	5.7 m sec.
	per 512 bytes

(Mass Memory to Calculator or vice versa)

Thermal Printer — For high-quality, hard-copy output the Model 9866A Thermal Printer operates at a fast, 250 lines/minute, equivalent to 3,600 words/minute. It's flexible, producing page-width, fully-formatted, alphanumeric text, tables, or simple plots. This option for the Model 9815, 9825 or 9830 carries a low price tag.

Typewriter — Tables, standard forms, letters, data listings — these are just a few of the data formats users can prepare with a Model 9861A Typewriter. And they can be produced with full alphanumeric capability, including upper/lowercase letters, punctuation marks, and symbols. The calculator, operating through a peripheral control block, automatically controls such things as tab setting and clearing, ribbon color, and vertical and horizontal spacing. But when the calculator is not running a typewriter program, the Model 9861A can be operated manually.

Tape Cassette — The high-speed Model 9865A Tape Cassette lets users store, update, and retrieve data and programs. A precision dual-motor drive protects irreplaceable data by eliminating the snarling and tape surge characteristic of capstan drive systems. And a fast bidirectional search feature lets users find any file on the tape . . . from any starting point . . . without rewinding. The 9865A has a minimum capacity of 6,000 registers; or 24,000 16-bit words for the Model 9830. Multiple cassette units can be used to speed data management and processing.

Specific Unit Descriptions — HP 9867B: Dual Platter (one removable, one fixed) Mass Memory Drive with interface cable (6 feet) and separate HP 13215A Power Supply.

HP 11305A; Controller. Provides the necessary interface to transfer data and programs bidirectionally between the HP 9830A Calculator and the HP 9867B Mass Memory.

HP 11273B: Read Only Memory, Calculator Interface Cable (10 feet) and Cassette for the HP 9830A Calculator. The ROM enables the HP 9830A Calculator to generate the necessary commands to write into and read from the Mass Memory. The cassette contains the program necessary to initialize a new memory cartridge and perform a system check out.

HP 12869A: Memory Cartridge has 2.4 million bytes capacity.

H-P 9000 Series Peripherals — Tape Punch users can add high-speed tape output to their HP system with a Model 2895B Tape Punch. The compact unit punches tape at 75 characters/second, permitting greatly improved throughput.

Card Readers — For big-batch processing capability, the high-speed Model 9869A Hopper Card Reader handles 80-column punched cards as well as mark-sense cards. It gives users speed and the versatility of formatted input. For smaller applications, the low-cost, hand-fed Model 9870A Card Reader optically reads mark-sense cards.

Paper Tape Readers — Data from analytical instruments, machine tools, and computer terminals goes directly into the Series 9800 calculator with paper tape readers. Model 9863A utilizes a pin-board programmer to make it easy to read a wide variety of formats at 20 characters/second. One Model 2748B Tape Reader is designed for high-speed, heavy-volume operations; it optically reads tapes at 300 characters/second.

Interfacing — With plug-in interface cards, the Series 9800 calculator takes on the ability to accept data from a large number of digital voltmeters, counters, and other instruments. By automating data entry users have a flexible lab processing center. The Model 9868A I/O Expander allows users to plug up to 13 peripherals or test instruments into the calculator.

X-Y Plotter — Histograms; pie charts; linear, log-log, and polar plots; circuit diagrams — these are just some of the things the Model 9862A X-Y Plotter can do. With a Peripheral Control Function Block, the plotter can automatically scale user data, generate words as well as numbers, and set up both axes complete with labels and tic marks — all in the designated units.

Line Printer — The HP 9881A Line Printer is a low-cost, 5 × 7 dot-matrix printer which enhances the throughput of any 9800 Series calculator. Its unique print mechanism makes it quite enough for business environment and provides up to 6 consistent, clean copies. It prints at 200 lines per minute, regardless of the line length, and has full 132-column line width.

Digitizer — This is a specific machine that reads a curve, or any irregular shape, as a series of discrete points and then converts these to a series of digital X-Y coordinates. To make these entries, users trace the shape and the HP calculator prints out dimensions and area of the line or contained shape. With the Model 9864A Digitizer users can directly process graphical data such as X-rays, blueprints, strip-chart recordings, cut-and-fill profiles, to name a few.

CRT Display — Terminal Automatic formatting of repetitive data, business form filling and tax form preparation are some of the tasks which are for the HP 9882A CRT Subsystem. When users couple the advanced features of this CRT with those of the 9830 Calculator, their scrolling, cursor sensing, addressability, tabulation and positioning make even the big jobs seem smaller. The 5 in. by 10 in. display has an 1,920-character capacity in 24 lines of 80 characters per line.

Outside Suppliers Provide Floppy Disk Replacement for HP Cassettes and Typewriter Interfaces

Infotek Systems (Covina, CA.) offers a floppy disk for the Hewlett-Packard 9830A scientific calculator that requires no new software and no installation. Called the FD-30, Infotek's floppy disk emulates the 9830 cassette system so that no changes in existing software are required. The cassette control commands and syntax of the 9830 are completely obeyed and all such programs operate without modification. The FD-30 stores five to seven cassettes at the cost of one cassette, and fifty times faster. The floppy provides 305K bytes of user area. According to Infotek, this specially designed unit is only four inches high and fits neatly into place between the calculator and printer.

Users just plug in the I/O connector and power cord and they are ready to use the FD-30 with the 9830.

Another important feature, the FD-30 provides data transfer to or from the 9830 much faster than the present mass memory system. The FD-30 stores a 10,000-word array in only five seconds via a simple store data. The HP mass memory requires 18 seconds to complete the same task.

The Tycom 9800 Interface Unit designed with the cooperation of Hewlett-Packard engineers, is a specially designed system to allow the use of an IBM Selectric Typewriter as an output writer for the Hewlett-Packard 9800 series calculators. The Tycom interface and the baseplate which attaches to the IBM Selectric typewriter not only provide an electro-mechanical interconnection between the calculator and the typewriter, it also converts the ASCII code from the calculator to the particular code of the typewriter, thereby making them compatible. This is unique to the Tycom system and is one of only a few interface systems available which can make this conversion. The buffer is the logic and the ROM which converts the ASCII to typewriter code. Also mounted on the unit are the electro-mechanical interfaces.

We have noted that for calculator users who need lots of storage, there are two mass memories for HP's 9830A programmable calculator. Users can have large data storage for such varied applications as general ledgers, accounts payable, personnel records, patient data, laboratory tests, real estate listings, structural design, and statistical analysis. The 9880A is a single disc memory subsystem that stores 2.4 megabytes; the dual-disc 9880B has capacity for 4.8

megabytes. Both have a photoelectric mechanism for fast, accurate read/write head positioning. It takes just 50 ms (average) to access and transfer a data item from the memory to the calculator. The subsystem is versatile, allowing users to connect up to 4 memory disks, in any combination (A or B), to one HP 9830A calculator through a controller — or connect up to 4 calculators to one mass memory subsystem. However, only one calculator can access the memory at a time.

HP Answers User Requests for more 9830 Calculator Memory

In early 1976, by using the new memory technology, the 9830B offers twice the memory of the largest 9830A. The 9830B has 15,808 bytes of read/write memory that can be increased to 30,144 bytes. HP also built additional functions into the 9830B — matrix manipulation and alphanumeric text and labeling capabilities. Users can choose from an array of optional peripherals, storage devices, software, ROMs and interfacing cards for either 9830. And the system can switch from one application to another quickly. Users just plug in the devices they need, load their program and go — all without help from computer experts. A 9830 computing system could be all the computing power a small company needs — for research, design, production, marketing, accounting, etc. Using the 9830's **optional mass** memory, random-access data bases can be created, including a management information system built with HP-supplied programs for accounts receivable, accounts payable, payroll, general ledger, inventory, order processing and financial reporting when coupled with HP programs for engineering, math and for data acquisition and control.

Within various departments there are all types of computing applications — applications as varied as quadratic equations and budget preparation; statistical analysis and report generation. With a 9830 computing system, members of various groups have immediate access to computing power. Users can easily and quickly write their own programs using the 9830's English-like BASIC language, and run them whenever the need arises.

The 9830 can also communicate with a company's **central computer** for remote batch, time-share and satellite operations, when not performing standalone applications.

Insertable ROMs for the HP 9830 Being Imitated by Other Suppliers

We have noted that external ROM inserts (plug-ins) add significant versatility and new capabilities to calculators — the Olivetti P6060, National's Hand-Held 7100, and others. Some brief detail of these devices as used in HP machines might be of interest to all calculator users because they can quite likely expect to see many more of them in future machines of many brands.

It was quickly apparent from initial successes soon after 1972 that the convenience and extra capabilities of insertable ROMs would be extensively used in advanced programmable calculators. An early example was the 9830A Calculator. It allowed the addition of up to 8 blocks of add-on Read-Only Memory. Five may be added as external plug-in, 3 as internal plug-ins. The below add-on ROMs provide additional capabilities to the Model 9830, permitting extension of the BASIC language with no change or lessening of the amount of read/write memory available to the user. Some of the capabilities of these specific ROMs are described.

1. The Matrix Operations ROM allows the user to add the matrix capability commonly found in BASIC to a 9830 calculator. This expands the language of the 9830 to include many matrix commands without sacrificing any of the 9830 special function keys or read-write memory.

2. The Plotter Control ROM provides the 9830 calculator with the additional commands that are necessary for the control of a plotter. It expands the language of the 9830 to include many plotter commands without sacrificing any of the special function keys or read/write memory.

3. The Extended I/O ROM allows the user to command a wide variety of peripheral devices with the 9830 calculator. It expands the language to include the I/O commands without sacrificing any of the special function keys or read/write memory. The two most important features in this ROM are the enter/output statements and an automatic code conversion capability.

4. The String Variable ROM provides the 9830 calculator with the ability to accept and manipulate alphabetic, as well as numerical information. It expands the language to include string variables without sacrificing any of the special function keys or read/write memory. The new commands provided by the Strings ROM are of three main types — input, manipulation, and output.

5. The addition of the ROM/data communication package enables the HP 9830 to act as an intelligent computer terminal. Included in the package are procedures for setting-up operations of the time sharing terminal, commands for the sending and receiving of programs and data, and the selection of the proper modem.

Additional ROM's are available to extend the language capabilities of the 9825A calculator for those who want to expand performance. Here are samples similar to those available for the 9830A:

- **String ROM** provides strings and string arrays whose lengths are limited only by available memory. A full set of string functions and operators allows users to easily manipulate alphanumeric data.

- **Advanced Programming ROM** provides for-next looping, split and integer number packing, parameter-passing functions and subroutines with local variables, and a variable cross-reference command.

- **Matrix ROM** adds standard matrix operators such as inversion and multiplication, plus a large number of multidimensional array operators.

- Others to be announced — four are insertable quick snap-ins on the bottom of the 9825A standard case.

A Typical 9830 Application Makes RF Network Measurements Automatically

Although applications are covered in the next few chapters, one 'sample' use of the 9830 might be appropriate here. Hewlett-Packard's 1.3 GHz network analyzer, the 8505A, brings strong capability to RF network characterization: 100 dB dynamic range, high-resolution digital data readout with analog display, direct measurement of group delay, and a unique electronic line stretcher to measure deviation from linear phase. The 8505A is also a programmable network analyzer permitting a combination with the programmable HP 9830 calculator through the Hewlett-Packard Interface Bus (HP-IB) to become a very powerful *automatic* network analyzer. Key advantages of automating the network analyzer include: extreme measurement accuracies (by virtue of the system's ability to measure, store, then subtract such vector errors as frequency response, directivity and source match). Ability to make many measurements quickly, and the ability to manipulate data and format results in a suitable form.

Unique to this new automatic analyzer is its **"Learn Mode"** of operation which makes it possible to automate measurements *without programming*. A single key stroke can cause the calculator to store (Learn) the front-panel control settings of the network analyzer. These can later be recalled which returns the analyzer to its original test conditions. An entire test procedure can be created without writing a single program line! A fully-configured automatic analyzer, Model 8507A, includes the 8505A analyzer, 8503A s-parameter test set, 9830 calculator (controller) with printer, necessary interfaces, cables, calibration kit, table and cassette programs permit users to start making measurements immediately.

The First IBM Calculator Competition

The IBM 5100 Portable Computer is the competition to advanced programmable calculators, but at about twice the cost. The IBM 5100 compact, portable computer is designed for personal use. It can be carried in its own case and used in office or home — wherever there is a 115 A.C. grounded wall outlet. The IBM 5100 unit weighs about 50 pounds, consists of an $8 \times 17\frac{1}{2} \times 24$-inch package containing a typewriter-like keyboard with 15-key numeric pad, a 5-inch diagonal CRT with 1024-character capacity and a drive for a 204,000-byte tape cartridge. Memory includes both read-write and read-only, with the former available in 16K, 32K, 48K and 64K bytes and the latter available in various sizes up to 190K bytes. The read-only storage (ROS) is based on new, higher density chips, according to IBM. The ROS contains language interpreters for APL and BASIC — the two interactive languages which the 5100 uses for handling special IBM software routines and for user programming.

Two IBM applications packages are offered in APL of BASIC: the mathematics library and statistical library. A BASIC only package is the business analysis library. Each library carries a one-time license charge of $500. And the 5100 can be equipped with optional communications equipment enabling communications with a host 370. Priced at $900, the communications option enables the 5100 to emulate a 2741 terminal, with transmission at either 134.5 or 300 bps using start/stop line discipline. Additional options are a Model 5103 80-character, 132-print position, bi-directional matrix printer, priced at $3,675, and other auxiliary products.

A standard feature on the system, is a TV monitor adapter that enables a user to attach external black-and-white monitors to the 5100 for dispersed display of CRT data at meetings, conferences or classes. The number of displays which can be attached depends on distance, monitor quality, cabling and other variables. Some users have run up to 12 monitors off the 5100.

Three Problem-Solver Libraries are available on tape cartridges. They contain the most often used analytical routines. These tested programs permit the user to concentrate on the solution of a problem rather than the operation of a computer. All models are equipped with a tape cartridge specifically designed for high-speed data handling as well as high-capacity data storage.

Options Available for the IBM 5100 Portable Computer — 5103 Printer — An 80 character per second, 132 print position printer.

5106 Auxiliary Tape Unit — Doubles the accessible storage capacity.

Communications Adapter — Permits access to remote data bases and program libraries.

Carrying Case — A case with a sturdy carrying strap is available.

The Mathematics Problem-Solver Library provides engineers and scientists with preprogrammed mathematical routines. The conversational nature of the programs enables the user to define a problem with a series of questions and answers. And to search for the solution with routines covering areas such as:

- Solutions to Simultaneous Linear Equations
- Matrix Eigenproblem

- Eigenvalues and Eigenvectors
- Integration
- Differentiation
- Interpolation, Approximation and Smoothing
- Zeroes and Extrema of Functions
- Ordinary Differential Equations
- Finite Fourier Transform
- Special Functions
- Linear Programming

The Business Analysis Problem-Solver Library consists of 30 interactive BASIC routines designed to provide business and financial analysts, product planners, economists and engineers with quantitative methods that might be impractical on a manual basis. Each routine can be used without the assistance of specialized data processing personnel.

The IBM 5100 enhances the problem-solving professional's capability to examine additional, alternative case studies . . . respond to requests for special financial studies . . . produce spread sheet, investment, break-even and time series analyses.

The Business Analysis Library provides the user with easy-to-operate procedures for:

- Leave vs. Purchase Analysis
- Cash Flow Analysis
- Forecasting
- Resource Projection
- Profitability Analysis
- Return-on-Investment Analysis
- Budgeting
- Financial Projection
- Spread Sheet Preparation

The Statistics Problem-Solver Library offers concise programs designed for the problem solver who uses statistical techniques. Each program guides users, at their own pace, through a set of procedural instructions. This interactive mode simplifies usage and enables the user to concentrate on problem solving.

The statistical analysis programs include:

- Regression and Correlation Analysis
- Multivariate Analysis
- Design Analysis
- Nonparametric Statistics
- Time Series Analysis
- Biostatistics

CHAPTER 9
PROGRAMMABLE CALCULATOR APPLICATIONS IN BUSINESS, INDUSTRY, EDUCATION

Prologue

The Broad Ranges of Advanced Calculator Applications:
Business, Industry, Education

Management in even the smallest service, trade, industrial, or professional office or shop is threatened with losing to competition if they do not automate most of their *paper work* their accounting, records management, plans and forecasts, and scores of other operating functions. Manufacturing, processing, fabricating, and other types of industrial processes can be significantly *economized* if the labor content is reduced, thereby decreasing costs, increasing per worker productivity and overall operations efficiency. Similar circumstances prevail in both the administration and tutorial activities in practically every educational institution. For most of these enterprises it is no longer a question of whether or not to automate as many functions as possible, but, rather, "What equipment do we need," "Can we afford to continue to operate inefficiently with slowly produced often inaccurate information," and "Have we already waited too long to stay abreast of our competitors?"

Most large companies are taking full advantage of sophisticated computer technology resulting in their increased shares of markets through improved operating methods, better information on which to base decisions, reduced overhead and labor costs, etc. It thus becomes almost impossible for small companies or institutions to continue burying their futures by using old-fashioned manual methods or complex, expensive computer service bureaus. Those forward-looking executives of smaller operations already using automated equipment and systems have quickly discovered that their biggest benefits are not merely in reduced clerical costs. The early users of programmable calculators have received even larger payoffs very early through: improved decisions and better planning; better customer service and satisfaction; increased profits due to stricter cost controls; better management and reduction of inventory and supply levels; tighter management procedures resulting in better personnel relations, and timely up-to-the-minute information and reports that provide sound, factual bases for swifter, more accurate, and realistic management decisions.

Programmable calculators are low cost alternatives to difficult-to-handle minicomputers and expensive, stringent controls of many business computer *systems*. Their chief attributes are versatility, programming simplicity, expandability, reliability, portability, and low first and follow-on costs. For a trucking firm, for example, a very low cost program provided the company with the capability of automatically selecting the best applicable freight rate for customers with the touch of a key. The same company experienced reduced billing errors, faster invoicing, increased amounts of work completed with fewer employees, etc. As we will note on pages ahead, companies with 200 or more employees complete their total payroll and tax accounting, control inventories, and do general ledger work with *canned* programs on their programmable calculator systems. Before making their calculator system purchase, new users should consider report requirements, applications areas, data volume, time constraints, future additional requirements, and comparative calculator system costs. Although a programmable calculator is a relatively simple system to operate and is similar in many ways to a manual calculator, it is a mistake to avoid planning for the full use of its power, versatility and *future system* capabilities. The pitfalls of both underuse and overexpectation must be considered. Manufacturers' representatives can be of great assistance in enlightening managers of current and coming new advantages of calculator peripherals. Until and unless management can clearly define the objectives desired, the full value of programmable calculator systems may not be realized. Some equipment is too simple, but seldom are these systems too sophisticated or too powerful. Prices of excellent desk-top exterior programmables run from $700 to upwards of $10,000. We have noted many of them — The Texas SR-60A. Tek 31, Victor 4900, Olivetti 6060, Wang 600, Hewlett-Packard 97, 9815A, 9825A, and the several models from Canon, Sharp, and others coming. As the prices extend above $5000, capabilities relate to mass-memory, expandable main memory, plotters, larger displays, communications devices, graphics added to alphanumeric keyboards, etc.

For the reader making a study of evaluation criteria or for a potential purchaser seeking a comparison checklist, the following few pages will be most helpful. Most units require no special programming language, lengthy employee training, or special environmental changes such as special wiring, floors, air conditioning, etc. But, at the outset at least the following check items should be considered:

- A programmable calculator that is easy to use and logically designed the way a person thinks
- User definable keys that instruct and lead the user with a natural language
- Expansion capabilities that let users increase memory and storage capacity as their needs grow
- A machine that interacts with peripherals
- A company that provides local service
- A company that backs its machines with experience in the business community
- A company that tailors programs to specific needs and provides access to ready-made programs for a variety of applications

Looking at the future both as to a company's future uses or requirements and to what capabilities may soon be available or some current models that may be far too costly is important. Because of the growing interest in programmable calculators and the technological advancements made in this area, the price of the basic hardware will be gradually declining. While price is going down the power of programmables will be going up as interfacing capabilities are expanded and mass storage added.

For small businesses, service, manufacturing or professional operations, the development of more ready-made programs and access to customized programming provides them with the benefits larger companies have been enjoying for some time. The wide range of applications analyzed in this and the following chapter built upon the equipment capabilities explained in previous chapters should provide a good base to use for selecting the correct system for individual enterprises despite their special characteristics. It is hoped that the examples provided on the pages ahead will be satisfactory for *breaking in* the reader to added utility of the unit he or she owns, uses or contemplates. Some may seem a bit too advanced, but even these — hopefully developed in a degree of clarity — should be at least read, if not studied, to gain further awareness of problems that can be resolved with these instruments.

The Directions

It is certainly true that the ranges of applications for programmable calculators are somewhat limited in comparison to full-service minicomputers, but the simplicity of operation and the many programming conveniences, as well as the reduced installation costs, make them most attractive, although many are also considerably slower. Quite a large majority of industrial processes do not require such great versatility that minicomputers offer, nor is speed an overriding factor, especially for supervisory control applications. The use of standard ASCII as the communication code, easily allows installation of conventional CRT terminals as input-output devices and status indicators, for larger systems. Most programmable calculators no longer lack an interrupt structure and, therefore, they can accept immediate response input *on line* or in *page* modes.* Conventional BASIC language time-sharing with these units is coming up strong, and only modular *engineering* is required to make them as easily adaptable to the system as specialized *intelligent* terminals are. A brief criteria evaluation review follows:

The decision to use programmable calculators rather than minicomputers is most favorable when some of these conditions are present: (1) When input-output rates do not require speeds too much higher than 100 characters per second, (2) when the people using the instrument are not particularly adept at minicomputer assembly language programming, (3) when plug-in convenience is paramount because of the lack of electronic wiring and fabrication needed for other computers, and (4) when the equipment will be used for specific applications which do not require frequent basic internal control program changes.

---

* As early as Oct. 1974 Hewlett-Packard made the following announcement: **Desktop calculator doubles as data terminal** Now data communications capability for the 9830A allows it to be used as an interactive or batch terminal. Thanks to a new interface, you can inexpensively and easily add data communications capability to 9830A desktop calculator systems. Now, you not only have a powerful programmable self-contained calculator, but you can also use the unit as an interactive terminal to communicate with a batch computer, timeshare system, or another 9830A calculator. The 11285A data communications set includes an interface cable and a read-only-memory (ROM). New BASIC statements in the ROM enable the 9830A to send and receive data and strings from a remote terminal or computer via telephone lines. Programmable asynchronous or synchronous transmission and data rates from 110 to 9600 bits/second are available, as well as programmable parity, automatic dialing and answering, "end-of-transmission" character, and half- or full-duplex mode. Two other ROMs add further capability. One provides remote batch capability using IBM binary synchronous line protocol. The other ROM provides timesharing capability and allows you to receive and transmit programs in other languages, such as FORTRAN. From: HP Measurement Computation News, Sept.-Oct., 1974. p. 1.

Programmable calculators are purchased by both large and smaller companies much more easily because the people who must approve the budgeting for them, conceive them to be *departmental* instruments instead of full-range computers and do not require approval of high-level managers or controllers. A purchase consideration equally as important is the simplicity of installation and the significantly reduced *extra* costs, including software and interconnection. Perhaps the most widely-used justification for purchasing these instruments is that they will be used by many people for *hands-on* experimentation, sampling and *what-if* demonstrations, training purposes for foremen and/or lower-level managers, or as a simulator for large-scale systems.

Because of the *convenience of purchase* calculator-based systems have become very successful in many of the following areas: (1) automated quality control in chemical, pharmaceutical, and other process applications; (2) all ranges of data acquisition and analysis programs, such as financial reports, medical tests, agricultural yield analysis, control of testing machines, water quality analysis, control of cement composition; (3) rapid determination of plant output and efficiency, production analysis, employee scheduling, etc.

Because many of the programmable calculators use the BASIC (or FORTRAN-like) language for data communications and remote control capabilities, many new ranges of applications are also available, such as monitoring and control of bulk storage terminals, inventory control in warehouses, centralized logging and monitoring of animal feed production, ready-mixed concrete, some sewage plants, etc. Using the BASIC language facilitates *calculator* control of batching and weighing operations, flow analyses, pipe line condition monitoring, supervisory data collection and monitoring, and control of large numbers and types of machine tools using remote counting techniques.

It becomes quickly obvious from the above that programmable calculators have become *beautiful* instruments for thousands of purposes and have broken the barriers and overcome the obstacles of the people problems which result when *regular* computer systems are installed. Many of these devices are in true definition *real computers,* but they don't sound like, look like, or act like the instruments most people have tended to fear. They are easily and quickly purchased and just as easily put to use by practically any employee in practically all types of businesses, industries, professions, educational institutions, or government bureaus. Many believe that the programmable calculator will be the primary unit responsible for a tremendous wave of computerization for a large proportion of all our small and medium-sized service and commercial operations.

Indeed, the great rise in popularity and expertise of users have resulted in techniques in which the pocket calculator can be converted to keyboard entry stations. For example, a low-cost data-entry device can be built from a pocket calculator, without disturbing its calculator functions, by connecting a few wires from easily located internal points to a few simple logic circuits. In a typical calculator, the keyboard is a matrix switch. When power is on, the rows of the keyboard are rapidly and continuously scanned in sequence. Depressing any key makes a connection from one row circuit to one column circuit; the particular combination of row and column identifies the key and, in the calculator, initiates a function such as entering a digit into a register or executing an arithmetic operation on previously entered numbers. Bringing the row and column signals outside the calculator to similar external logic circuits permits the key to be similarly identified and can initiate another function.

Putting Computing Equipment in Working Departments is a
Special Kind of Job Enrichment, An Example . . .

One Midwestern banker reports, "What we've done by putting computation equipment (programmable calculators) down into the working department of the bank is departmental enrichment. Job satisfaction has been increased and we can also get a job done without a lot of red tape."

He further reports, "This is a training ground in computation equipment, which will lead the staff to better use of our IBM 370's. That's our philosophy. Right now people are afraid of the computer. Getting simple computation equipment leads to development and preparation of other work for the main system."

"Now many different people are using the four programmables we have. All of these programmables have a typewriter, three have a high-speed printer, and three have disk units. We also have a tape drive which can be used on any of the machines. We duplicate all programs on tape for interchangeability. So if we are overloaded on one calculator, we can take the tape to another department and do the work there."

"We can discount a note in less than a minute with a programmable calculator, something that used to take two people about half an hour. It has greatly improved accuracy, which is the real savings. We've got an instruction book, and it's so simple that the employees can learn to program by themselves. We have people in our operating divisions — skilled clerical types and MBA's trained in calculating — to do the programming. Many MBA's today have basic training in programming and they have fun with it." (Programmable calculators mentioned are the Wang 700s).

Another Example of Multiple Calculator Efficiency

"About two years ago, we needed some sort of electronic calculating device during transition from a manual system to a completely computerized system," explains cost accounting manager of a container company. "Today we are still probably five to eight years away from a large computerized system encompassing a telecommunications network tied to an IBM 360 computer in New York. We decided we needed a programmable calculator or small desk-top computer for cost estimating, payroll, labor distribution, accumulation of production statistics and for smaller applications involving management and payroll efficiency standards. The billing program involves calculation of amounts which we record on invoices. Finally, in this operation, we summarize four elements of standard costs for orders shipped for presentation in the standard costs of goods sold section of our operating statements. This is now all done on programmables." A great many more applications are similar. Another follows.

"We purchased 15 programmables to install in 15 plant offices throughout the Northeast. Many of the machines are equipped with a typewriter for output to enable us to format reports and type them out automatically. the programs were developed jointly with the manufacturer. Initially, we wrote up specs, which we later refined and are now maintaining. It's necessary to make changes in payroll programs every year, for instance, since the tax structure changes. This applies to programs for cost estimating as well because the structure of data changes. The machine writes and records data on cards with ferrous oxide backing, which retains electrical impulses. It has the ability to record and accumulate final results on cards for external storage of data." (Programmables mentioned are the Olivetti P 101 and 203.)

When to Use a Programmable Calculator or a
Minicomputer to Automate Systems

Programmable calculators can serve as the brains of many types of automated systems. As noted, these systems do not need the top speed and memory capability of a minicomputer. The cost of the mini itself, plus the cost of its peripherals, plus the cost of its software development, many times represent *overkill* for many types of processing systems. The choice between calculator and minicomputer can be difficult. Some considerations to be taken into account are: (1) Execution speeds; (2) Memory characteristics; (3) Costs of peripherals; (4) Languages; (5) Program entry methods, and (6) Input/output features. Most of these factors must be weighed against specific system characteristics, user requirements, and future expansion concepts.

Preparing programs for minis usually is the most manpower-consuming and expensive phase of system implementation. A contributory factor is the need to use required software to translate the program into machine language before it can be executed. This alone can take up many hours; many more will be used up during the debugging cycle. However, when using calculator-based systems, programs are entered and edited through the keyboard and are interpreted directly by the hardware at execution time. In consequence, the assembly, or compilation phase is eliminated, and debugging time is almost always less than half. In further review in preparation for applications analyses:

Programmable calculators generally have three language levels:

1. The first may be called a keystroke language that resembles assembly-level computer language, but that problem was solved by the calculator designer. It is safely removed from the user.
2. Formula language, i.e., programs are entered in the form of algebraic statements to be evaluated. The statements are keyed in directly without needing to be translated by software. The hardware has the capability of interpreting statements in the order dictated by the well-known mathematical hierarchy. (RPN vs. AOS were analyzed previously.)
3. Full-fledged scientific programming language. The most common one is BASIC which has the great advantage of being implemented on many computers. Programs developed for calculators will also be useful for using micro or minicomputers.

Most manufacturers sell read-only memories (ROMs) for groups of special routines. Several manufacturers sell a considerable variety of basic *firmware* in the form of separately marketed, preprogrammed ROMs, which the user selects to fit either his unique or general requirements and plugs into special slots in the calculator housing or "mainframe." Many ROMs provide various mathematical and statistical functions as well as special input/output routines for mass-storage devices and other peripherals.

Comparative Speeds

Calculators were initially much slower than minicomputers. Advanced calculator speeds have improved significantly and now vary considerably. Generally, however, they have execution times in the same ranges of a few milliseconds to several hundred microseconds per instruction. Minicomputers, except for a few special instances, have instruction-cycle time of less than 5 microseconds or several hundred nanoseconds. Simple arithmetic operations, such as addition, require many instruction cycles in primitive micro or minicomputers, but only a single keystroke instruction in a calculator. So the actual differences in execution time for a complete operation are sometimes not large. Complex numerical calculation requirements generally eliminate calculators from consideration for high-data-rate applications. For example, much communication processing precludes their use, but not so for many measurement and control tasks where data is often limited in both amount of input and speed for processing.

Calculator memories usually distinguish between register memory, where data is stored, and step memory, where programs are stored. Various size combinations are available, ranging up to several thousand program steps and several hundred registers. The advantage to the user is the freedom to select the right memory size for his needs. The second type of calculator memory structure uses the same space for both instructions and data and can be either strings of instructions or strings of registers. Basic machine configurations range from hand-held units of 100 to 244 registers up to options providing 20 times as many registers. Many calculator users require extra storage, amd several mass-storage devices are available now for hand-held and desktop units. Most common are tape-cassette transports, which may be built into the mainframe or bought as separate units. They extend into the tens of thousands of instructions. Disk drives are also used. They range in size from 1.0 to 5.0 megabytes, as similar to many minicomputer systems. They and some ROM-RAMs allow the user to access files by name. All the required directory lookup procedures are handled by hardware. Minicomputers and microcomputers often require relatively bulky software packages to achieve the same performance.

Comparative Prices

Comparing the costs of programmable calculators and minicomputers is made difficult by differences in the principal cost-determining factors for the two classes of devices. In 1976, base prices for calculators, with card input, good language level, and adequate memory size were under $200. Under $30 was a starting price for keystroke-language machines. Between $1500 and $3000 were low prices paid for desktop formula-language machines, and $4000 to $6000 were prices for machines that used BASIC. Typical comparable minicomputer base prices are in the range of $3000 to $10,000, and different language levels are based on different software packages. Many cost more than $500. These prices are based on machines with a minimum-size central processing unit and at least one peripheral device, either hard-copy output or with low-priced CRTs. Byte for byte, the cost of sophisticated, advanced calculator and minicomputer memory was about the same. However, the tradeoff between register memory and program memory is important. In calculators numeric data storage formerly seldom increased beyond 1000 registers. This changed significantly in 1976-77. Important input/output considerations now include character-processing capabilities, character codes, faster data rates, and several transmission modes. Calculators emphasize numerical processing. Their ability to handle non-numeric data was not well developed initially. To process alphabetic data, a BASIC-level machine with string variables as an option was needed.

As calculator control expanded and different or more complex situations were met, calculator manufacturers quickly developed the hardware-interrupt capability. Most calculator manufacturers rely generally on asynchronous communications. In the asynchronous mode, data is only transmitted when the readiness of both devices has been established, usually by some form of handshake procedure. Bytes can be offered to external devices in two basic ways. All the bits may be transferred at once on different lines (parallel), or they may be transmitted one at a time on a single line (serial). The former method is commonly used between local system components, while the latter is useful for long-distance communications.

Calculator systems generally cost much less overall than minicomputers. The programmable calculators open up whole new areas of measurement and control for automation techniques. They can also be used to streamline automation instrumentation systems, many of which use inflexible hard-wired logic or relatively inflexible paper tape. The use of calculators in measurement instruments and automated control systems is expanding rapidly. Special-purpose calculators began to appear as early as 1974. They were not simple desktop instruments, and they extended their capabilities over large areas. Different versions were rack-mountable and made rugged to adapt to different environments. Calculators benefited greatly from computer technology. They adopted interrupt and special processing, and special calculator I/O structures to permit simpler and more efficient routing of information within the system, as well as to peripherals. Users and designers of these systems expanded their planning horizons,* and upward compatibility within calculator product lines grew quickly and significantly. Many wide-capability systems are explained on following pages. Several other competing systems are analyzed in the next chapter.

New LED-alphanumeric displays provide the lowest price per character unit for calculators. [Litronix, HP, others.] One type of display has four 0.16-in.-high characters preassembled for multiplex operation on a PC board with pins on 0.075-in. centers. Boards may be stacked end to end to create a display with any number of characters, all evenly spaced on 0.260-in. centers. The high-contrast characters are readable in daylight at distances up to 5 ft, within a 20-degree half angle. Characters are formed with a 16-segment star-burst pattern. Luminous intensity is 0.5 mcd/digit at 5 mA/segment. Litronix and H-P lead the way; others followed quickly.

Background and Basics

Before progressing to a large number of applications examples, some technical review is in order. Sophisticated electronic calculators were introduced to the business markets in 1969 and have swiftly risen to a new class of data acquisition and process control devices. This was accomplished by first adding *memory chips* and then microprocessor devices to many desktop models. Because the Read-Only Memory (ROMs) could be programmable (PROM) and because the microprocessors could be designed with wide versatility, the programmable calculator quickly became a true computer with specialized and limited capabilities. The primary characteristic that is now pushing the sale of these remarkable devices into the millions is that they are exceptionally cost-effective. Although hardware costs are somewhat similar to microcomputer systems, the programming costs are substantially smaller because of the simpler keyboard-oriented instruction set of the calculator. Installation costs are a low minimum due to the *plug-in* nature of interface and peripheral equipment.

We have noted that it is extremely simple to expand the memory capability of programmable calculators with more memory chips (ROMs or RAMs), or with low-cost peripherals, such as high-speed magnetic tape, cassette systems, cartridges, external semiconductor or core memory devices, disk drives, etc. Calculator manufacturers design their units to be very practical, not only for conventional processing but also for supervisory control of processes, *sensing* instrumentation for equipment control, and highly specific for distinct problem

---

*Two recent LED advances are noteworthy — Low-cost alpha and changeable multi-colored units.

solving, such as, statistics, real estate, engineering, finance, etc. Special plastic overlays for all keys or for individual keys of some calculators can change the basic unit to practically any specialized computing device imaginable when they are connected to programs contained in specific ROMs or RAMs which can be built in originally or added externally as *plug-in* printed circuit (PC) cards.

Most programmable calculators use external memory transfer instructions by having a simplified *program step/data register* orientation of the calculator language which is preserved and insures a low programming cost. The number of manufacturers has stopped expanding rapidly, and each of stronger firms, it seems, is bringing to the markets even more powerful calculators, many with high-level languages, such as APL, BASIC, FORTRAN, and others. These new larger units have alphanumeric displays and can be operated in the conversational mode or with their CRT display which is part of the system. These can be used for alarm signals, ennunciator panels, editing versatility, report-format checking, *handshaking* procedures for training beginners on *how to use* them. The BASIC language is a terminal or time-sharing language, learned by practically anyone within a week's time, and is easily used for telecommunication applications. Most calculators have serial input-output capabilities which allow data communication or process control, using simple *twisted pair* wires, low-cost modems, and the telephone system. The BASIC language compiler is hardwired in the built-in ROMs, and program execution by the most advanced calculator is very often almost as fast as that by minicomputer. Most of all, the calculator is easier to use by far, and practically no one is *afraid* of the programmable calculator, but as noted, millions are scared to death of regular computers. Several new types of calculators using BASIC are ideally suited to data transmission systems and are very practical for the industrial user who can install rather complex calculator-communication systems using his own in-house electricians.

Applications of Calculators in Financial Management

Typically, calculators can compute future value of a compounded amount in 10 seconds; discounted cash flow in about 35 seconds; series of loan payments in 10 seconds; rate of return in 15 seconds, and the list goes on and on. For all years past, financial people had to solve these and hundreds of other problems with cumbersome tables and interpolation, or with a distant computer, or through several intermediaries, and after a distressing wait. A brief chart (below) demonstrates a portion of the range of financial calculations that can be performed in seconds instead of the many minutes and many hours these tasks formerly consumed when performed manually.

Millions of workers in financial enterprises have been able to forget about using tables, formulas, and equations because with advanced calculators, they now merely press the key representing the answer desired and it appears, displayed in up to ten decimal places. This procedure often includes practically every specific financial answer needed (that can be programmed): mortgage payments and analyses, accrued interest, trend lines, mean and standard deviation, true equivalent annual yield, and a thousand others. Financial users can perform chain calculations, percentages, numbers as large as 1 followed by 99 zeroes, using some hand-held and desktop machines that contain a two-hundred year calendar. Most offer at least a four-location operational memory, constant storage memory, etc. Operation characteristics of the various machines have been covered in other sections. It is important for students and calculator users to fully appreciate the types and ranges of problem-solving applications to realize the full benefits of calculator capabilities. Brief descriptions follow.

Financial Management/Analysis
Capital budgeting, including rate of return
and discounted cash flow analysis.
Trend line for forecasting.
Depreciation calculations.
Statistics.
Annuities, especially sinking funds.
Compounded growth rate.

Loans
Payment amount.
Annual percentage rate.
Finance charges.
Loan amortization.
Interest rate conversions.
Interest rebates (Rule of 78's).

Securities/Securities Analysis
Bond price and yields, bond amortization.
Short term investment price and yields.
Accrued interest for the above.
Compounded growth rate.
Trend line analysis.

Real Estate
Rate of return.
Monthly mortgage payment amount.
Discounted cash flow analysis.
Depreciation calculations.
Mortgage amortization, accrued interest.
Trend line analysis for appraisal.

Life Insurance
On the spot calculation of:
Annuities.
Premiums.
Sinking fund.

Chart Publishing for the Commodities Market Customers

The commodities market provides excitement, surprises and plenty of action for investors. Wild price swings in traded commodities are commonplace — and fortunes can be made and lost with each swift change. Traders, brokers, and analysts find some order when they subscribe to chart services such as "Commodity Perspective" to receive timely information on price levels and number of contracts changing hands. But how do the publishers of these charts keep abreast of the action? "Commodity Perspective", a 40-page weekly, in 1975, used an HP desk calculator to prepare detailed charts of 60 of the most current options. It also printed mailing labels, subscription reminders, subscription billing — and kept books. The managers of the publication felt that the chart service would have been impossible without the power and efficiency of the calculator.

A Burroughs Calculator Specializes in Weight Calculations

A Burroughs technologically sophisticated calculator is designed to handle tedious and time-consuming calculations involving units of weight with a conversational simplicity not generally offered in a desktop calculator. The unit

(C 6451) features a Program Activator Panel. The user simply snaps the Program Activator Panel into place on the applicational keyboard. The versatile Program Activator Panel . . .

. . . activates the weight program.

. . . combines the functions of the applicational keyboard with the computing and listing keys of basic calculator.

. . . identifies the three common function keys (per, convert to and metric) and the nine unit entry keys which represent the units of weight for the applications.

. . . permits computations and conversions for a broad range of weight applications.

Weight problems are entered on the keyboard in the same manner as they would be stated by the user.

Burroughs Calculator is Specifically Oriented to Solution of Liquid Problems

The Burroughs C 6451 is also designed to handle tedious and time-consuming calculations involving units of liquid with a conversational simplicity seldom offered in a desktop calculator. As noted, it features a Program Activator Panel. The user simply snaps the Program Activator Panel into place on the applicational keyboard. The Program Activator Panel . . .

. . . activates liquid program.

. . . combines the functions of the applicational keyboard with the computing and listing keys of the basic calculator.

. . . identifies the three common function keys (per, convert to and metric) and the nine unit entry keys which represent the units of liquid for the applications.

. . . permits computations and conversions for a broad range of liquid applications.

Liquid problems are entered on the keyboard in the same manner as they would be stated by the user.

Some Wang calculator software is specifically designed for auto dealers resulted in sales of many thousands of their calculators throughout the world. For example, auto dealers needed a fast, accurate way to put together "deals" for prospects. Looking up rates in a number of different and hard-to-use books led to errors and customer impatience. Waiting for a bank to figure the deal often meant the prospect turned cold. The Wang 600, 700, and now also the System 2200 give the dealer a tool for working directly with each prospect; figuring out the best financial deal for every prospect and preparing all the paperwork (including all the state forms) in minutes. A special software system handles all of the dealer's "back office" accounting, also.

Programmable Calculator "Computer" Capability — By most definitions, a computer is a device or system capable of solving problems by accepting and retaining data, performing prescribed operations on that data, and supplying and/or storing the results of those operations. If the capability of accepting and retaining a planned program of operations is added to a calculator chip, then, in effect, the calculator/programmer combination becomes a basic computer.

Not too long ago, a programmable calculator required several LSI chips to provide the necessary calculation, memory and programming functions, keyboard debounce circuits to prevent false entries, separate segment and digit drivers for the display, a multidigit display, power supply regulation circuits and, of course, a suitable keyboard. However, commercial programmable calculators cost as little as thirty or forty dollars now due to integrated units.

Calculator-Based System Approaches — Firmly established as a valuable tool for the engineer, the calculator has recently found its way into systems. Programmable desk calculators, for example, offer small-scale data acquisition and process control systems. Many documents refer to Calculator Based Data Acquisition and Process Control Systems. They point out the advantages of the "intelligent" programmable approach as compared to hardwired systems and will assess the relative merits of the scientific desk calculator vs conventional minicomputers for those applications. In addition to detailing keyboard-oriented programming techniques and operator-interactive systems using programmable calculators, they also provide a checklist to aid in selection of the appropriate type of calculator, memory capacity, and peripheral equipment. Potential users will gain from evaluations of data acquisition, processing and display-type calculator-based systems. They should also examine hardware versatility and the ability to acquire information from a variety of sources; processing capabilities, low software requirements, easy speed-cost tradeoffs, and diverse utilization of processed information.

Business Management Calculator units are efficient management tools that enable managers to forecast the future faster, more easily and with greater certainty, using the same data they use now. The calculator's financial, statistical and mathematical capabilities help managers perform most time-value-of-money calculations and the statistical and mathematical calculations users need to forecast scientifically, e.g., linear regressions, curve fits. Most types also assist in extended percent calculations. They offer separate percent keys that let users make all sorts of percent calculations with a minimum number of keystrokes. Many units contain expanded memories, with many special registers. In addition to the many financial registers, and other operational stack registers, these units offer many that are addressable in which users can store and retrieve data.

Programmable Calculator Decisions — Decision-making capabilities are an essential requirement of all but the simplest kind of program. A programmable calculator must therefore handle programs that are constructed with decision (or branch) points. Different sequences of commands are performed depending on the value, or almost any other aspect of a number, or a logic condition at a specific branch point in a program. Many single condition decisions — negative numbers, zero, switch settings, greater than, less than, etc. — can be combined to create highly complex multi-branched programs, but overall simplicity is still retained. The programmer spells out, singly, each condition to be tested in a multiple-branch program no matter what the complexity.

Investment and Business Decision Calculators — Although a scientific calculator may be used for solving the more basic types of business problems, calculators especially designed for business and/or financial problems can soon pay for themselves in terms of time and effort saved because they are designed to solve specific business problems, giving the exact answers when and where they are needed. A business calculator should provide all of the fundamental financial functions to solve problems involving interest rates; rates of return and discounted cash flows; extended percent calculations; remaining balances, amortization and balloon payments. But in addition, a business calculator should help the modern business manager in planning, forecasting and decision analysis. For these problems, a business calculator should provide advanced statistical capability, mathematical functions, and extra memory power. "Advanced business" or "financial" calculators usually have all of the functions found in business calculators, but will also have more specialized capabilities to solve problems involving depreciation, bond prices and yields.

And because the latter require a calendar, these types of calculators will have one "built-in."

For specialized business or financial problems, involving extended calculations or unique and complex formulas, a programmable calculator can be a tremendous time-saver. Since problem-solving programs are entered just once, and then with one keystroke start an entire sequence, a user reduces error ratios and as a result has confidence in answers. Another point to consider when selecting a business calculator, is the basic financial concepts worked with daily as decision makers handle routine transactions. The calculator selected should help in making complex decisions. A user could very well make or save far more than the calculator costs the very first time it is used.

Data Processing Calculator System — When owners connect advanced programmable calculators to their computers they put full computing capability right on the user's desk — where it often belongs. They put an end to the data processing run-around because the calculator can be a remote batch terminal, timeshare terminal, and satellite processor, all in one unit. As a satellite processor, most types of powerful BASIC language calculators give fast solutions to most of the user's computational problems. And by keeping these small- or intermediate-size jobs out of the data processing stream, the calculator helps users make better use of all their computing resources. Data can be gathered from many sources because the calculator accommodates instrumentation and a complete line of input/output peripherals, including plotter, digitizer, and line printer. To convert the calculator to a computing data terminal, users simply add a Data Communications Interface and ROMs. Then it can communicate with another terminal or another calculator to function as a binary synchronous remote batch terminal to a large computer, or serve as a timeshare terminal. Users find that the calculator then becomes an economical alternative for connecting to remote batch or timesharing services — especially since it has so many of the features users need to improve their data processing capabilities.

Advanced Calculator Terminal Systems — As proven systems with many years of hard field use at many organizations, calculators have demonstrated abilities to disperse computing power to field offices for many tasks, sharply improving employee productivity while reducing operating costs. Many units are designed into fully programmable, multi-user systems using powerful processors and lines of peripherals to match user needs. Some units contain processors with 48k user memory. Users can simultaneously access the system and accomplish data entry, data processing, file management or report generation. Programming can be quickly accomplished in calculator BASIC language. Each user can run a separate program and access single or multiple public or restricted files. There's no "spinning of wheels" trying to make a limited system fit specialized needs. Advanced calculators with inherent flexibility and powerful software let the users at each remote site readily accomplish the task at hand.

Advanced Calculator Expansion Capabilities — After users establish their initial system, they can use special types of software to make it work or be tailored to provide them with increased effective problem-solving capability. Several hardware elements may be installed as part of the initial system. Or they may add any elements as their needs expand without sending the system to the factory: More memory for more jobs or more complicated jobs. Extra storage to process and file increased data loads. Additional workstations, all with access to new disk units. A card reader which reads punched and/or marked cards. A 9-track tape drive to interchange data with a central computer and maintain large data archives. The telecommunications option so they can use the system for daily computations as well as corporate reporting.

Alpha Prompting Capability — With the alpha capability in some units, the calculator or terminal actually communicates with the operator. Because the calculator can print instructions, ask for input and label results, an experienced operator is no longer a necessity. Any one who can press the start key can get the right answers after only a few days training.

CRT Subsystem, Programmable Calculator — One specific CRT subsystem is a special configuration of the HP 2640A intelligent terminal. It has been designed to interface with the HP 9830 BASIC language calculator to provide a high speed entry system for users who work with business forms: It can be operated in either a block or character mode for sophisticated data entry applications. The easy-to-read, 5 × 10 inch, inverse video (black on white) display is available with standard 128-character Roman font. The terminal generates characters with a high-resolution (7 × 9) dot matrix in a 9 × 15 dot character cell.

The microprocessor-controlled operating characteristics of the terminal, combined with its RAM semiconductor memory, provide a smart (dynamically allocated) memory that can store more than 200 lines of data that are viewable 24 lines at a time. The 9882A comes with 3K bytes of memory, which can be expanded in a 2K byte step ups. (H-P stands for Hewlett-Packard Co.)

Executive Graphics and Alphanumerics — Executives often need vivid descriptions of their math problems. Their concepts can be drawn on their personal graphic calculator system. The system becomes a combination of mathematician and problem designer. The programmable calculator has the computational power, and the Graphic Terminal has the artistic skill. With both machines sitting at an executive's desk, he has two keyboards to work with. The math keyboard of the calculator and the teletype keyboard of the terminal lets him draw the shape of his thoughts as he builds them. This lets him concentrate on ideas instead of mechanics. He can see his concepts take form on the bright screen. This permits him to work easier because the system is fast. For example, he can tap the calculator's remote key to send these commands to the terminal: Erase screen. Accept X-Y coordinate data. Enable graphics. Start or start alpha. Print alpha. Make hard copies with optional hard copy unit.

The Burroughs Preprogrammed System (6451)

A Burroughs C 7200 Program Product Example

Program 252 from the Burroughs Program Library

FORECASTING: TREND ANALYSIS AND TREND PROJECTION

EXAMPLE I

Company expenses for the first eight months of the year are:

JAN..................15,500	MAY..................17,500
FEB..................18,000	JUN..................20,000
MAR..................14,500	JUL..................19,000
APR..................19,600	AUG..................20,500
	TOTAL YEAR TO DATE=144,600

If expenses continue at the current rate, what will they be for the rest of the year?

INPUT

1. Number of periods for which results are available.
2. Monthly expenses.
3. Number of periods to be forecasted.

OUTPUT

I STATISTICAL DATA—indicates degree of fluctuation and consistency of previous results, and gives guidance in interpreting the forecast. (See section OUTPUT I for explanation.)

II SMOOTHED RESULTS—Results to date adjusted to fit the ideal straight line trend.

FORECAST—Projected monthly forecast based on current straight line trend.

TOTAL—Total expenses for the year—actual expenses to date plus forecasted expenses.

SUMMARY

(a.) The C7200 calculates the trend of results to date and accurately projects the increasing trend over the period concerned. Combining these easily produced results with knowledge of your business will help you to produce better forecasts.

(b.) It is more accurate than annually rating the total expenses to date which would not reflect the true trend.

	P 02	
1	8 •= ₥	
2	15500•= ₥	I
2	18000•= ₥	N
2	14500•= ₥	P
2	19600•= ₥	U
2	17500•= ₥	T
2	20000•= ₥	
2	19000•= ₥	
2	20500•=	

(i)	18075•000000000	O
(ii)	2155•2262062240	U
(iii)	•11923796438320	T
		P
(iv)	•54175728418390	U
(v)	•54175728418390	T
(vi)	15160•714290	I
(vii)	647•619050	

INPUT 3	4 •= ₥	
	1•0 15808•0	
	2•0 16456•0	
	3•0 17104•0	
SMOOTHED	4•0 17751•0	
RESULTS	5•0 18399•0	O
	6•0 19046•0	U
	7•0 19694•0	T
	8•0 20342•0	P
	9•0 20989•0	U
	10•0 21637•0	T
FORECAST	11•0 22285•0	II
	12•0 22952•0	
TOTAL	232443•0	

426 programmable calculators

EXAMPLE II

An advertising campaign has been introduced in July to increase the sales of a product which has not been selling at the desired rate. Sales for the first nine months of the year are as follows:

JAN.....................8490		JUN.....................8329
FEB.....................9104		JUL.....................11839
MAR.....................9283		AUG.....................8993
APR.....................8434		SEP.....................10570
MAY.....................9110		

If sales continue at this rate what is the outlook for the last three months of the year and the total year?

INPUT

1. Number of periods for which results are available.
2. Monthly sales.
3. Number of periods to be forecasted.

OUTPUT

I STATISTICAL RESULTS—(see section OUTPUT I for explanation) The determination Coefficients are different indicating the C 7200 has calculated that a curved trend best fits the past results.

II SMOOTHED RESULTS—Results to date are adjusted to get the ideal non-linear trend.

FORECAST—Monthly sales projected for three months ahead.

TOTAL—Total sales for the year includes total of actual plus forecasted sales.

SUMMARY

The C 7200 automatically calculates that a curved or non-linear trend program is best suited to the past results and projects the trend for the period required. As with any rapidly increasing or decreasing trend, local knowledge and business experience should be applied to interpret the results.

P02

1	9•=	INPUT
2	8490•=	
2	9104•=	
2	9283•=	
2	8434•=	
2	9110•=	
2	8329•=	
2	11839•=	
2	8993•=	
2	10570•=	

(i)	9350•2222222220	OUTPUT I
(ii)	1148•6226292580	
(iii)	•12284442037440	
(iv)	•26661817488620	
(v)	•28665474503580	
(vi)	8747•785710	
(vii)	45•467970	
(viii)	26•203460	

INPUT 3	3•=

SMOOTHED RESULTS	1•0 8729•0	OUTPUT II
	2•0 8762•0	
	3•0 8847•0	
	4•0 8985•0	
	5•0 9176•0	
	6•0 9418•0	
	7•0 9713•0	
	8•0 10061•0	
	9•0 10461•0	
FORECAST	10•0 10913•0	
	11•0 11418•0	
	12•0 11975•0	
TOTAL	118458•0	

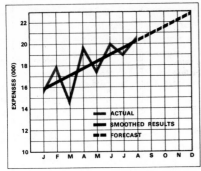 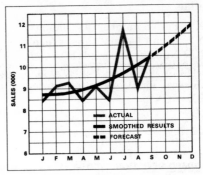

The above graphs show the actual results for the examples worked previously. Also illustrated are the trends and the projected trends which form the basis of the forecasts.

OUTPUT I

(i)   The MEAN—The average of the figures entered, i.e. the monthly average of expenses or sales to date.

(ii)   STANDARD DEVIATION—of the entered figures. This result is required to calculate the variation coefficient.

(iii)   VARIATION COEFFICIENT of the entered figures.

        Indicates the degree to which the figures entered have fluctuated. The less the variation of the indexed figures, the closer the Variation Coefficient will be to zero.

        A high variation coefficient (approaching or exceeding 1.0) indicates that the figures entered vary considerably. The forecasted results should be examined carefully and critically to ensure that they are viable.

        A high coefficient does not necessarily mean that the forecast is incorrect—it simply draws attention to the degree of variation of the input.

(iv) & (v)   DETERMINATION COEFFICIENTS
        Reflects how well the figures entered match the trend calculated by the C 7200.

        The coefficient can vary between 1.0 and 0. A perfect match would be indicated 1.0.

        (iv) is the Determination coefficient for a straight line.

        (v) is the Determination coefficient for a non-linear curve.

        The C 7200 automatically selects which of the two trend methods—straight line or non-linear curve—is the better trend to project, i.e. the determination coefficient which is closest to 1.0.

        If a straight line trend is selected, the C 7200 will print identical determination coefficients for both straight line and curve.

(vi, vii & viii) This information will only be of use if a projection is required for a partial period.

        The general formula for a second degree parabola is

$$Y = A + BX + CX^2$$

        In the case of a straight line the formula becomes $Y = A + BX$

        (vi) is the value of coefficient A

        (vii) is the value of coefficient B

        (viii) is the value of coefficient C

Formulae

X = Period number (e.g. January = 1, February = 2, etc.).
Y = Result (Actual sales, expenses etc. for a given period).
N = Number of periods of *actual* results being used for input.
General formula for linear representation is Y = A + BX.
General formula for second degree parabolic representation is Y = A + BX + CX².

(i) MEAN $\dfrac{\Sigma Y}{N}$

(ii) STANDARD DEVIATION $\sqrt{\dfrac{\Sigma Y^2 - \dfrac{(\Sigma Y)^2}{N}}{N-1}}$

(iii) VARIATION COEFFICIENT $\dfrac{\text{Standard Deviation}}{\text{Mean}}$

(iv) DETERMINATION COEFFICIENT—STRAIGHT LINE

$$\frac{\left[\Sigma XY - \dfrac{(\Sigma X)(\Sigma Y)}{N}\right]^2}{\left[\Sigma X^2 - \dfrac{(\Sigma X)^2}{N}\right]\left[\Sigma Y^2 - \dfrac{(\Sigma Y)^2}{N}\right]}$$

(v) DETERMINATION COEFFICIENT—SECOND DEGREE PARABOLA

$$\frac{B\left[\Sigma XY - \dfrac{(\Sigma X)(\Sigma Y)}{N}\right] + C\left[\Sigma X^2Y - \dfrac{(\Sigma X^2)(\Sigma Y)}{N}\right]}{\Sigma Y^2 - \dfrac{(\Sigma Y)^2}{N}}$$

(vi), (vii) & (viii) FOR STRAIGHT LINE

$$A = \frac{\Sigma Y - B\Sigma X}{N}$$

$$B = \frac{\Sigma XY - \dfrac{(\Sigma X)(\Sigma Y)}{N}}{\Sigma X^2 - \dfrac{(\Sigma X)^2}{N}}$$

FOR A SECOND DEGREE PARABOLA

$$A = \frac{\Sigma Y - B\Sigma X - C\Sigma X^2}{N}$$

$$B = \frac{\left[\Sigma XY - \dfrac{(\Sigma X)(\Sigma Y)}{N}\right] - \left[\Sigma X^3 - \dfrac{(\Sigma X)^3}{N}\right]}{\Sigma X^2 - \dfrac{(\Sigma X)^2}{N}}$$

$$C = \frac{\left[\Sigma X^2 - \dfrac{(\Sigma X)^2}{N}\right]\left[\Sigma X^2Y - \dfrac{(\Sigma X^2)(\Sigma Y)}{N}\right] - \left[\Sigma X^3 - \dfrac{(\Sigma X)^3}{N}\right]\left[\Sigma XY - \dfrac{(\Sigma X)(\Sigma Y)}{N}\right]}{\left[\Sigma X^2 - \dfrac{(\Sigma X)^2}{N}\right]\left[\Sigma X^4 - \dfrac{(\Sigma X^2)^2}{N}\right] - \left[\Sigma X^3 - \dfrac{(\Sigma X)^3}{N}\right]}$$

Burroughs Has Offered a PreProgrammed Electronic Calculator Designed for Financial Institutions

Burroughs Corporation has also announced a pre-programmed electronic printing calculator, the C 6203, which is designed especially for commercial banks, savings and loan associations, other financial institutions and financial management of large commercial organizations. The C 6203's versatile stored programs provide simple and rapid solutions to the complex computations which are part of the everyday work of departments handling installation loans, commercial loans, mortgages and savings accounts. The calculator's simplicity of data entry and rapid calculation eliminates the need for charts,

Burroughs C-6203 PreProgrammed Electronic Calculator Designed for Financial Institutions.

rate books, tables and formulas. For example, computation of monthly payments of a conventional mortgage loan is performed by entering the principal amount, the annual interest rate, and the number of years of the loan. The automatic result shows the monthly payment, including principal and interest. Monthly payments on installment loans including credit life insurance and accident/health insurance can be computed quickly and can include the "odd days" interest frequently lost by an institution because of the number of references that must be made to rate books and charts.

Single or multiple payment commercial loans and amortization schedules can also be computed quickly and easily. The calculator also makes it easy for a savings department to determine how much a customer needs to deposit on a periodic basis to achieve a specific savings goal. General financial applications include such routines as equity calculation on a mortgage loan, equivalent interest rate on discounted notes, calculation of investment required to yield fixed periodic withdrawal, calculation of periodic withdrawal from a known investment, and others. The unit has eleven application programs, which are activated simply by depressing program selection keys; they are stored permanently in read-only memory (ROM), consisting of large scale integrated circuit chips. Read-only memory contains all the program instructions required to permit fast, simple solution of the complex problems encountered by financial management and financial institutions. In addition, the calculator can be used for many general-purpose applications and as a standard four-function calculator with square-root capability.

The calculator has five storage memories used principally for storing of proof totals and/or accumulations, or both, resulting from executed programs. The "execute" key is an important feature which contributes to simplicity of operation. After data is entered on the keyboard, depression of the "execute" key triggers completion of the selected program steps. The calculator's output tape provides printed results, and also provides a complete audit trail of data entry and computations. The calculator, designed and manufactured by Burroughs, includes special internal diagnostic checkpoints and removable components, permitting fast, easy, maintenance in customers' offices.

Another Mortgage Loan Accumulated Interest, Remaining Balance Program

This program will allow the user to calculate the amount paid to interest, for one payment or over a number of payments, as well as the amount of principal still unpaid, i.e., the remaining balance. The user must input the following values: the initial amount of the loan, the periodic interest rate, and the periodic payment amount. He must then key in a beginning payment number, J, and an ending payment number, K. The program will compute the accumulated interest charge from payment J through payment K, inclusive, and the balance remaining after payment K. If one wishes to find the amount of interest paid in a single payment, he can simply set K = J.

The program can also be used to generate a limited amortization schedule showing the balance remaining after successive payments. This can be done by leaving J = 1 and increasing K by 1 at each iteration. Outputs will be the total amount paid to interest over the first K payments, and the balance remaining after payment K. (See formulas in appropriate manuals.)

The Burroughs Corporation offers a special businessman's calculator. All of the following frequently used, quite complex calculations are preprogrammed in the unit:

> Selling price from cost and gross profit
>   margin
> Compound interest with automatic
>   scheduling
> Forecasting with % increase/decrease
> Depreciation
> Commission
> Proration
> Distribution
> % Analysis
> Invoice extension with accumulation
> Job estimating
> Inventory extensions, count and average
> Costing (jobs or process)
> Area/volume
> Mark-up
> Sales analysis
> Price comparisons
> Gross profit margin
> % Increase/decrease
> Sequential comparison
> Growth over succeeding periods
> Two total prelisting
> Cost and sell extensions
> Logarithms and exponentials
> Standard deviations

Preprogramming eliminates over 80% of the work required to complete these calculations. Proof totals and grand totals are provided automatically. To activate any of these preprogrammed calculations, users simply press two keys, then enter the variables. Calculation is completed faster, more simply, and with less chance for error.

Another Example of a Financial System Interfacing Application ... Tax Administration Department of Mobil Oil Corporation (Wang 700 System)

"The 727 interface has solved Mobil's problem of linking their New York and Dallas departments together for transmitting pertinent data on a day-to-day basis."

Mobil Oil Corporation's Tax Administration Department is presently utilizing Wang equipment to perform certain tax functions which are pertinent to its everyday operations.

It began in the early part of 1971, when Wang Laboratories was asked by Mobil if their equipment could perform a simple task of accumulating columns of data and storing the totals of these columns to be further used for specific tax calculations which would be developed in a tax program. Mobil was convinced that the application could be performed on an Advanced Programmable Calculator Model 720C, together with a Disk Memory Unit — Model 710-1 and an I/O Tyewriter — Model 711. The equipment was purchased and work began immediately on programming what is now called the "Tax Results."

The "Tax Results" program is one that compiles certain financial data from Mobil's many Divisions for each month and generates various reports which in summary arrive at Mobil's income tax liability on a monthly basis and a cumulative basis.

The program then makes a comparison of the results with the same period of time of the prior year. The program also generates a reconciliation of the difference between the current year and prior year results. All of the data for each month, both current and prior years, are stored on the disk, which enables Mobil to prepare quarterly, semi-annual and annual reports as the year progresses.

In addition to the latter program, several other tax programs were developed by Mobil's Tax Department to relieve the burden of routine tax calculations, such as federal tax depreciation, state taxes, etc.

Having successfully found many uses for the equipment in New York, the Tax Administration Department felt that the 720C could be of comparable advantage in Dallas, Texas, where the Tax Compliance function is located. However, for optimum advantage, the equipment had to be coupled utilizing an interface device.

Mobil was then informed that such a device did not exist at the present time, but could be developed to satisfy their specific needs.

As a result, the Interface — Model 727, which couples directly to a Bell 103-A dataphone, was designed to perform the following three functions required by Mobil:

(1) Memory to memory transmission.
(2) Execute program in Dallas and New York simultaneously, and
(3) Typewriter to typewriter transmission.

The Interface has solved Mobil's problem of linking their New York and Dallas Tax Departments together for transmitting pertinent data on a day-to-day basis.

Software for Wang Programmable Calculators

Perhaps the biggest surprise to computer people regarding the competing programmable calculators was the speed with which the suppliers produced massive software versatility for their units. The competence of any programmable calculator depends on software — the programs that it uses and that are accurate — tested and proved. Calculator and software firms, user clubs and private parties are offering an abundance of programs. It's much easier to turn on a calculator and start operating than to turn on a computer, find or purchase expensive programs, and spend a day or more doing testing and debugging. For those times when users may want to do the programming, it's nice to have a machine which programs easily and quickly and does not demand special languages like FORTRAN or COBOL. Most programmable calculators can be programmed through their keyboards with relative ease and speed by pressing the appropriate keys in an appropriate sequence. As early as 1974 complete turnkey (ready-to-go) systems were available for the following applications for the Wang 700 calculator, and many more were added rapidly:

Civil engineering
Surveying
Bond trading
General statistical & miscellaneous
   mathematics
   Bond package for billing & analysis
Distribution functions & test
   stations
Analysis of variance & regression
   analysis
Extended analysis of variance & re-
   gression analysis
Geodetic surveying
Clinical pathology
Regression analysis with plotting
Bond billing (Corporate &
   Municipal)
Auto dealer contracts
Real estate
Extended mathematics
Education package
Investment analysis
Extended surveying
Gear package
Plotter utility package
Life insurance
Heating, ventilation & air condi-
   tioning
Government bond trading
Installment loans
Petro-chemistry
Medical histories

All other suppliers also provide wide range of programs fast and cheaply.

Production and Process Automation Calculators

Some desk-top calculators enable users to log, compare, and analyze data the moment it arrives and to eliminate all manual entries. These systems can store data and match many of the capabilities of minicomputers. Calculator

The Wang Model 600 Operating as the Input-Output and Control of Instrumentation.

systems combine stand-alone data recorders with the data analysis calculator. New systems are especially useful in quality control testing and monitoring; design engineering testing and documentation; production testing, monitoring and control; and in various scientific and medical laboratories. Systems include the calculator, a mainframe power source, and interface plug-in, analog-to-digital converters, standard software for data acquisition, and standard accessories and options. Actual data acquisition is accomplished by other instruments which are plugged into the calculator mainframe in any desired configuration.

In a typical application situation, the first step is to establish where measurements are to be made and for how long. The next step is the placement of suitable measuring devices, perhaps multimeters or counters. By interfacing these instruments, raw signals are converted into useful data. By plugging the programmable calculator into the system, the data can be collected, measured, processed and in certain cases stored. Review of the results permit the identification of trends. By the use of a graphic terminal or digital plotter with the calculator, it is possible to display or plot the information in a meaningful format such as XY plot, histogram or frequency distribution.

Calculator Communication Systems Use Plotters Effectively

A large number of programmable calculators now have the capacity to handle line-oriented telecommunications between other similarly programmed computer systems. With the addition of telecommunication options, programmable calculators can, under program control, transmit, receive, store, format, and convert information. Such calculators are now called *Systems* and many new advanced programmable calculators have *intelligent* terminal capabilities . . . and these especially have become computers in their own right.

Utilizing the BASIC statements of PRINT, PRINT USING, and INPUT, the calculators send and receive data over telephone or dedicated lines at user-selected data rates up to 1200 baud. Data, which may be read from or stored onto cassette or disk, can be accepted in unformatted lines of up to 64 characters or specially formatted lines of up to 192 characters on some machines. In addition, they have facilities for initiating a break signal and for decoding a selected input character as the terminating character. Also introduced by some firms are digital flat-bed plotters (31 × 42 inches) priced at about $3,000 or less. Driven by the programmable calculators, the plotters produce accurate continuous line or point plotting graphics of curves and data of problems solved on the calculator.

The market for peripherals is very big. Firms are racing to build products which will interface with them. For example, Houston Instrument's Complot series of digital plotters may now be interfaced to Hewlett-Packard's programmable calculators. The Model 11282A interface is priced at about $750, or lower, and can be used with the DP series of plotters. And this trend with other interfaced equipment will continue with new rapid introductions of products.

Industrial Measurement Control Systems

Measurement control systems made possible with the use of programmable calculators can, as noted, greatly improve productivity. Their applications include material handling, process control, information networks, and quality control. Industrial measurement and control systems can ensure materials are on hand when needed, in the right quantity. They can control the manufacturing process; and when the job is done, they can check the quality of the finished products automatically. The system can also be integrated into a plantwide information network for management reports and data processing.

As regards production data analysis, characteristics usually pertain to:

- output in engineering units
- transducer linearization and compensation
- average values and standard deviations
- trend analysis
- design computations
- real time process profile
- efficiency and fast time information
- go/no-go limit testing
- comparison with historical test data

Production System Calculator Example

One type of calculator system's computational power and interactivity has practically eliminated human error and double production of precision electronic components. It eliminates hours of test equipment stabilization time, hand logging and visual comparison of tables. The operator presses a key as each part is tested for voltage drop. The calculator's program applies a formula to compute the voltage reading and oven temperature relationship. Then it accepts or rejects the part. The alphanumeric printer labels results and groups acceptable parts into three grades. A typical quality control calculator application follows. A pharmaceuticals manufacturer of proprietary and ethical ophthalmic preparations develops products that range from contact lens cleaning solutions for both conventional and the new "soft" lenses to antibiotic ointments. In the manufacture of any pharmaceutical product, quality control is one of the most important functions of the organization. Automation of quality control procedures has a high priority and thus "AutoAnalyzer" I and II systems were teamed with interface systems and programmable calculators to provide a completely-automated active ingredient assay system for their products.

Production Calculator/Controller

If a user has been working with BASIC language programming, some calculators are optimum controllers. They combine the high level BASIC language with many unique programming and editing features to shorten usual programming time. The major portion of the keyboard duplicates that of a typewriter or Teletype. On one unit, twenty special function keys can be defined by functions or subprograms to simplify system programming. Program, data, and special function key storage are easily and quickly done on the built-in cassette memory with up to 40,000 word capacity (16 bit words). Operator system interaction is greatly simplified with the 32 character alphanumeric display and the 80 character thermal printer. Of several types of controllers, some typical units have a large memory option with 7.9k (16 bit words) of user read-write memory.

Process Control

1. Automatic control of industrial processes are those in which continuous material or energy is produced. 2. Pertaining to systems whose purpose is to provide automation of continuous operations. This is contrasted with numerical control, which provides automation of discrete operations. Industrial processing applications are as wide and varied as the degrees of control that individual processes may require. Some general process-control application

areas are: precious metals production, cement production, environmental control, pilot plants, chemical processes, petroleum refining and many others. The data acquisition and control system provides maximum flexibility in the types of process data that it can accept, and the variety of output signals and data format that a calculator may exercise. A system of feedback devices is usually linked together to control one phase of a process.

Process-Control-Oriented Programmable Calculator

More powerful and versatile than a programmable controller or a microcomputer, various advanced programmable calculators include many features usually found only on minicomputers. One type of desktop unit is easier to use than a minicomputer and can be operated as a calculator at the same time that control programs are running. Although intended as a controller for an instrument system or a pilot process application, for remote data collection, or for production control, the calculator can also be used as a stand-alone computer.

One firm has designed a medium-priced unit primarily for use in engineering, research, and statistics. Some of its features are interrupt capability, input speeds of up to 400,000 words/s and output speeds of up to 200,000 words/s put modules which accepts input from the system being controlled and transmits control signals to that system; a power supply and regulators; a communiand load, internal calculation range of $\pm 10^{511}$ to $\pm 10^{-511}$, and optional plug-in read-only memories.

A process-control system is a system whose primary purpose is to provide automation of continuous operations. One industrial microcomputer system consists of a Central Processor Unit (CPU) Module which provides system control and performs the various arithmetic and logical functions; one or more Programmable Read-Only Memories (PROM'S) which store the system instructions or program; one or more Random Access Memories (RAM) which are used for data storage; possibly an interrupt control module which is used to handle interrupt signals from devices being controlled; one or more input/output modules which accept inputs from the system being controlled and transmit control signals to that system; a power supply and regulators; a communications bus flat cable which provides the signal path to tie the various modules together; and the necessary mounting hardware.

Analog-to-Digital Conversion Techniques

Much of the information required by a calculator for the various computations necessary in the processing system may be available as analog input signals instead of digitally formatted data. These analog signals may be from a pressure transducer, thermistor or other type of sensor. Therefore, for analog data and A/D (analog-to-digital) converter must be added to the system. A typical unit is an 8 bit binary counter or 2 digit BCD A/D converter using a staircase scheme. The operation is similar to a digital sample and hold except digital outputs are taken off the counter output taps. In one circuit an input strobe pulse first resets then triggers the counters and sets the flip flop which enables the counter. The staircase from the op amp counts down until it reaches the analog input, at which time the comparator resets the flip flop and stops the count. The digital word at the 8 outputs is the complementary binary (or BCD) equivalent of the analog input. The maximum conversion time is again approximately 2.6 msec. The Q flip flop output is convenient to use as a data ready flag since its output goes high when the conversion is complete.

Industrial Process Control Variety

Industrial processing applications are as wide and varied as the degrees of control that individual processes may require. Some general process-control application areas are: precious metals production, cement production, environmental control, pilot plants, chemical processes, petroleum refining and many others. The data acquisition and control system provides maximum flexibility in the types of process data that it can accept, and the variety of output signals and data format that a calculator may exercise. A typical N/C system (numeric control) is one which uses prerecorded intelligence prepared from numerical data to control a machine or process. The N/C system consists of all elements of the control system and of the machine being controlled that are, in fact, a part of the servomechanism.

Numerical Control (APT)

An example of the APT (automatically programmed tools) system, developed by aerospace industry combine and currently supported by IITRIIS: Using APT, the designer describes his tool and the desired part in a high-level, geometrically oriented language. A preprocessor program accepts the high-level language and digests it into a simpler, formalized internal representation. The central program (tool independent) converts the material, tool, and geometrical information into tool motion commands. A postprocessor program prepares the tool motion information in a format suitable for the particular control mechanism being used. If desired, a simultaneous output for a numerical control drafting machine permits preparation of detail blueprints while the robot tool is making the part.

A direct numerical control system connects a set of numerically controlled machines to a common memory for a part program or machine program storage, with provision for on-demand distribution of data for the machines. Direct numerical control systems typically have additional provisions for collection, display or editing of part programs, operator instructions, or data related to the numerical control process. Typical N/C (numerical-control) machines use punched paper or plastic tape with magnetic spots to feed digital instructions to a numerical-control machine, i.e., an automated cutting or forming machine thus guided. Tolerances as fine as 1/10,000 of an inch are achieved on unattended units. Tapes are developed from digital computer programs.

The Wide Range of Convenient, *Safety-Specialized* or Calculated Result Audio Response

Several calculator production companies have solved the basic problems of design and manufacture of audio calculators. They have coupled an audible display to a conventional visual one; configured the talking display so it responds to each calculator keystroke, and — on command — reads out the result of each final calculation. These units provide four-function capability combined with 24- or larger numbers of words of vocabulary, stored in Read Only Memory (ROM). These units are applications-oriented for both blind and sighted people. One model developed by Telesensory Systems, Inc. (Palo Alto, CA) uses a microprocessor based interface to implement the system's calculation algorithm, drive the calculator's visual LED display, service the keyboard and send speech-command signals to the speech synthesizer. Each signal is a 5-bit parallel code that specifies a unit in the system's 24-word vocabulary, plus a strobe signal to initiate speech. The speech synthesizer contains a commercially available 16k ROM mask-programmed with a custom pattern, and a microcontroller, that contains the system's proprietary speech-synthesis algorithm. On command, the microcontroller reads the calculator chip's outputs and uses them to fetch control information stored in the ROM. Typical control information includes data on how long to say a word and how to say it. The system generates sound by selecting the ROM address of each required word and using the data at that address to produce a speech-equivalent signal in an A/D converter. Changing the calculator's language involves only replacing the ROM, and the company can and does produce a German speaking unit and doubtless can *customize* units to fit many languages, varying disciplines and other techniques for specific business and scientific applications. Adding another ROM to the system, for example, ups its vocabulary to 64 words. The designers predict use of these units in talking versions of such devices as clocks, typewriters, voltmeters, notetakers, computer terminals, and hundreds of other *calculate and vocally report and readout* devices. Quite likely the reader can add to a list of appliances, instruments, and other devices which could conveniently utilize audio response to results of calculations, signals, alarms, specially *sensed* (and compared/calculated) heat, light, smoke, and other environmental measurements).

Calculators have been proven efficient and reliable in application ranges that surprise a great many professionals, scientists, teachers and students. A few examples are briefly described below to suggest an almost endless list that could be compiled. Are there limits to pragmatic applications? Only insofar as imagination is limited!

Voice Response Calculator Application Example

Voice response traditionally has been used to provide information to people using telephones as computer terminals, but there are many other reasons why calculators should speak. Many suppliers list such applications as automatic wake-up systems for motels, monitoring vital signs in hospital patients, and aircraft warning systems. In each example, instead of answering inquiries, the computer speaks when certain conditions are met or tolerances exceeded. Developments by these companies make such applications as now economically feasible for the first time. Many new model voice generators similar to the voice annunciator have been introduced. Audio tapes of the human voice are digitized and the codes compressed by a computer. The codes then are stored in read-only memories (ROMs) and used to drive the synthesizer, resulting in speech so natural that it is often possible to identify the original speaker's voice. Vocabularies may include continuous phrases as well as separate words in either a male or female voice.

Codes are transmitted from memory to the synthesizer in bursts, which means that one memory can drive multiple synthesizers concurrently, each speaking a different message. Some models accept ASCII codes at various standard baud rates via either a parallel or a serial interface. Evaluation units with a preprogrammed 48-word vocabulary are available.

Low Cost Audio Response Calculator Operation

An audio response calculator announces each entry and the results of every calculation using a solid-state synthesized voice stored on ROMs after digitizing. The CMOS circuits pronounce the ten numerals and the four algebraic functions of the calculator. They include: inverse, square root, square, and percent plus memory. The calculator's use was for vocational education of the blind and in the early development, an audio reinforcement of basic math concepts for sighted students. Low cost audio response calculator modes include the Learning Mode — This mode is used until the operator becomes familiar with a keyboard. Each entry produces an audio output associated with that entry. It has a keyboard lockout feature which guarantees audio output before new entry. This will prevent loss or clipping of words. Fast Mode — Standard calculator mode except function entry and answers are audibly announced. Calculator Mode — Performs as a standard calculator and only provides audio output upon demand by depressing repeat (R) key.

Audio Response Calculators originally used in vocational education for the blind, continue to be used in this important field. Recent technological advances have permitted both cost and size reductions to extend its use into other applications. One unit is an 8-function calculator that provides both an 8 digit visual display and voice readout for the basic four functions plus all numeral entries and results. As noted, each spoken word is digitized and stored permanently in its own individual Read-Only Memory (ROM) for a clear, natural-sounding voice readout. The solid-state operation of the system provides years of maintenance-free operation and audio output. In addition to the numeric-words zero to nine, the voice system in the calculator includes the words "plus", "minus", "times", "divide", "equals", and "point" for decimal point. The operator inputs the data through a standard keyboard with easily-learned key positions with touch sensitivity. In the learning mode, as each key is depressed, the number or word associated with that key is announced through a speaker in a natural-sounding male voice. When the "equals" key is depressed, the voice announces "equals" and then voices the number of the total that has been calculated by the arithmetic section of the calculator. A "point" is included in the numeric callout for the decimal point when required.

Auto Response Calculator Characteristics

- Portable — Small package that is easily picked up with one hand and carried from one place to another.
- 8-Digit Visual Display — Large characters for good visibility by partially sighted and sighted operators.
- Keyboard — Human engineered for multiple finger data entry and ease of operation.
- Audio Repeat Key (R) — Used to announce information on display at any time.
- Audio Reset Key (AR) — Used to silence the audio output. This is particularly effective when users desire a two or three place floating decimal point; any numbers beyond this are meaningless.
- Jack for external speaker or head-set for private listening.
- Tone for overflow condition.
- On-off switch and Volume Control.
- 115 or 230 V operation.
- Operating instructions with each unit.
- Rechargeable battery operation. (See talking calculator features)

TEACHING MACHINES: THE PROGRAMMABLE CALCULATORS START MOVING IN

Most systems have the following characteristics: 1. A computer monitor or controller with continuous and active response to each unit of information presented or queried. 2. Immediate and recorded feedback from questions or the students' responses and an acknowledgment of correct or incorrect answers to the student with other alternative or remedial information and instructions. 3. A scheduling which allows the student to work at his own pace and a modular presentation allowing teacher-programmers to present materials sufficiently varied to suit individual student capabilities. The teaching machine consists of both programs and hardware. The programs are either linear or branching types, or a mixture of both. Linear programs usually consist of one or two sentences, followed by a sentence containing blanks. Progress through the program is linear in the sense that one follows the other in sequence, although skipping some frames, usually planned. Branching programs have larger units of information, such as two or three paragraphs. The student usually answers multiple-choice questions, the main path is followed if the student answers are correct. Branches provide remedial teaching or instructions for incorrect answers. The teaching machines physically have a storage unit, a display mechanism, a response panel, and communication with a central data line. On some interfaces this puts 16 characters on mag tape. Data blocks correspond to data frames of the tape recorder and an inter-record gap is supplied. At the beginning and end of tapes a file gap may be inserted manually. The tape recorders themselves supply parity bits; vertical, horizontal, and any cyclic character redundancy codes.

Teaching Calculator

As noted in Chapter 1, one of the first calculators specifically made for developing individual mathematical computational skills is called Classmate 88. The machine uses an individualized instruction approach to generate unlimited drill and practice exercises for more than 70 computational skills. It is used in conjunction with Operational Achievement, a skills program developed in Monroe's education center. The combination of the computer system and the skills program provide an innovative approach to developing a capability in addition, subtraction, multiplication, division, fractions, decimals and number concepts. Classmate 88 comes with survey and diagnostic testing to determine exact competence levels for individual students. With a flick of the switch, the system generates random exercises in any of the 70 skill areas. When a skill area is selected and entered on the keyboard, the Classmate 88 prints a problem for that specific skill on a tape. The student works it manually on scratch paper, enters his solution into the machine and presses a "go" button. The machine either accepts the answer as correct and automatically prints another problem or prints the student's answer and a red error indicator. The student then may do the problem again until he gets the correct answer or he may press a key to ask the machine for the right answer. Problems and student's answers are printed on the tape, providing the teacher with a record of the student's work.

Many Educational Systems Are Now Programmable Calculator-based

An educational system would conceivably include a programmable calculator with small memory, a string variable ROM, marked card reader, page printer, and plotter. In this configuration, it is most versatile — equally at home or in the science, mathematics, business, or computer science classroom. For both teacher and student, the programmable calculator can raise scientific education out of the tedium of routine calculation and into the challenging arena of abstract concepts, a process that is enhanced by offerings of complete packages of educational programs and teaching materials. Some current lines of educational software are available for many educational levels. Since budgeting is always an important educational systems consideration, most of the equipment and software can be leased annually, often for less than the price of a teaching assistant's monthly salary.

Monroe's Classmate IV Math Lab Educator Module

The Classmate IV math lab module is an integrated hardware/software approach to learning and understanding mathematics. The software consists of:
1. Fundamentals of Programming — an introductory manual which presents the basic concepts of programming in an easy to understand straightforward manner. It covers topics such as systems organization, flowcharting, jumping, branching, decision making and subroutines. 2. Conceptual Mathematics Through Programming — a complete instructor/student math resource package:

Intermediate Math	Analytical Geometry
Algebra	Trigonometry
Geometry	Numerical Analysis
Intermediate Algebra	Introductory Calculus

Volume I contains reproducible lesson sets. Each individual lesson has four parts.
1. **Statement** of the mathematical problem to be solved.
2. **Discussion** of the problem in terms of either the mathematics involved or suggested programming techniques.
3. Description of the program which the student is to write to solve the problem.
4. Test examples for the student to use in checking the program.

Volume II Appendix describes briefly flow charting symbols and how charts are used. There are selected flow chart solutions to aid the student in writing programs for difficult problems. Programming examples are given for the programming techniques introduced in each chapter. Also, program solutions to selected programs are presented in machine codes and commands are defined. The Classmate IV Math Lab Module hardware includes the Classmate IV desktop computer and a CR-2 Mark Sense Reader.

The Mark Sense Card Reader permits students to write and code programs using only a pencil, anywhere . . . in the classroom, during study period; as a homework assignment. To check a program a student merely enters the program cards and data; the Classmate IV will confirm the solution in a matter of seconds. The Classmate IV desktop minicomputer stresses simplicity, yet provides all the power students need to master the concepts of high school mathematics. It has an algebraic keyboard logically arranged for simple, straightforward calculation and requires a minimum of machine orientation time. The student writes problems on the keyboard as he would on paper. The Classmate IV requires no special computer language, thereby allowing students at various levels of math background to quickly learn and understand the techniques and logic of programming.

There are 27 hardwired keyboard functions enabling students to perform complex calculation with a minimum of effort. There are 512 steps in basic program memory; expandable in increments of 512. Data storage includes 10 scratch pad registers and 64 main data storage registers; expandable in increments of 64. Complete I/O capability is built into the unit to allow interfacing with a wide range of optional peripheral devices.

The Classmate IV Math Lab Module has been designed by educators at the Monroe Education Center to be an effective tool for the teaching of high school level mathematics. The Classmate IV adds a new dimension to the mathematics curriculum by featuring an alternate application: Operation Achievement. Operation Achievement is a proven software resource package designed to provide drill and practice in computational skills and mathematical applications for each of these areas:

Addition	Fractions	Applications in Math
Subtraction	Decimals	Algebra I
Multiplication	Inequalities	Geometry
Division	Number Concepts	Algebra II

Applications Summary

All totaled, there are over 200 individual skills on preprogrammed cassettes which are used with the Monroe 392 Cassette Reader to program the Classmate IV for Operation Achievement. Each skill is a self-contained unit offering a large number of unsequenced exercises tailored for the skill drill. Flowcharts have been designed to give the student all the information necessary to operate the Classmate IV and work through each lesson with little or no teacher supervision. With Operation Achievement, the Classmate IV generates exercises which the student solves with pencil and paper and enters on the keyboard of the Classmate IV. If the answer is correct, the Classmate IV will print a new exercise. If the answer is incorrect, ERROR will be printed on the paper tape. At this point the student simply clears the keyboard and tries the exercise again. If, after a few tries, he or she is unable to determine the correct answer, the student may push the BULL's EYE key to find the correct answer. An Automatic scoring of the student's performance is provided by the Classmate IV. The Instructor's Guide and the Diagnostic Tests complete the Operation Achievement resource package and define it as an excellent teaching aid.

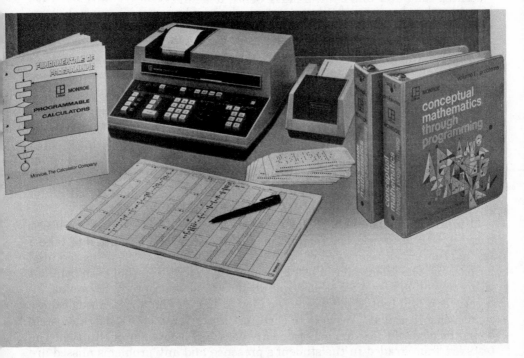

Classmate IV Math Lab Educational Module

SOME EXAMPLES OF PROGRAM ABSTRACTS USING WANG PROGRAMMABLE CALCULATORS

One-Way Analysis of Covariance With Three Covariates

by M. B. Barkley Jr. and M. C. Miller III, Ph.D., Department of Biometry, College of Medicine, Medical University of South Carolina, Charleston, South Carolina.

Abstract: Differences in results from various treatment groups can sometimes be explained (or obscured) by one or more "concomitant variables." The analysis of covariance (ANCOVA) combines regression and the analysis of variance to give a truer picture than either alone. In addition to providing the standard one-way ANCOVA with unequal group sizes, this program also allows testing for unequal regression coefficients and heterogeneous within-group variances. A Wang 600 Calculator System application.

A Laboratory Quality Control System

by J. David Sommer, Environmental Protection Agency, National Field Investigations Center, Denver, Colorado

Abstract: The National Field Investigations Center (NFIC) in Denver, Colorado is an enforcement arm of the Environmental Protection Agency supporting water pollution abatement. NFIC-D conducts field surveys to collect and chemically analyze water samples, evaluate analytical results, and prepare reports for enforcement action. Since this work is often the basis of court proceedings, the chemical laboratories must use exacting quality control.

The Laboratory Quality Control System contains two programs designed for the Wang 720 Programmable Calculator equipped with a Wang 702 Printer/Plotter. The programs have been written in "conversational mode" to simplify their use. One program applies statistics to compute the upper and lower limits necessary to construct a control chart. The other program computes the value of points to be plotted on the control chart.

The System helps insure that proper analytical procedures have been followed by the chemists and that data calculations have been accurately computed.

Generation of Exams on a Programmable Calculator

by Edward J. Gucker, Associate Professor of Physics, State University of New York, Brockport, New York

Abstract: Individualized examinations have been generated for the past three semesters using a Wang 720/702 calculator system at the State University of New York College at Brockport. The course was designed around this capability and uses such exams exclusively throughout the body of material covered. The course content includes a survey of several branches of mathematics which are appropriate to the study of physics, and use of a plotting calculator permits relatively sophisticated design of test materials.

In practice, students qualify for the tests by handing in assigned problems based upon class work. Having qualified, each student is permitted to take a test as often as necessary and without time limit, a grade of 100 being required for passing. Questions on the test are randomly selected so that each printout of the text differs from all others over about 80% of the content. Formulas, integrals and differential equations are plotted to give the appearance of these same items in a text. Answers to each test are printed on a perforated strip along the edge of the exam paper and are detached before administration. The tests are then graded in the student's presence and any problems missed are discussed. Thus the testing processes is directly integrated with the teaching process.

Current work includes transfer of the program scheme to a Wang 2200/2202 calculator system.*

Summary

Calculator System Applications: General and Specific

Advanced programmable calculators combine the easy keyboard operation of manual calculators with the sophisticated programmable calculators, a valuable combination for the scientific and business user. A complete set of fully interfaced peripheral equipment, including output writers, plotters, paper tape punch readers, on-line interfaces, high-speed printers, disk drives, dual tape drives, plus other input and output devices can provide flexibility for designing a calculating system. Some calculators feature several user-definable special function keys. In a given program these keys are readily assigned specific functions or subroutines which can be executed by a single keystroke. This can allow the user to write specific singlestroke programs in each application. A magnetic tape cassette drive can record programs for future reference. Programs can be chained together for automatic execution; specific programs can be loaded under program control. Most advanced calculators are supported by a library of programs which modify the machine for specific applications. Statistical, engineering, surveying, and medical programs can be entered into many calculators with a single keystroke, enabling the evaluation of data entered either manually or automatically from various instruments. Available investment and financing programs compute, and actually type out legal contracts. Other systems can be further enhanced for automatic letter writing.

An Advanced Programmable Desktop Calculator Example

A typical example of an advanced desktop programmable calculator is one well suited to a variety of scientific, engineering, research, and industrial applications. A specific unit contains a built-in thermal printer with alphanumeric, mathematic, and trigonometric functions and a high-speed bidirectional data cartridge. This almost standard model includes 472 program steps and 10 data registers. The memory can be expanded to 2,008 program steps. Input to the unit can be via the keyboard, which includes: 15 special function keys, 10-key numeric pad, program language and control keys, editing keys, and 28 scientific functions; or through the advanced series input peripherals. The units optional interface module provides the capability to interface to all of the supplies peripherals and various instruments.

Programmable Calculator Language Characteristics

We have noted that while minicomputers are binary in nature, most programmable calculators are decimal in nature, and many are programmable in a few high-level languages which range from algebraic types to BASIC. The hardware is quite fundamental: a keyboard, a numeric or alphanumeric display, a numeric or alphanumeric printer or both a printer and a display, and provisions for ROMs, tapes, strips, cards, etc., as programs. The keyboards are generally developed with four categories of keys: data entry, mathematics, program control, and on some calculators, edit keys. The programmable calculator is often used as a powerful stand-alone computational unit. All have several types of capabilities. These items qualify it as a system.

General mathematical languages are often used on many programmable calculators. The task of software development is thus quite arbitrary. Many pro-

---

*Excerpts from: The WANG Laboratories Programmer Dec. 1974, p. 24.

grammable calculators feature hard-wired functions such as the trigonometric functions, logarithmic and exponential functions, and a variety of other statistical and mathematical functions. Because they are decimal machines, there is no need to convert to and from binary or to incorporate algorithms to perform floating point operations. Programming mathematical functions into the calculator becomes almost as easy as copying equations from paper onto the keyboard. A great many current entries into the calculator market feature the high-level, easy-to-learn language BASIC. Each programmable calculator also has its own programming language. Most of these languages follow the rules and symbols of mathematics, whereby only a few of these calculators observe math hierarchy strictly. The majority still treat the various math operators on a first come, first serve basis. Many consider the calculator languages as high-level languages and as such carry the same ease-of-use as other standard high-level languages. Happily, most calculators do not require additional memory to support the math languages.

The high-level languages utilized on most calculators do generally result in slower speed and a lack of bit-manipulation capability. A few calculators do offer hidden instructions which allow bit manipulations. The decimal nature of the calculator thus means slower speed than is obtainable on the binary machines. Execution of single keystrokes on calculators generally is in the millisecond range. To accomplish the same functions on a minicomputer as on a programmable calculator often requires from several to over one hundred machine language instructions. No one-to-one comparison exists as far as timing is concerned. Therefore, execution times for various programs run on a mini will vary from 100 times faster to only twice as fast depending on whether the program is written in assembly language or in a higher-level language like BASIC. Calculator I/O speeds are not necessarily slow. A recently introduced unit can accept 16 BCD digits into its data registers at a rate of over 15,000 per second. Programmable calculators can and do capture and store data at rapid rates for later more leisurely analysis. They often do lack the computational speed for more critical applications. If the user cannot tolerate delays before he gets the answers, the application might necessarily exclude calculators while a micro or mini would meet their requirement.

When programmable calculators can do the job, users are money ahead. Programming in a high-level language is time-efficient and the use of BASIC in a programmable calculator doesn't require much extra memory expense. Maintaining the software in a high-level language also becomes more cost-effective. Users who program their systems for varieties of tasks have programming ease and low cost with calculators, and the ease with which it can be reprogrammed to perform different tasks, as well. Programmable calculator manufacturers supply memory options and usually some type of auxiliary magnetic storage, and the scope of the magnitude of these options is becoming greater with time. Several programmable calculator suppliers offer a line of peripherals which include practically all the items of standard X-Y plotters, typewriters, card readers, discs, etc.

Business System, Programmable Calculator-Components

A business system for small manufacturing concerns might consist of a programmable calculator with small memory, a string variable ROM, a peripheral tape cassette, a hopper card reader, and a typewriter. With this configuration, a user could automate many number-crunching tasks in his shop: payroll, billing, loan contracts, inventory control. The system can enable the businessman to get vital information to help make decisions for cutting costs, bidding jobs, planning investments, and the like. The system could also maintain a list of important customers, periodically mailing them "personal" letters describing new products and services.

Calculator Business System Typical Program 'Packages'

Complete business system calculator configurations can be delivered with all of the programs to handle the accounting and administrative needs for a particular business. For example, the package for wholesaler/distributor handles the order writing and invoicing, inventory accounting and control, accounts payable, aged accounts receivable, and sales analysis. Each of the functions generates all necessary reports and documents for both management analysis and day-to-day running of the business by some systems.

The cost always enters in the selection of calculators, minis, and micros which will do the job adequately at the best price. The hardware price and the software development are involved. Users must be careful and must consider the total cost of getting the processor into a working system as basic. The hidden costs of software development, interface design, service requirements, etc. are usually not significant with programmable calculators. High-speed and/or large memory are not part of the power and versatility of today's programmable calculators, but very often still fill the requirements of many systems.

Many calculator-based systems being sold today have been built by system houses for custom applications, or have been designed by companies for in-house use. Customized calculator-based systems have been developed and are currently operational in many manufacturing facilities. Many systems are selling fast because the speed, memory, and programming requirements all point to programmable calculators as logical choices. Being added to many units are new levels of versatility. These systems have additional programming for more conceived applications and are opening the door for future programs and for applications not yet conceived. The speed, memory, and software requirements are now very similar to the original requirements of the original small standard computer system. There is no doubt that the programmable calculator has the most economical and satisfactory solutions for the many thousands of systems in the accounting, engineering, educational, and general business fields. It's very easy to switch to other programs. The operator can simply press a key, cleanly labeled by the user-defined overlay on the keyboard to recall from the built-in ROM, strip, mag tape, etc. the desired programs. Or at the touch of another key, the operator can permanently record the results of various tests or the actual data on the mag tape. The ease of use, the flexibility, and the economic advantages of these systems are readily apparent. The calculators seldom stay idle. When calculator systems are not being used for testing, processing, etc. the calculator is still used as a stand-alone scientific calculator or as a terminal connectable to a large time-sharing remote system. Thus, the system costs can be divided and amortized quickly and fairly.

CHAPTER 10
ADVANCED PROGRAMMABLE CALCULATOR SYSTEMS IN ENGINEERING, SCIENCE, COMMUNICATIONS

Prologue

The Constantly Widening Ranges of Personal Fingertip Control Power

Engineering solutions at a moment's notice — network analysis, control systems, magnetics, microwave — whatever. There seem to be no limits to the capabilities of measurement, control, and reporting systems for engineers and scientists using programmable calculators which now are very effective *full computers* in their own right. Complex design and analysis problems that formerly required extensive computer programming, complex computer equipment, stringent computer procedures and difficult computer languages have now become simple, immediate, and direct calculator solutions. The class of calculators called *computing* calculators now utilize practically every peripheral that computers do — but with almost utter simplicity relative to the *old* data processing way. Accuracy and speed also approach computer capability — and memory expansion of calculators is now unlimited for all practical purposes. Calculator users routinely do their own programming — on cards, cassettes, PROMs, and a dozen other different devices and media. Branches, loops, logical comparisons, etc. are *old hat* for experienced calculator users. Cartridges contain a hundred programs and are speedily "clicked" or placed *in charge* by and for those who prefer to use *canned* programs. The experts in statistics, math, engineering, surveying, medicine, etc. have prepared upwards of 10,000 different programs that are available for sale, rent, lease, swap, or simply *free for the asking* in many cases.

Exotic displays, full alphanumeric output, graphics *wide-picture* visuals or hard copy are all automatically labelled, complete with immediate math conversions and programmed higher level languages. All this and more are becoming *standard* on advanced calculator systems. BASIC is an incredibly simple, effective *natural* language that is now available for many calculator models. Voice response systems are easy to operate, convenient to install, and very efficient in many applications. BASIC borrows its structure and most of its vocabulary from English. The remainder, most users recognize as familiar arithmetic and algebraic symbols and rules. Writing a BASIC program is much like writing a detailed and orderly set of instructions for normal routine business or engineering procedures. Instructions are composed in lines and are almost exactly like sentences, with subjects, verbs, and objects. Punctuation is with commas and quotes in place of a period. As the reader has noted in previous chapters, anyone can learn BASIC.

One of the nicest parts about working engineering problems with advanced calculators is that the user is in the loop every step of the way; he doesn't turn data over to an EDP center employee or contact a service bureau and wait around for hours or days for results. Personal, fingertip *computing* power is on the desk to use for tough complex tasks — to use for design experimentation, and to complete *what if* programs for any type of task or problem. Quite standard scientific and engineering applications number in the thousands, but some relatively routine types are noted on this short list:

OFF-LINE APPLICATIONS
- Digital filtering.
- Fast Fourier transforms.
- Root locus.
- DC bias analysis.
- Circuit optimization.
- Utility power flow analysis.
- Communication network analysis.
- Inventory control and costing.

ON-LINE APPLICATIONS
- Controllers.
- Data log and acquisition systems.
- Instrumentation interfacing.
- Manufacturering test.
- Factory operations.
- Traffic control.
- Air- and water-pollution monitoring.
- Pipeline, oil, and gas field operation.
- Water distribution, supply, and flood control.
- Medical monitoring.
- Railroad and truck distribution, weighing, and accounting.
- Process control.
- Other instrumentation and control systems.

Other advanced calculator capabilities coming on strongly relate to: data base systems, storage and logic technology design, and more ranges of calculator utilization in: petro-chemicals, energy, aerospace, retail sales, small business, transportation and distribution, health care, municipal government, banking and insurance, real estate, and stocks and commodities — as noted in previous chapters. In this chapter we are concerned with engineering, scientific, and communications applications. The communications capabilities of calculator systems, however, apply to and expand the previous business, financial, and educational applications discussions. And as we have noted, calculators are being increased in power and are getting both larger and smaller.

Calculators serve the engineer both at his desk and in the lab, providing rapid and easy solutions of many problems that otherwise might not be attempted. In the lab, calculators make speedy calculations, measurements and act as central processor units controlling automated test and reporting systems. Prices for these systems range from $800 to $20,000.

Dynamic Problem-Solving by Programmable Calculators by Engineers — All Types

The real business of programmable calculators is helping people solve control or analysis problems. Electronic computing products have become sophisticated systems in many markets today. Basic characteristics of these products are their dynamic problem-solving capabilities which are immediate and readily measurable. They permit direct problem-solving by the person with the problem. They are not *remote* like large computers often must be. Nor are they difficult to operate. Engineers and statisticians in government agencies as well as other enterprises, for example, spend hours every day examining pieces of data, searching for measurable interrelationships. Some are analyzing potential materials to be used in space; others are involved in large-scale drug studies . . . the list is almost endless. Programmable calculators give them the ability to personally perform computing and processing work with a large volume of data right in their own office. No time is wasted searching for or ordering computer programs or waiting for a computer run to be returned. High quality alphanumeric or graphic printouts are available at once. This frees up valuable hours for additional research.

There is more and more pressure on all engineering schools and college classes to educate students to be comfortable about basic computering concepts with calculators, and on most campuses to provide them with practical data processing skills as well. Calculator systems have enough memory and processing power to teach basic computer concepts, and they interface to TV-like screens to make them most convenient for instructional purposes. All this capability is competitively priced to meet the requirements of practically every school's budget.

Consulting engineers all over the world seek rapid, accurate calculations for solutions to problems when they undertake the design and construction of buildings. First they must accurately calculate their bid. In today's world especially, the rapidly changing costs of materials, labor, and energy make this process more critical. With so many items changing and inflating prices to consider, it is not possible to do a quick, accurate job *by hand* . . . it requires the power and ease of operation of an advanced calculator system. The administration and budget control involved in these projects also can no longer be performed manually. In this application, a programmable calculator is an especially powerful aid. Professional firms employing civil engineers either had to buy expensive computers to handle all their lengthy calculations or had to use computer time-sharing which often slowed their work flow. With programmable calculators the individual civil engineers and all other types, as well, can afford their own calculating and computing systems . . . even a convenient desk plotter that automatically prepares the most complicated plots. These calculating exams permit problem-solving from field notes to finished drawings, as we shall note on pages ahead.

Calculators as Versatile Controllers

Most advanced programmable calculators use a hardwired operating system and compiler of read-only-memory which allows the user to communicate with and program the calculator without diminishing the available read/write memory. Special functions and language enhancements are available for calculators in the form of plug-in read-only-memories (ROM's). The I/O software for instrumentation control is offered in convenient plug-in ROM's to provide input/output instructions which can be implemented either from the calculator keyboard or from a user-written calculator program. This programming feature, combined with a broad selection of interface cards, makes the calculator a friendly, easy-to-use controller. With a calculator as a controller, users have a virtually unlimited array of instrumentation applications available to them. Proven lines of calculator peripherals further enhance the capability of calculator-based systems. Results of test measurements and calculations can often be plotted on the plotters, stored on the internal tape cassettes, cartriges, RAM, PROM or stored on external tape cassettes. Additional output capability can be found in some typewriters, thermal page printers or line printers. Other peripherals include tape punch and reader, digitizer, punched marked card readers, and many more. Several offer powerful BASIC language capability that can be interfaced to various mass memory subsystems which provide up to 5 million bytes of additional storage. Advanced units can also communicate via telephone lines to large computers or other calculators using the data communications interface packages.

Typical types of instruments that can be controlled by calculators include: digital voltmeters, electronic counters, wave form analyzers and synthesizers, scintillation counters, clocks, capacitance meters . . . The applications are so broad that it is nearly impossible to describe them in detail. What is important is to understand the interface requirements between the calculator and the instrumentation equipment. Most suppliers offer many interface cards designed for those customers who desire to build custom, calculator-controlled instrumentation systems.

Before moving into the more formal and structured applications of calculator utilization in engineering, science and communication, we might briefly note a few that are effective and intriguing in various disciplines and enterprises. For example, to keep the National Radio Astronomy Observatory telescope at Green Bank, West Virginia locked onto radio sources far out in space, a calculator automatically issues new commands every half second to compensate for earth rotation. When it is not computer-controlled for special purposes, radio astronomers find that they can control the telescope most easily and economically with a programmable calculator.

An interesting application is an automatic cement plant in Mexico in which a programmable calculator controls the composition of cement going into the kilns. Other similar applications are: electrohydraulic fatigue testing, soil-testing data acquisition, sewage treatment and pollution monitoring, and remote data acquisition. The popularity for these and other test and control applications seems due to the fact that programmable calculators are very easy for most users to operate. If the calculator's speed and memory capacity are sufficient to do a given job, it is often the easiest and cheapest way to go. Systems generally include three areas: acquisition of information; processing the information; and display or use of the information. Acquisition of information is accomplished by such familiar information sources as cards, tape, keyboards, etc. Processing of information involves the programmable calculator and displays, and copy devices and a host of specific peripherals, many of which were listed above and will be discussed in some detail as covered in applications examples below.

The marriage of powerful calculators and smart instruments provides, for example, a truly flexible system and a standard bidirectional digital interface for controlling and communicating with all programmable instruments. Programmable calculators have built-in computing power that has opened up whole new areas of quite suddenly conceived new applications. Just a few examples of these new areas include geophysical data acquisition systems, navigational systems, and signal processing systems, etc. as the several write-ups below demonstrate.

Sampling, Student Training, TV Show Timing and File Searches, Radar Response Systems

Discovering elements in a sample and in what concentrations, can be efficiently accomplished by putting material in a Quantometer and pressing a button. Spectrochemical analyzers developed by Applied Research Laboratories, Sunland, California first excite the sample with x-rays or an electrical charge. Then they carefully measure the spectral intensities of the light produced to determine the exact composition of the sample. And in a very short time the Quantometer system prints a complete quantitative analysis. It identifies 40 elements in less than a minute — and neatly — no messy lab to clean up later.

Calculators Become *Mainframes* for Pilot Training Display Systems

Calculator-radar applications are already very widespread and are becoming more pragmatic and less complex. An example concerns the new mass memories that expand calculator storage. In a simulated radar exercise an HP storage display helps train pilots. Storage and variable persistence displays offer many advantages where information must be gathered over a relatively long period of time, then processed and presented for display. The bright stored information provides easy viewing in high ambient light, and highly burn-resistant CRTs ensure long life with no special operating precautions. A unique medical application for HP storage displays is in conjunction with an ultrasonic diagnostic system that provides a *picture* of internal organs or tissues in selected areas of the body. Storage allows build-up of the display by using as many scans as needed for the desired image detail. The application of the simulated radar acquisition system provides pilots with a realistic training environment. By having a calculator adjust the variable persistence in an HP 1331 storage display to match the scan rate, the pilot can see relative position trends that are not possible to view with long fixed-persistence phosphors.

Calculator Capable of Automatic Data Acquisition from Radar

The Naval Electronics Laboratory Center, San Diego, California, has developed a calculator which can automatically compute the point of closest approach between ships at sea. The system can calculate range, time, bearing, target speed, and target course at the point of closest approach for up to five target vessels. Radar-derived data from target ships such as range, bearing, and time for two sets of chronologically spaced readings are presently inserted manually into the calculator via keyboard. The calculator can then compute any or all of the desired parameters involved in finding the point of closest approach.

More significantly, however, human error in inputting typed data can be avoided by providing the radar display with an array of position sensors. Then by simply placing a probe over the target, its coordinates can be entered into the calculator. An audible alarm could be generated whenever the calculator detects a near-collision situation. In fact, algorithms have been worked out for determining corrective course changes to achieve a satisfactory closest point of approach. Work is also being done to increase the number of targets that can be handled simultaneously. The concepts inherent in this system may prove useful in other applications as well.

For example, another Marine Calculator has been designed and developed to quickly indicate the nearest approach distance of nearby ships when a planned change in the ship's own course or speed is made. The Nearest Approach Calculator is produced by Grundy & Partners of Gloucester, England. It is used with standard radar and is reported accurate to within 10%. The 6-kg (13-lb) cabinet is equipped with two groups of controls, one for the operated ship and the other for the threatening ship. When the bearing, speed, and any changes in course are entered into the machine, it produces the new nearest approach on a moving coil center zero meter.

The American Broadcasting Corporation (ABC) television network's "Password" program that appears every weekday for millions of viewers as a long-running game show, with thousands of dollars to guest contestants for naming the correct *word answer* uses an HP 9830 calculator. To make sure that there is no added drama due to technical difficulties, the producers of the show rely on the calculator to select the passwords from about 400 stored in its memory. It displays them to the TV audience to enhance their interest. Since it must perform very swiftly and flawlessly through taping sessions day after day, the calculator must be reliable, easily operated and quickly programmable for updated answers.

Engineers not only use programmables in their measure, control and lab test applications, but their accounting departments double up on them for payroll and other paperwork functions. One firm, keeping records for some 200 concurrent engineering and surveying projects does all the paperwork in just 15 to 20 hours a week. That includes job costing, accounting, billing, payroll — the works. The advanced programmable calculator doing the administrative work also takes on many engineering and surveying computations and thereby serves as a near ideal fast, low-cost computation service for a large number of key personnel. Again, reliability, easy operation, and programmability versatility wins easily over prior slow, error-prone manual methods and simplifies and performs at much lower cost work that would often be farmed out to computer service bureaus or be handled by expensive data processing equipment and personnel.

"CALCULATOR" COMPUTING POWER FOR DATA ANALYSTS

Many firms offer broad lines of calculating equipment and statistical analysis techniques which equal or exceed the capability of larger time-share or batch computing systems. It's "old hat" to plod through hand calculations and pencil annotations. Calculator users avoid consuming valuable time coding and punching cards and interfacing with the rigid hierarchy of computer input requirements. The advanced calculator systems combine with many large current statistics libraries and comprise very powerful and flexible data analysis systems. They are able to handle all but the largest problems. The interactive nature of these systems, along with their immediate accessability, combine to cut the time involved in sophisticated data analysis by at least one order of magnitude. Since most statistical analysis involves an iterative approach in converging upon a problem solution, the fact that these models work neatly on users desks is one of their outstanding features. When combined with data storage capability they permit many more ideas to be exercised in reaching conclusions in less time than would be possible using conventional computing facilities.

Systems Approaches to Statistics

Advanced desktop statistical analysis systems allow users the flexibility they need — whether it's solving a tough regression problem or analyzing the mathematical model of a complex situation. Users should specifically consider various input and output features:

• Data entry from punched cards. Variable format: Hollerith or mark sense.

- Data entry from internal cassette or an external cassette memory and the storing of data sets on separate cassettes.
- Data entry from typewriter-like keyboard.
- 80-column thermal printer output.
- Labeled plots of any pair of variables or plots of standardized residuals versus any variable using various printers.

Hewlett-Packard, for one, offers a Regression Analysis Pac that comes complete and ready for use. It consists of:

- A complete, prerecorded program cassette.
- A keyboard template overlay which defines program-dedicated special functions keys on the 9830.
- A comprehensive instruction manual that contains a general description of each program, detailed operating instructions, and complete program documentation. To utilize the Pac a user must have:
- A HP 9830A Calculator with 8k-word memory (for 35 variables) or with 4k-word memory (for 17 variables).
- A HP 9866A Thermal Printer or 9861A Typewriter.

For additional capability, these input and output peripherals are also recommended:

- Hp 9865A External Tape Cassette.
- HP 9862A Plotter and HP 11271B Plotter Control ROM.
- HP 9869A Hopper-Fed Card Reader and HP 11272B Extended I/O ROM.

Procedure for Stepwise Regression Analysis with the HP 9830
Data Entry Routine

Data is entered using the special functions key labeled **DATA ENTRY.**
Features:

- User has three data entry options: key, tape, cards.
- All original input data is optionally listed by the printer.
- All original input data is automatically stored on cassette. Additional analysis does not require data reentry.
- Program analyzes up to 35 dependent/independent variables.

Basic Data Analysis

By pressing the special functions key labeled **BASIC STATISTICS,** basic analysis for up to 35 dependent/independent variables is automatically provided.

In addition, a simple correlation matrix for the data is also automatically provided.

Multiple Regression Procedures

The complete multiple regression program is obtained by pressing the special functions key labeled **REGRESSION.**
Features:

- Any variable may be specified as the dependent variable.
- Tolerance level is specified. Protects against a very small value for the determinant of the data matrix.
- Four methods of regression analysis are provided: stepwise, forward, backward, and manual.
- Each step of the stepwise procedure is fully documented including: complete AOV table, R-squared for the step, partial correlations, and regression coefficients.
- The program automatically stops when the F levels grow smaller than those input at the beginning of the multiple regression procedure.

- When the final equation is computed, the coefficients can be stored for future use in the residual analysis.
- The analysis is easily restarted to try a different analysis procedure. In some examples, the backward procedure is used — forcing all variables, (except those that are suppressed) into the equation and generating coefficients for all variables.
- The program then permits addition or deletion of any variable in the equation in the manual procedure.

The 9830 Cross Tabulation Pac

The 9830 statistics library features a powerful and flexible cross tabulation program. It is based on a modified version of the University of California's BMD Series cross-tabulation program and is available from HP as Part Number 09830-70828.

The Cross Tabulation Pac comes complete and ready for use. It consists of:
- A complete, prerecorded program cassette.
- A keyboard template overlay which defines program-dedicated Special Functions keys on the 9830.
- A comprehensive instruction manual that contains a review of cross tabulation techniques and examples, detailed program operating instructions, and complete program documentation.

The system required for this program is a 9830A Programmable Calculator with 8k of read/write memory (Option 276), the 9866A Printer, and the 11274B String Variables ROM. Data entry and program running can be optionally enhanced with the use of the 9865A Cassette Memory and the 9869A Calculator Card Reader.

Up to 100 variables can be run with the cross tabulation program and up to ten tables can be specified for any run. The program is rerun with different tables specified if more than ten tables are desired on the variable set. Data need be entered only once since it is stored on the 9830's magnetic tape. Optional percentage tables are generated for row, column, and/or overall totals for any or all of the tables in the specified set. Three-way tables are also optionally generated for any three specified variables in the data set.

As previously noted the BASIC language 9830 Programmable Calculator has the power and memory of a minicomputer without the limitations and expense usually encountered. The 9830 uses a hardwired BASIC language compiler (the equivalent of 7,500 words) which allows the user to communicate with and program's read/write (R/W) memory without disturbing or diminishing the R/W memory itself. Also, the 9830 employs plug-in, read-only memories (ROM's) which perform additional user (or peripheral) functions with the main R/W memory — again, without reducing memory size or disturbing the user.

The R/W user memory is always reserved and ready for programs and data. There is no loading of compilers or use of valuable memory for functions other than programs or data. A maximum of 8,000 16-bit words of user R/W memory is available in the 9830 (in increments of 2,000 and 4,000 words). Additionally, a total of 8 plug-in ROM's provides up to 8,000 words of read-only memory over and above the R/W and compiler memories. (For more capacity, see 9830-B below.)

Further Examples of Calculator Statistics Capabilities

Because statistics is such a powerful and versatile tool, users have developed powerful and versatile statistics software for computing calculators which can handle almost any statistics application — from a simple determination of a mean to a four-way analysis of variance — without help from a statistician, computer programmer or a data processing service. That makes it easy for people in disciplines as diverse as analytical chemistry and mechanical engineering to reap the benefits of statistical analysis.

Many computing calculators can do a lot more than step-wise regressions of 35 variables. The newest models can interface to instruments for data acquisition and control. They can be used to budget, schedule and estimate. They can help people develop new components and systems. Some can also handle accounting functions. Combine this versatility with statistical analysis and users begin to appreciate the power of computing calculators. They can eliminate many steps between data acquisition and statistical analysis. If users analyze data generated by instruments, calculators can really save time. By interfacing one of the computing calculators to instruments, data acquisition becomes automatic — as does statistical manipulation of that data. They can directly interpret the results. And if they use some additional statistical techniques, they later can quickly recall the data from one of several storage devices and load appropriate program routines.

For instance, the new HP 9825 can interface to an array of thermistors to measure water temperature at a power plant outlet. This data is analyzed statistically on the same calculator to determine the frequency and extent of thermal blocks which could result in fish being unable to swim past the plant.

Advanced Numerical Analysis: Probability Distributions, Forward and Tabled Values

The Probability Distributions Pac, HP Part Number 09830-70855, is a collection of four programs that represent some of the most advanced programming and numerical analysis techniques yet to be seen for programmable calculators. The equipment necessary is a HP 9830A Programmable Calculator with 4k words of user memory and the HP 9866A Thermal Printer. The programs are concerned with two specific areas:
- Probability distributions: for continuous and discrete distributions.
- Generation of orthogonal polynomials: for balanced or unbalanced and equally or unequally spaced levels.

A great deal of mathematical research has been done to generate the algorithms for some of the distributions and, in many cases, these represent unique mathematical contributions.

These programs essentially eliminate the old set of statistical tables because they provide both *probability* and *tabled* values for most of the major continuous and discrete distributions. The keyboard templates are used to label the special functions keys of the 9830. Each key obtains a program (from a prerecorded cassette) which performs the function illustrated on the template. The completeness of these programs is best illustrated by studying the templates and the function accomplished with each key.

Continuous Distributions

The 9830 special functions keyboard template is shown on page 455.

Prob (Probability): When this key is used with any of the distribution keys, right-tailed probability values are supplied for that distribution, degrees of freedom, and value.

Table: This key can also be used with any of the distributions to provide the tabled value for any degrees of freedom and probability value.

Gamma: This key evaluates the right-tailed probability for a two-parameter gamma or finds the tabled value.

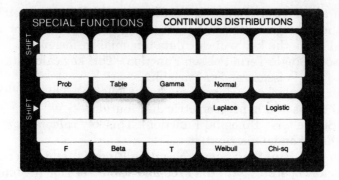

Normal: This key provides a rapid approximation to right-tailed normal probabilities or tabled values.

F (F-Distribution): This key calculates right-tailed probabilities for an F-distribution with degrees of freedom N and D or the tabled value when used with the table key.

Beta (Beta Distribution): This key calculates right-tailed probabilities or tabled values for a beta distribution specified by any values for the two parameters.

T (T-Distribution): This key calculates right-tailed probabilities or tabled values for a Student's t-distribution with any degrees of freedom.

Laplace and **Weibull** (Laplace and Weibull Distribution): This key will calculate either right-tailed probabilities or tabled values for the Weibull distribution and the Laplace distribution in the shifted mode.

Logistic and **Chi-sq** (Logistic and Chi-squared Distribution): This key will calculate either right-tailed probabilities or tabled values for the Chi-squared distribution and for the logistic distribution when in the shift mode.

Discrete Distributions

The special functions keyboard template is shown below.

Prob (Probability): This key selects the right-tailed probability mode for the binomial, hypergeometric and Poisson distributions.

Table: This key, when used with either the binomial, hypergeometric or Poisson distribution keys, will return a tabled value for associated parameters.

C-Beta and **N!** (Complete Beta): This key calculates N! It will also evaluate the complete Beta function for two parameters.

Neg-Bin (Negative Binomial): This key operates the negative binomial distribution and calculates the probability that A or more failures occur before the Nth success.

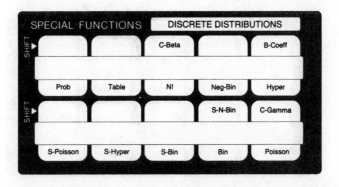

B-Coeff and **Hyper** (Binomial Coefficients and Hypergeometric): This key operates the hypergeometric distribution with either the Prob or Table key. In the shifted mode the key will calculate binomial coefficients.

S-Poisson (Single-Term Poisson Function): This key calculates the individual terms for a Poisson random variable.

S-Hyper (Single-Term Hypergeometric Function): This key calculates the individual terms of a hypergeometric distribution.

S-Bin (Single-term Binomial Function): This key calculates the individual terms of the binomial distribution.

S-N-Bin amd **Bin** (Single-term Negative Binomial and Binomial Distribution): This key operates with the Prob and Table keys for the binomial distribution. In the shifted mode, it will calculate individual terms of the negative binomial.

C-Gamma and Poisson (Gamma Function and Poisson Distribution): This key operates the Prob and Table keys for the Poisson distribution. In the shifted mode, it calculates $\Gamma(x)$ and $\log[\Gamma(x)]$ depending on the size of x.

High Accuracy Normal, Log Normal Distributions

All probabilities and tabled values are calculated with a minimum of five digits of accuracy and, in most cases, seven digits of accuracy. There is a separate program to provide high accuracy with the normal and log normal distributions. In these programs, if x is a normal deviate, then the absolute value of x must be less than 10^{33}. For tabled values, P must satisfy $1 - 10^{-49} > P > 10^{-49}$. The 9830 keyboard template for this program is shown below.

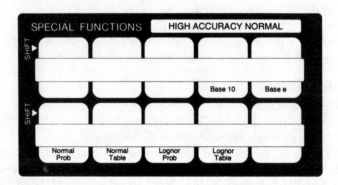

Orthogonal Polynomials

The fourth set of programs solve the problems of generating orthogonal polynomials of degree less than or equal to 10. The program will accommodate data sets of the following types:

- Equally spaced, equally replicated.

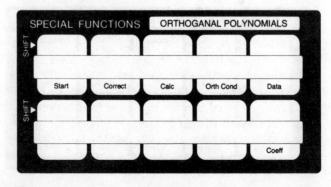

- Equally spaced, unequally replicated.
- Unequally spaced, equally replicated.
- Unequally spaced, unequally replicated.

The keyboard template for orthogonal polynomial generation is shown on page 456.

DATA ACQUISITION AND DESIGN SYSTEMS FOR ENGINEERS
Data Acquisition Systems

Data acquisition systems are used in three basic areas: research and development laboratories, process industries, and factory production. In laboratories they monitor electrical and physical parameters of experimental systems. In process industries they monitor process parameters, calculate and predict trends, and occasionally control the process itself on the basis of these calculations. Finally, in factory production, they permit more complete testing of the factory's product in less time — for example, testing printed circuit boards for faulty, incorrect, or missing components. Data acquisition is not necessarily complex. It can be as simple as a digital voltmeter and a printer, logging voltage measurements that represent other variables, such as pH or temperature. On the other extreme, it can involve data from multipoint transducers, periodically scanned under the control of a computer. The latter reduces data online and makes appropriate calculations to correlate data, test limits, and predict trends.

Data Acquisition Calculator Capabilities

Advanced rugged calculators provide a great shortcut to large-scale data gathering. Functionally, they are standardized data acquisition systems, under the control of a tiny microprocessor. These solid state integrated circuit "computers on a single chip," combined with RAMs (random access memory devices), ROMs (read-only memory devices), and PROMs (programmable ROMs), are keyboard programmed with one finger. Most are designed for the toughest industrial conditions where noisy signals are the rule, not the exception. Guarding and isolation are standard features to assure accurate measurement. The circuitry is generally reliable, readily serviced, and backed by nationwide service organizations. When users need a dependable data gatherer — in the laboratory, in the field, in the plant — wherever data originates, they consider the calculator to save from 20 to 80% of the alternative cost of any comparable hard wired system.

Data Acquisition Calculator Architecture

Basic system architecture is always a three-way tradeoff of versatility (how many functions?), capacity (how many channels?), and practicality (how costly?). Some specific advanced calculators provide the optimum combination of characteristics for 8 out of 10 applications in standard configurations; the others can be met optimally with special plug-in ROMs as noted above.

A field data gathering system calculator is a bit special. When users need to gather data in the field, away from power lines, they look for basic power and clocking systems that are designed for mobile or remote applications. The standard AUTO mode powers-down some units between scans to reduce battery drain. Users need a pre-set program, a customized ROM program that can tailor their system to specific requirements, reducing on-site hassle and time. An optional memory save feature lets the system "keep its wits" during a temporary engine generator outage. Self-calibration simplifies field checkout. If lightning or static electricity threaten the field setup, the calculator is made rugged up front for extra protection. A carrying case is usually available.

Calculator-aided Design Applications

Larger calculators equal the computer in data handling and calculating power. This is made possible by such features as increased key functions, printing capability, peripheral devices and computer-like compatibility with interfacing. Among the peripherals are X-Y plotters, card readers, tape readers and punches, typewriters, line printers, digitizing devices, magnetic-tape cassettes and disk memories. In perspective, a programmable calculator is an engineering tool designed for scientific usage with hands-on accessibility. Unlike computers, calculators are molded to fit typical engineering work spaces and provide on-the-spot solutions. Computational speed (a bench-mark factor used in assessing computer performance) is definitely a factor in large "number-crunching" programs. However, for most engineering design problems, the total engineering solution time overshadows the computational speed. A calculator also provides a capacity for dialogue, for iterations of solutions, and for direct hands-on interaction by the design engineer. As an extra advantage for calculator-aided design applications, some calculators are directly compatible with peripheral tape or disc memory and other capacity-building equipment. Graphic displays that effect the quickest interpretation of solutions are conveniently interfaced to calculators.

Various calculator-aided design (CAD) packages can slash days, even weeks, from an electronic design schedule. A user has complete interactive control of the design process. It is no longer necessary to interface with a time-sharing system or wait for a data processing center to run a job. The user enters component values and an X-Y plotter, can draw a Bode diagram that shows the effect of those changes. This entire process is done automatically — on the plotter or built-in printer, completely documented — before a design is committed to time-consuming breadboarding. As noted below there are CAD programs available for network analysis, filter design — all giving improved efficiency from concept to hardware.

CAD (Calculator Aided Design) AC Analysis Program

This program is patterned after the well-known ECAP circuit analysis program written by IBM. Features of the program are:
- Up to 9 nodes and 48 components can be analyzed concurrently.
- Components allowed are resistors, capacitors, inductors, and voltage-controlled current sources.
- The precision and dynamic range of the Calculator make it possible to transform other active elements, such as, op-amps, into the required form.
- Data input is simplified: users need only specify the element values and node interconnections.
- Circuit topologies can be stored on tape cassette for future recall.
- Analysis is available in the swept frequency mode with either log or linear sweep; components and circuits can be modeled and analyzed.

Various microwave circuit design calculator applications permit users to solve problems like these below with just a few keystrokes.
- Plot circles of constant noise, constant gain on the load plane.
- Calculate the stability factor, maximum available gain, and source and load reflection coefficients.
- Calculate the component values and topology of all possible 2-element reactive networks in an impedance matching design.

- Produce a Smith chart showing the dependence of the input impedance on load impedance in 2-port networks.
- Produce a Smith chart showing the effect of the series or parallel feedback in an active 2-port network.
- Reduce a complex network to an equivalent set of 2-port S-parameters.
- Convert from a given S, Z, Y, H-parameter set to any or all of the three remaining sets of 2-port parameters.
- Convert 2-port S-parameters from common emitter, common base, or common collector to either or both of the remaining configurations.
- Convert S-parameters referenced to a given characteristic impedance to a new set of generalized S-parameters referenced to arbitrary generator and load impedances.

Microwave Design Package (BAMP)

Hewlett Packard (HP) offers BAMP 30 (Basic Analysis and Mapping Program). The software package is available for designing or analyzing high frequency and microwave circuits. Originally developed for use on a time-shared computer system, the full power of BAMP is available for use on various HP Programmable Calculators.

BAMP 30 is a collection of programs for obtaining the frequency-domain response of linear electronic circuits that can be built up by interconnecting two ports. BAMP 30 is a two-port program. This means:

- Elementary two-ports are used as basic building blocks.
- The overall or composite circuit built up by BAMP 30 is in turn a two-port.

The first result of any analysis performed by BAMP 30 is the scattering, or S-matrix, for the overall circuit. The S-matrix is stored in the calculator as a function of frequency and can be used to compute, print, and plot numerous additional outputs. An analysis of the HP BAMP is developed below.

BAMP 30

Combining calculator-aided design (CAD) with S-parameter characterization of transistors affords a fast, efficient method for designing or analyzing high frequency and microwave circuits.

HP now offers a systematic approach to the frequency domain analysis of linear electronic circuits by providing the electrical engineer with a self-contained solution called BAMP. BAMP, Hewlett-Packard's proven electronic circuit analysis program, is now available as a software package for the HP 9830A. Originally implemented as an instructional and design tool for operation on a time-shared computer system, the full power of BAMP is now available to run on a 9830 Programmable Calculator. HP has used BAMP extensively in the U.S. and in Europe to provide instruction in microwave solid-state circuit design. Many laboratories, introduced to BAMP in this way, have subsequently found it highly useful for design applications. This new capability reduces the need for extensive breadboarding, costly trial and error testing, and eliminates the adjustments required to compensate for parasitic active devices, distributed elements, and circuit stability.

Software Description

BAMP 30 is a collection of programs for obtaining the frequency-domain response of linear electronic circuits that can be built up by interconnecting two-ports. The suffix 30 distinguishes the 9830 implementation from other closely related programs designed for time-share computer systems.

BAMP is a two-port program. This means:

- Elementary two-ports are used as basic building blocks.
- The overall or composite circuit built up by BAMP is in turn a two-port.

The first result of any analysis performed by BAMP is the scattering, or S-matrix, for the overall circuit. The S-matrix is stored in the 9830 memory as a function of frequency and can be used to compute, print, and plot numerous additional outputs, including:

- G-, H-, Y-, and Z-matrices for the overall circuit.
- Stability factor, maximum available gain, and source and load reflections for achieving maximum available gain.
- Delay.
- Transducer gain for arbitrary source and load reflection coefficients.
- Mapping of load impedance onto the plane of the input reflection coefficient and the source impedance onto the plane of the output reflection coefficient.

In addition to mapping load and source impedances onto input and output reflection coefficient planes, BAMP can also be used to map an internal impedance onto the plane of any one of the overall S-parameters.

The inputs to BAMP are:

- Component two-ports, parameter values, and interconnections.
- One explicit output request (optional — the computed S-matrix is the default output).
- Optional units and program parameters (default units are gigahertz for frequency; ohms for resistance; nanohenrys for inductance; picofarads for capacitance; and centimeters for length).

Frequencies Example

Elementary two-ports available for building up a composite circuit include resistances; inductances; capacitances; combinations of R, L, and C; transformers; gyrators; ideal linear amplifiers; a TEM transmission line; and a simple waveguide model. In addition to these standard elements, it is possible to include any linear element or component for which you have one- or two-port data whether measured, calculated, or hypothetical.

The size circuit that BAMP 30 can handle is determined by the following constraints:

- There can be, at most, 60 component two-ports.
- The total number of two-port parameters cannot exceed 150.

A circuit using nothing but single-parameter two-ports can include the maximum of 60 two-ports. At the opposite extreme, a circuit containing nothing but TEM lines is limited to a maximum of 25 two-ports because each transmission line has 6 parameters.

Twenty is the maximum number of frequencies allowed in any one run. However, a succession of analyses can be performed using different runs. There are no restrictions on the domain of frequencies except, of course, that frequencies must be real. Negative frequencies are acceptable.

System Requirements

In order to run BAMP 30, you will need the following equipment:

- HP 9830A or B Calculator with the optional 8k words of memory.
- HP 9866A Thermal Printer.
- HP 9862A X-Y Plotter.
- HP 11274B String Variables ROM.
- HP 11271B Plotter Control ROM.
- HP 11279B Advanced Programming I ROM.

Also the BAMP 30 software, HP Part Number 09830-71103, which includes a BAMP 30 Operating Manual and three program cassettes: BAMP (cassette with all analysis programs), BAMP DF (a program for creating your own data files and for converting configurations from common base to common emitter, etc.), and DEV (data cassette containing S-parameters for popular HP microwave transistors — space is available for adding your own data files).

No Special Functions keyboard overlays are necessary for program operation. All user prompts appear in the 32-character LED display of the 9830.

BAMP 30 — A Time Saver

BAMP 30 will help you design better circuits in less time. Circuit models can now be made as complex as necessary to accurately represent physical circuits, without danger of losing control over the design process. Analysis is more comprehensive and circuits can be as optimum as physical laws will allow them to be; that is, the comprehensive and convenient analysis through BAMP provides a far better trade-off between gain, stability, etc. All this is achieved in much less time than with manual methods. CAD drastically cuts down the trial-and-error breadboard phase. Circuit debugging is more systematic and much easier. If a circuit is not behaving in a desired fashion, the designer knows he has forgotten to tell the calculator something. Depending upon what the plot tells him, he can, in a matter of minutes, substitute one component for another or experiment with values of certain components until he gets the desired result.

In addition, circuits designed with BAMP usually require little or no critical adjustments. This is highly significant in a production situation. Whether it is a lab technician, manufacturing personnel, or the customer, not having to depend on fine tuning to get the circuit to work can mean big savings in time and money. The greater the circuit complexity, the greater the savings through BAMP.

CALCULATOR INTERFACE CONCEPTS, APPLICATIONS, AND SPECIFICATIONS

An interface usually refers to instruments, devices or a concept of a common boundary or matching of adjacent components, circuits, equipment, or system elements. An interface enables devices to yield and/or acquire information from one device or program to another. Although the terms adapter, handshake and buffer have similar meaning, interface is more distinctly a connection to complete an operation. It is a common boundary — for example, physical connection between two systems or two devices based on specifications of the interconnection between two systems or units. Thanks to the various interface busses, users can couple the speed and computational power of advanced calculators with the measurement capability of electronic counters and other state-of-the-art accessories. Many new application notes describe how these versatile low-cost combinations solve difficult measurement problems.

Applications ahead will note that thousands of electronic instruments are being used in many diverse applications throughout science, medicine, education, and industry. Automating these instruments involves interfacing them to a computational device. Because most instruments and controllers do not talk the same language, the function of an interface card is to convert the signals from one device into signals the connecting device understands and vice versa. Often in the past, the electronics required to do this was left up to the user. This involved building a special "black box", costing a great deal of time and money.

Now, with the introduction of many types of new computing controllers, the communications gap has been closed. Users have the required electronics to interface a wide range of instruments to their controllers. Various interface cards cover most of the standard, commonly-used instrument interfaces. So the electronics is done by the controller supplier. It has made interfacing easy.

Users simply plug the correct interface card into the back of the computing controller that fits their needs. They then connect their instrument to the other end of the I/O card. After programming the controller with a few simple instructions, they're ready to put the automated system to work. All this is done by users, not by an expensive systems analyst or computer programmer. One typical application note provides an example of a simple data acquisition system using low-cost counter modules, an interface, and some specific model calculators. A multimeter/counter measures frequency, ac volts, dc volts, or resistance and outputs these measurements to the calculator. The calculator computes the mean, standard deviation, and peak-to-peak deviation of the data and even plots a histogram.

An interface standard for products means users can conveniently interconnect a wide range of instruments, calculators, and other devices having stimulus, response, display, control or computational capabilities. Also, users can now assemble relatively low-cost systems with minimum engineering effort. Various interface devices accommodate high and low-speed devices in the same system. Some can interconnect as many as 15 devices — voltmeter, printer, signal source, calculator, digital clock, etc. — over a total distance of 20 meters and more. Devices are linked via a passive cable network having various signal lines. These signal lines carry all information (addresses, commands, program data and status data) at data rates up to 1 megabyte/sec on some units. Simple interface bus configurations do not require the use of a controller such as a calculator or computer. But in most cases, programmable calculators are the ideal controllers for customer-assembled systems whenever some degree of data manipulation is required.

Basic Calculator Interface Types

There are two main approaches to the dedicated interface and the general-purpose coupler. The dedicated interface connects a single peripheral device directly to the calculator's internal bus. Many times four or more interface cards are used. The calculator has full control over the bus, directing and routing data between itself and the peripheral, on most systems. The general-purpose coupler, however, provides its own external bus system, and couplers with as many as eight and more interface channels are available. Thus, up to eight different devices can be simultaneously connected to a standard calculator operation.

By using a general-purpose coupler with an ASCII input-output card and a programmable power supply, one can make an automatic stimulus source for testing. Combine this with a DVM and a data scanner (often part of the DVM), and have an automatic test system for circuit boards. The different functions of DVMs — such as ac or dc, volts or milliamperes, or ohms — and their ranges are also controlled by the calculator.

Other Interface Types

Various interfaces can be categorized into three distinct types for some systems. 1. Slave — This interface usually has no provision in its control logic to become Master. It will only transfer data onto and off the bus by command of a master device. 2. Interrupt — This interface generally has the ability to gain mastership of the bus in order to give the central processor the address of a subroutine which the processor will use to service the peripheral. 3. DMA — This interface has the ability to gain mastership of the bus in order to transfer data between itself and some other peripheral. A single interface may employ all three of the above types.

An example of interfacing for an advanced calculator is a specific interfacing capability that is provided calculators through an optional two-channel I/O module. It allows a choice of seven different peripherals to work with advanced calculator units including page printers. Users just plug them in, and they're ready to go. Specific interface cards and cables allow users to control, gather and process data from a variety of instruments. And by adding interface busses of various types, up to 14 instruments can be monitored simultaneously.

BCD — the Instrumentation/Measurement Interface

This interface will connect to most instruments produced today which have digital output. It accepts the standard four-bit parallel, binary coded decimal (BCD) data. The list of compatible instruments is very long: counters, digital voltmeters, multichannel nuclear analyzers. . . . This includes analytical instruments, medical instruments, and electronic measurement instruments.

Bit-Parallel — the General Purpose Interface

Depending on the controller, users can choose from an 8-bit parallel input bus and an 8-bit parallel latched output bus combination or a latched 16-bit input data bus and a latched 16-bit output bus for bidirectional transfer of information. This interface is used to connect to HP peripheral devices such as plotters, tape readers, tape punches, card readers, and printers. It can also be used to interface instruments or equipment such as scanners, multi-function units, scanning electron microscopes, or a user's own specialized circuits.

RS-232-C — the Communications Interface

There are many applications that call for transmitting data to teleprinters, CRT terminals, or telephone modems. This interface sends and receives serial data. The serial driver and receivers meet the EIA RS-232-C specifications. This simple plug-to-plug, wire-to-plug interface can save money by eliminating needless communication devices in most systems.

HP-IB — the IEEE Standard

Up to 14 instruments which have built-in HP-IB capability can be interconnected via a simple standard cable system. This easy-to-use hardware and software interface permits bidirectional, asynchronous communication between a wide variety of instruments. Because of its simplicity and flexibility, Hewlett-Packard is committed to this instrumentation/peripheral interface.

General Calculator Interfacing

Advanced units provide the capability of controlling the data flow to and from test instruments, gathering that data, and processing that data. For example, the optional interface bus is becoming standard for a majority of advanced units. I/O can accept up to 14 interconnected devices. Many units have available general purpose I/O cards to help make connections to calculators quickly and easily. Once users have set up their systems, they can develop exceptionally capable instrumentation controllers and processors.

As regards interfacing of peripherals, for many programmable calculators reading and writing operations can be performed with single or dual tape cassette drives. Peripherals such as Input-Output writers or teleprinter interfaces can be used with these systems, thus permitting alphanumeric information to be written or read. Also, using the proper interface, the units can be interfaced with an instrument acoustic coupler, line printer, teletype or CRT terminal and can accept or output numerical data, alpha strings of variable lengths or programs. Other calculator systems can use plotters, voice response units, etc.

Interface Plug-in Cards

With plug-in interface cards, some series calculators take on the ability to accept data from a large number of digital voltmeters, counters, and other instruments. By automating data entry users have a flexible lab processing center, as well as a powerful number cruncher. One Model I/O Expander allows users to plug up to 13 peripherals or test instruments into a calculator.

Interfaced Calculator Bus Architecture

Programmable calculators with a bus architecture are easy to interface with digital devices that use standard codes. Digital volt-meters, counters, X-Y plotters and tape-cassette units are only a few of the peripherals that may be used. In fact, a variety of standard packages are available for interfacing calculators with peripherals that use BCD and ASCII codes. A calculator, an interface card set and a DVM make an inexpensive measuring, data-processing and logging system. The voltages measured automatically by the DVM are fed into the calculator, and they can be converted to other units of measurement, if desired. A complete statistical analysis can be done. And a printer, usually part of the calculator, makes the system a data logger.

Further, while serving in such dedicated systems, the calculator can still be used for its basic purpose — calculating. Built into its language is the ability to disconnect from the interface; there is no need to physically reconfigure the system in any way.

Several suppliers offer many interface cards designed for those customers who desire to build custom, calculator-controlled instrumentation systems. These cards are, as noted:

- I/O Interface — an 8-bit parallel input/output card with TTL compatible drivers and receivers.
- BCD Input Card — 9 digits of 8421-coded BCD data, plus other functions (input from instrument to calculator only).
- Serial I/O Interface — bit serial input/output card conforming to RS-232-C recommended specification.
- Data Communications Interface — allows a calculator to communicate with other calculators and computers via telephone lines and modems which meet EIA Specification RS-232-C.
- Binary Synchronous ROM — when used with a bus allows a unit to act as a remote batch terminal emulating IBM 2780.
- Interactive ROM — when used with a bus allows a unit to act as time-sharing terminal emulating ASCII Teleprinter.

Specific Examples of Interfaces for Desktop Programmable Calculator Instrumentation Control

Many firms offer broad lines of programmable calculators, peripherals, instrumentation and interface cards. Combinations of these instruments allow the custom assembly of systems individually tailored to fit a particular need.

Various series programmable calculators are well suited to the task of being the central processors in automated instrumentation systems. They provide both a wide range of computing power and a flexible interfacing system, within low-cost, attractive desktop packages. Easy to use and understand calculator languages are built into each calculator, from the key-per-function language of some and the algebraic language of others to the popular BASIC computer language of some others. There are programmable calculators which will fit into almost any problem-solving situation or control performance.

Bus Interfacing

Physically, a bus is an etched board with rows of module connectors soldered to the board. The pin assignment can be the same on all connectors. One of the most popular busses consists of 96 signals which feed to 96 pins on the connectors. The user is generally only concerned with those signals that control data transfers, address memory, or contain the data to be transferred. However, additional signals, such as timing, are readily available on the bus to accommodate various tailor-made requirements in the event that the user should design and build his own interface module. A typical bus structure employs bidirectional data and control lines plus a few unidirectional control signals. Each bus line is a matched and terminated transmission line that must be received and driven with devices designed for that specific application. A module may have an unused bus driver for bus receiver circuits that can be used with TTL devices, provided the loading rules are observed.

General purpose interfaces are contained on individual plug-in I/O cards. In addition to the appropriate data registers, many interfaces have independent flag and control logic allowing two-way communication between the computer, and one or more external devices. Most interfaces operate under either program or direct memory access control. A wide choice of interfaces allows external connection via floating contact closures, DTL/TTL, transistor or differential logic.

Disk Interface, Power Expansion

The memory limits of advanced programmable calculators can be expanded to over 500 times standard capacity with the use of interfaces which link the calculator to flexible disks. The calculator flexible disk interface allows the disks to provide mass memory, dedicated either to data storage or programs or both. Single disk expands the memory capacity to 256 times the standard capacity and the dual disk doubles that capacity. Two different types of write protect can be utilized for securing the information on flexible disk. One, a tab which is inserted manually on the disk envelope, protects the entire disk; the other protects tracks 0 through 9 from erasure while allowing the remainder to be available for normal read-write operation.

RS-232-C I/O Interface Controller

This allows direct asynchronous input and output of data between a Teletype or other 8-level ASCII device and the host terminal. The controller is excellent for linking the host terminal to a local unit or for monitoring instruments. Laboratory or medical instrumentation which is RS-232-C and 8-level ASCII-compatible can be supported, as well as Teletype 33, 35's equipped with EIA, RS-232-C adapters. Operation is selectable at 110, 150, 300, 600 or 1,200 baud. The controller can often be used with the host terminal CPU alone, since the CRT is not required on some systems.

For unique user applications such as on-line installations which require specialized input/output equipment, engineering staffs will design the necessary interface units as part of services to their customers. Then, they will fabricate these units for particular systems under close supervision by the same engineers who designed them. These engineers, who are naturally quite familiar with the logic and requirements, are best qualified to do this important work. The EIA interface refers to a standard set of signal characteristics (time duration, voltage and current) specified by the Electronic Industries Association for use in communications terminals. Also included is a standard plug/socket connector arrangement.

Interface ROM

A special ROM enables the calculator to interface with any modem that conforms to EIA specification RS-232-C and with automatic dialers that meet EIA spec RS-366. Two BASIC statements are defined by the control ROM to allow the user to write or read messages in strings from a remote terminal or a computer via telephone lines. Other features include programmable parity, automatic answering, programmable end-of-transmission character, and either half- or full-duplex modes. Still other features can be added with two additional ROMs. One ROM allows the terminal to operate with a binary-synchronous protocol. It also adds error detection and ASCII-to-EBCDIC conversion so that the user can connect the calculator as a remote-batch terminal without modifying software drivers at the computer. One other significant feature is programmable error recovery. In a data-communications mode, errors (incorrect commands or codes, for example) can often be automatically remedied. The special ROM, therefore, includes the ability to take different actions for different types of errors.

The main storage in the interface is programmed with the actions to be taken, and the ROM includes the commands to jump to this area of storage after identifying the type of error. The ROM also allows use of transparent text in the binary synchronous protocol, so that special characters can be used, with appropriate coding that warns the receiving end of their presence.

Interfaces for Calculator Terminals

Several makers of programmable calculators now offer communications interfaces. Originally, these interfaces were designed simply to make the calculator operate as a remote printer for other calculators, but because many users indicated a desire to apply calculators as terminals, other terminal functions have been added. These features include alphanumeric character manipulation, an input-output structure that is compatible with other terminals and computers, at least 2,000 to 4,000 bytes of expandable buffer memory, and a page-width printer or similar output device. Mass storage such as disk or tape is also helpful for batch applications. For time-sharing applications, a typewriter-like keyboard is the most efficient keyboard format.

HP-IB Transfer and Interface Lines

Three DATA BYTE TRANSFER CONTROL (handshake) lines are used to effect the transfer of each byte of coded data on the eight DATA lines. The five remaining GENERAL INTERFACE MANAGEMENT lines ensure an orderly flow of information within the HP-IB system. One of these is called the "ATTENTION" line. The controller dictates the role of each of the other devices by setting the ATTENTION line low (true) and sending talk or listen addresses on the DATA lines. (Addresses are manually set into each device at the time of system configuration, either by switches built into the device as often diagrammed, or by jumpers on a PC board.) When the ATTENTION line is

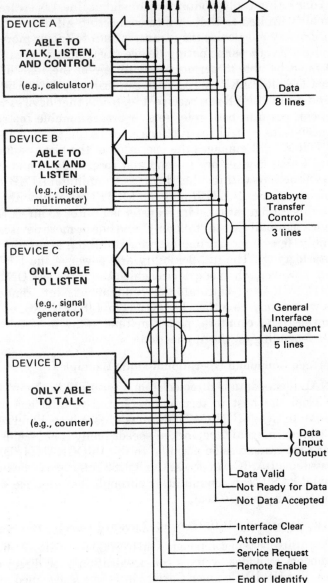

Data
8 lines

Databyte
Transfer
Control

3 lines

General
Interface
Management

5 lines

} Data
} Input
} Output

Data Valid
Not Ready for Data
Not Data Accepted

Interface Clear
Attention
Service Request
Remote Enable
End or Identify

INTERFACE CONNECTIONS AND BUS STRUCTURE

low, all devices must listen to the DATA lines. When the ATTENTION line is high (false), only those devices that have been addressed will actively send or receive data, while all others ignore the DATA lines. Several listeners can be active simultaneously, but only one talker can be active at a time. Whenever a talk address is put on the DATA lines (while ATTENTION is low), all other talkers are automatically unaddressed. It is not possible in this limited space to go into detail on each signal line's role. But users should note that every HP-IB device need not be able to respond to all the lines. As a practical and cost-effective matter, each HP-IB device will usually be designed to respond only to those lines that are pertinent to its typical function on the bus. (Appropriate details appear in each device's operating manual.)

HP Interface Bus Operation

All active interface circuitry is contained within the various HP-IB devices, and the interconnecting cable (containing 16 signal lines) is entirely passive. The cable's role is limited to that of interconnecting all devices together in parallel, whereby any one device may transfer data to one or more other participating devices. Every participating device (instrument, controller, accessory module) must be able to perform at least one of the roles of TALKER, LISTENER or CONTROLLER. A TALKER can transmit data to other devices via the bus, and a LISTENER can receive data from other devices via the bus. Some devices can perform both roles (e.g. a programmable instrument can LISTEN to receive its control instructions and TALK to send its measurement). A CONTROLLER manages the operation of the bus system primarily by designating which devices are to send and receive data, and it may also command specific actions within other devices. A minimum HP-IB system configuration consists of one TALKER and one LISTENER, but without a CONTROLLER. In this configuration, data transfer is limited to direct transfer between one device manually set to "talk only" and one or more devices manually set to "listen only" (e.g., a measuring instrument talking to a printer, for semi-automatic data logging). The full flexibility and power of the HP-IB become more apparent, however, when one device which can serve as CONTROLLER/ TALKER/LISTENER (e.g., calculator or computer) is interconnected with other devices which may be either TALKERS or LISTENERS, or both (e.g., frequency synthesizers, counters, power meters, relay actuators, displays, printers, etc.), depending on the application.

Terminal Interface Command Operational Mode Examples

In TERMINAL mode, data is directed from a terminal keyboard to the host computer, or from the host to terminal screen. The interface emulates a graphic terminal. In COMMUNICATIONS mode, data is sent and received via the terminal system internal tape unit, at speeds many times faster than keyboard or paper tape transmission permits. In the PROGRAMMED I/O mode, the terminal systems BASIC can access the RS232 interface as device number 40. In this mode, BASIC can communicate through the interface without operator intervention in some systems.

Common Carrier Interface HP-IB (Hewlett-Packard Corp.)

This offers separate system components up to 3000 feet using dedicated line. An optional modem provides systems communication over direct or dial-up telephone lines. The HP-IB/Common Carrier Interface is designed to overcome the older HP-IB length restriction of 50 feet. Up to 3000 feet of additional length can be obtained with just two CCI modules, while with the optional modem, length is limited only to the distance covered by available telephone networks. The CCI module converts all HP-IB data and control lines to a serial bit stream of digital information. This information can be sent in this form to another CCI up to 3000 feet away, or it can be fed into a modem for conversion to a data format that can be used over voice-grade telephone lines. The same CCI/Modem combination must be used at each end of the phone line.

Frequency Interface Bus

One type Hewlett-Packard (HP) interface bus can be used with HP 8620 sweepers to achieve calculator control of frequencies from 3 MHz to 18 GHz. The 8620A Opt E45 sweeper with appropriate RF plug-in becomes a source with 1000 points per band programmability. The HP 86290A, to 18 GHz plug-in, is ideal for HP-IB systems because of its flexibility, frequency accuracy and linearity. The bus-controlled 8620A/86290A can quickly step through as many as 3000 frequencies — typically with ± 5 MHz accuracy. For higher accuracy, add the HP 5340A counter plus D/A converter to automatically correct frequency to within 100 kHz. Even greater precision (to 25 Hz) can be obtained by phase-locking the sweeper to the HP 8660 synthesized signal generator and programming both the sweeper and 8660 via the HP-IB. Precision power level control of the sweeper is also possible using the 436A digital power meter.

Data Gathering Interface Bus

One type automatic data gathering and reduction is a compact low-cost system that scans up to 520 channels under calculator control; measures dc, ac and ohms at up to 4 readings/second; then calculates results either on-line or off-line. The interface bus teams a multimeter and a scanner with a programmable calculator. The system measures:

- dc in 5 ranges from 100 mV to 200 V with 1μ V resolution.
- ac in 4 ranges from 1 V to 200 V with 10μ V resolution over a frequency range of 20 Hz to 100 kHz.
- resistance from 100Ω to $10 M\Omega$ with $1 m\Omega$ resolution.

With the appropriate transducer, the system can also measure pressure, torque, velocity, acceleration, and weight.

Development of Interface Standards and Some Hewlett-Packard Specifics

In September 1974, the parent technical committee, IEC TC66, approved the main interface draft document for a formal ballot among the member nations of the IEC. Although final ballot results were not expected until the end of 1976, the present definition of the HP-IB is compatible with the current and approved IEC draft document.

Meanwhile, the IEEE Standards Board has approved IEEE Standard 488-1975, "Digital Interface for Programmable Instrumentation," as published in April 1975. The IEEE standard is based on work initiated by the IEC, and follows the general concepts of the draft standard document now under consideration by IEC member nations. The HP Interface Bus is Hewlett-Packard's implementation of IEEE Standard 488-1975.

HP-IB Connections and Structure

The 16 signal lines within the passive interconnecting HP-IB cable are grouped into three sets, according to their functions. Eight DATA lines carry coded messages in bit-parallel, byte-serial form to and from devices, with each byte being transferred from one TALKER to one or more LISTENERS as noted. Data flow is bidirectional in that the same lines are used both to input program data and to output measurement data from an individual device. Data is exchanged asynchronously, enabling compatibility among a wide variety of devices. All interface messages (to set up, maintain, and terminate an orderly flow of device-dependent messages) are 7-bit coded. Device-dependent messages may be from 1 to 8 bits; however, the codes containing printable characters of the ASCII (American Standard Code for Information Interchange) code set are most commonly used, and messages containing numbers are typically presented in scientific notation (FORTRAN-type) format.

HP-IB Specification Summary

Interconnected devices: Up to 15 maximum on one contiguous bus. Interconnection path: Star or linear bus network; total transmission path length 2 meters times number of devices or 20 meters, whichever is less (see HP 59403A for extending operating distance). Message transfer scheme: Byte-serial, bit-

INTERFACES FOR THE HP 9825A CALCULATOR

I/O Features	HP 98032A Bit Parallel Interface	HP 98033A BCD Interface	HP 98034A HPIB Interface⑤
Data input lines	16 latched⑥	43 not latched⑧	8 bidirectional
Data output lines	16 latched⑦	None	
Control lines to device	5⑦	2⑧	8 bidirectional
Control lines from device	5⑥	2⑥	
Interrupt capability	Yes ⑩	Yes ⑩	Yes ⑩
Type of data transfers	16-bit words or 8-bit bytes	16-bit character sequence⑨	8-bit bytes
Transfer rates extend to: with Gen. I/O ROM ⑪ with Ext. I/O ROM	1 ms/transfer 90,000 transfers/s	4 ms/transfer 4000 readings/s	1 ms/byte 45,000 bytes/s
DMA	Input 400k transfers/s ⑩ Output 225k transfers/s ⑩	No	No

⑤ Implements IEEE Standard 488-1975.
⑥ Input levels TTL compatible.
⑦ Open collector outputs, sink 40mA, 30V maximum voltage.
⑧ Open collector outputs with 2.2k Ω pullup resistors, sink 14 mA, 15V maximum voltage.
⑨ Capability to input up to 10 BCD digits with overload and sign information. Alternatively, two devices can be connected to the same interface.
⑩ Requires Extended I/O ROM.
⑪ The transfer rate can be increased, up to 15,000 bytes per second, by the use of strings.

parallel asynchronous data transfer using interlocked 3-wire handshake technique. Data rate: One megabyte per second maximum over limited distances; 250-500 kilobytes per second typical over full transmission path (depends on device). Address capability: Primary addresses, 31 TALK and 31 LISTEN; secondary (2-byte) addresses, 961 TALK and 961 LISTEN. Maximum of 1 TALKER and up to 14 LISTENERS at a time. Control shift: In systems with more than one controller, only one can be active at a time. A currently active controller can pass control to another, but only the designated system controller can assume control over others. Interface circuits: Driver and receiver circuits are TTL-compatible.

CALCULATORS AND INSTRUMENTS
Instrumentation, Calculators

Calculators generally cost much less than minicomputers. The programmable calculators open up whole new areas of measurement and control for automation techniques. They can also be used to streamline automation instrumentation systems, many of which use inflexible hard-wired logic or relatively inflexible paper tape. The use of calculators in measurement instruments and automated control systems is expanding rapidly. Special-purpose calculators began to appear in 1974. They were not simple desktop instruments, but extended their capabilities over large areas. Different versions were rack-mountable and made rugged to adapt to different environments. Calculators benefited greatly from computer technology. They adopted interrupt and special processing, and calculator I/O structures to permit simpler

INTERFACES FOR THE HP 9815A CALCULATOR

I/O Features	HP 98133A BCD Interface	HP 98134A Bit Parallel Interface	HP 98136A Serial Interface (12)	HP 98135A HP-IB Interface (13)
Data input lines	40 latched (14)	8 latched (14)	1	8 bidirectional
Data output lines	8 latched (15)	8 latched (15)	1	8 bidirectional
Control lines to device	3 (16)	4 (16)	2	
Control lines	2 (14)	1 (14)	1	
Interrupt capability	No	No	No	No
Type of data transfers	Flexible (17)	8-bit bytes	Bit-serial	8-bit bytes
Transfer rates extend to	2000 readings/s 5000 bytes/s	Output 2000 bytes/s Input 1200 bytes/s	Selectable 110-3600 band	2500 bytes/s

(12) RS-232-C compatible. Receive only current loop capability optional.

(13) Implements IEEE Standard 488-1975.

(14) Input levels TTL compatible.

(15) Open collector outputs, sink 40 mA, 30V maximum voltage.

(16) Open collector outputs, sink 16 mA, 15V maximum voltage.

(17) Up to 9 BCD digits with overload and sign information can be input. Alternatively, two devices can be connected to the same interface. 8-bit bytes may be output.

and more efficient routing of information within the system, as well as to peripherals. Users and designers of these systems expanded their planning horizons, and upward compatibility within calculator product lines grew quickly and significantly.

Production Data Analysis Calculator System

In the field of data acquisition, two general measurement solutions have been available. The simplest alternative is the basic data logger (voltmeter/scanner combination with printer or punched tape output) which has no on-site computational capability for analyzing data. When simultaneous data analysis or closed loop control based on measurement results are required, an online computerized voltmeter/scanner system is used. One major system enables users to move up to online data analysis for reliable real-time results without committing the money and support required for a highly capable and complex computer data acquisition system. In a typical application the system will:

(1) Control the system instruments,
(2) Acquire and convert analog data from physical sensors to digital form,
(3) Correct the data for nonlinearity and offset and convert it to meaningful scientific units,
(4) Determine test results,
(5) Control processes or set alarms,
(6) Perform high level statistical and historical analysis, and
(7) Log or display results.

The most significant effect is an increase in accuracy and dependability, while at the same time releasing skilled people from the costly routine of meter reading and performing other test procedures.

Instrument Control with Calculators

Instruments having a BCD output can be read by the calculator under program control. The calculators may also control external equipment. With these capabilities, the advanced units can automatically acquire and store data, perform statistical analyses of these data, and list the data on the optional calculator printer. These systems also have provisions for powering many of the standard plug-ins. Typical of the applications to which these systems may be applied are automatic data collection from laboratory experiments, automatic counting and sizing of produced goods, monitoring of heating and air conditioning efficiency, simulation and measurement of equipment or component performance, calibration of medical radiotherapy equipment and monitoring of pollutant levels (with limit alarm provisions).

Instrument Calculator Control Components

The system components generally include the advanced system calculator with any of the presently available options; a modified interface plug-in; and software for data acquisition and analysis. Among the basic features on some systems: up to two numerical inputs can be acquired from two digital multicuracy of one part to the 10^5 and provide additional timing intervals of 0.01, trolling external equipment; and a standard software package is provided that can be used for data logging (on printer) and data capture (in advanced calculator registers) with selectable sampling rates.

Capabilities vary depending on which version of some series calculator is used and the options that it incorporates. One type system with a printer can perform the following tasks: data logging on the printer at a preset sampling interval or under operator control; data monitoring and programmed decision making; mathematical operations on input data such as integration, differentiation, transformation, statistical reduction; and output stimulation and regulation of external equipment.

Another system with a printer can accomplish all of the above operations plus: direct data capture (3-4 samples per second) in registers, stored for later printout; graphic analysis or computation; extensive statistical reduction and regression analysis of input data; operator prompting and output labeling of interactive operator controlled measurements, such as in calculator based testing and evaluation; and long-term data monitoring and storage of data on mag tape. The software, recorded on magnetic media, allows the operator to select the number of samples to be taken, the sampling rate, and data limits to allow data collection to be terminated.

Instrument Digital Interface Units

Various digital interface units are designed for use in general purpose input/output systems for some electronic programmable desk calculators to allow these versatile highly-sophisticated systems to be used in a wide variety of data acquisition, process control, data collection, system control, and similar applications by putting the calculator "on-line" to the outside world. These units provide advanced calculators with the input/output versatility of conventional minicomputer systems while retaining the low cost, ease of programming, and computational ability characteristic of programmable calculators as a group. Many have been noted above.

Counting and Timing

The most common functions performed by men and/or machines today are counting and/or timing. Because of this, many firms have introduced very comprehensive lines of integrated circuits to perform these functions. Electronic timing, unit counting, frequency measurement, frequency/time base generation, clocking, and so much more can now be accomplished simply, with a minimum of cost. For maximum user convenience suppliers group the products into four categories: externally settable counter/timer; frequency and/or unit counter; complete timer/counter/stop-watch; and low power crystal frequency generators.

(A) Externally settable counter/timer circuits are a family of devices which can generate accurate, externally settable time delays from microseconds to five days.

(B) Frequency and/or unit counter is a 7-digit fully integrated circuit. To count units, users add an LED display, two resistors, a capacitor and control switches. For use as a timer or frequency counter, in addition to the above users also add an oscillator/controller circuit.

(C) A counter/timer/stopwatch comes complete in a single IC package. It works beautifully from a stack of three NiCad batteries. To make a system, users need to add only a quartz crystal, trimming capacitor, four switches and an 8-digit LED display.

(D) Low power crystal frequency generators provide low power operation plus the outstanding accuracy and stability of high frequency crystal circuits.

Programmable Timing Card

A typical programmable timing card is designed to provide a controlled interval signal to the calculator to allow synchronization or timing of measurements, output control signals, or the preparation of printouts. Various cards are available, which are designed for use in conjunction with time-of-day clocks. A typical card receives a 1 Hz input signal from the time base of the clock and provides 1, 2, 5, 10, and 30 seconds, 1, 2, 5, 10, and 30 minutes, and 1 hour timing signals. They often incorporate a crystal time base having an accuracy of one part of the 10^5 and provide additional timing intervals of 0.01, 0.02, 0.1, 0.2 and 0.5 second intervals. Intervals are generated by addressing the timing card. The calculator will then be disabled until a "go" command is triggered by expiration of the selected interval.

Estimating Calculator for Graphics Engineering

Various electronic estimating calculators are designed to measure linear and area dimensions and make quantity counts from drawings. In addition to performing the usual calculating functions, the units perform the electronic take-offs in just half the time with two specially designed probes for data entry. The electronic probes add automation to estimating. With the patented probes the user, for the first time, can automatically accumulate and display the lineal and area measurements and quantity counts which can then be used immediately for electronic extension by cost and labor factors. The ability to measure area and volume is a unique feature of the calculators. A typical estimating calculator combines all the standard calculating functions in the one unit. It adds, subtracts, multiplies, divides, performs mixed chain and constant calculations, repeats, squares, and raises to powers, automatic constants on all functions, floating decimal, overflow indications and so on. The many multiple features and greater flexibility of the calculator makes it useful to construction estimators and cost engineers of all types, surveyors, urban and regional planners, utilities, geographers, and many others involved with plans, maps and blueprints and the daily estimating function that is involved with many other diverse occupations.

Calculator-based Variables Monitoring System

Monitoring the pH and precisely controlling the amount of caustic that should be used to neutralize the acid in order to prevent damage to the bacteria in a municipal sewage plant is a complex process. A calculator helps control the effluents from some manufacturing plants. One specific data acquisition system is coupled with a programmable calculator providing a system that replaced multiple recorders previously required throughout the facility. The system is programmed for precise pH levels. It continuously monitors pH and indicates an alarm condition when the limits are not in specification. Measuring multipoint physical parameters to monitor or analyze phenomena and control devices will provide many varied applications of the system. Transmission of the data may be possible over thousands of miles using a common carrier interface and an optional modem.

Digitizer — Calculators

A digitizer is a device used to convert information in graphic (or actual) form into numerical intelligence suitable for processing, recording or transmission in a digital data system. While a line contains an infinite number of points, a digitized line is an approximation based upon a series of points no closer together than the resolution of the digitizer. In digitizing a line, the operator merely moves the stylus along the line and points are digitized at rates determined by the pulse rate of the digitizer.

Normally the pulse rate is such that, as a practical matter, coordinate sets are generated at distances equivalent to the resolution capability of the digitizer. It does this by generating a specific set of coordinates (X and Y) for every point on a plane area, the size of which is defined by the lengths of the axes from which the X distance and the Y distance are measured. Since a line is a series of points, a line or shape can be described by the coordinate measurements of all the points that make up that line. Digitizers operate nicely with advanced calculators. A typical digitizer reads a curve or any irregular shape as a series of discrete points into the calculator that prints out the dimensions of the line and the area of the contained shape.

Sonic digitizer advantages — An advantage of using sound as a ranging device is that digitization need not be confined to a plane. Rather, since sound waves travel in all directions from the stylus point, three-dimensional graf/ pens capable of digitizing shapes in space are both feasible and available. In such systems, three sensors are used to generate X, Y and Z coordinate sets.

Digitizer accuracy concerns the sum total of all factors which tend to cause deviations in coordinate outputs and actual point locations. The accuracy specification should assume that all factors are at their adverse limits. For the Graf/Pen accuracy is within 0.1% of full scale.

A digitizer calculator thus is a unique machine that reads a curve, or any irregular shape, as a series of discrete points, and then converts these to a series of digital X-Y coordinates. To make these entries, users trace the shape and their calculator prints out dimensions and area of the line or contained shape. With the digitizer users can directly process graphical data such as X-rays, blueprints, strip-chart recordings, and cut-and-fill profiles, to name a few.

Calculating Oscilloscope Advantages

These units give users the precision of a digital oscilloscope for data acquisition and display *plus* the built-in capability of a microprocessor for data reduction. Users can make exact calculations of rise times, integrals, differentials, peak areas, RMS values, peak-to-peak measurements, n-point averaging, and an almost unlimited range of other operations. This increases productivity by letting users measure, display, digitize, store, and process data faster and more accurately.

The unit will analyze data and, through conditional branching, function as a decision-making instrument. It is easily programmable — without computer instructions — so repetitive operations can be completely automated. Its mainframe, through modular design, has provisions for a wide range of plug-in modules to let users expand their system to meet individual requirements. Some units can be interfaced to control other equipment.

Low Cost A/D Systems Are Necessary for Many
Instrument Readouts — An Example

Providing up to 80 high level or 50 low level analog inputs, a series of low cost, standardized data acquisition systems for Hewlett-Packard 9815 programmable calculators is based on moderate speed (10 conversions per sec) isolated, dual-slope bipolar or high speed, unipolar successive approximation A/D converters. Optional time-of-day clocks, timers, event counters, and pseudo-interrupt cards are also available. Interface to the calculator is provided through an 8 bit TTL input/output control card. No other cabling between system components is required on the part of the user.

Circuit Network Analysis Program (CNAP)

Users can model a complex, active circuit design and have complete solutions automatically documented within a few minutes. They simply enter component values and node interconnections and define the plotter interval and bounds. The calculator takes it from there and quickly solves the problem using an HP (Hewlett-Packard) software routine patterned after the well-known ECAP circuit analysis program. User response data is printed in tabular form by the calculator while the plotter produces a Bode plot showing predicted amplitude and phase response. If circuit performance doesn't meet user specifications, it's a simple matter to modify component values and rerun the program until the user gets optimum results.

dc Analysis Program

Networks that are strictly resistive can be quickly and easily analyzed by this program. Additionally, active devices, provided they can be modeled by only resistive elements and voltage-controlled sources, can be analyzed.
Features of the program include:
- Networks with up to 7 nodes and 15 branches can be analyzed.
- Input requirements consist of element values and node connections.
- Networks may be stored on tape cassette for future recall.
- Networks may be edited easily to show the effect of different elements, values, or connections.
- Tabular output includes node voltages, element currents and power dissipation.

Users can easily determine nodal voltages, power dissipation, etc., for complex resistive networks and perform bias-point analyses at their desks. They also have the calculator printout to document their circuit configuration and analysis results.

Calculator Controlled Spectrophotometer

The "Super 700", from GCA/McPherson Corp., Acton, Mass., is a completely digital 700 Series spectrophotometer interfaced directly with a programmable statistical calculator. It features automatic spectrophotometer control, and unattended acquisition, storage, and reduction of data. With the Super 700, a user is able to input experimental parameters to the calculator by mag card program for digital control of the spectrophotometer. It will automatically start, stop, and slew the monochromator in either direction; control, monitor, and record elapsed or incremental time; and initiate and control peripheral devices.

In addition, the data acquisition, storage, and manipulation capabilities permit immediate calculations of first and second derivatives, peak locations, integration, and other high-level functions. The 735-50 simplifies statistical calculations, including regression and standard deviation.

Calculator Control System Design

Engineers assigned to develop control systems for STOL aircraft have overcome a host of highly complex aerodynamic problems. The control system designers often have turned to an advanced calculator. As they start they enter results from wind tunnel tests into the calculator, along with data on the aircraft's mass and inertia. The unit quickly computes the static and dynamic derivatives for various trim conditions required to set up a dynamic model of the aircraft for each flight condition. (There are approximately 120 different flight conditions.) The calculator also computes transfer functions and the roots of the characteristic polynomial. And then, using a root-locus plotting program, it designs single-loop control systems. These calculations that once took days are now done in about ten minutes.

LABORATORY CALCULATOR SYSTEMS
Laboratory Data Acquisition System Using Programmable Calculators

Data acquisition systems can make pressure, temperature, fuel flow and engine speed calculations, and provide personnel with a complete printout of this data. Data from the sensors, converted to digital form by a group of individual instruments can be placed in the memory of a calculator. Conversion to engineering units combined with standardization of data to compensate for variables such as air temperature, air density, and fuel density is accomplished and all of the corrected data can be printed out, completely formatted with alphanumeric headings and engineering unit indications by various automatic typewriters. Hardcopy output can become a permanent report of performance of a particular engine combination.

These systems perform laboratory data collection, logging and reduction. Programmable calculator users can eliminate most errors and drudgery associated with manually copying data generated by laboratory test equipment. Using available interfaces and data acquisition sub-systems with programmable calculators, chromatographs, auto-analyzers, spectrophotometers, universal testing machines and similar systems can be placed "on-line". Savings in labor costs often pay for the entire system in less than one year. No knowledge of computer programming languages or techniques is required. A system can be operating the same day it is received.

Laboratory Experiments and Tests

Many calculator users can make the general purpose calculator into a data acquisition system tailored to their project just by pressing the keyboard. For example, one day the system may be set up to handle 10 thermocouple channels, 10 MV channels, and 10 BCD channels, with alarms on 12 channels. The following day it could be keyed to handle 45 analog channels with low and high level alarms, outputing nonalarm readings into a tape recorder and printing out only when one or more channels go into alarm. Instant versatility benefits every lab. This is accomplished by programming and ROM customizing.

Thus, many users need a versatile data acquisition system that can be set up for one use, easily modified, and completely reprogrammed for another use — all by keyboard control. An advanced calculator general purpose data system can be easily adapted for specific experiments and tests.

If users need to handle a variety of input signals, measure at different rates — fast or slow scan, obtain direct outputs or use computerized reduction, a calculator is a most versatile input/output data formatting system. For program documentation, a program printout option automatically records the full keyboard setup for the various experiments.

Advanced Electronic Estimating Calculator, An Example

Recent literature available from the Keuffel & Esser Company describes what the company calls a revolutionary new estimating calculator. The brochure "Take-Off" describes the calculators in detail and shows how they are different from the standard units. They were designed with the architect, engineer, and estimator in mind. The calculators measure, calculate and display length, area, and volume directly from a drawing in either architect's or engineer's scale for immediate extension by cost or labor factors. In addition, the K&E estimating calculators count, mark and display individual items on a drawing for extension by other factors. Up to 50 per cent more output per take-off hour is possible with the easy-to-use calculators.

Two probes make the calculator unique — a counting probe and a measuring probe. To use the counting probe, the user simply touches the probe to the items being counted, presses down lightly and the count is displayed. To use the measuring probe, the user selects the appropriate scale, then places the probe at a starting point on the drawing and rolls the wheel along the distance to be measured. The actual length in feet will be displayed, and by setting a constant, such as height, into the calculator, square footage is automatically calculated, too.

According to literature, the K&E calculator does all this in addition to the normal functions of adding, subtracting, multiplication, dividing, calculating mixed, chain and constant totals, and so on. Three models are available: a 68-8000 which reads directly in either ¼-inch or ⅛-inch architect's scale; the 68-0801 which reads directly in either 1"-10' or 1"-20' engineer's scale, and the 68-0820 which reads in both scales and provides two memories and a printout.

Instrument Calibration System

A typical instrument calibration system brings to the calibration laboratory a cost-effective solution to calibrating the myriad complex instruments in use today. The system incorporates a wide variety of calibration-quality instruments, easily recognized by those involved in cal lab work as required for calibration purposes. The system calibrates a wide variety of passive meters, multimeters, electronic meters (voltage, current, VSWR, power, etc.), differential voltmeters, digital voltmeters, frequency counters, and oscilloscopes along with their plug-ins and amplifiers. In addition, the system can optionally calibrate signal sources and generators, oscillators, pulse generators, and function generators.

Laboratory Data Acquisition Calculator Capabilities

Some examples are:
(1) Lab applications, custom-designed.
(2) Easy setup, modification by keyboard.
(3) Digital inputs from specialized lab instruments, counters.
(4) Input flexibility, programming, versatility.
(5) Measurement method flexibility.
(6) Many different outputs.
(7) Special functions options simplify reduction.
(8) Program printout options.

Calculator-to-calculator communication can be employed simply to move data from one machine to another. In a typical system, a calculator interfaced to a blood analyzer in one clinical laboratory collects data on blood samples and stores this information on disk files. Another clinical laboratory 40 miles away performs the same data collection onto tape cassettes. This data is also forwarded via 300 bit/second acoustic couplers to the disk files at the first calculator. Thus, the calculator disk is used as a local data base for the two laboratories.

Calculator Data Acquisition Systems Analyze
Measurement Data in Laboratories

We have noted that various types of advanced desktop calculators enable users to log, compare, and analyze data the moment it arrives, and to thus eliminate all manual entries. These systems can store data and match many of the capabilities of minicomputers. These type calculator systems combine the abilities of stand-alone data recorders with data analysis computers. New systems are especially useful in quality control testing and monitoring; design engineering testing and documentation; production testing, monitoring and control; and in various scientific and medical laboratories. Systems include the calculator, a mainframe power source, and interface plug-in, standard software for data acquisition, and standard accessories and options. Actual data acquisition is accomplished by other instruments which are plugged into the calculator mainframe in any desired configuration.

In a typical application situation, the first step is to establish where measurements are to be made and for how long. The next step is the placement of suitable measuring devices, perhaps multimeters or counters. By interfacing these instruments, raw signals are converted into useful data. By plugging the programmable calculator into the system, the data can be collected, measured, processed and in certain cases stored. Review of the results permit the identification of trends. By the use of a graphic terminal or digital plotter with the calculator, it is possible to display or plot the information in a meaningful format such as an XY plot, histogram or frequency distribution. Some examples of plotter and graphics uses for data acquisition systems follow on pages ahead.

Some Calculator Systems with Communications Capabilities Use Plotters Effectively

The advanced programmable calculators systems have the capacity to handle line-oriented telecommunications between other similarly programmed computer systems. With the addition of telecommunications options, programmable calculators can, under program control, transmit, receive, store, format, and convert information. Such calculators are now called *Systems* because the new advanced programmable calculators have *intelligent* terminal capabilities . . . and have indeed become computers in their own right.

Utilizing the BASIC statements of PRINT, PRINT USING, and INPUT, the calculators send and receive data over telephone or dedicated lines at user-selected data rates up to 1200 baud. Data, which may be read from or stored onto cassette or disk, can be accepted in unformatted lines of up to 64 characters or specially formatted lines of up to 192 characters on some machines. In addition, they have facilities for initiating a break signal and for decoding a selected input character as the terminating character. Some telecommunications options are priced at $500.00 and over. Also introduced by some firms are digital flat-bed plotters (31×42 inches) priced under $4,000. Driven by the programmable calculators, the plotters produce accurate continuous line or point plotting graphics of curves and data of problems solved on the calculator.

The market for peripherals is very big. Firms are racing to build products which will interface with calculators. For example, Houston Instrument's Complot series of digital plotters may now be interfaced to Hewlett-Packard's programmable calculators. The Model 11282A interface can be used with the DP series of plotters. And this trend with other equipment will continue.

CALCULATOR PLOTTERS AND GRAPHICS INPUT AND OUTPUT
Calculator Digital Plotter Systems

Calculator's mathematical data users need accurate detail. A typical digital plotter can provide quick and digitally accurate presentation pieces: statistical data, histograms, schematics, sales and production curves. On some units Vectors are printed out at 15 to 22 inches per second. There's no lag. While the pen is moving the calculator is computing the next move.

Precision drawing means fewer misinterpretations of data. Digital plotting keeps lines vector straight and insures absolute repeatability to within .005

inch. On some units scale controls give full scale plots within a 10 × 15 inch plotting area. Each axis can be separately reduced to half scale by front panel controls. Users set their data zero point any place on the plot from the calculator or the plotter. Zero is set automatically for first quadrant operations on power up. Users may draw on any size paper they want — from sketch pad size to 11 ×17 inches easel-size. Electrostatic hold-down keeps it in place.

Engineering Graphics and Alphanumerics Terminals

The programmable graphic terminal calculator opens the skills of graphics with alphanumerics and provides added dimensions to calculator users. Fast X-Y plots are as easy as specifying X, Y coordinates. And alphanumerics is as simple as typing one's name. Users can program alphanumerics into the calculator from either the terminal or calculator keyboards. The terminal will format and print alphanumerics and data output under full program control. Rapid presentation of data or calculated results as well as graphical presentation of information for analysis or decision making is well within the capability of these devices. The various brands of graphic terminal combinations provide a powerful and versatile team for data analysis and presentation in the computational office or laboratory.

Graphic Calculator System Components

A calculator graphics system consists of two basic components: the advanced programmable calculator and the display terminal. Linked by an interface, the terminal provides the calculator with the capability of presenting data in alphanumeric and graphic form. Straightforward plots are possible. Several preprogrammed plot program tapes are supplied as parts of some systems. The programs take the mystery out of creating graphics while providing efficiency of system operations. Also offered are various function plots.

Designed to enable the user to plot any user-defined single variable function, automatic scaling routines assure good representation of data and optimum screen area usage. Interactive operation will, however, allow the user to specify minimum and maximum values for X and Y coordinates, the coordinate of axis intersection and the independent variable increment. Some systems offer optional function plots. Used with memory options, one package provides not only the above but also automatic scaling with axis labeling.

Calculator/Data Tablet Graphic Input Combination

A desktop graphic data-processing system designated the Calcutizer combines a data tablet with a programmable calculator to form a "smart" data-tablet system. Developed by Talos Systems Inc., the Calcutizer consists of an integrated hardware and software package. Data tablets and digitizers measuring from 11 by 11 inches to 44 by 60 inches of active area are available. A programmable calculator with a printer or, as an option, one of the more powerful series calculators is interfaced to the digitizer. Standard packages of statistical and graphic software are available.

The engineer or scientist can use the Calcutizer to perform calculations in seconds or minutes, in his office. Many previous data-reduction systems involved delays for batch-mode processing or connection to costly time-share systems. The input for the system is the Talos data tablet. Both tablets and digitizers developed by the company are based on closed-loop, all-electronic servo circuitry instead of the technique of pen-displacement detection used in other systems. In addition to the standard hardware of this system, an optional plotter for hard-copy graphics is available. The company also makes the Telenote system, which transmits handwriting over telephone lines.

Graf/Pen Data Entry

This technique enters both graphic and alphanumeric data automatically by requesting the user to simply trace a curve, circle a printed character or make a checkmark with a pen or cursor. If not restricted to a "tablet", the Graf/Pen can be mounted on a drawing table, a blackboard, a projection screen, a CRT display or any other flat surface. The system permits human judgement and cuts graphic data entry time. Many users have experienced time reduction of 90% compared with manual scaling and keyboard entry. It has become widely applicable and is currently used for such diverse purposes as planning radiographic treatment in medicine and for entering part numbers in order processing and inventory control. The technique is systems oriented and interfaces are available to almost every kind of minicomputer, programmable calculator of RS-232 device. Complete off-line systems use punched paper or magnetic media.

EXCERPTS FROM SUMMER 1975 ISSUE OF WANG LABORATORIES USERS SOCIETY MAGAZINE, THE PROGRAMMER . . .

A GRAPHICS USE CASE HISTORY "PROGRAMMABLE CALCULATIONS IN GRAPHICS AS INTRODUCTORY PHYSICS DEMONSTRATIONS"

by
T. R. Sandin
Associate Professor of Physics
North Carolina Agricultural and Technical State University
Greensboro, North Carolina

PREFACE: *This article synopsizes a presentation delivered by the author at the American Association of Physics Teachers (AAPT) meeting held at Boone, North Carolina, summer, 1974. Professor Sandin's presentation caused such an enthusiastic and large response among teachers for a written summary, that he prepared this information-packed item.*

Background

About a year and a half ago, we purchased a Wang 600-6-TP programmable calculator and a Wang 612 flatbed plotter. Why was this system chosen over a mini-computer system or a terminal to a large computer? First, we wanted portability. We leave the Wang system on a rolling table which can be moved from lab, to class, to lecture, to office as desired. I have also put it in the car and taken it to junior high schools and AAPT meetings. Secondly, we wanted low initial and monthly maintenance costs. Third, we wanted ease of access. That is, we wanted a system we could get to whenever we wanted to, not subject to the whims of another department or computer center. Also, we did not want to wait for hours or even minutes for the programs to run. Fourth, we wanted reliability. I had been frustrated as a result of problems with down time, transmission lines, and unpredictable turn-around times when the computer had been used in introductory courses. Fifth, we wanted graphical output. This I use mainly for class demonstrations, although students *do* run some of the programs.

The Graphical Approach

The reasons for using graphical output as a demonstration are:
(1) "The Lazarus effect" — some of the dead graphs in the text are brought to life and made to mean more.
(2) The parameters can be readily changed by the class, and the results can be predicted by them and then immediately and accurately seen.

(3) Graphical output provides a change in pace, which means an increase in student interest.

(4) The system awakens or increases many students' interest in computers.

There are two main types of plots that are used, the functional and the incremental. Functional plots are usually the easiest to program. The general solution that users receive with the Wang system contains programs for plotting with linear or logarithmic scales, in the first of all four quadrants, and in rectangular or polar coordinate systems. These programs are fed into the machine from a magnetic tape cassette, and then a subroutine is added for $y = f(x)$ or $r = f(\theta)$ (actually in the parametric form $x = f(t)$; $y = g(t)$ similarly, for r and θ). The program is then run, stopping to allow the operator to enter such things as the ranges of x, y, and t, the step size, the distance between the hash marks on the axes, and the values to be printed on the axes. The plot is then performed and then labelling of the graph must be done. This involves specifying the location of the letters, their size and spacing, and each letter to be printed. Naturally, you will not want to stand up in front of the class for a long period of time inputting all of this information. What one must do then, is to modify the company's programs so that pushing a very few buttons will execute the demonstration rapidly. That is, put all those ranges, step sizes, etc. into the program itself.

Incremental plots, on the other hand use a subroutine to calculate (Δy), plot, etc. Examples of incremental plots are those of the $F = ma$ type, where some method is used to determine the Δx and Δy during an interval of time, Δt.

A LABORATORY CASE HISTORY "AUTOMATED POTENTIOMETRY EMPLOYING A WANG 600"

by

Ivan Sekerka and Josef F. Lechner
Canada Center for Inland Waters,
Burlington, Ontario, Canada

ABSTRACT: *The use of Wang 600 calculator in connection with an automated system for multiparameter potentiometric measurements is described. The hardware includes a 600-2-TP and a Model 605-1A microface. The incorporation of a calculator into the system eliminates manual mathematical or graphical operations and gives a direct printout of desired concentration units together with an indexing of the sample and a labeling of the ions of interest.*

Introduction

Ion-selection electrodes are useful new analytical chemistry aids that can be expected to become measuring tools of general utility. These electrodes can be classified as direct potentiometric devices. This is a highly attractive attribute, since direct potentiometric analysis is, in principle, very simple and fast. It involves merely the immersion of a proper electrode set into a solution and the measurement of the resulting potential.

In recent years a variety of ion-selective electrodes have become available commercially and show great promise as fast and efficient tools for laboratory analysis as well as for "in situ" monitoring. The following electrodes are commercially available: ammonia, bromide, cadmium, calcium, chloride, cupric, cyanide, fluoride, fluoroborate, iodide, lead, nitrate, nitrite, perchlorate, potassium, silver, sodium, sulfide, sulfite, thiocyanate, and water hardness.

Description of the System

The idea for automation of direct potentiometric measurements is perhaps as old as the ion-selective electrodes themselves. A system, built in our laboratory represents a versatile apparatus, which is capable of employing from one to six different electrodes. Besides the direct potentiometry, it is capable of operating as a flow-through, known-addition, known-subtraction, and known-addition-known-dilution system. For example, the apparatus has been used for automated simultaneous determination of pH, water hardness, specific conductance, and ammonia, sodium, potassium, and fluoride ions concentrations in natural and waste-water samples. The system consists of individual instruments interfaced to a Wang 600 calculator. All signals necessary for timing and controlling of the assembly are generated by a control module. The block diagram of the apparatus is given.

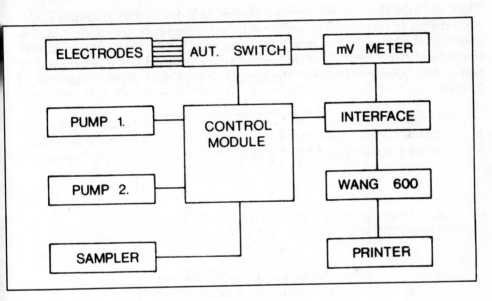

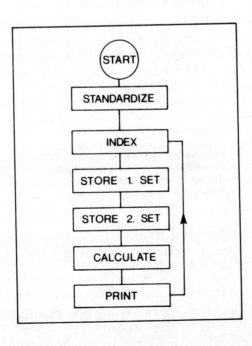

The on-line Wang 600 calculator accepts the data of the potentiometric measurements, indexes, computes, and prints out the results in any desired concentration units. Optimal sampling rate is about 30 samples (180 parameters) per hour. A flow chart for the calculator program is shown. The complete listing of the program is obtainable from the authors on request.

The calculation of the potentiometric data is based on solving the Nernstian equations:

$$E = D_o + \frac{RT}{nF} \ln a_i \qquad (1)$$

and the modified equation for the known increments technique:

$$C = C_1 \exp\left[\left(\frac{E_2 - E_1}{E_3 - E_2}\right) \log d - 1\right]^{-1} \qquad (2)$$

Thus, the procedures of calibration, manual calculation and graphical operations normally involved in potentiometric measurements are eliminated. The operator simply inserts the samples into the sampler and obtains the results in the form of direct printout of the desired unit of concentration or activity, together with proper indexing of the sample and labeling of the parameters of interest.

```
          1.              X
      245.62              A
      180.10              B
       65.52              C
        7.81              D
      576.00              E


          2.              X
      123.69              A
       23.00              B
      100.69              C
        7.49              D
      359.40              E


          3.              X
       12.98              A
        4.60              B
        8.38              C
        7.25              D
       85.40              E
```

X = Sample No.
A = Total water hardness (ppm CaCO₃)
B = Non-carbonate water hardness (ppm CaCO₃)
C = Carbonate water hardness (ppm CaCO₃)
D = -log activity of hydrogen ion (pH)
E = Specific conductance (μ m h o s)

Under consideration at the present time is the addition of statistical analysis routines to calculate standard deviations, means and other data required for the routine analysis of water samples.

Summary

The efficiency and versatility of the Wang 600 desk calculator have increased the capability of electrochemical measurements and made possible the further development of automated potentiometry for water samples analysis. The system provides automation of mathematical operations, eliminates tedious hours with tables, graphs and nomographs and improves the overall economy of serial analysis. The direct printout of the results in desired concentration units is an advantage very seldom achieved by other automated systems in analytical chemistry. We feel assured that the Wang system will continue to contribute to further research and development of multiparameter analysis via ion-selective electrodes as well as continuous monitoring of water quality parameters. Accordingly, it seems to be of great interest and importance to apply the system in other fields of chemical analysis.

A Laboratory Example: Hewlett-Packard's 9815A Calculator Offers an Economical Approach to Rapid RIA Data Reduction

Radioimmunoassay is one of the most powerful tools in modern laboratory medicine, and it is not surprising that the majority of clinical laboratories are now doing RIA's. Radioimmunoassay is also one of the researcher's primary investigatory methods into endocrine, metabolic, and reproductive functions. But only part of any RIA takes place chemically in a test tube. The other part is mathematical and consists of generating a standard curve, interpolating unknowns from the curve, doing error analysis and keeping quality control records. For most routine assays, this mathematical portion of RIA is tedious, repetitive, and prone to mistakes when done manually with pencil, ruler, and graph paper.

In fact, for a typical 100-tube assay, mathematics can consume over one hour of valuable technologist time. Any kind of exhaustive error analysis or quality control record-keeping may be ignored because it simply takes too much time.

Now, with the 9815A programmable calculator system and HP's latest and most comprehensive software, complete data-reduction of a 100-tube assay takes less than 5 minutes. This includes:

- Data entry with punched paper tape, eliminating transcription errors.
- Unweighted and iterative weighted least squares regression of % bound versus concentration, for an accurate standard curve.
- Interpolation of patient unknowns with correction for non-specific binding, aliquot factors, % recovery due to extractions, and quench correction from CPM to DPM for liquid scintillation counters.
- Exhaustive error analysis of standard curve and patient unknowns showing all observed data with associated coefficient of variations (C.V. %), standard deviations (S.D.), confidence limits, and figures of merit (NSB, B∅/T, ED 50, slope, intercept, correlation, etc.) for each assay.
- Storage of quality control data for each and every assay for listing and plotting upon command at any time.

The 9815 System and software will perform all of these calculations for each of the assays. It will also output neat, formal reports at a single keystroke in less time and with greater accuracy than any manual or graphical method and at substantially less cost per assay than computer or time share methods.

System Configuration

The 9815 Programmable Calculator System for RIA consists of:

- 9815A Programmable Calculator with Option 001 (2008 steps) and Option 002 (I/O capability)
- 9863A (or 9883A) Punched Paper Tape Reader (optional)

- 9871A Printer/Plotter (optional)
- P/N 09815-14250 software, prestored on one magnetic tape cartridge, with special function key overlay, "cookbook" user's manual, and 55 page RIA Theory Monograph.

The new 9815 calculator is an advanced version of the popular HP 9810A calculator which has become a traditional computational tool in today's clinical laboratory. The 9815 calculator is fully compatible with its "big brother", the 9830A BASIC language calculator for on-line data transfer and storage of laboratory data. For persons with limited computer knowledge and experience, the 9815 is a good laboratory calculator and serves as the cost-effective core of the new HP Radioimmunoassay Data Reduction System.

H-Ps Instructions for Setting up the 9815A RIA Data Reduction System in A Lab

The same assay (Digoxin, HTSH, B12, etc.) is performed many times using the same kit protocol and the same gamma (or liquid scintillation) counter. It is natural, then, that the 9815 Calculator permits storage of the common protocols for each of these assays as well as the data output format for each counter. Required only once for each assay and for each counter, the 9815 magnetic tape cartridge will store up to 15 assay protocols and up to 5 different counter punched paper tape formats, for automatic and repetitive access for any assay/counter combination used in the lab.

For each assay, is assigned, a code number from 1 to 15 and sequentially supply information to store the assay name, date of entry, number of total activity tubes used, number of non-specific binding (blank) tubes used, number of zero concentration standard tubes used, and the value and number of replicates for all other standard concentration tubes used. Whether the assay requires quench correction, aliquot correction, % recovery correction, and how many tube replicates are used for patient unknowns is entered. Where appropriate, these contents are stored. This is done only once for each assay routinely performed in the lab and the calculator's cartridge remembers.

Likewise, for each gamma or liquid scintillation counter used (up to 5), those numbers which relate to position and character length of tube number, time of counting, gross counts, and AES (or channels ratio) number are sequentially entered where appropriate. These stored values then permit access to the correct punched paper tape routine for whichever counter is used at any future date.

The assay code number and counter code number are all that are required to specify any assay/counter combination used in the lab. All these numbers and values can be updated at any time to adapt to changing circumstances in the lab (e.g., if new assays are adapted and/or counters are replaced).

CALCULATORS AS COMMUNICATION SYSTEMS
Data Processing Calculator Systems

Many owners connect advanced programmable calculators to their computers to put full computing capability on specific user's desks, where it often belongs. This puts an end to the data processing run-around because the calculator can be a remote batch terminal, time-share terminal, and satellite processor, all in one unit. As satellite processors, several types of powerful BASIC language calculators give fast solutions to most of these users' computational problems. And by keeping these small- or intermediate-size jobs out of the data processing stream, the calculator helps users make better use of all their computing resources. Data can be gathered from many sources because the calcu-

```
=================
SELECT KEY B-J.
=================

   PROTOCOL LIST

WHICH ASSAY #?
                1*


HTSH
ASSAY # 1
DATE: 8.18.75
-----------------
# TOTALS=        2
# NSB'S=         3
# B0'S=          3
RESPONSE=B/B0
# CONC.>0=       6
  CONC. 1=    0.60
  CONC. 2=    1.20
  CONC. 3=    2.50
  CONC. 4=    5.00
  CONC. 5=   10.00
  CONC. 6=   20.00
STD. REPL.=      3
UNKNOWN REPL.= 2
ALIQ. FTR.=1.000


USE BOUND COUNTS
NO QUENCH CURVE
RECOVERY=100%

=================
```

Typical assay protocol setup. Up to 15 protocols can be stored.

```
   PAPER TAPE
    SET-UP

PROGRAM?
  1=CALL
  2=STORE
                1*

WHICH COUNTER #?
  (1-5)
                1*

   PROGRAM FOR
COUNTER #1 IN
MEMORY.
=================

DATA ENTRY?
  1=MANUAL
  2=P-TAPE
                2*
```

Program option to accept/select appropriate paper tape format from gamma counter. Up to 5 different formats can be stored.

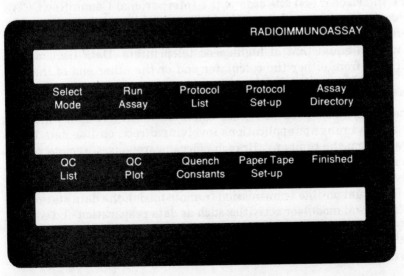

RADIOIMMUNOASSAY

| Select Mode | Run Assay | Protocol List | Protocol Set-up | Assay Directory |

| QC List | QC Plot | Quench Constants | Paper Tape Set-up | Finished |

lator accommodates instrumentation and a complete line of input/output peripherals, including plotter, disk, digitizer, line printer, etc. To convert the calculator to a computing data terminal, users simply add data communications interfaces and ROMs of various types. Then it can communicate with another terminal or another calculator to function as a binary synchronous remote batch terminal to a large computer, or serve as a time-share terminal. Users find that the calculator then becomes an economical alternative for connecting to remote bacth or time-sharing services — especially since it has so many of the features users need to improve their data processing capabilities.

Communications Calculators Using ROMs

Adding data communications capability to various desktop calculators, allows them to operate as programmable terminals accessed through BASIC instructions. By adding interface cables and plug-in read-only memory (ROM) modules, the units can communicate with another terminal, and some units can operate like a binary synchronous remote batch terminal using 2780 emulation mode on-line to an IBM 360/370 mainframe, or operate as a time-sharing terminal. By adding an on-line programmable BASIC capability, the calculator becomes a terminal input device for business and/or scientific applications. When attaching the interface and the interface control ROM, one type calculator/terminal can interface with RS-232-C modems, automatic dialers and other communications devices. Asynchronous or synchronous data rates from 110- to 9,600 bit/sec can be supported, and the terminals can have error detection and ASCII to Ebcdic conversion features depending on the ROM modems that are installed. Dual capabilities can be included so these devices can operate as both a binary synchronous batch terminals and interactive time-sharing devices depending on the application. Some specific calculators include thermal printers as a built-in capability. In addition, an 80-column card reader, 200 line/min printer and disk memory with up to 10M bits of memory can be installed on several systems.

Calculator Communications Interfaces

Practical remote use of most calculators is enhanced by the capability of the RS-232-C interface. We have noted use of systems with a variety of receivers and transmitters through land lines, a radio frequencies, literally and telemetering medium. The interface is a recognized standard of the Electronic Industries Association (EIA) and is the basis of all U.S. data communications. Further, the interface meets the code of the International Committee CCITT (Consultative Committee on International Telegraphy and Telephony). Advantages are that two-way interaction is possible in several modes, and transmission rates can equal that of high-speed teleprinters. Data transmission may be initiated from either the calculator end or the other end of the line.

Calculators as Data-Communication Stations

A data station is an all-purpose remote communication terminal which can be used for a broad range of applications involving direct, on-line data transmission to and from the company. Branch offices, warehouses, remote reporting locations throughout a plant, or any other company outpost can communicate directly with a centrally-located computer via the data station. When not being used for actual on-line transmission (remote mode), the data station can be used off-line (local mode) for activities such as data preparation and editing.

Programmable Calculators as Batch Terminals

Although designed as stand-alone machines, advanced calculators have several capabilities that allow them to be conveniently converted to terminals. These include alphanumeric character manipulation (strings), a general input/output structure, 4,000 to 16,000 bytes of expandable buffer memory, and page-width, high-speed printers. For time-sharing applications, their typewriter-like keyboards are easier to use than those which have the letters and numbers arranged in another format. For remote batch, the calculator mass memory allows efficient use of the communication link and provides ample storage for input and output data. Other functions performed by the batch calculator include data checking on received data and retransmission of improperly transmitted data. If line errors make data communication impossible or the connection is not maintained for some other reason, an error message is displayed at the calculator. Also, the number of message blocks transmitted or received is printed at the end of each transmission.

Batch Terminal Calculator Equipment

The following equipment is required for operation of one advanced calculator as a batch terminal:

- An advanced calculator with 4k or more word memory.
- String variables ROM.
- Thermal printer or equivalent.
- Data communications interface.
- Binary synchronous ROM.
- Modem.

Optional additions to the batch terminal environment may include one or more of the following groups of equipment:

- Mass memory subsystem.
- External cassette.
- Calculator card reader with Extended I/O ROM.
- Tape reader with option — extended IO ROM.
- Line printer subsystem (132-column output).
- Line Printer Subsystem (132-column output).

A larger calculator memory (8k words) and a wide variety of other peripherals can also be included in the calculator batch terminal environment. A user's particular application will determine which of the many series peripherals best suits user needs.

Telecommunication Calculators, an Example

Calculator-to-calculator communication provides a wide range of options. Full-precision data arrays can be transferred from one machine to another at rates up to 9,600 bits/second in either asynchronous or synchronous mode. BASIC programs can be transferred from the memory of one machine to the other, and for asynchronous rates up to 1,800 bits/second, one calculator can remotely control another. Programs can be loaded, run, or stopped and peripherals can be activated. If, for example, a calculator is connected to a disk containing several programs, a user at another calculator can call up and access programs from the disk via the first calculator. For data transmission where error immunity is required, two calculators can be configured as two remote batch terminals to use binary synchronous communication procedures.

Calculator-Host System, an Example

Some calculators can be used in both small and large control systems. Often they can be used in a large distributed-processing system. For example, a pipeline company that already has a master control center might want to expand the control network by buying several remotely-controllable systems from a supplier and linking them by telephone lines to the master control. Or, they might use a similar host-satellite organization with other serial data channels for master and local control in a large multiphase process plant. In one example, the OEM computer subsystem must communicate with the master control, calculate process-control parameters, transfer data to and from local controllers via d-a and a-d converters, accept information from a keyboard, and display system status. These requirements can all be met by variations of I/O configurations. So a single subsystem calculator board in each satellite system can implement all the required functions.

Calculators as Time-Sharing Terminals

Several types of programable calculators can emulate a time-sharing terminal once the appropriate ROM is plugged in and the programmable keys are labeled with their special functions by the template. The routines called up by the keys intervene in the operating system to add the communications functions. For example, on some units to send data, the "transmit" special-function key is pressed after the information has been entered into the display buffer. The "shift" and "control" keys emulate their counterparts on a teletypewriter to generate special control characters for signing on, editing, ending and input sequence, and breaking transmission. These user-definable keys can be made to provide access to frequently called sequences like the telephone number of a central computer and a user identification number. In some units, an entire sign-on sequence programed in BASIC and stored in the memory may be accessed through a single key. Besides saving time, this capability simplifies the use of the terminal by inexperienced operators — though of course it is not practical if security is a consideration.

Time-Sharing Keyboard Calculator Example

One unit has a keyboard that has 12 special function keys that can handle 24 different operations both for program writing and in peripheral and instrument control. The keys can serve as immediate-execute keys, as call keys for subroutines and as typing aids. With the time-sharing or "live keyboard" feature, the user can perform simple calculations, examine and change program variables and list programs while the calculator is performing other peripheral or control operations. The interrupt capability apportions these operations on a priority schedule determined by the operator. The unit comes with 8k bytes of internal read/write memory, which is expandable in 8k increments to a total of 32k bytes. The four optional ROM slots in the front of the machine accept ROMs that can do the following: an extended I/O which is required for interrupts and time-share features; a general I/O; a plotter; string arrays; and advanced programming. A tape cartridge can hold 250-000 bytes on two tracks (125k/track) and has a 2750 bytes/s transfer rate. The fast I/O speed, together with the simultaneous interfacing capabilities doubles for 16-bit parallel instruments and for instruments that use the IEEE Standard 488 bus, and makes this programmable calculator suitable as the controller of an instrumentation system.

CALCULATOR COMMUNICATIONS: A CASE HISTORY — WANG AT THE FIRE SCIENCE CENTER

by

A. J. Kayll, Director
Fire Science Center
The University of New Brunswick
Fredericton, New Brunswick, Canada

In the summer a forester in Atlantic Canada is concerned with the prevention, detection and suppression of forest fires.

One of the aids used in prevention is the Canadian Forest Fire Weather Index. This Index, which is representative of the likelihood of fires starting, and their intensity once ignited, is calculated by using the following data: air temperature, relative humidity, windspeed, and rainfall. These data are collected by provincial forest service personnel who then send the data to a central fire weather forecasting office operated by the Federal Government of Canada (Canadian Forestry Service, Department of Environment) at the Halifax International Airport.

Data are then sent by TWX to a computer situated at the University of New Brunswick. The responsibility of the Fire Science Center at U. N. B. entails twice daily receipt of data and computer compilation of the indices which are then sent back by TWX to the Halifax forecasting office for distribution to the news media, provincial agencies and private companies.

As a backup system, the Fire Science Center has a Wang 720C programmable calculator interfaced via a Wang 707 interface control unit to an ASR 33 Teletype. A special function key designed and installed by the New Brunswick Telephone Company allows the teletype to be used as either an I/O device for the Wang 720C or as a regular teletype.

When using the Wang equipment, data are sent from the Halifax forecast office by TWX to the Wang operator. Following automatic input (punched paper tape) of previously calculated indices, the operator then manually enters the new weather data and proceeds with compilation under program control. Calculations are output on punched paper tape and printed formats on the teletype. The new Fire Weather Indices are then sent to the Halifax forecasting office via the TWX network.

In all, for Atlantic Canada, 3941 program steps in 7 blocks utilize at certain stages all available core of the 720C. The program and operating procedures are the subject of an undergraduate thesis being completed in the Faculty of Forestry to U. N. B. by Mr. E. Bulley.

Programmable Calculator Systems for Automatic Gaging and Classifications (Some Examples from Fluidyne Instrumentation, Oakland, CA)

Automatic gaging and classification systems represent one of the most logical applications for on-line use of programmable electronic calculators. With the current trend to the use of electronic gaging devices having digital outputs, the next step is automatic processing of gage data for classification and statistical analysis of parts on the production line. It was this capability that led the Ross Gear division of TRW Incorporated to install a calculator-based automatic gaging system in their "Hydraguide" steering system production line at Lebanon, Tennessee. Fluidyne Instrumentation supplies interfacing systems for both optical and mechanical gaging systems for use with programmable calculators in both industrial and scientific applications. Complete operating systems including all software, installation and maintenance services can be provided by Fluidyne for single-source responsibility.

The TRW/Ross "Hydraguide" steering system consists of an engine-driven pump, relief valve, power cylinder or cylinders, reservoir, filter, fluid lines and a control unit to which an automotive-type steering wheel is attached. The metering section of the control unit for which the gaging system is designed consists of a commutator and bi-directional gearotor elements which contains an orbiting rotor and a fixed stator. The function of the metering section is to supply the oil to the power cylinder, maintaining the relationship between the hand wheel and the steered wheels. Since the closeness of fit of the elements of the metering unit determines the lost motion in the steering system, gaging of the rotor and stator units is crucial.

Prior gaging techniques involved two or three men utilizing a granite surface plate and a conventional air gage, scanning and parts off the production line searching for the high spots which determined the classification for fit. Although inspectors become adept at this procedure, the location and dimension of the high spot of the components was at best an educated guess. With the new, calculator-based system developed in conjunction with the Production Systems Service Center of the TRW Systems group in Redondo Beach, California, the highest projection or lowest point can be measured within 50 to 75 millionths of an inch on a routine basis. Where two men previously were necessary to categorize 160 pieces per day, one man now averages 1200 pieces per day.

According to the PSSC project manager for this system, a gage had to be developed which would operate reliably on the shop floor and which could easily be used by production personnel. A Wang model 700B programmable desk calculator was selected in preference to a minicomputer system not only due to its low initial cost but also because of its ease of programming — the arithmetic operations which the calculator is to perform are simply entered into the main memory of the system by a series of keystrokes. While computers appear to the operator of the equipment as an anonymous 'black box', a calculator represents an interactive system allowing the operator to comprehend the function of the machine for which he is responsible. Additional data concerning the type of parts being tested can be entered at the keyboard by the inspector and completely new programs can be stored in memory by means of the calculator's built-in tape cassette recorder.

The calculator itself performs a series of computation on the data supplied to it through the Fluidyne interface and control system. Data indicating the component design dimensions and tolerances for various classifications are entered into memory either manually through the keyboard or automatically by means of a punched card inserted into an accessory card reader. The entire calculation and classification takes place without operator attention in less than one-quarter of a second after the gage contacts the part. The next step, which has not yet been implemented, would allow this output information to be used to place the components in appropriate bins or packages if necessary for higher production rates.

The Wang 700 calculator also keeps track of the number of parts accepted in each classification and the number of rejects for out of parallelism, too high and too low. The ease of programming the calculator has permitted a number of operator convenient subroutines to be easily added in the field. Under consideration at this time is the addition of statistical analytical routines to determine standard deviations, means, and other data required by the quality control department.

Programming the calculator for gaging applications is a simple matter, especially in comparison with minicomputer programming techniques. The calculator-based system utilizes the techniques associated with the solution of arithmetic problems and requires no knowledge of any special programming languages. Programming costs for typical advanced programmable calculators represent $1/5$th to $1/10$th the investment of a similar program for a minicomputer system.

The gaging mechanism has two platens, one fixed and one floating. Placing a part between the two platens orients one platen to the other and measures their planar relationship to determine the thickness of the part in parallelarity of the two surfaces. Stators, rotors, and commutator rings represent the three typical groups of the 25-30 components the system is programmed to gage. Associated with the movable platen are three Bendix "Cordax" grading-type linear encoders which provide a six digit decimal height indication with a resolution of 0.00001 inch. Digital inputs from the three encoders and their associated electronic systems are interfaced directly to the calculator input/output connector by a Fluidyne 7200 universal digital interface which formats the data, transfers the information to the calculator and transmits control commands back to the gage.

The Fluidyne 7200 universal digital interface consists of a basic mainframe assembly equipped with a power supply, an input/output formatting card compatible with the I/O bus of the Wang 700 calculator, and provides for installation of a wide range of individual formatting and control cards which operate on command of the calculator.

In addition to its data transmission and formatting capabilities, the 7200 universal digital interface also incorporates programmable contact closures which are used in the TRW/Ross Gear automatic gaging system to indicate to the operator that he should reject or accept the part as well as to indicate proper operation of the gage. Additional alarm or control functions could be utilized for an audible warning or for automatic feedback control of the grinding machinery producing the parts being gaged.

Each specific function of the model 7200 universal digital interface is provided by separate plug-in printed circuit cards containing the appropriate integrated circuits, relays, etc., required for the specific function. As requirements change or additional data input or control functions are necessary, up to 8 cards may be installed in the standard mainframe assembly by the user.

Electrical connections are made to these cards at the back of the interface system by means of printed circuit "paddle cards", thus allowing simple removal of connections from the system if service should be necessary.

The entire 7200 universal digital interface system is designed to allow complete electronic trouble-shooting by either the replacement of printed circuit cards with a known good unit maintained as a spare at the site or, since all integrated circuits in the system are socket-mounted, simple substitution of a standard 930 series DTL or 7400 series TTL integrated circuit for units suspected to be defective.

The 7200 system is designed to allow complete trouble-shooting by experienced electronic technicians by means of a DTL/TTL-compatible logic probe. Extender cards can be provided to raise the circuit board for service out of the card cage assembly where it will be accessible to the technician.

Economic justification of the gaging system is based on a proven 15-to-1 reduction of gaging labor cost at the Lebanon, Tennessee plant of TRW/Ross Gear. Contributing to a rapid payout of the capital investment is the low acquisition cost of the calculator and the interfacing system combined with minimum programming costs. A rule of thumb for comparative programming costs of programmable desk calculators developed over several years of experience is that programming costs for minicomputers range from 1.5 to 5 times the hardware cost while programming costs for scientific calculators normally range from $1/5$ to $1/2$ the hardware cost for equivalent operations. These cost comparisons assume an application in which a substantial amount of arithmetic manipulation of decimal numbers is involved or where a significant amount of statistical analysis is required.

Fluidyne Instrumentation also manufactures a wide range of interface and peripheral systems designed for data acquisition and data logging applications, on-line operation of scientific and medical instruments, and production counting and control devices designed for real-time statistical quality control.

Calculator System Analyzes Jet Afterburner Performance Characteristics for U.S. Air Force

When the U.S. Air Force's Air Materiel Command engineering group at Tinker Air Force Base developed a field test program for J57-55 turbojet engine afterburners, they selected a Fluidyne 7200 series data acquisition systems to make all of the individual pressure, temperature, fuel flow and engine speed calculations and provide engineering personnel with a complete printout specifying the corrected thrust of the engine/afterburner assembly.

At Air Force bases throughout the world aircraft are tethered at isolated locations and sensors are attached to the various turbine stages as well as to fuel lines. The engine is started and operated at a number of different power settings and at different air temperatures during the test. Data from the sensors, converted to digital form by a group of 13 individual instruments, is placed in the memory of the calculator when equilibrium is established. Conversion to engineering units combined with standardization of data to compensate for air temperature, air density and fuel density variations is accomplished and all of the corrected data is printed out, completely formatted with alphanumeric headings and engineering unit indications by a modified IBM "Selectric" typewriter at 15 characters per second. This hardcopy output then becomes a permanent report on the performance of the particular engine/afterburner combination and is entered in the maintenance records of the equipment.

The complete system includes two Fluidyne model 7200 universal digital interfaces with a total of 13 digital input cards installed. Data from eight Doric DS100 digital strain gauge transducer indicators and three Doric DS100 digital thermocouple indicators combined with two Atec rate counters are transferred to the data input cards.

Individual instruments were used with the digital outputs multiplexed rather than multiplexing the analog signals so that test personnel could determine that equilibrium had been established for all variables prior to initiating the entry of data into the calculator memory. Although more costly than the analog multiplexing approach, individual Doric DS100-T2 strain gauge indicators were selected for pressure transducer and thrust measurements. These instruments include a microvolt level differential digital ratiometer, digital scaling and zero balance control, including provisions for tear. They also provide a floating excitation power supply for the strain gauge bridge and incorporate a special circuit for zero drift correction. The Doric DS100-T3 digital thermocouple thermometers used for measuring fuel, air and turbine temperatures include a microvolt level analog-to-digital converter, digital linearization of the thermocouple output, 4½ digit temperature display and reference junction compensation. Depending on the specific application, all of these features can be provided by low level multiplexing systems with compensation and linearization provided by the calculator.

The 7200 universal digital interface mainframe assembly is designed specifically for sequencing and formatting digital data from instruments whose output is in binary or binary-coded-decimal form. Data from up to 8 instruments may be accommodated by a single mainframe simply by inserting the appropriate card for the type of instrument involved. In addition, reed-relay output signals for warning or control purposes are also available with optional 7200 series plug-in cards.

Systems may start with one or two plug-in cards and be expanded with additional field-installed card assemblies as requirements increase. The cards may be installed by the user and it is not necessary to return the interface assembly to the factory to increase input or output capabilities.

Like all Fluidyne 7000 series interface systems, the 7200 universal digital interface is designed with maximum utilization of integrated circuit semiconductors. In the event of a field failure, either substitute printed cards known to be good can be installed in place of those suspected of failure or individual socket-mounted circuits can be replaced.

Printout Format for Data Acquisition

One of the major advantages of the use of programmable electronic calculators for data acquisition systems is their capability of providing completely-formatted output information printed out by a wide range of techniques. The most effective technique for moderate speed applications is typified by the Wang model 701 output writer which was selected by the Air Force for this application.

Accessories and Peripheral Systems

Other peripheral systems supplied by Wang Laboratories for their 700 series programmable calculators include the 721 high speed line printer capable of operating at 150 characters per second and 70 to 200 lines per minute, depending upon line length. Maximum line length for the model 721 is 132 characters. The model 712 flatbed plotter provides conventional X-Y plotting of test results. The flatbed plotter provides alphanumeric labeling of the plots. A dual magnetic tape cassette reader/recorder is available which contains two separately-controllable magnetic tape cassette units for recording from or reading data into the main memory of 700 series calculators. Up to 150,000 program steps or approximately 20,000 12-digit storage registers plus exponent can be stored on the model 709's cassettes.

Other Fluidyne 700 Series Data Acquisition and Process Control Systems

In addition to the systems based on the 7200 universal digital interface designed for timing and formatting of digital information from individual instruments, Fluidyne manufactures a wide range of precision, low level data acquisition systems with capabilities of up to several thousand individual sensor inputs. These systems, based on the 7100 series integrating digital multimeter components are used for a wide range of applications in data acquisition, data logging, and automatic test systems. A complete range of high speed, high level analog-to-digital conversion systems with up to several hundred inputs are also available in the 7150 series.

Summary
Minicomputers in Systems vs. Advanced Programmable Calculators

The decision to use a minicomputer in a system is usually dictated by one or more of the following advantages: (1) Satisfactory computational ability; (2) Extremely high speed and control capabilities; (3) Programming versatility, and (4) Considerably lower cost than *standard* computers. But, programming complexity is a handicap in many non-dedicated minicomputer applications. Even if the system is to be a dedicated system performing the same task for the next several years, the number of different successive items to be performed in order to complete the total task may justify the use of an easily programmable and versatile processor. If the system will be used for a variety of tasks, a processor without quickly-achieved programmability rapidly becomes cumbersome and expensive.

Minicomputers are usually programmed using an assembly language which is generally unique for each mini brand. Higher level languages are now available for most minis, and low-cost extra memory is always required. The fronts of most minis usually have series of switches to provide access (in a binary addressing scheme) to various registers and memory locations for the purpose of examining or changing their contents. The development of software required for special minicomputer tasks is not necessarily a small task. Some minicomputer suppliers offer free software or make it available at small costs to make applications tasks easier. This generally consists of editor programs which facilitate the actual writing of assembly language programs and assembler programs which convert the developed assembly language programs to machine language and produce a binary tape. The editor program is important because it allows users to develop their programs in assembly language with the added ability to insert and delete characters and search out character strings within the program. Once the program has been written in assembly language, the assembler program converts it to a usable machine language program code and generates a binary tape of the program. It is this program that is actually loaded into the minicomputer's memory and executed.

To program minis in assembly language requires a programmer with skill in the assembly language programming for that particular mini, and a knowledge of the actual binary or machine language is also useful for debugging and revisions. The above procedures will probably need to be repeated. To many, assembly language programming is cumbersome and unpopular. The advantages of assembly programming are few, but important. Because it is not far removed from the actual machine code, users essentially have control of each individual bit in the minicomputer's control memory. This provides good flexibility of bit handling usually available at the I/O ports, and control versatility in system control is the result.

As noted, extra memory is required to move to the alternative to assembly language programming, i.e., programming in a higher level language such as BASIC. The programming becomes much simpler as do the revisions of existing programs. There is also a reduction in operating speed, and it is often necessary to alter the language to handle the special I/O jobs, and the modifications are usually done in assembly language. In programming the mini, most users do not spend a significant part of their time hand-loading a binary program into the mini via front panel switches. Most have a minicomputer development system to do the software. The development system is often as simple as adding a teletype and punched tape attachment to the mini. Many mini-peripherals lists are quite extensive, including: high speed printers, high speed reader/punches, and disk or tape units. These added components greatly facilitate software development. The low cost of the stand-alone mini, however, rapidly increases in price when a complete system is developed — but it's still lower by 50% to 100% from standard computer systems.

Minicomputers, despite the awkward low level language problem, have two very significant characteristics which make them big sellers. They are fast, having cycle times into the high nanosecond regions, and they possess very desirable main memory options. Often these are the deciding factors in choosing minicomputers over standard systems.

But, for number-crunching applications, a calculator-based system is a good alternative to a mini-computer, if processing speed is not a major constraint. Logic designers must overcome the urge to use minicomputers everywhere merely because they happen to be in vogue. A minicomputer system can often result in design overkill. And the software needed may cost considerably more than the logic designer is prepared to invest.

In comparison, advanced programmable calculator systems now offer many peripherals capable of special functions, including: several types and sizes of internal control or external read-write memory, printers, plotters, tape cassette input, *floppy* disk storage and alterable input keyboards, with or without alphanumerics. Several brands and models offer a lot of capability for on-the-spot programming of complex problems. They offer very fast operation internally, with direct, immediate, effortless communication between user and the calculator. Users key in problems just as they would write them in Algebra and/or English. Calculators use simple instructions and offer labeled solutions that most can readily understand through unique alphanumeric displays and printers. Add to this many extensive error detecting and correcting features and multi-purpose memory, and users quickly find that calculators take them from concept to solution faster than many other systems do.

For input, users have choices of cassettes, ROM, RAM, marked card readers, paper tape readers, or digitizers; for storage, the tape cassettes, cartridges, etc.; and for output, typtwriters, X-Y plotters, and terminals that both draw and write. Support includes virtually every discipline of science and engineering, usually with products and with significant numbers of field engineers, etc. that bring solutions to problems with them.

Power, Peripherals, Price/Performance of Advanced Calculator Systems

Thus, with advanced programmable calculators problem solving was never so cost-effective, never so convenient. Many users have the computational power they need, where they need it most — right on their desks. This provides immediate solutions to the most complex problems . . . and users don't have to be computer experts to use them. They enter their data in practically any format they choose — through the calculator keyboard or through a score of devices as noted. Precise answers come swiftly in fully-formatted text, graphs, pie charts, histograms, etc. The BASIC language capability of many units couples with the alphanumeric displays and typewriter-like keyboard to permit users to operate and program the system in a relaxed, almost conversational manner. Many of these units or systems also offer big-machine power: 2k to 4k words of user memory, very high-performance cassettes, and standard 7.5k word, built-in operating system ROM. Other plug-in ROMs and user memory modules triple that power. One or more cassettes — or mass memories with up to 4.8M words and double this, are also available. Programmable cassettes allow users to program keys to do precisely what they want them to do. Or users can add programs from scores of extensive software libraries to automatically execute the functions needed. Either way, single keystrokes command these units to swiftly perform a complete series of steps . . . to complete the most sophisticated statistics and math functions; control instruments or whole laboratories. There is no limit to calculator capability . . . save the designer's imagination.

APPENDIX

Examples of Statistical, Mathematical, Financial and Engineering Programs, Formulas, and Procedures for Problem-Solving

This appendix is a compilation of a representative group of programs and procedural computation techniques for use with programmable calculators. Readers will discover some familiarity with most of the very common formulas and applications. Some of these mathematical and statistical procedures, listed in alphabetical order, will be helpful as tools and guides of calculator users as they either write specific programs or formulate their data into entry sequences to develop solutions to problems or proceed with data analyses.

All of the programs and procedures listed are available from various calculator suppliers and were selected from many of the manuals and compilations provided by manufacturers. No attempt was made to make the listing either exclusive to a few areas or disciplines or to include a significant percentage of the increasing number of programs currently available. The selections made were based on a determination to demonstrate the total range of products and procedures available and to include many of the most popular and heaviest used mathematics, statistics, and engineering techniques. Users may make inquiries to specific manufacturers for those programs desired.

accrued interest

Payment (PMT) is calculated as:

$$\text{PMT} = \text{PV}\left(\frac{i}{[1 - (1 + i)^{-n}]}\right)$$

Accrued interest (I_j) is computed as: $I_j = (\text{Bal}_{j-2}) \times i$

Payment to principal: $\text{Prin}_j = \text{PMT} - I_j$

Interest to date: $\Sigma I = \sum_{j=1}^{n} I_j$

Remaining balance: $\text{Bal}_j = \text{Bal}_{j-1} - \text{Prin}_j$

PV, i, n should be > 0

amortization schedule — balloon payments — This program prepares an amortization schedule for a loan with balloon payment, given the amount of loan, term, interest rate and monthly payment.

analysis of variance program — The one-way analysis of variance tests the differences between the population means of k treatment groups. Group i (i = 1, 2, . . . , k) has n_i observations (treatment group may have equal or unequal number of observations).

amortization with fixed payment on principal — This program determines the payment amount, interest amount, principal remaining and interest paid to date for a fixed payment loan (student loan), given the loan amount, fixed payment principal and interest rate per period.

angle between, norm, and dot product of vectors program — Let $\vec{a} = (a_1, a_2, ..., a_n)$ and $(b_1, b_2, ..., b_n)$ be two vectors. The norm of $\vec{a}$ is noted by $|a|$ and is calculated by the following formula:

$$|\vec{a}| = \sqrt{a_1^2 + a_2^2 + ... + a_n^2}$$

similarly,

$$|\vec{b}| = \sqrt{b_1^2 + b_2^2 + ... + b_n^2}$$

The dot product of $\vec{a}$ and $\vec{b}$ is denoted by $a \cdot b$ is calculated by the following formula:

$$\vec{a} \cdot \vec{b} = a_1 b_1 + a_2 b_2 + ... + a_n b_n$$

The angle between a and b is denoted by θ and calculated by the following formula:

$$\theta = \cos^{-1}\left(\frac{\vec{a} \cdot \vec{b}}{|\vec{a}| \cdot |\vec{b}|}\right)$$

area by double meridian distance program This program computes the area of a straight sided closed figure from the bearings and length of its sides. It is generally more accurate th methods which calculate area from the coordinates of the figure.

$$Area = \frac{1}{2} \sum_i DMD_i \times Latitude_i$$

$$DMD_i = DMD_{i-1} + Departure_{i-1} + Departure_i$$

where

$$Departure_i = Dist_i \sin Az_i$$
$$Latitude_i = Dist_i \cos Az_i$$

Note: Angles are input as bearing and quadrant code. The quadrant code is 1 for NE, 2 for SE, 3 for SW, and 4 for NW.

area of a triangle a, b, C program — Given two sides and an included angle of a triangle this program computes the area by the following formula:

$$Area = \frac{1}{2} ab \sin C$$

The angle C can be in any angular mode but if in degrees it is assumed to be in decimal degrees.

auto dealer contract calculations using add-on rate — This program calculates the monthly payment and insurance premium for each of five insurance options for an automobile dealer contract including APR, given the price of the car, trade-in allowance, amount owed on the trade, cash down, additional charges, add-on rate, contract term and odd days. When an option is selected, full contract details print.

auto dealer lease — This program calculates the monthly and total leasing fee, the termination value, total and monthly depreciation, sales tax, total monthly payment, security deposit and total cash required at time of lease, given the number of months, price, leasing charge, book price at termination, safety factor and license fee.

Bartlett's chi-square statistic program —

$$\chi^2 = \frac{f \ln s^2 - \sum\limits_{i=1}^{k} f_i \ln s_i^2}{1 + \dfrac{1}{3(k-1)} \left[\left(\sum\limits_{i=1}^{k} \dfrac{1}{f_i} \right) - \dfrac{1}{f} \right]}$$

where s_i^2 = sample variance of the ith sample
f_i = degrees of freedom associated with s_i^2
$i = 1, 2, ..., k$
k = number of samples

$$s^2 = \frac{\sum\limits_{i=1}^{k} f_i s_i^2}{f}$$

$$f = \sum\limits_{i=1}^{k} f_i.$$

This χ^2 has a chi-square distribution (approximately) with $k - 1$ degrees of freedom, which can be used to test the null hypothesis that s_1^2, s_2^2, ..., s_k^2 are all estimates of the same population variance σ^2 (H_0: Each of $s_1^2, s_2^2, ..., s_k^2$ is an estimate of σ^2).

base conversions — This program converts real positive numbers of any base r ($2 \leq r \leq 99$) to base 10 (decimal) or decimal to base r.

For numbers with bases greater than 10, two display digits will be used to represent each digit of the base r number. For example, $A1C_{16}$ is represented as 100112 by the display where A = 10, 1 = 01, and C = 12. Leading zeros are not displayed as $3B7_{16}$ appears as 31107 in the display. When an exponent appears for a base r > 10 number, any resulting exponent is in base 10 and only serves to locate the decimal point. To get a true value of the exponent, insure that the exponent is even by shifting the decimal point of the mantissa (if necessary) then divide the exponent by 2. The number $1.005 - 05_{16}$ is interpreted as $A.5 \times 16^{-3}$ or $.A5 \times 16^{-2}$.
Round off errors may result in numbers similar to 3.99999 decimal. For example, the number 118.222222_{23} should be interpreted as 119_{23}.

Behrens-Fisher statistic program — Suppose $\{x_1, x_2, ..., x_{n_1}\}$ and $\{y_1, y_2, ..., y_{n_2}\}$ are independent random samples from two normal populations with means μ_1, μ_2 (unknown). If the variances σ_1^2, σ_2^2 can not be assumed equal, then the Behrens-Fisher statistic

$$d = \frac{\bar{x} - \bar{y} - D}{\sqrt{\dfrac{s_1^2}{n_1} + \dfrac{s_2^2}{n_2}}}$$

is used instead of the t statistic to test the null hypothesis

$$H_0 : \mu_1 - \mu_2 = D$$

Critical values of this test are tabulated in the Fisher-Yates Tables for various values of n_1, n_2, α and θ, where α is the level of significance and

$$\theta = \tan^{-1} \left(\frac{s_1}{s_2} \sqrt{\frac{n_2}{n_1}} \right).$$

Notation:

$$x = \frac{\sum x_i}{n_1} \qquad s_1^2 = \frac{\sum x_i^2 - [(\sum x_i)^2 / n_1]}{n_1 - 1}$$

$$\bar{y} = \frac{\sum y_i}{n_2} \qquad s_2^2 = \frac{\sum y_i^2 - [(\sum y_i)^2 / n_2]}{n_2 - 1}$$

billing/invoicing — This program calculates an invoice allowing line discounting and back ordering. The net total, total tax, total tax plus freight, total profit, percent of net profit, total value of back ordered items, percent of item amount back ordered, total discount amount, total gross amount, percent of gross discounted and total cost amount will print.

binomial distribution program — This program evaluates the binomial density function for given p and n:

$$f(x) = \binom{n}{x} p^x (1 - p)^{n-x}$$

where n is a positive integer
$0 < p < 1$ and
$x = 0, 1, 2, ..., n.$

The recursive relation

$$f(x + 1) = \frac{p(n - x)}{(x + 1)(1 - p)} f(x)$$

$$(x = 0, 1, 2, ..., n - 1)$$

is used to find the cumulative distribution

$$P(x) = \sum_{k=0}^{x} f(k).$$

Notes:
1. $f(0) = P(0)$
2. When x is large, due to round-off error, the computed value for P(x) might be slightly greater than one. In that case, let $P(x) = 1$.
3. The execution time of the program depends on x; the larger x is, the longer it takes.
4. The mean m and the variance σ^2 are given by

$$m = np$$
$$\sigma^2 = np\ (1 - p).$$

biserial correlation coefficient program — The biserial correlation coefficient r_b is used where one variable Y is quantitatively measured while the other continuous variable X is artificially dichotomized (that is, artificially defined by two groups). It measures the degree of linear association between X and Y.

$$r_b = \frac{n\,(\Sigma'\,y_i) - n_1\,\Sigma y_i}{na\,\sqrt{n\,\Sigma y_i^2 - (\Sigma y_i)^2}}$$

Suppose X takes the value 0 or 1.

Define n^1 = number of x's such that x = 1
  n = total number of data points
  $\Sigma'y_i$ = sum of the y's for which x = 1
  Σy_i = sum of all y's
  a = ordinate of the standard normal curve at point z cutting off a tail of that distribution with area equal to

$$p = \frac{n_1}{n}.$$

Note:
Among the necessary assumptions for a meaningful interpretation of r_b are:
1. Y is normally distributed
2. The true distribution of X should be of normal form.

bivariate normal distribution program — This program evaluates the joint probability density function

$$f(x, y) = \frac{1}{2\pi\,\sigma_1\,\sigma_2\sqrt{1 - \rho^2}}\,e^{-P(x,y)}$$

where

$$P(x, y) = \frac{1}{2(1 - \rho^2)}$$

$$\left[\frac{(x - \mu_1)^2}{\sigma_1^2} - 2\rho\,\frac{(x - \mu_1)(y - \mu_2)}{\sigma_1\sigma_2} + \frac{(y - \mu_2)^2}{\sigma_2^2}\right]$$

Notes:
1. $\sigma_1 \neq 0, \sigma_2 \neq 0$
2. The program requires that $\rho^2 < 1$.

bond payments — interest and levy — This program calculates the interest due, given the principal, interest rate, levy and number of payments. It also allows for one odd levy amount at a first irregular payment date.

bond present value — This program calculates the present value (cost) of a bond with annual coupons using the following formula.

$$PV = I \sum_{j=1}^{N} (1 + YLD)^{-j} + MV\,(1 + YLD)^{-N}$$

where:
MV = Maturity Value
N = Number of years to maturity, j = 1,2 … N
I = Coupon Value
YLD = Bond Yield to maturity (in annual percent)
PV = Bond Present Value or cost

NOTES:
- PV is rounded and displayed to the nearest penny
- MV, I and YLD must be greater than zero
- N must be a positive integer

bond yield — An iterative method based on the following formula is used to determine the bond yield of an annual coupon bond.

$$PV = I \sum_{j=1}^{N} (1 + YLD)^{-j} + MV\,(1 + YLD)^{-N}$$

where:
PV = Present Value (bond cost)
I = Coupon Value
N = Number of years to maturity
MV = Maturity Value
YLD = Bond Yield (annual percent)

NOTES:
- Yield is displayed to four decimal places
- N must be a positive integer
- MV, PV and I must be positive
- MV must be greater than PV
- Yield range of this program is 0 to 25%. If larger yield is expected, change program location 4 to a smaller number as (.8 = 1/(1 + .25 for 25%).
- Execution time depends on N(for N = 20, time is several minutes)

calendar routines day of the week days between two dates program — This program calls March 1, 1700, day 1 and gives every succeeding day a corresponding number. The program works for days to and including February 28, 2100. However, for days from March 1, 1700, to February 28, 1800, 2 days must be added to the answer and for days from March 1, 1800, to February 18, 1900, day must be added.

Let M = month, D = day, Y = year, W = day of the week (0 = Sunday, 1 = Monday, etc.)

The day's number is calculated from the following formula:

$$N(M, D, Y) = [365.25\ g(y,m)] + [30.6\ f(m)] + D - 62104$$

where

$$g(y, m) = \begin{cases} y - 1 & \text{if } m = 1 \text{ or } 2 \\ y & \text{if } m > 2 \end{cases}$$

$$\text{and } f(m) = \begin{cases} m + 13 & \text{if } m = 1 \text{ or } 2 \\ m + 1 & \text{if } m > 2 \end{cases}$$

[m] represents the integer part of a number, i.e., n = 7.2 then [7.2] = 7. This must be put in by user

**California payroll, part 1, 1974, 1975, 1976 –
California payroll, part 2, 1974, 1975, 1975 –**
Part 1 of this program creates a magnetic card for

each employee containing the hourly rate, exemptions, deductions, tax constants and year-to-date totals. Part 2 performs the payroll calculations. Year-to-date totals are automatically updated on the employee card. This program can be modified to comply with the tax system of any state.

certificate of deposit — negotiable — This program calculates the number of days between the settlement and issue dates, dollar price, principal, accrued interest and total for negotiable certificates of deposit, given the settlement date, issue date, maturity date, coupon rate, yield and number of bonds.

chi-square distribution program — Given x, ν and f(x), this program uses a series approximation to evaluate the chi-square cumulative distribution

$$P(x) = \int_0^x f(t)\, dt$$

$$= \frac{2x}{\nu} f(x) \left[1 + \sum_{k=1}^{\infty} \frac{x^k}{(\nu + 2)(\nu + 4)\ldots(\nu + 2k)} \right]$$

where $x \geq 0$
    ν is the degrees of freedom, and density function

$$f(x) = \frac{x^{\frac{\nu}{2} - 1}}{2^{\frac{\nu}{2}} \Gamma\left(\frac{\nu}{2}\right) e^{\frac{x}{2}}}$$

The program computes successive partial sums of the series. When two consecutive partial sums are equal, the value is used as the sum of the series. Note: f(x) may be computed using Chi-square Density Function program.

chi-square evaluation program — This program calculates the value of the χ^2 statistic for the goodness of fit test by the equation

$$\chi^2 = \sum_{i=1}^{n} \frac{(O_i - E_i)^2}{E_i}$$

where O_i = observed frequency
    E_i = expected frequency.

The χ^2 statistic measures the closeness of the agreement between the observed frequencies and expected frequencies.

Notes:
1. In order to apply this test to a set of given data, it may be necessary to combine some classes to make sure that each expected frequency is not too small (say, not less than 5).
2. If the expected frequencies E_i are all equal to some value E, then E should be computed beforehand as

$$E = \frac{\Sigma O_i}{n}$$

and then input at each step as the expected frequency E_i.

circle determined by three points program — Let (x_1, y_1) (x_2, y_2) (x_3, y_3) be three points such that $x_1 \neq x_2$ and $x_1 \neq x_3$. If the points cannot be renumbered to satisfy this condition, the points cannot be

on a circle. Let the counter of the circle be (x_0, y_0) and the radius of the circle be r. Then

$$y_0 = \frac{k_2 - k_1}{n_2 - n_1}, \quad x_0 = k_2 - n_2 y_0,$$

and $r = \sqrt{(x_1 - x_0)^2 + (y_1 - y_0)^2}$

where

$$k_1 = \frac{1}{2}\left[(x_1 + x_2) + n_1 (y_1 + y_2)\right],$$

$$k_2 = \frac{1}{2}\left[(x_1 + x_3) + n_2 (y_1 + y_3)\right]$$

$$n_1 = \frac{y_1 - y_2}{x_1 - x_2}, \quad \text{and } n_2 = \frac{y_1 - y_3}{x_1 - x_3}$$

If $n_1 = n_2$ the points cannot form a circle.

circle, triangle and offsets from coordinates — This program calculates, given three points, (1) the center and radius of a circle (defined by these points) and the coordinate points equally spaced on the circle; (2) the lengths of the sides, the angles and the area of a triangle (defined by these points); and (3) the point of intersection of the offset perpendicular and the base and the distances from the intersection point to the three given points. The program utilizes the user-definable keys.

circular curve data — This program calculates sector area, triangle area and segment area, given the radius of a circle and any one of the following: central angle, arc length, chord length, tangent length or offset distance. The program automatically computes the other three data values not entered. The program utilizes the user-definable keys.

coefficient of correlation — The coefficient of correlation is widely used as a measure for the spread of a set of points about the line of regression. In turn, this will determine whether or not a linear relationship exists between two variables. If the points cluster about the line of regression, they indicate a linear relationship. If they are, however, widely scattered, the linear relationship is in doubt.

coefficient of determination, calculator use — To establish how well the data fits the linear regression, users may want to calculate the coefficient of determination (r^2). The coefficient of determination is a value between 0 and 1. At r = 0, there is no fit. At $r^2 = 1$, users have a perfect fit. The traditional equation for r^2 is:

$$r^2 = \frac{[\Sigma(x - \bar{x})(y - \bar{y})]^2}{[\Sigma(x - x^2][\Sigma(y - y)^2]}$$

On some units, however, the most efficient way to calculate r^2 is to use this equivalent equation:

$$r^2 = \frac{n\Sigma xy - \Sigma x \Sigma y}{n(n - 1)\, s_x\, s_y}$$

combination program — A combination is a selection of one or more of a set of distinct objects without regard to order. The number of possible combinations, each containing n objects, that can be formed from a collection of m distinct objects is given by

$$_mC_n = \frac{m!}{(m - n)!\, n!} = \frac{m(m - 1) \ldots (m - n + 1)}{1 \cdot 2 \cdot \ldots \cdot n}$$

where m, n are integers and $0 \leq n \leq m$.
This program computes $_mC_n$ using the following algorithm:
1. If $n \leq m - n$

$$_mC_n = \frac{m - n + 1}{1} \cdot \frac{m - n + 2}{2} \cdot \ ... \ \cdot \frac{m}{n}.$$

2. If $n > m - n$, program computes $_mC_{m-n}$.

Notes:
1. $_mC_n$, which is also called the binomial coefficient, can be denoted by C_m^n, $C(m,n)$, or $\binom{m}{n}$.
2. $_mC_n = {_mC_{m-n}}$
3. $_mC_0 = {_mC_m} = 1$
4. $_mC_1 = {_mC_{m-n}} = m$

complex arithmetic — Given two complex numbers in the form $a + bi$ and $c + di$, this program, with a, b, c, and d as inputs, calculates the following:

$$(a + bi) + (c + di) = a_1 + b_1 i$$
$$(a + bi) - (c + di) = a_2 + b_2 i$$
$$(a + bi)(c + di) = a_3 + b_3 i$$
$$(a + bi) \div (c + di) = a_4 + b_4 i$$

Where: $a_1 = a + c$
$a_2 = a - c$
$a_3 = ac - bd$
$a_4 = (ac + bd)/(c^2 + d^2)$
$b_1 = b + d$
$b_2 = b - d$
$b_3 = ad + bc$
$b_4 = (bc - ad)/(c^2 + d^2)$

compound amount program — This program applies to an amount of principal that has been placed into an account and compounded periodically, with no further deposits. The important variables in this case are the number of compounding periods n, the periodic interest rate i, the principal or present value PV, the future value of the account FV, and the amount of interest accrued I. Any of these may be calculated from the others by these formulas:

$$n = \frac{\ln (FV/PV)}{\ln (1 + i)} \qquad i = \left(\frac{FV}{PV}\right)^{1/n} - 1$$

$$PV = FV(1 + i)^{-n}$$

$$FV = PV(1 + i)^n \qquad I = PV[(1 + i)^n - 1]$$

compound interest — Knowing any three of the following variables in a compound interest situation,

Future Value, FV
Present Value, PV
Interest Rate per Period (%), i
Number of Periods, n

this program computes the remaining value.

$$FV = PV(1 + i)^n \qquad n = \frac{\log FV/PV}{\log (1 + i)}$$

$$PV = \frac{FV}{(1 + i)^n} \qquad i = 100\left[\left(\frac{FV}{PV}\right)^{1/n} - 1\right]$$

conversions (1) — This program provides length conversions by pressing the user defined keys as follows:

A inches to centimeters (2.54)
B feet to meters (.3048)
C yards to meters (.9144)
D miles to kilometers (1.609344)
E miles to nautical miles (.86897624)

Inverses of these conversions are obtained with t. second function of the above user defined key Area and volume conversions may be obtained pressing the conversion key twice or three tim respectively.
conversions (2) — This program provides volum weight, and temperature conversions by pressi the user defined keys as follows:

A °F to °C (Fahrenheit to Celsius)

$$C = \frac{5}{9}(F - 3$$

B fluid ounces to liters (.0295735296)
C gallons to liters (3.785411784)
D ounces to grams (28.34952313)
E pounds to kilograms (.45359237)

Inverses of these conversions are obtained with t. second function of the above user defined keys.
cosine integral program — The cosine integr is denoted by Ci (x) and is defined as follows:

$$Ci(x) = \gamma + \ln x + \int_0^x \frac{\cos t - 1}{t} dt$$

where $x > 0$, and $\gamma = 0.5772156649$ is Eule constant.
Also, a Taylor series expansions yields

$$Ci(x) = \gamma + \ln x + \sum_{n=1}^{\infty} \frac{(-1)^n x^{2n}}{2n(2n)!}$$

This program computes successive partial sums the series. When two consecutive partial sums a equal, the value is used as the sum of the seri
covariance and correlation coefficient pr gram — For a set of given data points $\{(x_i, y$ $i = 1, 2, ..., n\}$, the covariance and the correlati coefficients are defined as:

$$\text{covariance } s_{xy} = \frac{1}{n-1}\left(\Sigma x_i y_i - \frac{1}{n}\Sigma x_i \Sigma y_i\right)$$

$$\text{or } s_{xy}' = \frac{1}{n}\left(\Sigma x_i y_i - \frac{1}{n}\Sigma x_i \Sigma y_i\right)$$

$$\text{correlation coefficient } r = \frac{s_{xy}}{s_x s_y}$$

where s_x and s_y are standard deviations

$$s_x = \sqrt{\frac{\Sigma x_i^2 - (\Sigma x_i)^2/n}{n-1}}$$

$$s_y = \sqrt{\frac{\Sigma y_i^2 - (\Sigma y_i)^2/n}{n-1}}$$

Note:
$-1 \leq r \leq 1$
credit union — This program completely scribes a loan taken through a credit union th consists of equal payment at equal intervals. allows for the input of either the number of pa ments or an estimate of the payment amou Credit disability rates may be modified to fit t rates of any locale.
curve fitting-linear regression program When investigating the relationship between t variables in the real world, it is a reasonable fi step to make experimental observations of the sy tem to gather paired values of the variables, (x, The investigator might then ask the questic What mathematical formula best describes the

ationship between the variables x and y? His first guess will often be that the relationship is linear, i.e., that the form of the equation is $y = a_1 x + a_0$, where a_1 and a_0 are constants. The purpose of this program is to find the constants a_1 and a_0, which give the closest agreement between the experimental data and the equation $y = a_1 x + a_0$. The technique used in linear regression by the method of least squares.

The user must input the paired values of data he has gathered, (x_i, y_i), $i = 1, ..., n$. When all data pairs have been input, the regression constants a_1 and a_0 may be calculated. A third value may also be found, the coefficient of determination, r^2. The value of r^2 will lie between 0 and 1 and will indicate how closely the equation fits the experimental data: the closer r^2 is to 1, the better the fit. (See appropriate manuals for formulas)

curve, Gaussian (random-error concept) — A "random error of sampling" is a variation due to chance alone. If the sample is truly random, small errors will be more numerous than large errors and positive errors will be as likely as negative errors, thus giving rise to symmetrical, bell-shaped "normal curve of error." The concept was first investigated by the German mathematician, Karl F. Gauss, and the curve is often called the Gaussian curve.

cut and fill — This program calculates the cut and fill volumes given the cross sections (the existing and new profiles) of the volumes to be measured. A maximum of eighteen points per profile may be entered. The cumulative volumes are also calculated. The program utilizes the user-definable keys.

depreciation schedules straight line program —

Let PV = original value of asset (less salvage value)
  n = lifetime number of periods of asset
  B_k = book value at time period K
  D = each year's depreciation
  k = number of time period, i.e., 1, 2, 3, ..., or n

Then, B_k and D can be calculated by the following formulas:

1. $D = PV/n$
2. $B_k = PV - kD$

depreciation schedules sum-of-the-year's digits program —

Let n = life time number of periods of asset
  S = salvage value
  D_k = depreciation over time period k
  B_k = book value at time period k
  PV = original value of asset (less salvage value)
  k = number of time period, i.e., 1, 2, 3, ..., or n

Then, D_k and B_k can be calculated by the following formulas:

1. $D_k = \dfrac{2(n - k + 1)}{n(n + 1)} PV$
2. $B_k = S + \dfrac{(n - k) D_k}{2}$

depreciation schedule using any of four methods — This program computes the periodic depreciation charge by four methods, given the original cost, the scrap value and life of the asset. Methods: Straight Line, Declining Balance, Declining Balance with cross-over to Straight Line and Sum-of-the-Years-Digits.

depreciation schedules variable rate declining balance program —

Let PV = original value of asset (less salvage value)
  n = lifetime periods of asset
  R = depreciation rate (given by user)
  D_k = depreciation at time period k
  B_k = book value at time period k
  k = number of time period, i.e., 1, 2, 3, ..., or n

Then, D_k and B_k can be calculated by the following formulas:

1. $D_k = PV \dfrac{R}{n} \left(1 - \dfrac{R}{n}\right)^{k-1}$
2. $B_k = PV \left(1 - \dfrac{R}{n}\right)^{k}$

If R = 2 the program gives the double declining balance method. If R = 1.5 the program gives the 150% declining balance method.

determinant and inverse of a 2×2 matrix program —

Let $A = \begin{bmatrix} a_{11} & a_{12} \\ a_{21} & a_{22} \end{bmatrix}$ be a 2×2 matrix.

The determinant of A denoted by Det A or $|A|$ is evaluated by the following formula:

$$\text{Det A} = a_{22} a_{11} - a_{12} a_{21}$$

Also, the program evaluates the multiplicative inverse A^{-1} of A. The following formula is used:

$$A^{-1} = \begin{bmatrix} a_{22}/\text{Det A} & -a_{12}/\text{Det A} \\ -a_{21}/\text{Det A} & a_{11}/\text{Det A} \end{bmatrix}$$

determinant of a 3×3 matrix program —

Let $A = \begin{bmatrix} a_{11} & a_{12} & a_{13} \\ a_{21} & a_{22} & a_{23} \\ a_{31} & a_{32} & a_{33} \end{bmatrix}$ be a 3×3 matrix.

The determinant of A denoted by $|A|$ or Det A, is calculated by expanding A by minors about the first column. The formula is:

$$\text{Det A} = a_{11} \begin{vmatrix} a_{22} & a_{23} \\ a_{32} & a_{33} \end{vmatrix} - a_{21} \begin{vmatrix} a_{12} & a_{13} \\ a_{32} & a_{33} \end{vmatrix} + a_{31} \begin{vmatrix} a_{12} & a_{13} \\ a_{22} & a_{23} \end{vmatrix}$$
$$= a_{11} [a_{22} a_{33} - a_{23} a_{32}] - a_{21} [a_{33} a_{12} - a_{32} a_{13}] + a_{31} [a_{23} a_{12} - a_{13} a_{22}]$$

difference of two sample means programs — (1) Significance Test on Difference of Means. This program computes significance level on difference of Means of two samples with equal and known variance. (2) t-Statistic Test on Equality of Two Means with Unequal Variances. This program calculates the t-Statistic given two independent samples, each with random independent elements from normal populations, with unequal variances. An approximate number of degrees of freedom is also calculated. (3) t-Statistic for Independent Samples. This program calculates the t Statistic for testing the difference between two independent sample Means. It is assumed that both samples are drawn from populations having the same variance. The Means, Standard Deviations, and number of degrees of freedom are also calculated.

differences among proportions program — Suppose $x_1, x_2, ..., x_k$ are observed values of a set of independent random variables having binomial distributions with parameters n_i and θ_i ($i = 1, 2, ..., k$). A chi-square statistic given by

$$\chi^2 = \sum_{i=1}^{k} \frac{(x_i - n_i \hat{\theta})^2}{n_i \hat{\theta} (1 \hat{\theta})}$$

can be used to test the null hypothesis $\theta_1 = \theta_2 = .. = \theta_k$, where

$$\theta = \sum_{i=1}^{k} x_i \bigg/ \sum_{i=1}^{k} n_i .$$

This θ^2 has the chi-square distribution with $k - 1$ degrees of freedom.

differential — Either of a pair of symbols dy, dx associated with the functional relationship $y = f(x)$ in such a way that $dy/dx = f'(x)$ or $dy = f'(x)dx$. Therefore, it appears that when dy/dx is used as the notation for a derivative it may be treated as a fraction. While this gives consistent results in some circumstances, it is in general not true.

differential equation — Refers to an equation containing derivatives or differentials of an unknown function, i.e., the solution satisfies the equation identically throughout some interval of x. The general solution represents the set of functions that satisfy the equation. Related to physical problems, the arbitrary constants are determined from additional conditions which must be satisfied. Most differential equations result from mathematical relations and descriptions of motion and change.

differential equation — An equation which contains derivatives of differentials of an unknown function, i.e., the solution satisfies the equation identically throughout some interval of x. The general solution represents the set of functions that satisfy the equation. Related to physical problems, the arbitrary constants are determined from additional conditions which must be satisfied. Most differential equations result from mathematical relations and descriptions of motion and change.

differential equation, partial — Refers to differential equation which contains more than one independent variable and/or derivatives or differentials of more than one independent variable.

differential equations, first order — This program solves a number of differential equations of the form:

$$y' = f(x, y) \text{ with initial condition } x_0, y_0.$$

A numerical, third-order Runge-Kutta approximation is used.

$$y_{n+1} = y_n + (1/6)k_1 + (2/3)k_2 + (1/6)k_3$$
for $x_n = x_0 + nh_1$, $n = 1, 2, 3 ...$

where: h = an increment specified by the user.
$k_1 = hf(x_n, y_n)$
$k_2 = hf[x_n + (1/2)h, y_n + (1/2)k]$
$k_3 = hf(x_n + h, y_n - k_1 + 2k_2)$

NOTES:
- $f(x, y)$ is defined by a series of keystrokes as suming y is in R_8 and x is in R_9
- There are 30 program locations and 4 memory registers available for $f(x, y)$ input which is keyed into program memory
- $f(x, y)$ must be defined for all $n = 0, 1, 2, 3, ..$
- $h \geqslant 0$.

direct reduction loan accumulated interest remaining balance program — This program finds the accumulated interest and remaining balance of a mortgage.

Let I_{c-k} = the accumulated interest paid by payments c through k
PV_k = the remaining balance after payment k
n = number of payments
i = periodic interest rate expressed as a decimal, e.g., 6% is expressed as .06
j = c - 1

Then, I_{c-k} and PV_k can be calculated by the following formulas:

1. $I_{c-k} = PMT\left[k - j - \dfrac{(1 + i)^{k-n}}{i}(1 - (+ i)^{j-k})\right]$

2. $PV_k = \dfrac{PMT}{i}[1 - (1 + i)^{k-n}]$

direct reduction loan payment, present value number of time periods program — Calculate payment, present value, and number of time periods of a mortgage given two of the three and the interest rate.

Let n = number of payment periods
PV = present value or principal
PMT = payment
i = periodic interest rate expressed as a decimal, e.g., 6% is represented as .06.

Then, PMT, PV, and n can be calculated from the other three by the following formulas:

1. $PMT = PV \dfrac{i}{1 - (1 + i)_-^n}$

2. $PV = PMT \dfrac{1 - (1 + i)^{-n}}{i}$

3. $n = - \dfrac{\ln(1 - iPV/PMT)}{\ln(1 + i)}$

discontinued cash flow analysis program –
Let PV_0 = original investment
PV_k = cash flow of kth period
i = discount rate per period as a decimal e.g., 6% is expressed as .06
C_k = net present value as period k

Then

$$C_k = -PV_0 + \sum_{k=1}^{n} \frac{PV_k}{(1 + i)^k}$$

discounted cash flow net present value, internal rate of return program — The primary purpose of this program is to compute the net present value of a series of cash flows. In general, an initial investment V_0 is made in some enterprise which is expected to bring in periodic cash flows $C_1, C_2, .. C_n$. Given a discount rate i, which must be entered as a decimal, then for each cash flow C_k, the program will compute the net present value at period k, NPV_k. A negative value for NPV_k indicates that the enterprise has not yet been profitable. A positive NPV_k means that the enterprise has been profitable, to the extent that a rate of return i on the original investment has been exceeded.

The program may also be used iteratively to calculate an internal rate of return. The objective here is to find the discount rate i which will make the final net present value, NPV_n, equal to zero. The procedure, then, is to store V_0 and a first guess at the rate of return i, input the cash flows C_1 through C_n, and thus find NPV_n. If NPV_n is negative, the estimated rate of return was too high; if NPV_n is positive, the estimate for i was too low. Adjust the estimate for i accordingly, store the new i, and input the cash flows again. Inspect the new value of NPV_n to obtain a new estimate for i and repeat the process. The entire procedure is repeated until NPV_n is zero, or very close to it. The last value of i input is then regarded as the internal rate of return.

Each figure for net present value is found by

$$NPV_k = -V_0 + \sum_{j=1}^{k} \frac{C_j}{(1+i)^j}$$

ellipses of concentration — This program calculates, for entered values of X and Y, the values W (the ellipses of concentration), f (X, Y) (the density of a bivariate normal distribution) and P (the chi-square distribution with 2 degrees of freedom).

equally spaced points on a circle program — Given a circle with center (x_0, y_0) and radius r, this program calculates the coordinates of equally spaced points on the circle. The user inputs the coordinates of the center, the radius, the number of points n to be spaced on the circle, and an angle θ (measured from the positive x-axis) which describes the position of the first point on the circle.

The formulas used are:

$$x_{k+1} = x_o + r \cos(\theta + ck)$$
$$y_{k+1} = y_0 + r \sin(\theta + ck)$$

where

$$k = 0, 1, 2, \ldots, n - 1$$

and

$$c = \frac{4 \sin^{-1} 1}{n} = \frac{2\pi \text{ radians}}{n} = \frac{360°}{n} = \frac{400 \text{ grads}}{n}$$

The program works in any angular mode but if in degrees decimal degrees are assumed.

error function and complementary error function program

$$\text{Error function erf } x = \frac{2}{\sqrt{\pi}} \int_0^x e^{-t^2} dt$$

$$= \frac{2}{\sqrt{\pi}} e^{+h} \sum_{n=0}^{\infty} \frac{2^n}{1 \cdot 3 \cdot \ldots \cdot (2n+1)} x^{2n+1}$$

Complementary error function

$$\text{erfc } x = 1 - \text{erf } x$$

where $x > 0$.

This program computes successive partial sums of the series. The program stops when two consecutive partial sums are equal and displays the last partial sum as the answer.

Notes: 1. When x is too large, computing a new term of the series might cause an overflow. In that case, display shows all 9's and the program stops.
2. The execution time of the program depends on x; the larger x is, the longer it takes.

exponential curve regression program — Least Squares Fit, Exponential Curve. This program uses the least squares fit method to fit N pairs of (X, Y) data points to the exponential function $Y = AE^{bx}$. Y must be greater than zero.

exponential equation — A name given to an equation in which the unknown quantity enters as an exponent; thus $A^x = b$ is an exponential equation. Every exponential equation of the simple form $a^x = b$, may be solved.

exponential integral program — The exponential integral is denoted by Ei (x) and is defined as follows:

$$\text{Ei}(x) = \int_{\infty}^{x} \frac{e^t}{t} dt$$

where $x > 0$.

Using a Taylor's series expansion and letting $\gamma = 0.5772156649$ be Euler's constant:

$$\text{Ei}(x) = \gamma + \ln x + \sum_{n=1}^{\infty} \frac{x^n}{n(n!)}$$

This program computes successive partial sums of the series. When two consecutive partial sums are equal, the value is used as the sum of the series.

exponential probability program — Refers to an Exponential Distribution. This program calculates the probability distribution of a random variable with exponential distribution function.

factorial — Let n be a positive integer. The notation n! is read as "n factorial," and represents the product of all positive integers from 1 to n, that is n! = 1, 2, 3, ... n. Thus 4 factorial or 4! = 4 × 3 × 2 × 1 = 24. Factorial notation is used most importantly in combination, permutation, and other counting techniques.

factorial function key — Factorial function allows rapid calculations of combinations and permutations ... to reduce problem-solving time to seconds. Calculators can quickly find the factorial of positive integers.

factorial operator — An operator which applies to a number in a specific way, i.e., if n is the number being considered, then n factorial (written n!) is equal to n × (n − 1) × (n − 2) ... 1, it being understood by convention that 0! = 1.

factorial program — This program will compute factorials for positive integers between 2 and 69.

$$n! = n (n - 1) (n - 2) \ldots (2) (1)$$

Notes:
1. For large values of n, the program will take some time to arrive at a result, up to a maximum of about 20 seconds for n = 69.
2. The program does not check input values and will return incorrect answers for values of n < 2 or n > 69 or n non-integer.

factorial sign — The sign ! is placed after a number to indicate that it is a factorial.

factoring — The process of separating a quantity into its factors, e.g., to separate a monomial into its factors: the prime factor of $24x^2y^3z$ are $2 \cdot 2 \cdot 2 \cdot 3 \cdot x \cdot x \cdot y \cdot y \cdot y \cdot z$.

faction defective chart program — Computes the sample statistics, P Sub 1, Control Limits and other summary statistics needed for P charts. Considerable flexibility is provided by three main options and two sub-options. The main options permit a constant sample size, a variable sample size with common control limits based on the average of N, and A variable sample size with the associated variable control limits. The sub-options permit use of the average of P or P's for control limit computations as well as error correction and/or removal of unwanted data for computation of revised estimates of P and control limits.

F distribution program — This program evaluates the integral of the F distribution

$$Q(x) = \int_x^\infty \frac{\Gamma\left(\frac{\nu_1 + \nu_2}{2}\right) \, y^{\frac{\nu_1}{2} - 1} \left(\frac{\nu_1}{\nu_2}\right)^{\frac{\nu_1}{2}}}{\Gamma\left(\frac{\nu_1}{2}\right) \, \Gamma\left(\frac{\nu_2}{2}\right) \left(1 + \frac{\nu_1}{\nu_2} y\right)^{\frac{\nu_1 + \nu_2}{2}}} \, dy$$

for given values of x (> 0), degrees of freedoms ν_1, ν_2, provided either ν_1 or ν_2 is even. The integral is evaluated by means of the following series:

1. ν_1 even

$$Q(x) = t^{\frac{\nu_2}{2}} \left[1 + \frac{\nu_2}{2}(1 - t) + \dots \right.$$

$$\left. + \frac{\nu_2(\nu_2 + 2) \dots (\nu_2 + \nu_1 - 4)}{2 \cdot 4 \dots (\nu_1 - 2)} (1 - t)^{\frac{\nu_1 - 2}{2}} \right]$$

2. ν_2 even

$$Q(x) = 1 - (1 - t)^{\frac{\nu_1}{2}} \left[1 + \frac{\nu_1}{2}t + \dots \right.$$

$$\left. + \frac{\nu_1(\nu_1 + 2) \dots (\nu_2 + \nu_1 - 4)}{2 \cdot 4 \dots (\nu_2 - 2)} t^{\frac{\nu_2 - 2}{2}} \right]$$

where $t = \dfrac{\nu_2}{\nu_2 + \nu_1 x}$.

Note:
If both ν_1, ν_2 are even, the two formulas would generate identical answers. Using the smaller of ν_1, ν_2 could save computation time. For example, if $\nu_1 = 10$, $\nu_2 = 20$, then classify the problem as ν_1 is even to obtain the answer.

functions library (elementary) — A typical offering of many manufacturers is a set of subroutines to perform the most common mathematical functions using floating point number format. Some are: Square Root; Exponentiation; Hyperbolic Tangent; Arctangent; Sine; Cosine; Natural Logarithm; Common Logarithm; Base 2 Logarithm; etc.

functions of x and y program — Can be used to find: (1) y raised to the x power for any real y and x (if y is negative, x must be an integer); (2) logarithms of y to base x; (3) y (mod x) = y − x (integer part of [y/x]); (4) permutations of y things taken x at a time; (5) combinations of y things taken x at a time.

functions, trigonometric — Specific mathematical functions of an angle or an arc. The most common are: sine, cosine, tangent, cotangent, secant and cosecant. If θ is the angle formed by r and the x axis, and P is a point on r having "a" as its abscissa and "b" as its ordinate, then: sine $\theta = b/r$; cosine $\theta = a/r$; tangent $\theta = b/a$; cosecant $\theta = r/b$; secant $\theta = r/a$ and contangent $\theta = a/b$.

function table — 1. Refers to two or more sets of data so arranged that an entry in one set selects one or more entries in the remaining sets, for example, a tabulation of the values of a function for a set of values of the variable, a dictionary. 2. A device constructed of hardware, or a subroutine, which can either decode multiple inputs into a single output or encode a single input into multiple outputs.

function, transfer — 1. A mathematical expression frequently used by control engineers which expresses the relationship between the outgoing and the incoming signals of a process, or control element. The transfer function is useful in studies of control problems. 2. A mathematical expression or expressions which describe(s) the relationship between physical conditions at two different points in time or space in a given system, and perhaps, also describe(s) the role played by the intervening time or space.

gamma function program — This program approximates the value of gamma function $\Gamma(x)$ for $1 \le x \le 70$.

$$\Gamma(x) = \int_0^\infty t^{x-1} e^{-t} \, dt$$

1. $\Gamma(x) = (x - 1) \Gamma(x - 1)$
2. For $1 \le x \le 2$, polynomial approximation can be used.

$$\Gamma(x) \cong 1 + b_1(x - 1) + b_2(x - 1)^2 + \dots + b_8(x - 1)^8$$

where $b_1 = -0.577191652$, $b_2 = 0.988205891$
$b_3 = -0.897056937$, $b_4 = 0.918206857$
$b_5 = -0.756704078$, $b_6 = 0.482199394$
$b_7 = -0.193527818$, $b_8 = 0.035868343$.

Note: This program can be used to find the generalized factorial x! for $0 \le x \le 69$.

$$x! = \Gamma(x + 1)$$

gamma probability program — Refers to a Gamma Probability Distribution. Calculates the Gamma Probability Distribution for a given argument. Another program computes the probability of a random variable which has a Gamma probability distribution. It also computes the Mean and Variance of the specified Gamma Distribution. This distribution requires two parameters, Alpha and Beta, as input, both of which must be greater than zero.

generalized analysis program — Generalized Analysis of Variance. Computes the statistics needed to perform an Anova Test on a wide variety of experimental designs. To demonstrate its generality, sample problems illustrated in the write-up include a full factorial-two way crossed classification with replication, a randomized complete block with subsampling, a latin square, a nested-factorial with three factors and replication and a completely randomized design with an unequal number of samples and an unequal determinations per sample.

generalized mean program — For a set of n positive $\{a_1, a_2, \dots, a_n\}$, the generalized mean is defined by

$$M(t) = \left(\frac{1}{n} \sum_{k=1}^n a_k{}^t \right)^{\frac{1}{t}}$$

where t is any desired number.

Notes:
1. If t = 1, the generalized mean M (1) is the same as the arithmetic mean.

. If $t = -1$, the generalized mean $M(-1)$ is the same as the harmonic mean.

geometric mean program — For a set of n positive numbers $\{a_1, a_2, ..., a_n\}$, the geometric mean is defined by

$$G = (a_1 a_2 ... a_n)^{\frac{1}{n}}.$$

geometric progression program — Can be used to: (1) display the terms of a geometric progression; (2) find the value of a particular term of a geometric progression; (3) find the sum of the first n terms of a geometric progression; (4) find the infinite sum of a geometric progression if the ratio of two successive terms has an absolute value less than one.

histogram — A histogram is constructed to help interpret a set of data points (x_i). The points are segregated into a specified number of adjacent cells (CN) of width (CW).

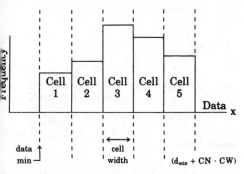

A minimum data limit (d_{min}) can be specified for the start of the first cell or the program will initialize the starting point to zero.

The data points are entered and assimilated into the data memories. Once all data have been input, the mean and standard deviation can be computed. The number of points in each cell can also be displayed.

histogram key — Calculates complete histogram on data set. Resulting printout includes cell number, lower bound of cell, number of occurrences in cell, relative percent frequency of cell. (some units)

histogram plot — In some calculators, a histogram package allows users to specify the minimum and maximum values and establish cell width. Some programs use consecutively entered values to establish mean, standard deviations, and percentage of occurrences per cell. Upon key command, accumulated cells are plotted on the x-axis. At any point, the user may return to input mode and add new data. In addition, a memory option offered by some manufacturers includes automatic scaling and labeling. Additionally, it allows cell plotting three ways: occurrences per cell, percentages per cell and pie charts.

histogram plot, calculator package — This package allows users to specify the minimum and maximum values and establish cell width. The program will use consecutively entered values to establish mean, standard deviations and percentage of occurrences per cell. Upon key command, accumulated cells are plotted on the axis. At any point, the user may return to input mode and add new data. Also available is an Optional Histogram

Package. In addition to the above, this memory option package includes automatic scaling and labeling. Additionally, it allows cell plotting three ways: occurrences per cell, percentages per cell and pie charts.

hydraulics program package — These programs include:
- Gravity Flow Programs: Round Pipes, Pipe-Arches, Elliptical Pipes, Trapezoidal Channels
- Water Surface Profile, (Backwater Curve Analysis) Direct Step Method, Standard Step Method
- Design of a Water Distribution Network, using the Hardy Cross Method
- Design of a Non-Looping Water Distribution Network
- Circular Culvert Design
- Box Culvert Design
- Pipe-Arch Culvert Design
- The Streeter-Phelps Equation
- Storm Sewer System Design
- Sanitary Sewer System Design
- Equivalent Pipe Calculations

hyperbolic functions — The calculator returns values for sinh, cosh, tanh, arc sinh, arc cosh, arc tanh.

hyperbolic functions program — This program evaluates the six hyperbolic functions by the following formulas:

1. $\sinh x = \dfrac{e^x - e^{-x}}{2}$

2. $\cosh x = \dfrac{e^x + e^{-x}}{2}$

3. $\tanh x = \dfrac{e^x - e^{-x}}{e^x + e^{-x}}$

4. $\operatorname{csch} x = \dfrac{1}{\sinh x} \quad (x \neq 0)$

5. $\operatorname{sech} x = \dfrac{1}{\cosh x}$

6. $\coth x = \dfrac{1}{\tanh x} \quad (x \neq 0)$

hypergeometric distribution program — This program evaluates the hypergeometric density function for given a, b and n:

$$f(x) = \frac{\dbinom{a}{x} \dbinom{b}{n-x}}{\dbinom{a+b}{n}}$$

where a, b, n are positive intergers
$x \leq a, n - x \leq b$ and
$x = 0, 1, 2, ..., n.$

The recursive relation

$$f(x+1) = \frac{(x-a)(x-n)}{(x+1)(b-n+x+1)} f(x)$$
$$(x = 0, 1, 2, ..., n-1)$$

is used to find the cumulative distribution

$$P(x) = \sum_{k=0}^{x} f(k).$$

Notes:
1. The program requires that $n \leq 69$.
2. $f(0) = P(0)$
3. The execution time of the program depends on x; the larger x is, the longer it takes.
4. When x is large, due to round-off error, the

computed value for P(x) might be slightly greater than one. In that case, let P(x) = 1.

5. The mean m and the variance σ^2 are given by

$$m = \frac{an}{a + b}$$

$$\sigma^2 = \frac{abn\,(a + b - n)}{(a + b)^2\,(a + b - 1)}.$$

hypergeometric program — Refers to a Hypergeometric Probability Function. Computes the individual and the cumulative hypergeometric distributions. The Mean, Variance, and Standard Deviation of the Distribution are also computed.

implicit function — An expression in which the form of the function is not directly expressed but which requires some operation to be performed, to render it evident. Thus, in the equation $ay^2 + bxy + cx^2 + dy + ex + f = 0$ y is an implicit function of x.

in-circuit symbolic de-bugging — The hardware and software aspects of the Intellec MDS (Intel. Corp.) ICE-80 offer prototyping and production test of user systems. ICE-80 is a unique development system that provides full emulation and debug features while operating inside the user system. The user can get extensive information on the interplay of his software and hardware without introducing extraneous hardware or special debug software into his working system.

income tax — 1040 form — This program calculates the income tax and totals required for completing page 1 and page 2 (part 3) of Form 1040 for individual income tax returns by any of three methods: (1) Tax Table, (2) Standard Deduction, and (3) Itemized Deduction.

incomplete gamma function program —

$$\gamma\,(a, x) = \int_0^x e^{-t}\,t^{a-1}\,dt$$

$$= x^a\,e^{-x} \sum_{n=0}^{\infty} \frac{x^n}{a(a + 1)\,...\,(a + n)}$$

where $a > 0$, $x > 0$. This program computes successive partial sums of the above series. The program stops when two consecutive partial sums are equal and displays the last partial sum as the answer. Note: When x is too large, computing a new term of the series might cause an overflow. In that case, display shows all 9's and the program stops.

installment loan — payment known — This program calculates the finance charge, amount financed, contract term and APR for an installment loan, given the amount borrowed, add-on interest rate, payment amount each period, service charge and insurance option.

intersection of lines and curves — This program calculates the coordinates (Northing and Easting) of the intersection between two lines, between two circles or between a line and a circle. The inputs required for the calculations are: (1) Lines: the bearing and the Northing and Easting of any point on the line and (2) Circles: their radii and the Northing and Easting of their center points. The program utilizes the user-definable keys.

inverse from coordinates program — This program uses coordinates to calculate distance and bearing between points of a traverse. The area in square feet and a summation of distance inverse are also computed.

$$H\ Dist = \sqrt{(N_i - N_{i-1})^2} + (E_i - E_{i-1})^2$$

$$Az = \tan^{-1} \frac{E_i - E_{i-1}}{N_i - N_{i-1}}$$

$$Area = \tfrac{1}{2}[\,(N_2 + N_1)\,(E_2 - E_1) + (N_3 + N_2)$$

$$(E_3 - E_2) + \,....\,(N_n + N_1)\,(E_1 - E_n)]$$

where N, E = Northing, easting of a point
Subscript i refers to current point
Subscript n refers to next to last point
Numeric subscript refers to point number
H Dist = Horizontal distance
Az = Azimuth of a course

inverse function, calculator — This key is used with trig, logs, conversions, sum and product to memories, fixed point and exponent keys.

inverse normal integral program — This program determines the value of x such that

$$Q = \int_x^{\infty} \frac{e^{-\frac{t^2}{2}}}{\sqrt{2\pi}}\,dt$$

where Q is given and $0 < Q \leqslant 0.5$.
The following rational approximation is used:

$$x = t - \frac{c_0 + c_1\,t + c_2\,t^2}{1 + d_1\,t + d_2\,t^2 + d_3\,t^3} + \epsilon\,(Q)$$

where $|\epsilon\,(Q)| < 4.5 \times 10^{-4}$

$$t = \sqrt{\ln \frac{1}{Q^2}} =$$

$c_0 = 2.515517$ $\quad$ $d_1 = 1.432788$
$c_1 = 0.802853$ $\quad$ $d_2 = 0.189269$
$c_2 = 0.010328$ $\quad$ $d_3 = 0.001308$

invert — Refers to various steps to place in a contrary order. To invert the terms of a fraction is to put the numerator in place of the denominator and vice versa.

invoice with line discount and automatic inventory updating — This program calculates an invoice so that each line can be discounted. The prices and inventory quantities for up to ten items are stored in memory with a running inventory kept on a magnetic card. If the inventory for any of the ten items falls below ten, the quantity remaining will print.

Kendall's coefficient of concordance program — Suppose n individuals are ranked from 1 to n according to some specified characteristic by k observers; the coefficient of concordance W measures the agreement between observers (or concordance between rankings).

$$W = \frac{12 \sum\limits_{i=1}^{n} \left(\sum\limits_{j=1}^{k} R_{ij} \right)^2}{k^2\,n(n^2 - 1)} - \frac{3(n + 1)}{n - 1}$$

where R_{ij} is the rank assigned to the ith individual by the jth observer. W varies from 0 (no community of preference) to 1 (perfect agreement). The null hypothesis that the observers have no community of preference may be tested using special tables or, if n > 7, by computing

$$\chi^2 = k\,(n-1)\,W$$

which has approximately the chi-square distribution with $n-1$ degrees of freedom.

least squares fit, $a_1 x^{b1} + a_2 x^{b2}$ — This program calculates the values $\hat{a}_1$ and $\hat{a}_2$ which minimize $\Sigma(Y_i - a_1 x_i^{b1} - a_2\,X_i^{b2})^2$, given data (X_1, Y_1), $(X_2, Y_2), \ldots (X_n, Y_n)$ and values of b_1 and b_2 with $b_1 \neq b_2$. The options offered calculate $Y_i - \hat{a}_1 x_i^{b1} - \hat{a}_2 x_i^{b2}$ using entered values of X and the residual values of $S_{y\,.\,x}$ and $S_{y\,.\,x}$.

least squares fit, $a_1 f_1(X) + a_2 f_2(X)$ — This Program calculates the values $\hat{a}_1$ and $\hat{a}_2$ which minimize $\Sigma(Y_i - a_1 f_1(X) - a_2 f_2(X_i))^2$ when given data $(X_1, Y_1), (X_2, Y_2), \ldots, (X_n, Y_n)$ and user entered functions $f_1(X)$ and $f_2(X)$. The options offered will also calculate values of residuals $Y_i - \hat{a}_1 f_1(X_i) - \hat{a}_2 f_2(X_i)$ and $\hat{a}_1 f_1 + \hat{a}_2 f_2(X)$ using entered values of X.

linear — 1. Relating to order in an algebraic equation in which all of the variables are present in the first degree only, i.e., an equation in which none of the variables are raised to powers other than unity or multiplied together. 2. Having an output that varies in direct proportion to the input.

linear, exponential and power equations regression program — Analysis of Ungrouped Data Using Various Regression Techniques. This program uses the least square fit method to fit N pairs of X, Y (X not equal to 0) data points to one of these three curves: (1) Linear Regression, (2) Exponential Curve, (3) Power Curve.

linear regression — The linear least-squares fit of input data points (x,y) is calculated using the following:

$$\text{Slope} = m = \frac{\dfrac{\Sigma x \Sigma y}{n} - \Sigma xy}{\dfrac{(\Sigma x)^2}{n} - \Sigma x^2}$$

$$\text{Intercept} = b = \frac{\Sigma y - m \Sigma x}{n}$$

The y' for entered x and x' for entered y are calculated as follows:

$$y' = mx + b$$
$$x' = (y - b)/m$$

The coefficient of determination is calculated as:

$$r^2 = m\left(\frac{\Sigma x \Sigma y}{n} - \Sigma xy\right) \Big/ \left(\Sigma y^2 - \frac{(\Sigma y)^2}{n}\right)$$

linear regression programs —

(1) Linear Regression (Grouped Data). This program calculates the Standard Deviation, Mean and Standard Error of Group Data X and Y and also calculates the correlation coefficient, slope and intercept of the linear regression. The maximum and average deviation and the bias are also calculated.

(2) Hypergeometric Probability Function. Computes the individual and the cumulative hypergeometric distributions. The Mean, Variance, and Standard Deviation of the distribution are also computed.

(3) Linear Regression with Correlation Coefficient and Standard Error of Estimate. This program fits the equation Y equals A plus the quantity B times X to variable data by the

linear unit — A device which follows the rules of mathematical linearity, i.e., in which the change in output due to a change in input is proportional to the magnitude of that change and does not depend on the values of the other inputs, i.e., adders, scalars, and integrating amplifiers, whereas multipliers and function generators are often designed as nonlinear.

logarithmic curve — A particular type of curve on which one coordinate of any point varies in accordance with the logarithm of the other coordinate of the point.

logarithmic functions — Many units compute both natural and common logarithms as well as their inverse functions (antilogarithms).

Mann-Whitney statistic program — This program computes the Mann-Whitney test statistic on two independent samples of equal or unequal sizes. This test is designed for testing the null hypothesis of no difference between two populations. Mann-Whitney test statistic is defined as

$$U = n_1 n_2 + \frac{n_1\,(n_1 + 1)}{2} - \sum_{i=1}^{n_1} R_i$$

where n_1 and n_2 are the sizes of the two samples. Arrange all values from both samples jointly (as if they were one sample) in an increasing order of magnitude; let R_i ($i = 1, 2, \ldots, n_1$) be the ranks assigned to the values of the first sample (it is immaterial which sample is referred to as the "first"). When n_1 and n_2 are small, the Mann-Whitney test bases on the exact distribution of U and specially constructed tables. When n_1 and n_2 are both large (say, greater than 8) then

$$z = \frac{U - \dfrac{n_1 n_2}{2}}{\sqrt{n_1 n_2\,(n_1 + n_2 + 1)/12}}$$

is approximately a random variable having the standard normal distribution.

mean, standard deviation, standard error for grouped data program —
Given a set of data points

$$x_1, x_2, \ldots, x_n$$

with respective frequencies

$$f_1, f_2, \ldots, f_n$$

the program computes the following statistics:

$$\text{mean } \bar{x} = \frac{\Sigma f_i x_i}{\Sigma f_i}$$

$$\text{standard deviation } s = \sqrt{\frac{\Sigma f_i x_i^2 - (\Sigma f_i)\bar{x}^2}{\Sigma f_i - 1}}$$

$$\text{standard error } s_{\bar{x}} = \frac{s_x}{\sqrt{\Sigma f_i}}\,.$$

mean-square successive difference program — When test and estimation techniques are used, the method of drawing the sample from the population is specified to be random in most cases. If observations are chosen in a sequence $x_1, x_2, \ldots, x_n$, the mean-square successive difference

$$\eta = \sum_{i=1}^{n-1} (x_i - x_{i+1})^2 \Big/ \sum_{i=1}^{n} (x_i - \bar{x})^2$$

can be used to test for randomness.

If n is large (say, greater than 20), and the population is normal, then

$$z = \frac{1 - \eta/2}{\sqrt{\dfrac{n-2}{n^2-1}}}$$

has approximately the standard normal distribution. Long trends are associated with large positive values of z and short oscillations with large negative values.

moments — This program calculates the first four moments about the origin and the first four central moments about the arithmetic mean, given N sample values, $X_1, X_2, \ldots, X_N$. In addition, it calculates indices of skewness, a_1 and of kurtosis, a_2.

moments and skewness program — The program computes the following statistics for a set of given data $\{x_1, x_2, \ldots, x_n\}$:

$$1^{st} \quad \text{moment} \quad \overline{x} = \frac{1}{n} \sum_{i=1}^{n} x_i$$

$$2^{nd} \quad \text{moment} \quad m_2 = \frac{1}{n} \Sigma x_i^2 - \overline{x}^2$$

$$3^{rd} \quad \text{moment} \quad m_3 = \frac{1}{n} \Sigma x_i^3 - \frac{3}{n} \overline{x} \Sigma x_i^2 + 2\overline{x}^3$$

moment coefficient of skewness

$$\gamma = \frac{m_3}{m_2^{3/2}}$$

moments, skewness and kurtosis program — This program computes the following statistics for a set of given data $\{x_1, x_2, \ldots, x_n\}$:

$$1^{st} \quad \text{moment} \quad \overline{x} = \frac{1}{n} \sum_{i=1}^{n} x_i$$

$$2^{nd} \quad \text{moment} \quad m_2 = \frac{1}{n} \Sigma x_i^2 - \overline{x}^2$$

$$3^{rd} \quad \text{moment} \quad m_3 = \frac{1}{n} \Sigma x_i^3 - \frac{3}{n} \overline{x} \Sigma x_i^2 + 2\overline{x}^3$$

$$4^{th} \quad \text{moment} \quad m_4 = \frac{1}{n} \Sigma x_i^4 - \frac{4}{n} \overline{x} \Sigma x_i^3 + \frac{6}{n} \overline{x}^2 \Sigma x_i^2 - 3\overline{x}^4$$

moment coefficient of skewness

$$\gamma_1 = \frac{m_3}{m_2^{3/2}}$$

moment coefficient of kurtosis

$$\gamma_2 = \frac{m_4}{m_2^2}$$

mortgage loan calculations — This program generates a mortgage amortization schedule for any portion of the loan term selected by the user. The balance and interest paid as of the beginning of the schedule and as of the end of the schedule will also print. If unknown, the monthly payment is calculated, given the amount of loan, interest rate and contract term.

multinomial distribution program — This program evaluates the joint probability function of k (k can be 2, 3, ..., or 8) random variables having the multinomial distribution

$$f(x_1, x_2, \ldots, x_k) = \frac{n!}{x_1! \, x_2 \ldots x_k!} \, \theta_1{}^{x_1} \theta_2{}^{x_2} \ldots \theta_k{}^{x_k}$$

where $\displaystyle\sum_{i=1}^{k} \theta_i = 1, \quad \sum_{i=1}^{k} x_i = n, \theta_i > 0$ and

$$x_i = 0, 1, 2, \ldots, n \ (i = 1, 2, \ldots, k).$$

The parameters of this distribution are n, θ_1, $\theta_2, \ldots$ and θ_k.

Note: The program requires that $n \leq 69$.

multinomial program — Refers to a Multinomial Distribution. For an experiment in which there are K mutually exclusive possible outcomes $E_1, E_2, \ldots E_k$ where P_1 is the probability that event E_1 will occur at trial of the experiment; this program will calculate the probability that event E_1 will occur X_1 times, event E_2 will occur X_2 times, etc., in N trials of the experiment, according to the multinomial distribution. Also calculated are the Mean and Variance of the distribution.

multiple regression program — (1) This program calculates the coefficients of the normal equations which are required for determining the regression equation. The program is done in two parts, Part 1 is for the data entries and the summations for the normal equations; Part 2, a modified version of solution of N-Simultaneous equations, determines the coefficients of the regression equation. (2) Multiple Linear Regression Analysis. Given a set of user-defined transformation function, sets of observed values for several independent variables X, and the corresponding values for the dependent variable Y, this program uses a least square fit method to perform a linear regression on the transformed independent variable, finding the coefficients A_j in the equation. As many as 15 independent variables can be accommodated in a − 44 memory configuration; as many as 9 different transformation functions can be applied to each of the independent variables. (3) Multiple Regression, Three Variables. Makes the necessary computations for a multiple regression study between two independent and one dependent variable. Program computes the coefficients of the model, $Y = AX_1 + BX_2 + C$, along with the multiple and partial coefficients of correlation to enable significance testing via t tests or Anova.

normal distribution — In order to calculate the standard normal distribution, the following probability function is used:

$$Z(x) = \frac{1}{\sqrt{2\pi}} e^{-x^2/2}$$

Then: $Q(x) = Z(x) [b_1 t + b_2 t^2 + b_3 t^3 + b_4 t^4 + b_5 t^5] + \epsilon(x)$

where: $t = \dfrac{1}{1 + px}$

$p = .231642$
$b_1 = .319382$
$b_2 = -.356564$
$b_3 = 1.78148$
$b_4 = -1.82126$
$b_5 = 1.33027$

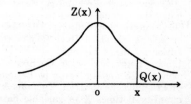

NOTES:
- $Z(x)$ is calculated before $Q(x)$
- $0 \leq x \leq 21.1$
- $Z(-x) = Z(x)$

ordinary annuity (1) — This annuity program is used when the periodic interest rate (i) is known. Given values for two of the other variables (PV, PMT, or n), the value for the remaining variable will be computed from the following relationships:

$$PV = PMT\frac{1 - (1 + i)^{-n}}{i} \quad (i > 0)$$

$$= (PMT)n \quad (i = 0)$$

$$PMT = PV\frac{i}{1 - (1 + i)^{-n}} \quad (i > 0)$$

$$= \frac{PV}{n} \quad (i = 0)$$

$$n = -\frac{\ln\left[1 - PV\left(\dfrac{i}{PMT}\right)\right]}{\ln(1 + i)} \quad (i > 0)$$

Where: PV = present value
PMT = payment per period
n = number of periods
i = periodic interest rate (decimal)

ordinary annuity (2) — This annuity program calculates the periodic interest rate using an iterative method given the present value (PV), payment per period (PMT), and the number of periods (N). Input variables may be entered directly or may be picked up from other programs BA 1-09-1 when these programs are run sequentially. Input variables may be entered in any order and only the necessary changes need be made for subsequent calculations; that is, previous input arguments need not be re-entered.

partial correlation coefficients program— The partial correlation coefficient measures the relationship between any two of the variables when all others are kept constant. For the case of 3 variables, the partial correlation coefficient between X_1 and X_2 keeping X_3 constant is

$$r_{12 \cdot 3} = \frac{r_{12} - r_{13}\,r_{23}}{\sqrt{(1 - r_{13}^2)\,(1 - r_{23}^2)}}$$

where r_{ij} denotes the correlation coefficient of X_i and X_j. Similarly, for the case of 4 variables, the partial correlation coefficient between X_1 and X_2 keeping X_3 and X_4 constant is

$$r_{12 \cdot 34} = \frac{r_{12 \cdot 4} - r_{13 \cdot 4}\,r_{23 \cdot 4}}{\sqrt{(1 - r_{13 \cdot 4}^2)\,(1 - r_{23 \cdot 4}^2)}} =$$

$$\frac{r_{12 \cdot 3} - r_{14 \cdot 3}\,r_{24 \cdot 3}}{\sqrt{(1 - r_{14 \cdot 3}^2)\,(1 - r_{24 \cdot 3}^2)}}.$$

Any partial correlation coefficient can be computed by means of these formulas (using this program) if correlation coefficients r_{12}, r_{13}, r_{23}, ... are given.
Note: This program finds $r_{13 \cdot 2}$, $r_{23 \cdot 1}$ by similar formulas.

partial correlation program — Given the simple correlation coefficients of three variables, X, Y and Z, this program computes the partial correlation coefficients for each combination of two variables.

partial product — A particular result developed by multiplying the multiplicand by one of the digits of the multiplier, i.e., there are as many partial products in a multiplication operation as there are significant digits in a multiplier, as partial sums are shifted and added to obtain the final product.

partial sum — A particular result obtained from the addition of two or more numbers without considering carries, i.e., in binary numeration systems, the partial sum is the same result as is obtained from the exclusive OR operation.

payroll: commissions — This program computes an employee's salary including a commission and a base amount.

payroll: incentive program — This program computes an employee's salary based on an incentive hourly rate.

payroll: labor cost distribution — This program computes the salary of employees who work on different tasks at different hourly rates.

payroll: piecework — This program computes the salaries of employees who work for an hourly wage and on a piecework basis.

payroll: quarterly summary report — This program computes all the necessary information required on the employer's quarterly federal tax return form.

payroll: salary plus bonus — This program calculates an employee's salary including a bonus and a base amount.

payroll: time card calculations — This program calculates total hours worked during the week.

permutation — The number of possible sequences of n items taken c at a time:

$$p\binom{n}{c} = \frac{n!}{(n - c)!}$$

permutation program — A permutation is an ordered subset of a set of distinct objects. The number of possible permutations, each containing n objects, that can be formed from a collection of m distinct objects is given by

$$_mP_n = \frac{m!}{(m - n)!} = m(m - 1) \ldots (m - n + 1)$$

where m, n are integers and $0 \leq n \leq m$.
Notes:
1. $_mP_n$ can also be denoted by P_n^m, $P(m,n)$ or $(m)_n$.
2. $_mP_0 = 1$, $_mP_1 = m$, $_mP_m = m!$

PERT, early start dates — Used in an optimistic time estimate in which each job is started as early as possible to estimate the duration of the entire task.

PERT, free float — Certain stops used to halt particular tasks where no action would have resulted in an overall delay in the project.

PERT, latest start dates — Used in estimating the completion date of a particular task. Each job is arranged to start as late as possible so that the entire task is completed on the required date.

PERT (program evaluation and review technique) network — Use of PERT requires an extensive analysis of an overall project in order to list all the individual activities, or jobs which must be performed in order to meet the total objective. These activities are then arranged in a network that displays the sequential relationship among them. This analysis must be extremely thorough and detailed if it is to be realistic. PERT provides a means of reporting and analysis for project administrators. Information required can be developed and areas which impose the greatest time restrictions on the completion of a product can be high-lighted. Areas with an excess of time for completion, called slack areas, are also high-lighted.

PERT, start dates — Used in estimating the completion date of a particular task. Each job is arranged to start as late as possible so that the entire task is completed on the required date.

PERT start dates, latest — Refers to various calculations used in estimating the completion date of particular tasks. Each job is arranged to start as late as possible so that the entire task is completed on the required date.

Poisson distribution program —
Density function

$$f(x) = \frac{\lambda^x e^{-\lambda}}{x!}$$

where $\lambda > 0$
and $x = 0, 1, 2, \ldots$.
Cumulative distribution is

$$P(x) = \sum_{k=0}^{x} f(k).$$

This program evaluates $f(x)$ and $P(x)$ for a given λ using the recursive relation

$$f(x + 1) = \frac{\lambda}{x + 1} f(x).$$

Notes:
1. $f(0) = P(0)$
2. When x is large, due to round-off error, the computed value for $P(x)$ might be slightly greater than one. In that case, let $P(x) = 1$.
3. The execution time of the program depends on x; the larger x is, the longer it takes.
4. Mean = variance = λ

polynomial cyclic code — A very practical code which achieves perfect detection of single, double, and odd number of errors and very good detection of bursts of errors is the polynomial code. Given an integer r, the data is multiplied by 2^r (left shifted r places) and divided by a polynomial P. The remainder is appended to the original message. Upon receipt, the total message is divided by P. If the remainder is non-zero an error has occurred. This division is implemented in a shift register, thus providing an automatic low cost check sum. If the data is recycled through the shift register the process is called a cyclic sum check.

polynomial evaluation program —
A polynomial of the form

$$f(x) = a_0 x^n + a_1 x^{n-1} + \ldots + a_{n-1} x + a_n$$

is evaluated by writing it in the form

$$x (\ldots x (x (a_0 x + a_1) + a_2) + \ldots + a_{n-1}) + a_n$$

n can be any positive integer.

polynomial regression program — This program calculates the regression coefficients for a polynomial in one variable. The program is done in two parts: Part 1 is for entries and summations used to obtain the normal equations; Part 2 uses a modified solution of the N Simultaneous Equations, and determines the coefficients of the re-

gression equation (with a few modifications, this program can be executed in one pass on a larger capacity machine).

power curve fit — Given a set of data points:

$$\{(x_i, y_i), i = 1, 2, \ldots, n\}$$

Where: $x_i > 0$ and $y_i > 0$, this program will fit a power curve:

$$y = ax^b \qquad (a > 0)$$

The problem may be interpreted as a linear regression problem by using the equation in the form:

$$\ln y = b \ln x + \ln a$$

The computed statistics are:
1. Regression coefficients

$$a = \exp\left[\frac{\sum \ln y_i}{n} - \frac{b \sum \ln x_i}{n}\right]$$

$$b = \frac{\sum (\ln x_i)(\ln y_i) - \frac{(\sum \ln x_i)(\sum \ln y_i)}{n}}{\sum (\ln x_i)^2 - \frac{(\sum \ln x_i)^2}{n}}$$

NOTE: n is a positive integer $\neq 1$.
2. Correlation coefficient

$$r^2 = \frac{\left[\sum (\ln x_i)((\ln y_i) - \frac{(\sum \ln x_i)(\sum \ln y_i)}{n}\right]^2}{\left[\sum (\ln x_i)^2 - \frac{(\sum \ln x_i)^2}{n}\right]\left[\sum (\ln y_i)^2 - \frac{(\sum \ln y_i)^2}{n}\right]}$$

3. Estimated value x' for given y

$$x' = \sqrt[b]{y/a}$$

4. Estimated value y' for given x

$$y' = ax^b$$

Example:

x_i	3	6	8	11	13.5	15	18.5	20
y_i	.8	1.12	1.3	1.53	1.95	2.4	3.0	3.7

$a = .2901902009$
$b = .7759169351$
$r^2 = 0.921727263$
for $x = 9$, $y' = 1.596230726$
for $y = 2.8$, $x' = 18.56904361$

present value or amount of an annuity of 1 — This program solves either for the present value of an annuity of 1 or the amount of an annuity of 1, given the annual effective rate of interest in percent, number of periods per year, and total number of periods.

probability of no repetitions in a sample program — Suppose a sample of size n is drawn with replacement from a population containing m different objects. Let P be the probability that there are no repetitions in the sample, then

$$P = \left(1 - \frac{1}{m}\right)\left(1 - \frac{2}{m}\right) \cdots \left(1 - \frac{n-1}{m}\right)$$

Given integers m, n such that $m \geq n \geq 1$, this program finds the probability P.
Note: The execution time of the program depends on n; the larger n is, the longer it takes.

progressions, arithmetic, geometric, harmonic — This program may be used to calculate the following:

1. The nth term A_n of the arithmetic progression
$$A_n = A_1 + (n - 1) d$$

2. The sum S_n of the first n terms of the arithmetic progression
$$S_n = (n/2)(A_n + A_1)$$

3. The nth term G_n of the geometric progression
$$G_n = G_1 r^{n-1}$$

4. The sum S_n of the first n turns of the geometric progression
$$S_n = G_1 \left(\frac{1 - r^n}{1 - r} \right)$$

5. The nth term H_n of the harmonic progression
$$H_n = \frac{a}{b + (n - 1) c} \quad b + (n - 1) c \neq 0$$

where: n = Number of terms $(n \geq 1)$
d = Common difference
r = Common ratio $(r \geq 0, r \neq 1)$

quadratic equations program — A general quadratic equation is of the form
$$a x^2 + b x + c = 0$$

The equation has two roots x_1 and x_2. Let
$$D = \frac{b^2 - 4ac}{4a^2}$$

If
$$D \geq 0 \quad \text{then} \quad x_1 =$$
$$-\frac{b}{2a} + \sqrt{\frac{b^2 - 4ac}{4a^2}} \text{ and } x_2 = \frac{c}{ax_1}$$

If
$$D < 0 \quad \text{then} \quad x_1, \ x_2 =$$
$$-\frac{b}{2a} \pm i \sqrt{\frac{4ac - b^2}{4a^2}} = u \pm iv$$

The coefficient a cannot be zero.

random number generator program — This program calculates uniformly distributed pseudo random numbers u_i in the range
$$0 \leq u_i \leq 1$$

using the following formula:

u_i = Fractional part of $[(\pi + u_{i-1})^5]$.

The user has to specify the starting value u_0 (the "seed" of the sequence) such that
$$0 \leq u_0 \leq 1.$$

random walk — A statistical term which relates to the movement of a body to its next position, in such a way that it is likely to move in any direction with equal probability by a specified fixed distance from its current position, i.e., numbers can be involved which correspond to the distances. Mathematics techniques such as Monte Carlo are used in developing random walks.

random walk method — A variation of the Monte Carlo statistical system or method in which a problem is developed for a probabilistic solution. The "walk" factor consists of a series of traverses of long line segments. The directions; and often-times lengths, vary at random. The probability of reaching a defined point by a walk of this type at a given time is often given by a function that is for other interests.

real estate appraisal — **basic ellwood formulas** — This program uses Ellwood Formulas to determine the basic capitalization rate, the composite capitalization rate, the building value and total value, given a yield rate and basic input data.

rectangular coordinates — A set of three lines called axes, the intersect at a common point in space in a way that each line, or axis, is perpendicular to the plane containing the other two.

rectangular probability program — Given a and b of the probability density function $f(x) =$ registers to rectangular x and y coordinates.

regression — This is the rate at which an output changes in relation to the changes in inputs; more specifically, it represents the slope of a line which graphs the comparable values of inputs (independent variables) and the output (dependent variables).

regression, multiple — A special type of mathematical regression analysis.

regressions, statistic package — Concerns overlays individualized to polynomial regression and multiple linear regression problems. Almost totally interactive variable selection procedures permit plotting any variable against any other; calculating and plotting residuals; calculating Durbin Watson statistics; and descriptive statistics that calculate variable means, standard variances, and correlation matrices.

simple accrued interest — This program calculates the interest earned in a certain number of days (n) on a given amount of money (PV) knowing the annual interest rate (i). The number of days in a year (DPY) that the annual interest rate is based on must also be known. Compounding is not considered.

$$\text{Interest earned} = \frac{PV \times n \times i}{100 \, (DPY)} \text{ where } PV, n, i > 0$$

simple interest calculated between two dates This program calculates the exact number of days between two dates, the interest amount for these days, and the number of years, months and days in the interest period. Adjustments for leap years are incorporated.

simultaneous equations for 2 unknowns — Given the coefficients of two simultaneous equations with two unknowns each:

$$a_{11} x_1 + a_{12} x_2 = c_1 \qquad a_{21} x_1 + a_{22} x_2 = c_2$$

the values for x_1 and x_2 can be calculated.

$$x_1 = \frac{a_{22} c_1 - a_{12} c_2}{\text{Det}} \qquad \text{Det} = a_{11} a_{22} - a_{12} a_{21}$$

$$x_2 = \frac{a_{11} c_2 - a_{21} c_1}{\text{Det}}$$

sinking fund (interest rate known) — A sinking fund is an annuity where a future value is accumulated by equal payments at equal intervals at a certain interest rate. This program will calculate the future value, payment per period or number of payments knowing the interest rate (i) and the two remaining known values.

$$FV = PMT \times \frac{(1 + i)^n - 1}{i} \text{ for } i > 0$$

$$n = \frac{\ln\left(\frac{FV \times i}{PMT} + 1\right)}{\ln(i + 1)} \text{ where } i \neq 0$$

$$PMT = \frac{FV \times i}{(1 + i)^n - 1} \text{ for } i > 0$$

$$= \frac{FV}{n} \quad \text{ for } i = 0$$

NOTES:
- Input variables can be stored in any order. Only values that change between problems need be re-stored.
- Store a zero in the proper memory register for the unknown value.
- After program execution, the unknown value is stored in its assigned memory register.
- Memory register contents from this program can be used for input to program "SINKING FUND (Interest Unknown)."

sinking fund (interest rate unknown) — A sinking fund is an annuity where a future value is accumulated by equal payments at equal intervals at a certain interest rate. Knowing the future value (FV), payment per period (PMT) and number of periods (n), this program calculates the periodic interest rate using Newton's method.

$$\frac{f(i)}{f'(i)} = \frac{\frac{PMT[(1 + i)^n - 1]}{i} - FV}{\frac{PMT[n(1 + i)^{n-1}]}{i} - \frac{PMT[(1 + i)^n - 1]}{i^2}}$$

with a first estimate $= \frac{FV}{PMT(n^2)} - \frac{PMT}{FV}$

NOTES:
- Input variables can be stored in any order. Only values that change between problems need be re-stored.
- FV, PMT and n > 0.
- After program execution, the display will contain the interest rate rounded to the nearest one hundredth of a percent.
- Memory register contents from this program can be used for input to program "SINKING FUND (Interest Rate Known)."

statistics, descriptive: three variables — This program calculates the means, standard deviation and correlation coefficients, given n triplets of numbers, $(X_{11}, X_{21}, X_{31}), (X_{12}, X_{22}, X_{32}), \ldots (X_{1n}, X_{2n}, X_{3n})$. In addition, the elements of the variance-covariance matrix, its inverse and determinant, the squares of multiple correlation coefficients of each variable and the partial correlation coefficients are also determined.

structural engineering program package — The package consists of 12-programs. The programs included in this package are:

Rigid Frame Analysis (7 Story, 5 Bays)
Frame Analysis (1 Story, 8 Bays)
Beam Analysis — Continuous Prismatic
Wind Analysis by Cantilever Method
Beam Analysis — Simple
Section Properties — Concrete
Section Properties — Steel and Aluminum
Steel Beam Design
Steel Column Design
Rectangular Concrete Beam Design
Rectangular Concrete Columns
Retaining Wall Design

student's t for independent samples — This program calculates the values of the sample means, the values of the sample standard deviations, the "pooled" (or averaged) variance and the t-statistic comparing the sample means, P, the significance level is also determined for the corresponding t-statistic.

test statistics for correlation coefficient program — Under the assumptions of normal correlation analysis, the following t statistic can be used to test the null hypothesis $\rho = 0$,

$$t = \frac{r\sqrt{n - 2}}{\sqrt{1 - r^2}}$$

where r is an estimate (based on a sample of size n) of the true correlation coefficient ρ. This t statistic has the t distribution with $n - 2$ degrees of freedom.

To test the null hypothesis $\rho = \rho_0$, the z statistic is used.

$$z = \frac{\sqrt{n - 3}}{2} \ln \frac{(1 + r)(1 - \rho_0)}{(1 - r)(1 + \rho_0)}$$

where z has approximately the standard normal distribution.

3 × 3 matrix inversion program — If a_{ij} indicates a number in the ith row, j^{th} column then a 3 × 3 matrix A can be represented as

$$\begin{array}{ccc} a_{11} & a_{12} & a_{13} \\ a_{21} & a_{22} & a_{23} \\ a_{31} & a_{32} & a_{33} \end{array}$$

then the multiplicative inverse of A is denoted by A^{-1} and is calculated as follows:

$$A^{-1} = \begin{array}{ccc} \dfrac{\begin{vmatrix} a_{22} & a_{23} \\ a_{32} & a_{33} \end{vmatrix}}{\text{Det } A} & -\dfrac{\begin{vmatrix} a_{12} & a_{13} \\ a_{32} & a_{33} \end{vmatrix}}{\text{Det } A} & \dfrac{\begin{vmatrix} a_{12} & a_{13} \\ a_{22} & a_{23} \end{vmatrix}}{\text{Det } A} \\[3ex] -\dfrac{\begin{vmatrix} a_{21} & a_{23} \\ a_{31} & a_{33} \end{vmatrix}}{\text{Det } A} & \dfrac{\begin{vmatrix} a_{11} & a_{13} \\ a_{31} & a_{33} \end{vmatrix}}{\text{Det } A} & -\dfrac{\begin{vmatrix} a_{11} & a_{13} \\ a_{21} & a_{23} \end{vmatrix}}{\text{Det } A} \\[3ex] \dfrac{\begin{vmatrix} a_{21} & a_{22} \\ a_{31} & a_{32} \end{vmatrix}}{\text{Det } A} & -\dfrac{\begin{vmatrix} a_{11} & a_{12} \\ a_{31} & a_{32} \end{vmatrix}}{\text{Det } A} & \dfrac{\begin{vmatrix} a_{11} & a_{12} \\ a_{21} & a_{22} \end{vmatrix}}{\text{Det } A} \end{array}$$

For the ith, j^{th} position of A^{-1} use the minor of the jth, i^{th} position of the original matrix. The minor is the two by two matrix left after crossing out the ith row and j^{th} column of A.

three factor analysis programs — (1) - Analysis of Variance for the completely randomized three-factor design. This program produces the statistics for the Anova table for the three-dimensional case of factors A, B, C. The sum of squares, degrees of freedom, mean of squares and F statistic are calculated for each factor and the interaction of each factor. The number of cells allowable is machine register dependent. All cells are assumed to have N samples each. Total, standard deviation and mean are determined for each cell.

(2) - Mixed Model Experimental Design. This program calculates the sum of squares, degrees of freedom and mean square ratio for a three-factor mixed design. The model used represents a three-factor experiment in which the first and third factors are fixed, the second factor is random and nested within the first, and the third factor is crossed with the first and second.

translation and/or rotation of coordinate axis program — Let (x, y) be coordinates in the old system and let (x_0, y_0) be the center of a new coordinate system rotated through an angle of θ. The new coordinates are (x', y') and are calculated by the following formulas:

1. $x' = (x - x_0) \cos\theta + (y - y_0) \sin\theta$
2. $y' = -(x - x_0) \sin\theta + (y - y_0) \cos\theta$

For no rotation put in $\theta = 0$.
For no translation put in $(x_0, y_0) = (0, 0)$

traverse adjustment — compass rule — This program calculates the bearings, latitudes and departures for each leg, corrects the angles, and determines the closing error, using the Compass Rule, given the coordinates of a known point, an initial bearing and a surveyed traverse consisting of distances and field angles. The program utilizes the user-definable keys.

traverse adjustment — Crandall's Rule — This program calculates the bearings, latitudes and departure for each leg, corrects the angles, and determines the closing error, by Crandall's Rule, given the coordinates of a known point, an initial bearing and a surveyed traverse consisting of distances and field angles. The program utilizes the user-definable keys.

trend line analysis — The linear least-squares fit of points (x, y) where y is input and x is integrally incremented beginning with 1.0 is determined by this program using the following calculations:

$$\text{slope} = m = \left(\frac{\Sigma y \Sigma x}{n} - \Sigma xy\right)\Big/\left(\frac{(\Sigma x)^2}{n} - \Sigma x^2\right)$$

$\text{intercept} = b = (\Sigma y - m\Sigma x)/n$
Where: n is the number of data points
The y' and x' for entered x and y are calculated as follows:

$$y' = mx + b \qquad x' = (y - b)/m$$

The coefficient of determination is calculated as:

$$r^2 = m\left(\frac{\Sigma x \Sigma y}{n} - \Sigma xy\right)\Big/\left(\Sigma y^2 - \frac{(\Sigma y)^2}{n}\right)$$

The value of r^2 measures the "degree of fit" of the given points to the least-squares straight line. When $r^2 = \pm 1$, the correlation is said to be exact. When $r^2 = 0$, the variables are said to be uncorrelated with a linear equation.

triangle solution a, A, C program —

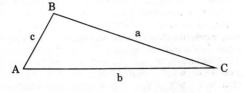

Given two angles and an opposite side this program solves the triangle for the remaining parameters by the following formulas:

$B = 2 \sin^{-1} 1 - (A + C) = \pi$ radians −
$\qquad\qquad\qquad (A + C) = 180° - (A + C)$
$\qquad\qquad = 200$ grads − $(A + C)$

$$b = \frac{a \sin B}{\sin A}$$

$$c = \frac{a \sin C}{\sin A}$$

The program works in any angular mode. However, if in degree mode all angles are assumed to be in decimal degrees.

triangle solution a, b, c program —

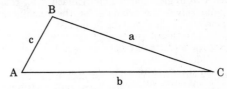

Given three sides of a triangle this program solves the triangle for the remaining parameters by the following formulas:

$$C = \cos^{-1}\left(\frac{a^2 + b^2 - c^2}{2ab}\right)$$

$$B = \sin^{-1}\left(\frac{b \sin C}{c}\right) \qquad A = \sin^{-1}\left(\frac{a \sin C}{c}\right)$$

Reletter if necessary to make c the largest side. The program works in any angular mode. However, if in degree mode decimal degrees are assumed.

triangle solution a, b, C program —

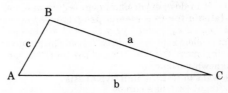

Given two sides and their included angle this program solves the triangle for the remaining parameters by the following formulas:

$c = \sqrt{a^2 + b^2 - 2ab \cos C} \qquad A = \sin^{-1}\left(\frac{a \sin C}{c}\right)$

$B = 2 \sin^{-1} 1 - (A + C) = \pi$ radians −
$\qquad\qquad\qquad (A + C) = 180° - (A + C)$
$\qquad\qquad = 200$ grads − $(A + C)$

Reletter if necessary, to make a the smaller of a and b. This program works in any angular mode. However, if in degrees decimal degrees are assumed.

triangle solution a, B, C program —

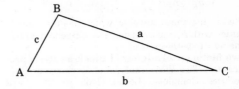

Given two angles and their included side this program solves the triangle for the remaining parameters by the following formulas:

$A = 2 \sin^{-1} 1 - (B + C) = \pi$ radians −
$\qquad\qquad\qquad (B + C) = 180° - (B + C)$
$\qquad\qquad = 200$ grads − $(B + C)$

$$b = \frac{a \sin B}{\sin A}$$

$$c = \frac{a \sin C}{\sin A}$$

The program works in any angular mode. However, if in degrees the program assumes decimal degrees.

triangle solution B, b, c program —
Given two angles and a non-included side, this program solves the triangle for the remaining parameters by the following formulas:

1. $C = \sin^{-1}\left(\dfrac{c \sin B}{b}\right)$

2. $A = 2 \sin^{-1} 1 - (B + C) = \pi$ radians —
$$(B + C) = 180° - (B + C)$$
$$= 200 \text{ grads} - (B + C)$$

3. $a = \dfrac{b \sin A}{\sin B}$

If B is acute $(< 90°)$ and $b < c$, a second set of solutions exists and is calculated by the following formulas:

4. $C' = 2 \sin^{-1} 1 - C$

5. $A' = 2 \sin^{-1} 1 - (B + C')$

6. $a' = \dfrac{b \sin A'}{\sin B}$

This program works in any angular mode. However, if in degrees, decimal degrees are assumed.
t statistic for two means program — Suppose $\{x_1, x_2, ..., x_{n_1}\}$ and $\{y_1, y_2, ..., y_{n_2}\}$ are independent random samples from two normal populations having means μ_1, μ_2 (unknown) and the same unknown variance σ^2.
We want to test the null hypothesis

$$H_0 : \mu_1 - \mu_2 = D$$

where D is a given number.
Define

$$\overline{x} = \frac{1}{n_1} \sum_{i=1}^{n_1} x_i$$

$$\overline{y} = \frac{1}{n_2} \sum_{i=1}^{n_2} y_i$$

$$t = \frac{\overline{x} - \overline{y} - D}{\sqrt{\dfrac{1}{n_1} + \dfrac{1}{n_2}} \; \sqrt{\dfrac{\Sigma x_i^2 - n_1 \overline{x}^2 + \Sigma y_i^2 - n_2 \overline{y}^2}{n_1 + n_2 - 2}}}$$

We can use this t statistic, which has the t distribution with $n_1 + n_2 - 2$ degrees of freedom, to test the null hypothesis H_0.
two factor or randomized block analysis program — Two Way Analysis of Variance or Randomized Complete Blocks. This program will produce the Means and the Analysis of Variance for any number of entered groups with up to R replications each. The program may be used for a randomized complete block design.
two × K contingency programs — Two-by-K Contingency Table. This program calculates CHI-Squared for a 2 × K contingency table. The number of degrees of freedom, $V = K - 1$, is also calculated.

2 × k contingency table program — Contingency tables can be used to test the null hypothesis that two variables are independent.

	1	2	3	...	k	Totals
A	a_1	a_2	a_3	...	a_k	N_A
B	b_1	b_2	b_3	...	b_k	N_B
Totals	N_1	N_2	N_3	...	N_k	N

Test statistic χ^2 has $k - 1$ degrees of freedom.

$$\chi^2 = \frac{N}{N_A} \sum_{i=1}^{k} \frac{a_i^2}{N_i} + \frac{N}{N_B} \sum_{i=1}^{k} \frac{b_i^2}{N_i} - N$$

Pearson's coefficient of contingency C measures the degree of association between the two variables.

$$C = \sqrt{\frac{\chi^2}{N + \chi^2}}$$

2 × 2 contingency table program (with Yates correction) — This program calculates χ^2 for a 2 × 2 contingency table containing observed frequencies. Yates correction for continuity is used.

	1	2
Group A	a	b
Group B	c	d

$$\chi^2 = \frac{(a + b + c + d)\left[|ad - bc| - \tfrac{1}{2}(a + b + c + d)\right]^2}{(a + b)(a + c)(c + d)(b + d)}$$

2 × 2 matrix multiplication program —

Let

$$A = \begin{bmatrix} a_{11} & a_{12} \\ a_{21} & a_{22} \end{bmatrix} \quad \text{and} \quad B = \begin{bmatrix} b_{11} & b_{12} \\ b_{21} & b_{22} \end{bmatrix}$$

be two 2 × 2 matrices. The matrix product of A and B is calculated as follows:

$$AB = \begin{bmatrix} a_{11} b_{11} + a_{12} b_{21} & a_{11} b_{12} + a_{12} b_{22} \\ a_{21} b_{11} + a_{22} b_{21} & a_{21} b_{12} + a_{22} b_{22} \end{bmatrix}$$

Let the answer be denoted by:

$$C = \begin{bmatrix} c_{11} & c_{12} \\ c_{21} & c_{22} \end{bmatrix}$$

two variable descriptive statistics — This program calculates the means, $(\overline{X}$ and $\overline{Y})$, the standard deviations $(S_x$ and $S_y)$ and the correlation coefficient, r, when given the observations (X_1, Y_1), $(X_2, Y_2), ... (X_n, Y_n)$. The largest and smallest values of X and Y are also determined.
uniform, exponential or normal random number program — Random Number Generation, Uniform, Exponential or Normal. Computes sequences of random numbers with optional choice of distributions, VIZ: (1) Uniform over the interval (0, 1), (2) Exponential with specified Mean, or (3) Normal with Mean Zero and specified standard deviation.

ector cross product program — If $A = (a_1,$ $a_2, a_3)$ and $B = (b_1, b_2, b_3)$ are two three dimen-ional vectors then the cross product of A and B is enoted by $A \times B$ and is calculated as follows:

$$A \times B = \left(\begin{vmatrix} a_2 & a_3 \\ b_2 & b_3 \end{vmatrix}, - \begin{vmatrix} a_1 & a_3 \\ b_1 & b_3 \end{vmatrix}, \begin{vmatrix} a_1 & a_2 \\ b_1 & b_2 \end{vmatrix} \right) =$$

$$(a_2 b_3 - a_3 b_2, a_3 b_1 - a_1 b_3, a_1 b_2 - a_2 b_1)$$

Let the solution be represented by (c_1, c_2, c_3).

vectors in three dimensions — This program performs the following three-dimensional vector operations: vector addition, vector subtraction, dot product, cross product, cartesian coordinates to spherical coordinates, angle between two vectors, vector magnitude and parallel unit vector. The user-definable keys are utilized.

Weibull distribution parameter calculation program — The Weibull probability density function is given by

$$f(x) = \frac{bx^{(b-1)}}{\theta^b} e^{-\left(\frac{x}{\theta}\right)^b}$$

where $\theta > 0,$ $b > 0,$ $x > 0.$

The cumulative distribution function is

$$F(x) = 1 - e^{-\left(\frac{x}{\theta}\right)^b}$$

For a set of data $\{x_1, ..., x_n\}$, the Weibull parameters b and θ are to be calculated for these functions. A common application is to use Weibull analysis for failure data where all samples are tested to failure. To use the program, list the items in order of increasing time to failure. The median rank (M. R.) is calculated by

$$\frac{R_i - 0.3}{n + 0.4}$$

where R_i is the rank of failure data x_i. Using this median rank as an approximation of $F(x_i)$, a least squares fit is performed to the linearized form of the cummulative distribution function

$$\ln \ln \left(\frac{1}{1 - F(x)} \right) = b \ln x - b \ln \theta.$$

The solution is similar to the linear regression problem, and estimates of b and θ are obtained.

INDEX

1300 p.B.